D0146018

Juvenile Delinquency

HISTORICAL, CULTURAL AND LEGAL PERSPECTIVES

3RD EDITION

ARNOLD BINDER
UNIVERSITY OF CALIFORNIA - IRVINE

GILBERT GEIS
UNIVERSITY OF CALIFORNIA - IRVINE

DICKSON D. BRUCE JR.
UNIVERSITY OF CALIFORNIA - IRVINE

anderson publishing co.
2035 Reading Road
Cincinnati, OH 45202
800-582-7295

Juvenile Delinquency: Historical, Cultural and Legal Perspectives, Third Edition

Library of Congress Cataloging-in-Publication Data

Binder, Arnold.
    Juvenile delinquency : historical, cultural, and legal perspectives / Arnold Binder, Gilbert Geis,
    Dickson D. Bruce, Jr.--3rd ed.
        p.   cm.
    Includes bibliographical references and index.
    ISBN 1-58360-503-7 (pbk.)
    1. Juvenile delinquency. 2. Juvenile delinquency--United States. I. Geis, Gilbert.
    II. Bruce, Dickson D., 1946-   III. Title.
    HV9069 .B59 2000
    364.36'0973--dc21

                                                            00-038040

Cover digital composition and design by Tin Box Studio, Inc.
Cover photo credit: © Susan Johann/Tony Stone Images

EDITOR Ellen S. Boyne
ASSISTANT EDITOR Genevieve McGuire
ACQUISITIONS EDITOR Michael C. Braswell

Preface

We have been gratified by the response of students and faculty to the first two editions of this book. This text has sought to highlight core insights into acts that are defined by the law as juvenile delinquency and to extend them by adding and integrating the most recent statistics, theoretical statements, and the results of a wide range of quantitative and qualitative studies. The book also places developments in juvenile law and responses to it into a historical context. We like to believe that each edition improves on its predecessor because we have the added advantage of student and faculty comments and the time to refine points that we think are important for a thorough understanding of the subject.

Revising a textbook is an intriguing task and it might be worth a few paragraphs to convey some sense of the process—at least as it bears upon this book. Even as an individual edition is finished, we continue to collect lists of articles and books that might add new and relevant information. At revision time, we gather this material and read it carefully. We also monitor major newspapers because the sophistication of investigative and beat reporters has increased so dramatically in recent decades that what they write on the scene can provide important insights that supplement formal research probes.

Cutting material—that is, eliminating discussions that appear in earlier editions—is perhaps the most difficult part of revising because what was included earlier was done so with the belief that it was essential information. It sometimes is a hard choice between retaining what is in the book and adding new material; there is a tendency to incorporate something more recent even if it is a bit less significant than something older. Part of that tendency resides in the aim to be current. We have tried hard to use an "importance" calculation rather than a "newness" standard. Certainly, discussions of topics such as the amount and shape of delinquency have to be updated, but how much history and past theory do you sacrifice for the newer information and ideas? In the end, it becomes a judgment call, rooted in the understanding that a textbook can only be so long lest it become overwhelming.

A sizeable portion of the current edition differs from the previous one because in addition to statistical reports, a great deal has been written and researched in regard to delinquency as society, entering a new millennium, finds its youth increasingly precocious—that is, doing more things (some good and some not so good) that in the past usually were not done until people were many years older.

Most important, we have attempted to make this a student-friendly textbook. We have avoided stringing out an array of research endeavors, each of which adds only in a very minor way to a major idea about delinquency. Indeed, quite often such studies contradict one another, in part because they use different definitions of the concepts they are examining and in part because of how they go about their task. Our aim has been to do the best we can to integrate such research into a general statement of its contribution to our understanding of delinquency.

It is a cliché of the field that juvenile delinquency can best be understood from an interdisciplinary perspective. Nonetheless, there tends to be little cross-fertilization among the scientific efforts to comprehend delinquency. This book, recognizing the need for a variety of perspectives in order to better interpret delinquent behavior, is written by three persons with very different academic backgrounds.

Arnie Binder was trained at Stanford University in engineering and received his doctorate there in mathematical psychology. For many years since, he has been specializing in studies of delinquency. In addition, he inaugurated and operated the Youth Studies Project in southern California, an intervention project so successful that its current director received a presidential award for outstanding contributions to human welfare.

The second author, Gilbert Geis, was trained in sociology at the University of Wisconsin, and has carried out research on delinquency and cognate matters for almost half a century. He is a former president of the American Society of Criminology and has received its Edwin H. Sutherland award for distinguished research.

Dickson Bruce, a professional historian, brings to this book a background that provides a deeper understanding of the development of the concepts of delinquency and juvenile justice. This reminds us that understanding aspects of the way we have dealt with delinquent behavior over time is essential to an adequate understanding of current conditions and arrangements.

It was Bruce who alerted us to the fact that in the field of history there has been a decided trend to produce textbooks that do not, almost reflexively, acknowledge by name those who have produced the knowledge that marks the discipline. Historians have decided that while the names and sources are essential to those at work in the discipline, frequent reference to sources often are distracting to students who (understandably) have little need of or interest in knowing who contributed this or that insight (although, of course, they should be aware of major figures and the names of those who are connected to particularly important ideas).

So that students can focus on ideas, we have sought to reduce the number of citations and similar references that proliferate in most textbooks. We nonetheless still probably have too much scholarly paraphernalia, perhaps out of habit. We have been warned that our tactic might turn off professors who (like us) are pleased to find their authorship acknowledged when an element of their work is presented, but we decided that textbooks must be written to convey as clearly as possible what students ought to learn about the subject.

There are a number of persons whose assistance was crucial to our work. As she has with earlier editions, Carol Wyatt proved to be a superb coordinator of our materials. She has come to be able to interpret our awful handwriting, to pick up on things that might not be as clear as we had hoped, and to perform the critical word processing tasks associated with revising the text.

We also owe thanks to Judy Omiya, long a sustaining force in our writing lives, and to her assistant, Marilyn Wahlert. Gratitude also is due to Helena Rene for tracking library materials and to Steve Reynard, Julia Gelfand, and Corina Oliver.

Table of Contents

1

Defining Juvenile Delinquency and Determining Its Extent

Every culture has a broad set of regulations and expectations that define proper behavior for children. These regulations and expectations take such forms as codes, laws, and rules, and are conveyed to children either explicitly or by implication, as when they are told that certain behavior is "good" and other behavior is "bad." Supplementing the broad set of regulations and expectations of the general culture are the regulations and expectations of its various subcultures. Thus, in the United States, there are general laws regarding school attendance and working conditions for children. But each school district and each school in a given district has regulations that apply to children within its domain. The pattern extends down to one of the smallest subunits in our culture, the family, in which there may be rules such as that one does not stay out past a certain hour without parental consent or that one does not hit a brother or sister.

The layers of regulations and expectations have evolved in their respective domains to serve many purposes. Some are aimed at preventing a child from directly hurting himself or herself, or someone else; others are aimed at preventing damage to or loss of property; others are oriented toward inculcating habits and patterns of behavior that prepare a child for a style of life in the mode of those in authority; others attempt to make the child-rearing process as minimally disruptive to the social or family system as possible; and still others are aimed at controlling or inhibiting behavior that people in authority find annoying or personally offensive.

1

Associated with many of the regulations and expectations are sanctions or consequences that will, or may, result if behavior deviates significantly from prescribed paths. To illustrate at the family level, a boy may be deprived of his weekly allowance if he strikes his sister, or a girl may be sent to her room if she uses an obscenity at the dinner table. At another cultural level, an adolescent may be suspended from school if he or she has deliberately smashed a window or insulted a teacher.

At the general cultural level, we have developed complex systems to deal with the large array of children who show significant behavioral aberrations. Two prominent systems are the mental health system and the juvenile justice system. Generally speaking, the mental health system handles youngsters who show such disturbances as excessive anxiety or perhaps a fear of riding in a car—disturbances that are assumed to result from "illness of the mind." The juvenile justice system primarily handles youngsters who violate laws designed to protect the personal and property rights of others and the youngsters themselves from abuse and from misdirected behavior. A child who assaults another person or who steals is, thus, a candidate for the juvenile justice system—at least initially.

That there may be ambiguity as to which system is appropriate in a given instance is illustrated in the following news item:

> A 15-year-old boy who was determined to be rid of his braces pulled a gun on an orthodontist and told him to remove them, the doctor said Friday.
>
> Police said the youth entered a dentist's office in Grosse Pointe Woods armed with a .45-caliber automatic pistol and asked to see a dentist to have his braces removed. The dentist refused because the boy did not have proof of parental permission, so the boy cocked the pistol and aimed it at the doctor, who immediately took the boy to a dental chair while a nurse called police.
>
> When the police arrived, one officer spoke to the boy, and when he turned to look, the other officers rushed him. In the ensuing scuffle, the boy allegedly fired one shot that hit the floor, then grabbed an officer's pistol, causing another shot to be fired into the floor.
>
> Jack Patterson, Grosse Pointe Woods director of public safety, said the boy spent a few hours at a psychiatric center after the February 8 incident.[1]

There were no further media reports about this episode, so we do not know whether the boy was found to be without need for further mental health care or whether he continued to receive treatment. It is obvious that the boy might have been dealt with as a juvenile delinquent who had committed a serious offense, especially if the dentist had so insisted. It should also be noted that the boy is not identified in the newspaper story, whereas an adult involved in a similar incident probably would have been.

In the United States, a book devoted to the topic of juvenile delinquency is generally considered to encompass youngsters who show behavioral patterning that could activate the juvenile justice system.[2] Behaviors such as assault and stealing are included, of course, but various other behaviors and conditions also may trigger intervention by the system. For example, children who are truant, who run away from home, or who disobey their parents are candidates for intervention by the juvenile justice system as a result of the historical development of the system. Such children are almost always considered to be in a designated category that differs from the one used for criminal-type offenders, though they are equivalently subject to justice system intervention. Children who are below a certain age (e.g., age 10) are sometimes included in this category even when they commit criminal offenses.

Because the two types of behavior (criminal-type behavior and behavior defined as unacceptable when shown by a child) differ substantially on practical and theoretical grounds, they will be treated separately in the analyses of this chapter. That substantial difference has led many people and advocacy groups to recommend that only criminal-type behavior should be in the domain of the juvenile justice system; truancy, running away from home, disobedience, and other such behavior (as well as conditions of dependency), they argue, should be dealt with by mental health professionals.

CRIMINAL-TYPE BEHAVIOR

Defining "Juvenile Delinquent"

The Oxford dictionary defines a juvenile delinquent as "a person below the legal age of [criminal] responsibility and above a certain minimum age, who is held punishable for breaking the law."[3] The age of criminal responsibility, meaning the youngest age at which a person can be tried in a criminal court, has been moving downward in recent years in the states, especially in cases of serious criminal offenses. For such youngsters, the initial hearing for an alleged offense usually occurs in a juvenile court, but that court (as we shall see), may waive its jurisdiction under certain conditions and order transfer to a criminal court for trial. The phrasing "above a certain minimum age" in the foregoing definition means that children below a certain age, perhaps 8 or 10 or 12, may not be considered juvenile delinquents.

There are laws in the statute books of each state that specify when and how a juvenile court in that state may intervene in the life of a youth. The set of such laws is commonly referred to as juvenile court law. One of the components in the juvenile court law of many (but certainly not all) states is a definition of an expression such as "juvenile delinquent," "delinquent youth," or "delinquent child." In general, the definition will be in some such form as: "a juvenile delinquent is a youth in a certain age range who has committed an offense which, if committed by an adult, would be a crime." That form makes it clear that when an adult would be labeled as a criminal offender for a certain act, a youth committing the same act would be labeled as a juvenile delinquent, delinquent youth, or some other term that contains no direct reference to criminality.

As indicated in the preceding section, however, the jurisdiction of the juvenile court extends beyond youths who have committed criminal-type offenses. The jurisdiction includes youths who are considered in need of help on the basis of such unacceptable behavior as truancy or because of an absence of parental care. The broad inclusion of these types of youths is based on the founding principle of juvenile court law: *parens patriae*, which envisions the state as a protective parent with a goal of caring for and correcting wayward and unprotected children of all sorts (see Chapter 8).

The following juvenile codes define juvenile delinquency and differentiate delinquents from other youths subject to juvenile court jurisdiction. The first is from Minnesota:[4]

> Subd. 2a Child in need of protection or services. "Child in need of protection or services" means a child who is in need of protection or services because the child:
>
> (1)   is abandoned or without parent, guardian, or custodian;
>   . . .
>
> (3)   is without necessary food, shelter, education, or other required care for the child's physical or mental health or morals because the child's parent, guardian, or custodian is unable or unwilling to provide that care; . . .
>
> (12)   has committed a delinquent act or a juvenile petty offense before becoming ten years old;
>
> (13)   is a runaway;
>
> (14)   is an habitual truant . . .
>
> Subd. 5 Delinquent child (a) Except as otherwise provided in paragraph (b) [specifying that a child of 16 or older who commits first degree murder may not be considered a delinquent child], "delinquent child" means a child:

(1) who has violated any state or local law [except for traffic offenses and those defining a "child in need of protection or services"].

(2) who has violated a federal law or a law of another state and whose case has been referred to the juvenile court if the violation would be an act of delinquency if committed in this state or a crime or offense if committed by an adult.[4]

The second illustrative juvenile code is from Pennsylvania. It presents that state's definition of a juvenile delinquent, with clear differentiation from what is referred to as a "dependent child," but also illustrates the recent tendency (as mentioned above) to move serious young offenders from juvenile hearings to criminal trials.[5]

"DEPENDENT CHILD." A child who:

(1) is without proper parental care or control, subsistence, education as required by law, or other care or control necessary for his physical, mental, or emotional health, or morals; . . .

(4) is without a parent, guardian, or legal custodian;

(5) while subject to compulsory school attendance is habitually and without justification truant from school;

(6) has committed a specific act or acts of habitual disobedience of the reasonable and lawful commands of his parent, guardian or other custodian and who is ungovernable and found to be in need of care, treatment or supervision;

(7) is under the age of ten years and has committed a delinquent act.

"DELINQUENT CHILD." A child ten years of age or older whom the court has found to have committed a delinquent act and is in need of treatment, supervision or rehabilitation.[5]

A "delinquent act" in that code of 1999 is not just any act that would be considered a crime if carried out by an adult; there are exclusions. In earlier years, the only crime so excluded was murder but now such serious crimes as the following are not considered delinquent acts for youths who were 15 or older at the time of the alleged conduct: rape, kidnapping, aggravated assault, and voluntary manslaughter. Currently, Pennsylvania requires prosecution under criminal law and procedures for the older youths accused of those serious crimes (as well as murder); they are no longer assigned to the jurisdiction of the juvenile court.[6]

Suppose, now, that two boys commit identical criminal acts, but only one of them is arrested and later adjudicated a delinquent (that is, found to be a delinquent by a juvenile court) under the relevant state statute, and perhaps sent to an institution. One might feel fully justified in calling that boy a juvenile delinquent, but what about the boy who was never arrested? He committed a criminal act identical to that of the adjudicated boy and may not have been taken into custody for entirely fortuitous reasons—perhaps for no reason other than that there was an absence of witnesses or a busy caseload kept the police from a thorough investigation in his case.

Are detection, arrest, and adjudication necessary criteria for specifying that a given youth is a "delinquent" for research and general discussion purposes? If that were the case, only a very small proportion of youngsters who commit criminal offenses would be considered juvenile delinquents. While that is indeed the case in state codes, as the definition for Pennsylvania illustrates, legal and scholarly needs differ.

This issue was faced by Wolfgang, Figlio, and Sellin in their longitudinal study of boys born in 1945 who lived in the city of Philadelphia from their tenth to their eighteenth birthdays.[7] The goals of the investigation were to determine the age when delinquency started, its progression or cessation, and the relationship of the delinquent behavior to various personal and social characteristics of the delinquents. The comparison of the characteristics of delinquents with boys who never behaved in a delinquent manner was also important for the study. To accomplish those ends, it was necessary to identify the delinquents so that they could be studied and compared with the remaining group of nondelinquents. The investigators considered specifying as delinquents those youngsters who had been adjudicated (found "guilty") by a court but rejected that approach because they

> would have had to ignore police data except when they applied to boys whose involvement in delinquent events was subsequently affirmed by a court decision, which in nearly all cases would have been handed down by a judge of the juvenile court. Another consequence of using such official judicial decisions for defining the delinquents in the cohort would necessarily have been the inclusion of all other boys, with no matter how many police contacts, among our nondelinquents.[8]

Accordingly, they decided to identify delinquents on the basis of police contact. Using police records, they argued, "we are closer in time to the offender's specific conduct and are not disturbed by the series of often unpredictable administrative decisions which intervene between the discovery of any given offender and his ultimate disposition by a court."[9] The investigators were well aware that a vast array of juvenile offenses never come to the attention of the police and that arrests (and official records) do not follow in many of the cases that do come to their attention. They took the following position on that point:

> When one relies on police data for a study of delinquency, one realizes, therefore, that the delinquencies charged to boys apprehended by the police represent only the visible illegal conduct, that the total record of their delinquencies during their juvenile years contains only their officially recorded misbehaviors, and that an unknown number of illegal acts which they may have committed have escaped official notice. At present, we have no satisfactory way of estimating this number with confidence. Our research is based, then, on the officially recorded delinquencies of the cohort. We have been compelled to adopt this policy, fully conscious of the fact that its effect on the findings of our research is not calculable. We do know that there are differences in the willingness of victims to bring an offender to public notice, depending on the social class of the offender, the degree of tolerance toward delinquent conduct in different areas and social groups in a community and toward different kinds of delinquency, the relative strength of the victim's belief in the ability or desire of the police to find the offender, and so forth. If, for instance, a delinquent's family indemnifies the victim for his loss of property and as a result the offense is not reported, a juvenile from a wealthy family would not have as full an official record of delinquency as one from a poor family, who lacks this means of covering up his misconduct. On the other hand, if poor people have less confidence in the police than have the middle and upper classes, they will fail to report offenses that would be reported by the well-to-do. We can only point to the existence of differential reporting of delinquency and admit that we cannot estimate its effect on our research.[10]

There is, then, a dictionary definition of the expression "juvenile delinquent" and a specification of its meaning (or that of a closely related form) in most state laws. Those definitions provide a broad conceptualization but are of limited value when it is necessary for research or other purposes to specify whether an individual is—or a group of individuals are—delinquent. For a purpose of that sort, one must appreciate the sequence of criminal offenses, possible reporting of the offense to police, possible arrest, possible referral to court, possible adjudication, and possible placement in an institution, and then decide on the definitional point in the set of transitions in a manner responsive to the purpose. That means that individuals designated as delinquent for one purpose may not be delinquent for another one.

Methods of Measuring Delinquent Behavior

Official Data

The expression "official data" refers to information that has come to the attention of officials of the justice system, which has been properly recorded. The primary national source for summaries of such data is a publication called the Uniform Crime Reports (UCR), which is assembled on an annual basis by the Federal Bureau of Investigation. Data in the UCR include numbers of offenses known to the police, numbers of offenses cleared by arrest, and characteristics of arrested people. Other major sources of crime data are the reports of state bureaus or divisions of criminal statistics. Beyond those major sources of official data, records are maintained by such public entities as county governments, city governments, police departments, probation departments, and courts. A prime illustration of the use of this type of source is the research of Wolfgang, Figlio, and Sellin, which was discussed earlier in the chapter. These investigators used the records of the Philadelphia Police Department to determine which youngsters in their pool had official contacts with the police (and were, accordingly, designated delinquent).

The existence of official records depends on the process whereby some person reports an event to an official who enters it on an appropriate form or in a computer memory. Clearly, there is no entry in official records when a police officer disregards a violation on the part of a minor, or when a youngster steals candy from a supermarket and the loss is never discovered, or when a woman is raped and does not report the incident.

Self-Report Data

The method of self-report is an attempt to obtain information about offenses that may never make official records. The self-report was introduced in 1957 as a systematic approach to measuring delinquency. In the self-report method, youngsters of the general population are questioned about offenses they may have previously committed. Questioning is in oral or written form and usually occurs in a school setting.

The self-report approach was widely used in the years following 1957 and became firmly established for measuring and evaluating delinquency. It is important to note, however, that the approach depends upon two characteristics of the youngsters reporting that may or may not actually exist: (1) good memory, and (2) honesty in responding to the items. One might reasonably expect some reluctance on the part of people to report their involvement in offenses, particularly if those offenses are serious crimes.

Victim Data

Another method of measuring crime is worthy of mention, although its implications for assessing delinquency are limited. The method consists of determining the characteristics of crimes from the victims of those crimes. A high level of sophistication in the overall approach has been achieved in the National Crime Victimization Survey (NCVS), sponsored by the Bureau of Justice Statistics and conducted by the U.S. Census Bureau since the program started in 1973. In the survey, randomly selected people are asked if they have recently been victims of crime and, if they answer affirmatively, they are asked questions about various characteristics of themselves, the crimes, and the offenders, including the perceived ages of the offenders. In the 1995 survey, for example, about 90,000 people (above age 11), living in 47,750 housing units, were interviewed.

As in the case of the self-report approach, success with this method depends upon both accurate memory and a willingness to respond honestly.

Measurement Complications

As one might expect, the picture one gets of delinquency and its distribution is a function of the measurement method used. To illustrate, if official data such as those in the UCR are used in the evaluation of delinquency, one is likely to infer that criminal behavior is concentrated among young males of low socioeconomic status living in cities and that there is particularly heavy concentration among African-Americans. On the other hand, the use of self-report data is associated with the inference that criminal offending is so widespread throughout the population that it is artificial to associate it primarily with certain socioeconomic, racial, or ethnic groups living in urban areas.

It is important to note that a given theory is often a direct function of the data source used, accepted, selected, or preferred by the theorizer. For example, Shaw and McKay (see Chapter 6) used police, court, and correctional records in a study of delinquency in Chicago over the period 1900-1940. Their resulting theory is that the path toward juvenile delinquency starts with urban deterioration and proceeds as follows: Urban deterioration produces socially disorganized communities that lack control over children; the lack of social control encourages the formation of street gangs, which in turn develop and transmit delinquent behavioral patterns. Minority-group involvement is high, not for any biological or genetic reason but because minority-group members tend to be poor and live in inner (deteriorating) cities.

In contrast, Hirschi (see Chapter 7) depended very heavily on self-report data in the formulation of his theory, a theory based on universal human characteristics rather than such factors as socioeconomic status, race, and area of residence. According to Hirschi, the tendency toward delinquent behavior is a component of human nature and is held in check by various processes of social control. Thus, given delinquent behavior, one infers that there is a problem in such sources of control as emotional attachment to parents; involvement in school; and commitment to the values enunciated by parents, schools, and other social institutions.

Official Statistics—Uniform Crime Reports

Sources and Types of Data

The UCR depends on the monthly reporting of law enforcement agencies throughout the country. The information goes to the FBI either directly from a reporting agency or through an intermediary at the state level. Many of the state-level programs have reporting requirements that exceed those of the FBI in scope of data collected.

The UCR's primary emphasis is on crimes that compose the Crime Index. These are murder and nonnegligent manslaughter, forcible rape, robbery, aggravated assault, burglary, larceny-theft, motor vehicle theft, and arson. There are two components to Index crime listings: violent crime (murder and nonnegligent manslaughter, forcible rape, robbery, aggravated assault) and property crime (burglary, larceny-theft, motor vehicle theft, arson).

The number of "actual offenses known" (from sources that are primarily citizen reports and observations by officers) are crimes reported, whether or not arrests or prosecutions follow the knowledge, but excluding those in which the police find the complaint unfounded or false. A central part of the monthly submission is the number of Index offenses cleared by arrest for adults and for youths below the age of 18.

In addition, the UCR program collects data on persons arrested for various offenses—those in the Crime Index as well as less serious offenses. These data are reported in terms of the age, sex, and race of arrestees.

Results by Sex and Age

In 1997, of 576,848 Index arrests reported for youths under the age of 18, 74.0 percent (427,036) were males. That produces a male-to-female ratio of 2.8 to 1. The ratio is even more lopsided if one looks only at violent crimes; it is 5.3 to 1 (on a percentage basis, 84.1% of arrestees for violent crimes were males).

According to the UCR for 1997, 30.2 percent of all people arrested for Index crimes were minors below the age of 18. However, estimates based on census figures indicated that the percentage of people in the United States in the age range 10 to 17 was 11 percent. In other words, about 30 percent of all arrests for the most serious crimes were youths who accounted for only about 11 percent of the population.

It is abundantly clear, then, that youths are arrested for serious crimes far out of proportion to their percentage in the population (by almost a 3 to 1 ratio) and that boys are arrested for those crimes at an overwhelmingly higher rate than are girls. As noted above, 74 percent of the arrests of youths for serious crimes are boys and 84.1 percent of the arrests of youths for violent serious crimes are boys.

Results by Race

In 1997, 67.5 percent of arrestees under the age of 18 for Index crimes were whites and 29.2 percent were blacks (the remainder were Native Americans, Asian-Americans, or Pacific Islanders). In the case of violent crimes, the percentages were 53.4 for whites and 44.2 for blacks. To appreciate the large percentage of blacks in those figures, consider that estimated population figures indicated that about 75

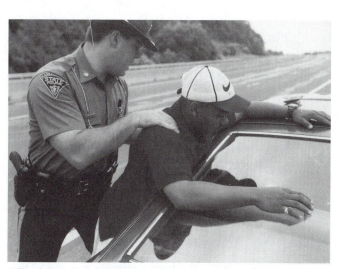

Official data show that black youths are arrested at a considerably higher rate than white youths, although self-report studies indicate little difference between the groups in law-violating behavior. *(Photo by Mark C. Ide)*

percent of youths under 18 were whites and about 15 percent were blacks.

Results by Population Concentration

Tables in the UCR make it apparent that the rate of arrests for serious crime increases as the population becomes more dense. To illustrate at the extremities, the arrest rate for Index crimes in cities was 1,229 per

100,000 inhabitants, while the comparable arrest rates were 684 for suburban counties and 531 for rural counties. Thus, the ratio of arrest rates in cities to those in suburban counties is 1.8 to 1, and the ratio of rates for cities versus rural counties is 2.3 to 1.

The Broad Picture

In summary, according to official recordings of arrests for Index crimes, younger males, particularly if they are black, contribute to the numbers far beyond what is expected on the basis of their numbers in the population. Furthermore, arrests are predominantly phenomena of the cities, particularly the large cities.

Although the UCR was used to establish those results, the conclusions would be essentially the same no matter what the source of arrest data. It is hardly surprising, then, that theorists who have relied primarily on official data have developed theories that have explanatory constructs based on the struggles of inner-city boys, such as gang theories, theories based on deterioration of neighborhoods, and theories derived from organizational patterns of lower-class, urban cultures.

Self-Report Data—The Seattle Youth Study

Principal Features of the Study

The report of the Seattle Youth Study by Hindelang, Hirschi, and Weis was based on data collected in the city of Seattle during the academic year 1978-1979. Their self-report instrument consisted of 69 items grouped into five categories for purposes of analysis: official contacts with the juvenile justice system, serious crimes, general delinquency, drug offenses, and school and family offenses. The full list of items may be seen in Table 1.1. The table also contains the percentage of respondents who indicated that they had, at one time or other, behaved in the designated fashion for each item (as, for example, 35.2 percent of white males and 10.9 percent of black females answered "yes" to the question, "Have you ever been questioned as a subject by the police about some crime?").

The sample of participants was obtained from three distinct populations: (1) students enrolled in Seattle public schools who had never been arrested or referred to the juvenile court, (2) youths with a record of Seattle police contact, and (3) youths who had been referred to the Seattle juvenile court. A stratified sampling approach was used within each of the populations to assure that there was appropriate representation by race, sex, and socioeconomic status (SES).

Table 1.1
Percent Responding "Yes" to Question "Have You Ever . . .?" on Seattle Survey Instrument

	White Males	Black Males	White Females	Black Females
Official Contact Index				
1. Been questioned as a suspect by the police about some crime	35.2	38.6	11.4	10.9
2. Been held by the police or court until you could be released into the custody of your parents or guardians	16.8	21.2	5.4	9.8
3. Been placed on probation by a juvenile court judge	8.7	18.8	2.1	9.3
4. Been caught shoplifting by the clerk or owner of a store	32.8	29.3	23.8	23.8
5. Been sentenced to a reformatory, training school, or some other institution by a judge	2.4	2.3	0.3	1.0
Serious Crime Index				
6. Sold something you had stolen yourself	18.4	19.5	3.6	3.0
7. Broken into a house, store, school, or other building and taken money, stereo equipment, guns, or something else you wanted	16.8	12.9	4.9	4.3
8. Broken into a locked car to get something from it	16.5	11.6	1.7	0.9
9. Taken hubcaps, wheels, the battery, or some other expensive part of a car without the owner's permission	16.3	12.4	1.0	0.0
10. Taken gasoline from a car without the owner's permission	14.4	8.0	3.0	0.0
11. Taken things worth between $10 and $50 from a store without paying for them	13.5	14.2	14.2	15.2
12. Threatened to beat someone up if they didn't give you money or something else you wanted	12.8	17.8	4.0	10.0
13. Carried a razor, switchblade, or gun with the intention of using it in a fight	12.7	17.5	1.1	11.6
14. Pulled a knife, gun, or some other weapon on someone just to let them know you meant business	12.6	17.1	3.1	9.5
15. Beat someone up so badly they probably needed a doctor	10.2	15.4	3.1	8.9
16. Taken a car belonging to someone you didn't know for a ride without the owner's permission	9.7	7.3	0.8	1.7
17. Taken a tape deck or a CB radio from a car	9.0	6.7	0.1	0.6
18. Broken into a house, store, school, or other building with the intention of breaking things up or causing other damage	7.3	3.6	2.1	3.4
19. Taken things of large value (worth more than $50) from a store without paying for them	5.2	5.6	1.4	3.7
20. Tried to get away from a police officer by fighting or struggling	4.9	4.5	0.6	0.4
21. Used physical force (like twisting an arm or choking) to get money from another person	4.1	7.9	0.7	5.3
22. Used a club, knife, or gun to get something from someone	3.7	7.1	1.0	3.0
23. Taken things from a wallet or purse (or the whole wallet or purse) while the owner wasn't around or wasn't looking	17.4	19.4	11.9	17.3
24. Hit a teacher or some other school official	11.6	17.1	3.2	12.6
25. Taken a bicycle belonging to someone you didn't know with no intention of returning it	11.0	16.0	1.8	0.7
26. Tried to pass a check by signing someone else's name	3.0	3.9	1.8	0.6
27. Intentionally started a building on fire	2.4	2.4	0.0	1.7
28. Grabbed a purse from someone and run with it	0.5	1.9	0.0	1.0
29. Forced another person to have sex relations with you when they did not want to	0.5	1.0	1.0	0.0
Delinquency Index				
30. Taken little things (worth less than $2) from a store without paying for them	62.8	52.4	55.8	37.2
31. Broken the windows of an empty house or other unoccupied building	48.6	58.0	11.0	16.6
32. Let the air out of car or truck tires	40.7	35.1	12.8	7.5
33. Used a slug or fake money in a candy, coke, coin, or stamp machine	39.7	35.7	12.8	9.8
34. Fired a BB gun at some other person, at passing cars, or at windows of buildings	34.9	39.7	7.0	7.3
35. Taken things you weren't supposed to take from a desk or locker at school	31.6	40.0	15.0	24.4
36. Bought something you knew had been stolen	31.1	35.2	5.1	14.7
37. Broken the windows of a school building	29.0	30.0	10.0	9.2
38. Taken material or equipment from a construction site	26.0	11.9	4.6	6.1
39. Refused to tell police or some other official what you knew about a crime	22.5	30.8	10.7	15.2
40. Purposely broken a car window	16.4	17.8	2.8	4.3
41. Picked a fight with someone you didn't know just for the hell of it	15.2	15.4	4.1	11.6
42. Helped break up chairs, tables, desks, or other furniture in a school, church, or other public building	10.6	6.5	1.7	0.6

Table 1.1—*continued*

	White Males	Black Males	White Females	Black Females
43. Jumped or helped jump somebody and then beat them up	8.9	23.4	2.1	18.4
44. Slashed the seats in a bus, a movie house, or some other place	8.5	11.3	1.8	5.2
45. Punctured or slashed the tires of a car	7.9	6.8	0.4	1.3
46. Destroyed things at a construction site	13.0	8.4	1.8	1.7
47. Destroyed mailboxes	12.3	1.9	0.9	0.0
48. Kept money for yourself that you collected for a team, a charity (like the March of Dimes), or someone else's paper route	11.6	11.8	15.2	13.1
49. Driven away from the scene of an accident that you were involved in without identifying yourself	10.8	7.6	6.2	1.3
50. Taken mail from someone else's mailbox and opened it	10.1	10.1	5.1	3.6
51. Broken into a parking meter or the coin box of a pay phone	3.6	5.4	0.2	2.0
Drug Index				
52. Drunk beer or wine	93.1	85.0	93.0	73.7
53. Drunk whiskey, gin, vodka, or other "hard" liquor	79.4	61.1	80.4	62.2
54. Smoked marijuana (grass, pot)	75.3	70.9	71.6	74.6
55. Gone to school when you were drunk or high on some drugs	54.2	46.6	43.2	34.6
56. Pretended to be older than you were to buy beer and cigarettes	42.9	37.6	38.9	22.5
57. Sold illegal drugs such as heroin, marijuana, LSD, or cocaine	41.5	31.3	13.2	15.5
58. Driven a car when you were drunk or high on some drugs	36.6	29.6	27.2	13.6
59. Taken barbiturates (downers) or methedrine (speed or other uppers) without a prescription	22.4	8.0	21.9	9.9
60. Used cocaine	21.6	18.8	15.7	12.1
61. Taken angel dust, LSD, or mescaline	16.9	9.6	14.7	7.0
62. Used heroin (smack)	0.8	0.6	0.8	1.0
School and Family Offenses Index				
63. Been sent out of a classroom	73.2	71.1	39.3	57.4
64. Stayed away from school when your parents thought you were there	60.0	60.2	59.3	55.4
65. Gone out at night when your parents told you that you couldn't go	51.2	39.6	32.1	22.5
66. Been suspended or expelled from school	38.0	64.6	15.0	51.3
67. Cursed or threatened an adult in a loud and mean way just to let them know who was boss	34.7	33.7	23.1	19.6
68. Run away from home and stayed overnight	16.5	13.6	16.0	19.8
69. Hit one of your parents	13.4	4.4	10.9	9.6

Source: Hindelang, Michael J., Travis Hirschi, and Joseph G. Weis, *Measuring Delinquency*, pp. 223-226. Copyright © 1981 Sage Publications. Reprinted by permission of Sage Publications, Inc.

In order to test for the effects of mode of administration, the instrument was given in four ways: anonymous questionnaire, nonanonymous questionnaire, anonymous interview, and nonanonymous interview. The various ways permitted the determination of whether youths were more honest in answering the items when they were not identified, as well as the relative efficacy of oral and paper-and-pencil approaches to the questioning.

Interestingly, data from the study indicate that results of self-report approaches are independent of manner of administration—questionnaire or interview—and of whether the process is or is not anonymous. According to the investigators, all methods of administration produced equally high reliability and validity measures. Other studies in the United States and abroad have produced confirming results. In the words of a participant in a series of very recent studies, "self-report instruments are surprisingly robust."[11]

The Extent of Violating

Earlier research using the self-report method had established that juvenile law violation is more widespread than official data or general observation would lead one to expect. In one pioneering work using self-reports, for example, Short and Nye reported that delinquent behavior was "extensive" among the high school students studied. In the report of a subsequent study, one that compared delinquent and "nondelinquent" (in the sense of never having been caught) boys, Erickson and Empey stated, "The number of violations which respondents admitted having committed was tremendous."[12] To illustrate, in that study, 92 percent of the nondelinquents admitted minor thefts; 66 percent, "destroying property"; and 32 percent, "breaking and entering." Still more recently, on the basis of overall figures derived from interviews with a probability sample of boys and girls in the age range 13 to 16, Williams and Gold state, "Eighty-eight percent of the teenagers in the sample confessed to committing at least one chargeable offense in the three years prior to their interview." They add, interestingly, "It is clear that, if the authorities were omniscient and technically zealous, a large majority of American 13- to 16-year olds would be labeled juvenile delinquents."[13] Actually, less than 3 percent of the reported offenses were detected by the police, and only 9 percent of the youths had any contact with the police in the three years preceding the survey. Note that Table 1.1 has several entries in the range of 45 percent to 65 percent for general offenses and 75 percent to 95 percent for drug abuse.

Results showing similar patterns of offending have been obtained in many other and more recent studies. Particularly noteworthy among them is the International Self-Report Delinquency Study in which a self-report instrument was translated from English into eight other languages and administered to adolescents in 13 western countries. As in the United States, the results indicated a picture of high offense rates. For example, 81.1 percent of the youths in Spain and 90.3 percent in Switzerland admitted to delinquent behavior during their lives. That was interpreted to mean that "some delinquent or deviant behavior forms part of the growing-up process of western children."[14]

Results by Sex and Race

As the previous discussion in this chapter shows, there are substantial differences in arrest rates across years of age and between the sexes. Significant age and sex differentials have also been widely reported with self-report data, but the sizes of the differences are much smaller than with official data.

The Seattle data were analyzed in terms of sex differences, but not on the basis of age. The investigators used the ratio of proportion of males admitting the offense to proportion of females admitting the offense—called a sex ratio—to gauge sex differences. To illustrate, if .75 of the males admitted to a certain offense, as did .25 of the females, the sex ratio would be .75:.25 or 3.00. Similarly, if .45 of the males and .45 of the females admitted to an offense, the ratio would be .45:.45 = 1.00. The obtained sex ratios varied widely over the 69 self-report items. Table 1.2 shows several of the items with high sex ratios and several with low ratios.

Table 1.2
Offenses with High Sex Ratios and Offenses with Low Sex Ratios Controlling for Race

Offense	Total Population	White	Black
Taken hubcaps, wheels, the battery, or some other expensive part of a car without the owner's permission	18.80	1.55	12.42*
Destroyed mailboxes	10.01*	12.30*	1.89*
Broken into a locked car to get something from it	9.97	9.55	11.65*
Taken a car belonging to someone you didn't know for a ride without the owner's permission	9.10	9.71*	4.36
Taken a tape deck or CB radio from a car	8.48	8.98*	6.70*
Taken a bicycle belonging to someone you didn't know with no intention of returning it	7.92	6.23	16.01*
Destroyed things at a construction site	6.79	7.25	4.98
Drunk beer or wine	1.03	1.00	1.15
Stayed away from school when your parents thought you were there	1.03	1.01	1.09
Taken barbiturates (downers) or methedrine (speed or uppers) without a prescription	1.00	1.02	.81
Drunk whiskey, gin, vodka, or other "hard" liquor	.99	.99	.98
Run away from home and stayed overnight	.94	1.03	.69
Taken things worth between $10 and $50 from a store without paying for them	.94	.95	.93
Kept money for yourself that you collected for a team, a charity (like the March of Dimes), or someone else's paper route	.79	.76	.90

*Female percent less than 1, male percent shown.
Source: Hindelang, Michael J., Travis Hirschi, and Joseph G. Weis, *Measuring Delinquency*, p. 226. Copyright © 1981 Sage Publications. Reprinted by permission of Sage Publications, Inc.

It is clear that boys heavily predominate over girls in the more serious and destructive offenses, while there is little difference in lesser offenses, such as the use of certain types of drugs and in minor shoplifting. Girls clearly predominate in keeping collections for charities and other uses for themselves.

It was seen above that official data like those in the UCR show considerable racial differences. Early self-report studies, on the other hand, found very little difference between black youths and white youths in the prevalence of law-violating behavior. The investigators in Seattle constructed a table showing the black-to-white crime ratios from a number of studies based on official data. Using that table, they comment:

> As is evident, in all comparisons available, the black rate of delinquency is equal to or greater than the white rate. Although there is considerable variation in ratios, apparently depending on the sample and on seriousness of offense or extent of official processing, there can be no doubt that marked differences in rates are to be expected in official data, with ratios in the 2-4 range common among boys and no ratio smaller than 3 in samples restricted to girls.
>
> In sharp contrast to these findings are black-to-white ratios in published studies based on self-reported delinquency. . . . The range of ratios in self-report samples restricted to a single sex (males, .8 to 1.3; females, .9 to 1.7) does not overlap with the range of ratios found in official data similarly restricted to single-sex groups. . . . The very strong relation between race and delinquency in official data is not present in these self-report data. In fact, the self-report relation would have to be characterized as weak or very weak, with a mean 1.1:1 expected on the basis of previous research.[15]

The investigators then reported the black-to-white ratio from each of the 69 items in the Seattle survey (in the manner shown in Table 1.2 for sex ratios). There was not much difference in the percentages of whites and blacks admitting offenses, leading the investigators to state:

> Consistent with virtually all previous research, the overall impression from [the table showing black-to-white ratios for the 69 items] is that blacks are only slightly more delinquent than whites, somewhat more so among females than among males. Overall, the black-to-white ratio in the Seattle data does not exceed the ratio of 1.1: 1 mentioned earlier as the best guess of the ratio.[16]

Moreover, conjecturing that the "abundance of trivial items" may have depressed the "relationship between race and self-report delinquency" the investigators computed ratios for a group of 17 serious items. The resulting ratios remained small: total sample, 1.16; male, 1.08; female, 1.37.

Given that official data show that black youths are arrested at a considerably higher rate than white youths, while self-report studies indicate little difference in law-violating behavior, one can appreciate the following comment, made in 1970:

The Racial Context of Arrest. Considerable evidence suggests that the police have long had differential arrest policies in regard to race. It is apparent that police have tended to arrest Negroes on slight evidence in comparison to the amount of evidence required to arrest whites. Furthermore, Negroes have been exposed more than others to the misuses of police power. Selective enforcement according to racial factors results in part from long-held prejudices of individual policemen. But also important is the fact that the Negro tends to fit the stereotype that police have of the criminal. Through the use of certain cues, a probabilistic model of law violation, and their past experiences, the police are more likely to arrest the Negro than the white man in a similar offense situation.[17]

Despite that argument, there remains some uncertainty in the matter, stemming from an observation of the Seattle investigators who had access to the official records of the Seattle Police Department and the local juvenile court. They compared self-report and official records and found a "strong tendency of black male official delinquents to underreport substantially the offenses in the official records."[18] They illustrate the process as follows:

For example, the Seattle police or court records list four offenses in the vehicle theft category: auto theft, take motor vehicle without permission, take and ride or joyride, and ride in a stolen vehicle. Respondents were classified as reporting such an offense if they responded positively to the item "have you ever taken a car belonging to someone you didn't know for a ride without the owner's permission?". . . 19 percent of the white males with an official record of this type did not respond positively to the self-report auto theft item; among similarly situated black males the rate of nonreporting was 57 percent. For serious offenses as a whole (burglary, robbery, vehicle theft, person offense, and weapons offense), the white [male] nonreporting rate was 20 percent compared to the rate of 57 percent among black [males].[19]

On the basis of that type of evidence, despite their negative findings using the ratios, they conclude that "there are true black/white differences in offending behavior" as indicated by official measures.[20] That position has been supported in the results of more recent research, which indicate that while whites and blacks may not differ in having committed offenses at some time in their lives, they do differ in the frequency of those offenses and their seriousness, with blacks in the more frequent and more serious position. That provides another explanation for the differential arrest rates: youths who commit offenses more frequently and of a more serious nature are of course more likely to get arrested.

It is important at this point to define two relevant terms that are widely used in the literature: *prevalence of offenses* and *incidence of offenses*. Prevalence is the percentage of youths who indicate they have committed the offense or offenses in question. Incidence, on the other hand, is based on the number of offenses that youths indicate having committed. In these terms, blacks and whites do not differ much in prevalence over offenses; that is, individuals in both groups have committed at least one offense at high rates. On the other, they do differ in incidence, as studies indicate that blacks commit offenses more frequently than whites.

Results by Socioeconomic Status

As the final possible correlate of delinquency, we consider socioeconomic status (SES). Although the UCR does not report the SES of those arrested, it does have indirect information indicating higher crime among those in lower SES areas. That is, we have seen that the UCR shows arrests as predominantly phenomena of large cities and a strikingly disproportionate involvement of black youths in serious crime. However, where SES data are available in official records, a negative correlation between SES and amount of crime involvement is invariably found.

The Task Force Report of the President's Commission on Law Enforcement and Administration of Justice, arguing on the basis of official crime statistics for slum improvement, states:

> Delinquency in the slums . . . is a disproportionately high percentage of all delinquency and includes a disproportionately high number of dangerous acts. . . . And besides delinquency rates, the other familiar signs of trouble—truancy, high unemployment, mental disorder, infant mortality, tuberculosis, families on relief—are all highest in the inner city.[21]

In their study of a birth cohort in Philadelphia, based on official police data, Wolfgang, Figlio, and Sellin found that race and SES were associated with the offender-nonoffender classification after examining the relationship of delinquency and various background variables. More specifically, they found the rate of offending for lower-SES boys to be 548 per 1,000 subjects and the comparable rate for higher-SES boys to be 140 per 1,000 subjects—that is, a ratio of nearly four to one.

In contrast, as in the case of race, the early self-report studies found little or no difference in delinquent behavior due to SES. As might be imagined, the markedly variant results between official and self-report data regarding the delinquency-SES relationship led to vigorous debate in the literature.

For the Seattle study, Hindelang, Hirschi, and Weis brought SES into the picture in two ways. First, white males were sampled on the basis of median income of their residential areas. Second, an additional SES indicator was developed on the basis of the report of each respondent regarding the occupation of the primary family wage earner. They found that the differences in reports of offending were very small.

Moreover, when correlational measures of association were used between delinquency indexes and SES, the resulting table of correlations showed "that by neither measure of social class and by no measure of delinquency is there even a moderate relation between the two."[22]

Perhaps more convincing evidence on the relationship between SES and delinquency may be found in a subsequent report by Elliott and Huizinga, who used three sets of self-report scales, including those that were specific to a type of offense, those that included more general classes of behavior, and those that encompassed a broad, heterogeneous grouping of offenses. An example of the most specific is "felony assault," which included aggravated assault, sexual assault, and gang fights. An example of the middle category of specificity is "crimes against persons," which included the items under "felony assault" as well as "hit teacher, parent, or students" and "strong-armed students, teachers, or others." Finally, the most general scales included "school delinquency," "index offenses," and "general delinquency."

They found that middle-class youths, girls as well as boys, are less likely to commit serious offenses than working- and lower-class youths, and that when middle-class youths do commit serious offenses, they do so less frequently than youths in the two lower SES categories.

In the words of the investigators, "When the focus is shifted from serious offenses to delinquent acts in general, there are few significant class differences in the proportions of youth reporting one or more delinquent acts."[23] However, working- and lower-class males do commit substantially more general acts of delinquency than do middle-class youths; on the other hand, "there is no consistent pattern of class differences in female . . . rates."

As in all previous studies, females in all classes had lower rates of offending than working- and lower-class males without a clear pattern of differences over classes.

Because there is an obvious relationship between race and SES and because African-Americans generally show more involvement in serious crime, they controlled for the possible effect of race by repeating their analyses for whites only. They report, "With few exceptions, the same pattern of class differences was found."[24]

The Broad Picture

What does the pattern of results for self-report studies tell us about the extent and nature of juvenile offending? In truth, the pattern tells us much about the evolutionary measurement processes, a little about the people who produce and interpret the results, and perhaps a bit about the law-violating tendency of youths as a whole and of subgroups of these youths.

We are inclined to agree with arguments that actual differences in occurrence of serious criminal acts are reflected in official statistics, although the picture is certainly not as dramatic as those data make it seem. Support for that position comes from the work of Elliott and Ageton, which used national survey data. They argued that their findings:

> provide some insight into the mechanisms whereby official actions produce exaggerated race and class (as well as age and sex) differences in delinquent behavior when compared with self-reported differences in normal adolescent populations. On both logical and empirical grounds, it seems reasonable to argue that the more frequent and serious offenders are more likely to be arrested, and that the youth population represented in official police statistics is not a representative sample of all youth.

> Self-report studies are capturing a broader range of persons and levels of involvement in delinquent behavior than are official arrest statistics. Virtually all youth report some delinquent activity on self-report measures, but for the vast majority the offenses are neither very frequent nor very serious. Police contacts, on the other hand, are most likely to concern youth who are involved in either very serious or very frequent delinquent acts. Police contacts with youth thus involve a more restricted segment of the general youth population.

> The findings discussed previously indicate that race and class differences are more extreme at the high end of the frequency continuum, that part of the delinquency continuum where police contacts are more likely.[25]

The National Crime Victimization Survey (NCVS)

Principal Features of the Survey

In 1967, the President's Commission on Law Enforcement and Administration of Justice issued its report, which stated:

> Although the police statistics indicate a lot of crime today, they do not begin to indicate the full amount. Crimes report-

ed directly to prosecutors usually do not show up in the police statistics. Citizens often do not report crimes to the police. Some crimes reported to the police never get into the statistical system. Since better crime prevention and control programs depend upon a full and accurate knowledge about the amount and kinds of crime, the Commission initiated the first national survey ever made of crime victimization. The National Opinion Research Center of the University of Chicago surveyed 10,000 households, asking whether the person questioned, or any member of his or her household, had been a victim of crime during the past year, whether the crime had been reported and, if not, the reasons for not reporting.[26]

The initial crime victimization survey indicated that actual crime was several times that indicated in the UCR. For example, the rate of violent crime reported in the survey was almost twice that reported in the UCR and the rate of property crime more than twice as high. Those sorts of observations led to the inauguration of a regular and formal survey, on a national basis, of criminal victimization in 1973. It was originally called the National Crime Survey, and then became the National Crime Victimization Survey (NCVS).

The survey has focused on the personal crimes of rape, robbery, and assault, and the property crimes of household burglary, larceny, and motor vehicle theft. Clearly, there is close similarity to the UCR's Index crimes (even closer than at first appearance, given that the direct victims of murder and manslaughter cannot be interviewed). The interviews are conducted semiannually. Each person at least 12 years of age in a randomly selected household is asked a series of screening questions at the start of an interview to determine whether he or she has been a victim of a crime during the preceding six-month period. If the person responds affirmatively to one or more of the screening questions, thus indicating that he or she has been a crime victim, the interviewer asks questions regarding characteristics of the victim, the crime itself, and the offender, where relevant. Details include age, race, and sex of the victim; place and time of occurrence of the crime; extent of injury or economic loss; relationship between victim and offender, if any; and perceptions regarding the offender on the part of the victim.

It is the last item that is used to obtain estimates of juvenile offense rates. Given the difficulty of estimating age, especially in the context of occurrence of a crime, it is obvious that the victimization survey cannot be regarded as a powerful contributor to the measurement of juvenile delinquency.

Offender Characteristics

In the NCVS report for 1998 (the most recent available for these data), offender characteristics are reported for personal crimes of violence: rape, robbery, assault. In 20.7 percent of the victimizations in which there was a single offender in each case, the offenders were perceived to be between the ages of 12 and 17. This may be compared with adjusted census figures showing that about 11 percent of the United States population was between the ages of 10 and 17 (even fewer, of course, between 12 and 17).

Unfortunately, age-based data are not available for differentiating offenders on the basis of gender or race. However, over all ages, the perceived single offender in a crime of violence was white in 74.8 percent of the cases and black in 14 percent of the cases. The adjusted census figures indicated a population that was approximately 80 percent white and 12 percent black.

One last bit of information provided in NCVS data is noteworthy: the finding that the violent crimes of youths are overwhelmingly directed at other youths.

While the crime victimization survey cannot be considered a major contributor to knowledge of the offending characteristics of youngsters, it does provide information not available elsewhere, such as victim-offender age relationships, information on single- and multiple-offender crimes, and the perceptions of victims. Although interesting in its own right, the last of these produces difficulties in interpreting actual criminal involvement. In the words of a Survey report:

> As with most [Survey] information, offender attributes are based solely on the victim's perceptions and ability to recall the crime. However, because the events often were stressful experiences, resulting in confusion or physical harm to the victim, it was likely that data concerning offender characteristics were more subject than other survey findings to distortion arising from erroneous responses. Many of the crimes probably occurred under somewhat vague circumstances, especially those at night. Furthermore, it is possible that victim preconceptions, or prejudices, at times may have influenced the attribution of offender characteristics. If victims tended to misidentify a particular trait (or a set of them) more than others, bias would have been introduced into the findings, and no method has been developed for determining the existence and effect of such bias.[27]

NONCRIMINAL MISBEHAVIOR

As stated above, the possible offenses by youths include not only such crimes as murder, rape, and robbery but also such phenomena as truancy, ungovernability, and disobedience. An adult could not be arrested for the offense of truancy no matter how many classes were missed, nor could an adult be charged with ungovernability or disobedience no matter how he or she behaved toward a parent or a teacher (or even a spouse).

It is interesting to note that some state codes include status offenses along with criminal offenses in the specification of "delinquency," while others use separate categories for criminal and status offenses. In many of these latter cases, a youth who commits a status offense is designated by expressions like "child in need of supervision" (frequently abbreviated as CHINS or CINS), "person in need of supervision" (or PINS), "youth in need of supervision" (or YINS), or even a "dependent child."

The term "status offense" in juvenile court law derives its meaning from the fact that the behaviors embraced within the category apply only to persons whose status within the society is that of a minor. Similar behavior on the part of adults is regarded as the adults' own business. Adults are presumed to be old enough to suffer or to enjoy, without state interference, the consequences of what they choose to do, so long as the behavior is not criminal. For them, with some exceptions, what is denoted as crime involves acts that threaten or hurt others, or illegally deprive persons of their property. For juvenile status offenders, the forbidden acts include those that concern control by others and the presumed long-range well-being of the child.

Juvenile status offenses have been separated into three types. First, there are behaviors that are proscribed because the person doing them is considered to be under the age of discretion and in need of protection. This would include such things as use of tobacco. Then there are deviations from behaviors that are believed to be necessary for the proper upbringing of a young person and that person's training for assumption of a satisfactory social role. These include obedience to parents and guardians. Young persons who are brought to the attention of the authorities on the grounds of failure to adhere to parental discipline typically are labeled "incorrigible" or "unruly." Often, they will have attempted to escape from the home environment and have come under the "runaway" heading. Finally, there are pervasive behavioral patterns indicating generally maladaptive functioning; youngsters showing such patterns will be considered "wayward" or "growing up in idleness or crime."

Turning once again to Pennsylvania codes, the definition of "dependent child" includes: "while subject to compulsory school attendance is habitually and without justification truant from school," and "has committed a specific act or acts of habitual disobedience of the reasonable and lawful commands of his parent, guardian, or other custodian and who is ungovernable and found to be in need of care, treatment or supervision."[28]

There are, of course, no restrictions on persons over the age of 18 using tobacco, regardless of the possible consequences for them or for those who depend upon them or upon whom they depend. Nor does, for example, a 27-year-old woman or man need to heed the admonishments of her or his parents, regardless of how sound they might be or how disastrous their own course of conduct might seem to be. Equally well, any person over the age of 18 can live as idly and parasitically as he or she chooses, if the person can figure out a way to manage it without committing criminal acts. Nor will the law interfere if an adult college student chooses to be habitually truant from his or her classes, although the college may take administrative action.

Disobedience to parents, one of the conditions that gives rise to a juvenile status offense, has been of serious social concern throughout the history of Western civilization. In Roman times, fathers exercised what (at least in precept) were totally dictatorial powers over their children (see Chapter 2). Moreover, the Old Testament leaves no question about how serious filial disobedience was considered in the religious community:

> If a man's son is stubborn and rebellious against the voice of his father and of his mother, refusing to listen to and to obey them when they discipline him, then his father and mother must lay hold of him and bring him to the gate of his city, to the elders of his town, and they shall say to the elders of his city, "This our son is stubborn and rebellious; he refuses to listen to us; he is a spendthrift and a drunkard." Then all the men of the city shall stone him to death. Thus you shall exterminate evil from you.[29]

As is discussed in Chapter 2, a similar rule was included in the statute book of colonial Massachusetts, though there is no record of its draconian penalty ever being invoked. Juvenile court laws, following a tradition established early in the nineteenth century, incorporated control provisions from their outset in 1899. It is notable that little attention was paid to the nature of the dictates of parents that led to the "rebelliousness" of offspring: the disobedience might have been related to serious kinds of infractions or it could have involved petty disputes over use of cosmetics, curfew, friends, and cleaning up one's room. Often nothing was said about whether the commands were reasonable or whether they represented arbitrary and tyrannical impositions on the child.

Not until the 1950s and 1960s was there any serious challenge to the legal treatment of status offenders. The assumption was that the juvenile court was benign, always seeking the best interests of the young person before it, even if that young person did not understand its concern or see the justice of its judgment. There also was a virtually unchallenged belief that the behaviors classified as status offenses were strong signs of predelinquent behavior, that is, that they were satisfactory indicators of the likelihood that the young persons were well on their way to involvement in criminal behavior. It took some years for it to be appreciated that there might be "situations . . . in which the child beyond control is sound and healthy, and the lack of control is due to attempt at excessive control, or to some ignorance or neurotic need on the part of the parent that the child may naturally resist."[30]

For reasons such as that one, many critics argue that the juvenile court should not be allowed to exercise any control over status offenders. They insist that status offense behavior, such as parental disobedience and truancy, is at worst immoral, and that it is "transitional deviance" through which youths can be expected to pass without difficulty. Indeed, an important report of the Institute for Judicial Administration and the American Bar Association recommended that noncriminal behavior should be excluded from juvenile court jurisdiction because those courts have been ineffective in dealing with noncriminal behavior, while other institutions, such as schools and social service agencies, are appropriate for handling them. The report also took the position that when a misbehaving juvenile is treated in the same coercive manner as a delinquent, the process makes the entire system seem unfair in the eyes of the misbehaving juvenile.

On the other side, most justice officials seem persuaded that there are young persons in difficulty who, if identified, can be helped and kept from more serious trouble. They are unwilling to abandon the coercive power of the state in what they regard as an important and helpful mission. They argue that it is the very lack of effective coercive powers of schools and social service agencies that has limited their ability to deal with the misbehavior of the young.

The UCR presents arrest data in 1997 for only two types of status offense: (1) curfew and loitering offenses, and (2) runaways. The data on curfew and loitering offenses show the usual predominance of males over females: 69.2 percent versus 30.8 percent. There is a reversal in the case of runaways: 58.2 percent of such arrests were females, while only 41.8 percent were males.

The percentages of arrests for white youths and black youths for these offenses were closer to the corresponding percentages in the population than were Index offenses, particularly of the violent variety. In the case of curfew and loitering offenses, the percentages of arrests were 74.8 for whites and 22.6 for blacks; the corresponding percentages for runaways were 77.2 and 18.1.

Two items in the instrument of the Seattle survey clearly refer to status offenses: "Stayed away from school when your parents thought you were there" (Item 64) and "Run away from home and stayed overnight" (Item 68). The proportions of youngsters who responded "yes" differed only slightly over the four categories of white males, black males, white females, and black females.

The different results found for the offense of running away between UCR and self-report analyses is likely due to the greater tendency of the police to take runaway females into custody.

SUMMARY

In every society, there are regulations and expectations regarding acceptable and unacceptable behavior that are aimed at protecting people and property and at minimizing disruptions to social processes. To encourage conformity, sanctions may be imposed if there is significant deviation from the standards set by the regulations. In the United States, behavior that is thought to be particularly harmful or disruptive is regulated by laws that specify sanctioning by the criminal justice system (in the case of adults) or by the juvenile justice system (in the case of children).

A juvenile delinquent is a youth who violates one of those laws (called criminal laws) and becomes subject to sanctioning by the juvenile justice system. The task of defining the concept "juvenile delinquent" is difficult for two major reasons: first, a youth who may be a juvenile delinquent in one state may not be one in another state because of a differing set of laws; second, most violations of laws by youths are never detected, and few of those detected make it through the court procedures that establish the equivalent of guilt. To illustrate the difficulty, a youth may have been adjudicated a delinquent in Mississippi for behavior that is not even a violation of law in Montana. Moreover, if one defines "juvenile delinquent" on the basis of detection and arrest and several gang members commit a criminal offense for which only one is caught, that gang member alone would be a delinquent even though others may have participated fully in the criminal act.

Children are, of course, subject to the same criminal laws that adults must obey. In addition, there are laws that are applicable only to the behavior of children. Among these are laws that mandate school attendance, obedience to parents, and compliance with curfews. Because offenses of the latter type can be committed only by those who have the status of children, they are called "status offenses."

There are three principal ways to measure the extent of juvenile offending: using official data, using self-report data, and using information from the victims of crime. The central source for official data is the Uniform Crime Reports (UCR), which contains tabulations of offenses reported to police departments and characteristics (age, sex, race, etc.) of people who have been arrested. The picture one gets from the UCR is that the heaviest contributors to serious crime are black youths in later adolescence who live in geographical areas of high population density.

The self-report technique indicates that offending is more widespread than one assumes on the basis of UCR data, though boys do indicate many more of the serious, more destructive offenses than girls. Some studies have shown racial differences in self-reported crime of a magnitude approaching those obtained from UCR data, but the majority of studies have shown much less or no difference. On the issue of socioeconomic status (SES) and delinquency, there is evidence from self-report studies that indicates greater and more serious offending rates at the lowest SES levels but no pattern when comparison is over all SES levels.

Victimization data on a nationwide basis come from the National Crime Victimization Survey (NCVS). The results indicate that youths are perceived as committing offenses (where there was a single offender) by victims at a rate just under two times their population proportion. However, the results of victimization surveys must be used with great caution because they are dependent on the observations of people under stress who most often have little time for careful scrutiny.

Finally, UCR data indicate that females are arrested as runaways more than males, but that males are arrested for curfew law violations more than two-to-one over females. Self-report results, on the other hand, show no greater tendency on the part of females to run away. Some think that the difference between UCR and self-report results stems from a greater tendency for the police to arrest runaway females.

REFERENCES

Braithwaite, John (1981). "The Myth of Social Class and Criminality Reconsidered." *American Sociological Review* 46:36-57.

Criminal Victimization in the United States, 1995 (1998). Washington, DC: U.S. Department of Justice, Bureau of Justice Statistics.

Elliott, Delbert S. (1994). "Serious Violent Offenders: Onset, Developmental Course, and Termination." *Criminology* 32:1-21.

Elliott, Delbert S., and Suzanne S. Ageton (1980). "Reconciling Race and Class Differences in Self-reported and Official Estimates of Delinquency." *American Sociological Review* 45:95-110.

Elliott, Delbert S., and David Huizinga (1983). "Social Class and Delinquent Behavior in a National Youth Panel." *Criminology* 21:149-177.

Empey, LaMar T., and Maynard L. Erickson (1966). "Hidden Delinquency and Social Status." *Social Forces* 44:546-554.

Erickson, Maynard L., and LaMar T. Empey (1963). "Court Records, Undetected Delinquency, and Decision-making." *Journal of Criminal Law, Criminology and Police Science* 54:456-469.

Federal Bureau of Investigation (1997). *Crime in the United States: Uniform Crime Reports, 1996.* Washington, DC: U.S. Government Printing Office.

Gold, Martin (1966). "Undetected Delinquent Behavior." *Journal of Research in Crime and Delinquency* 3:27-46.

Gould, Leroy C. (1969). "Who Defines Delinquency: A Comparison of Self-reported and Officially-reported Indices of Delinquency for Three Racial Groups." *Social Problems* 16:325-336.

Heimer, Karen (1997). "Socioeconomic Status, Subcultural Definitions, and Violent Delinquency" *Social Forces* 75:799-833.

Hindelang, Michael J., Travis Hirschi, and Joseph G. Weis (1981). *Measuring Delinquency.* Beverly Hills, CA: Sage.

Hirschi, Travis (1969). *Causes of Delinquency.* Berkeley: University of California Press.

Jackson, Patrick G. (1990). "Sources of Data." In *Measurement Issues in Criminology*, edited by Kimberly L. Kempf. New York: Springer-Verlag.

Junger-Tas, Josine (1994). "Delinquency in Thirteen Countries: Some Preliminary Conclusions." In *Delinquent Behavior Among Young People in the Western World. First Results of the International Self-Report Delinquency Study*, edited by Josine Junger-Tas, Gert-Jan Terlouw, and Malcolm W. Klein. Amsterdam: Kugler Publications.

Klein, Malcom W. (1994). "Epilogue." In *Delinquent Behavior Among Young People in the Western World. First Results of the International Self-Report Delinquency Study*, edited by Josine Junger-Tas, Gert-Jan Terlouw, and Malcolm W. Klein. Amsterdam: Kugler Publications.

Maguire, Kathleen, and Ann L. Pastore, eds. (1998). *Sourcebook of Criminal Justice Statistics.* Washington, DC: U.S. Government Printing Office.

National Crime Survey Report (1983). *Criminal Victimization in the United States, 1981.* Washington, DC: U.S. Department of Justice, Bureau of Justice Statistics.

Navasky, Victor S. (1971). *Kennedy Justice.* New York: Atheneum.

President's Commission on Law Enforcement and Administration of Justice (1967). *Task Force Report: Juvenile Delinquency and Youth Crime.* Washington, DC: U.S. Government Printing Office.

Quinney, Richard (1970). *The Social Reality of Crime.* Boston: Little, Brown.

Reiss, Albert J. (1975). "Inappropriate Theories and Inadequate Methods as Policy Plagues: Self-reported Delinquency and the Law." In *Social Policy and Sociology*, edited by Nicholas J. Demerath III, Otto Larsen, and Karl F. Schuessler. New York: Academic Press.

Ringel, Cheryl (1997). *Criminal Victimization 1996*. Washington, DC: U.S. Department of Justice, Bureau of Justice Statistics.

Rubin, Sol D. (1960). "Legal Definition of Offenses by Children and Youth." *University of Illinois Law Forum* 1960:512-523.

Shaw, Clifford R., and Henry D. McKay (1942). *Juvenile Delinquency and Urban Areas*. Chicago: University of Chicago Press.

Short, James F., and F. Ivan Nye (1958). "Extent of Unrecorded Juvenile Delinquency: Tentative Conclusions." *Journal of Criminal Law and Criminology* 49:296-302.

Tittle, Charles R. and Robert F. Meier (1990). "Specifying the SES/Delinquency Relationship." *Criminology* 28:271-299.

Tittle, Charles R., and Wayne J. Villemez (1977). "Social Class and Criminality." *Social Forces* 56:474-502.

Williams, Jay R., and Martin Gold (1972). "From Delinquent Behavior to Official Delinquency." *Social Problems* 20:209-229.

Wolfgang, Marvin, Robert M. Figlio, and Thorsten Sellin (1972). *Delinquency in a Birth Cohort*. Chicago: University of Chicago Press.

NOTES

[1]   *Los Angeles Times*, February 16, 1985, Part I, 8.

[2]   Navasky [in Navasky, Victor S. (1971)]. *Kennedy Justice*. New York: Atheneum, p. 17] has pointed out, interestingly, that J. Edgar Hoover, the former head of the FBI, had suggested that the expression "juvenile delinquency" be eliminated from national usage. Navasky quotes the following written statement by Hoover:

> There are still among us muddled-headed sentimentalists who would wrap teenage brigands in the protective cocoon of the term "juvenile delinquency"; with emphasis upon all its connotations of youthful prankishness... As a representative of law enforcement, I would like to see the term "juvenile delinquency" banished forever from our language as a description of vicious acts. Such teenager gangsterism should be labeled for exactly what it is—"youthful criminality."

[3]   *The Oxford English Dictionary*, 2nd ed., 1989, prepared by J.A. Simpson and E.S.C. Weiner. Oxford, England: Clarendon Press.

[4]   Minn. Stat. § 260.015 (1998).

[5]   42 Pa. C.S. § 6302 (1999).

[6]   42 Pa. C.S. § 6355 (1999) (E).

[7]   Wolfgang, Figlio & Sellin (1972).

[8]   Ibid., 14.

[9]   Ibid., 15.

[10]   Ibid., 17.

[11] Klein (1994), 383.

[12] Erickson & Empey (1963), 458.

[13] Williams & Gold (1972), 213.

[14] Junger-Tas (1994), 379.

[15] Hindelang, Hirschi & Weis (1981), 159.

[16] Ibid., 169.

[17] Quinney (1970), 129-130.

[18] Hindelang, Hirschi & Weis (1981), 180.

[19] Ibid., 171.

[20] Ibid., 130.

[21] President's Commission on Law Enforcement and Administration of Justice (1967), 42.

[22] Hindelang, Hirschi & Weis (1981), 196.

[23] Elliott & Huizinga (1983), 165.

[24] Ibid.

[25] Elliott & Ageton (1980), 107.

[26] President's Commission on Law Enforcement and Administration of Justice (1967), 20-21.

[27] National Crime Survey Report (1983), 11.

[28] 42 Pa. C.S. § 6302 (1999).

[29] Deut. 21:18-21.

[30] Rubin (1960), 514.

2

Children and Their Offenses in History

Juvenile delinquency in America is complex in meaning and character. In part, this is because the very concepts of childhood and youth, basic to the idea of juvenile delinquency, are themselves complex. These concepts have changed significantly over time, and the changes have had much to do with the way people understand and respond to juvenile delinquency. They even have had much to do with the very idea that there is such a thing as juvenile delinquency. In this chapter, we will look at the background and development of modern attitudes toward children, focusing on the history of childhood and youth in Western civilization and the relationship of ideas about childhood with the evolving understanding of juvenile delinquency.

If it is possible to speak of an overall tendency in Western history, it has been toward an increasing "child-centeredness" in family and social life. This means several things. First, family life has become increasingly oriented toward childrearing as its primary function. For many centuries, the family was mainly an economic unit. Roles within the family were understood in terms of the family's economic mission. In recent centuries, there has been a tendency to elevate the domestic, emotional focus of the family and, particularly since the early nineteenth century, to understand that focus in terms of the effort to raise children properly (and even happily). Second, this child-centeredness has also meant an increasing stress on the distinctiveness of childhood. Although people have always acknowledged that children are different from adults, recent centuries have seen an increasing conviction in Western society that there are distinctive characteristics and needs associated with childhood that that should be addressed by childrearing practices. Finally, recent times have seen an increasing value placed on childhood and youth as in themselves good. This notion has had much to do with the emergence of a concept of juvenile delinquency, a concept that can be dated to the period around 1800. It has also had much to do with the complexity of even contemporary approaches to delinquency. The background behind contemporary concepts of childhood and youth is, thus, far from irrelevant to an understanding of juvenile delinquency.

EARLY APPROACHES TO CHILDHOOD AND YOUTH

There has been some controversy among historians concerning the emergence in Western history of the idea of childhood presently in effect in the United States. In the past, the understanding of age categories has been very different from today's; in ancient Rome, for example, the category of "youth" could be applied to individuals between the ages of 17 and 46, and such breadth continued to characterize the term through the Middle Ages. Most historians have also agreed that social and family practices tended to center on the adult's world rather than the child's. For much of Western history, parents had (at least theoretically) absolute power over their children and a right to demand absolute obedience from them. For example, in Rome, from ancient times through the early Christian era, the most salient characteristic of the child was his or her membership in a family. Fundamental to that characteristic, as noted in Chapter 1, was subjection to *patria potestas*—essentially the power of the father over his family for as long as he lived. This included the power of life or death over his children—even his grown children (although he might be punished for exercising that power arbitrarily).

According to this view, there was no appreciation for the child's "special nature" and no sense of a "childhood" that demanded cultivation in its own right, for its own sake. This state of affairs characterized Western society from classical times through the Middle Ages and into the Early Modern period, beginning in about the sixteenth century. Some commentators have emphasized the extent of conscious brutality toward children in the past, as children were often used to further the family's economic ends in ways that are shocking to us today. Adult needs (and not those of the child) were at the center of family concern.

Other historians have, however, considered such a picture to be at least slightly overdrawn. Even in Rome, for example, *patria potestas* was increasingly undermined by doctrines of *patria pietas* (fatherly love), especially during the late empire. Moreover, throughout Western history, bonds of affection unquestionably have united parents and children, even if those bonds have not been defined or given centrality in the ways that they are today.

Moreover, in the classical civilizations of Greece and Rome, and continuing through Medieval times, people were strongly aware of what were called the "stages of life," each with its own characteristics— "youth," for example, being traditionally understood as a kind of testing time, a time of transition when individuals did not always show the greatest self-restraint.

People were also aware of the need for special institutions and special efforts to help prepare young people for the demands of adult life, including schools as well as apprenticeships (especially in the Medieval and Early Modern periods), in which young people were expected to the learn a trade. From ancient times, moreover, "youths" displayed their own self-awareness through organized festivals and guilds, and as students and apprentices, and through less organized occasions of revelry and sport that came to be associated with their peculiar stage of life.

There is a wealth of conflicting evidence from earlier times and a continuing debate in which both sides have strength. It can be said, though, that the main lines of development in the Western world through much of its history did not focus on the child in the terms that have become so familiar by the end of the twentieth century. Above all, and at the very least, it appears that childhood was not understood to comprise a world that was somehow separate from the life of adults. At a very young age, children were required to meet the demands posed by adult social and economic life. The ancient and Medieval worlds were clearly adult worlds to which children were, for the most part, expected to conform.

Such an adult focus to social institutions characterized approaches to crimes committed by young people in earlier times. As we shall see in more detail in Chapter 8, during the ancient and Medieval periods, there were no special codes defining anything like "juvenile delinquency." Children were subject to the same criminal codes as adults. The only real concession to childhood was a general recognition that children below a certain age, usually seven, should not be held criminally responsible for their actions. The idea that juvenile lawbreaking represented a distinctive social problem (the very basis of those issues discussed in Chapter 1) had little place in ancient or Medieval social thought.

THE EMERGENCE OF MODERN IDEAS

The Significance of Colonial America

The background underlying ideas of childhood similar to those of today became more obvious beginning in the sixteenth and seventeenth centuries, as many people began to think in new ways about childhood and youth, celebrating—even as they worried about—the distinctive nature of the child. Although this thought did not carry over immediately into major developments in the treatment of young offenders, it did set the stage for an understanding of childhood and youth that ultimately resulted in the basic assumptions that continue to lie behind much of the juvenile justice system in the United States.

One of the first clear indications of the strength and meaning of these emerging notions of childhood appeared in the English colonies of North America. In New England, under the influence of Puritanism, there existed a great deal of concern and awareness about children and childrearing. Some historians have even suggested that the Puritans, in England as well as America, were among the first to "discover" the child, at least in the modern sense of the term. This discovery provides an essential background for understanding subsequent developments in American concepts of childhood and youth.

From the time of colonization into the late 1700s, the family was the center of life in Puritan New England, and childrearing was a central activity. The Puritan concern for the child had important religious roots. Puritan belief focused above all on the salvation of individual souls. Puritans saw proper childrearing as an essential element in the process of salvation. As strict Calvinists, the early New England settlers believed that all humans, including children, were innately sinful and given to evil, but this only increased their concern about childrearing. Because children were born, in the words of the great Puritan minister Cotton Mather, "defiled, depraved, horribly polluted, with original sin, and fearfully perishing under the wrath and curse of God," they had to be taught as soon as possible to seek salvation.

Within the Puritan family, efforts at proper childrearing involved inducing a combination of fear and love in the child toward its parents. Puritan thinking about childrearing emphasized the importance of breaking the child's will and enforcing its subordination to the instruction of the parents. Corporal punishment was common—"Better Whipt, than Damn'd," Cotton Mather declared[1]—and Puritans believed that children should not be spoiled or indulged.

Still, in important ways, the Puritans brought a new attitude to child rearing, one that emphasized the importance of children as ends in themselves. This new focus on the child spread well beyond the boundaries of New England, notably through the impact of the first and most widely influential early American schoolbook, the *New England Primer*. With more than six million copies in print, between 1680 and 1830, and in use throughout the British North American colonies, in England, and Scotland, it did much to spread Puritan ideals throughout the English-speaking world.[2]

Puritan innovations were significant. It might be suggested that the Puritans helped initiate thinking about juvenile offenses in a new way, too, by legislating the first American status offense, based on incorrigibility. The law (see Chapter 1) provided that if any son, age 16 or over (daughters, presumably, being less headstrong) should habitually refuse to obey his parents, he could be taken before the magistrates. Should the magistrates find sufficient evidence of incorrigibility, according to the law, "such a son shall be put to death." Hence, Puritan youths were given good reason to obey the biblical commandment to honor their parents. Fortunately, however, as mentioned in Chapter 1, there is no indication such a sentence was ever carried out.[3]

Still, for the most part, older approaches to juvenile offending continue to be observed. That is, there was no differentiation in treatment, either in New England or elsewhere, for children or young people involved in criminal acts.

The Revolution in Sentiment in the Nineteenth Century: Toward a Child-Centered Family

At the close of the eighteenth and the opening of the nineteenth century, ideas about childrearing were in flux. For a variety of reasons, the authoritarian, patriarchal Puritan ideal was undergoing increasing challenge, and new modes that stressed the bending rather than the breaking of a child's will (while emphasizing the pliability of the child's nature) were beginning to emerge. Children, especially young children, were seen as a source of pleasure, and good behavior as a product of affection rather than fear. Among middle- and upper-class Americans, in particular, people were beginning to place an extraordinary emphasis on domesticity and intimacy. Love and reverence were to bind family members together, and the family was seen as set apart, a place of refuge in which love and tranquility contrasted with the harshness of society at large.

The emphasis on domestic ties was to provide a main theme in the development of ideas of family life and childhood in the nineteenth century. Families became increasingly aware of themselves as emotional units, united by ties of love. Modes of childrearing viewed as authoritarian, or likely to produce confrontations between parents and their children, were increasingly rejected, and the very nature of the child, as such, was reevaluated. Gone was the old Puritan idea of the child as innately sinful and depraved. Nineteenth-century thought increasingly considered the child as innately good, with a nature to be molded and encouraged instead of subdued.

Certainly, obedience was important in a child, but the new mode of childrearing emphasized that children should be obedient because they wanted to be, not because they were forced to behave. One of the most influential figures in developing these new ideas, the Congregationalist minister Horace Bushnell, wrote that those parents who, "only storm about their house with heathenish ferocity" were hardly performing their proper parental duties. "It is frightful to think," he said, "how they batter and bruise the delicate, tender souls of their children, extinguishing in them what they ought to cultivate." In the place of such a harsh family setting, Bushnell urged an atmosphere of "order, and quiet, and happy rule," firm, to be sure, but based on love and gentleness.[4]

Bushnell's view of the child was in keeping with his prescriptions for family life. He urged parents not to place too many prohibitions on their children, stressing the importance of giving the child an opportunity to realize his or her own possibilities and virtues. He was even willing to accept a bit of mischief now and again, as a product of "exuberant life and playfulness"[5] and as something to be corrected but not dwelled upon or treated with undue severity. Such ideas became widespread through the first half of the nineteenth century, leading to a celebration of childish impulses and a sense that the basis for a proper upbringing lay in the children themselves. The distinct nature of the child was coming to be a key premise in thinking about childrearing and family life.

THE BIRTH OF JUVENILE DELINQUENCY

The changes taking place in the first half of the nineteenth century had much to do with the first steps in the development of a concept of juvenile delinquency, a term that appears to have originated in the century's second decade. The earliest formulations about delinquency should not be viewed as systematic theories of delinquency. Such theories did not begin to develop until the late nineteenth century when scholars in the United States and elsewhere began to create explanations of delinquency that sought to meet the criteria of theory building (to be discussed in Chapter 3).

The concept of juvenile delinquency, as it developed in early nineteenth-century America, was mainly a product of emerging concepts of childhood and family life. The notion, so long established, that children and adults should stand identically before the law was anathema to those who celebrated childhood's special nature and who had turned from punishment to nurture in their ideas about childrearing. Later we will examine the legal and institutional implications of this shift. For now, it is important to see how the emergence of a belief in the distinctive nature of the child also encouraged the idea that the juvenile offender was something more than simply a young criminal.

The Stimulus of Urbanization

Among the more important catalysts leading to a concept of juvenile delinquency was the urbanization of the American population. After the American Revolution, many American cities began to grow at remarkable rates. New York, for example, had been a city of only about 12,000 at the close of the Revolution in 1783, but by 1790 had grown to a population of more than 33,000. By 1825, only 35 years later, the city's population had reached more than 166,000. Other cities did not match New York's spectacular growth, but they also grew quickly, drawing population from rural areas of the nation and abroad.

The cities were horribly unprepared for such growth. Municipal services were slow to expand and reach all the newcomers, leading to difficulties in sanitation, water supply, and public health. Many of those moving to America's cities, looking for opportunity, brought little with them, and there soon appeared a sizable underclass of poor people, all congregated in filthy and crowded slums.

The earliest conceptions of juvenile delinquency were built on perceptions of the incompatibility of urban conditions with the ideals of childhood taking shape during the early nineteenth century. The early nineteenth century did see a rise in crimes on the part of young people, including a rise in property crimes on the part of young men, prostitution among young urban women, as well as the appearance of a kind of "streetcorner" society of young people who were unemployed and apparently independent of family life and adult supervision.

At one level was the issue of how society should respond to the crimes of juveniles as those crimes became more visible in America's cities, especially among those who, increasingly cognizant of childhood's special character, were turning from punishment to nurture in response to youthful behavioral problems generally.

However, another emerging concept of delinquency focused not only on juvenile crime but on what were taken to be, more generally, deviations from proper norms of childhood and family life because of the inability of children to live as children in the setting of the urban slum. From the perspective of many observers, the lives of children in the urban slums were too far from those ideals of gentility and domesticity that were coming to be prized. "Search out their homes," one writer asserted, "and if you find cheerlessness and discomfort, ignorance and wretchedness, there you will see children ripening daily into habits of evil and driven into sin as by dire necessity."

Delinquency, such observers suggested, was the product of environment, and, most especially, of the difficulty of maintaining a proper family environment in a setting of urban poverty. Delinquents were frequently characterized as "precocious," meaning that such children were, or at least tried to be, adults before their time because they were insufficiently exposed to the guidance of loving adults. One reformer of the era referred to juvenile delinquents as "stunted little men."[6]

At the same time, even as reformers emphasized environmental factors in producing delinquents, they also emphasized what they saw as major moral issues in juvenile delinquency. Poverty, most reformers believed, originated in the deficient moral stature of the adult poor; it was perpetuated by the inability of the poor to give their children a proper upbringing. The English educator Mary Carpenter, who had great influence on American thinking, wrote in the 1850s that delinquents came from families in which "vicious indulgence, the gratification of the lowest animal tastes, hardened the heart against all good and holy influences,—stifled the voice of conscience,—deadened all natural affections."[7] From this perspective, the proper relationship between parent and child, based on reverence and love, simply did not exist for delinquents; hence, reformers concluded, they fell into crime.

Thus, among those who helped develop juvenile delinquency as a concept, there was an anxiety not only about juvenile crime but also about what they took to be "wayward" tendencies in young men and women. The "delinquent" label was attached at least as often to young people who appeared to lack adequate adult supervision—apparent "vagrants," for example—as to those who were actually accused of criminal offenses. The labeling was tied to the norms of childhood and youth taking shape during the period.

It is revealing that the urban character of delinquency was taken for granted during the early nineteenth century. Children of the slums were not the only ones to engage in what would today be considered criminal behavior. Violence was common, particularly among young men, throughout the United States before the Civil War. In rural areas, children were pretty much left on their own, and there was no great concern over fighting and what were called "pranks." On university campuses, fights, even duels, were also common, and campus riots were widespread. At Brown University, students stoned the president's home almost nightly in the 1820s. Harvard University saw riots in 1766, 1805, and 1823. Such riots were not tame affairs: a professor at the University of Virginia, perhaps the most eminent legal scholar in the state, was shot to death by a student when he interfered with a student riot on that campus.

Despite such occurrences, juvenile delinquency was treated, from the beginning, as a problem of the urban poor. There can be little doubt that this bias on the part of reformers narrowed their perceptions of the problem and their approaches to its solution. Nevertheless, it was a bias rarely questioned until the late years of the nineteenth century; some would suggest that it continues to inform much in the American juvenile justice system (as discussed in Chapter 1) as well as in the theories of some contemporary scholars of delinquency that will be discussed in Chapters 3 through 7. Moreover, this bias was a guiding influence on Americans' earliest institutional approaches to the problems of delinquency (see Chapter 8).

THE DISCOVERY OF ADOLESCENCE

The ideas that began to take shape in the early nineteenth century formed an important backdrop against which subsequent American thinking about delinquency has continued to develop. Toward the close of that century, still further elaborations took place that were also to have continuing significance. Chiefly, men and women from a variety of backgrounds came to take a less moralistic, more scientific approach to delinquency, viewing it not so much as a matter of moral deficiency but rather as a product of inherent problems in the maturation of the child, problems that could be exacerbated by environmental factors. A major key to this shifting view was the identification of "adolescence" as a distinctive phase in the process of child development.

The Prolongation of Childhood

Just as the concept of "childhood" has been debated by historians, so too has the concept of "adolescence." In the adult-centered world of Western society prior to the early modern era, the recognition of "stages of life" never seems to have hardened into clear categories based on age. This is true despite the fact that young people in the roles of apprentices, students, or even as novices in monastic communities developed a consciousness, accompanied by customs and traditions that conformed to a widespread sense of youth as a time of unusual exuberance and recklessness.

Nevertheless, for many historians, the latter part of the nineteenth century represents a key period in the development of the idea of adolescence as a distinct stage of life. The main factor leading to this development was what has been described as the "prolongation of childhood" during that period. Through the eighteenth century, it was quite common for children to leave the household somewhere between the ages of 10 and 14, either for schooling or (more commonly) to enter an apprenticeship, moving into the household of a skilled worker in order to learn a trade.

For a variety of reasons, apprenticeship became obsolete during the nineteenth century. Among working-class Americans, industrialization and the demand for wage labor lessened the importance of the skills fostered by apprenticeships; for the middle class, the educational requirements of an industrial, commercial economy had little to do with traditional forms of learning a trade. Young people tended to remain in their parents' homes longer, until well into their late teens.

The great interest that had already been directed toward young children came to be increasingly directed toward older ones. Though they had been thrust out in the past, young people between 14 and 20 were coming to be seen as part of the emotional complex the family had become. To be sure, some were still sent away. Poorer youths might be put to work; those from the upper and middle classes, sent to boarding schools. Nevertheless, the relationship to the family was becoming qualitatively more complex, even for those sent away. No longer were they believed to be in the world by themselves. Now they remained closely tied to their own homes, living there or (if away at school) dependent on their parents for support. Those who worked did so to contribute to the family income, not to embark on their own independent lives. Work itself was increasingly frowned upon for children in nineteenth-century America. Thus, the late nineteenth century saw the passage of the first "child-labor laws" designed to remove young people from the economic sphere. If not everyone could afford to meet the ideal—and, obviously, not everyone could—the ideal took on compelling importance as the nineteenth century ended.

G. Stanley Hall: The Psychology of Adolescence

This prolongation of childhood and dependence was the basis for what came to be defined as a new "stage of life": adolescence. It was a stage about which people quickly developed some fairly clear ideas. For much of the nineteenth century, it was understood to be a time when the more "ardent passions" began to rise in young people, producing peculiar problems, both moral and intellectual. Young people between puberty and adulthood were seen to be striving for independence and maturity, just at the time when they needed the firmest guidance.

The result was that adolescence was identified not simply as a distinct stage of life but as one that was both particularly dangerous to and crucial for the formation of character. This point of view was put into systematic form by one of the most significant pioneer psychologists in nineteenth-century America, G. Stanley Hall. Although Hall did not publish his encyclopedic *Adolescence: Its Psychology and its Relations to Physiology, Anthropology, Sociology, Sex, Crime, Religion and Education* until 1904, the impact of his work began to be felt as early as the 1880s. This achievement was important for bringing the new science of psychology to bear on the study of adolescence, summarizing and reshaping many of the popular ideas about youth that had begun to develop during the 1800s.

Hall viewed the adolescent as neither fully child nor fully adult. He argued that the psychological costs of being in such a position could be quite large. Prior to about age 12, he said, the child tended to be "well adjusted to his environment and proportionately developed"; with adolescence, this relationship broke down, and the young person entered a "long pilgrimage of the soul" that was marked by many psychological difficulties, including "intense states of mind" and powerful and sudden "shifts of mood." Adolescents were often overaggressive in asserting their individuality; they were willful, given to folly, prone to envy, and overeager for independence.[8]

Still, while adolescence was a difficult stage of life, it was also one in which the character could most easily and properly be molded into the right shape. There were real possibilities for influencing the individual between the ages of 14 and 20, and Hall viewed exerting such proper influence as a key task for parents—as well as for society.

The Extent of Hall's Influence

Early in the twentieth century, many of Hall's ideas were adopted and put into practice by those who felt a special need to shape the lives of adolescents. Fearful of the turbulence of adolescence in the lives of young women, many reformers sought to develop "Girls Clubs" to encourage properly virtuous behavior at a time when "desires" were most difficult to control. Hall was no less influential on those "boys-workers" who tried to create organizations to shelter adolescent boys from the difficulties—and temptations—of public life, while also bringing order to what they had learned was an unstable stage of life. Thus, by combining military and civic educational elements with an emphasis on physical activities, they sought to tame what was not quite civilized in the adolescent breast. In Britain, one of the leaders in such "boys-work" was General Robert Baden-Powell, who established the

Boy Scouts in the United States in 1910. Marked by rigid organization and a focus on physical toughness, the Boy Scouts were founded by leaders who looked directly to Hall's writings for inspiration.

Adolescence and Delinquency: Early Ideas

Ideas about adolescence had great influence on thinking about juvenile delinquency. Although explanations of delinquency emphasizing the importance of urbanization remained central themes, toward the close of the nineteenth century, many scholars turned to psychological explanations based on theories of adolescence that saw the instability of that stage of life as a major cause of delinquent tendencies.

The most systematic analysis of the relationship between adolescence and delinquency was carried out by Hall himself. Hall might, in fact, be considered the first real American psychological *theorist* of delinquency. His understanding of juvenile crime was grounded to some extent in the work of hereditarian criminologists such as Cesare Lombroso, whose ideas are discussed in detail in Chapter 4. Hall wrote, "Juvenile criminals, as a class, are inferior in body and mind to normal children."[9]

However, Hall was no less convinced that delinquency was closely related to the nature of adolescence as such. Describing it as an "essentially antisocial" stage of life, he argued that being a good citizen was not easy for the adolescent; turning to crime, not unnatural. He wrote, for example, of "a chronic illusion of youth that gives 'elsewhere' a special charm" and that, if not controlled, "must lead to vagrancy." He noted, too, that "all boys develop a greatly increased propensity to fight at puberty," as well as an increased readiness to feel violent anger. The antisocial tendencies of adolescence, in Hall's view, were themselves a major factor in producing delinquent behavior.[10]

One important implication of this view was, thus, to redefine juvenile delinquency in terms of the stages of life. Previously, delinquents were described by nineteenth-century men and women as "precocious," that is, as too adult for their ages. Hall and others in the latter part of the century tended to focus more on the *immaturity* of the delinquent, on the young offender's not having developed sufficiently mature restraint over natural adolescent tendencies. It was a view that made the delinquent seem to be much more of a child.

Environmentalism, Adolescence, and Delinquency in Turn-of-the-Century Thought

One result of this connection between adolescence and delinquency was not only to make the delinquent more of a child but also to "decriminalize" the concept of delinquency itself. In the view of many, the delinquent was not a criminal but rather a victim of his or her own natural—and not entirely controllable—impulses.

Moreover, it was felt that this was especially the case for those young people whose fall into delinquency had been encouraged by the problems of urban life. The late nineteenth century was a period of massive urban growth in America, largely as a result of unprecedented levels of immigration from poorer regions of Europe. This growth brought an increase in urban problems and in urban delinquency, including the appearance of youth gangs, which often crossed over into criminal activities.

In the late nineteenth century, however, there was an increasing sense that the sources of delinquency lay less with urbanization or even urban family problems than with the inability of cities to supply needed services, particularly schooling, in urban slum neighborhoods. In one New York school district, for example, more than 1,500 children were turned away from public schools simply because there was no room for them.

Psychology provided an important basis for understanding the process. This was apparent in the thought of one of the most influential reformers of late nineteenth and early twentieth centuries, Jacob Riis. For Riis, juvenile delinquents were preeminently the victims of the inability of cities to supply needed services, particularly schooling, in urban slum neighborhoods. Decrying the overcrowding in New York's schools, for example, Riis wrote that children had "practically been referred to the street for such education as they could pick up there."[11] Such children, he wrote, would quickly progress from being truants by circumstance to being truants by choice. From there, it was a short step to crime and delinquency.

The adolescent character of the young people was seen as contributing to the process. Discussing urban gangs, Riis wrote that they were organizations that responded "to a real need of the [boy's] nature. The distinguishing character of the American city boy is his genius for organization . . . Unbridled, allowed to run riot, it results in the gang."[12] No lover of gangs, Riis nevertheless believed that they were a natural direction in which youthful tendencies could run. Environmentalism thus combined with the discovery of adolescence to create a view of delinquency as a symptom of society's failure to deal adequately with a significant and difficult element in the American population—not as a moral deficiency in the delinquent.

Views such as Riis's were dominant by the beginning of the twentieth century. They served as the foundation for the creation of the juvenile court (noted in Chapter 1 and discussed in more detail in Chapter 8). Hence, they provided major premises that have characterized American juvenile justice to our own time.

THE TWENTIETH CENTURY

Much that we have seen from nineteenth-century developments continues to guide the twentieth century and beyond. For one thing, the appreciation for the distinctive nature of childhood and adolescence has remained strong. This has led not only to certain ideas about how children should be treated but also to dedicated efforts to investigate child and adolescent development in order to identify their characteristics as fully as possible.

This is not the place in which to survey the vast body of literature produced by these efforts. Here we will offer only an overview of twentieth-century ideas, stressing those that have had the greatest influence on American culture and society, and on American concepts of juvenile delinquency.

Child Rearing and Friendship: A Twentieth-Century Theme

In regard to childrearing, twentieth-century American thought was generally built on nineteenth-century ideas of encouraging affection within the family as the basis for relationships between parents and their children, modeling those relationships on ideals of companionship and even friendship. Parents and children, like good friends, have been encouraged to enjoy each other's company by having fun together. Adjustment and good psychological health were increasingly believed to come from a family life that was more democratic than authoritarian, in which parents and their children got along well with each other.

Perhaps the most influential statement of these democratic ideals came from the work of Benjamin Spock. Spock's views on child rearing have often been exaggerated by commentators on American culture; he has frequently been described as a champion of excessive permissiveness in the raising of children. In fact, Spock placed great stress on bringing up mannerly and obedient children, and at several points advised that, in order to be successful, parents must be firm in responding to misbehavior, even in the very young. Nevertheless, in his emphasis on tailoring child rearing to the individual child, Spock took earlier trends in significant directions.

According to Spock, a key to child rearing was the recognition of how much children differ from each other and of how individual children require different methods of disciplining. The good parent, he wrote, must make "allowances" for each child's "individuality," developing methods accordingly.[13] The chief goal of any method

The theories of Dr. Benjamin Spock were a great influence on twentieth-century child rearing. His *Baby and Child Care*, originally published in 1946, became a widely accepted "bible" on child rearing, and is still popular today. Spock encouraged new parents to use common sense and to treat children with respect. This led some critics to call him the "Father of Permissiveness," in spite of Spock's protests to the contrary. *(Photo by Ellen S. Boyne)*

was to produce a child who was well adjusted and to develop family relationships in which parents and children were happy and friendly. The ideal child (and this applied to adolescents as well) was to be sociable and popular, with high standards, but not standards observed at the expense of getting along with others.

The Twentieth-Century Child and the Weakening of the Family

The ideas of Benjamin Spock are important to note because they represent one influential statement of a set of views that was to become especially important in the period following World War II. This set of views emphasized individuality and sociability and rejected moralism in thinking about childhood and youth. This point of view has dominated thought on childrearing, at least at the level of theory that has reached the general public. One result has been a progressive lessening of the role of the family itself in bringing up children.

This development has been especially significant in regard to adolescents. Adolescence has retained a crucial place in thinking about childhood down to the present time. There remains a strong belief in the

formative significance of the adolescent years, but approaches to adolescence have undergone significant changes since World War II.

There has been increasing stress on individuality and identity, consistent with the recognition of the individuality of the child. This has
had great impact on the understanding of adolescence itself, particularly
through the influential work of Erik H. Erikson, a psychoanalyst. Erikson argued that adolescence is preeminently a time of identity confusion
and crisis, as the adolescent searches for both a sense of self and a legitimate social role. Much contemporary thought about how to deal with
adolescence retains Erikson's focus on the importance of identity to
adolescent development.

The focus on identity has also led to a considerable broadening of
the definition of adolescence. In G. Stanley Hall's time, and for some
time thereafter, adolescence was identified with the onset of puberty.
The physiological changes of puberty were used to explain the psychological and emotional changes associated with adolescence. More
recent scholars have emphasized, however, that much that has been
observed about adolescence cannot be correlated with physiology. For
some young people, traits associated with adolescence occur well before
puberty; for others, much later. As a result, recent studies have extended the age of adolescence downward to about 11 years old and have
considered that adolescence continues to about age 19. The kinds of
identity concerns associated with adolescence tend to appear during
those years.

Perhaps the most notable development in regard to adolescence in
recent years has been the way the general weakening of the role of the
family has affected adolescent socialization. For the most part, parents
have played a decreasing role in bringing up their adolescent children.
Peers, it is argued, rather than adults are setting the standards and
defining the rules for contemporary adolescents.

This has led some scholars to argue that adolescents have sought to
create a subculture, a "youth culture," asserting their separation from
the adult world. Although some feel that such a characterization is too
strong, most agree that the alienation—expressed by everything from
music to language to styles of dress—felt by adolescents with regard to
adult institutions and role models has been increasingly strong.

Twentieth-Century Conceptions of Delinquency: An Overview

The views of childhood and delinquency we have been reviewing
have not had an inevitable impact on delinquency theory. However, as
we shall see in Chapters 8 through 11, their impact on social policy has
been enormous. As noted in Chapter 4, delinquency theory has its
own intellectual tradition, and has developed in many ways quite inde-

pendent of concepts of childhood and youth. This is true of the hered-
itarian arguments that may be traced to the early theories of Cesare
Lombroso, which continue to play a role in the works of a few theorists
(Chapter 4).

In the case of other theories, however, the connections between theory and more general concepts of childhood are strong. Conceptions of
childhood and youth are for some theories the dominant assumptions
upon which the theory is based. This is especially true of theories
developed after about 1910. Most continued to stress environmental
causes for delinquency, as will be seen in Chapters 6 and 7, while
drawing on the insights of an individualistic psychology (Chapter 5).
Particularly important were approaches that stressed an individualized,
holistic approach to the understanding of delinquent behavior, suggesting that each juvenile offender must be understood on his or her
own terms. Such approaches were encouraged through the efforts of the
Federal Children's Bureau, founded in 1912, and the Commonwealth
Fund, founded in 1918, which through the 1920s and 1930s supported programs of psychological research and treatment aimed at preventing and responding to delinquency. Such conceptions have also
focused on a range of causal factors, including the inability of urban settings to provide a stable environment in which children and youth
may come of age, as well as the lack of opportunities for adolescence to
move in predictable paths toward adult roles (the lack, that is, of
meaningful jobs).

No less important have been "subcultural" explanations for delinquency, which see delinquency as one manifestation of a powerful,
deviant youth culture (Chapter 6). While social scientists have hotly
debated whether delinquency rests on a distinctive, deviant set of values, the debate itself has reflected the major role of peers in the socialization of adolescents. Enormously complicated by issues of color and
gender in American society, these explanations have emphasized the
power of both alienation and peer pressure in the formation of delinquency, including the severe problem of urban gang violence and forms
of sexual "delinquency" such as teenage promiscuity and pregnancy
among teens. Emphasizing the lack of family influence on young people, these explanations view delinquency as rooted in an adolescent subculture that inculcates values and standards that tend to antisocial,
often delinquent behavior.

Finally, as the age categories associated with "childhood" and
"adolescence" have become increasingly vague in recent years, at least
a few scholars in law and the social sciences have begun to question
their relevance for thinking about juvenile crime and delinquency.
Indeed, many have gone so far as to suggest that "juvenile delinquency," with its connotations of a distinctive "nature" of the child or
adolescent, is no longer a useful concept for understanding more serious forms of criminal behavior, regardless of the age of the offender.

Thus, as we shall see in more detail in the chapters to come, an appreciation for changing views of childhood and youth is essential to understanding many of the crucial directions that the thinking about delinquency has taken historically and in our own time.

SUMMARY

The ideas about delinquency that have developed in the United States are firmly based in conceptions of childhood and youth. These conceptions have not been static. For much of Western history, adult society formed the focus of social concern; people were not indifferent to childhood but children were expected to find their way in the adult world. Only in the early modern era, beginning in about the sixteenth and seventeenth centuries, did adults begin to believe that society had a duty to respond to special needs of the child.

During the time of English colonization in North America, these ideas were given significant shape by the Puritans, who gave much thought to proper modes of childrearing. Although they did not take a clearly positive view of childhood, their great concern for salvation led them to stress the unique vulnerability of children and youths and the need for special care in the formation of character in the child. Though their methods were not those of today, their concern for the child anticipated the child-centered focus of family life that has come through to the present day.

The nineteenth century was marked by a revolution in sentiment that promoted more positive views of childhood. Many Americans began to emphasize not only the child's vulnerability but also the basic goodness of children—a goodness that had to be encouraged by the family and by the environment.

This revolution in sentiment had much to do with the emergence of a clear-cut concept of delinquency. When many people compared the needs of childhood with the conditions under which urban children had to mature, they saw clear reasons why such children could become delinquent. This was an important step in the development of the idea of juvenile delinquency.

There have been other important developments as well. With the prolongation of childhood and the creation of a concept of adolescence (also datable to the nineteenth century), distinctly psychological approaches to the understanding of childhood and youth became prevalent, as did a focus on adolescence. In addition, twentieth-century America has witnessed what many scholars consider a weakening of the family, both in terms of childrearing practices and socialization. Increasingly, children and youths look more to their peers than to their parents as they grow and mature.

These developments have had an impact on the way many Americans think about delinquency. Theories and popular conceptions that stress not only environmental factors but the apparently inevitable problems of "adjustment" have come to play an important role in the understanding of juvenile delinquency. So, too, have subcultural theories that view delinquency as an aspect of a youth culture that sets itself apart from the adult world. The theoretical ideas about juvenile delinquency that have emerged from such conditions will be the subject of the next five chapters.

REFERENCES

Alexander, Ruth M. (1995). *The "Girl Problem": Female Sexual Delinquency in New York, 1900-1930*. Ithaca, NY: Cornell University Press.

Ariés, Philippe (1962). *Centuries of Childhood: A Social History of Family Life.* Translated by Robert Baldick. New York: Vintage.

Beales, Ross W. (1985). "The Child in Seventeenth-Century America." In *American Childhood: A Research Guide and Historical Handbook*, edited by Joseph M. Hawes and N. Ray Hiner, 17-56. Westport, CT: Greenwood Press.

Bernard, Thomas J. (1992). *The Cycle of Juvenile Justice*. New York: Oxford University Press.

Bushnell, Horace (1947). *Christian Nurture*. New Haven, CT: Yale University Press.

Clement, Priscilla Ferguson (1985). "The City and the Child, 1860-1885." In *American Childhood: A Research Guide and Historical Handbook*, edited by Joseph M. Hawes and N. Ray Hiner, 235-272. Westport, CT: Greenwood Press.

Clement, Priscilla Ferguson (1993). "The Incorrigible Child: Juvenile Delinquency in the United States from the 17th through the 19th Centuries." In *History of Juvenile Delinquency: A Collection of Essays on Crime Committed by Young Offenders, in History and in Selected Countries*, 2 vols., edited by Patricia F. Clement and Albert G. Hess, II: 453-490. Aalen, Germany: Scientia Verlag.

Coleman, James S. (1961). *The Adolescent Society: The Social Life of the Teenager and Its Impact on Education*. Reprint. Westport, CT: Greenwood Press, 1981.

Crouzet-Pavan, Elisabeth (1997). "A Flower of Evil: Young Men in Medieval Italy." In *A History of Young People in the West*, vol. I, *Ancient and Medieval Rites of Passage*, edited by Giovanni Levi and Jean-Claude Schmitt, translated by Camille Naish, 173-221. Cambridge, MA: Harvard University Press.

Cunningham, Hugh (1995). *Children and Childhood in Western Society Since 1500*. London: Longman.

Erikson, Erik H. (1963). *Childhood and Society*, 2nd ed. New York: W.W. Norton.

Eyben, Emiel (1993). *Restless Youth in Ancient Rome*. Translated by Patrick Daly. London: Routledge.

Friedman, Lawrence M. (1993). *Crime and Punishment in American History*. New York: Basic Books.

Gillis, John R. (1974). *Youth and History: Tradition and Change in European Age Relations, 1770–Present*. New York: Oxford University Press.

Golden, Mark (1990). *Children and Childhood in Classical Athens*. Baltimore: Johns Hopkins University Press.

Graff, Harvey J. (1995). *Conflicting Paths: Growing Up in America*. Cambridge, MA: Harvard University Press.

Grant, Julia (1998). *Raising Baby by the Book: The Education of American Mothers*. New Haven, CT: Yale University Press.

Greven, Philip J., Jr. (1977). *The Protestant Temperament: Patterns of Child-Rearing, Religious Experience, and the Self in Early America*. New York: Knopf.

Hall, G. Stanley (1904). *Adolescence: Its Psychology and Its Relations to Physiology, Anthropology, Sociology, Sex, Crime, Religion and Education*. 2 vols. New York: Appleton.

Hanawalt, Barbara A. (1993). *Growing Up in Medieval London: The Experience of Childhood in History*. New York: Oxford University Press.

Hawes, Joseph N. (1971). *Children in Urban Society: Juvenile Delinquency in Nineteenth Century America*. New York: Oxford University Press.

Hawes, Joseph N. (1997). *Children Between the Wars: American Childhood, 1920-1940*. New York: Twayne.

Kett, Joseph (1977). *Rites of Passage: Adolescence in America, 1790 to the Present*. New York: Basic Books.

Lindenmeyer, Kriste (1997). *A Right to Childhood: The U.S. Children's Bureau and Child Welfare, 1912-46*. Urbana: University of Illinois Press.

Lystad, Mary (1980). *From Dr. Mather to Dr. Seuss: 200 Years of American Books for Children*. Boston: G.K. Hall.

McDannell, Colleen (1986). *The Christian Home in Victorian America, 1840-1900*. Bloomington: Indiana University Press.

Macleod, David I. (1983). *Building Character in the American Boy: The Boy Scouts, YMCA, and Their Forerunners, 1870-1920*. Madison: University of Wisconsin Press.

Mennel, Robert M. (1973). *Thorns and Thistles: Juvenile Delinquents in the United States, 1825-1940*. Hanover, NH: University Press of New England.

Mohl, Raymond A. (1971). *Poverty in New York, 1783-1925*. New York: Oxford University Press.

Morgan, Edmund S. (1966). *The Puritan Family: Religion and Domestic Relations in Seventeeth-Century New England*, Rev. ed. New York: Harper.

Nicholas, David (1991). "Childhood in Medieval Europe." In *Children in Historical and Comparative Perspective: An International Handbook and Research Guide*, edited by Joseph M. Hawes and N. Ray Hiner, 31-52. New York: Greenwood Press.

Passerini, Luisa (1997). "Youth as Metaphor for Social Change: Fascist Italy and America in the 1950s." In *A History of Young People in the West*, vol. II, *Stormy Evolution to Modern Times*, edited by Giovanni Levi and Jean-Claude Schmitt, translated by Carol Volk, 281-340. Cambridge, MA: Harvard University Press.

Rawson, Beryl, ed. (1991). *Marriage, Divorce, and Children in Ancient Rome*. Oxford: Clarendon Press.

Riis, Jacob (1892). *The Children of the Poor*. Reprint. New York: Garrett Press, 1970.

Riis, Jacob (1894). "The Making of Thieves in New York." *Century* 49 (n.s. 27): 109-116.

Ryan, Mary P. (1981). *Cradle of the Middle Class: The Family in Oneida County, New York, 1790-1825*. Cambridge, England: Cambridge University Press.

Shorter, Edward (1975). *The Making of the Modern Family*. New York: Basic Books.

Sommerville, C. John (1992). *The Discovery of Childhood in Puritan England*. Athens: University of Georgia Press.

Spock, Benjamin (1957). *The Common Sense Book of Baby and Child Care*, Rev. ed. New York: Duell, Sloan and Pearce.

Springhall, John (1986). *Coming of Age: Adolescence in Britain, 1860-1960*. Dublin, Ireland: Gill and Macmillan.

Strickland, Charles E., and Andrew Ambrose (1985). "The Baby Boom, Prosperity, and the Changing Worlds of Children, 1945-1963." In *American Childhood: A Research Guide and Historical Handbook*, edited by Joseph M. Hawes and N. Ray Hiner, 533-585. Westport, CT: Greenwood Press.

Sutton, John R. (1988). *Stubborn Children: Controlling Delinquency in the United States, 1640-1981*. Berkeley, CA: University of California Press.

Watkins, John C., Jr. (1998). *The Juvenile Justice Century: A Sociolegal Commentary on American Juvenile Courts*. Durham, NC: Carolina Academic Press.

Watson, Alan (1970). *The Law of the Ancient Romans*. Dallas: Southern Methodist University Press.

Wishy, Bernard W. (1968). *The Child and the Republic: The Dawn of Modern American Child Nurture*. Philadelphia: University of Pennsylvania Press.

Youcha, Geraldine (1995). *Minding the Children: Child Care in America from Colonial Times to the Present*. New York: Scribner.

Zelizer, Viviana A. (1985). *Pricing the Priceless Child: The Changing Social Value of Children*. New York: Basic Books.

NOTES

[1] Morgan (1966), 103.

[2] Lystad (1980).

[3] Friedman (1993).

4   Bushnell (1947), 44, 278.

5   Ibid., 262.

6   Gillis (1974), 138.

7   Ibid.

8   Hall (1904), vol. II, 71-76.

9   Hall (1904), vol. I, 401.

10   Ibid., 349, 356.

11   Ibid., 110.

12   Riis (1892), 215.

13   Spock (1957), 49.

3

Thinking Theoretically

All of us think and talk in theoretical terms, though when we do so we are not likely to characterize what we say with such a high-sounding designation. We use theoretical ideas when we offer general explanations for particular phenomena. Female college students who tell their dorm mates about the aggressive behavior of a male student they dated may get the response: "Well, that's the way guys are; they're like that." The explanation being offered is that there is something characteristic of young men that pushes them—or at least some of them—into behavior that was called "making advances" in days when language was more delicate.

Behind that explanation may lie a deeper one: that the aggression is the result of male hormones, or because of the way men think, or the manner in which they have been brought up, or the standards that they acquire from their fraternity brothers. Or perhaps the behavior is believed to result from drinking or drug use. Each of these ideas represents an attempt to explain *why* something happened. To reach the level of a sophisticated theory, such explanations have to be susceptible to proof and should be able to predict not only the particular event but others as well. That is, males would display aggressive traits in other realms besides the world of dating.

Lower-level explanations can be called axioms, postulates, or a variety of other names. There is very little agreement, at least in the social sciences, about what kinds of explanations qualify as theories rather than as more humble interpretations. Most people in the academic world value theoretical thinking highly—more highly, for example, than research that correlates matters such as the age structure of a society and its delinquency rate. This latter work is regarded as necessary fodder for theoretical interpretation, but it is the quality of the interpretation that tends to take precedence. Scholars often construct theories that are based not on research but on what they know or think they know. Others then support or repudiate these theoretical constructs on the basis of their own research.

Sophisticated theories have to be susceptible to proof or falsification. The idea that good people go to heaven, for instance, however valid, cannot be proved or discredited; therefore, it is a belief, not a theory. In the realm of juvenile delinquency and criminology theory, rarely has a theory been thoroughly falsified. When research demonstrates that the facts do not mesh with the ideas in the theory, people supporting the theory have been able to claim, with some success, that the test does not truly cut to the core of the theoretical ideas. In large part, this happens because the theories themselves are not stated in so exact a manner that a precise test can be carried out and the fate of the theory can come to rest on the results of such a test.

It has not been possible as yet (and it may never be possible) to formulate totally satisfactory theoretical explanations for juvenile delinquency because it involves behaviors as different as murder, arson, shoplifting, sale of dangerous drugs, vandalism, rape, and (occasionally) incorrigibility. The only element that these things seem to have in common is that they are against the law and that people of a certain age caught doing them can be brought before a juvenile court. Robert Rice underlined the complexity of trying to locate a formula that would allow us to interpret all delinquency with a single theory by pointing out that matters defined as juvenile delinquency have about as much in common as the words "quail," "deliquescence," "pique," and "kumquat"—all of which can be said to be similar because each contains the letter "q."

The very different kinds of behavior that make up the world of juvenile delinquency sometimes lead those who study the subject to despair at the idea of discovering any general propositions about the behavior. The President's Commission on Law Enforcement and Administration of Justice maintained in regard to both crime and juvenile delinquency that every single act "is a response to a specific situation by a person with an infinitely complicated psychological and emotional makeup who is subject to infinitely complicated external pressures." The causes of illegal behavior, the commission report observed, "are numerous and mysterious and intertwined."[1]

Others have deplored what they see as the tendency for overblown theoretical statements to ignore the vast and complicated research information that is available about juvenile delinquency. "The history of social theory is too largely a record of generalizations wrung from insufficient facts," Huntington Cairns has maintained.[2] Box 3.1 indicates the longstanding consideration of whether delinquency can be interpreted by a single cause or whether there are different causes for delinquent behaviors.

Box 3.1
How Many Explanations for Delinquency?

> Nigel Walker, Wolfson Professor of Criminology at Cambridge University, taught a course during the summer of 1973 at the Yale Law School, in which he told students that crime and delinquency, like medical disease, could only be understood as the product of many different considerations. The students resisted this idea, insisting that there must be one basic factor that produced delinquency. Walker, normally a very mild-mannered man, became irritated at what he saw as their failure to think clearly.
>
> Later, as he left the classroom with the students, he apologized to them for losing his cool.
>
> No, not at all, one student replied, "It showed that you cared."
>
> The student was Hillary Rodham. Her husband-to-be, Bill Clinton, was also a member of the class.

DELINQUENCY AND THE LAW

Some scholars have concluded that it is only the fact that there is a law against committing acts that are defined as juvenile delinquency that distinguishes the behaviors from other acts and that offers an opportunity to make a statement that applies specifically to them. However, this is true only if the difference between those who commit acts of delinquency and those who do not is related to the laws themselves (or at least the perpetrator's response to such laws). In many cases of delinquency, though, the offender does not care whether the behavior is legal or illegal. There are persons who will drive 80 miles an hour in the United States, where such a speed is illegal, and no slower or faster on a German autobahn where it is permissible. Some juveniles will make obscene telephone calls regardless of whether the law declares that this is delinquent conduct or that it is protected and lawful behavior under the freedom of speech doctrine of the First Amendment to the Constitution. There are many laws of which few of us are aware, so that if we were to violate them their existence could hardly be said to be of any importance in producing our behavior. Nonetheless, the old legal adage, "Ignorance of the law is no excuse," will usually (though not always) prevail, and we will be declared guilty.

Persons who commit delinquent acts often believe that they will not be caught or punished. They also may commit the acts not in defiance of the law but because they have reasons to do so that seem more important to them than what the law may say. Reasons can include a search for thrills and excitement, financial gain, being one of the crowd, or going along with friends.

As an illustration of the law's weak effect in terms of discouraging or encouraging delinquent behavior, think about the case of 15-year-old Lamont Cherry. On the casual suggestion of a 17-year-old friend, Cherry set out to rob someone. The victim, a 47-year-old Russian immigrant house cleaner, was encountered by chance under the Coney Island boardwalk in Brooklyn as she was jogging. The incident resulted in the rape and severe beating of the victim. Cherry, interviewed after he was caught, called the crime "instant and insane," an act that did not make sense to him then and does not make sense to him now. Cherry says that he has recurrent flashbacks about the anguish of the victim. "It's just dark, and I'm the only one out there," he says of the nightmares. "It's just dark, dark, dark. I just wish I could go back to before it happened. Just go back." The fact that what they were doing was illegal, and they knew that it was, had little meaning for Lamont Cherry and the four teenagers with him that night.[3]

In many regards, everyone organizes their actions without particular attention to laws. For example, very few of us would murder, whether or not it was against the law. A good test of this last proposition is to consider the following scenario. Suppose you had good reason to believe the following set of facts: There is an impoverished peasant living in some spot on the globe far distant from you. The peasant is quite old and feeble, and probably has relatively little more time to live. He has no close relatives or friends. If you press a button on your desk, that action will kill the peasant. You are guaranteed that nobody in an official position ever will learn that you were the one who pressed the button. You are to be paid $2 million by those who for their own reasons—perhaps only as part of an experiment—want the peasant dead. Would you press the button?

One could also consider the case of Larry Clark, producer of the film *Kids*, a story of inner-city teenage delinquents heavily involved in skateboards, casual theft, fighting, and smoking marijuana. Clark himself started using drugs when he was 16 years old in what he now calls his "outlaw years." He went to prison for shooting a man. Today, absorbed in filmmaking, Clark has abandoned drugs and given up smoking cigarettes. Why had he behaved as he did when he was a teenager? "Because I wanted to," Clark says today. "I was totally ugly on drugs. Thought it was the right thing to do." Speaking of his present life, he says: "I get up early, touch my toes, do some push-ups. Feel good in the morning. All because I want to work."[4]

Sometimes the fact that a behavior is against the law is exactly what makes it exciting. Note the observations below of a heroin user interviewed by Jeremy Larner:

If narcotics was easy to come by, there wouldn't be half as many addicts. To take narcotics right now, it is cloak-and-dagger, it's spy work, it's something out of television, believe me. You have to walk the street, you have to secure a pusher, you have to locate the money to buy these narcotics, you have to check in dark hallways, on roofs, go through cellars, all this running about, all the time, keeping one eye on the police. This is an adventure for a young man. And when you finally get your narcotics back to your pad where you can use it, you say to yourself: Man, I did it, I beat the fuzz. I made the scene.[5]

A careful reading of the young addict's words indicates that the common belief that heroin use represents a withdrawal from society may be far from the truth. It might be argued that ordinary life is much less demanding than existence in the world of heroin, with its imperative demands. Indeed, it is possible that the inability to adjust to the looser requirements of everyday work and play is what impels some youngsters to take up heroin use, and thereby to severely curtail their freedom of action.

Making theoretical sense out of vignettes such as these presents a challenge to those who study juvenile delinquency. Not surprisingly, few people hazard guesses about particular individual delinquents; a person may, for reasons such as those offered by Clark, defy the odds. The predictions almost invariably are statistical ones. For instance, of 100 young people who have a particular profile, so many (say, 79) are likely to do this or that. Natural science predictions, of course, can be considerably more precise: Drop 100 similar baseballs from 100 feet off the ground and, if you know the atmospheric conditions, you can predict when all 100 will make their first bounce on earth.

The Role of Law

Some people (sometimes half jokingly) suggest that the truest cause of delinquency is the existence of laws defining it. Abolish the laws, they say, and we will have solved the problem of delinquency. It is true that such a step would cure the society of a phenomenon that now bears the name "juvenile delinquency," but it is also obvious that virtually all (and very likely more) of the same kinds of acts will continue. Laws do not cause delinquency, except in the relatively rare cases in which youths get particular satisfaction out of doing the forbidden. Laws only specify delinquent acts, as defined in Chapter 1. Without the laws, however, most of the behaviors condemned under them would still remain taboo. After all, few stores would permit their merchandise to be taken without payment by anyone who so chooses, and few of us will amiably allow others to kill us. People would have to band together to create some kind of a system under which they could be protected from the more outrageous kinds of injury and loss.

The Function of Law

To summarize material in Chapter 1, the major function of the law of juvenile delinquency is to set forth in a formal manner a roster of forbidden acts and to thereby add a moral dimension and a formal punishment to these behaviors. Regardless of the law's stand, many acts of delinquency will elicit strong informal sanctions. People who steal things, hurt others, or engage in any number of behaviors that are deemed to be offensive or unacceptable will come to learn that they are not welcome in some circles. Parents often will nag, scold, and impose penalties. Offenders are forbidden to use the car, denied an allowance, grounded, or may have their "wings clipped" in dozens of other ways.

Nonetheless, it is the law—and the law alone—that allows the state to take action against a person who is adjudicated as a juvenile delinquent. The law makes it very different to sell cigarettes than to sell marijuana. Vicious gossip may be more injurious than a simple assault, but the legal status of the first (within certain limits) and the illegality of the second give additional meanings to the behaviors. In the Bible, Paul notes that the laws brought him knowledge of sin (Romans 3:20), indicating the force of legal doctrine in both reflecting and establishing moral principles. In later American scholarship, Jerome Michael, a criminal law professor, and Mortimer J. Adler, an eminent philosopher, noted that "the criminal law is the formal cause of crime. That does not mean that the law produces the behavior which it prohibits. It means only that the criminal law gives the behavior its quality of criminality."[6]

THEORY DEFINED

Despite the considerable difficulty involved, it is essential to try to organize the information we possess about delinquency so that we can interpret it more satisfactorily, come to appreciate meaningful regularities, and predict on the basis of our theories the likelihood that certain kinds of persons will become delinquent and that certain social conditions and arrangements will produce certain levels of delinquent activity. Theory is like a magnet that draws filings together. Nonetheless, it is not necessary to have a theoretical understanding of the roots of delinquency in order to deal with it effectively. For example, quinine was employed to treat malaria long before physicians came to appreciate the crucial role of stagnant water and the anopheles mosquito in transmitting the disease. Theoretical understanding, such as the rules of disease transmission, allows us to operate with something more than a pragmatic and intuitive approach to the problems we seek to solve.

A particular difficulty with theories lies in their tendency to induce a kind of blindness among their advocates and supporters about information that does not fit with their assumptions. Thomas Huxley, a famous scientist, once remarked that nothing is more tragic than the murder of a grand theory by a little fact. However, he hastened to add that nothing proved more surprising than the way in which a theory will continue to survive long after its brains have been knocked out. Nonetheless, the pursuit of sound theory has a strong appeal. The eminent psychologist William James outlined the character and value of theory in words that should be kept in mind as we review various propositions in the following four chapters:

> Investigators have become accustomed to the notion that no theory is absolutely a transcript of reality but that any one of them may from some point of view be useful. Their great use is to summarize old facts and lead to new ones. They are only a man-made language, a conceptual shorthand in which we write our reports of nature; and languages, as is well known, tolerate much choice of expression and many dialects.[7]

At the same time, while appreciating the value of theory, Frank Williams made a point about the limits of current theoretical thought in regard to delinquency:

> Our theories variously paint a picture of criminals [and delinquents] who had too many bad friends, or who were under too much pressure to succeed, or who were not given the proper values as a child. While we can all nod our heads sagely saying "those indeed are the critical variables of criminality," most of us do not really believe that. Humans are too complex to be affected so simply, and *not one of the theorists and researchers would attribute his or her own behavior to something so simple*. Where is a picture of the excitement, the pump of adrenaline, the breathlessness, we know from our own small transgressions. Existing theory is dangerously *sterile*; street life is not.[8]

THEORIES OF DELINQUENCY

Theories Keyed to Behaviors

There are various approaches to an understanding of delinquency. Among them, we can differentiate sociological, psychological, and anthropological formulations. Other theoretical realms also will be considered in subsequent chapters.

Sociological Insight

Sociologists have contributed a great deal of theoretical understanding regarding the formation and behavior of juvenile gangs. Investigation of gangs fits well with long-standing sociological concern with interactions among groups of persons and with the need of almost all of us to affiliate with groups. But theories of gang behavior, however sophisticated, will not carry us very far toward understanding a lone 12-year-old arsonist with no friends who is found to have a brain lesion that impairs social judgment.

The Psychological Approach

Psychologists offer theories that account for individual behavior, but their work usually is insensitive to matters such as the impact of social values on delinquent behavior. The work of social psychologists will not help us very much when we try to learn why one part of a city—often a slum enclave—has a great deal of gang activity, while another part—perhaps the affluent suburbs—is marked by different kinds and apparently lesser amounts of delinquency.

Anthropological Insight

Margaret Mead's early anthropological studies illuminate the limitations of work that focuses on individual personality traits without taking into account the social setting in which the person operates. Mead points out, for instance, that the Arapesh people disapprove of personality traits that Western cultures find admirable. In Arapesh culture, it is not aggression that is deplored but rather behavior that rouses anger and violence in another person. If a young man refuses to reveal something, for instance, and this brings forth a violent response from an adult, the young person would be viewed as being in the wrong. Traits that would be related to success in our society are considered deviant in the world of the Arapesh. As Mead notes:

There were individuals among the Arapesh who were capable of good, clear thinking and some of the little boys did a fine job on the "ball and field" test of the Stanford-Binet intelligence test. These were, however, deviant individuals who had difficulty in dealing with the soft, uncertain outlines of the culture, in which no one did skilled work.[9]

Because they were "deviants" among the Arapesh, such individuals found themselves isolated from the mainstream and at times pushed into behaviors that the Arapesh ruling group regarded in much the same manner as we regard juvenile delinquency.

Problems with Constructing Delinquency Theories

In short, as a concept in search of theoretical integrity, the construct "juvenile delinquency" leaves an enormous amount to be desired from a scientific viewpoint. The difficulty of defining it has been noted in Chapter 1. It is anchored in law and legal processes, and the law varies from jurisdiction to jurisdiction. It is inconstant in the sense that today's forbidden act can be tomorrow's permissible behavior (note how the laws against gambling and homosexuality have changed in the last few generations) and vice versa. Delinquency also is restricted to an age span that varies from place to place and rests on an arguable proposition: that there is something significantly different about youth crime in contrast to illegal acts committed by adults.

This last item is particularly disconcerting when we come to review the parade of ideas that have been advanced in attempts to explain juvenile delinquency. Many of the theories draw exclusively upon studies that have been done on adult criminals and presume that the same things are true of their underage counterparts; after all, what could be different about the reasons why a person just short of his eighteenth birthday committed a burglary and another person a few days or so past that birthday also did so? Unless perhaps (though unlikely) it was the prospect of being able to face a juvenile court judge rather than an adult tribunal that triggered the former offense.

Some major distinctions, however, between adult criminals and young offenders can be found in the nature of the offenses that are perpetrated by those in each category. Juveniles, for example, do not commit white-collar offenses such as insider trading and antitrust violations because they have not attained the positions in the business world necessary for the launching of such illegal behavior. Similarly, as noted earlier, adults cannot be found guilty of school truancy or similar kinds of behaviors defined as impermissible only for those under a specified age.

Just as many theories of delinquency result from studies of adult criminals, many of the most highly regarded theories of crime emerge from investigations of juvenile law-breaking. Among the particular reasons for this is that studies of delinquents are somewhat easier to carry out than studies of adult offenders. Young persons often are more readily available and much less threatening personally than mature offenders. What sensible scholar, for example, would seek to penetrate the ranks of organized crime in order to obtain a fuller understanding of the operations of the Mafia? If we were to restrict our inventory only to theories that are directly related to delinquency, we would overlook a very large part of the roster of attempts to understand the behavior. Therefore, we will scrutinize a variety of theories of crime and delinquency that appear to have merit, though we will attend much more closely to those that deal directly with juvenile miscreants.

Broken Homes and Delinquency

The fact that so many theories of delinquency exist—and persist— is a sign of the problems connected with providing satisfactory inter- pretations of the behavior. Most sophisticated sciences have a dominant theory or, at least, a very few competing theories that deal with their subject matter. The study of crime and delinquency, however, is marked by adherents to this or that of the very many schools of thought, with little consensus about which offers the best prospect for a comprehen- sive understanding of the roots of delinquent activity.

Take, by way of illustration, the belief that "broken homes" (fam- ilies in which one parent is absent) cause juvenile delinquency. A few decades ago, this idea, standing alone, was particularly popular. In those earlier times, when divorce was much less common than it is now, there was even greater emphasis on the terrible effects for children of split families. Delinquency would be reduced, it was claimed, only if moth- ers and fathers could be persuaded to remain together, if only "for the sake of the children." Today, the theme of broken homes has been incorporated into other theories that stress the inadequacy of family training in personal values and the alleged sorry consequences of dual- income families in which children are farmed out to child-care workers and day-care centers from a very early age.

There is some surface plausibility in the idea that broken homes pro- duce wayward adolescents. For one thing, children of divorced or sep- arated parents usually live with the mother, and she is seen as having less control and authority, particularly over her sons, than would have been the case if the father had remained in the home. Also, a split fam- ily usually has to reduce its standard of living and sometimes falls to levels of poverty that tend to be associated with delinquent behavior.

There are, however, innumerable inadequacies in the theoretical proposition that "broken homes cause delinquency." First, there has been a dramatic increase in the percentage of broken homes, well ahead of the escalating rate of delinquency. Second, it is obvious that millions of youngsters have been raised in homes broken by divorce, separation, or death without having committed delinquent acts other than the pranks that are engaged in by almost every youngster. Finally, it is obvious that just as many girls as boys are the product of broken homes, but significantly fewer girls than boys engage in delinquent acts. Obviously, it is something other than—or in addition to—broken homes that might explain the genesis and nature of delinquency.

Numerous studies have sought to pinpoint more precisely what might be the destructive aspects of broken homes. Patricia Van Voorhis and her coworkers found that it is the quality of home life that leads to delinquent behavior, regardless of whether the family is intact. Physical abuse, conflict, lack of affection, minimal supervision, and little enjoyment in the home are correlated with delinquency. Lack of affection and supervision relate to drug and property offenses, while abuse is tied to later delinquent behavior. Others have focused on the age of the children when the parents separated, the sex of each sibling, how many children there are and their age differences, and the dating and remarriage patterns of the parents. One researcher concluded that the intelligence of the child is an important factor in determining the effect of a broken home: the more intelligent the child, the better that child is able to cope with troubles at home.

Obviously, many other matters besides the breakup of parents will play into delinquency. For example, the outcome is apt to differ if a divorced mother marries a wealthy second husband who adores her and her infant child, or if a divorcée is forced onto welfare in order to care for two junior high school boys already experiencing difficulty in school. How involved each of the divorced parents remain in the upbringing of their children likely will also have an influence on how the children turn out.

That the broken home-delinquency link is not merely past history is indicated by a 1995 report by Nicholas Kristof that suggested that the explanation of the strikingly low rate of delinquency in Japan is to be found in the much larger number of intact families in that country. Only 1.1 percent of Japanese children are born to unmarried mothers, compared to 30.1 percent in the United States.[10] The report drew a sharp retort that pointed out, as we have, that "there is certainly no consensus among sociologists about whether it is the absence of a father or the absence of economic opportunity that leads children of broken families to commit crimes in greater numbers." Then the critic offered her own theory of delinquency, insisting that it was the product of the fact that "increasing numbers of Americans are impoverished, alienated and desperate, and society offers them little assistance, compassion or hope."[11] The low Japanese crime rate also may be the result of rigorous inculcation of principles of good behavior in Japanese children. Tellingly, in the Japanese version of "Goldilocks and the Three Bears," the story does not end with Goldilocks fleeing after she is discovered eating the bears' porridge and sleeping in their beds. Instead, she apologizes profusely and then she and the bears sit down together for a friendly meal.

The broken-home theory, we can see, provides at best only some possible clues to the kind of disturbances that might be related to delinquency under certain circumstances for certain kinds of people to whom other things might happen. It is by no means a powerful or a persuasive statement. It fails to meet satisfactorily any of the three attributes for a satisfactory causal statement set forth by Harold Kelly:

1. *distinctiveness*—the degree to which the effect (delinquency) occurs primarily in the presence of one causal candidate (broken homes) and not in the presence of others;

2. *consistency*—the degree to which the effect is observed reliably when a particular causal candidate is present; and

3. *consensus*—the degree to which people other than the target actors show the effect.

Families in which both parents are away from home during the day or those that are broken by separation, divorce, or death may (or may not) have a relationship to juvenile delinquency. The evidence indicates, though, that such a relationship, where it exists, is very much more complicated than simple-minded attempts to relate one phenomenon directly to the other. Innumerable additional considerations come into play and many of these are very much more significant than the broken homes and working families that are alleged to produce the delinquency.

THEORY AND RESEARCH

The eminent physical anthropologist, Mary Leakey, noted that she preferred field work in the hot African sun to theorizing in the shade. "Theories come and go," she maintained, "but fundamental data always remain the same."[12] Leakey's observation can be taken as a headnote on the issue of the relationship between theory and research. The goal of science always has been to derive theories from observation, field work, and experiments and to test the theories that are advocated by the same kind of tactics. Sometimes the research that gave birth to a theory will be duplicated to see if the same results emerge; at other times, different approaches will be used to determine whether the theory holds up and how far its reach may be extended.

The study of juvenile delinquency often has strayed far from the ideal blueprint of the way a scientific enterprise should proceed. For one thing, academic journals are disinclined to publish material that is not theory-driven and, in more recent years, reports that are not heavily quantitative. It has been said that economics is now a branch of applied mathematics and that the social sciences are headed in the same direction. Persistently reducing the reality of juvenile delinquency to simple equations and single alleged causal concepts (for instance, self-control) can result in the loss of adequate comprehension of the complex and many-sided aspects of this form of human behavior.

For our part, we yearn for a balanced menu in which all kinds of knowledge—quantitative and qualitative—are equally valued if they serve to provide insight into any aspect of juvenile delinquency and the response to it. The building and testing of research and theory are not cookbook enterprises. Generally, as a good cook does, a researcher will have favorite recipes and a thorough basic knowledge of techniques and rules, and of the intricacies of induction, deduction, and logical thinking. In the final analysis, though, imagination and ingenuity will be the touchstones of truly valuable research work and theoretical developments. Good researchers ponder the most effective tactics they can use to understand the complicated considerations underlying juvenile delinquency, trying to leave themselves open for any interpretation that may be conveyed to them by their field experience.

Some years ago, Eugene Webb, Donald Campbell, and two other authors, in a classic book on social science research, used a statement by Arnold Binder (one of the authors of this text) as a whole chapter. In its entirety it reads:

> We must use all available weapons of attack, face our problems realistically and not retreat to the land of fashionable sterility, learn to sweat over our data with an admixture of judgment and intuitive imagination, and accept the usefulness of particular data even when the level of analysis for them is markedly below that available for other data in the empirical area.[13]

A similar view has been expressed by Percy Bridgman, a Nobel Prize winner:

> I like to say that there is no scientific method as such, but that the most vital feature of the scientist's procedure has been merely to do his utmost with his mind, *no holds barred*. This

means in particular that no special privileges are accorded to authority or to tradition, that personal prejudices and predilections are carefully guarded against, and that one makes continued check to assure one's self that one is not making mistakes, and that any line of inquiry will be followed that appears at all promising.[14]

Today's social scientists, unfortunately, are often a good deal more sophisticated in statistical techniques than they are in the gathering of information in the precincts where the behavior they are concerned with takes place. Careers are being made by the secondary analysis of large data sets, without the research worker having had any direct contact with the people and the issues that are translated into numbers and fed into the computer. There may be a more compelling need at the moment to go out and sweat (and freeze) in order to better comprehend the nuances of various forms of delinquent behavior so that such information can better ground theoretical statements.

Causation

It is important to examine further the concept of causation that has been raised in the preceding pages. A theory placing emphasis on broken homes cannot be discarded only on the ground that a single exception can be found to the postulated cause, or even because there are quite a few exceptions. We downgrade the theory because it is so loose, because it omits so many important considerations, and because it explains so little and turns attention away from what could prove to be more meaningful factors associated with delinquent behavior.

Social science theories, including those related to juvenile delinquency, commonly fall far short of a perfect alignment between suggested causal factors and an invariant outcome. In good causal postulations, however, the gaps are susceptible to empirical inquiry, and the nature of such inquiry can be determined readily from the theoretical statement. "What we call a cause typically is, and is recognized as being, only a partial cause," John Mackie has noted. The stated cause, Mackie observes, is what makes the difference.[15] David Hume, an eighteenth-century philosopher, put the matter this way: "We may define a cause to be an object to be followed by another and where all the objects similar to the first are followed by objects similar to the second. Or in other words, where, if the first object had not been, the second had never existed."[16]

John Stuart Mill, a preeminent philosopher of the nineteenth century, suggested that instead of cause we ought to employ the term "condition." In a famous statement, Mill noted: "Nothing can better show the absence of any scientific ground for the distinction between the cause of a phenomenon and its conditions, than the capricious manner in which we select among the conditions which we choose to denominate the cause."[17] More simply put, Mill is saying that when there are many circumstances involved in the production of a phenomenon such as delinquency, interpreters often select as "the cause" the one that best fits with their personal or political biases and preferences.

Suppose that during an intense storm, lightning strikes a hotel and it catches fire. We ordinarily would say that the fire was "caused" by the lightning. Some, though, may insist that the fundamental cause of the destruction of the hotel was the failure of the owner to install lightning rods on the structure. Philosopher Daniel M. Hausman, using the same kind of illustration, shows how, with human behavior, we ignore many aspects of cause because we assume that these matters operated as we would guess they would in producing the particular result:

> Suppose a fire breaks out in a hotel and hundreds flee. The fire explains why they fled. It is silly to explain their flight by pointing out that the occupants noticed the fire alarm, that they believed that they might be in danger, and they preferred not to be burned. The claims about beliefs and preferences are scarcely worth making. But the correctness of the explanation depends upon their truth. If the occupants did not notice the fire or fire alarm and would not have cared if they had, then the fire does not explain their flight.[18]

To take another example: if a police officer shoots and kills a juvenile who threatens him with a rifle, we may say that the youngster's death was "caused" by the officer's bullet. However, we also could maintain that the true cause was the officer's failure to keep his cool and deal with the offender in a less lethal manner or, alternatively, that it was due to the carelessness of the boy's parents in allowing the youngster to have a rifle.

As Mill indicated, one often has one's pick of causes; the one that is selected reflects the point that the chooser wants to make. The lightning and bullet examples also convey the general understanding that we can say that A caused B if the occurrence of A led to the occurrence of B, and that if A had not occurred, B would not have happened. In addition to the time sequencing, we use the term "cause" only when we have some idea or explanation of why the occurrence of A led to the occurrence of B. Nonetheless, the precise meaning of "cause" remains complicated.

The complexities and uncertainties of pinpointing causality in crime and delinquency are forcefully indicated by Bruce DiCristina:

Although many criminologists appear to believe that the causes of crime can be discovered with a significant degree of certainty, there is no logical foundation for the position. If a researcher claims to have discovered a causal relationship, or to have demonstrated that a special causal relationship is highly probable, there is good reason to be skeptical. The obstacles that surround the issues of causation, temporal relations, and the elimination of rival causal factors suggest that such claims are little more than constructs of the imagination. Some causal assertions may be true. But how can we ever know for certain which ones?[19]

In a survey of "The Concept of Cause," two well-known psychologists, Thomas Cook and Donald Campbell, offered the following verdict: "The epistemology [that is, the basis] of causation . . . is at present in a state of near chaos. We are far from satisfied with our treatment of it here and find in it no completely satisfying resolution of the major problems of causation."[20]

There is another difficulty with thinking in causal terms, one involving interpretation of sequential events. It is perhaps best illustrated by the story (hopefully only a story) of the professor who holds a frog and says loudly: "Jump!" The frog jumps, then the professor cuts off the frog's legs and again yells "Jump." The frog remains inert. "So you see," the professor proclaims, "when you cut the legs off a frog, it grows quite deaf."

If, then, students of juvenile delinquency have difficulty dealing comfortably with issues of causation, they can take satisfaction in the fact that this frustration is shared by some of the best minds of current as well as earlier times. For present purposes, the principles noted in the foregoing paragraphs and recourse to the dictionary definition should suffice. *Merriam-Webster's Collegiate Dictionary*, Tenth Edition, defines cause as "something that brings about an effect or a result; a person or thing that is the occasion of an action or state, especially: an agent that brings something about." This is how we will use the term "cause" in our review of theories of delinquency.

Determinism and Free Will

The aim of theories of juvenile delinquency is to provide a better understanding of the behavior by showing how it is the product of particular conditions and processes. Once these matters are understood, it is reasoned, then the behavior can be predicted and handled. This assumes, of course, that delinquents do not possess an ability to do something besides what circumstances dictate. Can a person who seems without question doomed to become involved in delinquent activities make up his or her mind not to do so? This is an exceedingly complicated question to which no one has an answer with which everyone else will agree.

Determinism

Determinists believe that everything we do is ordained by what we are and what happens to us; we have no choice in the matter. They maintain that every event, from the most trivial collision of two billiard balls to the most considered decision to start a new career—or to commit a delinquent act—is the product of prior causal conditions that necessitated that event. It is the belief, as Lawrence Fraley put it, that "given the conditions surrounding an event, nothing but it *could* have happened."[21] If others were smart enough, they could anticipate everything we do and everything we say, though it is granted that this is never likely to happen, at least in the near future. The psychologist William James stated the principles of determinism in these words:

> It professes that those parts of the universe already laid down absolutely appoint and decree what other parts shall be. The future has no ambiguous possibilities hidden in its womb. Any other future complement than the one fixed from eternity is impossible. The whole is in each and every part, and welds with the rest into an absolute unity, an iron block, in which there can be no equivocation.[22]

Using the rationale of determinism, defense attorneys have argued before the courts that accused delinquents and criminal offenders should not be held responsible for their illegal behavior because what they did was predetermined by their being an abused child or a battered spouse, or because they were caught up in neighborhood violence. It has been said (and jurors have sometimes been persuaded) that such experiences rendered the defendant incapable of choosing not to castrate her husband, bury a brick in a victim's skill, or blow off his mother's face with a shotgun.

Free Will

A contrasting viewpoint is the free will doctrine, insisting that human beings uniquely have the ability to choose to do or not to do something, regardless of the forces that press upon them. Free will is a doctrine deeply rooted in religious traditions. Its defenders believe in the human ability to choose between good and evil, despite a history of child or spousal abuse or the strongest temptation. Free will is considered to be the key element of human nature.

A compromise position, one that likely represents the view of most social scientists, is that our behavior is ruled by soft determinism. According to this belief, many actions are beyond our control because they are determined by what we are and our experiences, but we still retain the power to make choices in important areas of our life, though things such as disease draw in the boundaries of free will.

Theoretical thinking has to presume that human behavior can be predicted from prior circumstances. We know (or at least are very certain) that a dropped cannonball, given specified circumstances, will not "decide" to float upward rather than fall downward, but we are less convinced that a young person with a certain personality and background, placed into particular circumstances, will not decide to behave in ways other than those we believed he or she would behave. In a valiant attempt to use delinquency data to determine whether wayward acts are a matter of choice or are predetermined, Robert Agnew concluded that delinquency by an individual who has a large number of behavioral options is less readily predictable than that by a person with fewer options. However, Agnew had to grant that it remained impossible to truly adjudicate the fundamental matter of determinism and free will.

The issue of free will and determinism, as Richard A. Wright has indicated, is pivotal to criminology. A person's position on this question influences his or her thinking about the purposes of criminal law, the explanations for crime, the fairness of punishment and the prospects for treatment. Determinists, for instance, find it difficult to justify punishments for behaviors that are beyond human control. They are caught in an odd intellectual trap, though, because their own views (if their premise is correct) are themselves predetermined by prior circumstances.

What Does it Come To?

That those who study juvenile delinquency cannot agree on whether the behavior is the product of free will decisions or is driven by deterministic principles reflects an ongoing impasse that also characterizes more scientifically sophisticated fields of investigation such as physics. In physics, at least, we are dealing with objects that do not possess a brain. Nonetheless, there is a considerable split among the leading theoreticians in physics about determinism and free will.

For instance, chaos theory in physics (first enunciated in the early 1960s) is based on the fact that many phenomena do not unfold in a predictable way but act in what appears to be a random manner or, as one wry scientist has said, in a predictably unpredictable way. Nonetheless, Francis Crick, who with James Watson won the Nobel Prize in 1953 for having unraveled the twin-corkscrew structure of DNA, is quite certain that determinism rules: "What you are aware of is a decision. It seems free to you, but it's the result of things you're not aware of."[23] The opening paragraph of Crick's *The Astonishing Hypothesis* reads:

> Is that "You," your joys and your sorrows, your memories and your ambitions, your sense of personal identity and free will, in fact no more than the behavior of a vast assembly of nerve cells and their associated molecules?

Watson thinks the answer to his question is "Yes, it is you." In physics, the soft determinism position has been stated by Ilya Prigogine, a 1977 winner of the Nobel Prize: "What we have to find is a middle way," he believes, "to find a probabilistic statement [about behavior]." Prigonine appreciates the extraordinary difficulty of predicting human behavior. "When you decide whether you take coffee or not, that's already a complicated decision. It depends on what day it is, whether you like coffee, and so on."[24]

Noam Chomsky, a linguist, summed it up in a statement claiming that scientists have made absolutely no progress in investigating the issues of determinism and free will. "We don't even have bad ideas," he says.[25]

ON THEORETICAL THINKING

The causes of delinquency are considerably more complicated than the explanations of physical phenomena, and this, among other things, has led to the production of a considerable range of theories, all competing for endorsement. The competition will be resolved only when there is agreement that one or another theory offers the best understanding of delinquency. This, Charles Hartshorne and Paul Weiss have observed, is the definition of truth: "The opinion which is fated to be agreed to by all who investigate."[26]

Though we remain a long way from production of a satisfactory theory of juvenile delinquency, there is no question that the attempt is thoroughly worthwhile. A good theory can organize an enormous amount of scattered facts into a coherent and impressively informative shape. Consider, for instance, the theory of gravity, which is able to provide a single explanation for such varied knowledge as the movement of tides, the erect posture of trees, and the difficulty of writing on the ceiling with a ballpoint pen. A child might say that a stone dropped because it "wanted to." A profound thinker in Aristotle's time probably would have said that the stone dropped because it possessed the property of gravity. It was only after Isaac Newton propounded his theory that we could declare that the stone dropped because it existed in a field of forces of which the most relevant were the mass of the stone, the earth's gravitational pull, and the relative insubstantiality of the intervening medium (in this case, air). The theory of gravity allows us to understand the extraordinary demands for blood circulation that are made upon the human body when it is standing, and it explains why some quadrupeds not adapted to the upright position may be killed merely by suspending them vertically. "The supreme goal of all theory," said Albert Einstein, one of the most renowned theorists of all time, "is to make the irreducible basic elements as simple and as few as possible without having to surrender the adequate representation of a single datum of experience."[27] Einstein accomplished this feat (called parsimonious explanation) for the phenomenon of relativity by representing its essential elements in the famous formula $e = mc^2$.

Human behavior, such as juvenile delinquency, seems much more resistant to reduction to theoretical shorthand. As we have noted, this in large part may be because humans can think creatively and apparently can exercise some degree of choice in how they elect to behave. Sociologist Anthony Giddens has observed that "theories and concepts emerge in social science like popcorn, puffed up by their own steam" and that they are defended by "warring factions which group themselves under the umbrella of their own singular visions."[28] Richard Nisbett and Lee Ross point out that many theories, particularly in the realm of human conduct, are no more than flimsy ideas, uncritically passed from one person to another. They note in this regard:

> Many causal theories originate not from summaries of scientific theories or informed expert opinion, or from close and systematic observation, but rather originate from much more haphazard and uncertain sources. Many causal theories seem to have come from maxims, parables, myths, fables, epigrams, allegories, well-known songs or novels, and anecdotes about famous people or personal acquaintances.[29]

The same writers point out that many popular ideas contradict each other—just as some theories of delinquency do—but that such logical inconsistency seems to have no effect on their support. Thus, for instance, some people are told that "absence makes the heart grow fonder," while others are equally seriously forewarned that "out of sight, out of mind." We are informed that "a penny saved is a penny earned," advice that is contradicted by the idea that you have got to spend money to make money.

Nonetheless, what the theories of juvenile delinquency most importantly have to offer is a crude blueprint of the kinds of approaches that might begin to increase our understanding of the roots of delinquent behavior. They call our attention to ways to try to comprehend what is going on and, if nothing else, they provide targets and building blocks that can be used to advance further in our interpretative efforts.

Sometimes though, current theories seem to be no more than ideas "puffed up like popcorn by their own steam." When dealing with complicated theories, one is sometimes reminded of the response of Lord Byron, the famous British poet who listened to a complicated theoretical talk and then said: "I wish he would explain his explanations." Theories of delinquency, though, often represent the product of good minds grappling with very complicated issues, and in that regard they have much to offer. They also stand as challenges to the current crop of students from whose ranks future theoretical insights regarding delinquency will emerge.

THE PUBLIC'S VIEW OF CAUSES OF DELINQUENCY

The General Nature of Popular Ideas

Though most people will grant that they do not quite understand the principles that underlie space flight, much less how a television set works, they often are convinced that they know for certain why kids get into trouble. Two research workers found that in the United States and the United Kingdom a majority of people believe that delinquency primarily is the result of a lack of parental discipline. Older persons more than younger ones also think that the decline of religion is a major contributor to delinquent behavior. A study in Britain examined the views of 300 respondents who were asked to evaluate 30 common explanations for delinquency and to rate each on a seven-point scale. Political beliefs were found to be closely related to a person's ideas about delinquency. Conservatives explained delinquency primarily in terms of a failure in social and moral education, while liberals were likely to blame it on the injustices of society. Women more than men fixed on faulty parental practices as the major cause of wayward youngster behavior. Three items were particularly prominent in the responses: (1) the high level of unemployment among youths, (2) the perils of life in high delinquency neighborhoods, and (3) the absence of satisfactory recreational and leisure activities for young people.

Despite the possible accuracy of such explanations, they do not cut to the core of the problem of delinquency. Youth unemployment is a social evil on its own merits, but studies suggest that it is at best only mildly related to delinquency. For one thing, when youths are unable to obtain jobs because of depressed economic conditions, it is likely that many of their parents also are unemployed. In such instances, parents forced to remain at home often are able to supervise their children more closely than when they are at work. In addition, employment means extra spending money for adolescents, and such money can provide them with independence from parental care and the wherewithal to get into trouble. A youth's income can finance the purchase of a car, and, as Jackson Toby has pointed out: "In the age of the automobile, an adolescent's home may be the place where he sleeps and little else." A car, Toby observes, is a notably "effective instrument for escaping the eyes of adults."[30] Without work and the money it provides, youths generally have less freedom and therefore less opportunity to get into trouble. Overall, the relationship between factors such as youth employment and delinquency can be seen to be quite complex.

The Case of the Subway Vigilante

A striking illustration of popular ideas about the causes of delinquency arose in what became known as the "Case of the Subway Vigilante." Bernhard H. Goetz, an electronics engineer living in New York City, was riding on the subway early on a Saturday afternoon in 1984. He had been attacked on the subway four years earlier and now carried an unlicensed gun because, he said, he feared another attack. On this particular Saturday, four youths approached Goetz and asked him for the time, then for a match, and finally for $5.00. Goetz pulled out his .38-calibre handgun, fired several times, and wounded each of the youths. Later, the young men were discovered to have screwdrivers in their pockets, which they could have used as weapons, although (as the following story indicates) the youths apparently intended to employ the screwdrivers to rob slot machines.

Public support for Goetz's action was generally very strong. However, some persons condemned it, saying that the use of a gun to deal with panhandling and the seemingly remote possibility of violence was a form of vigilantism, much like imposing the death penalty on a wrongdoer for a minor offense and without due process of law. A newspaper poll found that 49 percent of New Yorkers approved Goetz's actions compared to 32 percent who disapproved. Seventeen percent believed he should be awarded a medal for shooting the four teenagers; 58 percent disagreed with the charge of attempted murder that was filed against Goetz; 75 percent thought he had acted in self-defense.[31]

Of particular interest here are the explanations for behavior offered by the mother of one of the four youths. Her son was the most seriously injured. He was in a coma with a severe brain injury when she was interviewed, and later he would be confined to a wheelchair for life and have the mental capacity of an eight-year-old. In the following *New York Times* story, we have placed in italic type the causes for the juvenile delinquency of her son indicated by the offender's mother, as well as one explanation (the absence of "constructive outlets for energy") offered by the news reporter on the basis of talks with neighbors of the youth's family.

Victim's Mother; Worry and Self-Doubt

When Darrel Cabey was arrested for armed robbery and possession of a weapon last October, his first serious offense, he called his mother from the police station and asked her to post bail.

Mrs. Cabey was reluctant to put up the money. "I thought if he had to stay in jail, *he would choose his friends more carefully*," she said.

Mrs. Cabey said she doubts even more now whether she did the right thing by letting relatives persuade her to bail Darrel out. He is in a coma now and paralyzed from the waist down, one of four teenagers who were shot last month by Bernhard Hugo Goetz after they asked him for $5.

"I was really mad when he called," said Mrs. Cabey. "But everyone was saying, 'He's a good boy, don't be so hard.'"

There were signs that Darrel was heading for trouble, Mrs. Cabey said, signs that are familiar to people from the Claremont Village neighborhood in the South Bronx, where the four teenagers live.

"*He was staying outside a lot, and I didn't know what he was doing*," said Mrs. Cabey, a food-services worker who has five other children. "Knowing *the situation out there and the area around here*, I just should have known."

The concrete buildings of Claremont Village are on litter-choked lots, covering block after block of the South Bronx. About 13,500 people live in the city housing complex, and more than half are under 21.

Teenagers who grew up there have *few constructive outlets for their energy*, said many people who live there. Many youngsters, they said, revert to petty crime—shoplifting, breaking into vending machines and video games.

"Kids who live here are under *a lot of peer pressure*," said Mrs. Cabey. "I tried to talk to him, I told him, 'You have two strikes against you, *you're black and you're poor*, so you better get back to studying.' I told him there's more to life than hanging out in the streets. If only he had used *a little common sense*."

Teenagers in the Claremont Project talked knowledge-ably about the risk and sentences for various crimes. "Most guys just hit videos because they're easy and it won't be so bad, like mugging, if they get caught," said Junior Mendez, a 17-year-old. "But it's bad to bust machines around here, or say, up in Harlem, because the owners go after you. Down-town they just call the cops."

Mrs. Cabey said that she encouraged her six children to entertain themselves at home, but she never allowed them to have friends visit because she was afraid they would later return to rob the apartment.

She said she was careful about what she would allow her children to display outside the home. She said she never bought them expensive jackets or bicycles or radios because, she said, "lots of kids have been killed for a 10-speed bike."

Mrs. Cabey said it was difficult to instill values in *a neigh-borhood where wrongdoing and lawbreaking abound. It was easier*, she said, when Darrel was young, and *his father, Ray-mond Eugene Cabey, was alive*.

The family lived in Far Rockaway, Queens, then, but in 1973 Mr. Cabey was crushed to death by a car while trying to wrest his taxi from a thief. A year later, the family moved to Claremont." Everyone said *the change was too much*," said Mrs. Cabey.

Darrel *dropped out of high school* when he was a junior, she said, adding, "I knew by the different things he was doing that something would be up."

But she said he remained a polite and affable young man, and she did not realize *the extent of his predilection for trou-ble*. It is difficult, she said, *to control a teenager who "want-ed to be a man too fast*."

Friends and relatives have given her strength, said Mrs. Cabey, even as she and the families of the other three teenagers have received letters condemning the youths and applauding Mr. Goetz. Some of the letters are from people who have been the victims of crime. Some are very cruel.

"Drop Dead" was written in a greeting card that someone sent to Darrel Cabey.

"I'm not angry," said Mrs. Cabey, who presses the letters between pages of a Bible. "A lot of people have been victims and are boiled up to the boiling point. I am hurt, though, that people would take the time to be so mean. Time is so precious these days."[32]

Darrel Cabey was judged incompetent to testify at the Goetz trial because of his mental condition after the shooting. So as not to preju-dice the jury by letting it know the great extent of injuries inflicted on Cabey, jury members were told only that he was "unavailable." One of

Goetz's victims flew into a rage when cross-examined, hurling obscenities at the judge and defense attorney. This outburst led to 11 charges of contempt of court that added six months to his prison sentence. Some courtroom observers thought that the young man frightened jurors, thus lending credibility to Goetz's position that he had acted out of fear. Goetz had said that the four youths had surrounded him: "They wanted to play with me. You know, it's kind of like a cat plays with a mouse."

After a seven-week trial, Goetz was acquitted of 12 of the 13 counts in the indictment. Conviction was only for illegal possession of a weapon. He was given a sentence of one year and released after two months. George Fletcher, a Columbia University law professor who followed the case closely, disagreed with the ver-

Darrell Cabey sits in his wheelchair at the civil trial against Bernhard Goetz in April 1996. The court ordered Goetz to pay Cabey $43 million for having paralyzed him by gunfire in 1984. The criminal case for the trial convicted Goetz only for illegal possession of a weapon. *(AP Photo/Ralph Ginzburg, New York Post/POOL)*

dict. Fletcher thought that racial attitudes, hostile to the youths, pervaded the trial, even though they never were voiced openly. He was not convinced that "the four young men were about to mug Goetz. If Goetz had said, 'Listen, buddy, I wish I had $5, but I don't,' and walked to the other side of the subway car, the chances are 60-40 nothing would have happened." Why? "Street-wise kids like that," Fletcher said, "are more attuned to the costs of their behavior than Goetz was."[33]

The Bernhard Goetz case did not end with the criminal trial. Nine years later, in April 1996, a six-person civil jury rejected Goetz's claim of self-defense and ordered him to pay $43 million to Darrel Cabey for having paralyzed him by gunfire. Cabey's victory was more moral than material, however, because Goetz has little money. In such instances, it is common for the court to garnish 10 percent of the person's wages for the next 20 years. Notably, the criminal jury that gave Goetz little more than a slap on the wrist had been largely made up of whites, while four blacks and two Hispanic jurors made up the civil jury.

The wide range of explanatory ideas offered in the Goetz case by Darrel Cabey's mother (each one seemingly sensible) form a portrait that generally coincides with popular notions about the roots of juvenile delinquency. We should keep these ideas in mind as we examine the more elaborate formulations of academic scholars and see how their theories line up with the interpretations of persons directly affected by juvenile delinquency and with your own views. We should also bear in mind Donald Shoemaker's general appraisal of theoretical thinking in regard to juvenile delinquency:

> The explanations of delinquency vary widely in substance and empirical verification. Certainly, no one theory can be used to explain all delinquency, or even certain types of delinquency. Furthermore, there is no unifying trait that can be used to connect the diverse and often competing theories. Each explanation has its own strengths and weaknesses, and some theories are, overall, more persuasive than others.[34]

SUMMARY

Theoretical interpretations of the causes of juvenile delinquency abound, but there is no agreement at this time regarding which interpretation offers the most promising path to a fuller understanding of the misbehavior of young persons. Debate also continues concerning whether there is a single, overarching explanation of delinquent activity or whether its various manifestations each require a particular explanatory approach.

A considerable part of the problem lies in the fact that the concept of juvenile delinquency embraces many different forms of activity—some of them aggressive acts, others passive—some done alone, others carried out by small or large groups. It becomes very difficult to formulate an explanatory scheme that provides understanding of matters as different as cold-blooded murder and running away from home.

Theorists today often settle for explanatory outlines that concentrate on some of the major forms of delinquent behavior and ignore the more unusual acts. They also focus on why youngsters get into trouble with the law—regardless of what kind of trouble it may be—and do not attempt to explain why the trouble took the form that it did. In this regard, the theories seek to distinguish conformity to the law from illegal behavior, or at least to differentiate those who get caught from those who do not.

Theories of delinquency offered by persons in universities, colleges, and research institutes often collide with popular explanations. Many persons believe that they understand perfectly well why youngsters misbehave. They have friends, brothers or sisters, or children—or their personal experiences—to provide them with what they regard as telling insight into the roots of "good" and "bad" behavior. In many ways, they undoubtedly possess some worthwhile ideas about delinquency. However, as is often true with academic theories, these ideas begin to fall apart when examined in light of the considerable amount of evidence available about delinquents and their behavior. As with the idea of "broken homes" as the cause of delinquency, other explanations usually prove to have too many exceptions or to be altogether too elementary to offer much hope of being useful as predictors of behavior or as guidelines to public policy.

Nonetheless, the pursuit of useful theoretical formulations remains a preeminent goal in the study of delinquent behavior. Theory offers the possibility of explaining more clearly acts that otherwise appear to be random and incomprehensible. Sophisticated theories can be employed to guide efforts to reduce the extent of the danger that delinquent behavior poses to its victim (and often to perpetrators as well).

REFERENCES

Agnew, Robert (1995). "Determinism and Indeterminism: An Empirical Exploration." *Criminology* 33:83-109.

Banks, C., E. Maloney, and H.D. Willcock (1975). "Public Attitudes to Crime and the Penal System." *British Journal of Criminology* 15:228-240.

Bridgman, Percy W. (1950). *Reflections of a Physicist.* New York: Philosophical Library.

Cairns, Huntington (1935). *Law and the Social Sciences.* New York: Harcourt, Brace.

Cook, Thomas D., and Donald T. Campbell (1979). *Quasi-Experimentation: Design and Analysis Issues for Field Settings.* Chicago: Rand McNally.

Davis, April (1995). Letter to the Editor. *New York Times* (May 18):14.

DiCristina, Bruce (1995). *Method in Criminology: A Philosophical Primer.* New York: Harrow and Heston.

Einstein, Albert (1933). *On the Method of Theoretical Physics.* New York: Oxford University Press.

Fein, Esther (1985). "Victim's Mother; Worry and Self Doubt." *New York Times* (Jan. 12):23.

Fletcher, George (1988). *A Crime of Self-Defense: Bernhard Goetz and the Law on Trial.* New York: Free Press.

Fraley, Lawrence E. (1994). "Uncertainty about Determinism: A Critical Review of Challenges to the Determinism of Modern Science." *Behavior and Philosophy* 22: 71-88.

Giddens, Anthony (1976). *The New Rules of Sociological Methods: A Positive Critique of Interpretative Sociologies*. New York: Basic Books.

Golden, Frederic (1996). "First Lady of Fossils." *Time* (December 23):33.

Gottfredson, Michael R., and Travis Hirschi (1990). *A General Theory of Crime*. Stanford, CA: Stanford University Press.

Hartshorne, Charles, and Paul S. Weiss, eds. (1934). *The Collected Papers of Charles F. Pierce*. Cambridge, MA: Harvard University Press.

Hausman, Donald M. (1992). *Essays on Philosophy and Economics*. New York: Cambridge University Press.

Hirschi, Travis (1973). "Procedural Rules and the Study of Deviant Behavior." *Social Problems* 21:159-173.

Horgan, Paul (1996). *The End of Science: Facing the Limits of Knowledge in the Twilight of the Scientific Age*. Reading, MA: Addison-Wesley.

Hume, David (1777). *Enquiries Concerning Human Understanding and Concerning the Principles of Morals*, 2nd ed. Reprint. Oxford, England: Clarendon Press, 1966.

Huxley, Thomas (1894). *Collected Essays*. New York: Appleton.

James, William (1909). *The Will to Believe and Other Essays in Popular Philosophy*. New York: Longmans, Green.

James, William (1907). *Pragmatism: A New Name for Some Old Ways of Thinking*. New York: Longmans, Green.

Kelley, Harold H. (1967). "Attribution Theory in Social Psychology." In *Nebraska Symposium on Motivation*, vol. 15, edited by David Levine, 192-238. Lincoln: University of Nebraska Press.

Kristof, Nicholas D. (1995). "Japanese Say No to Crime: Tough Methods at a Price." *New York Times* (May 14):D71.

Larner, Jeremy, ed. (1964). *The Addict in the Street*. New York: Grove Press.

Mackie, John L. (1980). *The Cement of the Universe: A Survey of Causation*. Oxford, England: Clarendon Press.

Maslin, Janet (1995). "A Ratings To-Do Over a Raw Tale of City Teen-Agers." *New York Times* (May 23):C13-C14.

Mead, Margaret (1972). *Blackberry Winter: My Earliest Years*. New York: Morrow.

Merriam-Webster's Collegiate Dictionary, 10th ed. (1993). Springfield, MA: Merriam-Webster.

Michael, Jerome, and Mortimer J. Adler (1933). *Crime, Law and Social Science*. New York: Harcourt, Brace.

Mill, John Stuart (1843). *A System of Logic*. London: Longmans, Green.

Nisbett, Richard, and Lee Ross (1980). *Human Inference: Strategies and Shortcomings of Social Judgment*. Englewood Cliffs, NJ: Prentice Hall.

President's Commission on Law Enforcement and Administration of Justice (1967). *The Challenge of Crime in a Free Society*. Washington, DC: U.S. Government Printing Office.

Rice, Robert (1956). *The Business of Crime*. New York: Farrar, Straus & Cudahy.

Rubin, Lillian B. (1986). *Quiet Rage: Bernie Goetz in a Time of Madness*. New York: Farrar, Straus & Giroux.

Sexton, Joe (1995). "Jailed Youth Recalls Whim That Led to a Robbery and Gang Rape." *New York Times* (May 14):29, 32.

Shoemaker, Donald J. (1984). *Theories of Delinquency: An Examination of Explanations of Delinquent Behavior*. New York: Oxford University Press.

Toby, Jackson (1985). "Affluence and Adolescent Crime." In *Delinquency, Crime, and Social Process*, edited by Donald R. Cressey and David A. Ward, 285-311. New York: Harper and Row.

Van Voorhis, Patricia, Francis T. Cullen, Richard A. Mathers, and Connie C. Garner (1988). "The Impact of Family Structure and Quality of Delinquency: A Comparative Assessment of Structural and Functional Factors." *Criminology* 26:235-261.

Webb, Eugene J., Donald T. Campbell, Richard D. Schwartz, Lee Sechrist, and Janet Belew Grove (1981). *Nonreactive Measures in the Social Sciences*. Boston: Houghton Mifflin.

Williams, Franklin P., III (1999). *Imagining Criminology: An Alternative Paradigm*. New York: Garland.

Wright, Richard A. (1995). "Where There's a Will There's No Way: Treatment of the Choice Debate in Criminology Textbooks, 1956 to 1965, 1983 to 1992." *Teaching Sociology* 23:8-15.

NOTES

[1] President's Commission on Law Enforcement and Administration of Justice (1967), 1-2.

[2] Cairns (1935), 20.

[3] Sexton (1995), 29.

[4] Maslin (1995), C14.

[5] Larner (1964), 100.

[6] Michael & Adler (1933), 5.

[7] Mead (1972), 198.

[8] James (1907), 55-58.

[9] Williams (1999), 103.

[10] Kristof (1995), D71.

[11] Davis (1995), 14.

[12] Golden (1996), 33.

[13] Webb et al. (1981), 329.

14   Bridgman (1950), 370.

15   Mackie (1980), xi.

16   Hume (1777), 104.

17   Mill (1843), 215.

18   Hausman (1992), 56.

19   DiCristina (1995), 15.

20   Cook & Campbell (1979), 10.

21   Fraley (1994), 71.

22   James (1909), 150.

23   Horgan (1996), 162.

24   Ibid., 219-220.

25   Ibid., 152.

26   Hartshorne & Weiss (1934), 408.

27   Einstein (1933), 10-11.

28   Giddens (1976), 7.

29   Nisbett & Ross (1980), 119.

30   Toby (1985), 303.

31   Fletcher (1988), 64.

32   Fein (1985), 23.

33   Fletcher (1988), 132.

34   Shoemaker (1984), 225.

4

From Beccaria Forward:
Classical, Rational Choice, Lifestyle, and Constitutional Theories of Juvenile Delinquency

Richard Feynman, a Nobel Prize-winning theoretical physicist, has offered a perceptive criticism of the tendency in social science to cloak commonplace ideas in grand language, thereby obscuring matters rather than clarifying them. Feynman tells of attending a conference in which a paper was read that contained the sentence: "The individual member of the social community often receives his information via visual, symbolic channels." Feynman puzzled his way through this verbiage and concluded that what the social scientist was trying to say was: "People read."[1] The tendency of theorists to employ language in ways that camouflage common understanding sometimes seems to be an occupational disease or a standard that they have come to believe they must meet if they are to be taken seriously. Fancy language can never compensate for sloppy thought; we will try to reduce the theoretical positions regarding juvenile delinquency to clear statements that convey their essential meaning.

Feynman also emphasized that theorists often become so attached to their positions that they strongly resist ideas that might disprove what they have maintained. He points out that good theorists ought to be especially diligent to seek out any possible criticism of their work and to subject that work to intense logical scrutiny. Feynman notes:

Details that could throw doubt upon your interpretations must be given, if you know them. You must do the best you can—if you know anything at all wrong, or possibly wrong—to explain it. If you make a theory, for example, and put it out, then you must also put down all the facts that disagree with it. There is also a more subtle problem. When you have put a lot of ideas together to make an elaborate theory you want to make sure, when explaining what it fits, that those things it fits are not just the things that gave you the idea for the new theory, but that the finished theory makes something else come out right, in addition.[2]

Theories seeking to explain juvenile delinquency generally fall short of such criteria. They are sometimes adept at ignoring contradictory evidence. However, there are many critics alert and ready to pounce upon a vulnerable theory and to point out its shortcomings. It is this critical literature that we will combine with our review of the theoretical statements to provide a full portrait of the ideas.

Two major theoretical schools of an earlier period offer an understanding of the intellectual structure upon which many later ideas were constructed. The first is the classical or utilitarian school of thought, represented by Cesare Beccaria of Italy and Jeremy Bentham of England. Classical theory is in large part based on the assumption that human beings voluntarily choose between good and evil after calculating the costs and benefits of different ways of behaving.

The second theoretical current was dominated by Cesare Lombroso, an Italian physician, who believed that he had located the causes of lawbreaking within the biological traits of the offender. Lombroso's ideas are essentially deterministic, insisting that persons with certain traits (preeminently biological deficiencies) are foreordained to commit criminal acts. This school is known as positivistic because of its attempt to relate certain conditions to certain behaviors experimentally (that is, by direct observation). Both the classical and the positivist theories focused almost exclusively upon adult crime because, as our earlier historical review has shown, the concept of juvenile delinquency had not yet been clearly differentiated. Many students will already have met these older theories in criminology classes. We will seek to make them a bit more sprightly for those revisiting them by providing details about their progenitors and by relating them to the research about delinquency that they foreshadowed.

THE CLASSICAL SCHOOL: UTILITARIANISM

Recent scholarship has seriously disputed the traditional textbook tactic of covering the history of theories of crime and delinquency beginning with the classical school. One reason for this is because the classical school's leaders—Beccaria and Bentham—were interested almost exclusively in issues of penology and social control, not in criminology. Additionally, as Piers Beirne maintains, much of what they wrote has been misrepresented as focusing on free will as opposed to their considerable reliance on deterministic doctrines. The recent chorus debunking the prestige accorded to Beccaria over the last three centuries also notes that there was a strong element of retribution in Beccaria's thinking, and that it was only Bentham's selective use of his material that led to his being regarded as a pure utilitarian. Graeme Newman and Pietro Marongiu write about what they call the Beccaria "myth." They maintain that Beccaria's work is "reactionary" and replete with "irresolvable contradictions." "The adoration afforded Beccaria," they insist, "far outweighs the actual contribution he made."[3] Philip Jenkins contends that Beccaria played a conservative role, defending authority and private property while ignoring the unsettling themes that challenged established power.

These are persuasive points. Moreover, they demonstrate that ideas will be reexamined (maybe hundreds of years later) and might be viewed very differently than when first presented. Only after considerable hesitation did we as authors decide to keep the classicists in their usual place in the line of theoretical development. We did this partly in conformity to tradition, and mostly because utilitarianism (as we shall see) constitutes a strong element in many present-day theories of juvenile delinquency. This said, we now can look at the views of the two leaders of the classical school.

Cesare Beccaria

Cesare Beccaria (1738-1794), a member of the Italian nobility, was the heir of a down-on-its-luck aristocratic Milan family. His training was in law, and his famous *Dei delitti delle pene* [*On Crimes and Punishments*], which ran to fewer than 100 pages in its original edition, was published anonymously in 1764 when Beccaria was just 26 years old. The book gained him worldwide fame and provided the basis for the laws enacted by the Constituent Assembly in France after the Revolution. It also was quoted in 1770 by John Adams (later to become the second President of the United States) in his defense of British soldiers involved in the Boston Massacre. Thomas Jefferson's reading notes also contain extensive quotations from Beccaria. The enduring nature of Beccaria's contribution is testified to by the republication of his book in 1996 in the United States—232 years after it first appeared. The reissue has a Foreword by Mario Cuomo, then Governor of New York, who wrote ("[Beccaria's] work remains one of the best guides we have for what criminal laws and penalties should look like").[4]

After he wrote *Dei delitti della pene*, Beccaria, a timid and reserved man, worked briefly as a university professor. He then settled down in Milan for the remainder of his life to work in bureaucratic jobs with the Austrian government (which controlled Italy), grinding out dry reports on rather inconsequential economic issues.

Beccaria's essential theme in regard to crime and punishment is that laws should follow one major rule: They should seek the greatest happiness for the greatest number of people. However, he was aware that one of the major problems of his pleasure principle is that people vary in what delights them:

> The attraction toward one pleasure instead of another is one of the main reasons for the difference in human characters. These different tendencies are probably a consequence of the first pleasant feelings received by infants; grown-ups will look for the pleasures they first experienced as infants.[5]

Some intellectual double-talk was employed by Beccaria that sought to overcome the problem of differing personal ideas about what is pleasurable. He notes that the ancient Spartans were known for their austerity and their avoidance of most things that we find pleasurable. For Beccaria, this is not a contradiction of his general principle. For the Spartan, he argues, their greatest pleasure consisted in being enclosed in heavy armor and being involved in fiery battles. However clever such an argument may (or may not) be, it fails to deal satisfactorily with the problems involved in passing laws based on deterring the pursuit of pleasure if pleasure is not defined in reasonably similar ways by all people.

Beccaria stressed that for a punishment to attain its end, the evil that it inflicts has only to exceed the advantage derivable from the crime. On this ground, he maintained that both capital punishment and the torturing of criminals are pointless because these inflictions are needlessly too harsh to cure the ills that lead to their use; milder penalties would result in just as great a reduction in the outlawed behavior. Beccaria also argued that the abolition of cruel and ferocious punishments would contribute to making the people of a nation more humane and sensitive, and thereby would reduce the number of (and the horrible nature of) crimes of violence. He also believed that suicide should not be a crime (in his time, the goods of a person who committed suicide were confiscated by the government).

In particular, Beccaria stressed the importance of speed and certainty in order for punishment to prove effective, a theme that continues to occupy scholars who seek to determine the relative importance of these two considerations in deterring delinquency. Beccaria also insisted that punishment ought to be at the minimum level possible in any given circumstances. This doctrine would stand as a major element in the formation of special court for juvenile offenders almost a century and a half later.

Jeremy Bentham

Following in Beccaria's footsteps, Jeremy Bentham (1748-1832) became the leading proponent of utilitarianism in the English-speaking world. His tribute to Beccaria is fulsome, though he often disagrees with his predecessor and travels far beyond him in his thinking. "Oh, my master, first evangelist of reason, you who raised Italy so far above England. You who have made so many useful excursions into the path of utility, what is there left for us to do?"[6] This last sentence is interesting in light of the fact that Bentham went on to produce a prodigious library of his own. The collection of his published writings amounts to 15 hefty volumes.

Bentham was an odd human being. His body can be viewed today by any curious passerby because, in accord with his will, it was mummified and sits at the entrance of University College in London. Because he was a man of exceptional intellect, Bentham reasoned, his remains ought to be publicly exhibited to inspire future generations. He called the body an "autoicon" and decreed that it should be seated in his favorite chair in his own clothes in the attitude in which he was sitting when in thought. He also insisted that his body should be placed at the table during faculty discussions.

A lifelong bachelor, Bentham spent virtually his entire life writing reams of manuscript pages suggesting programs for the reform of English criminal law. "He shrank from the world in which he was easily browbeaten to the study in which he could reign supreme," Sir Leslie Stephen said of Bentham.[7] Many of Bentham's papers, housed in English archives, remain unread today. His published works alone contain nearly six million words, some of them inventions that have become part of the English language (for example, words such as "codify," "rationale," "international," and "demoralize").

Outstanding theorists tend to be eccentric. It takes distinctive human beings to see things truly differently from the rest of us and to dedicate themselves to enlightening us about new ways of looking at reality. Bentham abhorred the criminal law of his time, which was both chaotic and mercilessly brutal. As late as 1833, for instance, a boy of nine would be hanged for stealing. The laws were so barbarous that juries often would declare offenders innocent rather than permit them to undergo the harsh punishment mandated by law for what jurors deemed was a minor offense. Bentham tried to introduce some logic in determining how serious an offense might be, and he insisted that behaviors that harm no one but their perpetrators ought to be eliminated from the statute books. He thought that laws should not be enforced if the result of enforcement produced more harm than good. He would not, for instance, prosecute the son of an ambassador from a foreign country for a trivial shoplifting offense if such a prosecution would cause strained relations between England and the country represented by the ambassador.

Fundamentally, Bentham, like Beccaria, believed that people act in a calculated manner to advance their own good. "Men calculate," he said, "some with less exactness, indeed, some with more; but all men calculate."[8] Therefore, the aim of criminal law was to fix penalties so that they would make calculators conclude that the illegal behavior was not worth the risk.

Evaluating Utilitarianism

A major problem with utilitarianism is that there is considerable evidence that people do not always act rationally and do not carefully calculate the pleasure and the likely pain if they do one thing instead of another. They rarely have sufficient information to evaluate clearly their own best interests. Even with adequate information, most of us cannot look deeply enough into the future to make an accurate prediction about the odds of one outcome or another. A potential delinquent might well guess that a given act of shoplifting will secure for him 50 "units" of pleasure (however such pleasure might be measured) and that being caught and having to serve three months on probation will cause him 75 units of pain. Obviously, he ought not to undertake the shoplifting excursion, but the equation is relevant only if he is going to be caught and brought before the juvenile court. How does he accurately figure the chances that this will happen?

Because one person's pleasure is another's pain, some witty observers point out that the wisdom of the precept "Do unto others as you would have them do unto you" will not work with masochists, because by definition they enjoy having pain inflicted on them. In the realm of juvenile delinquency it seems apparent that for some people one of the pleasures of the behavior is to get caught and by this means to draw attention to oneself in order to develop the "reputation" often so highly prized by gang members. A few nights in juvenile detention is abhorrent to some kids, a lark to others. In addition, as Daniel Kahnemon and his coauthors noted, systematic errors in judging earlier experiences do not lead to sound decisions about future outcomes.

In a rather strange way, the contributions of a great thinker can be evaluated by the criticisms the thinker evokes from others. Bentham may well hold the record for being hated by persons with first-rate minds. Goethe, the eminent German philosopher, called him "that frightfully radical ass," while John Maynard Keynes, a leading British economist, considered Bentham's ideas "the worm which has been gnawing at the insides of modern civilization and is responsible for its present moral decay." Karl Marx, founder of communist thought, called Bentham "the insipid, leather-tongued oracle of commonplace bourgeois intelligence."

RATIONAL CHOICE THEORY

The relevancy of the viewpoints of Beccaria and Bentham to current theories of juvenile delinquency can be seen in what is called "rational choice theory." Rational choice precepts found their way into theorizing about juvenile delinquency through the work of economists who have sought to comprehend in marketplace terms how human behavior works and how it might be changed. Simply put, without the paraphernalia of the numerical formulas economists attach to their ideas, rational choice theory says that humans are goal-oriented (with money being a particularly powerful goal) and that their behavior can be manipulated by changing situations so that acts that disobey the law will not have satisfying outcomes.

Rational choice theory has become deeply ingrained in social science research in fields adjacent to the study of juvenile delinquency. In 1957, for instance, there was no mention of the theory in political science journals; but by 1992, 40 percent of the articles in these journals were built around rational choice premises.

Most rational choice theorists today appreciate that at best they are supporting an approach that in the language of social science is a "sensitizing" principle: that is, it suggests things that you might look at if you are trying to understand delinquency. For rational choice, the two major items to consider are what the person who did the act sought to achieve and what that person believed were the circumstances that would enable him or her to get away with the outlawed behavior. Derek Cornish and Ronald Clarke, leading criminological exponents of the rational choice approach, are well aware of the complications involved in seeking a clear understanding of matters that play into any delinquent act. They write:

Offenders seek to benefit themselves by their criminal behavior. This involves the making of decisions and choices, however rudimentary on occasion these processes might be. These processes exhibit a measure of rationality, albeit constrained by limits of time and the availability of relevant information.[9]

An illustration of the operation of rational choice insight in the field of juvenile delinquency is provided by Martin Jankowski. He indicates that in chronically poor neighborhoods, many parents encourage their children to belong to the same gangs to which they belonged when they were younger, much as parents with Ivy League educations encourage their children to attend their alma maters.

Cornish and Clarke stress that their approach emphasizes the similarities instead of differences between criminals and noncriminals. It does not deny the existence of irrational and pathological behavior in some delinquencies. However, if most delinquency is seen as the result of rational behavior based upon consideration of anticipated costs and benefits, Cornish and Clarke observe, then we must stop looking at delinquency as a single kind of behavior and focus instead on specific forms of delinquency: shoplifting, arson, armed robbery, sex offenses, and other kinds of illegal acts. Closer attention must be paid to the particular delinquent event itself and to the situational factors that play into its commission.

A psychologist, Robert P. Abelson, offers a vignette to underline the fact that human beings sometimes will behave in ways that defy the self-interest perspective of rational choice theories. People, Abelson argues, do not always seek to optimize their material self-interest; "applied to ordinary citizens," he writes, "rational choice is manifestly incomplete and at worst, seriously misleading." Take, for instance, this behavior:

> Every autumn, John Doe traveled a long distance for something he claimed was important, and this aroused the curiosity of a rational choice theorist. "What do you do there?" he asked.
>
> "I dote," John replied. "I dote on Sally, my granddaughter."
>
> "You go all that way to dote? How do you benefit from it?"
>
> "Benefit?" asked John, puzzled. "I dunno. I just dote on her. Little Sally, she's really something. She'll do great things some day—make money, be famous, maybe even be president."
>
> The theorist considered this. "Well, do you think your doting makes a difference?"
>
> "Difference? How do you mean? I guess Sally likes to be doted on. When she's a teenager, she might not. Those teenagers . . ."

"No, no. I mean does your doting make it any more probable that she'll do the great things than if you don't dote?"

"More probable? Never thought about it. She'll do great things anyway."

John's questioner became exasperated. "You spend a lot of money and effort to go and dote, without expecting your doting to make a difference?"

"Should I?" "Oh, yes," said the rational choice theorist. "It's a law of human nature. Your action is anomalous."

Troubled, the theorist pondered the matter for many years. In the meantime, John Doe had died without knowing his grand-daughter's achievements. The theorist, further perplexed, wondered whether Doe had considered the possibility that he would die before the benefits of his doting could be enjoyed.

The rational choice theorist never solved the riddle.[10]

Beyond the fact that "different folks respond to different strokes," the rational choice theory does not reach very far into the brain of the individual offender as that offender calculates any given situation. Individuals vary dramatically in how much they feel the need for things that can be secured from delinquent acts: money, property, peer acclaim, excitement, and challenge to their own sense of what they are capable of doing. Nor are we altogether similar in the risks that we are willing to run, as any look at hang gliding enthusiasts, surfers, auto racers, boxers, and cowards will quickly demonstrate. In addition, individuals may at times follow the dictates of a moral code though what they do is clearly not a pursuit of self-interest. Finally, the theory offers no insight into how interests arise and how and why they change.

LIFESTYLE THEORY: THE ROUTINE ACTIVITIES APPROACH

The routine activities approach to understanding delinquency complements rational choice by suggesting that the conditions that propel persons into delinquent behavior are largely the product of the availability of illegal opportunities. Developed by Lawrence Cohen and Marcus Felson, routine activities theory basically focuses on predatory crimes and suggests that three conditions promote such offenses: (1) motivated offenders, (2) suitable targets, and (3) the absence of adequate guardians.

Consider burglary, for instance. Those who carry out the offense—often juveniles—are attracted by an awareness of the availability of items that are important to them (e.g., stereos, jewelry, cash, weapons, etc.). Any alteration that makes such items more readily available will increase the appeal of burglary, so that if smaller, more portable television sets were to flood the market, the theft of television sets would increase. Similarly, the theory suggests that an increase in homes left vacant during the day by working couples will inevitably lead to higher levels of offenses against the home. As persons commute each morning from their residences to their places of work, nobody remains to monitor street activity, to inhibit house thefts, or to control other delinquent activity through neighborhood surveillance.

The idea that neighborhood "routine activities" can be related to delinquency rates recently has been expanded through research by Wayne Osgood and his coworkers to include drug use, dangerous driving, and many deviant acts. Such acts are seen as the result of unstructured socializing activities with peers that occur in the absence of authority figures.

THE POSITIVIST SCHOOL: CONSTITUTIONAL THEORIES

Distinctions between the classical school and the positivist school have been drawn by Ray Jeffrey in the following terms:

> The Classical School focused attention on crime as a legal entity; the Positive School focused attention on the act as a psychological entity. The Classical School emphasized free will; the Positive School emphasized determinism. The Classical School theorized that punishment had a deterrent effect, the Positive said that punishment should be replaced by a scientific treatment of criminals calculated to protect society.[11]

The earliest positivists focused on constitutional (that is, bodily) characteristics of criminals. Later positivists keyed their approach to the methods of natural science, and also dealt with demographic and behavioral considerations.

Cesare Lombroso

The positivists, under the leadership of Cesare Lombroso (1835-1909), a physician and professor of forensic medicine at the University of Turin for most of his career, are generally credited with being the first to regard criminal behavior within a scientific context. Hermann Mannheim, a prominent criminologist, noted that Lombroso "saved criminal science from the shackles of merely academic abstractions and fertilized it with the rich treasures of the natural sciences."[12]

In 1876, when the first edition of Lombroso's treatise on crime, *L'umo delinquente* (*The Criminal Man*), was published, the intellectual climate of the day was dominated by the ideas of Charles Darwin. In keeping with the evolutionary doctrine, Lombroso maintained that he could identify physical characteristics of criminals and delinquents in terms of facial, cephalic (head shape), and bodily abnormalities. He believed that offenses against the law were an "atavistic" form of human behavior. By atavistic he meant that criminals were a reversion to a primitive or subhuman type, characterized physically by a variety of traits otherwise found only in apes and lower primates and among those Lombroso called "savages" (that is, members of preliterate tribes). Criminals, Lombroso insisted, "talk differently from us because they do not feel in the same way; they talk like savages because they are veritable savages in the midst of this brilliant European civilization."[13]

These physically retarded types constituted Lombroso's "born criminals," individuals destined by their deficient heredity to enter into criminal activity. Lombroso granted in his later writings, however, that not all criminals were "born." He came to believe that more than half either were insane or criminaloids, that is, individuals who by their physical and psychological constitutions were predisposed toward crime in the face of certain eliciting circumstances. This idea is comparable to the medical concept of diathesis—a predisposition toward a given disease with no certainty that the disease will result.

A quotation from Lombroso's address at the Sixth Congress of Criminal Anthropology indicates the initial stage of his ideas about law-breaking behavior:

> I was carrying out research in the prisons and asylums of Pavia upon cadavers and living persons in order to determine upon substantial differences between the insane and criminals, without succeeding very well. At last I found in the skull of a brigand a very long series of atavistic anomalies, above all an enormous middle occipital fossa [a hollow in the back part of the head] and a hypertrophy [morbid enlargement] of the vermis [the connecting mass between the two hemispheres of the brain] analogous to those that are found in inferior vertebrates. At the sight of these strange anomalies the problem of nature and the origin of the criminal seemed to be resolved; the characteristics of primitive men and of inferior animals must be reproduced in our times. Many facts seemed to confirm this hypotheses, above all the psychology of the criminal; the frequency of tattooing and of professional slang; the passions as much fleeting as they are violent, above all that of vengeance; the lack of foresight which resembles courage and which alternates with cowardice, and idleness which alternates with the passion for play and activity.[14]

Though he subsequently paid attention to matters such as the relationship of crime to climate and rainfall, marriage customs, banking practices, and religious beliefs, at the heart of Lombroso's thought was a commitment to a determinism that saw offenders as a group apart, virtually predestined by their biology to their behavior. On delinquency, he wrote that "all great criminals have given proof of their perversity in their youth, especially at the age of puberty and even before." Then he catalogued the early sins of some of the more notorious European malefactors of the time:

> At age 7, Dombey was already a thief, and added sacrilege to his theft at age 12. At age 3, Crocco tore out the feathers of living birds. Lasagne cut out the tongues of cattle at age 11; at the same age Cartouche stole from his schoolmates, while Mme. Lafargue, as a child of 10, strangled fowls.[15]

So strong an impact did Lombroso's ideas have that Count Dracula, the blood-sucking fictional vampire, is described in the 1897 novel by Bram Stoker in terms taken directly from Lombroso's case histories. A person who encounters Dracula says: "His eyebrows were massive, almost meeting over the nose" and "his ears were pale and at the tops extremely pointed."[16] Lombroso's born criminal, for his part, had "eyebrows that are bushy and tend to meet across the nose" as well as "relics of the pointed ear."[17] It also was in pure Lombrosian terms that A. Mitchell Palmer, director of the Federal Bureau of Investigation in the 1920s, described alleged "subversives": "Out of the sly and crafty eyes of many of them leap cupidity, cruelty, insanity, and crime; from their lopsided faces, sloping brows, and misshapen features may be recognized the unmistakable criminal type."[18] On the other hand, renowned novelists such as Joseph Conrad and Leo Tolstoy have contributed comments, usually bitingly critical, on Lombroso's ideas. In Conrad's *The Secret Agent* (1907), for instance, a character proclaims: "Lombroso is an ass."[19]

Evaluation of Lombroso's Work

Lombroso scorned the armchair and employed the medical laboratory in his work, but Lombroso's caricatured and anecdotal case histories of prostitutes ("a demi-type. Her ears stand out, she has big jaws and cheek bones and very black hair, besides other anomalies, such as gigantic canine teeth and dwarf incisors"),[20] and his torturing of logic (such as his attempt to relate the fatness of prostitutes, which "strikes those who look at them en masse," to the obesity of Hottentots, and then to relate both of these to a theory of atavism) represents a sorry twisting of the scientific approach. Steven Jay Gould's assessment of Lombroso identifies his major scientific shortcoming:

> Lombroso constructed virtually all of his arguments in a manner that precluded their defeat, thus making them scientifically vacuous. Whenever Lombroso encountered a contrary fact, he performed some mental gymnastics to incorporate it into his system.[21]

One criticism of Lombroso came from French anthropologist Paul Topinard, who, according to some, gave criminology its name. When Topinard was shown a collection of Lombroso's pictures of allegedly atavistic criminals, he remarked that the pictures were no different than those of his own friends. Similarly, during the Congress of Criminal Anthropology in Paris in 1889, a French doctor took the participants to the reformatory in which he worked to show them young children who were delinquent but who, he said, showed no physical stigmata or degeneracy. Lombroso, part of the visiting group, undertook to measure the youths and pointed out various "abnormalities" that he declared "were not noticeable to the naked eye."[22] Of course, had Lombroso been measuring a group of young saints, variations from the norm in some of their physical characteristics would also readily have been located.

It took many decades, unfortunately, before the main body of criminological theory accepted the validity of Topinard's perceptive appraisal of Lombroso's theoretical position. Yet there remains a germ of importance in Lombroso's approach; otherwise we would not have tarried so long to set it forth. Biological conditions clearly play some part (and perhaps sometimes a very prominent part) in conditioning delinquency. There is little doubt that what you look like, your physical abilities, your intelligence and, your energy level, among other traits, will influence in some ways how you behave and how you are viewed by those who have an influence on you. Moreover, how you are treated inevitably will influence how you act, and sometimes whether you choose to engage or not engage in delinquency. Unattractive people, for instance, often are treated less well than attractive ones. Their work is more likely to be judged less favorably, they are more likely to be blamed for their transgressions, and those transgressions are more likely to be seen as indicating antisocial characteristics. This process may indeed more readily push them into delinquency.

Post-Lombroso Constitutional Theorists

The heritage of Lombroso's views about people with hereditary conditions that doom them to violate the law continues to occupy a place in theories of juvenile delinquency. There seems to be something attractive about the idea that biological factors exist that, once determined, can be linked to behavior outcomes. Nonhumans, following inherited instincts, do exactly what we know they will do when they swim upstream to spawn, fly north or south with the seasons, and build their nests in a predictable manner. They do not (as least as far as anyone knows) change their mind and decide not to swim upstream, fly in a different direction, or construct a totally different kind of nest this year. Some persons are certain that humans are much the same, and they keep seeking to locate the biological key to the cause of juvenile delinquency. A particular appeal of constitutional theory is that it allows its adherents to establish themselves as a breed apart (and above). We know of no theorists who located physical traits determining wrongdoing that they themselves possessed.

Charles Goring

An Englishman, Charles Goring (1870-1919), a physician in His Majesty's prisons and author of *The English Convict* (1913), often is regarded as the prime debunker of Lombroso's ideas. Actually, although he attacked Lombroso harshly for the sloppiness of his methods and thinking, Goring ended up taking a position that was not very different from Lombroso's. Piers Beirne has noted that in refuting certain aspects of the notion of "born criminality," and in lending support to others, *The English Convict* advanced an ambiguous position not in opposition to Lombrosianism but parallel to it. What Goring did was replace Lombroso's genetically inscribed atavistic offender with a preordained convict born with inferior weight, stature, and mental capacity. Goring's aim was not to debunk Lombroso, but rather to support the burgeoning eugenics movement that advocated controlling the birth rate of "defectives" and encouraging the bearing of children by the "fittest."

Basing his conclusions on the examination of 43 traits as they were shown in some 3,000 prisoners, Goring constructed a theory called criminal diathesis. Criminal diathesis, Goring proclaimed, is a constitutional proclivity, either mental, moral, or physical, that is present in all individuals but so potent in some as to determine for them, eventually, the fate of imprisonment.

Precisely how a general constitutional "moral" deficiency is transmitted biologically remains unstated. Given the enormous variation in moral codes throughout the world, such an idea appears highly dubious. It might also be noted in regard to moral sentiments that researchers find prison inmates more likely than the average citizen to support conventional morality. Goring's theme, like so much early theorizing, is beyond science because, as it is stated, it cannot be tested. If he had maintained that all persons born with spinal ganglia of a certain length eventually will be imprisoned, we might be able to determine the accuracy of such a position, but how do we measure "constitutional moral proclivities," and how can we be assured that what we have measured, even if we can determine it, is not the product of experience?

One of the giant steps that Goring took beyond Lombroso was to use a control group in his work, that is, a group of persons with the same background as his study group except for an absence of criminal behavior. These persons could be compared to the criminals studied so that located differences could be said to be true not of all humankind but only of criminals. Unfortunately, however, Goring's control group hardly represented a cross-section of males similar, except for their law-breaking, to the criminal population he studied. He recruited the controls from such diverse groups as Cambridge, Oxford, and Aberdeen university students; University of London professors; mental hospital patients; German army recruits; and members of the British royal engineers. There were, in fact, greater differences between men from one university and those from another in regard to the physical items Goring measured than between the university students and the prisoners.

Earnest Hooton

Earnest Hooton (1887-1954), another major figure in the debate on constitutional correlates of delinquency, was responsible for a brief revival of Lombrosian theory. Hooton was a preeminent physical anthropologist at Harvard University, and his status made it particularly likely that his excursion into criminology, late in his career, would be well regarded. Like Bentham, Hooton had his eccentricities. He would insert whimsical poems as footnotes in tedious scholarly tomes that he wrote regarding humankind's physical attributes. Though he had authored the ditties himself, he would say that he had found them in a washroom and that they undoubtedly had been written and discarded by a building janitor. Hooton had completed his doctoral dissertation at the University of Wisconsin on early Roman literature, dance, and song before he earned a diploma in anthropology at Oxford University. He was a witty, engaging classroom lecturer and wrote books for the popular market with titles such as *Apes, Men and Morons*; *Why Men Behave Like Apes and Vice Versa*; and *Young Man, You Are Normal*. There even was a story that he had considered naming one of his children Newton; thus he would have been Newton Hooton.

Like Lombroso's, Hooton's study of crime and delinquency attempted to identify bodily characteristics linked with criminal behavior. Hooton examined 14,873 male convicts in prisons in 10 states, using 107 different measures. He reported that he had found that criminals were inferior to civilians in nearly all their bodily measurements and that they were marked by things such as low foreheads, high pinched nasal roots, excess of nasal deflections, compressed faces, and narrow jaws. These, he insisted, were indications of constitutional inferiority and such inferiority was due to heredity. Hooton's major conclusion was forcefully stated:

> Criminals are organically inferior. Crime is the resultant of the impact of environment upon low grade human organisms. It follows that the elimination of crime can be effected only by the extirpation [elimination] of the physically, mentally, and morally unfit, or by their complete segregation in a socially aseptic environment.[23]

There is something chilling in a prescription such as this, especially when we look back now on the killings by the Nazis of those who they deemed to be "unfit." By no means do Hooton's findings lend satisfactory scientific support to the idea that criminals are organically inferior human beings and, even if they did, the "cure" is morally obscene. It can be presumed that Hooton never would have been so remorselessly punitive had he been talking about white-collar criminals, such as income tax cheaters and corporate officers convicted of illegal dumping of toxic waste—or of college professors who misappropriate grant money or fake experimental results.

Biting criticisms of Hooton's work abound. For one thing, he was studying convicts, persons who represent the failures of crime and delinquency. Hooton's control group, those persons to whom he compared the prison inmates, was hardly, if at all, any better than Goring's. Its 3,203 members included firefighters in Nashville, hospital outpatients, patrons of a Massachusetts bathing beach, and members of a militia company. Persons in the last group were likely to be in unusually good physical shape, and a group who elects to allow their physiques to be viewed publicly on a beach is likely to be overrepresented by the physically impressive. If a study design is not scientifically satisfactory, the results will be suspect. It is often better that such work not be done at all than that it be done poorly.

Other reservations about Hooton's work have been catalogued by George Vold and Thomas Bernard, who note that Hooton was guilty of circular reasoning. He assumed that the traits that he declared to be characteristic of criminals were marks of inferiority, while he defined such inferiority on the basis of his subjects' criminality. Like Goring, Hooton often found (and ignored) much greater differences between inmate groups at various sites at which he worked than those between the inmates and persons in the groups to which they were being compared.

William Sheldon

Ten years after Hooton's contribution had met with almost total rejection by the criminological community, constitutional criminology made another attempt at an intellectual comeback. This effort involved studies by William Sheldon (1898-1977). Sheldon had formulated a theory of somatotypes (body types). He designated three major human shapes: the roundish endomorph (soft body, short neck, small hands and feet), the spindly ectomorph (slender and delicate), and the squarish mesomorph (firm body with rugged muscles), with many intermediate shapes between these distinctive forms. Each body type was said to correspond to a kind of temperament. Endomorphs were declared to be good-natured, relaxed, and gluttonous, and to love comfort and to crave affection. This was because, of the three types, they had the greatest amount of body exposure to the sensory stimuli of the outer world. Mesomorphs were said to be vigorous and active, and ectomorphs to be inhibited, self-conscious, and marked by feelings of inadequacy.

In his role as clinical director of the Hayden Goodwill Inn School for Boys in Massachusetts, Sheldon examined 200 young males who had been placed in the facility for various behaviors—some serious and many not notably serious (for example, runaways). Thirty years later, a number of Sheldon's colleagues restudied the same sample. The finding that stood up most consistently was the association of a mesomorphic (vigorous, active) body build with delinquency.

Edwin H. Sutherland, the dean of sociological studies of crime, whose differential association theory will be discussed in Chapter 7, was pitiless in his condemnation of Sheldon's work. Sutherland maintained that Sheldon "declares dogmatically that his is the only way to study personality and behavior and insists that it is the Messiah for a world rushing into social chaos."[24] Sutherland believed that Sheldon's work was "useless" as a demonstration of the value of constitutional psychology and that this "should have been obvious from the previous failure of analogous studies." Sutherland also maintained that "Sheldon's most general conclusion, which he expresses with something approaching religious hysteria, affirms the necessity of selective breeding." Such a conclusion, Sutherland insisted, was "completely unrelated to his data."[25] Sutherland itemized the following deficiencies in Sheldon's work:

> His definition of delinquency cannot be used in empirical research; his selection of cases prevents him from generalizing about any given population; his method of scoring delinquency is subjective and unreliable; his varieties of delinquent youth are meaningless, because no one of his variables differs from any other somatotypical or psychiatric indexes; and his findings on these indexes have no evaluative significance.[26]

It must be noted that the accuracy of Sutherland's critique does not demonstrate that constitutional factors are not related to delinquency, but only that Sheldon had been scientifically inept in his attempt to prove such a thesis.

Glueck and Glueck: Incorporating Sheldon's Work

Sheldon's work was incorporated into the mainstream of research on juvenile delinquency when in the late 1930s Sheldon Glueck and Eleanor Glueck decided to adopt his schema as one of the numerous measures they would employ in the most comprehensive examination of matched groups of delinquents and nondelinquents to date. Glueck and Glueck's approach was fundamentally eclectic: they were interested in studying anything that might show a relationship to delinquent behavior. Besides physical traits, they also focused on numerous social correlates, some of which we will look at in a subsequent chapter.

Glueck and Glueck exerted a very strong influence on the study of delinquency, but it was an unusual kind of influence. Sheldon Glueck was based at the Harvard Law School, where he held the Roscoe Pound Chair. His teaching was primarily in the field of criminal law, so that his and his wife's research on delinquency represented work in an area far afield from his academic training and responsibilities. Eleanor Glueck was a social worker. Few law students and faculty at the Harvard Law School cared a whit about the monumental research program that Glueck and Glueck undertook; it had nothing to do with passing a bar examination. Social scientists, with rare exceptions, tended to scorn Glueck and Glueck, to regard them as rather inept and amateurish intruders into a field that they were ill prepared professionally to comprehend. Their books were reviewed in social science journals with biting condescension. At the same time, Glueck and Glueck were lionized overseas, where the study of delinquency was not dominated by sociologists but largely fell within the domain of lawyers and physicians.

Glueck and Glueck's study sample was made up of 500 delinquent boys who were matched with 500 nondelinquents. In their work with Sheldon's body types, Glueck and Glueck found that 11.8 percent of their 500 delinquents were endomorphs, as were 15.0 percent of the nondelinquents. For mesomorphs, the percentages were 60.1 for the delinquents and 30.7 for the nondelinquents, while 14.4 percent of the delinquents and 39.6 of the nondelinquents were ectomorphs. No dominant body type was found in 14 percent of the sample.

That mesomorphs so disproportionately dominated the ranks of delinquents testifies to no more than the importance of a good body build to cope with the rigors of the delinquent life style. Put another way, physically inadequate persons would be well advised to avoid delinquency; they are likely to do poorly in gang fights and to lack the strength and the stamina for stealing and other gang activities. Persons with less satisfactory body makeups might well retreat to the library or to other settings where they will be less likely to become involved in street delinquency.

On the surface, the Sheldon-Glueck data on body type make sense, but they tell us very little. Youngsters with other body types become involved in delinquency and enormous numbers of mesomorphs avoid delinquency. Obviously, other considerations interact with whatever influence body build exerts to determine the behavior that will result. In addition, the Sheldon measurement of body type is rather crude, and with passing years persons will change from one category to another. The tie between body type and personality also is primitive.

Like Lombroso, Sheldon also drew the attention of the literary world. W.H. Auden, an eminent British poet and essayist, joked about Sheldon's classification system in a 1950 verse: "Footnotes to Dr. Sheldon." Auden's verdict was that Sheldon's research was "pseudo-science rubbish."[27]

Sheldon Resurfaces

The work of Sheldon, carried out between 1940 and 1960, seemed to have been relegated to well-earned obscurity by the critical judgment of the scientific community. Sheldon himself, according to his research assistant, had turned into a lonely old man who did nothing in his last years but sit in his room and read detective stories. In 1995, however, on the basis of work by an investigative journalist, Sheldon's materials gained momentary national notoriety when it was reported that a stash of nude photographs of Yale, Mount Holyoke, Vassar, Smith, and Princeton students, among others, were housed in the National Anthropological Archives. Sheldon had prevailed upon colleges to tell students that they had to pose for "posture photos" as a part of their first-year orientation program. Hillary Rodham Clinton, Diane Sawyer, George Bush, and Meryl Streep were among those who had unwittingly participated in Sheldon's research. The 1995 news stories recalled that Sheldon's aim, like so many of the constitutional theorists, was to improve the breed. Included in the archives was a 1924 study that Sheldon had published in which he paraded as scientific truth the notion that "Negro intelligence comes to a standstill at about the tenth year," and that of Mexicans at about age 12. In a stinging critique of the colleges and universities that had allowed their students to be photographed, the journalist concluded: "In the Sheldon rituals, the student test subjects were naked—but it was the emperors of scientific certainty who had no clothes."[28]

Chromosomal Theories: The XYY Type

The idea that delinquents possess genetic traits that distinguish them from nondelinquents did not die out in the wake of scholarly antagonism to the positions of Lombroso and his followers. For a time, the belief flourished that there was a distinctive chromosomal pattern that predisposed some males to low intelligence and to aggressive behavior and—because of this—to crime and delinquency of a violent nature. Normally, individuals possess 23 pairs of chromosomes that determine their inherited traits, such as gender. Females have an XX chromosomal combination, males an XY. In some instances, however (a common estimate is one person in 236), male infants are born with an extra Y chromosome, sometimes known as the forty-seventh chromosome. These XYY persons have been alleged to be destined to engage in acts of violence to a much greater extent than their XY fellows.

In one of the most sophisticated tests of the XYY syndrome, Alice Theilgaard looked at the records of 31,348 males born in Copenhagen in Denmark between the first day of 1944 and the last day of 1947. She drew a sample of the tallest 15 percent, as the extra chromosomal pattern tends to be located within this group. Of the 4,591 persons who were examined, 12 were identified as XYY and 16 as XXY. Members of the latter group possess what is known as Klinefelter's syndrome and are alleged, in contrast to XYYs, to be "feminized." Theilgaard used as her contrast group 52 male XYs. She concluded that the XXYs and the XYYs were "more alike than different" and that they showed a wide spectrum of intelligence scores and no evidence of variations in cognitive styles. The XYYs did not appear to be in any greater danger of committing criminal offenses than XY men of a similar background. Summarizing her work, Theilgaard made this eminently sensible observation:

> As in all human beings, the XYYs and the XXYs are the result of an interplay of genetic, environmental and psychological processes. It follows that there is no ground for anticipating that a person with a certain cytogenic [chromosomal] status will demonstrate a preordained, inflexible and irremediable personality or pathology.[29]

Twin and Adoption Studies

A large research enterprise has examined the criminal records of identical (MZ, for monozygotic) and fraternal (or DZ, dizygotic) twins. The studies show that identical twins, reared together or separately, show a higher similarity in their delinquency records than might be expected by chance. The difficulties with taking such findings as conclusive evidence of a genetic push toward illegal activity are that, as the researchers grant: (1) there is no way to explain, except by environment and training conditions, why for a very considerable number of identical twins one had engaged in delinquent acts while the other had not; and (2) there are no studies in which there is not some evidence that the identical twins were raised in similar circumstances that might have contributed significantly to their troubles with the law.

Research purists interested in pursuing this topic can look forward to further development of genetic research techniques that will allow DNA material to be extracted and cloned, even from people long deceased. The process involves taking a sample of the person's DNA, available from any cell of the body, and placing it in the nucleus of an egg or embryo, which then would be implanted in the uterus and brought to term like any other child. It would be vastly informative if we could reproduce the identical genetic characteristics of a notorious delinquent and have a saintly couple parent the child without the couple knowing its genetic background. Of course, enormous ethical difficulties surround such a research enterprise, but those interested in gathering satisfactory data on the age-old debate of the contributions of nature and nurture to behavior could not help but be delighted with such an endeavor. That the idea itself is neither new or novel is shown by the fact that the eighteenth century French philosopher Denis Diderot suggested that delinquents be consigned to stud farms, where they would be allowed to procreate under controlled conditions in order to demonstrate that crime is not hereditary.

Other Biological Measures

Many other constitutional correlates of delinquent behavior have been explored, again with interesting but far from conclusive results. Figure 4.1 illustrates graphically the attempt to locate the cause of violence in a brain condition. Our biological heritage presses us toward certain kinds of behavior and some of these forms are defined as illegal. Work has been done with an electroencephalogram, which looks at brain waves; cardiovascular and electrodermal measures; hormone research; and brain dysfunction studies. That these measures correlate with certain kinds of activity that are illegal is unarguable.

Characteristic of research on the hormonal basis of delinquency is Lee Ellis's genetic-environmental, neurologically mediated interactionist (GENMI) approach to the understanding of delinquency. Ellis notes that his ideas assume that the physical-chemical functioning of the brain is directly responsible for all human behavior, just as it is for the behavior of other animals. Brain functions are believed to be the result of genetic and environmental factors, the latter including such things as drugs, poisons, and physical injuries, as well as learning.

Figure 4.1
Does the Brain "Trigger" Violence?

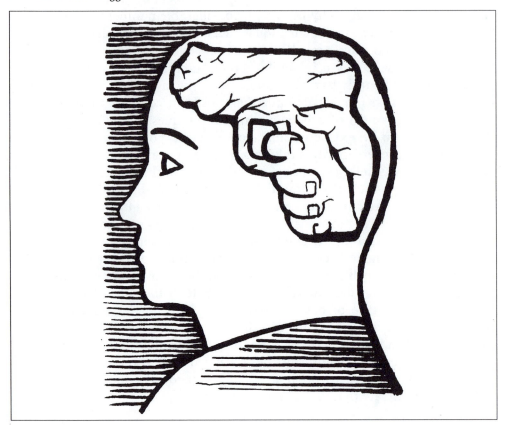

Work on testosterone levels highlights some of the unresolved problems concerned with relating hormonal conditions to delinquency. Men normally have 300 to 1,000 nanograms of testosterone per deciliter of blood, while women have only 40 nanograms of the hormone. Testosterone has been blamed not only for the disproportionate representation of males in the ranks of delinquents, but also for war, the violence of football and hockey, and Genghis Khan, to name a few matters. Yet a report by Christin Wang at the 1995 meeting of the Endocrine Society insisted that excessive levels of testosterone are not what drive men to behave aggressively but rather that testosterone deficiency (a condition labeled hypogonadism) produces male aggressive behavior. Wang maintained that regular levels of testosterone are related to calmness, happiness, and friendliness.[30] Other scientists commented that the report tended to demonstrate that testosterone has been given an undeserved knock and that the commonly held belief that testosterone produces antisocial behavior may be a misconception.

A key question remains unanswered in biological approaches to interpretation of delinquency: How often do these theories predict such behavior when it does not take place (the false positives)? The same question also has to be raised, of course, with social science theories of delinquency. All people who are defined as lacking social control hardly end up manifesting delinquent and criminal careers. There are other factors that work upon the stipulated conditions; it remains for each theory to seek, if possible, to identify such items so that a satisfactorily predictive statement can be made. At the moment, studies of delinquency have far to go to reach such a goal.

The work of Sarnoff Mednick, a contemporary student of the relationship between biology and illegal behavior, illustrates the much greater sophistication of scholars currently working in the field. In one of his research probes, Mednick concluded that electrodermal responses may be predictive of delinquent behavior. He followed the careers of 313 Danish youths who had been intensively examined in 1962 and found that 36 came to have "serious disagreement with the law." These men demonstrated electrodermal responses significantly slower than those of members of the control group. This rate is regarded as an indication of autonomic nervous system function. Electrodermal inadequacy is said to produce a deficit in the ability to experience fear, resulting in an incapacity or a lag in curbing aggressive impulses.

Mednick suggests that electrodermal inadequacy is transmitted by heredity, so that it might well be "a characteristic that a criminal father could pass to a biological son, which (given the proper environmental circumstances) could increase the probability of the child failing to learn adequately to inhibit asocial responses."[31]

Neuropsychological Factors

Representative of newer work on the relationship between brain functions and delinquency is the study by Terrie Moffitt, Donald Lyman, and Phil Silva of neuropsychological items as they relate to subsequent delinquent behavior. The research tested a cohort of several hundred males in New Zealand at age 13 and determined their delinquency from official records and self-reports, finding that poor neuropsychological status that began before age 13 and persisted at high levels thereafter correlated with delinquent behavior. However, neuropsychological test results were not related to delinquency that began in adolescence. The neuropsychological tests included a considerable variety of batteries, such as the Wisconsin Card Sort Test and the Rey Auditory Verbal Learning Test. What the authors thought most significant was that poor test scores indicated difficulty the children had in expressing themselves and remembering things. This, they maintain, leads to poor communication with parents, peers, and teachers, creating "one of the most critical risk factors for childhood conduct problems that grow into persistent antisocial behavior in young adulthood."[32]

SUMMARY

Two major theoretical schools marked pioneering attempts to determine the wellsprings of juvenile delinquency and adult crime. Both schools still exert an influence on current theoretical thinking. The classical school, represented by Cesare Beccaria and Jeremy Bentham, was based on armchair theorizing. It maintained that offenders calculate potential gains and losses before they decide to break the law. The classical school argued that what was required to deter delinquency was a schedule of penalties slightly in excess of the perceived gains from the behavior.

The vitality of the classical school's basic premise that human beings act in their own interest—and will only cease misbehaving when they come to understand that it is not in their best interest to do so—underlies the rational choice and routine activities theories of delinquent behavior. Rational choice theory assumes that we calculate our potential gains and at the same time evaluate the risks before we decide to act. Routine activities theory focuses on the way changes in the society play into the rate of delinquency. If better techniques of car-proofing are developed, the rate of car thefts will decrease; if neighborhoods are stripped of older people who "patrol" the streets from their house windows, delinquency will increase (all other things being equal).

The second theoretical school, the positivistic, founded by Cesare Lombroso, pushed the study of illegal behavior in the direction of experimental investigation. It sought to locate distinctive biological and physical traits that differentiated the law-abiding from the delinquent. Early positivists were pessimistic about the likelihood of reforming delinquents because inherited traits were believed to be the cause of their lawbreaking.

Theories of delinquency that focus on heredity can represent an elitist view that places the theorist in a superior position and the delinquent in an inferior position. In this chapter, we saw how Goring used more sophisticated experimental techniques to rebut Lombroso, but nonetheless reached essentially the same conclusion, insisting that he was able to identify a distinctively different person: a physically predetermined delinquent. Subsequently, Hooton, in work as seriously questionable from a scientific viewpoint as Goring's, added his name to the Lombrosian roster. Since then, other investigators have looked at XYY chromosomes, EEG brain patterns, intelligence test scores, left-handedness, and an array of other items, seeking the interpretative grail in regard to delinquent behavior.

More recent work on biosocial correlates of delinquency seems to confirm the view that human beings with certain forms of bodily and genetic structure are likely to be more susceptible to social difficulty in certain kinds of environments, just as persons who stand seven feet tall have a better chance of being basketball stars than those under five feet, and those with a slow pulse rate have an edge toward becoming better distance runners than those with higher pulse rates. We know that height has strong genetic components, and pulse rate probably does as well. The strength of genetic relationships, however, does not appear to be so overwhelming as to suggest the value of any kind of intervention program designed to prevent delinquency. The problem with such interventions is that they inevitably overpredict and overtreat and that they come to embrace far too many young people who, left alone, would never encounter any difficulty with the law.

David Rowe and Wayne Osgood claim that social science explanations of delinquency have "ignored or ridiculed" genetic factors, though they too grant that such factors "can only be the first stage of any causal sequence leading to social behavior."[33] Their own work, conducted with a sample of twins in all Ohio school districts (except inner-city districts, where access proved too difficult), found that genetic factors contributed more to delinquency than either general or specific environmental influences.

Other scholars prominent in the study of biological contributions to crime and delinquency note that unless the background factor of genetic predisposition is adequately taken into account, society will never know which environmental factors are most important in triggering lawbreaking, particularly violence. Writing shortly before his death in 1994, Richard Herrnstein summed up his view on the constitutional aspects of crime and delinquency: "There is, in short," he wrote, "a scientific consensus that criminal and antisocial behavior have genetic, as well as environmental sources. The disagreements among experts concern the size of the genetic factor." Then he added: "Some say it is negligible, others, that it may account for as much as 50 percent or more of the variance in criminal behavior."[34] As a statement of the issue as it now stands, there seems no disputing Herrnstein's position. See Figure 4.2 for an assessment of theories by Ellis and Walsh.

Figure 4.2
**Theories Judged By Criminologists to Have the Greatest Explanatory Power for
Serious/Persistent Criminality and for Delinquency/Minor Adult Criminality**

Theory	Delinquency & Minor/ Adult Offending	
	N	%
Social control	8	5.6
Self-control	33	23.1
Differential association	16	11.2
Conflict	6	4.2
Adolescent-persistent	5	3.5
Traditional anomie	8	5.6
Social learning	12	8.4
Strain	8	5.6
Routine activities	9	6.3
Feminist	2	1.4
Developmental	2	1.4
Marxist/radical	1	0.7
Biosocial	3	2.1
Social disorganization	4	2.8
Differential opportunity	3	2.1
Labeling	7	4.9
Critical	5	3.5
Integrated	3	2.1
Classical	3	2.1
Criminal personality	0	0.0
NeoDarwinian	1	0.7
Ecological	4	2.8
TOTAL	142	100.1

Source: Ellis & Walsh, 1994:4

References

Abell, Peter, ed. (1991). *Rational Choice Theory*. Aldershot, England: Elgar.

Abelson, Robert P. (1995). "Rational Choice Theory" *Critical Review* 1-30.

Angier, Natalie (1995). "Does Testosterone Equal Aggression? Maybe Not." *New York Times* (June 20):Al, B6.

Beccaria, Cesare (1764). *On Crime and Punishments*. Reprint. Translated by Henry Paolucci. Indianapolis: Bobbs-Merrill, 1963.

Beirne, Piers (1993). *Inventing Criminology: Essays on the Rise of Homo Criminalis*. Albany: State University of New York Press.

Beirne, Piers (1988). "Heredity Versus Environment: A Reconsideration of Charles Gor-ing's *The English Convict* (1913)." *British Journal of Criminology* 28:315-339.

Bentham, Jeremy (1838–1843). *The Works of Jeremy Bentham.* Edited by John Bowring. Edinburgh: Tait.

Cohen, Lawrence E., and Marcus Felson (1979). "Social Change and Crime Rate Trends: A Routine Activities Approach." *American Sociological Review* 44:588-608.

Conrad, Joseph (1907). *The Secret Agent: A Simple Tale.* New York: Harpers.

Cornish, Derek B., and Ronald V. Clarke (1986). *The Reasoning Criminal: Rational Choice Perspective on Offending.* New York: Springer-Verlag.

Cuomo, Mario (1996). "Foreword" In Cesare Beccaria, *On Crimes and Punishments,* v–viii. New York: Marsillo.

Davenport-Hines, Richard (1995). *Auden.* London: Heinemann.

Ellis, Lee, and Harry Hoffman, eds. (1990). *Crime in Biological, Social and Moral Con-texts.* New York: Praeger.

Ellis, Lee, and Anthony Walsh (1999). "Criminologists' Opinions About Causes and Theories of Crime and Delinquency." *The Criminologist* 24(4):1, 4-5.

Feynman, Richard (1985). *Surely, You're Joking Mr. Feynman! Adventures of a Curi-ous Character.* New York: Norton.

Glueck, Sheldon, and Eleanor Glueck (1968). *Delinquents and Nondelinqents in Per-spective.* Cambridge, MA: Harvard University Press.

Glueck, Sheldon, and Eleanor Glueck (1950). *Unraveling Juvenile Delinquency.* New York: Commonwealth Fund.

Goring, Charles (1913). *The English Convict: A Statistical Study.* London: His Majesty's Stationery Office.

Gould, Stephen Jay (1981). *The Mismeasure of Man.* New York: Norton.

Hechter, Michael, and Satoshi Kanalawa (1997). "Sociological Rational Choice The-ory." *Annual Review of Sociology* 23:191-214.

Herrnstein, Richard (1993). "Crime and Punishment in American History." *National Review* 45:68-70.

Holton, Robert J. (1995). "Rational Choice Theory in Sociology. *Critical Review* 9:519-537.

Hooton, Earnest (1939). *The American Criminal: An Anthropological Study.* Cam-bridge, MA: Harvard University Press.

Jankowski, Martin S. (1991). *Island in the Street. Gangs and American Urban Society.* Berkeley, CA: University of California Press.

Jeffrey, C. Ray (1960). "The Historical Development of Criminology." In *Pioneers in Criminology,* edited by Hermann Mannheim, 364-394. London: Stevens.

Jenkins, Philip (1984). "Varieties of Enlightenment Criminology: Beccaria, Godwin, de Sade." *British Journal of Criminology* 24:112-130.

Kahneman, Daniel, Peter Wakker, and Rakesh Sarin (1997). "Back to Bentham? Expla-nations of Experience Utility." *Quarterly Journal of Economics* 112:375-396.

Kurella, Hans (1911). *Cesare Lombroso: A Modern Man of Science*. Translated by M. Eden Paul. London: Rebman.

Lombroso, Cesare (1911). *Crime: Its Causes and Consequences*. Translated by Henry P. Horton. Boston: Little, Brown.

Lombroso, Cesare (1905). *L'Homme criminel: Etude anthropologique et medicolegale*. Translated by G. Regnier and M.A. Bornet. Paris: F. Alcan.

Lombroso, Cesare, and William Ferrero (1895). *The Female Offender*. New York: Appleton.

Lombroso-Ferrero, Gina (1911). *Criminal Man According to the Classification of Cesare Lombroso*. New York: Putnam.

Mannheim, Hermann (1955). "Lombroso and His Place in Modern Criminology." In *Group Problems in Crime and Punishment*, edited by Hermann Mannheim, 69-84. London: Routledge and Kegan Paul.

Mednick, Sarnoff (1977). "A Biosocial Theory of the Learning of Law-Abiding Behavior." In *Biosocial Bases of Criminal Behavior*, edited by Sarnoff Mednick and Karl O. Christiansen, 1-8. New York: Gardner Press.

Moffitt, Terrie E., Donald R. Lyman, and Phil A. Silva (1994). "Neuropsychological Tests Predicting Persistent Male Delinquency." *Criminology* 32:277-300.

Newman, Graeme, and Pietro Marongiu (1990). "Penological Reform and the Myth of Beccaria." *Criminology* 29:325-346.

Osgood, D. Wayne, Janet K. Wilson, Patrick M. O'Malley, Jereld G. Bachman, and Lloyd B. Johnson (1996). "Routine Activities and Individual Deviant Behavior." *American Sociological Review* 61:635-655.

Perkus, Cathy, ed. (1975). *Cointelpro: The FBI's Secret War on Political Freedom*. New York: Monad Press.

Rosenbaum, Ron (1995). "The Great Ivy League Nude Posture Photo Scandal." *New York Times Magazine* (January 15):26-31, 40, 46, 55-56.

Roshier, Bob (1989). *Controlling Crime: The Classical Perspective in Criminology*. Philadelphia: Open University Press.

Rowe, David C., and D. Wayne Osgood (1984). "Heredity and Sociological Theories of Delinquency: A Reconsideration." *American Sociological Review* 49:526-540.

Shah, Saleem A. (1967). "The 47, XYY Chromosomal Abnormality—A Critical Appraisal with Respect to Antisocial and Violent Behavior." In *Issues in Brain/Behavior Control*, edited by W. Lynn Smith and Arthur A. Kling, 49-67. New York: Spectrum.

Sheldon, William H., Emil M. Hartl, and Eugene McDermott (1949). *Varieties of Delinquent Youth: An Introduction to Constitutional Psychiatry*. New York: Harper and Row.

Stephen, Leslie (1900). *The English Utilitarians*. New York: Putnam.

Stoker, Bram (1893). *Dracula*. New York: Grosset and Dunlap.

Sutherland, Edwin H. (1956). "Varieties of Delinquent Youth." In *The Sutherland Papers*, edited by Karl Schuessler, Alfred Lindesmith, and Albert Cohen, 279-290. Bloomington: Indiana University Press.

Theilgaard, Alice (1984). A Psychological Study of the Personalities of XYY- and XXY-Men." *Acta Psychiatrica Scandinavia* (Supplement No. 35):69:1-33.

Vold, George B., and Thomas J. Bernard (1979). *Theoretical Criminology*, 2nd ed. New York: Oxford University Press.

NOTES

1   Feynman (1985), 281.

2   Ibid., 341.

3   Newman & Marongiu (1990), 325.

4   Cuomo (1996), VIII, and an introduction by Marvin Wolfgang, a preeminent scholar of crime and delinquency.

5   Beccaria (1764), 104.

6   Bentham (1838-1843), 10.

7   Stephen (1900), vol. I, 175.

8   Bentham (1838-1843), 328.

9   Cornish & Clarke (1986), 1.

10   Abelson (1995), 27-28.

11   Jeffrey (1960), 366.

12   Mannheim (1955), 70-71.

13   Lombroso (1905), vol. I, 497.

14   Lombroso (1911), xiv.

15   Ibid., 78.

16   Stoker (1893), 46.

17   Lombroso (1911), 112.

18   Perkus (1975), 32.

19   Conrad (1907), 185.

20   Lombroso & Ferrero (1895), 113-114.

21   Gould (1981), 54.

22   Kurella (1911), 33.

23   Hooton (1939), 309.

24   Sutherland (1956), 280.

25   Ibid., 286.

26   Ibid., 289.

27   Davenport-Hines (1995), 269.

[28]   Rosenbaum (1995), 27-28.

[29]   Theilgaard (1984), 108.

[30]   Angier (1995).

[31]   Mednick (1977), 5.

[32]   Moffitt et al. (1994), 296.

[33]   Rowe & Osgood (1984), 526-527.

[34]   Herrnstein (1993), 45.

5

From Freud to *The Bell Curve*:
Psychiatric, Psychological, and Intelligence Theories

The theories of Cesare Lombroso represent an extreme point on the continuum of explanations of juvenile delinquency. In Lombroso's early writings, heredity played out as destiny. The delinquency was there at birth, just waiting to manifest itself after the passage of years. At the other extreme of the continuum are theories that regard all human beings as totally unformed at birth, so that social experience alone will determine how they will behave. Both sets of ideas about delinquency—those stressing heredity exclusively and those solely emphasizing environment—are lopsided. It is more likely that it is the interplay of what we are with the things we experience that will determine what we do—or what we choose to do—and will decree whether we perform certain acts that come under the definition of juvenile delinquency.

At the same time, we know that the blend of heredity and experience that plays into human behavior can be unevenly mixed. In some cases, hereditary factors appear to dominate the causal process; in others, environmental influences seem to play the most important role. In still others, traumas visited on a human organism, such as brain disease, offer persuasive evidence that they have been prominent in the production of delinquent acts. Take, for instance, the disease of encephalitis, whose name literally means "brain inflammation." Sufferers experience sleepiness, difficulties in swallowing, strabismus (a

115

vision disorder marked by an inability to direct both eyes to the same object), and bizarre personality changes. A case history of a juvenile who contracted encephalitis has been supplied by John Pfeiffer:

> An epidemic of encephalitis broke out among horses in southeastern Massachusetts and three weeks later the malady spread to human beings. The patients included a 10-year-old boy, a model child with an IQ of 145. He continued to be well-behaved and obtained his usual good marks until more than a year after passing through the crisis of the disease, when he began getting restless and noisy. He struck his mother, gouged holes in the walls with his pocket knife and had screaming tantrums followed by fits of remorse. In this case there was no question about the most likely cause. The boy's symptoms were brought under control with benzedrine and have not flared up again.[1]

Obviously, if a young person was behaving in exemplary fashion and after a bout of encephalitis got into constant difficulty with the juvenile authorities because of brawling aggressiveness, it might reasonably be argued that the disease was the major cause of the delinquent behavior. Note how Pfeiffer sensibly calls the disease "the most likely cause" rather than insisting that it was without question the cause. It always should be kept in mind that we are talking about statistical not universal consequences; that is, there are plenty of people with any one of the conditions identified as related to delinquent behavior who never get into any difficulty.

In the present chapter, we will scrutinize theoretical frameworks that are important to a complete understanding of how various specialists try to explain juvenile delinquency. The psychiatric approach—the first to be addressed—has occupied a very significant niche in the thinking of ordinary people as well as those who make a career of interpreting how humans live out their lives. Psychiatry has the rather unusual characteristic of combining an elaborate theoretical underpinning with a recommended form of treatment—the so-called "talking cure." Therapists, many of whom adopt a psychiatric perspective, abound in our contemporary society—a society in which personal problems often overcome the individual's ability to cope without the assistance of someone credentialed to offer aid. Whether the therapeutic intervention brings about the result sought by the client may have little to do with the validity of its theoretical underpinnings. The treatment could succeed for any number of other reasons. In the realm of delinquency, where it is far easier to try to change an individual rather than to deal with the social system, treatments with psychiatric overtones always have been popular.

Psychological theories of delinquency, the second topic in this chapter, have tended to take a back seat to sociological interpretations, not necessarily because they are less persuasive or powerful but because the people who conduct research on delinquency typically have been trained in sociology, which has for many years been marked by sibling rivalry with psychology, its older kin. Psychological theories cannot by themselves provide totally comprehensive and satisfying explanations of delinquency. If, for instance, frustration is presumed to produce aggression, we would like to be able to pinpoint the characteristics of social situations that give rise to frustration. On the other hand, when sociologists earmark certain social conditions as basic to illegal youthful behavior, they often fail to attend to the processes by which such conditions work their way into the thinking and behavior of the young miscreant. The incorporation of both psychological and sociological explanations into a theoretical system increasingly preoccupies theorists at work today.

The final segment of this chapter takes up the issue of the relationship between intelligence (typically as measured by IQ tests) and delinquency. Fiery debate on the question has captured the attention not only of those who do research on delinquency but also of the general public. Close attention to the debate can provide an understanding of its particular ingredients as well as the political processes through which certain ideas catch the attention of the mass media—and through it, the interested citizen.

PSYCHIATRIC THEORIES

Sigmund Freud

Sigmund Freud (1856-1939) was born in Moravia and completed his medical training in Vienna. He first worked as a research scientist, dissecting fish and coming close to discovering the value of cocaine as an anesthetic for eye operations. Freud himself used cocaine, sometimes heavily, for about 10 years, but stopped completely in 1896. In a recent study of Freud's work, bearing the provocative title *Why Freud was Wrong*, Richard Webster notes that Freud's failure to discover that cocaine was an excellent local anesthetic grew out of his compulsive need to achieve world fame by locating a cure-all for all human ills. In his work with cocaine, Webster observed, Freud was looking for a forest and missed the only significant tree. Webster goes on to discuss Freud's recommendation to a friend, an opiate addict, that he cure the addiction by using cocaine—a prescription for disaster, as the drugs do not counter one another but produce a more addictive high.

Freud contended that a triad of forces constitute the human personality; they are the id (biological urges and wants), the superego (the learned dictates of the social system), and the ego (the "I," the forces that mediate the demands of the id, the obstacles of the environment, and the pressures from the superego). According to Freudians, all of us are forced to control biological urges from childhood on, and we often develop frustrations and insecurities as a result. We are conflicted creatures, torn by contradictory yearnings for love and death, and besieged by unconscious impulses only barely held in check by the rules of civilized life. In a person not sufficiently healthy emotionally, such setbacks can trigger illness or antisocial behavior such as delinquency. We often do not ourselves understand why we act as we do, because the reasons, too hurtful to be faced directly, lie buried in our unconscious. Particularly important among the conflicts we must resolve is that identified for men as the Oedipus complex and for women as the Electra complex. The basis of these conflicts is said to be that boys lust for the exclusive love of their mothers and girls for that of their fathers. This brings them into conflict with the competing parent. An inability to resolve the conflict—to move beyond parental attachment and hostility—can, Freudians insist, cause problems in social living.

The Freudian system is appealing because it is a closed framework of thought; that is, once the premises are granted, it becomes impossible to rebut a Freudian conclusion. In this sense, it is different from science—perhaps better, perhaps worse, but different. For this reason, the eminent philosopher of science Karl Popper dismissed Freudian psychoanalysis (along with Marxism and astrology) as made up of self-confirming, nonscientific tenets. For Popper, the difficulty was that the theories could not be falsified; that is, there was no conceivable behavior that would contradict them. Psychological theories can be abstract, Popper notes, but they must have consequences that are observable. A mental process, such as repression, he maintained, cannot be observed.

The self-confirming aspect of Freudian theory is exemplified by the diagnosis of a probation officer that a delinquent under her supervision showed "neurotic tendencies." The boy had been late for his appointment with the officer, who interpreted the tardiness as "hostility," with the alleged hostility forming the basis for a diagnosis of neurosis. However, had the boy been precisely on time, the officer, using a Freudian approach, might well have interpreted this as "compulsivity." Similarly, had he been early, this could have been viewed as "defensiveness." Both of these also could be translated into neurotic manifestations.

Freud has been subject to scathing criticism in recent years. Summarizing a considerable body of literature, Daniel Goleman wrote that "new revelations depict a Freud who seems at times mercenary and manipulative, who sometimes claimed cures when there were none, and who on occasion distorted the facts of his cases to prove his theoretical points." Goleman nonetheless says that "the new revelations do not demean Freud's brilliance." Instead, he observes, "they portray a Freud far more prone to human failing than the legend of the man has allowed."[2] If, as some social commentators observe, fame is like a tennis ball, only kept aloft by being hit from opposing sides, Freud clearly remains a very famous person.

The major scientific problem with the Freudian system as it applies to juvenile delinquency is that it is not predictive. It is one thing to proclaim that a young boy who kills his father after the father had beaten his mother is acting out an unresolved Oedipal fixation, but it is quite another thing to predict which young men will murder their fathers. Interpreters often fall back upon psychiatric explanations because they provide ready-made, "easy" answers in the face of interpretative confusion. This, however, does not necessarily make them accurate.

Arson

Take, for instance, the crime of arson. About 40 percent of the somewhat more than 100,000 confirmed or suspected arsons each year (which kill about 700 people) are carried out by juveniles, and about 7 percent of the juveniles arrested for arson are under 10 years of age. Males commit almost nine out of 10 arson offenses.

Why do these delinquents select fire-setting as their crime of choice? Freudian theory would suggest a big-bang-for-your-buck theory; that is, an inadequate youngster needs only a match to make a huge impression. Therefore, arson, it is maintained, will be carried out by youths with inadequate personalities who are frantic for attention. Freudians also assert that fire-setting is symbolically expressive of sexual desires. They note that young men sometimes set fires and then attempt to extinguish them with their own urine, thereby, in the words of Jessica Gaynor and Chris Hatcher, "engaging in homosexual struggle with another phallus."[3] Arson also is a crime that allows its perpetrator to stand by and observe the destruction that has been wrought; thus, arson investigators often monitor the bystanders at a fire to see if they can identify a suspicious person.

Nolan D.C. Lewis and Helen Yarnell believe that compulsive fire-setters show symptoms of an "irresistible impulse" when they embark on fire-setting (though others point out that such impulses are readily resisted if a cop is standing behind their possessor). Arsonists, they maintain, report mounting tension, restlessness, and an urge for motion, as well as symptoms such as headaches, ear ringing, and heart palpitations. The great number of baby carriages set on fire by arsonists in urban apartment houses is interpreted as symbolic hostility against infants, although it is equally possible that the carriages are the most flammable objects in the hallways of tenements. Lewis and Yarnell illustrate the theoretical approach of the psychiatric school in a summary statement about the arsonists they examined:

> A desire for exhibitionism is the fact most common to each, as though they began life with an exaggerated wish to become leading participants in the contemporary drama, and then, when it was realized that fate had relegated them to insignificant roles, they secretly staged a drama of their own, in which they were author, stage-director, and leading actor.[4]

The language associated with fire is seized upon by Freudians to show its emotional content. In our society, the color of fire (red), is considered the most exciting of the shades of the spectrum. Theologically, hell is portrayed as a fiery place. The American language is replete with fire symbols to express strong emotions. An angry person is said to "see red" and to be "burned up"; a person in love "carries a torch" and the object of his or her affection may be "a ball of fire"; a person with deep convictions has a "burning zeal."

Shoplifting

Shoplifting is another act of delinquency that often produces psychiatric theorizing. That a male offender steals a fountain pen or a flashlight will be linked to fears of castration, with the stolen items said to represent "phallic symbols." Things stolen, whether lingerie, sweaters, or pup tents, are believed to possess meaning for the pilferer. In addition, shoplifting can be interpreted as an unconscious attempt to punish parents for real or imagined grievances the delinquent bears toward them. According to Freudians, the offense also is committed to obtain attention that is not forthcoming when the delinquent behaves satisfactorily. Delinquency also might reflect a desire for punishment growing out of a sense of guilt or an interest in obtaining help.

In Freudian thinking, individuals with weak superegos are presumed to be particularly likely candidates for delinquency. Ego defects also are said to impair accurate interpretation of the environment in a way that can produce law-violating behavior. Such personality defects generally are ascribed to distressed parent-child relations, usually resulting from the mother's psychological problems. This position is one of several psychiatric postulations that has put the theory into disrepute with many feminists. Herbert Quay's summary of psychiatric theories in regard to criminal and delinquent behavior is well put:

In many ways these explanations are appealing, if only for their simplicity. Weak superegos can often be "found" in criminals, particularly if criminal behavior is accepted as evidence for the weakness. Also, many criminals seem to show unconscious desires for punishment by leaving fingerprints or other incriminating evidence at the scene of the crime; but this may also be explained by the empirical finding that a high level of anxiety impedes deliberate thinking. Psychoanalytical theory, in addition to the unobservable nature of its basic explanatory concepts and its reliance on instinctual drives, does not provide adequate room for environmental factors and the process of learning.[5]

Despite these reservations, Quay points out that long-forgotten early events in a person's life, as noted by psychiatrists, certainly can have lasting effects. In recent years, considerable controversy has been aroused by claims by young women—often heavily prompted by a therapist—that they now recall being sexually abused by their fathers when they were infants or youngsters. They say that they have "repressed" the memory of the experience until now. Such claims rarely can be proved or disproved. In some instances, the allegations seem to have some basis; in many, they appear to be ill-founded.

PSYCHOLOGICAL THEORIES

Psychologists were paramount in the study of juvenile delinquency during the opening decades of the twentieth century. Subsequently, however, the study of delinquency was preempted in the United States by sociologists who often promoted theories of delinquency that basically rest upon psychological premises (that is, ideas about the nature of individual human behavior), such as social learning. Arnold Binder in the *Annual Review of Psychology* offered an explanation for this development:

> First, the work of the sociologists has been more imaginative than that of the individual-oriented scholars and, second, the American intellectual climate is more receptive to theoretical positions that overtly blame society for an individual's (particularly a young individual's) transgressions than to those that seem to blame the individual. Related to the latter is the particular antipathy in American scholarship (and the culture generally) to notions of the born delinquent or even to the milder notion of individual predisposition toward delinquency.[6]

Only after World War II did multidisciplinary academic units develop that were devoted to studying and teaching about crime and delinquency. They represent a response to the belief that to understand a phenomenon such as delinquency it is essential to spread its study among a variety of specialists—sociologists, economists, psychologists, historians, medical specialties, jurisprudents, social workers, and others. It must also be appreciated that different kinds of explanations of delinquency each may contain some element of truth and be of some value. Psychological explanations of delinquency can coexist with physiological and sociological explanations, because each can be logically independent.

All too often, psychological work on delinquency has taken the route of paper-and-pencil tests that attempt to distinguish cohorts of delinquents and nondelinquents on the basis of their responses. In part, this is the result of the accessibility of the samples. Like students (another favorite target for psychological experimentation), delinquent offenders can be induced rather easily to participate in such exercises. They do so partly out of boredom, partly out of curiosity, and partly because they are agreeable to the solicitations of the experimenters. Sometimes, though, "subjects" resent the intrusions, a matter that obviously can affect the test results. Lars Gorling, writing from the perspective of the delinquents, noted of psychologists and their tests:

> They wanted to know everything, the likes and dislikes, interests, what it had been like when we were kids. About our parents, brothers, and sisters. And then we had to interpret various words. It was like eating yourself up in daily portions. Afterwards, you felt gnawed to pieces and hollowed out, squeezed dry and quite empty. It almost hurt you all over.[7]

Much psychological testing has depended upon the Minnesota Multiphasic Personality Inventory (MMPI). In a typical inquiry, for instance, researchers found that delinquents scored significantly higher on a scale said to measure "sensation-seeking" than did nondelinquents. The result could, of course, be the product of delinquent behavior rather than its cause, yet the researchers recommended that it might be useful to fight delinquency by providing persons who register high sensation-seeking scores with socially approved opportunities to meet their expressed need for thrills.

Hans Eysenck: Conditioning Theory

Hans J. Eysenck (1916-1997) was the leading proponent of *conditioning theory*, one of the more sophisticated psychological approaches to the understanding of juvenile delinquency. Eysenck believed that the major explanation for delinquency is that some youngsters fail to incorporate the rules of society in their minds. This is congruent with Freud's idea that an inadequate superego can cause delinquency, but Eysenck discards Freudian theorizing as little more than idle speculation; in fact, he has been one of the severest critics of psychiatric treatment, insisting that those who receive it improve no more than those who forego treatment.

Eysenck maintains that conscience, in the main, makes us behave in a socially acceptable manner and that the acquisition of a satisfactory conscience is the result of a long process of conditioning. According to Eysenck, his own research demonstrates that extroverted persons (those whose interests are centered on outside stimuli) are more difficult to condition (that is, to train) than those who are introverted (persons who tend to be more self-contained). He then points out that extroverts tend to get into more trouble than introverts. A study of 963 male first-year students at the University of Minnesota, for instance, found that extroverts were involved in more automobile accidents than introverts. Similarly, pilots in South Africa who had flying accidents while in training were much more extroverted than those who completed training without trouble. Eysenck also cites a study that found the same distinctive personality difference between young women who had been involved in sexual delinquency and those who had not—a matter that often is at the root of cases filed against them in juvenile court.

To his credit, Eysenck regarded his theory as very tentative, requiring much more confirmation before it can be fully accepted. He posed the question that we earlier noted as essential (and often absent) for sophisticated theorists: "Are there any contradictory data that might lead us to doubt the validity of our theory?"

Dollard and Miller: Frustration-Aggression Theory

The ideas about conditioning advanced by Eysenck represent a global theory of delinquency; that is, if correct, they could account for all forms of the behavior. Other psychological theories focus only on certain aspects of delinquency. The *frustration-aggression theory*, which is particularly prominent, deals almost exclusively with acts of violence.

The idea that frustration produces an aggressive response was first formulated in 1939 by John Dollard, Neal Miller, and their associates. Frustration was defined as an interference with the occurrence of an integrated goal-response at its proper time in the behavioral sequence. More simply put, the theorists said that a person becomes frustrated if he or she is kept from attaining the satisfaction expected at the time the person thought it would be achieved. Such frustration arouses aggression against the source inflicting it or, perhaps, against a more convenient object. Thus, a youngster frustrated by a teacher might take his or her anger out on a weaker classmate. The expression of aggression alleviates the frustration and allows the person to return to a more comfortable state. Laboratory studies confirm this notion. One study, for instance, showed that male subjects displayed a sharp increase in systolic blood pressure when angered and had a more rapid return to their regular blood pressure if they could punish the person who had insulted them than if they could behave only in a nonaggressive manner.

Reviewing the scientific status of the frustration-aggression theory some 40 years after its initial statement, one psychologist has pointed out that the theory does not account for all aggression. A soldier might kill an enemy without anger, seeking to end the war and to protect himself or herself, and a Mafia "hit man" might kill on order with no emotional involvement. Some commentators also have suggested that prior learning might influence whether the response to frustration will be aggressive or whether the person thwarted will withdraw or retreat. Berkowitz, citing animal experiments, believes that aggression may be an inborn response to frustration. He concludes that frustration is translated into pain and that, while responses to pain may take many forms, pain generally "elicits fairly specific reactions that incline the organism to be aggressive."[8]

The frustration-aggression theory can provide significant insight into the wellsprings of delinquency. It helps explain why deprivations suffered by lower-class children may fuel a higher level of openly aggressive forms of delinquency. The theory suggests that it is not a particularly good idea to frustrate a person needlessly if that person does not have a legal means to respond to such frustration. Frustration can also be enabling, though, in the sense that it can propel persons to seek ways to solve their dilemmas. Frustration is inevitable because none of us is going to be able to have everything we want when we want it, no matter how effectively we manipulate the world and keep our desires in check. Therefore, we need to learn how to deal with frustration, which is usually and understandably an easier task if we have many ways to compensate for the frustrations we experience.

Glueck and Glueck Revisited

In the previous chapter, we examined the work of Sheldon Glueck and Eleanor Glueck, which used William Sheldon's typologies of physical traits to differentiate delinquents from nondelinquents. Glueck and Glueck tended to employ in their research every kind of characteristic that might in some way distinguish young people who had trouble with the law from those who did not. In addition to physique and health, their research probes also analyzed conditions in the home, school experiences, and character structure. Their major study involved the comparison of 500 delinquent boys with 500 nondelinquents of the same sex. Glueck and Glueck avoided theoretical positions—indeed, they had an aversion to overarching generalization.

Most of Glueck and Glueck's work has been superseded by later, more sophisticated inquiries, but their contribution remains impressive if only for its compilation of a huge mass of data. Scrutiny of their work on psychiatric and psychological aspects of delinquency provides a flavor of their enterprise and some of their findings, as well as insight into the controversial construction of their tables that were alleged to predict which youngsters were likely to get into trouble so that something could be done about it before they did.

Glueck and Glueck employed a psychiatric consultant to look at various characteristics that might be related to lawbreaking. The psychiatrist did not know which of the 1,000 boys were in the delinquent group and which were not. He judged one-half as many of the delinquents as other boys (15 percent against 31 percent) to be "adequate" in their ability to conduct or express themselves reasonably. By contrast, he found that twice as many delinquents (28 percent versus 14 percent) were dynamic (that is, forceful and energetic). A great many more delinquents (55 percent against 18 percent) were reported to have a thirst for adventure, change, excitement, and risk.

In terms of personality, the delinquents were found to be less conventional than the nondelinquents (25 percent versus 49 percent) and much less conscientious (9 percent versus 54 percent). Rorschach tests, which consist of 10 symmetrical inkblots (most black, some colored), were interpreted to show that one-half of the delinquents, as compared to one in 10 of the nondelinquents, were marked by the trait of defiance. On the contrary, the feeling of not being wanted or loved was reported by a very large percentage of members of both groups: 92 percent of the delinquents and 97 percent of the nondelinquents, a rather surprising result. Finally, a significantly higher proportion of delinquents than nondelinquents were characterized by feelings of not being recognized or appreciated and by feelings of resentment.

These findings, however intriguing and suggestive, have to be viewed with some skepticism because they were found after the boys had been engaging in delinquent behavior and may well represent their altered self-perceptions after having been caught. Nonetheless, the results of Glueck and Glueck's work, particularly in regard to the family conditions of delinquents, often line up with later and more sophisticated inquiries, as shown in a recent reanalysis and reinterpretation by Robert Sampson and John Laub. Nonetheless, the extensive work of Glueck and Glueck has been largely ignored in discussions of the roots of juvenile delinquency. Part of this must be traced to their academic location in a law school, far from the precincts in which scholars of juvenile delinquency work. Part can be attributed to the considerable infusion of out-of-fashion moralizing that pervades their research reports.

Glueck and Glueck were deeply interested in social reform—in the prevention and control of juvenile delinquency. One of their major proposals was that there ought to be a program of early intervention to head off future delinquency:

> The selection of potential delinquents at the time of school entrance or soon thereafter would make possible the application of treatment measures that would be truly crime preventive. To wait for the certain manifestation of delinquency before applying therapy is to close the barn door after the horse has been stolen.[9]

The "prediction table" constructed by Glueck and Glueck relied on five factors: (1) discipline of the boy by father; (2) supervision of the boy by mother; (3) affection of father for boy; (4) affection of the mother for the boy; and (5) cohesiveness of the family. Glueck and Glueck's five factors reflect the emphasis on parent-child relationships that dominated the literature of the period during which they were writing and which has returned to center stage today.

Numerical ratings were given for each of the five items on the basis of a formula. The total number of possible points ran from a low of 116.7 to a high of 414, with the higher scores representing the greater likelihood of subsequent delinquent behavior. If a youth at age six had a score between 300 and 349, for instance, Glueck and Glueck maintained that he would have an 86 percent chance of becoming a juvenile delinquent. It was said that trained social workers could readily gather and interpret the materials required to predict a delinquent outcome.

Criticism of Glueck and Glueck's prediction table has concentrated on a concern about intervening early in a youngster's school career on the basis of what at best is a statistical likelihood that he or she might be headed for delinquency. Under such an approach, numerous "false positives" (persons not destined for delinquency) would invariably have their lives disrupted. In addition, some scholars, as we shall note later, maintain that the process of officially labeling a six-year-old as a "predelinquent" makes it more likely that the youngster will actually embark on a delinquent career.

Wilson and Herrnstein: Operant-Utilitarianism

Crime and Human Nature, by James Q. Wilson (born in 1931) and Richard J. Herrnstein (1930-1994), was one of the most widely heralded contributions to theories of delinquency (perhaps, in part due to its considerably overstated book jacket blurb that proclaimed the work as "the most significant social science study in the decade"). The volume was immodestly subtitled: "The Definitive Study of the Causes of Crime."

Crime and Human Nature reviewed studies of crime and delinquency but remained blind to investigations that seriously challenged its own conclusions. Consider, for instance, the issue of gender and delinquency. Studies worldwide persistently demonstrate that girls commit fewer acts of delinquency than boys. Wilson and Herrnstein believe that the basis for this outcome is biological. The roots of property crime by boys, they maintain, go so deep into the biological substratum that they are hard to change. Wilson and Herrnstein grant that most women commit crimes for essentially the same reason as most men, but they fail to appreciate, as John Braithwaite has observed, that a satisfactory explanation of gender differences in delinquency may be that girls are less exposed to the reasons that prompt both girls and boys to crime. As a simple example, boys may commit a criminal act because they desire the approval of their peers. Girls may learn that their friends will grant less approval to their delinquent behavior; therefore, there is less impetus to engage in it. Braithwaite also notes that girls are less likely than boys to be weakly attached to their parents, to be unconcerned about the respect of their parents, and to have delinquent friends. Their dependency on the family for approval may also be a part of the socially integrative role into which girls are socialized from very early in life.

Wilson, a public policy political scientist, and Herrnstein, a psychologist, introduce different and often refreshingly distinctive disciplinary perspectives into the study of delinquency. In addition, Wilson is something of an academic media star, in part because his views are in tune with the conservative trend of the times, and in part because he is notably articulate.

Wilson and Herrnstein cover a wide array of items that they maintain are significantly related to explanations of delinquency—most notably race and intelligence—but their basic theoretical position follows the line of psychological theorizing. That position is largely eclectic. First, they set out a menu of items that correlate with delinquency. Then they offer a summary statement that reflects the utilitarianism of Beccaria and Bentham, discussed in the previous chapter, and the social control position of Travis Hirschi, which we will examine later. The Wilson and Herrnstein theoretical position comes to this:

> The larger the ratio of rewards (material and nonmaterial) of noncrime to the rewards (material and nonmaterial) of crime, the weaker the tendency to commit crimes. The bite of conscience, the approval of peers, and any sense of inequity will increase or decrease the total value of crime; the opinions of family, friends, and employees are important benefits of noncrime, as is the desire to avoid the penalties that can be imposed by the criminal justice system. The strength of any reward declines with time, but people differ in the rate at which they discount the future. The strength of a given reward is also affected by the total supply of reinforcers.[10]

This is a grab bag of diverse ideas. The first sentence is pure utilitarianism. The authors, well aware of the deficiencies of so bald a statement standing alone, buttress it with an inventory of matters that incline toward and against delinquency (desire to avoid punishment, opinions of family and friends, etc.). Such things as the opinions of friends can keep people from acting contrary to the law or encourage people to do so, depending on who the friends are and what they value. Wilson and Herrnstein hedge their theory with a pair of reservations that would make testing extraordinarily difficult. People are different, they say, and the strength of any reward declines with time. Finally, the theoretical statement moves into even more abstract territory: "The strength of any reward is affected by the total supply of reinforcers." This comes very close to saying: "Well, it depends . . ."[11]

Wilson and Herrnstein grant that there is a great deal of tautology in their position. Tautology is defined as the needless repetition of meaning, such as in the phrase "audible to the ear." In science, the word takes on the added meaning of circular reasoning—of the kind we saw in the work of Lombroso discussed in the previous chapter. Some theorists have been prone to insist that delinquents were defective creatures and then to "prove" their defectiveness by pointing to their delinquency. According to Wilson and Herrnstein, the idea that "a person will do that thing the consequences of which are perceived by him or her to be preferable to the consequences of doing something else" is not only self-evident and tautological but defines itself. If people consistently hit their heads against a wall, using Wilson and Herrnstein's approach, we can say that they do so because they prefer the pain and what they are doing beats being bored. However, this is rather pointless from a scientific viewpoint, because it applies to everything that is done. Wilson and Herrnstein take the odd position that they can salvage a tautological statement by "plausibly" describing its ingredients. Most scientists would insist that you have to restate the idea in a way that can be tested and determined to be correct or inaccurate (in short, in a way that is not tautological).

Wilson and Herrnstein have been criticized for using their research materials in a self-serving manner, that is, rejecting those findings that do not suit their preconceptions and utilizing those that do. In a telling counterpunch, Leon Kamin makes the following point:

> Tiny snippets of data are plucked from a stew of conflicting and often nonsensical experimental results. Those snippets are then strung together in an effort to tell a convincing story, rather in the manner of a clever lawyer building a case. The data do not determine the conclusions reached by the lawyer. Instead the conclusions toward which the lawyer wants to steer the jury determine which bits he presents.[12]

Other commentators add further criticisms to Wilson and Herrn-stein's revisionist views. Jack Gibbs praised the authors for being able to "avoid the usual shrillness" found in interdisciplinary warfare, but believes that Wilson and Herrnstein might have done better to carry out original research to try to support their theoretical ideas rather than relying on materials published with other aims. He finds that their work fails to set forth a series of carefully enunciated premises or to demonstrate "the slightest concern about the empirical applicability of their terms." Gibbs considered the 20 pages devoted by Wilson and Herrn-stein to constitutional theories of the cause of delinquency to lie beyond the bounds of their major theoretical position and considered it to be a "puzzling" detour. He echoes the general response to Wilson and Her-rnstein by the scholarly community:

> It is unfortunate that Wilson and Herrnstein did not devote the space and energy invested in [a number of the chapters] to a clarification of their theory by stating explicit premises and deducing testable conclusions. Instead, we have another dis-cursive, untestable theory, something that has never been in short supply. Hence, despite Wilson and Herrnstein's serious scholarship, their book will not lead criminologists out of the wilderness in which they now wander.[13]

INTELLIGENCE THEORIES

Shortly after the beginning of the present century, scholars began to point their fingers at defective intelligence as the prime cause of delin-quent behavior. This idea went hand in hand with a movement calling for eugenics measures to improve the human breed in the manner in which better horses and livestock are produced by mating those with desired traits and limiting the fertility of those with unwanted characteristics.

Henry H. Goddard

The first major figure in this development was Henry H. Goddard (1866-1957), superintendent of a school for mental defectives, who wrote two major books—*The Kallikak Family* (1912) and *The Crimi-nal Imbecile* (1915)—in which he argued that feeblemindedness (or, in today's language, "developmental disability") was inherited and that it leads those who suffer from it to become juvenile delinquents because they do not adequately appreciate the requirements of the law. Goddard campaigned against unrestricted immigration, alleging that members of certain nationalities had unusually high proportions of feebleminded persons. Goddard invented the term "moron," a harsh new word with a Greek stem meaning "foolish," to replace Alfred Binet's French *debiles*, a milder word that literally means "weak ones"; these were persons scoring in the eight-to-12 year range on IQ tests. A case history employed by Goddard demonstrates his thinking:

> Fred Tonson lived in Portland, Oregon for two years and in that time he held seven different positions as an elevator man. He became infatuated with Emma Ulrich, a stenographer. He asked her to marry him, but she refused. On November 16, he waited for her outside of her home with two loaded revolvers. When she stepped off the streetcar, he again asked her to marry him. She became frightened and ran toward her home. He followed her into her own house and there shot her down. . . . Binet intelligence tests showed him to have a mentality of nine years. When his confession was read in court, Tonson asked a clergyman on the jury, "Well, what do you think of it?" When the verdict was given, he did not understand what it meant. His only remark was that he didn't think there was much of a crowd out for the trial. This man had been an imbecile at least since he was 12 years of age, and he could have been cared for, and thus this atrocious murder prevented. Shall we learn the lesson and take care of the other Fred Tonsons who are now in our public schools and on our streets?[14]

Goddard's position, however, fails to stand up under empirical scrutiny. Mentally defective persons as a group commit no more and, according to some studies, even fewer acts of delinquency than persons with average and higher intelligence. This finding would be even more striking if white-collar offenses such as embezzlement and insider trading were considered. Mentally defective persons tend to lack the aggressive initiative that often underlies crimes of violence, and they are protected by their condition from behavior conflicts and tension, which can lie at the core of delinquent acts. Moreover, low intelligence can insulate a person from being caught up in the whirl of ambition and greed that often propels others into illegal acts. Rather than committing crimes because of a failure to appreciate the law, as Goddard presumes, mentally defective persons often lack the intelligence to plan and coordinate acts of delinquency.

A full-length biography of Goddard notes that his ideas ultimately came to be ridiculed and that his study of families with extended histories of feeblemindedness were, in the words of one writer, "laughed out of psychology." An important question, though, is why such obviously flawed research received worldwide acclaim when it was published and for decades afterwards. The study of the Kallikaks went through 11 editions and as late as 1933 the Nazis published *Die Fram-*

ilie Kallikak, a German translation of a book that was then more than 20 years old and widely repudiated

The answer, in large part, is said to lie in the social and political prejudices of the time. Anti-immigration views fed into a willingness to equate poverty with mental deficiency uncritically. The religious dictum that the sins of fathers are passed on to their offspring also was employed to legitimate Goddard's view.

On the basis of work such as Goddard's, IQ testing became notably fashionable as a diagnostic tool in the early years of this century. It was administered during World War I to all military recruits, with the startling result that nearly one-third of the draftees were found to be "feebleminded." This result was later amended by altering the scoring procedure, and IQ testing remained popular for the following two decades. Its importance in criminology began to fade, however, when sophisticated research showed little significant difference between offenders and the general population. Typical of such work is Deborah Denno's longitudinal study of 800 persons born in Philadelphia between 1959 and 1966. She found that intelligence scores demonstrated no direct effect on delinquency for either sex, though for males poor verbal ability had an indirect impact because of unsatisfactory school achievement. What makes the result particularly reliable is the fact that the intelligence tests were administered before there was any involvement in delinquency. Denno believes it likely that test scores are strongly influenced by both behavioral and environmental circumstances.

Only one discordant note appeared to challenge the apparent demise of the focus on intelligence as it related to delinquency. Travis Hirschi and Michael Hindelang revisited the question in an article and concluded that several factors underlay what they regard as the inadequate attention being paid to intelligence in delinquency research. These included: (1) the shift in research focus from a medical to a sociological perspective; (2) the failure of later research to support the exorbitant claims of earlier work on intelligence; (3) reservations about the validity of measurements of both intelligence and delinquent behavior; and (4) a professional ideology held by most sociologists that a focus on individual differences is dangerous. Instead, Hirschi and Hindelang claimed that textbook writers were likely to quote anecdotal observation that inmates in some midwestern institutions were more intelligent than their guards and to leave the matter at that. Hirschi and Hindelang argued that IQ scores were stronger than either race or class variables in predicting the difficulties of delinquents with the law. Nonetheless, they also cautioned that IQ itself needed considerable modification as an explanation of delinquent behavior. They observed that there is no evidence that IQ has a direct impact on delinquency, though it may be tied to poor school performance and adjustment.

Despite the Hirschi and Hindelang manifesto, IQ testing had become so out-of-style in the field of delinquency that one scholar matter-of-factly noted in 1995: "Today very little if any research tries to explain crime as a result of feeblemindedness."[15] Understandably, he failed to anticipate the impact that a 1994 book, *The Bell Curve,* would have on ideas about delinquency.

Herrnstein and Murray: *The Bell Curve*

Intelligence as a cause of crime (and innumerable other personal and social problems) rose to fiery prominence with the appearance in 1994 of *The Bell Curve,* written by Richard J. Herrnstein and Charles Murray. In this book, persons with low intelligence, as measured by IQ score, were labeled "cognitively disadvantaged" and were said to be destined to commit crime, fail at school, be unemployed, end up on welfare, produce illegitimate children, and, in all, to be rather wretched citizens. Furthermore, IQ was said to be genetic, that is, largely fixed and unchangeable.

The Bell Curve also plunged into a notoriously controversial arena, that of differences in intelligence among racial and ethnic groups, and

the presumed implications of such alleged differences. Herrnstein and Murray made an enormous, unwarranted leap to the assumption that intelligence tests were accurate portrayals of an ability to cope in life, including an ability to avoid delinquent behavior, and that the quality measured was not capable of being altered much by various educational and other kinds of programs. They expressed concern about "dysgenesis" or what

Charles Murray, coauthor of the controversial book *The Bell Curve,* relaxes in the office of his Maryland home. *(AP Photo/The Frederick News-Post, Sam Yu)*

others have less elegantly called "the dumbing down of America." They did, however, grant that single individuals categorized in any of the tested groups could perform exceptionally well.

In the scientific community, J. Blaine Hudson offered a view that was seconded by most others. "The vast preponderance of social science and genetic research over several generations," Hudson wrote, "indicates that this [the Herrnstein-Murray conclusion on race and intelligence], when examined closely, is inherently illogical and baseless—and that differences in test score patterns reflect differences in how racial groups are educated and/or are treated."[16] Others noted that Herrnstein and Murray had totally ignored one of the more meaningful IQ testing studies, reported by Otto Klineberg in his *Race Differences*, which showed that black recruits to the U.S. Army from the northern part of the United States scored higher than blacks from the South and, more interestingly, higher than whites from the South. The result was attributed to the schooling the recruits had received.

Critics of *The Bell Curve* called attention to what they regarded as the misuse of science to advance a conservative political crusade. Among the arguments against the book was David Perkins's claim that there were at least three dimensions of intelligence: the first, the neural kind on which Herrnstein and Murray focus; the second, experiential intelligence, which represents the contribution of the storehouse of personal experience; and the third, reflective intelligence, which is marked by knowledge, understanding, and attitudes about how to use our minds to make intelligent decisions. Perkins contends that at least the second and third clearly are learnable.

Francis Cullen, a highly regarded criminologist, shows that of 17 crime predictors, intellectual functioning is the third weakest. Further, IQ was shown to account for only 3.4 percent of the variation in any crime measure in Cullen's reanalysis of the National Longitudinal Survey of Youth, the data that provided a considerable part of the basis for many of Herrnstein and Murray's conclusions. Cullen found that more than 96 percent of crimes remained to be explained by factors other than the offenders' intelligence. According to Cullen, Herrnstein and Murray "have exaggerated the importance of IQ as a predictor of crime and their own empirical data do not support their immodest conclusions." In short, he maintains, "their social science is poor, though their ideology is strong." Then he writes whimsically: "In any case, there is at least one comfort. If you see Forrest Gump walking in your neighborhood, you don't have to call the police or even cross the street."[17]

The summary judgment of Robert Hauser on *The Bell Curve* seems accurate: "*The Bell Curve* is a massive, ideologically driven, and frequently careless or incompetent assemblage of good science, bad science, and pseudo-science that is likely to do great damage both in the realm of public policy and in the conduct of social research."[18] A Princeton University scholar offers another biting critique. *The Bell Curve*, he argues, is marked by "faulty reasoning, faulty inferences, incorrect data analysis, selective citing of literature and totally ignoring pertinent research and literature, some arithmetically incorrect calculations and inferences and implausible assumptions used in certain calculations, particularly those cited in estimating IQ inheritability."[19]

For a book so flawed, *The Bell Curve* received enormous press and television coverage. Murray (Herrnstein had died prior to the book's publication) appeared on *Nightline ABC* and the *Larry King Show* on the CNN network. This outpouring of attention strongly suggests that the public will pay close attention to heavily advertised books that provide an aura of scientific respectability and legitimacy to ideas that are in line with its political biases. The ideas in *The Bell Curve* have been with us a long time, and long have been effectively discredited in the scientific community, but it was the receptive climate of the present time, plus some intense promotional efforts, that enabled the book to garner the attention that it did.

Learning Disabilities

A clear correlation exists between youthful learning disabilities and delinquency, probably because youngsters unable to learn too often engage in behaviors that isolate them from their peers, and because they experience considerable difficulty in school and in making other social adjustments.

Current research estimates that the learning disabled population in school classes is between 10 and 20 percent. Pupils with such disabilities usually have average or higher intelligence, but they show inconsistent academic achievement. They may excel in some subjects while failing others or may do very well at some times and very poorly at other times in the same subject during the same semester, for no apparent reason. They can show that they understand the material, yet fail a test on it. School records often describe such students as lazy, unmotivated, inattentive, "daydreaming," and "not working up to their potential."

An illustration of the operation of a learning disability is provided by novelist Agnes Rossi, who portrays the efforts of a sister to help her younger brother:

> It wasn't that Chris had the ability and not the will. He had plenty of will. When I was in eighth grade and he was in fourth, I'd help him study for spelling tests. I'd sit him down at the kitchen table, and browbeat him. "Fifteen lousy words?" I'd groan. He wanted an A badly and figured I knew what had to be done. The spelling tests were on Friday. After school on Monday I'd demand to see his paper. He'd bring it to me dutifully, sorrowfully, a big red F. "But you knew these words," I'd say, looking down at *definitely* and *receive*. "I

Figure 5.1
Letter from a Learning Disabled Youth Sentenced to Prison

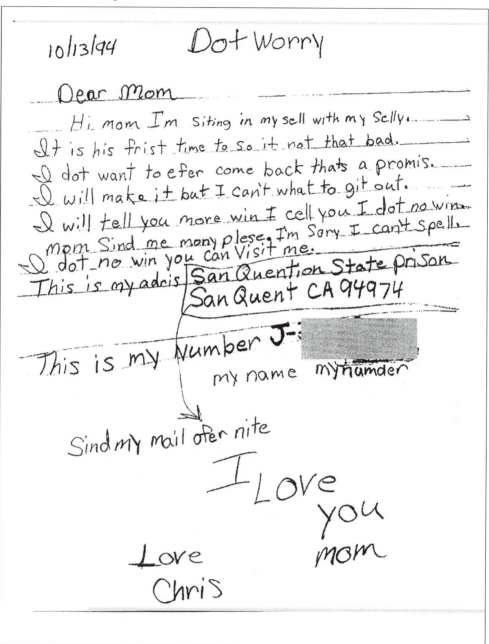

know them until the second she says them. Then I don't know them anymore." His voice would be higher-pitched than usual and reedy.[20]

Youngsters with learning difficulties come to absorb definitions of themselves. Some come to believe that they are irreparably brain-damaged and develop a feeling of hopelessness. Some hide their hurts behind aggressive behavior because they fear being perceived as dumb. They may repel most everyone. Exemplifying the problems of a learning disabled youngster is a letter (reproduced in Figure 5.1) from an adolescent to his mother after he was sentenced to state prison for a serious crime. Those who reviewed the adolescent's case maintain that throughout his life he had been pushed outside the mainstream because no one had adequately addressed his inability to do the kind of work demanded by the schools.

SUMMARY

Psychiatric and psychological theories of delinquency, like those that are biologically based, have focused on the individual rather than the group or the social system. Their reasoning is this: Whatever attitudes a group holds, reinforces, or transmits ultimately are effective only when these attitudes penetrate into the mind of an individual. Examining what a social system values, they say, will never tell you what any particular person within that system holds dear and what set of ideas any person will respond to. There are so many ideas available and so many contradictory things stressed in the United States that what any given person believes and acts upon can be determined only through study of that person.

Freudian psychiatry and its contemporary offshoots have exerted a deep influence on attempts to understand delinquent behavior. At the moment, psychiatry is under serious attack—particularly as a theoretical system, less so as a treatment modality, as "talk" therapy has yielded to some extent to the use of drug treatments for neuroses and psychoses. Psychiatry has the advantage of being able to "explain" virtually anything but has the considerable disadvantage of not being predictive or susceptible to testing (two essential attributes of a body of knowledge seeking scientific repute).

Psychological theorizing has yet to provide ideas that have gained widespread support in the study of delinquency, in part because of academic turf arrangements. The study of delinquency largely is undertaken and in some regards controlled by persons with sociological training. Many of these people, as we shall see, despite their academic backgrounds, advance theories that have strong psychological elements, though they very infrequently draw upon mainstream psychological research and theory. In this chapter, we focused on Eysenck's conditioning theory, the theory of frustration-aggression, and the relatively recently enunciated operant-utilitarian approach of Wilson and Herrnstein as representative of the insights that psychology can bring to an understanding of delinquent acts. Other, more comprehensive psychological views undoubtedly will emerge during coming decades.

We have devoted considerable space to *The Bell Curve* because it has had so strong and controversial an impact on ideas about delinquency and other kinds of lawbreaking. Its themes that IQ is genetic and unchangeable, that IQ accurately measures intelligence, and that we can predict the kind of life persons with certain IQs will lead and the behavior in which they will engage all have been challenged on various fronts (including one that argues that research that the authors ignored demonstrates otherwise). Warren C. Whatley's judgment of *The Bell Curve* seems to us accurate: "It is the kind of book that gives social science a bad name. It is a loosely argued set of propositions that rest on weak empirical foundations—propositions which are then crafted for maximum shock value."[21]

REFERENCES

Berkowitz, Leonard (1978). "Whatever Happened to the Frustration-Aggression Hypothesis?" *American Behavioral Scientist* 21:691-708.

Binder, Arnold (1988). "Juvenile Delinquency." *Annual Review of Psychology* 39:253-282.

Braithwaite, John (1987). "Review Essay: The Mesomorphs Strike Back." *Australian and New Zealand Journal of Criminology* 20:45-53.

Cullen, Francis T., Paul Gendreau, G. Roger Jarjoura, and John P. Wright (1997). "Crime and the Bell Curve: Lessons from Intelligent Criminology." *Crime & Delinquency* 43:397-411.

Denno, Deborah (1990). *Biology and Violence: From Birth to Adulthood*. New York: Cambridge University Press.

Dollard, John, Neal E. Miller, Leonard W. Doob, O.H. Mowrer, and Robert Sears (1939). *Frustration and Aggression*. New Haven, CT: Yale University Press.

Eysenck, Hans (1964). *Crime and Personality*. Boston: Houghton Mifflin.

Fischer, Claude S., Michael Hout, Martin Sanchez, Jim Kowski, Samuel Lucas, Ann Swindler, and Kim Wass (1996). *Inequity by Design: Cracking the Bell Curve Myth*. Princeton, NJ: Princeton University Press.

Fraser, Steven, ed. (1995). *The Bell Curve Wars*. New York: Basic Books.

Freud, Sigmund (1961). *Civilization and Its Discontents.* Translated by James Strachey. New York: Norton.

Freud, Sigmund (1935). *A General Introduction to Psycho-Analysis.* Translated by Joan Riviere. New York: Liveright.

Gaynor, Jessica, and Chris Hatcher (1986). *The Psychology of Child Firesetting: Detection and Intervention.* New York: Brunner/Mazel.

Gibbs, Jack (1985). "Review Essay: Crime and Human Nature." *Criminology* 23:381-388.

Glueck, Sheldon, and Eleanor Glueck (1950). *Unraveling Juvenile Delinquency.* New York: Commonwealth Fund.

Goddard, H. (1915). *The Criminal Imbecile.* New York: Macmillan.

Goleman, Daniel (1990). "As a Therapist, Freud Fell Short, Scholars Feel." *New York Times* (March 6):C1-C2.

Görling, Lars (1966). *491.* Translated by Anselm Hollo. New York: Grove Press.

Hauser, Robert M. (1995). "Review of The Bell Curve." *Contemporary Sociology* 24:149-153.

Herrnstein, Richard J., and Charles Murray (1994). *The Bell Curve: Intelligence and Class Structure in the United States.* New York: Free Press.

Hirschi, Travis, and Michael J. Hindelang (1977). "Intelligence and Delinquency: A Revisional Review." *American Sociological Review* 42:571-587.

Hudson, J. Blaine (1995). "Scientific Racism: The Politics of Tests, Race and Genes." *Black Scholar* 25:1-10.

Jacoby, Russell, and Naomi Glauberman, eds. (1995). *The Bell Curve Debate: History, Documents, Opinions.* New York: Times Books.

Kamin, Leon (1986). "Is Crime in the Genes? The Answer May Depend on Who Chooses What Evidence." *Scientific American* 254:22-27.

Klineberg, Otto (1935). *Race Differences.* New York: Harper.

Lewis, Nolan D.C., and Helen Yarnell (1951). *Pathological Firesetting (Pyromania).* New York: Nervous and Mental Health Monographs.

Lilly, J. Robert, Francis T. Cullen, and Richard A. Ball (1995). *Criminological Theory: Content and Consequences.* Thousand Oaks, CA: Sage.

Perkins, David (1995). *Outsmarting IQ: The Emerging Science of Learnable Intelligence.* New York: Free Press.

Pfeiffer, John (1965). *The Human Brain.* New York: Harper and Row.

Popper, Karl R. (1950). *The Open Society and Its Enemies.* Princeton, NJ: Princeton University Press.

Quay, Herbert (1983). "Crime Causation: Psychological Theories." In *Encyclopedia of Crime and Justice,* edited by Sanford H. Kadish, 330-342. New York: Free Press.

Quay, Herbert, ed. (1987). *Handbook of Juvenile Delinquency.* New York: Wiley.

Rossi, Agnes (1992). *The Quick: A Novella and Stories.* New York: Norton.

Sampson, Robert J., and John H. Laub (1993). *Crime in the Making: Pathways and Turning Points Through Life*. Cambridge, MA: Harvard University Press.

Taylor, Howard F. (1995). "Book Review, The Bell Curve." *Contemporary Sociology* 24:153-158.

Webster, Richard (1995). *Why Freud was Wrong: Sin, Science, and Psychoanalysis*. New York: Basic Books.

Whatley, Warren C. (1995). "Wanted: Some Black Long Distance Runners." *Black Scholar* 25:44-46.

Wilson, James Q., and Richard J. Herrnstein (1985). *Crime and Human Nature*. New York: Simon and Schuster.

Zienderland, Leila (1998). *Measuring Minds? Henry Herbert Goddard and the Origins of American Mental Testing*. New York: Cambridge University Press.

NOTES

1   Pfeiffer (1965), 116-117.

2   Goleman (1990), C1.

3   Gaynor & Hatcher (1986), 114.

4   Lewis & Yarnell (1951), 154.

5   Quay (1983), 382.

6   Binder (1988), 259.

7   Görling (1966), 145.

8   Berkowitz (1978), 205.

9   Glueck & Glueck (1950), 269.

10   Wilson & Herrnstein (1985), 261.

11   Ibid., 43.

12   Kamin (1986), 24.

13   Gibbs (1985), 387.

14   Goddard (1915), 65.

15   Lilly, Cullen & Ball (1995), 46.

16   Hudson (1995), 1.

17   Cullen et al. (1997), 384.

18   Hauser (1995), 149.

19   Taylor (1995), 155.

20   Rossi (1992), 43.

21   Whatley (1995), 45.

6

A Sociological Potpourri:
Ecological, Strain, Anomie, Subcultural, Labeling, and Shaming Theories

The dominance of sociology in the teaching and study of juvenile delinquency is reflected in the wide range of theoretical contributions rooted in concepts that are important to the sociological enterprise. Sociologists are concerned primarily with group processes rather than with individuals when they seek explanations of behavior. Their theories attend to matters such as slum conditions, racism, and the formation, structure, and behavior of juvenile gangs—among many other matters having to do with the influence of the society and groups within it on lawbreaking by young people.

THE ECOLOGICAL SCHOOL: SHAW AND MCKAY

Serious sociological study of juvenile delinquency began in the city of Chicago, which in 1899 was the site of the establishment of the country's (and the world's) first juvenile court. The sociology department at the University of Chicago, largely under the impetus of Robert E. Park (a journalist turned academic), undertook the examination of the environment surrounding the university, with particular emphasis on problems and persons not in the mainstream of American life. Universities traditionally have been located in remote places, away from metropol-

141

itan areas, presumably so that their students can pursue learning unimpeded by urban distractions. The University of Chicago, however, founded with Rockefeller money, contradicted this ancient tradition, and its sociologists elected to exploit their situation. The result was a series of brilliant monographs that endure as classics of urban study; Nels Anderson's *The Hobo* (1923), Ruth Cavan's *Suicide* (1928), Louis Wirth's *The Ghetto* (1928), Harvey Zorbaugh's *The Gold Coast and the Slum* (1929), and Paul Cressey's *Taxi-Dance Hall* (1932) were among the more prominent investigations.

The subject of juvenile delinquency in Chicago became the particular province of Clifford R. Shaw and Henry D. McKay, both trained in the University's sociology department (though neither completed his Ph.D. because of an inability, or unwillingness, to pass the foreign language requirement). Shaw was gregarious and charismatic—a leader. More than half a century later, Charlotte Kobrin, the wife of one of Shaw's coworkers, remembers thinking when she first met Shaw: "This must be what Abraham Lincoln was like." McKay was soft-spoken, modest, and retiring. Both men were rural products, part of the great migration from the surrounding countryside into the hub city of the midwest. Shaw was from Luray, Indiana, a crossroads town with a few houses; McKay was from Orient, South Dakota. They worked together at Chicago's Institute for Juvenile Research, established in the late 1920s.

Areal Studies

The major thrust of Shaw and McKay's effort was to plot the ecological distribution of juvenile delinquency within Chicago. There was great concern at the time (as there is today) regarding what was deemed to be the extensive lawlessness of members of immigrant groups. Pamphleteers deplored what they claimed was a decline in national standards of conduct, maintained that newcomers undercut the wages of citizens by working for less money, and said that they were "strange." Immigrants were criticized for retaining allegiance to their native lands—for refusing to jump into the melting pot to be refashioned into a shape more like that of the majority population. Children of immigrants often found themselves caught between the demands of two cultures—that of their new homeland and the "foreign" values of their parents. In a particularly vivid field study, Pauline Young showed how Molokan children, transplanted from the Russian steppes to Los Angeles, became confused. Their parents, devoutly religious, glorified manual labor, noting that Christ was a carpenter, but their non-Molokan friends scorned such work, looking for quick and easy money. Older brothers, arrested as delinquents, wrote home from reform school extolling the freedom and food of institutional life—compared to the bleakness of home—and advising younger siblings that all this was theirs if they got caught stealing a car or robbing a store.

Shaw and McKay demonstrated two basic points: first, that rates of delinquency varied significantly in different parts of the city; and second, that these rates remained the same over time in a given locale regardless of which ethnic group made up the bulk of the area's residents. The highest rates of delinquency were in areas next to centers of commerce and industry, and particularly on the fringe of the downtown section. These were slum neighborhoods, crammed with immigrants, derelicts, and the downtrodden. Absentee landlords were unwilling to rehabilitate decaying property because they assumed that in time it would be ripped down to make way for the outward expansion of the core of the city. Dwellings often were "railroad flats," large, old mansions converted into apartments in which access to the rear units was through the quarters of other families. The dwellings were overcrowded and disease-ridden; sometimes persons working different shifts (for instance, in places such as the cattle slaughterhouses) would share a bed, one sleeping in it while the other worked.

Successful immigrants quickly moved out of these high-delinquency neighborhoods for reasons of self-protection and self-improvement. It therefore was not race or ethnicity, Shaw and McKay insisted, that led to delinquency but rather life in a deteriorated section of the city where each day a variety of examples of wayward activity unfolded before the youngsters' eyes and where illegal acts represented a means of overcoming the grim reality of a marginal existence. When a group edged its way into the suburbs (as the Swedes, the Irish, and the Jews had done), its rate of delinquency dropped to the level already manifested in the place where the group now came to live.

The theoretical implication of the mapping strategy employed by Shaw and McKay was that delinquency is learned in a youngster's surroundings and is a consequence of examples of lawbreaking and a function of distress. Shaw and McKay's work also emphasized that a delinquent career was a response to the culture rather than an individual phenomenon resulting from inborn tendencies or psychological abnormalities. The theory did not, however, pinpoint why certain boys and (many fewer) girls in an area became delinquents while others did not. Also, as Shaw and McKay themselves pointed out, there were exceptions, most notably Asian-Americans:

> In communities occupied by Orientals, even those communities located in the most deteriorated sections of our large cities, the solidarity of Old World cultures and institutions has been preserved to such a marked extent that control of the child is still sufficiently effective to keep delinquency at a minimum.[1]

An extension of the ecological work of Shaw and McKay was undertaken by Robert Bursik, who reanalyzed their data using more modern statistical techniques. Bursik's major finding was that the pattern of delinquency for 1940, 1960, and 1970 remained much as Shaw and McKay had seen it, with particular neighborhoods demonstrating consistently high rates regardless of population changes. For 1950, however, Bursik found a very different situation. Between 1940 and 1950, as a result of a United States Supreme Court decision outlawing racial discrimination in home sales, blacks moved into white areas in unprecedented numbers. Racially mixed census tracts in Chicago (those having more than 1 percent and less than 97.4 percent black composition) increased from 135 in 1940 to 205 in 1950. For a time, this black population movement generated violent opposition that was reflected in much higher than ordinary delinquency rates. Gangs of white delinquents were one of the major forces at work against what was defined as a black invasion.

New residential patterns that have significantly altered the pre–World War II layout of cities have played havoc with the Shaw and McKay conclusions. Cheap public housing sometimes is scattered throughout an urban area, rather than placed downtown exclusively, and satellite shopping centers and malls draw juveniles, who now often have access to automobiles. The new mosaic urban form disperses delinquency much more widely.

Autobiographies of Delinquents

Shaw and McKay also collected biographical statements by juvenile delinquents, "the boys' own stories," which resulted in the publication of three books: *The Jack-Roller: A Delinquent Boy's Own Story* (1930), *The Natural History of a Delinquent Career* (1931), and *Brothers in Crime* (1938). Shaw and McKay allowed the youngsters in their autobiographical statements to convey how they felt about things, rather than having the researchers impose their judgments on the stories.

The Jack-Roller is illustrative of the books. In it, Stanley tells of his intense hatred for a stepmother, his constant efforts to run away from home, and his involvement with other boys in jack-rolling (that is, robbing drunks who are too incapacitated to resist). Shaw made a number of efforts to redeem Stanley, including several foster home placements. Stanley, though, describes feeling ill at ease in one rather splendid setting into which he is placed, and he consistently gets into difficulty in a series of menial jobs because of his chronic inability to suffer the smallest slight, real or imagined. Ultimately, Shaw finds a traveling sales job for Stanley that appears to provide the freedom from direct supervision and the ability to exploit his extraordinarily ingratiating personality. Forty years after *The Jack-Roller* was published, when Stanley was reinterviewed in Los Angeles, he reported that he had continued to remain out of prison, though he had spent some time in a mental hospital. He remained painfully touchy about any infringement on his emotional territory; he would explode if he thought that someone looked at him "wrong" or otherwise slighted or insulted him.

An obvious lesson from Stanley's story is that theoretical interpretations of delinquency can be extremely complicated. Was Stanley doomed by his personality to continuing social difficulty? Was there something in Stanley's genetic structure that preordained him to the problems he experienced, given the environment in which he was raised? Had Shaw salvaged him from a career in crime, or was it Stanley's timidity with regard to really serious lawbreaking that kept him from trouble? Was his stepmother as influential in corroding his life as Stanley maintained or had the neighborhood placed an indelible scar on him? And how typical was Stanley of young men who embark on careers of delinquency? In one respect, at least, he was unusual: he was very articulate, and able to put together in dramatic form the story of his life both as a young delinquent and as an elderly man.

The Chicago Area Project

For Shaw and McKay, action was primary and theory secondary in their agenda for dealing with delinquency. Their main effort was to upgrade the neighborhoods that produced high levels of delinquency by involving the local population in self-improvement campaigns.

Chicago was divided into areas designated by concentric circles drawn from the core of the city (see Figure 6.1). Their approach was based on the belief that the most serious problem leading to delinquency was the failure of family life and social institutions to fill the needs of impoverished slum residents. As Ruth Kornhauser, summarizing Shaw and McKay's work, has written:

> Family, school, and community lack the money and skills with which to attract and hold the child to a conventional course of action. They cannot provide the channels that lead to successful achievement. Poor families cannot bind their children because they lack the means with which to help them realize valued goals. The slum family is also unable to communicate or enforce its special needs through organizations linked to conventional institutions. As a result, institutions outside the family are not pressured to serve the child more adequately.[2]

Figure 6.1
Concentric Zone Model

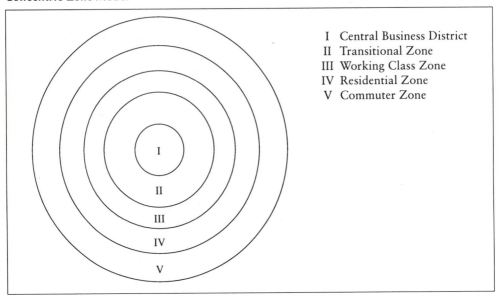

I   Central Business District
II   Transitional Zone
III   Working Class Zone
IV   Residential Zone
V   Commuter Zone

This view formed the basis for Shaw and McKay's Chicago Area Project (CAP), which was undertaken during the 1930s and 1940s. On the basis of a review of archival materials regarding Russell Square in South Chicago, a neighborhood in which the CAP operated, Steven Schlossman and Michael Sedlak concluded that the program likely was effective in reducing delinquency and that its ending represented a significant setback in delinquency prevention work.

Russell Square was primarily a Polish neighborhood, geographically separated by steel mills and railroad tracks from places surrounding it. Juvenile delinquency was rampant when the CAP moved in: 15 different youth gangs were active. Gang delinquency in Russell Square, however, was less violent than it is in today's impoverished areas. Petty theft was the most common delinquent act, involving things such as raiding fruit stands, stripping cars, and snatching purses. Typical of the area's gangs were the Aces, which were described by Schlossman and Sedlak in the following manner:

> The Aces always looked for and managed to discover excitement in anything that devilled someone else. They pulled trollies off the wires routinely [trolley cars, attached to overhead electrified wires, were a common form of urban transportation at the time]; snatched purses in broad daylight; were so adept at lifting fruit from peddlers' wagons that on one adventure they succeeded in running off with three bushels of apples, tossing fruit back at the storming peddler. The Aces shinnied up trees in the park, reached into the nests of sleeping spar-

rows, and popped them into paper bags. They took the spar-
rows into St. Michael's gym where a basketball game was in
progress and released the birds, one by one. They delighted in
burning homemade stink bombs at social gatherings.[3]

Shaw assigned several community workers to Russell Square. Their
task was to hang around with gang members and to develop informal,
trusting relationships. The workers were to be alert to boys with serious emotional problems; these youngsters would be referred to the project headquarters, where they would be given help. The workers were
expected to offer a model of conventional moral and social values to
Russell Square youths. The CAP also sponsored an athletic program
that was used as a vehicle to enlist adults in neighborhood improvement
projects. The CAP, Shaw often said, did not wish to impose itself on the
community; it sought to mobilize local residents to analyze their own
problems and to engage in appropriate remedial efforts.

Those running the program tried to explain to representatives of
governmental agencies (such as the police, the schools and the probation department) why troublesome children in Russell Square behaved
as they did. Emphasis also was placed on reducing school truancy in the
belief (later elaborated on by other theorists) that continuing attachment to traditional institutions and values is an especially important
inhibitor of delinquency. The CAP also established close relationships
with the Illinois Parole Board and exercised considerable control over
the conditions placed upon Russell Square residents when they were
released from prison.

Opposition to the CAP focused on a number of issues. Initially there
was a strong distrust of the outsiders, particularly academicians from
the University of Chicago. Some believed that the CAP was too accom-
modating to vested interests, while government officials thought that
the program was too tolerant of misbehavior and thereby encouraged
more of it. Professional social workers were not pleased with what they
regarded as the amateur efforts of local leadership.

At the end, Shaw and McKay remained uncertain as to whether
their attempt to translate some loose theoretical concepts into a practical action program had been successful. They were convinced, however, that residents in high-delinquency areas could organize themselves effectively to address common problems and that, because of
their intimate knowledge of local conditions, they could mobilize support in ways not available to outsiders.

Projects similar to Shaw and McKay's continue to operate today in
Chicago to reduce gang delinquency by hiring workers living in the
affected communities. "Modest" success was reported for the Crisis
Intervention Project (CRISP), which employed former gang leaders,
conventional citizens, police, and university graduate students to work
with gang members.

THE GANG THEORISTS

One of the most important discoveries of Shaw and McKay was that juvenile delinquency is something of a social event. Lone offenders were relatively rare; much more often it was a pair of youths or a group that became involved in lawbreaking. Unlike adult crime, in which associates are sometimes necessary to maximize the likelihood of success, delinquent groupings seem to be a reflection of the need for comradeship and a matter of more passive youngsters following the lead of aggressive peers.

Groups of delinquent youths—gangs—also have served as a means for protection and identification in American cities. Typically, gang members consort with those who share a similar heritage, usually of a racial or ethnic nature. There are white gangs, Asian gangs, Latino gangs, and black gangs. Their conflicts at times seem choreographed, much like the action in the well-known theatrical play and motion picture *West Side Story*. Quarreling erupts over "turf" (that is, which group has "rights" to which particular segment of a ghetto neighborhood). Conflict also is likely to arise over girls and women, with gang members manifesting a stereotypical possessive posture in regard to "their" women. The term "gang" is very infrequently used by teenagers to describe their group; rather, it is the "clique," the "club," the "team," or the "boys." The names employed seem to represent an attempt to differentiate their association from that of "gangsters."

A former gang member in Mesa, Arizona, is involved in an intervention program for gang members. The Mesa unit is considered to be so successful at steering young people away from gangs that the government has granted the city about $1.7 million for the program. *(AP Photo/Tribune Newspapers, Andy Sawyer)*

Frederic Thrasher: Chicago Gangs

All paths involving the sociological study of gang behavior fan out from the pioneering investigation in the 1920s by Frederic M. Thrasher, another of the scholars connected with the University of Chicago. Thrasher's *The Gang* (1927) was based on an investigation of 1,313 juvenile gangs in Chicago (an amount believed by Thrasher to be exhaustive). Skeptics wonder how Thrasher could have determined with such exactitude the number of juvenile gangs. Folklore has it that 1,313 was the address of a notorious house of prostitution in the Chicago slums and that Thrasher's whimsical research assistants chose it to represent the number of gangs that they thought existed in the area.

Thrasher's study emphasized that juvenile gangs were training groups for adult crime. He further noted that putting gang members into jails and prisons usually failed to reduce gang activity because it lent further prestige to the delinquent, who, after release, could claim a toughening experience that would be admired by others of the group. Like Shaw and McKay, Thrasher's primary aim was to portray a social phenomenon so that something could be done about it. He believed that because gangs were seen as a normal and reasonable response to prevailing slum conditions, they should not be eliminated. Rather, thought Thrasher, the push should be to change the underlying conditions in order to lead gang members into more law-abiding ways of behaving.

William Foote Whyte: Street-Corner Society

A second book, William Foote Whyte's *Street Corner Society* (1943), notably advanced the theoretical understanding of juvenile gangs. Whyte (1914-2000) had moved into a working-class North End Italian neighborhood in Boston, where he did field research under a four-year fellowship at Harvard University. Later, he would turn his study into a Ph.D. dissertation at the University of Chicago (despite the fact that it lacked the usual paraphernalia of footnotes and a literature review).

Whyte gained acceptance from gang members by obtaining the sponsorship of the group's leader, and he proceeded to take copious notes on the group's activities, much like an ethnographer in an alien tribe. Status in the gang was determined to be a key ingredient in a wide range of members' behavior. Good bowlers, for instance, would do poorly when they played against group leaders, but would improve considerably when matched against persons with standing in the gang lower than their own.

Whyte had asked his sponsor, Doc (later identified at Ernest Pecci), to let him know if he did anything wrong. What Doc tells him conveys one of the insights gained by Whyte about gangs—the ability of the leader to fashion the group's acceptance or rejection of an outsider: "You won't have any trouble," Doc said. "You can take a lot of liberties, and nobody will kick. There's just one thing to watch out for. Don't spring [treat] people. Don't be too free with your money."[4]

Whyte also noted how distinctive language styles and words used by the "in group" fostered a sense of separateness and pride among the members. He thereby pinpointed a particularly important theoretical issue regarding gangs: they offer to their members rewards that may not otherwise be available to them—acceptance, achievement, excitement, money, and a sense of belonging.

Albert Cohen: Strain Theory

Albert K. Cohen's *Delinquent Boys* (1955) stands as a monumental contribution to the theoretical understanding of gangs. The book provided the impetus for a parade of exciting work that continues to this day.

Cohen's study followed an earlier sociological tradition of research that sought to discover the values that determined how Americans live and the things for which they stand. Working in "Middletown, U.S.A." (which actually was Muncie, Indiana), Robert Lynd and Helen Lynd had noted an extraordinary emphasis on success and the way that those who had not achieved it were held in low esteem. W. Lloyd Warner and Paul Lunt, conducting their research at a site they called "Yankee City" (actually Newburyport, Massachusetts), demonstrated the importance of class structure in American life and showed how and for what reasons a person was regarded as belonging to one or another of the social classes in the community.

According to Cohen's *strain theory*, the nature of our culture leads to the formation of delinquent gangs. His theme is highlighted in the following sentence: "The same value system, impinging on children differently equipped to meet it, is instrumental in generating both delinquency and respectability."[5] Consider the matter of social class and automobiles. Middle-class youths yearn for their own car because the possession of an automobile is an important element of self-esteem in America. Plush upholstery and state-of-the-art stereo equipment are accorded respect almost everywhere, and ownership of such a vehicle indicates success and importance. Some youths are given brand new cars by affluent parents. Youths from the middle class who have to postpone ownership of a classy car have numerous compensating satisfactions, and those things that they have would be seriously jeopardized if they were to violate the law and steal a car. The risk for them is not worth the gain.

Lower-class youths, including gang members, also have been efficiently and almost mercilessly tutored by advertising and word of mouth regarding the importance of owning a car. They are less likely to have other sources of self-esteem and self-importance. Nor, particularly in the case of gang boys, are they as fearful as middle-class and upper-class youths of the consequences of illegal behavior or as hopeful about their future prospects. Stealing a car becomes a reasonable way to achieve what most everybody in the society believes is important.

Cohen maintains that for some youths, delinquency constitutes a solution to adjustment problems for which the established culture provides no satisfactory answer. Delinquency is a gang member's response to problems with status and self-respect. The gang provides "moral reassurance" against "gnawing doubts" and gives "repeated, emphatic and articulate support" to its members.[6] The gang also justifies the use of hostility and aggression against those in the outside society who are seen by the gang members as the sources of the status frustration.

Cohen asks: How can we change the norms of the middle-class world so that a youngster's working-class characteristics do not relegate him or her to an inferior status? Moreover, what price are we willing to pay for this or that change? Cohen compares this dilemma with that confronting schoolteachers: do they reward those who are doing particularly well and by doing so implicitly humiliate those who are doing poorly? Or do they abandon competition and the inevitable discrimination involved in it (someone must lose) and in doing so give up a very powerful spur to achievement? What Cohen's analysis indicates is that theoretical insight—correct or not—does not necessarily point the way to corrective actions.

Cohen's ideas found support in a study of juvenile delinquency in the Netherlands. The study concludes that the much higher rate of delinquency among boys compared to girls is a function of boys' emphasis on autonomy and independence compared to girls' stress on emotional ties with parents and family. The Dutch writers found that when boys fail in conventional efforts, they, more so than girls, will seek to compensate for their loss of status. One way is to turn away from society. They report that failure in school was a particularly powerful precursor of delinquency. It resulted in frequent truancy and the development of a "tough guy" attitude. The Dutch research team recommended that remedial efforts be concentrated on school reforms because education is "an open and accessible system" compared to the "private sphere of the family."

A study of delinquency in Argentina, however, did not support Cohen's thesis, presumably because the culture of the country does not emphasize success and status-seeking for all. Argentina, like most South American countries, is characterized by a social structure that encourages people to remain contentedly in the class into which they have been born.

Cloward and Ohlin: Anomie Theory

Albert Cohen's idea of a delinquent subculture—a distinctive way of life lived by certain boys (and fewer girls)—formed the basis for several succeeding theoretical statements. A major difference between

Cohen's position and the work of those who followed him lies in the later writers' focus upon different forms of delinquent adjustments and styles as well as their disagreement with Cohen that delinquency is primarily a reaction against middle-class values. It is argued, for instance, that the example of the prosperous drug merchant, with an elegant automobile, fine clothes, and what seems to be an exciting lifestyle, is reason enough to attract slum youths who have the skills to make them successful dope peddlers.

The second major postwar contribution to the theoretical understanding of gangs, *Delinquency and Opportunity* (1960), by Richard Cloward and Lloyd Ohlin, seeks explanations for the various patterns of delinquency—some involving theft, others marked by violent episodes, and some concerned with drug use. These behaviors are said to be the result of *anomie*, which is defined as the tension between specified social goals (particularly the acquisition of money) and the limited legitimate means available to achieve them. Once a slum youngster gets caught up in the quest for things, the "opportunity structure" determines the precise form the behavior will take. Most notable is the idea that delinquent and criminal roles are not universally available. As Francis Cullen has noted, "aspiring offenders are barred from professional thievery unless selected for tutelage in the technical expertise of the role and allowed to perform this role by existing thieves."[7]

For Cloward and Ohlin, it is the character of the delinquent neighborhoods and the abilities of the youths that lead youngsters to adopt particular lawbreaking lifestyles. In some neighborhoods, gangster activity is limited and only the most qualified youngsters are recruited into organized criminal groups; others may engage in petty theft or become drug users. For all, though, the impetus to delinquency and adult crime lies in the absence of adequate opportunities to succeed in a manner other than that offered by illegal behavior. To change this pattern, Cloward and Ohlin suggest the following:

> The major effort of those who wish to eliminate delinquency should be directed to the reorganization of slum communities. Slum neighborhoods appear to be undergoing progressive disintegration. The old structures, which provided social control and avenues of social ascent, are breaking down. Legitimate but functional substitutes for these traditional structures must be developed if we are to stem the trend toward violence and retreatism [i.e., drug use] among adolescents in urban areas.[8]

Cloward and Ohlin believed, as had Cohen, that working-class boys aspire to higher social levels and that their lawbreaking behavior is in large part a response to the frustration of such desires. Support for this view comes from a study by Ramon Rivera and James Short, who asked a group of delinquents and nondelinquents the question: "Thinking realistically, what sort of work do you actually think you'll be doing 10 years from now?" Responses fell into two major patterns. First, all youths expected to attain a position well above their present status. Second, racial differences were the reverse of what might be expected. Within both the gang and the nongang groups, blacks anticipated greater achievement than whites.

The conclusions of Cloward and Ohlin echo themes from the Chicago Area Project:

> What is necessary is to introduce a measure of variety into the occupational horizons of these youngsters. They must be taught that better worlds exist and that these worlds are populated with flesh and blood people with whom they may interact. The problem lies in the task of getting close enough to the boys to be taken seriously and in encouraging a sense of emulation and a willingness to make a final separation from the neighborhood milieu.[9]

Cloward and Ohlin see delinquency as a response to the actual opportunities available to lower-class youth and emphasize that delinquents behave in a perfectly sensible way by making choices in an environment in which such choices are limited. Lee Steiner has pinpointed this view:

> In studying the delinquent, we must face the reality that he is responding in the best way he knows how, with the only set of emotions he has, and to the only surroundings he knows. If we accept the truism that within the limits where we have a choice, each of us selects that behavior which is most pleasing and rejects that which is most distasteful, we must conclude that the delinquent's behavior seems logical to him.[10]

Looking at the same situation from a different angle, Malcolm X, a renowned black leader in the 1960s, came to essentially the same conclusion:

> Ghetto teenagers see the hell caught by their parents struggling to get somewhere. The ghetto teenagers make up their own minds that they would rather be like the hustlers whom they see dressed "sharp" and flashing money and displaying no respect for anybody or anything. So the ghetto youth becomes attracted to the hustler worlds of dope, thievery, prostitution, and general crime and immorality.[11]

The speculations of Cloward and Ohlin about delinquency and gangs was adopted as the guideline for intervention programs during the years when the national government poured funds into what it labeled the "War on Poverty." Nationally, Attorney General Robert Kennedy became convinced that delinquency was a cover word for poverty and that poverty, in turn, was a cover word for racial discrimination.

In a subsequent review of the use of the Cloward-Ohlin position as a guideline for federal efforts to combat delinquency, Daniel P. Moynihan, a Harvard sociologist and then United States Senator from New York, argued that the theory was inadequate as a basis for reforms. Moynihan acidly noted that "the government did not know what it was doing," and that it was "no more in possession of confident knowledge of how to prevent delinquency than it was in possession of a dependable formula to deal with the ill-fated Vietnamese war." Moynihan noted that, "an afternoon of library research would have established that the Cloward-Ohlin thesis of opportunity structure, though eminently respectable, was nonetheless rather a minority position, with the bulk of delinquency theory pointing in a quite different direction."[12]

Moynihan overstated the marginal position of the Cloward-Ohlin position. In truth, delinquency theory was pointing (and still points) in a considerable variety of different directions. Cloward and Ohlin's thesis was one of the more prominent of those thrusts. Indeed, the theories that we will be reviewing might well be compared to the horse rider portrayed by the Canadian mathematician-humorist Stephen Leacock: the rider got on his mount and rode off wildly in all different directions.

Moynihan faulted Cloward and Ohlin for neglecting the role of the family in the genesis of delinquent acts. He cited with approval the observations of David Bordua that although opportunity structures may be blocked for delinquent youths, "this seems, often, the end product of a long history of their progressively cutting off opportunity and destroying their own capacities which may begin in the lower-class family."[13]

Present-day researchers have added to Cloward and Ohlin's strain theory. Robert Agnew, in the best-known extension of the earlier work, sets out what he calls General Strain Theory (GST), which locates the roots of delinquency not only in a failure to achieve desired goals, but also in the taking away by others of something that the potential delinquent values and the loser's attempt to confront this disagreeable circumstance. Such "negative affect" stems from disappointments, anger, and frustration. The condition can be produced by events such as excessive demands, school changes, a father or mother moving in or out of the household, or a serious accident.

In a test of GST theory based on reports from 1,380 New Jersey adolescents, Agnew and Helene Raskin White found that strain was much more powerful in inducing delinquent acts and drug use among adolescents if they had delinquent friends. Lisa Brody and Agnew subsequently used GST to establish possible explanations for the lower rate of delinquency by young women compared to young men. They believe that females experience just as much strain as males, but that the stressors are of a different nature. Male strains are more conducive, they say, to serious violent and property crime; female stress produces escape attempts such as running away and more self-directed forms of deviance, such as drug use. Though both males and females react to stress with anger, females are more likely to become depressed because of their anger and to feel guilt, anxiety, and so on. Males are more likely to express their anger with aggressive acts.

Walter Miller: Subcultural Theory

The third of the major postwar contributors to delinquency theory was Walter Miller, a social anthropologist who worked with delinquent gangs, primarily in Roxbury, Massachusetts. For Miller, gang behavior represents a lower-class culture that prevails in the slums, a delinquent *subculture* that is oriented to the deliberate violation of middle-class norms.

Miller insists that delinquency is engaged in repeatedly, systematically, and regularly by rational, understandable people as a routine part of their ordinary lives. The lower-class culture that Miller describes is said to be marked by female-based households and a pattern of serial monogamy (that is, many marriages, one after the other). Lower-class boys expect to get into trouble; they assert their toughness, display "smartness," emphasize their ability to outwit or con others, and seek excitement. These are what Miller calls their "focal concerns." They also are accepting of the dictates of what they see as "fate" and are constantly concerned with the maintenance of their individual autonomy. According to Miller, gangs are built around individuals who belong to four social subcultures: they are males, adolescents, urban residents, and persons equipped for only low-skilled manual work.

Miller's ideas have been the most severely criticized of the early gang theorists. One commentator maintained that the subculture of the lower class, as portrayed by Miller, existed only in his imagination. Moreover, whatever their status in fact or fancy as components of a subculture, the traits described by Miller are not related to delinquency.

The strongest attack on Miller's position came from William Ryan, who blasted what he believes is the lamentable habit of "blaming the victim." Ryan said that we tend to regard social problems as if they were the fault of the person who suffers from them rather than the responsibility of those circumstances or individuals that cause the suffering. For instance, a rape victim is often blamed for hitchhiking or for wearing "provocative" clothing, but Ryan maintains that all the blame should be affixed onto the rapist, who flagrantly broke the law. Caricaturing victim-blaming tactics, Ryan tells of a United States Senator during an investigation of the beginning of World War II, who bellowed: "What was Pearl Harbor doing there?" when inquiring about the 1941 Japanese attack on that Pacific naval base.[14] Ryan argues that the "focal concerns" that Miller identifies with the lower class actually are values shared by all Americans. Who among us, he asks, prefers the opposite of such concerns—boredom, stupidity, subjugation, and weakness?

Gang Theories in General

The early "gang theories" were very important in rejuvenating and focusing attention on the explanation of processes that contribute to juvenile delinquency. Indeed, it is one of the ironies of scholarship that there is more sophisticated theory dealing with juvenile lawbreaking than there is with adult crime, though the latter by most reasonable standards is a larger problem. This situation may be attributable to the unusually great importance that Americans attach to youthfulness and to our deep concern with waywardness within that age group. Those outside the United States often comment on the intense identification of Americans with the young and on Americans' own interest in "staying young" as long as possible. There also exists a national spirit of optimism, a belief that youngsters gone astray can be "saved" and that, with help and a bit of luck, they too can realize the American dream of success.

LABELING THEORY

Essentially, *labeling theory* rests upon the supposition that human beings respond to the definitions placed upon their behavior by others (especially those who have power). If a child is called a "bad boy" and treated as such, he comes to accept that image of himself and behaves in the manner that others have maintained is his mode. This happens particularly when there are no other definitions available to him; that is, when nobody tells him that he is good, decent, and acceptable, or provides rewards for such behavior. Thus, the labeling process amplifies the phenomenon it is intended to suppress.

An illustration of the impact that labeling can have on a youth is provided by Jean Genet, who at 10 years of age was already an accomplished thief but who later became one of France's leading writers:

> At ten, I felt no remorse when I stole from people whom I
> loved and whom I knew to be poor. I was found out. I think
> the word "thief" wounded me deeply. Deeply, that is to say

enough to make me want, deliberately, to be what other people made me blush about being, to want to be it proudly, in spite of them.[15]

As an explanation of juvenile delinquency, labeling theory enjoyed a decade-long period of prominence before reservations began to undercut belief in its ability to capture effectively the essence of causal patterns for delinquent acts. Nonetheless, some research indicates that the pronounced demise of labeling theory may have been premature. Raymond Paternoster and Leeann Iovanni maintain that those who criticize labeling theory do not truly understand it and tend to caricature its ideas. They insist that labeling has its most devastating consequences on those, most notably African-Americans, who do not have other self-esteem resources to fall back upon.

Labeling theory is built upon early work by two prominent students of crime and delinquency, Frank Tannenbaum and Edwin Lemert. Tannenbaum had served time in prison as a conscientious objector during World War I. Partly because of this experience, he began his career at Columbia University specializing in criminology (later he would become a leading authority on South American history). Tannenbaum coined the phrase "dramatization of evil" to describe the tendency of authorities to paint deviants in a light that thrusts them outside the stream of conventional life. He said that we treat people in terms of the categories into which we place them rather than in terms of the fullness of their humanity. A boy may be a Catholic, a dog lover, an ardent baseball fan, someone who is kind to his sister, reflective, a nature lover, and a delinquent caught committing a burglary, but it is the last label that will suffocate the others, and the one in terms of which most people will regard him. The label may keep him from staying in school (teachers and other pupils are likely to shy away from him), from getting a good job, and from associating with conforming youngsters. The only route left open may be that into the world of delinquency.

Tannenbaum believed that the amount of crime in America is a response to the essential nature of the way we live. Delinquency, he maintained, "is just as much one aspect of America as is a baseball or divorce or antiunion industry or unemployment or Ford or movies." Tannenbaum pinpointed the element in our culture that often would be regarded by later theorists as particularly important:

> The individual has to succeed or be lost, forgotten, thrown upon the scrap heap. The individual who could not make a fortune or secure a niche for himself has to face poverty, isolation, neglect, unemployment, and possibly scorn and abuse. Therefore friction is the essence of life. Against such a background of experience law is a feeble instrument indeed, and custom has no roots.[16]

Lemert, the second of the major early labeling theorists, differentiated between "primary" and "secondary" labeling processes. He granted that there is little or no labeling of a youngster by the authorities until that youngster does something that gets him or her into difficulty. The secondary labeling process occurs after the initial encounter with law enforcers, and it is this phenomenon that is considered to have the potential for strengthening commitment to antisocial actions.

Labeling theory was employed to justify reducing the stigma placed on persons who have contact with law enforcement. It was argued that it would prove more useful in the long run to release youngsters or to ignore their behavior rather than to place the label "delinquent" on them—at least unless the harm was so severe that it could no longer be overlooked. Policies of benign neglect and "radical nonintervention" were advocated to deal with delinquency. The analogy was sometimes made to the temper tantrums of infants, about which the wisdom offered is that ignoring the behavior will prove the most effective way of eliminating it.

Criticisms of Labeling Theory

With delinquency, as opposed to temper tantrums, the situation is likely to prove a good deal more complicated. Delinquent behavior is undertaken to achieve a good many more things than the attention of one's parents (though sometimes that can be one of its goals). In addition, if delinquent acts result in the acquisition of some sort of fame and fortune, it hardly seems likely that they will be abandoned if the authorities overlook them. Moreover, at least some persons who are labeled do not passively accept the designation but rather set out to demonstrate its inaccuracy. For instance, if I am called cheap by my friends, there is some likelihood that I will become more generous in order to gain their approval.

Labeling, in such terms, can be seen to be considerably more complex than indicated by its advocates, who see all delinquents as fundamentally decent persons who have been thrust into nastiness by their oppressors. In this sense, the labeling theory (as do many theories) fits well with the tenor of the political period in which it came into strong favor—during the Vietnam War period, a time of especial hostility to authority. The roots of a theory and its political character, though, do not in any way speak to its accuracy. For labeling, decline of its acceptance seems to lie primarily in a growing belief that it greatly oversimplifies the process producing juvenile delinquency. Labeling is an unavoidable process; it occurs constantly through individual and group disapproval as well as through official mechanisms. Delinquents are usually aware of the definitions others make of their behavior. In many cases, in fact, they are their own severest critics.

A Swedish review of labeling theory noted that its ideas are particularly popular with college students. The author believes that this may be because the theory somewhat relieves persons of moral responsibility for their actions. "As viewed by labeling theory in its most popular form," the author writes, "the deviant starts by doing what everybody else does but has the bad luck to get caught and labeled." He finds the theory "unclear and dubious" but grants that it has provided "interesting insights into the deviant's behavior as seen from his own viewpoint."[17]

The fact that the label is not imposed until some wayward behavior occurs represents a notably weak link in the theory. One critic has noted that labeling theory conveys the idea that people go about their own business and then society suddenly comes along and slaps them with a stigmatized label. Labeling theorists respond by saying that all of us engage in acts that could be negatively labeled, but only a portion of us are selected out for such treatment—and those so selected are largely from the economically depressed segments of society.

A particularly sophisticated review of labeling theory was done by Nigel Walker, a British scholar, who distinguished seven forms of the process. These are:

(1) suspicion, whereby the offender may become more likely to be suspected of subsequent offenses, especially those resembling the original offense;

(2) employment disqualification;

(3) ostracism, whereby the offender may lose friends and family support;

(4) damaged self-image, in terms of which offenders might be inclined to regard illegal behavior as consistent with their "nature" or to believe that they have little to lose by further lawbreaking;

(5) antilabel reaction, whereby an offender may reject the label as unfair and become determined to prove that this is true;

(6) antilabeler reaction, in terms of which the labeled person might reject the values of society as unfair and seek to expose the shortcomings of the society;

(7) martyrdom, in which the labeling could be defined by others as a moral wrong and could enlist support for the person and the person's cause.[18]

Walker pointed out that the last three reactions tend to be ignored by labeling theorists and that the evidence for the first five effects is equivocal. He noted that studies demonstrating that prosecuted juvenile delinquents are more likely than unprosecuted delinquents to commit further delinquent acts could support Items 3 and 4 in the list, but they also could be explained by the idea that many of the prosecuted delinquents come to realize that the results of their being caught were mild.

SHAMING

Public Shaming

Social scientists have tried, without much success, to distinguish among embarrassment, humiliation, guilt, and shame. In the fields of criminology and juvenile delinquency, these various conditions generally are subsumed under the umbrella of *shame*. Shame is a standard element in the repertoire of parents, and it has a long history of use against those who violate the law. Perhaps the best known application is that depicted fictionally by Nathaniel Hawthorne in *The Scarlet Letter*, in which the main character, Hester Prynne (but not her male partner) is ordered to wear a large "A" on the outside of her garments as punishment for an act of adultery. Other early tactics included the pillory and stocks, where offenders were exposed to the public gaze and, depending on the nature of the people who gathered, were subjected to scorn or to raucous merriment.

Today, shame as punishment appears to be enjoying a revival. In Illinois, an offender placed on probation after an assault was made to post a sign at the entrance to his property that read: "Warning; A Violent Offender Lives Here, Travel at Your Own Risk." Drunken drivers sometimes must display special colored license plates that proclaim their violation, and some shoplifters have been sentenced to take out advertisements in local newspapers that include their picture and an account of what they did.

Advocates of public shaming believe that such penalties allow the community to become involved in the punishment process. Otherwise, offenders will resume their position in the social system without visible signs of loss or will disappear into a state facility. Fines, another possibility, are often regarded as merely buying one's way out of a law-breaking situation.

For John Whitman, a Yale law professor, shaming penalties are unacceptable. Whitman does not base his opposition on their ability to deter an offender—he says that there is no certain evidence one way or the other on this matter—nor does he rely on the consequences for the offender. He believes that the public should not become involved in things such as public shaming because it represents a kind of "lynch justice." "The chief evil in public humiliations sanctions," Whitman argues, "is that they involve an ugly and politically dangerous complicity between the state and the crowd."[19]

Reintegrative Shaming

A great deal of attention has been paid in recent years to the redemption of youngsters by use of what John Braithwaite, an Australian scholar, calls *reintegrative shaming*. Braithwaite's position reflects the wisdom that has guided parenting for many: parents may object to their child's behavior but at the same time convey that it is only the behavior and not the child that offends them. Braithwaite's is a more sophisticated version of labeling theory, arguing that the most effective response to undesired behavior is strong group disapproval of the act accompanied by sympathetic acceptance of the person.

The failure of a culture to shame satisfactorily those who violate its legal codes underlies for Braithwaite the failure to control such behavior. He sees crime as a symptom of underlying social ills and, most importantly, the absence of moral force among citizens about what is right and what is wrong.

Braithwaite notes that high moral expectations, publicly expressed, will deliver superior crime control compared to inflicting pain on wrongdoers. Disapproval by shaming can be conveyed in verbal and nonverbal ways. The aim is to make the offender feel remorseful by subjecting him or her to the distaste of those who are important: family, friends, workmates, and authorities. Braithwaite grants that shaming is a double-edged sword: it can also be used to encourage delinquent behavior among gang members by gang leaders. Therefore, he holds that the offender must be isolated from that kind of reinforcement.

The approach advocated by Braithwaite has been employed with reported success in New Zealand and among the Aborigines of Australia. It also is a tactic that works strikingly well in Japan and China. It is arguable whether a country such as the United States can muster enough moral force to carry out the delicate mission of forcefully condemning the wrongful behavior yet compassionately embracing its perpetrator.

The absence of a satisfactory process of shaming was pinpointed in a 1995 essay by James Q. Wilson as the fundamental flaw in delinquency control efforts in the United States. Wilson pointed to the spectacularly low delinquency and crime rate in Japan despite the fact that pornography is readily available, violence pervades the arts, and children are raised with extraordinary permissiveness. "The reason that

Japanese can behave so properly," Wilson insists, "is that they have a culture that powerfully induces a sense of shame in its members." Americans, on the contrary, "have become shameless." Wilson believes that people in the United States no longer are shocked or scandalized by the conduct of others; they have adopted individualism—not responsibility to the group—as their standard.[20]

Reintegrative shaming has been enacted into law in regard to Maori youth in New Zealand. The police are mandated to refer law-breaking Maori juveniles (the Maori being the indigenous tribal people) to a youth coordinator who arranges family conferences that seek to condemn the behavior yet embrace the offender as an essentially decent person who temporarily erred and now is forgiven. Reports indicate that the process has enjoyed some success, though victims are said to be less than thoroughly pleased with the abandonment of punitive responses.

In a critique of the technique, particularly as efforts have been made to use it with Aboriginal juveniles in Australia (the so-called Wagga model), one writer insists that the youth coordinators are but another authoritarian force whose interests are not necessarily those of the native peoples, and that the youth conferences seek to impose mainstream values upon people who would prefer to hold on to their own values and ways of life.

He also insists that reintegrative shaming often falters because of the Aboriginal lifestyle. Many of the offenders are migratory and are long gone from the place where the offense was committed before a family conference can be scheduled. He also believes that Aboriginal people will not be shamed by having Western values proclaimed to them as the most desirable way of life.

Braithwaite found this critique visionary and notes that the shortcomings alleged are remediable. "If we think it inevitable," Braithwaite writes, "that we have police, and inevitable that their power is temptation to domination of the oppressed, then we might be better served with something more than simply circumventing their gatekeeping when we can." Braithwaite indicates that the early results from the first 548 family conference cases in Canberra (Australia's capital city) showed that, compared to a randomly selected control group, both victims and offenders believed that the police respected their rights better during the conference process than in court proceedings. Braithwaite adds an anecdotal report to support the value of conferencing resolutions:

> I have seen conferences where mothers criticize the police for excessive force or victimization of the child in a way that they would never be allowed to do in court. This makes the police more accountable, especially in a system where the offender is advised of the right to walk out of the conference at any time and take their chances in court.[21]

The most strident attack on Braithwaite's position is noted more as an illustration of the tactics sometimes employed to attempt to bring down a theory of crime and delinquency than for its intellectual strength. It has been argued that Braithwaite adopted an unacceptable definition of crime, seeing it only as acts that have been condemned by the law. Within that definition, the writer says, there are many noble behaviors, such as those by freedom fighters in a fascist country. He also notes that numerous ignoble acts, such as those by the Ku Klux Klan in the United States in the early 1900s, are not officially defined as crimes. Braithwaite also is accused of equating consensus (that is, general agreement on what is illegal) with morality (that is, a reasoned determination of what should be illegal). He also is charged with failing to tap into the offenders' self-expressed motivations for their delinquency: if he were to do so, it is suggested, he would look at their behavior with more accepting eyes.

These points nonetheless fail to grant that at least for certain crimes—murder, rape, robbery, and burglary, for instance—there is widespread agreement among people that, if possible, reasonable measures ought to be taken to reduce their numbers. There undoubtedly is an adequate moral underpinning to regard such acts as deserving of a social response.

The intensity of his criticism might be read from the observation that Braithwaite's book on reintegrative shaming "is a text of uncommon complexity—and marred by uncertain editing." But how does this comment square with sentences in the critical article, such as the one that begins: "We need to take seriously the deconstruction of epistemological meta-theory. . . ."[22] Perhaps it all adds up to the lesson that the formulation of theories of delinquent behavior can be a hazardous enterprise.

NEUTRALIZATION AND DRIFT

Neutralization

What tactics do juvenile delinquents employ to maintain their self-esteem and counteract negative labels? This question was addressed by Gresham Sykes and David Matza in a classic inventory of the *neutralization* techniques delinquents use to blunt judgments that will be made about the lack of compassion shown in acts of violence and property crimes. Sykes and Matza suggest five major self-justifications: (1) Delinquents condemn the condemners, that is, they insist that those who denounce their behavior are themselves no better than they are (consider white-collar criminals, such as tax evaders or judges who take bribes); (2) they deny responsibility, claiming that their act was due to forces beyond their control, such as drug use or unloving parents; (3) they deny injury, maintaining that what they have done harmed no one (e.g., after all, the store they stole from has insurance and, besides, it will pass the loss on to customers); (4) they deny the victim, claiming that the person robbed or hurt got only what he or she deserved; and (5) they appeal to higher loyalties, stating that the views of friends and the gang are more important than anything else. The theory indicates that these explanations are in place before the delinquent act takes place. However, it may be more plausible to presume that they usually are brought forth following the law-breaking behavior—in order to seek to justify it.

That delinquents employ such techniques of neutralization indicates that they have incorporated into their thinking the usual definitions of acceptable behavior and feel the need to ease their consciences for what they have done. Of course, virtually none of us—delinquent or otherwise—is likely to put the worst face on what we do, however reprehensible. It is unlikely that someone would say forthrightly: "I robbed that crippled old woman because I'm a no-good kid and I wanted to have some fun at the arcade and she was an easy target, so I stole her money. I enjoy robbing old women almost as much as beating blind old men and young, helpless kids."

In studies of neutralization, a question such as the following typically is asked: "Would you feel guilty cheating on a test if the instructor deliberately gave an overly difficult or tricky test?" Those willing to cheat are being supplied with neutralizing excuses (that is, an "unfair" instructor and a "tricky" test).

In an interesting study of the Sykes-Matza propositions, Herman Schwendinger and Julia Schwendinger asked delinquents and nondelinquents to respond to a vignette, which read as follows:

> I want you to act out this story: some teenagers are arguing over whether they should beat up an Outsider who insulted their club. An Outsider is someone outside their circle of friends. Those who are in favor of beating him up argue with the others about it. The others are convinced that the Outsider should be beaten up by the entire group.[23]

Schwendinger and Schwendinger suggest that if Sykes and Matza are correct, the delinquents should voice neutralizations to justify the beating of the Outsider. The delinquents, however, were almost entirely concerned with tactical rather than moral issues. They worried about the intrusion of the Outsider's friends or police apprehension, or maintained that the gain was too small for the risk. Nondelinquents were the ones who raised moral issues. Schwendinger and Schwendinger grant that the delinquents may have been expressing views that would carry weight with their fellow gang members and that group decision processes can differ significantly from individual explanations of behavior.

Delinquency and Drift

David Matza has put forward the view that delinquents *drift* into their waywardness, that they usually behave in a satisfactory manner but on some occasions will release themselves from social constraints and break the law. To test his view, Matza asked 100 institutionalized delinquents to respond to vignettes showing situations such as a mugging, fighting with a weapon, armed robbery, auto theft, stealing from a warehouse, vandalism, and stealing a bike. On the average, 2 percent of the respondents approved of the acts, 40 percent were indifferent, 30 percent were mildly disapproving, and 28 percent were indignant. Matza finds in these responses evidence that adherents of the subculture of delinquency seem little committed to the misdeeds prominent in it.

Attacks on this conclusion raise a point that we have encountered before: Matza failed to employ a control group. It also has been said that delinquents confined in institutions will be wary about expressing anything but conventional views because their opportunity for release might be affected. Contrary to Matza's findings, Michael Hindelang, using a population in Oakland, California, found that delinquents approved of what they had done much more so than persons who had not committed such acts. Hindelang claimed that his result supports the positions of Cloward and Ohlin and of Cohen, which hold that delinquents have distinctively different attitudes from nondelinquents. "It is not necessary to postulate the mechanism of 'drift' or of 'techniques of neutralization,'" Hindelang maintains, "if in fact delinquents do not have moral inhibitions which normally restrain them from delinquent activity."[24] There are a number of questions that can be raised about Hindelang's results as well. When research combines two pencil-and-paper measures, the first of delinquent activity and the second of attitudes, we have at best only secondhand measures of those matters. A natural experiment would provide more believable evidence on the issue; even better, observations on how delinquents actually use or do not use neutralization tactics would advance the debate on this aspect of delinquency theory.

SUMMARY

The dominance of the study of juvenile delinquency by sociologically trained scholars has led to a wide range of theoretical statements that focus on group processes and social values as the key elements that produce wayward behavior by young persons. The work began at the University of Chicago as part of an effort by its sociology faculty to determine the ecological patterns of the city in which the university was located. Ecology, a biological term, refers to the relationship between an organism and its environment. Chicago sociologists assumed that different parts of a city create and support special kinds of lifestyles, just as a rain forest nurtures special kinds of animal and plant life.

Shaw and McKay stressed that so long as such neighborhoods remain slums they will produce large numbers of lawbreakers regardless of which ethnic group resides there, be it Scandinavians, Germans, African-Americans, Hispanics, or other newcomers. The exception has been Asian-Americans, whose especially close-knit family patterns and high achievement motivation may save youngsters from involvement in delinquency.

Work with inner-city dwellers by Chicago sociologists was largely based on efforts to improve conditions rather than on explicit theoretical grounds. Shaw and McKay placed particular reliance on law-abiding adults living in the area to establish programs that would keep youths out of trouble. This reliance conflicted with the convictions of trained social workers and other professionals who believed that special kinds of skills were essential to redirect the behavior of youth.

Chicago sociologists, led by Frederic Thrasher, began to study juvenile gangs, a line of research that has produced particularly sophisticated and provocative theoretical reasoning. Thrasher saw gangs forming as adolescent play groups and then, in certain settings, becoming more troublesome and isolated from mainstream life as the members threatened the well-being of law-abiding citizens and fought with members of other gangs. Albert Cohen, a pioneer in the contemporary study of gangs, declared that gang members find solace in such groups because they are severely handicapped in efforts to achieve the kind of things valued by middle-class society. If you cannot obtain recognition by having a good car, a nice home, expensive clothes, good grades, or a star position on an athletic team, you can spurn these things and set up your own rules. The most lucrative shoplifting heist, the greatest display of courage in gang warfare, the snazziest gang costume and hairstyle, and similar badges of achievement make gang life important for those who cannot succeed in more conventional life.

Cohen's theory, involving what psychologists call reaction formation, was challenged at some points and refined by Cloward and Ohlin, who held that entrance into delinquency is not merely a passive surrender to an inability to achieve middle-class values but is dependent upon a young person's own traits and the opportunities offered in the neighborhood. Some youths lack the qualities to achieve either middle-class or gang status; they might fall into what Cloward and Ohlin call a retreatist pattern, marked by withdrawal from social striving and typified by drug usage. Opening up avenues to middle-class achievement, particularly through educational and job opportunities, represented for Cloward and Ohlin the most promising method to control delinquency.

A different theoretical pronouncement emerged from Walter Miller's study of gangs in the Boston area. Miller did not believe that middle-class values dictated gang activity but rather that such behavior represented the product of a set of values found only in lower-income areas. Miller listed a core of "focal concerns" (including matters such as toughness and a desire for excitement) that he believed underlay juvenile gang activity. According to his critics, however, Miller's ideas do not accurately depict exclusively lower-class values.

Labeling theory came into prominence at a time when American society was in a particularly critical mood about the trustworthiness of persons exercising authority. The theory maintains that youths who are officially declared to be delinquent will be pushed even more deeply into such behavior because they will come to define themselves in terms of what they are said to be, and because other channels of behavior will be closed to them. Labeling theorists argue that teachers who insist that certain pupils are "bad" reinforce the very badness they supposedly want to suppress. However, labeling theory has not fared well in research efforts to test it. Its most prominent shortcoming lies in its inability to explain the first delinquency—the act that elicited the label. It may well be that it is not the labeling but rather the causes of the original delinquency that push the youth toward later delinquency. Furthermore, persons can adapt to being labeled in a variety of ways, one of which is to change their behaviors so that the label is refuted.

Other work has focused on the neutralization techniques employed by delinquents to avoid having to deal with negative feelings and blame for their behavior. Gresham Sykes and David Matza identified a number of such responses (e.g., condemning the condemners) that they claim are used by delinquents. Research, however, has failed to provide much support for the idea that delinquents feel any special need to redefine their acts in more "acceptable" ways before they engage in it.

That delinquents "drift" into their lawbreaking, a view advanced by Matza, is another theoretical notion reviewed in this chapter. Matza maintains that delinquency is not caused by any particular constellation of circumstances but that most youngsters commit a large number of different acts, a few of which are against the law. Many of the illegal acts essentially are chance occurrences—a response to an opportunity or a routine involvement that is common to all persons of a particular age. Sometimes these acts will be repeated, perhaps because the experience was enjoyable or perhaps because the opportunity is readily at hand. In time, some persons "drift" deeper and deeper into patterns of delinquency, although throughout their lives most of the things they do are perfectly lawful.

Finally, John Braithwaite's theory of reintegrative shaming suggests that the failure of society to embarrass the juvenile offender satisfactorily for the delinquent act is what allows wrongdoing to continue. Shaming, in Braithwaite's view, should focus on condemning the wrongful act but encouraging the actor to take a proper place in the life of the society.

REFERENCES

Agnew, Robert (1992). "Foundations for a General Theory of Crime and Delinquency." *Criminology* 30:47-87.

Agnew, Robert, and Helene Raskin White (1992). "An Empirical Test of General Strain Theory." *Criminology* 30:475-499.

Blagg, Harry (1997). "A Just Measure of Shame: Aboriginal Youth and Conferencing in Australia." *British Journal of Criminology* 37:481-503.

Bordua, David J. (1961). "Delinquent Subcultures: Sociological Interpretation of Gang Delinquency." *Annals of the American Academy of Political and Social Science* 338:119-136.

Braithwaite, John (1989). *Crime, Shame and Reintegration*. Cambridge, England: Cambridge University Press.

Braithwaite, John (1997). "Conferencing and Plurality: Reply to Blagg." *British Journal of Criminology* 37:502-506

Brody, Lisa, and Robert Agnew (1997). "Gender and Crime: A General Strain Theory Perspective." *Crime & Delinquency* 34:275-306.

Bursik, Robert J., Jr. (1984). "Urban Dynamics and Ecological Studies of Delinquency." *Social Forces* 63:393-413.

Cloward, Richard A., and Lloyd E. Ohlin (1960). *Delinquency and Opportunity*. New York: Free Press.

Cohen, Albert K. (1955). *Delinquent Boys*. New York: Free Press.

Cullen, Francis T. (1988). "Were Cloward and Ohlin Strain Theorists? Delinquency and Opportunity Revisited." *Journal of Research in Crime and Delinquency* 30:245-256.

DeFleur, Lois B. (1970). *Delinquency in Argentina: A Study of Cordoba's Youth*. Pullman: Washington State University Press.

Hindelang, Michael J. (1970). "The Commitment of Delinquents to Their Misdeeds: Do Delinquents Drift?" *Social Problems* 17:502-509.

Junger-Tas, Josine, and Marianne Junger (1984). *Juvenile Delinquency: Backgrounds of Delinquent Behavior*. The Hague: Ministry of Justice.

Knutsson, Johannes (1977). *Labeling Theory: A Critical Examination*. Stockholm: National Swedish Council for Crime Prevention.

Kornhauser, Ruth R. (1978). *Social Sources of Delinquency: An Appraisal of Analytic Models*. Chicago: University of Chicago Press.

Lemert, Edwin M. (1951). *Social Pathology*. New York: McGraw-Hill.

Lynd, Robert S., and Helen Lynd (1929). *Middletown: A Study in Contemporary American Culture*. New York: Harcourt, Brace.

Malcolm X. (1965). *The Autobiography of Malcolm X*. New York: Grove Press.

Matza, David (1964). *Delinquency and Drift: Do Delinquents Drift?* New York: Wiley.

Miller, Walter B. (1958). "Lower-Class Culture as a Generating Milieu of Gang Delinquency." *Journal of Social Issues* 14:5-19.

Moynihan, Daniel P. (1969). *Maximum Feasible Misunderstanding: Community Action in the War on Poverty*. New York: Free Press.

Paternoster, Raymond, and Leeann Iovanni (1989). "The Labeling Perspective and Delinquency: An Elaboration of the Theory and an Assessment of the Evidence." *Justice Quarterly* 6:359-394.

Rivera, Ramon J., and James F. Short, Jr. (1967). "Occupational Goals: A Comparative Analysis." In *Juvenile Gangs in Context*, edited by Malcolm W. Klein and Barbara Meyerhoff, 70-90. Englewood Cliffs, NJ: Prentice Hall.

Ryan, William (1976). *Blaming the Victim*, Rev. ed. New York: Vintage Books.

Schlossman, Steven, and Michael Sedlak (1983). "The Chicago Area Project Revisited." *Crime & Delinquency* 29:398-462.

Schwendinger, Herman, and Julia Schwendinger (1967). "Delinquent Stereotypes of Probable Victims." In *Juvenile Gangs in Context*, edited by Malcolm W. Klein and Barbara Meyerhoff, 91-105. Englewood Cliffs, NJ: Prentice Hall.

Shaw, Clifford R., and Henry D. McKay (1942). *Juvenile Delinquency and Urban Areas: A Study of the Rates of Delinquency in Relation to Differential Characteristics of Local Communities in American Cities*. Chicago: University of Chicago Press.

Steiner, Lee (1960). *Understanding Juvenile Delinquency*. Philadelphia: Chilton.

Sykes, Gresham M., and David Matza (1957). "Techniques of Neutralization: A Theory of Delinquency." *American Sociological Review* 22:664-670.

Tannenbaum, Frank (1938). *Crime and the Community*. Boston: Ginn.

Walker, Nigel (1980). *Punishment, Danger, and Stigma: The Morality of Criminal Justice*. Totowa, NJ: Barnes & Noble.

Warner, W. Lloyd, and Paul S. Lunt (1941). *The Social Life of a Modern Community*. New Haven: Yale University Press.

Watts, Rob (1996). "John Braithwaite and *Crime, Shame, and Reintegration*: Some Reflections on Theory and Criminology." *Australian and New Zealand Journal of Criminology* 29:121-141.

White, Edmund (1993). *Genet: A Biography*. New York: Knopf.

Whitman, James Q. (1998) "What is Wrong with Inflicting Shame Sanctions?" *Yale Law Journal* 107:1055-1092.

Whyte, William F. (1943). *Street-Corner Society: The Social Structure of an Italian Slum*, 4th ed. Reprint. Chicago: University of Chicago Press, 1993.

Wilson, James Q. (1995). "Capitalism and Morality." *The Public Interest* 121(Fall):42-60.

Young, Pauline V. (1932). *Pilgrims of Russian-Town*. Chicago: University of Chicago Press.

NOTES

[1]   Shaw & McKay (1942),440.

[2]   Kornhauser (1978), 80.

[3]   Schlossman & Sedlak (1983), 424.

[4]   Whyte (1943), 276.

[5]   Cohen (1955), 137.

[6]   Ibid., 133.

[7]   Cullen (1988), 253.

[8]   Cloward & Ohlin (1960), 211.

[9]   Ibid., 193.

[10]   Steiner (1960), 181.

[11]   Malcolm X (1965), 315.

[12]   Moynihan (1969), 170.

[13]   Bordua (1961), 134.

[14]   Ryan (1976), 153-154.

[15]   White (1993), 114.

[16]   Tannenbaum (1938), 54.

[17]   Knutsson (1977), 53.

[18]   Walker (1980), 143.

[19]   Whitman (1998), 1088.

[20]   Wilson (1995), 53.

[21]   Braithwaite (1997), 504.

[22]   Watts (1996), 123, 134.

[23]   Schwendinger & Schwendinger (1967), 96.

[24]   Hindelang (1970), 508.

7

Further Interpretations of Delinquency:
Conflict, Learning, Control, and Integrated Theories

The first theory examined in this chapter—conflict or Marxist theory—finds its vitality in economic and political factors (particularly modes of production) and it argues that such factors lie at the root of juvenile misbehavior. The second schema discussed, the differential association theory, is based on learning principles. Differential association theory maintains that persons learn delinquent behavior from others who are important to them. In the third approach, control theory, delinquency is seen as a falling away from the grip of forces that produce conformity, in particular the loosening of the hold of the family's values on the pre-delinquent. In its most recent statement, control theory has been construed to involve a single factor—self-control—the absence of which is said to be the cause not only of delinquency and crime but also a variety of other acts considered aberrant.

Integrated theories attempt to select the best predictive items from the other theories of delinquency and to construct an interpretative approach embracing them. The use of concepts from diverse theories at times offers deeper understanding of delinquency than that provided by an individual theory. Nonetheless, when researchers adapt different portions of different theories, it becomes exceedingly difficult to build cumulative knowledge rather than a hodge-podge of conclusions.

MARX: CONFLICT THEORY

Much of the contemporary world was ruled by the ideology of Marxism from the end of World War II in 1946 until the last decade; indeed, during the 1950s, for the first time in centuries the Bible was replaced by Karl Marx's *Das Kapital* as the best-selling book in the world. A German-born political economist, Marx (1818-1883) lived most of his adult life in London in genteel poverty. He eked out a livelihood for his family writing pieces for the *Tribune* in New York and was subsidized at times by his collaborator, Friedrich Engels (1820-1895), whose father owned a mill in Manchester, England.

Marxist or *conflict theory* maintains that delinquency is rooted in inequalities in the distribution of wealth in capitalist countries. Such inequities are said to lead to a struggle among members of different economic and social classes. The leaders under capitalism (members of the grand bourgeoisie class) are said to exploit the working masses (the proletariat). The essence of the Marxist position lies in the idea of surplus value. Workers produce wealth. Under a fair system, Marx maintained, they ought to share fully in the wealth they produce. In capitalistic societies, however, much of what they produce goes to those who control the resources and who thereby exert power over the government and the way it does things. If, for instance, I own 1,000 shares of stock in General Motors, I will receive cash dividends on a regular basis, although I may have inherited the stock and done nothing to earn this money. If I own enough stock, I can endlessly cruise the seas in my yacht as I receive funds made available through the labor of others. Conflict theorists insist that those others, the workers, receive less than they deserve, while I am getting more than I deserve. This situation puts me and them into conflict, because I would prefer to get even higher dividends—by reducing salaries, for instance, or by making workers labor as hard as possible to increase their productivity. They, on the other hand, have an interest in securing

Members of the leftist People's Liberation Front carry placards of communist icons Karl Marx, left, Friedrich Engels, center, and Vladimir Lenin, in a procession to commemorate international workers on May Day in Sri Lanka in 1998. Since the end of World War II until recently, much of the contemporary world has been ruled by Marxist ideology. (AP Photo/Gemunu Amarasinghe)

more of the wealth they have produced and reducing my share. The dramatic shift in wealth distribution in the United States during the past decade illustrates that these processes are currently at work. Between 1980 and 1996, the share of household income going to the richest 5 percent of the families in the country increased from 15.3 percent to 20.3 percent, while the share of the income going to the poorest 60 percent of families fell from 34.2 percent to 30 percent. Each shift of one percent, it should be noted, represents about 38 billion dollars.

Marx is now in disrepute, largely because of the dismal failure of Soviet-style communism, but his major interest was not in establishing a communist state. He wrote little about this and what he did write was notably vague. His concern was to highlight flaws of capitalism. Marx believed that capitalism made human beings greedy. Money formed the essence of a people's work and being, dominating them until they came to revel in fiscal success. Marx believed that capitalist values debilitated a society, and he predicted (quite incorrectly, at least so far) that in the end, this misguided perspective was doomed—destined to disappear as the proletariat came to appreciate the inherent injustice of their position.

Conflict Theory and Delinquency

Delinquency is said by some to be generated by this built-in conflict between capitalists and workers. In earlier days, manufacturing companies preferred to hire women for menial jobs, because before affirmative action and comparable worth campaigns, women would accept lower wages than men would demand. Conflict theorists contend that moving women out of their homes and into factories contributed to the number of delinquent acts committed by their unsupervised children. At that time, some young persons who might have engaged in delinquent acts were kept from doing so by being employed six days a week, 10 or more hours a day in agriculture, manufacturing, and mining. A journalist visiting a cotton mill early in the nineteenth century noted that all the machinery was operated by waterwheels that were kept moving by children ranging from four to 10 years old. In 1820, 43 percent of all textile workers in Massachusetts were children.

Catherine Sinclair suggests that the juvenile justice system originated in the wake of the decline in child labor because of a fear among persons in the upper classes of youngsters who were neither in school nor employed. Juvenile delinquency, she maintains, was "invented" in order "to ensure the perpetuation of the rule of the bourgeoisie and its concept of childhood." The following represents part of her reform agenda:

> There can be but one real solution to our juvenile justice
> problem, the radical/Marxist theorists agree—a humane
> socialist society which would eliminate the feeling of power-
> lessness and inadequacy of the young. No one group would be
> predestined to occupy the lowest paying, most menial jobs.
> Every job in society would be given dignity and all members
> of society would share in those jobs which must be performed.
> The elimination of competition, the guarantee of a decent
> living, the elimination of excessive accumulations of private
> property and wealth would create a true democracy.[1]

Mark Colvin and John Pauly offer what they label a "structural-
Marxist" theory of "serious patterned delinquency"—delinquency that
is repetitive and involves more than petty offenses. They suggest that
under capitalism the lives of lower-class youths are marked by oppres-
sion in the home and in the workplace, which produces feelings of alienation (that is, feelings that they do not belong and do not count for anything). Colvin and Pauly believe that this alienation is produced
deliberately and subtly. In school, intelligence tests for tracking are said
to be ruling-class methods of keeping working-class youths down. The
tests, Colvin and Pauly argue, measure not innate ability but "initial
bonds," which are weaker in lower-class families. Youths in this situation are programmed to fail and they come together with others who
are in the same position, and almost inevitably come into conflict with
the law. Under a true Marxist regime, conflict theorists insist, delinquency would disappear because there would be no reason for persons
to commit acts against others or against the state, because they would
not themselves be victimized and the state would essentially be themselves.

In a test of the Colvin-Pauly postulates using a national youth
sample, Sally S. Simpson and Lori Ellis found that the effects noted by
Colvin and Pauly did not hit hardest at the most alienated groups in the
society but instead at those somewhat above them on the social ladder.
They also found that the theory did a better job of predicting violent
crime than property crime. The authors concluded that it is not unlikely that the variables considered in Colvin and Pauly's theory fail to tell
the whole story of delinquency production.

Conflict Theory in Practice

Difficulties abound in seeking to prove or disprove the claims of conflict theorists. Some attempts have focused on depicting what took
place in nations that maintained that they operated under Marxist principles. If such efforts show that delinquency was far from absent in these
places, the rebuttal argument has been that the regimens did not adhere

to fully realized Marxist ideas. Nonetheless, the delinquency levels in communist countries, though far from nonexistent, were indeed lower than those in the United States—though probably not as low as in Japan (whic is also a capitalist nation). The breakup of the Soviet regime and the independence of countries such as Poland, Lithuania, and Latvia (among many others) were accompanied by what appears to be an ever-increasing rate of criminal activity. Juvenile theft is now rampant in Moscow, for instance. Can this be said to be one of the prices to be paid for democracy? Was it the strong fear of the brutality of the communist regime or was it the benefits and social arrangements of communism (which have been rejected by the people on other grounds) that kept the delinquency rate relatively low? It may be that a high level of delinquency is an inevitable outcome of a free society. If so though, how do we explain the extraordinarily low level of such behavior in Japan?

Cuba: An Illustration

The situation in Cuba illustrates the difficulties communist authorities and scholars face when seeking to explain why delinquent behavior persists. Typically, Cuban authorities insist that those who break the law fail to appreciate that there is no reason for them to do so. The fact that remnants of capitalist thought have not yet been satisfactorily overcome is often blamed for delinquency. It also is maintained that Cuban youths are the target of efforts by the United States to corrupt them. This is said to take place via rock music and similar "bourgeois trash" on Miami radio and television that is available in Cuba. Fidel Castro, long-time leader of the Cuban government, addressed what he regarded as the moral laxness in Cuban families, which he believed to undermine state attempts to eliminate social distinctions and to fuel delinquency:

> Sometimes too much is allowed and faults are tolerated. There are some parents who, if their child comes home with a towel or some other object which is not theirs, force him to return it, make him apologize and criticize his actions. There are other parents who do not yet have this consciousness, so that we sometimes have cases of theft in schools.
>
> Another way that families influence their children negatively is that because they made a foreign trip, or because a friend brought them some gift, immediately adorn the child with the foreign gift. Leave it home and don't allow the child to come to school with this super special gift which the others do not have and cannot have.[2]

The data available from Cuba on juvenile delinquency are far from complete but it seems that delinquency differs very little in kind (though not necessarily in degree) from what is found in capitalist societies. Delinquency is reported to be concentrated among lower-class, urban, male youths with low educational achievement. Property offenses constitute the largest category of juvenile crime, with consumer goods such as clothes, radios, and tape recorders the most sought after by offenders. The overrepresentation among lawbreakers of adherents of African-Cuban religions seems to indicate that race and prejudice probably play important roles in Cuban delinquency, just as they do in the United States. Cuba also is reported to have juvenile gangs that are apparently similar to those found in capitalist societies.

Evaluating Conflict Theory

Some conflict theorists believe that all delinquents and criminals should be regarded as victims of the mean-spirited and exploitative political and economic systems that are said to characterize most Western societies. This view, which called lawbreakers "political criminals," was evident when the feminist movement turned its wrath against sex offenders who prey upon women and children. Most writers of the conflict school brought their views into line with the feminists by no longer regarding offenders as martyrs, but as "lumpenproletariat," the German term used by Marx to describe most criminals as thugs who prey upon members of the working class. Paul Hirst notes that, for Marx, criminals form a "parasitic class" that lives off productive labor "by theft, extortion and beggary, or by providing 'services' such as prostitution and gambling." Under communism, said Marx, such people would be forced to work.[3] Because of issues of deep importance to the feminist movement, this change in conflict theory included a repudiation of the romanticized "Robin Hood" image of juvenile delinquents and a recognition that decent people in working-class communities were overwhelmingly the most common victims of the offenses of such delinquents.

Growing support has being given to the "left realist" approach to interpreting crime, a movement originating in the United Kingdom. Left realists formed a sympathetic alliance with the victim movement. They dropped their original interest in focusing on delinquents' perspectives in regard to why they behaved as they had, and instead coined the slogan "taking crime seriously" to reflect their new emphasis. Policy proposals call for greater democratic control of the police and deeper community participation in the formulation of programs to prevent crime.

The postulates of conflict theory, like those of psychiatry, have not been readily adaptable to the demands of science. Some rather crude empirical tests challenge the theory. One British scholar discovered that the Marxist insistence that capitalism and crime go hand-in-hand does not hold up when the level of lawbreaking in precapitalist and capitalist England are compared. The rates do not seem to have changed much between the fourteenth century and 1860.

The final verdict on the relationship between economic and political systems and their effect on the type and level of juvenile delinquency has not yet been rendered. Delinquency may in part be a consequence of more glaring discrepancies between the "haves" and the "have-nots." The observation of Norval Morris and Gordon Hawkins, two distinguished criminologists, is worth bearing in mind:

> The evidence is substantial that social, industrial, and commercial progress is accompanied by an increase in criminal activity. For as you expand the bounds of human freedom and economic and social potential, you equally expand the bounds of potentiality for nonconformity and delinquency and crime. As legitimate opportunities increase so do illegitimate opportunities.[4]

LEARNING THEORY

Edwin Sutherland: Differential Association

The theory of *differential association* is the hardiest survivor among the explanations offered in the United States for criminal behavior and delinquency. It first appeared as a systematic formulation in the third edition of *Principles of Criminology*, by Edwin H. Sutherland. Sutherland regarded differential association as a comprehensive scheme that could account for virtually all lawbreaking. The problem with such an aim, as we have seen, is that it requires extraordinarily general ideas if you try to "explain" such varied phenomena as arson, murder, and riding a motorcycle without a helmet.

Differential association theory contains nine points. It begins by asserting that *criminal behavior is learned*. The chief objection to this first point is use of learning to account for a variety of casual, occasional, or episodic delinquent behaviors. Does a youthful arsonist need to "learn" how to set fires? Or is it more reasonable to presume that he knows how to light a match and on his own makes the connection between a legal lighting of a candle and the illegal torching of a dwelling?

Sutherland's second point is that *criminal behavior is learned in interaction with other persons in a process of communication*. The proposition is totally dismissive of biological or genetic approaches to the explanation of crime. When confronted with the example of a youth whose behavior was exemplary, but who turned mean after contacting a brain disease, Sutherland's answer was that it was not the disease, but rather the way people responded to the person manifesting it that pushed that person into episodes of violence. The theoretical statement may be reasonably accurate, but only in the most general sense. Delinquent acts can be learned from the mass media or from other stimuli. There is a considerable body of thought that maintains that television and pornography both inculcate ideas of delinquent behavior. (See Chapter 15 for additional discussion on this issue.)

While there can be little doubt that delinquents learn a variety of things from others, learning seems to have different outcomes for different people. Solomon Kobrin showed that in depressed urban areas, youngsters are exposed to a variety of conflicting types of interactions—some with delinquent emphases, others nondelinquent, and still others antidelinquent. It seems to be almost an accident which learning circumstances create delinquent behavior. Indeed, a standard criticism of differential association is that it ought to predict very high levels of criminal behavior by prison guards, because they associate so much with criminals. Sutherland, as we shall see, indicates that more is needed than a mere count of interactions with other persons to predict delinquent activity.

If individuals acquiring delinquent propensities were exposed only to situations, circumstances, and interactions of a delinquent nature, it would be easy to comprehend how the process of communication brings about delinquent behavior. In view of the enormous variation in standards and personalities to which each of us is exposed, it becomes exceedingly difficult to determine the critical elements that induce delinquency.

Sutherland's third point is that *criminal behavior is acquired through participation in intimate personal groups*. This suggests that the roots of delinquency must be sought in the socializing experiences of an individual. By processes such as role playing, it is assumed that a person will develop characteristics of family and peer groups with whom that person has the closest connection, but we cannot detail how and to what extent that process takes place. The problem becomes especially troublesome when it is recognized that the behavior to which a developing individual is exposed is often highly inconsistent.

The fourth point of differential association theory is that *the criminal learning process includes not only techniques of committing crime but also the shaping of motives, drives, rationalizations, and attitudes*. Techniques for delinquency can involve high levels of skill. Picking pockets (without getting caught at it) demands a considerable adroitness. Most pickpockets will use the fingers next to the thumb of their strongest hand, usually the right one, and lift up their whole body once they have grasped a wallet rather than moving only the arm. Being a successful juvenile prostitute demands knowing how to hustle customers, collect money, buy protection, deal with a drunk or violent john, and a considerable number of other employment qualifications.

Fifth, Sutherland stipulates that the *specific direction of motives and drives is learned from definitions of the legal codes as favorable or unfavorable.* The broad reference to "direction of motives and drives" leaves almost as many questions unanswered as it clarifies. Besides, the development of delinquent attitudes appears not to be the formal process that Sutherland describes. For example, before a person accepts the view that "only suckers work," a variety of other reinforcing attitudes have to be absorbed (into which a knowledge of legality and illegality may not figure prominently).

Sixth, Sutherland postulates that a *person becomes delinquent because of an excess of definitions favorable to violation of the law over definitions unfavorable to violation of the law.* This doctrine, lying at the heart of the theory, is extremely difficult (if not impossible) to prove or disprove. It is doubtful whether any standard of behavior to which an individual is exposed may be assessed wholly in terms of attitudes favorable or unfavorable to law. It is one thing to look at persons who committed crimes and say that they did so because they possessed an excess of definitions favorable to doing so; it is quite another thing to take 10 people and seek to determine how they feel about any given law and then to predict accurately which of them will commit a particular crime.

To demonstrate with more clarity the character of the associations that subsequently affect behavior, Sutherland offers his seventh point: that *differential association may vary in frequency, duration, priority, and intensity.* There is no suggestion regarding which of these elements is likely to be more important than the others. Frequent contacts may promote feelings of boredom and indifference, or one intense experience may overwhelm all prior learning—or it may not.

Sutherland's eighth point states a common behavioral science principle: *learning criminal and delinquent behavior involves all the same mechanisms that are involved in any other learning.* But what are these mechanisms? If delinquency is learned like anything else—for example, basketball skills, cooking, patriotism, and flirting—then any theory that can unravel its ingredients will at the same time have to provide an interpretation of all human action. As Sutherland's propositions cannot approach so stunning an intellectual achievement, in that regard they can be seen as overambitious or, perhaps, simplistic.

As his next-to-last proposition Sutherland stressed that *learning differs from pure imitation.* His last point is a reminder that *while criminal behavior is an expression of general needs and values, it is not explained by these general needs and values because noncriminal behavior is an expression of the same needs and values.* This final injunction indicates that the oversimplified generalizations sometimes employed to account for delinquency (such as the idea that a youth steals because he or she "craves esteem," kills because he or she is "unhappy," or robs because he or she "wants money") have no real scientific merit. Persons, both delinquent and nondelinquent, are motivated by much the same needs and values. They become or do not become delinquents on the basis of their individual responses to common drives for prestige, happiness, success, power, wealth, and other human aspirations. I may feel a pressing need for money and take an extra weekend job pumping gas, or try to borrow some from a friend, or shrug my shoulders and figure that this time I will do without. Another person, feeling the same need, may hold up a fast food outlet.

Those who read Sutherland's work are likely to be impressed with the quality of intellectual honesty and rigor that it shows. It is not surprising that the severest criticism of differential association appears in a manuscript (not published until after Sutherland's death) written by Sutherland himself, whimsically titled "The Swan Song of Differential Association." In it, among many other things, he points out that the theory neglects consideration of opportunities to commit delinquent acts. Consequently, Sutherland wrote, criminal behavior is not caused entirely by association with criminal and anticriminal patterns, and differential association is not a sufficient cause of criminal behavior.

For others, the most severe handicap of the theory lies in its inability to lend itself to research probes. Researchers have concluded that the theory is at such a high level of abstraction that it is not possible to test it directly with empirical data. In addition, the theory is unable to account for the processes by which individuals respond differently to similar situations. There is no way out of this dilemma unless we take into account differences in human perceptions of seemingly similar experiences. John Mays has said that differential association "takes us a little way and then abandons us to doubt."[5] Nigel Walker, perhaps the harshest critic of differential association, believes that it and many other theories of crime and delinquency "begin with the observation of the obvious, generalize it into a principle, and are eventually reduced again to a statement of the limited truths from which they originated."[6] Sir Leon Radzinowicz has pointed out that it would be impossible to collect, weigh, and compare all the associations favorable or unfavorable to crime that even one offender had encountered in his or her life, and concluded that the main tide of criminology has "passed by" differential association. It is noteworthy that none of these critics are Americans: Mays and Walker are Scottish, while Radzinowicz, who was born in Poland, lived most of his life in England before retiring in the United States. American scholars tend to be much more respectful of Sutherland's work, perhaps because he exerted so strong an influence on American criminology and on their own studies.

Ronald Akers: Social Learning Theory

The major attempt to refine Sutherland's theory of differential association was made by Ronald L. Akers, whose *social learning theory* posits that the primary mechanisms driving social behavior are the stimuli that are the consequences of the behavior. If, for instance, people ask me how I feel and I tell them at some length, and then observe that their eyes glaze over, if I have any sense I will learn to respond to such inquiries with the short and superficial answer that they actually expect. My subsequent behavior in this regard has been conditioned by the response to my earlier behavior.

Imitation of others' acts also may help determine how I will behave, as will positive reinforcement (such as praise or other rewards) and negative reinforcement (such as punishment, the failure to secure something that I sought, or harm that comes to me as a result of what I have done). Differential reinforcement—the amount and strength of what ensues from my behavior—lies at the heart of social learning theory.

Delinquency in Akers's terms occurs when favorable definitions of the behavior overpower those definitions that are set against it. For example, progression into more frequent and sustained use of drugs would "be determined by the extent to which a given pattern is sustained by the combination of the reinforcing effects of the substance with social reinforcement, exposure to models, definitions though association with using peers," as well as by the degree to which "it is not deterred through bad effects of the substance and/or negative sanctions from peers, parents, and the law."[7]

A review of Akers's theory suggests that the time sequencing of matters such as peer association and delinquency are not well specified. Reinforcement is said to occur when the behavior has been strengthened, but this is true by definition and cannot be demonstrated by scientific experimentation.

CONTROL THEORY

Travis Hirschi: Social Bonding Theory

The control theory advanced by Travis Hirschi, often called *social bonding theory*, is built on a series of "if-then" statements: if something exists, then it foretells that something will happen. Such formulations allow for confirmation or rebuttal, which is the essence of the scientific enterprise.

Social bonding theory grew out of Hirschi's study of delinquents and nondelinquents in northern California (see the discussion in Chapter 1 on his use of the self-report technique). Hirschi, who was born in Rockville, Utah, took his theoretical cue from Emile Durkheim's *Suicide* (1897), in which the famous French scholar wrote:

> The more weakened the groups to which [an individual] belongs, the less he depends on them, the more he consequently depends on himself and recognizes no other rules of conduct than what are founded on his private interests.[8]

Control theory maintains that societies strive to press their members into patterns of conformity. Schools train for social adjustment, peers typically advance ideas of success and conventional behavior, and parents (even parents who themselves play fast and loose with the rules) seek to inculcate law-abiding habits in their children. The theory says that to the extent that a youngster fails to become attached to the control agencies of society (for instance, the family and the schools), the youngster's chances of engaging in delinquency are increased. This doctrine edges very close to the self-evident in its insistence that close attachment to law-abiding people, groups, and organizations is predictive of law-abiding behavior, but it is rich in subordinate statements and findings, many of them far from obvious.

Four aspects of social bonding are addressed by the theory: (1) attachment, (2) commitment, (3) involvement, and (4) belief. (For students interested in a mnemonic device to help them remember these, they can be recalled as words beginning with "a," "b," "c," and then "i.")

Attachment refers to affectional ties with persons such as parents, teachers, and peers. *Commitment* refers to the costs of being caught in delinquent activity. For example, a person seeking college admission and a professional career will have a strong stake in avoiding delinquency. *Involvement* concerns participation in activities related to future goals and objectives (e.g., time spent on homework). *Belief* has to do with feelings about the legitimacy of conventional values, such as law in general and criminal law in particular.

Hirschi insists that there is not an important relationship between social class and delinquency. Persons in any class—lower, middle, or upper—who fail to form ties with important elements of conforming society will be much more likely to find themselves on a path that ends in delinquent activities.

Control theory stresses the importance of "the bond of affection for conventional persons" as an inhibitor of delinquent behavior. "The stronger this bond, the more likely the person is to take it into account when and if he contemplates a criminal act."[9] What happens, the theory suggests, is that juveniles confronted with the possibility of breaking the law are likely to ask themselves: "What will my mother—or my father—think if they find out?" To the extent that persons believe their parents will be disappointed or ashamed, and to the extent that they care that the parent will feel so, they will not engage in the prohibited behavior. Positive answers to the following two family-related items were found to correlate with nondelinquent behavior: "When you come across things you don't understand, does your mother (father) help you with them?" and "Does your mother (father) ever explain why she (he) feels the way she (he) does?" In regard to items such as these, Hirschi reaches the following conclusion:

> The intimacy of communication between child and parent is strongly related to the commission of delinquent acts. Only five percent of the boys who often discuss their future plans and often share their thoughts and feelings with their fathers have committed two or more delinquent acts in the year prior to administration of the questionnaire, while 43 percent of those who never communicate with their fathers about these matters have committed as many delinquent acts.[10]

Hirschi goes on to say that it is not communication alone that matters. Delinquents talked almost as much with their parents as nondelinquents. It is the nature of what is discussed that matters. One difficulty with this formulation, however, has to be that the testing was done after many of the boys had committed delinquent acts. It could well be that the misbehavior of the children had distanced their parents from them and that whatever kind of close communication had existed no longer prevailed.

Similarly, in control theory, school is said to be related to delinquent behavior. The better a student does in school, the less likely is the student to commit a delinquent act. "The boy who does not like school and does not care what teachers think of him is to this extent free to commit delinquent acts," Hirschi argues. He proceeds to make the more general point: "Positive feelings toward controlling institutions and persons in authority are the first line of social control. Withdrawal of favorable sentiments toward such institutions and persons neutralizes their moral force."[11] Hirschi's control theory suggested that other theorists tend to romanticize gang existence. Hirschi believed that delinquents are not likely to make sacrifices to the requirements of the group, and that delinquent gangs are marked by "distrust and suspicion." Other researchers report, however, that Hirschi's portrayal of the "cold and brittle" image of delinquents' friendships and the kind of "intimate fraternity" enjoyed by nondelinquents is considerably oversimplified.

Control theory says that things such as smoking cigarettes, "riding around in a car," and early dating are all predictors of delinquent behavior. Hirschi believes that such behaviors indicate a premature striving for adult status, an inappropriate shedding of adolescent behavior. Smoking, for Hirschi, is equivalent in causal significance to the tattoo, a starting point for the development of a delinquent self-image, and the earlier smoking begins, the more likely the child is to commit delinquent acts. Among those youngsters who spend five or more hours a week riding around in a car, the proportion having committed a delinquent act was found to be twice that for those who spend no time in such activity. Similarly, those who found adolescence "boring" were more likely to be in the ranks of the delinquents.

Critiques of Hirschi's Control Theory

There are a number of questionable aspects of control theory. It relies exclusively on responses to questionnaires and not on behavioral measures. If I say that I am respectful of teachers' opinions, Hirschi has

to assume that I really am so and that I will in fact think twice or more about what a person in authority might believe of me before I commit a delinquent act. It is arguable whether this assumption is accurate.

Similarly, the measure of delinquency on which control theory is based is a self-report measure. Again, there has to be uncertainty about the correspondence between what persons say they have done and what in fact is their behavior. So, in essence, control theory is a statement about the relationship between two sets of questionnaire responses, both of which may be only partially accurate indicators of the behavior that they are presumed to determine (see the discussion in Chapter 1 on the validity of self-report studies).

Travis Hirschi's control theory considers smoking cigarettes to be equivalent in causal significance to getting a tattoo. His theory, proposed in 1969, saw both behaviors as starting points for the development of a delinquent self-image. *(Photo by Ellen S. Boyne)*

In addition, Hirschi does not consider how the four elements of his theory—attachment, belief, commitment, and involvement—might act simultaneously and independently in regard to delinquent behavior. One study found that attachment to parents, patterns of dating, attachment to school, belief, and involvement are far more important than the other postulated items. Another study concluded that control theory did not stand up as an explanation of either illegal or nonconforming behavior of fifth graders. It found that belief was correlated with such behavior but in the opposite direction that Hirschi had indicated in the theory. Hirschi also has been challenged for assuming causal relationships among his variables, when only longitudinal data (information gathered over a period of time) would support his conclusions.

There also has been some dispute over the manner in which school performance bears on delinquency. Delbert Elliott and Harwin Voss claim that their data show that after dropping out of school a person's rate of delinquency declines significantly. As they see it, it is not the absence of attachment to school that causes delinquency but rather the painful experiences of discomfort and failure that occur while in school. Elliott and Voss believe that school is the critical context for the generation of delinquent behavior. They disagree with Hirschi's observation that peer involvement reduces delinquent activity. Instead, they maintain that a strong commitment to one's peers is conducive to delinquency, regardless of the extent of delinquency in that group. They suggest that the peer culture itself is conducive to delinquency. Other research has concluded that considering delinquent companions to be a causal explanation statistically overwhelms the remainder of Hirschi's ideas about the causes of the behavior.

Hirschi has extended control theory into the arena of youth employment. He insists that if a youth holds a job while going to school, that youth is more likely to engage in delinquency because parents lose a degree of control and there is less dependence. Denise Gottfredson, however, has reported that working does not have an effect on delinquency. Nor, she maintains, does it have a detrimental effect on commitment to education, involvement in extracurricular activities, time spent on homework, attachment to school, or attachment to parents. Though working did decrease school attendance for some students, this did not translate into increases in delinquent behavior in Gottfredson's study.

Finally, after reanalyzing Hirschi's own data with more sophisticated statistical methods, David Greenberg concluded that the sources on which Hirschi built the theory provide only "modest" support for its claims. He suggests that the conservative ideological implications of the theory—its emphasis on bonding to existing social and institutions rather than reforming such institutions to make them more just—may account for the theory's high standing.

Gottfredson and Hirschi: Self-Control Theory

Michael Gottfredson and Travis Hirschi have recently advanced what they declare to be a general theory of crime and delinquency, as well as an explanation of matters that are not against the law (such as alcoholism and cigarette smoking). They argue that poor family upbringing produces low self-control. Poor upbringing is said to be lax, with punishments that are light, and short-term.

According to Gottfredson and Hirschi, unsatisfactory self-control is broken into several components, including:

1. failure to defer gratification;

2. absence of diligence and tenacity;

3. adventuresomeness rather than caution;

4. physical activity preferred to cognitive behavior;

5. self-centeredness and indifference to the suffering of others; and

6. minimal tolerance of frustration.

These components lead to engagement in behaviors that are exciting and risky, that provide meager long-term benefits, that require little skill or planning, and that often result in pain or discomfort for victims who are hurt or robbed by such behavior.

There is something a bit awesome about the hubris of theorists who seek to provide understanding not only of delinquent and criminal behavior but also of a wide variety of other kinds of activity in terms of a single word: self-control. One is reminded of the elegant conceptualizations that are advanced in theoretical physics in which all elements of a very complex issue are reduced to a short formula. The difference, however, is that in theoretical physics the formulations gain the acceptance (or rejection) by all trained persons working in the field—those who have an opportunity to examine its elements and carry out experiments to ascertain its accuracy. The idea that the absence of self-control adequately accounts for the phenomenon of juvenile delinquency hardly elicits that kind of universal support.

Most criminologists and scholars of delinquency regard the self-control theory as tautological or as a gross oversimplification. Those maintaining that the concept is tautological say that the absence of self-control merely explains a range of activities that, in order to be avoided, require self-control; that is why they are outlawed in a society that seeks to contain certain impulses of its citizens. All delinquent and criminal acts may not be mediated by self-control, and some delinquent acts (e.g., well-planned gang maneuvers) require as much self-control as those behaviors that mark conforming behavior. It has been pointed out that it was precisely the trait of self-control that propelled corporate executives and politicians into their upper-status positions and yet a number of them engage in criminal acts such as bribery, false reports, insider trading, antitrust violations, and similar crimes. In this regard, one review of the Gottfredson-Hirschi theory concludes that "too much of crime falls outside the boundaries of their definition for this general theory to be of much use."[12] Another reviewer indicated that he believed the theory was on occasion marked by "intellectual contortions."[13] A third critic was put off by the Gottfredson and Hirschi monograph's style (what he called its "excessive chest-thumping about how correct they are and how incorrect everybody else is") and he thought that supporting data for the theory was "insufficiently persuasive at this point."[14]

Seeking to relate delinquency to the possession of self-control (as it is defined in a paper-and-pencil test), Harold Grasmick and his colleagues found that, while there was some correlation, the most important consideration was the theory's lack of detailed attention to criminal opportunity. This, it may be remembered, was the same consideration that led Sutherland to critique his own theory of differential association. According to Grasmick and his coworkers, self-control theory needs expansion, refinement, and elaboration. Gottfredson and Hirschi, for their part, agree that self-reported delinquency represents a poor measure of actual behavior. They note that they would prefer to gauge self-control by actual behavior (such as whether a person uses a seat belt while driving) rather than by what the person told researchers.

The criminological industry has seized upon self-control theory as a research topic. This body of research can be readily summarized by noting that the investigators typically find that there is a better-than-average chance that persons who commit traditional kinds of criminal and delinquent acts lack self-control, however it is defined. They also have learned that there are many persons who do not fit the criteria used to define low self-control but who nonetheless violate the law. The published papers debate the adequacy of diverse measures of self-control but most do not bother to scrutinize the theory in terms of logic and common sense before they embark on their work. What we see might be represented by the observation: Ours is not to question why, ours is to quantify.

There are also those who question the sense of the policy positions that Gottfredson and Hirschi adopt and who argue that those who take such positions seriously are rather like "proper geese following their propaganda."[15] All theories carry with them implicit or explicit policy recommendations but it is important that such recommendations be tied in a reasonable fashion to the ingredients of the theory. Recommendations offered by Gottfredson and Hirschi seem notably unanchored. Note, for instance, the following statement:

> We see little hope for important reductions in crime through modification of the criminal justice system. We see considerable hope in policies that would reduce the role of the state and return responsibility for crime control to ordinary citizens.[16]

First, look at the phrase "important reduction." How "important" are the reductions that now keep showing up in statistical reports about crime and juvenile delinquency in the United States? While they may not altogether represent the efforts of the criminal justice system, they are quite unlikely to be the product of the inculcation of additional self-control in children by parents. The term "ordinary citizens" (who are the "extraordinary citizens"?) is a political buzzword that implies the ineptitude of the so-called elite. Equally ideological is the insistence that "policies that seek to reduce crime by the satisfaction of theoretically derived wants (e.g., equality, adequate housing, good jobs, self-esteem) are likely to be unsuccessful."[17]

To test their theory, Gottfredson and Hirschi believe efforts should be made to relate such childhood behaviors as whining, pushing, punching, and shoving to later delinquent careers. Parents must be trained to understand the rudiments of early childhood socialization, particularly to recognize signs of low self-control and punish children who exhibit them.

INTEGRATED THEORY

As the name indicates, *integrated theory* seeks to select from each of the numerous theories of juvenile delinquency those elements that are substantiated by research results. A principle of differential association might be blended with one from social control theory, with an added element from strain theory. Such a combination, it is claimed, will provide a more accurate and comprehensive understanding of the illegal behavior than will any of the particular theories alone.

"New theories [of crime and delinquency] appear on the scene with astonishing frequency," George Vold, Thomas Bernard, and Jeffrey Snipes observe. They add: "The abundance of theories does not enrich the field but impedes scientific progress. Theory is supposed to direct research and to accumulate into a coherent understandable product."[18] Bernard and Snipes maintain that the disparate theories of delinquency will much better serve our understanding if the strengths of the various approaches are abstracted and combined.

In a study by John Hagan and Bill McCarthy, for instance, it was noted that youths from large families are more likely to be on the streets because of difficulties and disruptions in parenting. Uncontrolled youths are less likely to be committed to school work and more likely to be in conflict with teachers. The authors suggest that, taken together, findings such as these encourage the integration of control and strain theories.

In another such effort, Terence Thornberry and several colleagues sought to learn about the importance for delinquent behavior of individual beliefs and relations with peers. They noted that learning or socialization theories view peer associations and beliefs as causes of delinquency, whereas other models maintain that after becoming involved in delinquent activity, a youngster develops contacts with others who also are behaving illegally and adopts a set of beliefs that allow the behavior to be defended. This "birds of a feather flock together" view is built on the idea that delinquents seek out others like themselves for companionship.

Using data from the Rochester (NY) Youth Development Study, the researchers concluded that both theories were accurate; for instance, some youngsters moved into delinquent behavior through associations, while others developed such associations afterwards, as they drifted away from the mainstream. For Thornberry and his colleagues, the results favored what they called an interactional model of delinquency, built on the recognition that an adequate explanation cannot be limited to either a social control or a social learning perspective but should incorporate elements of each into a broader body of explanatory principles.

Integrated theory also forms the basis of Janice Joseph's examination of juvenile delinquency among 333 male and female African-American youths in two New Jersey cities: Atlantic City and Pleasantville. Joseph examined the importance of five variables extracted from various theoretical positions: (1) socioeconomic status, (2) attachment to parents, (3) perceptions of blocked or limited opportunities, (4) attachment to schools, and (5) delinquent companions.

Socioeconomic status was found not to be related to delinquent behavior; neither was lack of attachment to parents or blocked opportunities. Joseph speculates that perhaps, unlike whites, African-Americans are socialized to expect blocked and limited opportunities to mark their lives. Lack of attachment to school proved to be strongly significant as a correlate of delinquency, while the presence of delinquent companions was found to be slightly significant. Joseph noted that by taking from diverse theories the items that seemed likely to prove important, she was able to examine a much wider range of elements than she could have done had she confined herself with what she calls a "restricted focus" on any single theory.

In an attempt to shed light on the roots of delinquency, Hennessey Hayes also found that integrated theory best served his ends. He discovered that weakened social controls increased opportunities for associating with delinquent peers, learning delinquency behaviors, and committing delinquent acts. Initial delinquency then increased the likelihood of being observed and labeled negatively by parents. These labels in turn escalated the likelihood of further delinquency.

Integrated theory, however, has exhibited a variety of problems in the attempt to offer a coherent explanation of delinquency. Logical incompatibility is a major issue; that is, the different elements often can form a rather disorganized set of postulates. Equally serious are problems of a lack of agreed-upon definitions of common terms, the imprecise measurement of key variables, and empirical indeterminacy (by which is meant the use of the same variables in different ways in different theories).

SUMMARY

This chapter has considered a number of major theories that play a significant role in present-day discussions of the causes of juvenile delinquency: (1) conflict theory, (2) differential association, (3) social learning theory, (4) control theory, (5) self-control theory, and (6) integrated theories. Each theory type has strong adherents—those who are persuaded that it offers the best understanding of juvenile waywardness.

Conflict theorists insist that it is pointless to look at the individual delinquent in an effort to explain his or her behavior. Delinquency's fundamental cause, they maintain, lies in the economic and political arrangements of the social system. They see capitalism and the profit motive as the culprits in the creation of social ills. According to them, class warfare underlies contemporary life in capitalist societies and results in the exploitation of those who are shut off from realizing the benefits that the society offers. These outcast persons resort to delinquent behavior in order to survive and maintain a satisfactory self-image. Their fate is the inevitable consequence of pressures exerted on them to be satisfied with less than their fair share of the benefits of the system and of what they produce. In this sense, delinquents are seen as political protesters, demanding that they too be allowed to enjoy an adequate income, free access to education and medical care, regular employment at decent wages, and similar satisfactions. For them to gain such benefits, those who have more than they reasonably need would have to have things taken from them, because it is not likely that they will readily give up what they have. Thus, conflict theorists often call for major social change that would allow for rule by the "people" and the confiscation of what are seen as the "ill-gotten" gains of the upper class.

On the specific issue of juvenile delinquency, conflict theorists would argue that the educational system is deliberately geared to create failures because it is fashioned in the interests of the upper class. Low-income-area schools get the least talented teachers. Counselors in such schools push minority students into dead-end work and aim to create a placid, tractable work force. Deliberate creation of a "satisfactory" rate of unemployment means that those who obtain work are careful to labor hard and uncomplainingly because of their fear of being laid off. Delinquents cannot adjust to an unappetizing lower-class existence and break the law to improve their conditions and add a bit of zest to their lives. They are punished in order to teach a lesson to those who might also be inclined to rebel, so that they can appreciate that delinquency has hurtful consequences.

Conflict theorists are particularly adept at being critical. They point out with considerable insight the shortcomings of the political-economic systems in which human beings are destined to enjoy very different fates, often primarily because of the chance circumstance of who their parents are. Opponents claim that where conflict theory falls flat it is in its blueprint for reform. There has been difficulty in finding any noncapitalist society (existing or past) that has become the paradise said by the theorists to be the product of the elimination of capitalism. Indeed, while improvements have been made in aspects of life in places such as China and Cuba, few persons would argue that they represent utopias. Communist countries have restricted human freedoms—most particularly the freedom to dissent and the freedom to travel—and they have not been willing to open up the political process to competing parties.

Recently, many conflict scholars working in the field of delinquency have moved toward a more centrist position, abandoning what they label as the "left idealist" position for one called "left realist." They now argue for reforms typically advocated by liberals rather than revolutionaries—reforms such as tighter control of the police by citizen groups and making life inside prisons as free and normal as possible.

Differential association, the second of the positions discussed, is essentially a social learning theory. Formulated by Edwin H. Sutherland, differential association is made up of a string of postulates that attribute attitudes favorable to lawbreaking to be the root of delinquent acts. Major criticism of differential association has focused on its inability to demonstrate either its accuracy or falsity experimentally. It also has been argued that the idea that criminal behavior is learned would be true only if all behavior were totally learned (that is, if there were no genetic correlates of human action).

Social learning theory attempts to shore up the weaker attributes of differential association precepts by pinpointing much more specifically the manner in which people come to incorporate in their behavior those things that they learn, either directly or by observation. The theory also indicates more precisely than differential association the elements of human experience that exert pressures toward lawbreaking and those that inhibit it. The downside of the theory is that, like differential association, it is very difficult to test in any thorough manner and it tends to lack predictive strength.

The fourth position, control theory, was originated by Travis Hirschi. It is built upon the idea that the more attachments a youngster has to law-abiding persons and ideas, the more likely that youngster is to conform. In this sense, the theory represents an extension of differential association. Its particular strength, though, is that it pinpoints those elements of personal and social existence that appear to play a particularly powerful role in immunizing a person from delinquent acts. Such things as concern for the opinion of others, the desire to succeed, and doing well in school are set out as matters that inoculate a young person against delinquency. In this regard, the postulates of control theory are readily susceptible to testing. Such tests have refined and occasionally rebutted the tenets set out by Hirschi.

Self-control theory represents a repudiation—or at least a proposed advance—on Hirschi's social control model. This theory, prompted by Gottfredson and Hirschi, suggests that the absence of self-control in the perpetrator offers the key to a thorough understanding of delinquent behavior and that this character deficiency is the result of faulty parenting. The theory fits very well with the political mood of the times. It points a finger at welfare families and at families in which both parents turn a significant amount of childrearing responsibility over to live-in caretakers or day-care centers. The theory's weak side is that it virtually takes the definition of the behaviors that it seeks to explain and then offers that definition as the explanation. More simply put, it suggests that people who lack self-control will commit delinquent acts, and then it demonstrates the absence of self-control by pointing to the acts that they have committed.

The use of integrated theories represents an attempt to extract from each of the manifold theories some aspects that provide insight into delinquent behavior. It grows from research endeavors that have found that any given theory by itself falls far short of adequately accounting for delinquency but that selecting items from a number of theories can strengthen our overall understanding. The problem with integrated theory, noted Hirschi, is that there is a tendency not to have a very neat explanatory schema but rather, using his term, to have "a stew."

REFERENCES

Akers, Ronald L. (1985). *Deviant Behavior: A Social Learning Approach*, 3rd ed. Belmont, CA: Wadsworth.

Brodsky, Stanley (1991). "Book Review." *Contemporary Psychology* 63:104-105.

Cassidy, John (1997). "The Return of Karl Marx." *The New Yorker* (October 20):250-259.

Colvin, Mark, and John Pauly (1983). "A Critique of Criminology: Toward an Integrated Structural-Marxist Theory of Delinquency Prediction." *American Journal of Sociology* 89:513-551.

Durkheim, Emile (1897). *Suicide*. Translated by John A. Spaulding and George Simpson. Reprint. New York: Free Press, 1951.

Elliott, Delbert S., and Harwin L. Voss (1974). *Delinquency and Dropout*. Lexington, MA: Lexington Books.

Geis, Gilbert (2000). "On the Absence of Self-Control as the Basis for a General Theory of Crime: A Critique." *Theoretical Criminology* 4:35-53.

Gottfredson, Denise C. (1985). "Youth Employment, Crime, and Schooling: A Longitudinal Study of a National Sample." *Developmental Psychology* 21:419-432.

Gottfredson, Michael, and Travis Hirschi (1990). *A General Theory of Crime*. Stanford, CA: Stanford University Press.

Grasmick, Harold G., Charles R. Tittle, Robert J. Bursik, Jr., and Bruce J. Arneklev (1993). "Testing the Core Empirical Implications of Gottfredson and Hirschi's General Theory of Crime." *Journal of Research in Crime and Delinquency* 30:5-29.

Greenberg, David (1999). "The Weak Strength of Social Control Theory." *Crime & Delinquency* 45:66-81.

Hagan, John, and Bill McCarthy (1992). "Streetlife and Delinquency." *British Journal of Sociology* 43:533-561.

Hayes, Hennessey D. (1997). "Using Integrated Theory to Explain the Movement into Juvenile Delinquency." *Deviant Behavior* 17:161-184.

Hirschi, Travis (1969). *Causes of Delinquency*. Berkeley: University of California Press.

Hirst, Paul Q. (1972). "Marx and Engels on Law, Crime, and Morality." *Economy and Society* 1:28-56.

Joseph, Janice (1995). "Juvenile Delinquency among African Americans." *Journal of Black Studies* 25:475-491.

Kobrin, Solomon (1951). "The Conflict of Values in Delinquency Areas." *American Sociological Review* 16:653-661.

Leonard, Kimberly Kempf, and Scott H. Decker (1994). "The Theory of Social Control: Does It Apply to the Very Young?" *Journal of Criminal Justice* 22:89-105.

Marx, Karl, and Friedrich Engels (1867-1894/1906). *Capital: A Critique of Political Economy*. Translated by E. Aveling. Chicago: Charles Kerr Press.

Mays, John B. (1963). *Crime and Social Structure*. London: Faber and Faber.

Meier, Robert F. (1993). "Integrated Theories of Crime." Unpublished paper.

Morris, Norval, and Gordon Hawkins (1970). *The Honest Politician's Guide to Crime Control.* Chicago: University of Chicago Press.

Polk, Kenneth (1991). "Book Review." *Crime & Delinquency* 37:575-579.

Radzinowicz, Leon (1965). *Ideology and Crime: A Study of Crime in its Social and Historical Context.* London: Heinemann.

Salas, Luis (1979). *Social Control and Deviance in Cuba.* New York: Praeger.

Sharpe, J.A. (1984). *Crime in Early Modern England, 1550-1750.* London: Longman.

Simpson, Sally S., and Lori Ellis (1994). "Is Gender Subordinate to Class?: An Empirical Assessment of Colvin and Pauly's Structural Marxist Theory of Delinquency." *Journal of Criminal Law and Criminology* 85:453-480.

Sinclair, Catherine M. (1983). "A Radical/Marxist Interpretation of Juvenile Justice in the United States." *Federal Probation* 46 (June):20-28.

Sutherland, Edwin H. (1956). "Critique of the Theory: The Swan Song of Differential Association." In *The Sutherland Papers*, edited by Karl Schuessler, Albert Cohen, and Alfred Lindesmith, 30-41. Bloomington: Indiana University Press.

Sutherland, Edwin H., and Donald R. Cressey (1978). *Criminology*, 10th ed. Philadelphia: Lippincott.

Thornberry, Terence P., Melanie Moore, and R.L. Christenson (1985). "The Effect of Dropping Out of School on Subsequent Criminal Behavior." *Criminology* 23:3-18.

Tittle, Charles R. (1991). "Book Review." *American Journal of Sociology* 96:1609-1611.

Vold, George B., Thomas J. Bernard, and Jeffrey B. Snipes (1998). *Theoretical Criminology.* New York: Oxford University Press.

Walker, Nigel (1965). *Crime and Punishment in Britain.* Edinburgh: University Press.

Winfree, L. Thomas, Jr., Finn-Aage-Esbensen, and D. Wayne Osgood (1996). "Evaluating a School-Based Gang Program: A Theoretical Perspective." *Evaluation Review* 20:181-201.

Young, Jock (1986). "The Failure of Criminology: The Need for Radical Realism." In *Confronting Crime*, edited by Jock Young and Roger Matthews, 4-30. London: Sage.

NOTES

1   Sinclair (1983), 25.

2   Salas (1979), 26-27.

3   Hirst (1972), 41.

4   Morris & Hawkins (1970), 49.

5   Mays (1963), 67.

[6]   Walker (1965), 95.

[7]   Akers (1985), 34.

[8]   Durkheim (1897), 209.

[9]   Hirschi (1969), 83.

[10]   Ibid., 91.

[11]   Ibid., 127.

[12]   Polk (1991), 576.

[13]   Tittle (1991), 1609.

[14]   Brodsky (1991), 104.

[15]   Geis (2000), 47.

[16]   Gottfredson & Hirschi (1990), xvi.

[17]   Ibid., 256.

[18]   Vold, Bernard & Snipes (1998), 302.

8

The American Juvenile Justice System:
Precedents and Development

With this chapter, we turn from ideas about the causes of juvenile delinquency to a consideration of the ways in which society has responded to it. Much of our focus in this chapter will be on the development of the American juvenile justice system. We shall examine the early precedents for that system, looking mainly at the nineteenth century and at the institutions that served as a background for much that characterizes the juvenile justice system in our own time.

We noted in Chapter 2, as a main theme in the development of ideas about juvenile delinquency, the increasing sense of the distinctive nature of the child. Institutionally, this process led to a growing belief that juvenile crime demands distinctive institutional responses and that the laws and facilities designed for adult offenders are inappropriate for young people. In this chapter, we shall see how this belief was put into practice in ways that led to the creation of a distinctive juvenile justice system. In Chapter 10, we shall explore the creation, evolution, and operations of the central institution of the modern American juvenile justice system: the juvenile court.

APPROACHES TO JUVENILE CRIME IN EARLIER AGES

To gain some perspective on the evolution of a juvenile justice system, it is useful to look back into history. For most of Western history, systems of criminal justice provided no separate laws or institutions for juveniles, even through the early modern period.

The Ancient World

The most informative accounts of ancient responses to juvenile crime come from Greece and Rome. In neither society did age diminish criminal responsibility. In Greece, young people accused of breaking the law were thought to be just as culpable as adults. Under the terms of the early codification of Roman Law, known as the Twelve Tables (c.488-451 B.C.E.),[1] the same was true. In the criminal justice system, juvenile offenders were to be dealt with in the same way as adults, although some allowance was made for youths in the severity of punishment imposed for certain crimes. Theft, for example, might result in death or enslavement for an adult, but an offender under the age of puberty would receive a flogging. Otherwise, no distinctions were made.

By about the fifth century (C.E.), Roman law had become more precise with regard to the age of criminal responsibility. Children under the age of seven were exempt from criminal liability; boys above 14 and girls above 12 were considered adults for purposes of criminal liability; those in between were to be judged individually, based on the apparent capacity of the child to distinguish right from wrong. Such an approach was widespread throughout Europe during the Middle Ages, with some variations according to time and place.

The English Common Law

English medieval judgments and practices showed a similar understanding of relationships between age and criminal liability. These judgments were ultimately crystallized in the common law tradition, the body of law, going back to the Middle Ages, that grew out of judicial decisions rather than specific legislation. Common law was the tradition of legal thought and practice that guided jurisprudence not only in Britain, but (with British colonization) in America as well.

For much of the medieval period, English law held children criminally liable for offenses, theoretically, from birth. However, few children under the age of seven actually faced legal penalties, as pardons after conviction were the usual response in such cases. Ultimately, by the

1300s, many English courts excused young children from prosecution, and by the 1600s, such younger children were no longer required to appear for trial on criminal charges.

For older children, English common law evolved much in the manner of Roman law. Medieval courts did not provide blanket pardons for those between seven and 14, but looked mainly to considerations other than age in the disposition of cases: apparent maturity, the severity of the crime, and the capacity to choose between right and wrong. Into the nineteenth century, such an approach would be an established part of the common law in both England and America. Chancellor James Kent, a great American scholar of the common law, wrote in 1827 that "the responsibility of infants for crimes by them committed depends less on their age, than on the extent of their discretion and capacity to discern right and wrong."[2]

Such an understanding of juvenile crime, though it recognized at least the potential legal incapacity of the young offender, was very different from the popular and theoretical ideas about juvenile crime that have developed in more recent times. The focus on the young offender and his or her capacity, which is central to the common law, implied an utter lack of recognition of juvenile crime as a special *category* of offending. In addition, it implied no duty on the part of society to respond in a distinctive institutional way to a young person held liable for the commission of an offense.

The Early Modern Era

One measure of the criminal justice system's unawareness (under the common law) of any special problems posed by juvenile crime may be seen in the fact that juvenile offenders were subject to the same punishments as adults. Before 1800, incarceration was almost unknown as a sentence; convicted juveniles, like their adult counterparts, were often subject to harsh corporal punishment. Into the nineteenth century, whipping and burning in the hand were the most common forms of corporal punishment, imposed regardless of the offender's age and exercised frequently as a part of English and American justice.

Also common as a response to crime was the removal of the offender, adult or juvenile, from his or her old environment, chiefly through what was known as "transportation." In the seventeenth and eighteenth centuries, this generally meant sending the offender to America or Australia. Paupers as well as criminals faced transportation during this period; the British Empire populated at least some of its dominions by sending its "undesirables" to new homes.

About the only sanction specifically aimed at juveniles was the decision to bind a young offender out as an apprentice, a practice pursued in the colonies as well as in England. English law had long provided for the binding out of paupers; it was easy to extend the practice to delinquents as well. However, binding out seems to have been less frequently used by the courts than the more common forms of corporal punishment.

Capital Punishment

In the early modern era, courts could impose capital punishment on any young offender over the age of seven, including those between seven and 14. Moreover, before 1800, English and American law recognized as many as 200 crimes as capital offenses. Children were subject to those laws and could be sentenced to death.

Occasionally, they were. In 1690, for example, a 14-year-old boy, found guilty of picking pockets and of robbery, was sentenced to die and was hanged. In 1735, a 10-year-old girl, an apprentice who stole some money from her master's house, was killed. Such executions do not appear to have been common, however. Very young offenders, those of nine or younger would usually have their sentences commuted to transportation; many others were simply pardoned. For older youths, though, the carrying out of a sentence of death was not unusual. In 1785, for example, 18 of 20 offenders executed in London were under 18 years of age. One recent study suggests that more than 100 offenders under the age of 18 were put to death in the United States between 1800 and 1899, most in the South and West. Therefore, executions were not unknown for young offenders, even into the nineteenth century.

Thus, in the English common law tradition, young offenders could receive lenient treatment, but for those over the age of seven leniency was by no means guaranteed. Those who were accused of crimes and prosecuted for them went through the same court procedures and, if found guilty, faced the same punishments as adults. In keeping with what we saw in Chapter 2, such an approach to juvenile crime, even if it recognized at least the potential legal incapacity of the very young offender, was something very different from the ideas about childhood and delinquency that were beginning to take shape in early nineteenth-century America.

TOWARD A LEGAL RECOGNITION OF JUVENILE DELINQUENCY

Early in the nineteenth century, this similarity of treatment began to be modified. In keeping with the increasing celebration of childhood, many people found it unthinkable, as we have noted in Chapter 2, that children—even those who had committed crimes—should be treated no differently from adults before the law. As we noted, these early nineteenth century reformers had begun to focus on the moral and environmental dimensions of juvenile crime, particularly as it appeared among the children of the urban poor. They sought to incorporate their new understanding of juvenile crime into their efforts to respond to it.

For many of these early nineteenth century men and women, the best approach to juvenile delinquency was a preventive approach, and they gave great attention to creating institutions that would help prevent children deemed to be at risk of running afoul of the law. Creating "charity schools," "infant schools," and similar institutions, they hoped to inculcate discipline and moral character in the children of the poor, providing those children with the virtues they believed were unlikely to come from home and family.

This effort took its most ambitious form, beginning very early in the nineteenth century, in the creation of public school systems, chiefly in the urban centers of the northeastern United States. From the beginning, public schools were seen as important not only because of the education they could provide, but also because they could help "civilize" poorer children by helping them learn the ideals Americans were supposed to prize. Hence, many felt, schools could serve as the first line of defense against juvenile crime and delinquency.

The Houses of Refuge

Early on, every reformer learned the hard lesson that, whatever the potential of public education, juvenile crime could not be wholly eradicated. There remained "vicious" youths, as they were often termed, who turned to criminal behavior. However, the reformers' approach to the problem was not what had been addressed in the common law, which focused on legal issues of capacity and prosecution. For many men and women, the question had become one of how to respond to juvenile offenders in a way that respected the unique character of the child. One of the earliest answers—and one of the most influential—lay in the early nineteenth-century movement in various cities to create what were called "houses of refuge."

To understand this movement, it is necessary to remember that juveniles guilty of crime were subject to roughly the same punishments as those facing adult offenders. This continued to be the case in the early nineteenth century, when imprisonment came to replace corporal punishment in the criminal justice systems of both England and America. Imprisonment was viewed as more humane and as offering the possibility of rehabilitation for those embarking on criminal careers.

In the early days, this approach was readily applied to juveniles and adults alike. As new prisons were built, they housed young offenders as well as adults. Thus, in New York in 1820, an eight-year-old boy was convicted of burglarizing a jewelry store, and the judge sentenced him to three years in the state prison. Although he may have been younger than most, such a sentence was common for offenders under 16 during the decade. Similarly, when Philadelphia's innovative and noted Eastern State Penitentiary was completed in the late 1820s, it housed inmates as young as 12. Although there were some differences in the treatment of children in prison (e.g., boys were not put to hard labor), they were still allowed to mix with adult convicts as members of the general prison population.

Reformers, given their environmentalist and moralistic approaches to delinquency, found this last issue to be especially repugnant. Mixing with adult convicts meant that young offenders were being exposed to the worst possible influences. As one group declared, "it is vain to expect that a sentence condemning a child to the Penitentiary will have any beneficial effect on his morals; on the contrary it is probable that his vicious inclinations will be strengthened by association with experienced Villains."[3] Despite the "viciousness" of some young delinquents, they needed to be separated from adult criminals. Only in this way could children who had gone wrong be removed from an evil environment and, thus, remade into good and useful citizens.

Although there were some English precedents for institutions for juvenile offenders, dating back to about 1730 (notable particularly in the efforts of John Howard in the 1770), these had been isolated at best and had not been adopted in America. Nevertheless, in the early years of the nineteenth century, an interest began to develop in founding such institutions, ultimately to be embodied in the creation of the houses of refuge.

The New York House of Refuge

The pioneering effort to create a house of refuge took place in New York where, under the leadership of John Griscom and Thomas Eddy, a group began serious discussions of what they called the "perishing and dangerous classes" of the city. The group quickly turned its attention to the problem of juvenile delinquency and the need to save juvenile delinquents from the influences that led to crime.

By 1823, Griscom had developed enough public concern about the issue to found the Society for the Reformation of Juvenile Delinquents, intended to agitate politicians at both the city and the state levels for the establishment of institutions devoted solely to the correction of juvenile offenders. A house of refuge would provide "a course of treatment, that will afford a prompt and energetic corrective of their vicious propensities, and hold out every possible inducement to reformation and good conduct,"[4] its proponents said. Their efforts met with success, and on January 1, 1825, with six boys and three girls, the New York House of Refuge began its operations.

Within a few years, comparable houses were established elsewhere. Boston established a House of Reformation in 1826; Philadelphia established its own House of Refuge in 1828. All these institutions were similar in organization and purpose. Each was founded by private individuals and, though receiving some state support, was primarily dependent on private money and management. In addition, while all of these houses of refuge began by taking in as inmates only young people convicted of crimes or vagrancy, they broadened their scope within a few years to accept those who appeared likely to fall into crime—orphans or abandoned children—and, in a few cases, children found unmanageable by their parents. Children could be assigned to the houses by police courts, public agencies, or even at the request of their parents. They were given indeterminate sentences. They were to stay until the managers believed a reformation had been accomplished, and not for any predetermined length of time.

Order and Discipline in the Houses of Refuge

In the houses of refuge, inmates were housed according to what was called the "congregate" system, in large dormitories with separate wings for boys and girls. Daily life was regulated by a strict, regular order of discipline, both as a measure designed to assist in rehabilitation and as one necessary to keep the institution functioning. Sponsors believed that all inmates needed to learn regular habits of labor. Boys were set to work caning chairs or making nails, among other tasks; girls were taught to perform "domestic" tasks. Part of the day was also set aside for academic education.

Inmates were also classified according to their conduct, various "grades" receiving differing privileges and privations. Those in the lowest grade in the Boston house, for example, were limited to a diet of bread and water, forced to wear shackles, or placed in solitary confinement. A few even received more imaginative sanctions: A child making "improper use of his hands" might have them bandaged; one with a roving eye might have them bandaged, as well. Those whose behavior placed them at the top, by contrast, were actually allowed to leave the house on their own, to wear "the undress uniform," and to receive other privileges.[5]

A variety of children were committed to the houses of refuge. Some were guilty of crimes (for boys and girls alike, mostly theft). Some were viewed as potential criminals. The guiding principle behind any committal was a belief on the part of city officials that the child could not receive a proper upbringing from his or her own parents. This may have been the most significant feature of the house of refuge, and the one with the farthest-reaching implications.

Parens Patriae

A key assumption made by the house-of-refuge system was that the state, in certain situations, had a right to intervene in the life of a family and assume responsibility for raising a child. Based on the recommendation of police and other agencies, or even on the wishes of their parents, children could be committed to an institution without regard to due process of the law and certainly without regard to the usual right of trial by jury. Moreover, because sentences to the houses of refuge were indeterminate, parents were forced to relinquish all control over their children. The state thus assumed enormous powers under the house of refuge system.

The justification for this assumption of powers was both formal and traditional, elaborated in the United States in the invocation of a legal doctrine known as *parens patriae*. A doctrine of uncertain origin, but with roots in the Middle Ages, *parens patriae* was an assertion of the right of the state to assume the wardship of a child when the natural parents or testamentary guardians were adjudged unfit to perform their duties. The doctrine had developed mainly in response to litigation having to do with the rights of infants to inherit property, and was invoked to allow state intervention to protect those rights.

During the sixteenth and seventeenth centuries, the doctrine was greatly extended. England had passed numerous laws for the regulation of the poor during this tumultuous period of history, and the king as *pater patriae* was given the duty of protector of charities in the country. The so-called English "poor laws" of this period empowered the state to separate children from parents who were unable to support them and to apprentice those children. The British colonies in North America usually incorporated such statutes into their bodies of laws as well. This role was subsequently extended into many areas of English life, even recreation. By the eighteenth century, *parens patriae*, understood as the right of the state to intervene in private affairs, was well established, and it continued to be applied with increasing scope to family matters. This meant that, "The Crown, as *parens patriae*," it was declared, "was the Supreme Guardian and the Superintendent over all Infants," and, hence, could intervene in the family on a child's behalf.[6]

Ex Parte Crouse

Parens patriae remained an important doctrine in English law. After the United States won independence, it was incorporated into legal tradition in the laws of the nation, informing much of the effort to create a distinctive body of American family law regarding inheritance, custody, and other issues. It was in America, moreover—in part as an extension of these developments—that *parens patriae* was first invoked in relation to juvenile delinquency. Its invocation grew directly out of a case involving one of the early houses of refuge. The decision in the case, rendered in 1838, was known as *Ex parte Crouse*. Briefly, the decision arose when the mother of a young girl named Mary Ann Crouse had her daughter committed to the Philadelphia House of Refuge as an incorrigible child. Mary Ann's father, upon learning of this, immediately filed a petition of *habeas corpus*, which was denied. He thereupon sued on constitutional grounds, charging that his daughter had been imprisoned without jury trial and should be released. The court denied the suit, approving Mary Ann's committal, and, more significantly, denying that rights of due process applied to children. The court justified its denial on grounds of *parens patriae*.

According to the court, the state had a major duty to children under the doctrine of *parens patriae*. Mary Ann, the judges declared, "had been snatched from a course which must have ended in confirmed depravity: and not only is the restraint of her person lawful, but it would have been an act of extreme cruelty to release her from it." The court added, "May not the natural parents, when unequal to the task of education, or unworthy of it, be superseded by the *parent patriae*, of common guardian of the community?" Its decision answered that the community could.

As we shall see later, *parens patriae* did not go unchallenged. In the post-Civil War years, in particular, the doctrine received strong criticism, and there were even a few judicial decisions undermining its authority. In our own time, as we shall also see, the doctrine has been severely tested. However, in the era in which the foundations were laid for an American juvenile justice system, *parens patriae* provided a strong legal justification for developing practices.

SOME APPROACHES TO JUVENILE DELINQUENCY

The houses of refuge in New York, Philadelphia, and Boston thus played an important role in the development of an American juvenile justice system. This development was to expand through the first half of the nineteenth century, as other states followed the house-of-refuge model by creating such institutions as "reform schools" to deal with their own juvenile offenders. Most states outside the South had established reform schools prior to the Civil War; the southern states followed suit by the beginning of the twentieth century. These schools also housed inmates in dormitories, employing what was called the "congregate system," operating in a structured environment that offered both vocational and academic educational programs. All of them relied on indeterminate sentencing and had the moral uplift of the inmate as a central goal. However, by mid-century, some major problems had begun to appear with the house-of-refuge model, and severe criticisms were leveled against it.

Criticisms focused on a number of issues. For one, although these institutions were supposed to be rehabilitative, they often appeared to be more like prisons than places of refuge. In the Boston House of Reformation, the proportion of juveniles adjudged guilty of crimes, as opposed to those considered incorrigible or otherwise "at risk," grew steadily. The New York House of Refuge, within a few years of its opening, became distinctly prison-like, surrounded by high stone walls and including buildings with individual jail cells.

More troubling was the apparent failure of these institutions to bring about high levels of reformation. All were characterized by severe disciplinary problems, including frequent escapes and abusive, even violent behavior toward teachers. As a result, house staff became increasingly dependent on corporal punishment to enforce discipline, and despite the intentions of the founders, such punishment was often brutal. One fugitive from the New York House of Refuge, after being recaptured, was whipped and then placed in solitary confinement on a bread-and-water diet for three days. No less common was the use of the "cat" (cat-o'-nine-tails, a whip used for corporal punishment) or a rattan on recalcitrant young inmates, much as occurred in adult prisons. In Boston, the House of Reformation's reputation for brutality became so noteworthy that city magistrates refused to commit children to it.

Finally, these institutions did an inadequate job of separating criminal inmates from those who had been admitted for other reasons. Thus, the prison-like refuges and reformatories, contrary to intent, were perpetuating the same problems they had been intended to solve because they mixed the corruptible with the already corrupt. They were becoming schools for crime rather than for reformation.

In large part, the failure of the early institutions for juvenile offenders grew out of the difficulties inherent in the emerging conceptions of childhood and youth discussed in Chapter 2. They were built on a growing admiration for childhood's natural virtues, but their clientele rarely conformed to the ideals presented by childrearing literature. When they failed to respond as ideals had predicted, the houses' managers reacted harshly. The various problems associated with the houses of refuge and their descendants, the reform schools, led many Americans to seek solid alternatives to the house-of-refuge model.

The Cottage System

One of the most significant of such alternatives was developed in the 1850s, taking shape in what was known as the "family system" or "cottage system." Introduced in the United States with the Massachusetts Industrial School for Girls (which began operation in 1854) and the Ohio Reform School (1857), the cottage system sought to depart from the prison-like "congregate system" prevalent in older institutions. Rather than house delinquents in large dormitory facilities, bringing them together under strict routines in classrooms and workshops, the family system placed from one to three dozen inmates with similar characteristics in separate small houses under the supervision of a surrogate father or mother. The "family" thus created was to work, live, and attend school together, mixing only rarely with the inmates placed in other "families."

Proponents of the cottage system believed it would provide opportunities for closer supervision of inmates and for better quality attention. Because the congregate system appeared to be highly impersonal, despite the best intentions, proponents of the cottage system argued that their approach would more closely approximate the kind of family atmosphere and guidance delinquents needed most. In the language of *parens patriae*, they argued that the cottage system would enable the state to come as near the idea of a well-regulated, honest family as possible, under the circumstances.

The cottage system had great impact on American approaches to delinquency. By the end of the nineteenth century, it had become the dominant model for institutions aimed at juvenile reform. It was not, however, an unalloyed success. In the pioneering Massachusetts Industrial School for Girls, problems became apparent fairly quickly.

The Massachusetts institution, in Lancaster, began with the kinds of ideas about delinquency that had been developing for 50 years, coupled with the idea that girls from poor families faced special dangers because of the weakness of their sex. The cottage system was thought to be especially suited to respond to such dangers because of its family-like structure.

The issue soon arose, however, of how to group the girls in the various cottages. Girls were sent to Lancaster for many reasons. Some were abused children, sent to Lancaster for their own safety. Others were "incorrigibles," placed into custody at the request of their parents. Still others had been found guilty of crimes, usually stealing or prostitution.

In theory, all were children and, thus, reformable. Thus, they were grouped together without regard to background.

The predictable problems appeared. Some of the girls appeared to be "hardened" when they arrived, and, thus, likely to corrupt the more innocent among them. This made the philosophy behind Lancaster difficult to maintain. Relatively soon after the school's founding, those responsible for it began to see its inmates more as delinquents than as children and to stress the punitive, custodial character of the institution over its redemptive purposes. The cottage system, as an institutional alternative to older house-of-refuge models, ultimately did not go very far in the direction that its proponents had envisioned.

The Reformatory-Prison

One final institutional alternative that should be noted (though it, too, was to meet with scant success) was the reformatory-prison model pioneered by reformer Zebulon Brockway at Elmira, New York, in 1876. The Elmira reformatory actually bridged the gap between juvenile and adult offenders, focusing on first-time offenders between the ages of 16 and 30 years, those deemed too old for juvenile reformatories and too young for prison. However, for much of its history, prior to 1899, Elmira should probably be considered a juvenile institution, because the majority of those it treated were between the ages of 16 and 20.

Brockway's philosophy in establishing Elmira was to focus more on the offender than the offense, and more on treatment than punishment in addressing the problems of juvenile crime. The Elmira system, as developed in the late 1870s and early 1880s, involved the use of a diagnostic interview with every new inmate, which attempted to identify the sources of each individual's criminal behavior. Treatment included basic education, religious instruction, and labor, in an effort to instill good habits of discipline and industry. Upon release, each inmate was to spend a period on parole, proving his ability to function in the world outside the prison's gates.

Between 1877 and 1899, the Elmira system was widely copied, with reformatories for "youthful offenders" opening in at least 10 states and Elmira methods coming to play a role in the correctional institutions of other states. This system appeared to offer a useful alternative to the failed methods put into place in earlier years of the century. Here, too, however, problems quickly emerged. For one thing, despite the reformers' intentions, inmates were never so tractable as they had hoped. As had happened in other institutions, corporal punishment— sometimes quite brutal—came to be a primary form of discipline, heightening inmate resistance and further diverting the institutional focus away from reformation and toward simple control. Nevertheless, as we shall see, the reformatory's focus on the offender rather than the offense was to have significant influence on thinking about juvenile crime as the nineteenth century drew to a close—despite the practical failure of the Elmira model itself.

Charles Loring Brace: The "Placing-Out" System

Given the failures of the institutional models, other reformers of the period went somewhat further in their efforts to move away from a prison-like approach to dealing with juvenile delinquency. Among the most influential was Charles Loring Brace, founder of the Children's Aid Society of New York. Among its many projects, the society (incorporated in 1856) organized workshops for teaching trades and establishing lodging houses for homeless "street boys" in the city. Its most ambitious project, though, was an elaborate "placing-out" system designed to remove unfortunate young men and women from the urban slums, placing them in new homes in which they might be subject to more wholesome influences. These young people were to be removed from the urban environment altogether and placed in the homes of rural families, some living quite far to the west.

Although his motives were complex, and have aroused some controversy among historians, Brace clearly believed that the nature of a child's family had much to do with the fate of the child, and that poor, urban parents were by and large unfit to raise their children. In addition, Brace felt that there was and would always be a need for agricultural labor. Those boys and girls placed in farm families would not only be saved from their present environment, but would enter useful lives and learn skills that would stand them well in the future. Brace believed that there was virtue in rural life, which he saw as a simpler life, uncorrupted by the economic and social problems of America's cities. Finally, he was happy to get what he saw as a class of potential troublemakers out of the city.

The importance of this last motive should not be underestimated. Though he found much to admire in individual slum children, Brace titled his account of his life's work "The Dangerous Classes of New York," and he meant the appellation to be taken seriously. Juvenile delinquents, in his view, were not simply unfortunate but positively dangerous to the very fabric of society. "Let but law lift its hand from them for a season, or let the civilizing influences of American life fail to reach them," he declared, "and, if the opportunity offered, we should see an explosion from this class which might leave this city in ashes and blood."[7] He likened people in New York to those who had led a mid-century "communist outbreak" in France; even if such a cataclysm was unlikely in the United States, he said, it was enough to note that young delinquents, reaching adulthood, would have the right to vote. Hence, to him, their reform was essential and their presence in the city a cause for concern.

Brace's program was not the only placing-out effort at mid-century. It had been anticipated (on a modest scale) by youth workers in Boston as early as the mid-1830s. It was followed by similar efforts in Philadelphia and in Boston. All such efforts were aimed at sending young people to rural areas in midwestern states such as Missouri, Iowa, Michigan, and Indiana. Some were sent as far south as Florida and as far west as Texas and California. In all, during the nineteenth century, more than 92,000 young people were "placed out" by Brace's society alone.

Most of those sent west under various placing-out programs were deemed to be at risk rather than guilty of criminal acts, although a few juvenile offenders were part of the mix. For many, the experience was a good one. A number grew up to be independent and prosperous farmers, and some went beyond that. By 1901, Children's Aid Society records showed that its alumni included 19 clergy members, 17 physicians, 26 bankers, 34 lawyers, and three governors of states or territories.

Still, the placing-out system was not without problems. There is evidence that some poor parents used the program as a quasi-employment agency for their children (which is an interesting commentary on Brace's own ideas about the lack of motivation in the urban poor). From the other side, it also seems that many of the farm families who received children from what came to be known as "orphan trains" saw the placing out-program as a way to get cheap help. One veteran likened the arrival of the children into their new community to a "slave auction." He recalled how, upon arriving at their destination, the young people "stood on the courthouse steps . . . and people felt their muscles," concluding that "a lot of folks were looking for free farm labor."[8]

The program also aroused opposition. Some western communities felt they were being asked to absorb the big cities' criminal element, and (not surprisingly) a few of those sent west did commit crimes, ending up in western reform schools or even prison. More opposition came from the Catholic Church, which feared efforts on the part of the society to draw urban Catholic young people into the rural Protestant fold. Despite such problems, placing-out continued through the nineteenth century and, on a reduced scale, into the third decade of the twentieth.

Other Nineteenth-Century Experiments

The placing-out system was not the only nineteenth-century approach to juvenile delinquency that might be labeled "anti-institutional." Influential efforts by such reformers as Samuel Gridley Howe and William R. George similarly sought new directions in responding to juvenile offenders and young people at risk.

Howe was among those troubled by the character of houses of refuge and of state-funded reform schools, which he saw as little better than prisons. He felt that most juvenile offenders committed to such institutions were more likely to be harmed than rehabilitated. Beginning in the 1860s, Howe proposed several alternatives to existing approaches. Working in Massachusetts, he initially sought to create a plan for leasing small farms to be colonized by young offenders. Failing this, he proposed that the state place juvenile offenders with families who would agree, for a stipend, to give them a proper upbringing.

Another institution that gained importance during the latter part of the nineteenth century was the military school. Unlike other institutions, which focused primarily on the needs of the urban poor, military schools served essentially as private reform schools for the children of middle- and upper-class families—children whose behavioral problems caused difficulties at home. Few were actually delinquents; the presence of tough cases was something the schools themselves did not want (although it is likely that, had some of them *been* poor, they probably would have been characterized as delinquent in the setting of late nineteenth-century America). The schools were often advertised as institutions that could prevent problem children from becoming delinquents, and this had much to do with their success.

Perhaps the most innovative response to juvenile delinquency was developed near the end of the century. William R. "Daddy" George was a New York businessman whose work in the city's slums gave him an interest in the growing problem of youth gangs. At one point, he recruited his own "Law and Order Gang" to try to combat the problems he saw on the streets. In 1890, he founded a "fresh air camp" in rural New York for the benefit of Manhattan street children. However, he soon came to believe that the camp promoted dependence rather than the self-discipline and self-reliance that could serve as antidotes to delinquency. By 1895, he had changed the camp into a year-round "junior republic" in which everything was to be paid for by the campers' labor and the campers were given the responsibility of electing their own representatives to devise and administer the laws.

The George Junior Republic was administered like a self-contained little village. There were stores, a post office, a farm, a courthouse, and a "capitol." All were run by the campers, who achieved varying levels of wealth based on their own individual "industry." Those who broke the rules were forced to answer to a court of their peers; those found guilty were sentenced to hard labor without wages, or to a camp prison guarded by other "citizens" of the republic.

The George Junior Republic was not without its detractors. Anti-institutional and contrary to the dominant, paternalistic ideologies of the houses of refuge and the reform schools, the junior republic received strong criticism and opposition from state charitable institutions and agencies. Internal troubles also plagued the republic. It did not survive in anything but name beyond the end of World War I.

Nevertheless, during its heyday around the turn of the century, the George Junior Republic attracted a great deal of interest. President Theodore Roosevelt was an ardent admirer of the republic, and the program inspired others in the United States. A few traditional reformatories introduced forms of self-government derived from George's model. Whatever the ultimate failure of George's republic, it was an important expression of the continuing sense among many Americans of a need for genuinely distinctive measures in the handling of juvenile delinquency.

Probation

Another approach to juvenile delinquency was developed during the first half of the nineteenth century: probation. Although probation became a major component of the juvenile justice system in the twentieth century, its beginnings were inauspicious. In the early 1840s, shoemaker John Augustus was visiting one of Boston's municipal courts and met a man who had been brought before the court as a "common drunkard." Augustus, convinced of the man's desire to reform, urged the judge to release him to Augustus's care, which was done. At Augustus's urging, the man "signed the pledge" and adopted an "industrious and sober" life. Augustus then began, as a regular practice, bailing out and supervising others brought before the court on charges of drunkenness.

During 1843, Augustus began to broaden his efforts to those charged with other offenses. This included two little girls, ages eight and 10, and an 11-year-old boy, all of whom had been charged with stealing. In these cases, too, Augustus's supervision was successful. Despite some opposition from the police, he began to deal frequently with juvenile offenders. By 1846, he had arranged with the Police Court in Boston to continue the cases of about 30 children from nine to 16 years of age, placing them under his supervision and (with the court's cooperation) administering a regular system of probation. Boston authorities were pleased with the scheme: the children showed improvement and Augustus's efforts were less expensive than building new institutions. By 1852, he had supervised the probation of 116 boys under the age of 16, and about 80 percent of them had avoided further trouble with the law.

Augustus died in 1859, but other volunteer probation officers carried on his work until 1869, when the state of Massachusetts began to supervise the practice. The legislature created the office of the state visiting agent, and gave its officer ultimate responsibility for supervision of all children who had come under the care of the state. This included the responsibility to appear "in behalf of the child" at hearings held for the purpose of committing children to state reform schools. In a related action in 1870, the state provided for separate trials for juvenile offenders. Probation thus became a regular part of Massachusetts's approach to juvenile delinquency; by the end of the century, five other states had passed similar probation laws to address juvenile crime, creating an important precedent for practices soon to be widely institutionalized in the United States.

THE FOUNDING OF THE JUVENILE COURT

Although the development of a distinctive juvenile justice system started with the house of refuge movement, some of the most significant practices and approaches to juvenile crime did not take shape until the end of the nineteenth century, during the period historians call the Progressive era. Extending roughly from the 1880s to the beginning of World War I, the Progressive era saw an unprecedented wave of immigration and a quickening pace of urbanization that made many Americans feel a need for significant broad-gauged reform, including reform in regard to juvenile crime and delinquency. Intellectual developments, especially the "discovery" of adolescence, made the need for such reforms seem all the more pressing.

As we saw in earlier discussions, whatever the strength of innovations in juvenile justice dating from the beginning of the nineteenth century, such institutions as the houses of refuge underwent mounting criticism through that century, prompting a series of alternative responses to juvenile crime. By the close of the century, most reformers were convinced that existing approaches, including reform schools, were ineffective. Increasingly, they sought to "decriminalize" delinquency, still further treating the offender instead of the offense, and removing young men and women from the criminal justice system altogether. Their efforts ultimately culminated in the

Judge Reggie Walton describes his experience as a young man in the juvenile justice system during a news conference in 1999 celebrating the 100th anniversary of the Illinois juvenile court. *(AP Photo)*

founding of special "juvenile courts." The first of these, founded in Chicago in 1899, was the predecessor of the juvenile courts now operating in every state in the union.

The Problems of Juvenile Justice in Illinois

In the 1890s, Chicago was a city of more than one million people, its population having more than doubled in the preceding decade (chiefly as a result of immigration). Urban growth had brought about a shocking increase in juvenile delinquency, and the city demonstrated a poor ability to respond to that increase.

Chicago faced special difficulties in regard to juvenile delinquency. Its reform school, established in 1855, had been destroyed by the great Chicago fire of 1871. The school had already been in trouble, plagued (like many others) by a bad reputation. Its efforts had also come under scrutiny as a result of one of the few nineteenth-century court decisions actually to challenge *parens patriae*: *People ex rel. O'Connell v. Turner* (1870). This was a decision by which Daniel O'Connell, committed to the reform school for preventive reasons rather than as a result of having been accused of a crime, was ordered released on the ground that the state had no right to interfere in the relationship between parent and child in the absence of any criminal act.

After *O'Connell*, Illinois courts lost all jurisdiction over young people deemed to be at risk, and delinquents had to be treated within the confines of the criminal justice system. Those arrested were held in jail with adult prisoners and were subject to the same criminal proceedings as adults; those found guilty were sentenced to either the city prison or the Cook County jail. There was a state reform school at Pontiac for more serious cases, but even that institution was considered little more than a "minor penitentiary." In 1898, the year before the juvenile court was founded, 575 boys were in the county jail and 1,983 in the city prison.

Reformers saw several reasons to be concerned about the situation. For one thing, by all accounts, conditions for children held in jail were appalling. Not only was there the traditional problem of mixing children with adult criminals, but reformers found problems of filth, vermin, and psychological terror as well. Because they could not bring themselves to commit a young person to such conditions, many judges let young offenders off with no sentence at all. Children became brutalized by a stint in jail. They might also be encouraged in crime by knowing that, even if convicted, there was a good chance of facing no punishment at all.

In keeping with the developing ideas about juvenile delinquency discussed in Chapter 2, reformers sought not only to change the conditions of custody for juvenile offenders, but argued that severe problems were created by young offenders' having to face the criminal justice system at all. Doing so, they claimed, was to place the "foul taint of the convict" on those who had, perhaps temporarily, run afoul of the law. The problem was, then, to find ways of treating young offenders without putting the taint of criminality on them.

Agitation for major change came as early as the 1880s, led chiefly by the Chicago Woman's Club, which sought, initially, to add matrons to the jail staff and sponsored a school for boys awaiting trial or serving sentences in jail. As early as 1892, the Woman's Club's Jail Committee suggested a special juvenile court, and by 1895, they sponsored a bill to provide for a separate court and probation staff. By 1898, the movement had become quite strong, and, in early 1899, a juvenile court bill passed the Illinois legislature. The court went into operation later that year.

The Illinois Juvenile Court Act of 1899 gave the court broad purposes in keeping with *parens patriae*. The obvious constitutional problems posed by the earlier *O'Connell* decision were simply ignored, raised by neither the legislature nor the legal community. The act specified that "any reputable person" having knowledge of a child under 16 "who appears to be either neglected, dependent, or delinquent" could have the child taken before the court to determine the necessity of state supervision. Dependent or neglected children could be committed to an appropriate institution or to a foster home. Delinquents could be placed on probation or committed to one of several training institutions for delinquent boys or girls or to a reformatory. The act forbade the confinement of children in any institution that also housed "adult convicts."

No less important was the nature of court proceedings embodied in the Illinois juvenile court. In the court itself, procedure was to be very different from that accorded adult defendants in a criminal proceeding. Procedural informality was to mark the court. What one advocate called the "solemn farce" of a jury trial was to be avoided. Hearings were to involve a judge, the child, his or her parents, and a probation officer who served as an expert on the specific needs of the individual. The usual criteria of "due process" did not apply because, in the words of one of the court's founders, no longer did the court ask the juvenile, "Are you guilty or innocent. . .? We ask at this time, 'What are you? How have you become what you are? Whither are you tending and how can we direct you?'"[9] The purpose was to be less a matter of determining a juvenile's guilt than a matter of addressing the need for the state to assume guardianship. Accordingly, the juvenile court relied heavily on reports not only from probation officers but also from social workers, psychologists, and other professionals.

As the act also made clear, the new juvenile court sought to make heavy use of probation rather than incarceration in the disposition of cases. Ideally, a young offender would be returned to his or her family but, rather than being left to the care of the family alone, that care would be supervised by a probation officer with broad powers of surveillance and intervention. Thus, the probation officer came to play a crucial role in the Chicago juvenile justice system, both in the proceedings of the court and the efforts at treatment and rehabilitation that the court hoped to apply.

One should not overemphasize the uniqueness of the Illinois juvenile court. Historians have noted that its significance resides mainly in the way in which it codified and elaborated on existing ideas and practices, giving an unprecedented legal sanction for *parens patriae* and coordinating the efforts of existing agencies within a single structure. Nevertheless, the creation of the court was a major episode in the history of American delinquency, one with profound and continuing implications.

The Diffusion of the Juvenile Court

Ben Lindsey and the Denver Juvenile Court

The Illinois court, once established, was one important inspiration for the diffusion of the juvenile court idea to other states. Perhaps equally important was the influence of one of the most significant proponents of the juvenile court, Ben B. Lindsey, a Denver judge noted for his use of a personal touch with juvenile offenders and his missionary zeal for the juvenile court idea. In 1901, Lindsey was appointed judge of the county court and was confronted with a case of larceny involving a frightened young boy. Placing the boy on probation, Lindsey began, as he said, to "think over this business of punishing infants."[10] Locating a section of a Colorado school law defining the habitual truant and the incorrigible child as "a juvenile disorderly person," Lindsey decided he had found the basis for a new approach: "A juvenile disorderly person! Not a criminal to be punished under the criminal law, but a ward of the state as *parens patriae*."[11] Lindsey requested the district attorney thereafter to file complaints against children under the Colorado school law. Thus began the Denver juvenile court.

Lindsey's court captured many of the ideals that had informed the Illinois act, and Lindsey himself was influenced by the Chicago model. The hallmark of his court was its informality, as Lindsey sought to establish rapport with the young people brought before him. His goals were to keep children out of the institutions of the criminal justice system, including the state reform school, and to rely heavily on probation. He even established his own Saturday morning "report sessions," in which he met with probationers and discussed reports on their behavior from probation officers and even teachers. Through such mechanisms, Lindsey sought to turn the legal doctrine of *parens patriae* into a mandate for a "parental" approach to those he viewed as society's victims rather than as criminals.

The Establishment of the Juvenile Court in Other States

Drawing on the Chicago model, and encouraged by such ardent champions as Lindsey, juvenile courts spread rapidly throughout the United States. Wisconsin and New York established juvenile courts in 1901; Ohio and Maryland in 1902. By 1912, 22 states had juvenile court laws, and by 1928, only two states lacked some kind of juvenile court system. The last of these, Wyoming, finally fell into line in 1945.

Juvenile court systems were not uniform throughout the states. Most states sought to define delinquency, neglect, and dependency in their juvenile court acts, but the definitions were often vague and contradictory. This lack of clarity ultimately became a major issue in juvenile justice policy. Separate detention was provided for with the establishment of juvenile courts in many states, but not everywhere. North Dakota did not require separate detention until 1969; Maine waited until 1977. Provisions for separate hearings and the encouragement of probation were, however, prevalent everywhere.

The early years of the juvenile courts were marked by great optimism about their potential. Some historians, influenced by conflict theory perspectives (discussed in Chapter 7), have raised some questions about the extent to which, in Chicago and elsewhere, those who tended to work hardest for the courts' creation came primarily from the affluent and powerful part of the community. At least a few have suggested that the juvenile court movement might best be understood as an effort by the wealthy to control the urban poor, to preserve the existing class system, and to create a more manageable labor force.

Such charges are not without merit, given the composition of the main body of juvenile justice reformers and what they themselves said about their motives and purposes. However, they clearly represent only one side of the story. The conditions to which reformers were responding were genuinely bad, and while some were motivated by a kind of social conservatism, others were clearly driven by justifiable humanitarian concerns. Moreover, whatever the source of the movement, the Illinois court (and others) achieved popularity in the urban communities toward which they were directed. Many of the earliest referrals to the court in Chicago, as would be the case elsewhere, came from the parents themselves.

EARLY DEVELOPMENTS IN THE JUVENILE COURTS

Not only were the courts popular wherever they were established, but they also seemed to offer a genuine alternative to the treatment of delinquency as a species of criminality—and to provide a field for the reform of young people and even of society. As the courts began to evolve, they continued to build on the assumptions and ideals that lay behind their creation, particularly by strengthening the doctrine of *parens patriae* and its influence on American responses to delinquency.

The juvenile court laws were often supported by other legislation based on *parens patriae*. The first decade of the twentieth century saw the passage of "parental delinquency" laws that specified "contributing to the delinquency of a minor" as offenses for which parents could be held liable. Colorado, with Lindsey's encouragement, provided jail sentences and fines for parents who neglected their children. Kansas parents could be fined up to $1,000 or imprisoned for contributing to delinquency in their children.

This period also saw the rise of family courts in several American cities and states. These courts were intended to deal not only with delinquency but also with the family problems that seemed to contribute to delinquency. Here, too, supported by *parens patriae*, the state asserted its right to intervene in (and even supervise) the affairs of individual families.

The doctrine of *parens patriae* was also established more fully in the legal community, legitimizing the deliberate rejection of adult due process concerns that served as the foundation for the Chicago model. A 1905 Pennsylvania decision, *Commonwealth v. Fisher*, cited *parens patriae* as the doctrine upholding the legal foundations of the juvenile court in that state. Similarly, in 1908, the Supreme Court of Idaho in *Ex parte Sharpe* upheld the state's juvenile court act in language clearly based on *parens patriae*, noting that the "protection of 'inalienable rights,' guaranteed by the Constitution" could in no way apply to a minor in a situation characterized by "idleness, ignorance, crime, indigence or any kindred dispositions or inclinations."[12] Although there were a few contrary opinions, for the most part, the courts supported both the juvenile court idea and the doctrine of *parens patriae* on which it was based. The idea, as put forward in a 1933 New York case, *People v. Lewis*,[13] was that because the goal of the juvenile court was one of helping rather than punishing, constitutional safeguards of due process were unnecessary.

Problems of the Early Juvenile Courts

This consensus does not mean, however, that the early juvenile courts lacked critics. Several major concerns appeared frequently in discussions of the courts. One of these was that the courts, whatever their ideals, really did little to change the treatment of juvenile offend-ers. Despite the reliance on probation, many delinquents continued to be sentenced to state institutions, and these were little affected in their character or operations by the establishment of juvenile courts. Beyond that, an investigation conducted in 1918 by the United States Children's Bureau (created in 1912 to address matters affecting the welfare of American children) found that many young offenders continued to be confined with adult prisoners in adult facilities, even where such con-finement was in violation of state law.

Moreover, given the need to deal with alleged criminal activity, most courts did in fact focus mainly on questions of guilt or innocence, though without the guarantees of due process found in adult criminal proceedings. In many places, the atmosphere of the juvenile court was far from familial, as juvenile court judges relied heavily on threats, coercion, and short-term imprisonment in trying to render juveniles cooperative.

Many critics argued that the juvenile courts were failing to achieve their primary purposes: the prevention of delinquency and the refor-mation of youths who had already been found guilty of delinquent behavior. The problem of recidivism was hotly debated in the early days of the courts, and continued to be in subsequent years. Surveys from the 1930s showed recidivism rates as high as 88 percent among those who had been through juvenile court.

Criticism focused on the juvenile courts' inability to engage in the proper treatment of delinquents, especially as sociologists developed more sophisticated ideas about deviance and delinquency. Despite the consensus in the higher courts on the legitimacy of *parens patriae* as embodied in the juvenile courts, a few legal scholars had already begun to condemn the resulting denial of due process to juveniles accused of crime.

Finally, despite the goal of removing the taint of criminality from juvenile offenders, a few scholars found that a real stigma was often attached to boys and girls who were taken before the courts. This issue was especially important in the research of sociologist-lawyer Paul Tappan, whose work in the New York City court not only raised due process issues but also demonstrated how a loose administrative application of legal classifications to young people coming before the court led to their stigmatization throughout the city's welfare system.

Criticism of the juvenile courts mounted during the 1930s and 1940s, as academic social scientists and others turned increasingly more attention to the problem of juvenile delinquency.

The Great Juvenile Delinquency Scare

Beginning during World War II, the juvenile court system underwent still closer and more skeptical investigation from many directions, and underwent modifications that had noticeable effects on the courts' bases and operations.

One reason for increasing scrutiny directed toward the juvenile courts during World War II and after was a heightened sense of juvenile delinquency as a serious problem in the United States. Beginning in late 1942 and early 1943, many Americans began to believe that juvenile crime was on the rise. There appeared to be evidence for such a belief. "Zoot suiters" (youths—especially minority youths—known for their extravagantly cut "zoot suits") in such major cities as New York, Los Angeles, and Detroit; a rise in sexual promiscuity among adolescent women; and the presence of other apparently rootless adolescents shocked many Americans. FBI statistics appeared to indicate a growing rate of juvenile crime. Popular magazines picked up such evidence and made it appear to prove the existence of a virtual crime wave among American youth. Although the figures were debatable, public concern was high, fueled by such visible figures as J. Edgar Hoover, director of the FBI, and the U.S. Attorney General, Tom Clark.

What appeared to be a mounting juvenile crime wave during the war continued to attract attention in the post-war years, prompting both popular concern and governmental interest. Governmental interest translated into a range of activities, including a 1946 National Conference on the Prevention and Control of Juvenile Delinquency, a Senate Continuing Committee focusing on the problem, a 1950 White House Conference on Children, and a series of FBI-sponsored conferences designed to reach workers in the field.

Popular concern was enhanced in the 1950s by a focus in the media on the problem of delinquency. Mounting gang violence attracted widespread attention. No less important were such forms as the "JD [juvenile delinquent] films" of the mid-1950s, including classics as *The Wild Ones* (1954), *Rebel Without a Cause* (1955), and the extremely popular *Blackboard Jungle* (1955). With their striking portrayals of alienated and rebellious teenagers, these films both played on and increased popular concern about American delinquents.

This popular consciousness of delinquency also had more formal manifestations, particularly in the work of the United States Senate Subcommittee to Investigate Juvenile Delinquency (which was established in 1953 and became prominent after 1955 when Senator Estes Kefauver of Tennessee assumed its chair). The subcommittee investigated a range of causes of delinquency, heightening the public's sense of the significance of delinquency and of the inadequacy of dominant approaches to bringing delinquency under control. Subsequent commissions at the federal level met in 1961 and 1966.

A Sense of Crisis: Mounting Criticism of the Juvenile Court

Criticism of the juvenile court mounted with the delinquency scare of the 1950s. It became a prominent feature of American thinking about delinquency during the 1960s and, as we shall see, has continued to the present. The failure of the juvenile court was seen to involve something more than the court's not living up to its own ideals. *The Challenge of Crime in a Free Society*, a 1967 report by the President's Commission on Law Enforcement and the Administration of Justice, concluded, after a sweeping investigation of juvenile court practices, that the courts had neither reduced the "tide of delinquency" nor succeeded in "bringing justice and compassion to the child offender." The real problem, the commission concluded, lay in the fact that delinquency appeared to involve more complexities than the juvenile courts could address.[14] Juvenile crime, that is, appeared to be resistant to the best-intentioned efforts of the juvenile courts to prevent it.

DUE PROCESS

Several important developments in the American juvenile justice system may be traced to the turmoil and pessimism that had become so visible by the 1960s. The Kennedy-Johnson years saw, for example, increasing federal involvement in issues of juvenile crime, including the institution of federally sponsored efforts to create a variety of alternative approaches to responding to delinquency, particularly approaches emphasizing diversion from institutionalization and community-based treatment. These approaches will be discussed more fully in Chapter 12.

Probably the most significant of these developments was an increasing focus on the issue of due process in the juvenile courts themselves. To some extent, the concern over the absence of due process in juvenile courts goes back to the earliest days of those courts, when, in their efforts at informality, they failed to guarantee such benefits of due process as the rights to counsel, trial by jury, and (in many states) appeal. Despite the decisions of higher courts to uphold the constitutionality of juvenile proceedings and of *parens patriae*, the continuing series of cases to reach those courts, even today, shows that the issue itself was never entirely laid to rest.

Due process in the juvenile courts was also encouraged by a more general focus on due process in state criminal justice systems for adult and juvenile offenders alike. For much of American history, including the period during which the juvenile courts were established, the U.S. Supreme Court had consistently held that due process guarantees in the Bill of Rights applied only in federal courts. Beginning in 1925, however, the Court started reversing itself, and by 1969, virtually all guarantees of the Bill of Rights were made applicable in the states. The expanded application of the Bill of Rights influenced the juvenile justice system.

Some of the pressure for change in juvenile court practices came from within the states themselves. These were especially visible in the California Juvenile Court Act of 1961 and the New York Family Court Act of 1962.

The California Act was based on the 1960 recommendations of a governor's special study commission on juvenile justice. Existing law at the time embodied the main features of *parens patriae*, providing that a juvenile offender should receive "care, custody, and discipline" that would "approximate as nearly as possible that which should be given by his parents."[15] The commission found that, in practice, the court was far from approaching the ideal. Court procedures were inconsistent, as was the disposition of cases. Basic legal rights were unprotected, detention appeared excessive, and treatment was ineffective.

The commission did not question the juvenile court's foundation in *parens patriae*—in the right of the state to "provide some of all parental guidance" to children in trouble, nor did it favor any change in the informality that was supposed to distinguish the juvenile court. However, it did recommend some changes, which were adopted into the 1961 law. The new law identified three distinct classes of minors subject to law, it established a two-stage hearing process in the courts, and it delineated certain rights to counsel.

Previous law had lumped together young people from "unfit" homes, those found begging (including those "singing or playing on any musical instrument" as a pretext to begging), habitual truants, and those accused of criminal activity. The revised code distinguished among neglected children, status offenders, and those who violated criminal laws, and provided different dispositions for each category.

The new code also made provision for due process. Prior to 1961, California law, consistent with *parens patriae*, allowed for a mixture of "social data" and testimony relating to issues of innocence and guilt ("jurisdictional facts") in a hearing. Court decisions were often rendered before any charges had been substantiated. The 1961 law provided for a two-stage procedure consisting of an adjudicatory (or jurisdictional) hearing to be followed by a dispositional hearing. In the first stage, the court was to consider only the allegations that had brought a youth before the court. Only then would the court consider how to dispose of the case. Although standards of proof were still not as strict as those in an adult court (allowing for disposition based on a "preponderance of evidence" rather than on a determination of guilt that must be "beyond a reasonable doubt"), the 1961 act did provide for the right to counsel for juvenile offenders charged with felonies.

The New York Family Court Act of 1962 made similar changes but went beyond California in regard to due process. The New York act established a statewide Family Court with power over a wide range of cases, including those involving child neglect, marital disputes, and crimes and offenses (other than felonies) committed by or against children.

Like California, New York adopted a system distinguishing among three kinds of juveniles subject to the Family Court's jurisdiction: (1) criminal children, (2) those brought before the court because of neglect or abuse, and (3) those who engaged in troublesome but noncriminal behavior. This last category included boys under 16 or girls under 18 who were habitually truant or who were considered beyond the control of their parents or guardians. Those in the last category were described as "persons in need of supervision" (PINS).

The New York Act also provided for a two-stage hearing process. Going beyond California law, however, the act asserted the importance of the right to counsel for all juveniles brought before the court, establishing a system of "law guardians" to represent not only juveniles accused of crime but those in court for other reasons as well. One effect of this system has been to shift much of the focus of Family Court hearings to encompass issues of due process.

Supreme Court Decisions

The changes in California and New York came mainly from private attorneys and legal aid societies dissatisfied with the juvenile courts' operations. These internal forces for change were buttressed, beginning in the mid-1960s, by a series of U.S. Supreme Court decisions that called for the provision of due process in juvenile court cases.

Kent v. United States

The first Supreme Court decision to call for due process was *Kent v. United States* (1966). Since age 14, Morris Kent had come to the attention of the District of Columbia juvenile court for a variety of reasons. At 16, under probation, he was arrested on charges of theft and rape. He not only admitted guilt on those charges but acknowledged having committed several other crimes.

The District of Columbia allowed a juvenile court judge to waive jurisdiction to adult criminal court in the case of a minor age 16 or older charged with a serious crime, a provision common in many state codes (as we shall discuss in Chapter 10). This was done in Kent's case, without so much as a hearing. The judge did not confer with Kent or

Kent's attorney and gave no reasons for the waiver. Kent was subsequently found guilty on several of the charges and sentenced to a total of 30 to 90 years in prison. Had his case remained in juvenile court, he could have been institutionalized for no more than five years.

Kent's appeal reached the U.S. Supreme Court. The Court, though approving the practice of waiver as such, agreed that the juvenile court's action in waiving jurisdiction in the case had been arbitrary and was, thus, invalid. According to the Court's decision, a juvenile accused of crime is entitled to certain minimum rights and procedures before a waiver may be granted. Because Kent had not been accorded those rights, the case was remanded to the District Court for a new hearing on waiver.

In re Gault

The action in Morris Kent's case was followed in 1967 by *In re Gault*,[16] which, along with *Ex parte Crouse* (the 1838 case establishing *parens patriae*), is one of the two most notable decisions in the history of American juvenile justice.

In Gila County, Arizona, 15-year-old Gerald Gault and a friend were arrested for making an obscene phone call. Gault, on probation at the time for having stolen a wallet, was taken to a detention home where he was held for several days. At the subsequent adjudicatory hearing, Gault was not given the right to counsel, nor to confrontation and cross-examination (the offended woman never even appeared). Gault admitted guilt and was committed to an institution for six years. It should be noted that the penalty in the Arizona for an adult found guilty of the same offense was a fine of $5 to $50 or imprisonment for not more than two months. Furthermore, for an adult, in contrast to Gault, even that comparatively slight punishment could be imposed only after a trial with due process protections.

Gault's case reached the U.S. Supreme Court, where a majority of the justices expressed outrage. Justice Abe Fortas, writing for the majority, declared, "Under our Constitution, the condition of being a boy does not justify a kangaroo court."[17] The Court found that Gerald Gault had been unconstitutionally confined in a state institution because he was denied his right to due process. In its ruling, it made the following rights and privileges mandatory in juvenile adjudicatory hearings that could result in confinement to a state institution for "delinquents": (1) timely notice of specific issues, (2) notification of right to counsel and appointment of counsel if the family cannot afford an attorney, (3) protection against self-incrimination, and (4) sworn testimony subject to cross-examination.

The Court's decision was not unanimous. In a strong dissent, Justice Potter Stewart objected to how *Gault* undermined *parens patriae*, and argued that *parens patriae* should remain a fundamental part of juvenile court hearings. Arguing that *Gault* would mean "a long step backwards into the nineteenth century,"[18] he emphasized the continuing appeal of the basic principles behind the juvenile court since its founding.

Subsequent Decisions

Since *Gault*, the effort to balance procedural fairness with the spirit of *parens patriae* has resulted in a series of decisions that, in many ways, have seemed contradictory. In 1970, in *In re Winship*[19] the Court decided that the standard of proof in juvenile court for delinquency hearings must be "beyond a reasonable doubt" instead of the far less stringent "preponderance of evidence" (a requirement that even the 1961 revised California code had accepted). In a dissenting opinion, however, Justice Warren Burger questioned whether such an emphasis would endanger what he saw as a necessary degree of flexibility in the institution.

In *McKeiver v. Pennsylvania* (1971), by contrast, the Court tilted in the direction of *parens patriae* by ruling against the requirement of a jury trial in juvenile court proceedings. Subsequently, however, in 1975, in *Breed v. Jones*, the Court again upheld due process by holding that a juvenile defendant had been unconstitutionally placed in double jeopardy by being waived for trial to a criminal court after an adjudicatory hearing in which allegations against the defendant had also been sustained. Such decisions reflect a continuing division about the bases for juvenile justice in the United States legal community.

The Impact of Due Process

The Supreme Court decisions had a somewhat ambiguous impact on state juvenile court systems. In theory, many states have adopted juvenile codes that seek to incorporate due process into their courts' proceedings. At the federal level, the comprehensive Juvenile Justice and Delinquency Prevention Act of 1974, covering federally assisted juvenile delinquency programs, also seeks to incorporate the requirements of *Gault*.

At the same time, though, operationally, juvenile courts continue to retain broad powers over those who come under their jurisdiction, and proceedings in many jurisdictions tend to try to preserve older juvenile court styles. Many juvenile courts have been haphazard in informing offenders of their rights, especially the right to counsel. Most juvenile court systems allow young offenders to waive those rights in the interest of receiving a more "paternalistic" treatment from the court, and many of the courts have been noted for their aggressiveness in encouraging waivers. (See the more comprehensive discussions of due process rights in Chapter 10.)

There are areas in which due process decisions have had significant influence on the operations of the courts, particularly (despite inconsistencies from jurisdiction to jurisdiction) in the provision of counsel during juvenile court proceedings. In some states (notably California, New York, and Pennsylvania), attorneys appear in most cases coming before the juvenile courts, even if, in some others, attorneys are present only about one-third to one-half the time. Here, too, however, the record is mixed, as most attorneys who take juvenile court cases tend to operate within older frameworks, assuming the role of negotiator between judge and family rather than molding the proceedings in the direction of adversarial criminal jurisprudence. There is some evidence, moreover, that the presence of an attorney may actually lead to a more severe sentence for a young offender.

"GETTING TOUGH" IN THE 1980S

To some extent, the lack of clarity in regard to due process is connected with other changes in the juvenile justice system. Since at least the 1960s, even as Supreme Court decisions were moving in favor of due process, the juvenile courts in some locations were developing an increasing focus on juveniles accused of criminal acts, with other problems (such as neglect or incorrigibility) being referred to other agencies for treatment.

This change has been particularly important with regard to preventive efforts on the part of the juvenile justice system. By the early 1980s, almost all states had removed noncriminal acts from the category of delinquency. Drawing on earlier efforts in California and New York, at least 25 other states had created their own categories of "CINS" or "CHINS" (Child in Need of Supervision) or "JINS" (Juvenile in Need of Supervision) to match New York's PINS. In some states, noncriminal offenders were removed from the jurisdiction of juvenile courts altogether. Thus, treatment—even institutionalization—of such young people may continue to occur without the need to observe the due process guarantees of *Gault* and other decisions.

So far as juveniles accused of crimes have been concerned, the issue has been more complex. One reason for this is that since about the mid-1970s, there has been, and continues to be, what has been described as a "get tough" movement in thinking about juvenile delinquency. In light of the apparent failure of the juvenile courts to stem what some see as a tide of juvenile crime, many people have argued that the courts need to take a more punitive, criminal justice–based approach to the problem. These arguments have been still further encouraged through the 1990s by an increase in violent crimes committed by juvenile offenders. If the first juvenile courts represented an effort to "decriminalize" juvenile delinquency, more recent approaches have proposed a "recriminalization" of juvenile crime.

One of the most important steps in this direction was made in 1977, with the recommendations of a joint committee of New York University's Institute of Judicial Administration and the American Bar Association. The committee argued that sanctions for juvenile offenders should be "based on the seriousness of the offense committed, and not merely the court's view of the juvenile's needs," a clear rejection of the child-centered philosophy underlying the founding of the juvenile courts.[20] At the same time, the committee's view of procedural protections was strong, further reflecting its criminal justice–based approach to the problem. Although it also made the argument that juvenile court judges should seek to impose "the least restrictive alternative" in the disposition of cases, the thrust of its report was to treat juvenile delinquency as juvenile crime.

The report had great impact. As early as 1977, the state of Washington used it as the basis for redrafting its juvenile code. In 1977 and 1978, New York took a similar but more modest step with a series of bills that required confinement (including a mandatory period of secure confinement) for anyone over the age of 13 found guilty of committing certain felonies. A continuing series of statutes also provided for the exclusion of some serious crimes, including murder, from the jurisdiction of the juvenile courts, and an automatic waiver to adult criminal courts for juveniles as young as 13. Similar legislation has been implemented in other states in subsequent years.

In point of practice, approaches to juvenile crime have also tended to move in the direction of recriminalization, especially during the 1980s. At this time, what was sometimes described as a "just deserts" philosophy came to play an increasing role in thinking about the disposition of juvenile criminal cases, a role reinforced by the development of a model juvenile code using the same approach that was developed during the Reagan administration.

This approach was particularly evident in an increasing reliance on incarceration in response to juvenile crime during the 1980s. Statistics from 1977 show an incarceration rate for juvenile offenders of about 17 per 100,000; during the 1980s, the rate went as high as 76 per 100,000— a major increase and one found nationwide. The period also saw the increasing incidence of detention of juveniles in jails and police lockups, in some cases mixing status offenders with juveniles accused of serious crimes, or even with adult criminals, despite state law and federal efforts (initiated in 1980) that were intended to prohibit the practice. Although a few states, notably Massachusetts and Utah, tended to buck the trend toward institutionalization in addressing juvenile crime, the "get tough" movement played a powerful role in evolving state approaches to juvenile crime.

The debate over the juvenile court reached significant proportions by the mid-1990s. Serious proposals, including formal discussions in the American Bar Association, were made to abolish the courts altogether, a position argued most forcefully by Barry C. Feld. Problems of procedural rights remain unresolved, and in many places, the increasing focus on juvenile crime in the courts, coupled with efforts to observe due process, have made the distinctiveness of the courts themselves ambiguous.

A group of youthful offenders is instructed in juvenile court. *(Photo by Mark C. Ide)*

Thus, while almost everyone agrees that the courts need reexamination and reform, even now, the directions such actions should take are far from clear. We shall look more closely at some of the specifics of these issues in Chapter 10.

SUMMARY

The early history of juvenile justice paralleled the histories of the concept of childhood and of emerging concepts of delinquency. At a time when Western civilization was becoming increasingly "child-centered," approaches to juvenile delinquency similarly aimed to set young offenders apart from adult criminals, focusing on ways to address the unique characteristics of the child in order to produce moral reform.

Through the early modern period in Western history, there were no such efforts. Although allowances were made for age, children accused and convicted of crime were generally treated like adult offenders. With the opening of the nineteenth century, this began to change through the creation of a range of institutions designed to deal specifically with juveniles. These included houses of refuge and reform schools, which separated young offenders from adult convicts, and a variety of anti-institutional responses focused directly on young people, including "placing-out" systems and "junior republics" as well as forms of probation.

No less significant were the legal precedents created in the nineteenth century, particularly the establishment of *parens patriae* as a fundamental basis for approaches to juvenile crime, which justified state intervention into families. With the founding of the Illinois juvenile court at the close of the nineteenth century, and for the first two-thirds of the twentieth century, *parens patriae* served as the cornerstone of the juvenile justice system—the culmination of attempts to define juvenile delinquency as a special category of legal concern.

Still, the history of the courts themselves has not been a story of unbroken development. Almost from the beginning, the juvenile courts have faced strong criticisms and challenges from several fronts. When the courts, in their daily operations, have been held up to the ideas that led to their establishment, they have often been found lacking. Expected to play a parental role for delinquents and other troubled children, the courts have often tended more toward an abrupt, unsympathetic treatment of young people coming under their jurisdiction.

Other criticisms have focused on the courts' apparent inability to reduce juvenile crime. Referring to what appear to be high rates of recidivism, critics have claimed that the treatment focus of the juvenile court is inadequate in the face of juvenile crime, and that a more punitive, criminal justice–oriented approach is necessary. Others, seeing the same problem of recidivism, have felt that the courts have not been parental enough and that more effective, treatment-based approaches are necessary to reduce juvenile crime. The debate goes back to the earliest days of the juvenile courts and has continued into our own time.

The major issue in the recent history of the courts has been that of due process. Although there were early challenges to the courts on due process grounds, these were generally unsuccessful. The constitutionality of the courts and the principle of *parens patriae* were generally upheld in the higher courts of the United States.

The 1960s, however, saw increasing legislative and judicial concern for the role of due process in juvenile court proceedings. In part, this may have been the product of a more general recognition during that period of the rights of defendants (adult as well as juvenile) in criminal proceedings. In part, it may have resulted from the increasing concentration of the juvenile courts themselves on criminal offenders.

These due process concerns were brought into the juvenile court systems in two major ways. First, in such states as California and New York, pressure from various sources led to major revisions in juvenile court statutes. These revisions clearly encompassed due process concerns, including a clearer distinction between criminal and noncriminal cases and provisions for the right to counsel and other rights previously deemed unnecessary in the informal, treatment-oriented setting of the juvenile court.

Second, from the middle of the 1960s through the 1970s, the U.S. Supreme Court handed down a series of decisions that required the observance of due process in juvenile court cases. Most notable were the *Kent* decision of 1966 and the *Gault* decision of 1967, each of which addressed substantive aspects of juvenile court operations and suggested major changes in them.

The larger ramifications of these decisions remain unclear. The Supreme Court itself has not fully rejected the older juvenile court model and has continued to hand down decisions seeking to balance that model with constitutional concerns. In the states, the impact of these decisions and of other forces for change has been piecemeal, leading to adjustments in juvenile court operations but not to any real revolution in the nature of juvenile justice proceedings. We shall consider several of these points in more detail in Chapter 10.

REFERENCES

Abbott, Grace, ed. (1938). *The Child and the State.* 2 vols. Chicago: University of Chicago Press.

Bernard, Thomas J. (1992). *The Cycle of Juvenile Justice.* New York: Oxford University Press.

Binder, Arnold, and Susan L. Polan (1991). "The Kennedy-Johnson Years: Social Theory and Federal Policy in the Control of Delinquency." *Crime & Delinquency* 33:242-261.

Brace, Charles Loring (1880). *The Dangerous Classes of New York, and Twenty Years' Work Among Them,* 3rd ed. Reprint. Montclair, NJ: Patterson Smith, 1967.

Bremner, Robert, et al., eds. (1970). *Children and Youth in America: A Documentary History.* 3 vols. Cambridge, MA: Harvard University Press.

Brenzel, Barbara M. (1983). *Daughters of the State: A Social Portrait of the First Reform School for Girls in North America, 1856-1905.* Cambridge, MA: MIT Press.

Caldwell, Robert G. (1961). "The Juvenile Court: Its Development and Some Major Problems." *Journal of Criminal Law, Criminology and Police Science* 51:493-511.

Campbell, D'Ann (1985). "Judge Ben Lindsey and the Juvenile Court Movement, 1901-4." In *Growing Up in America: Children in Historical Perspective,* edited by N. Ray Hiner and Joseph M. Hawes, 149-160. Urbana: University of Illinois Press.

Clement, Priscilla Ferguson (1985). "The City and the Child, 1860-1885." In *American Childhood: A Research Guide and Historical Handbook,* edited by Joseph M. Hawes and N. Ray Hiner, 235-272. Westport, CT: Greenwood Press.

Clement, Priscilla Ferguson (1993). "The Incorrigible Child: Juvenile Delinquency in the United States from the 17th through the 19th Centuries." In *History of Juvenile Delinquency: A Collection of Essays on Crime Committed by Young Offenders, in History and in Selected Countries.* 2 vols, edited by Patricia F. Clement and Albert G. Hess, II:453-490. Aalen, Germany: Scientia Verlag.

Cogan, Neil (1970). "Juvenile Law, Before and After the Entrance of '*Parens Patriae*.'" *South Carolina Law Review* 22:147-181.

Cohen, Esther (1990). "Youth and Delinquency in the Middle Ages." In *History of Juvenile Delinquency*, edited by Albert G. Hess and Priscilla F. Clement, I:207-230. Aalen, Germany: Scientia.

Feld, Barry C. (1993). "Juvenile (In)Justice and the Criminal Court Alternative." *Crime & Delinquency* 39:403-424.

Feld, Barry C. (1999). *Bad Kids: Race and the Transformation of the Juvenile Court.* New York: Oxford University Press.

Fox, Sanford J. (1970). "Juvenile Justice Reform: An Historical Perspective." *Stanford Law Review* 22:1187-1239.

Fox, Sanford J. (1996). "The Early History of the Court." *The Future of Children* 6(3):29-39.

Friedman, Lawrence (1993). *Crime and Punishment in American History.* New York: Basic Books.

Gilbert, James (1986). *A Cycle of Outrage: Reaction to the Juvenile Delinquent in the 1950s.* New York: Oxford University Press.

Golden, Mark (1990). *Children and Childhood in Classical Athens.* Baltimore: Johns Hopkins University Press.

Grossberg, Michael (1985). *Governing the Hearth: Law and the Family in Nineteenth-Century America.* Chapel Hill: University of North Carolina Press.

Grossberg, Michael (1996). *A Judgement for Solomon: The d'Hauteville Case and Legal Experience in Antebellum America.* Cambridge, England: Cambridge University Press.

Hale, Donna C., ed. (1991). Special Issue: "Juvenile Justice: History and Policy." *Crime & Delinquency* 37:2.

Hawes, Joseph M. (1971). *Children in Urban Society: Juvenile Delinquency in Nineteenth Century America.* New York: Oxford University Press.

Hawes, Joseph M. (1991). *The Children's Rights Movement: A History of Advocacy and Protection.* Boston: Twayne.

Holl, Jack M. (1971). *Juvenile Reform in the Progressive Era: William R. George and the Junior Republic Movement.* Ithaca, NY: Cornell University Press.

Holloran, Peter C. (1989). *Boston's Wayward Children: Social Services for Homeless Children, 1830-1930.* Rutherford, NJ: Farleigh Dickinson University Press.

Holt, Marilyn Irvin (1992). *The Orphan Trains: Placing Out in America.* Lincoln: University of Nebraska Press.

Hurley, Timothy D. (1925). "Origin of the Illinois Juvenile Court Law." In *The Child, the Clinic and the Court*, 320-330. Reprint. New York: Johnson Reprint, 1970.

Jackson, Donald Dale (1986). "It Took Trains to Put Street Kids on the Right Track Out of the Slums." *Smithsonian* 17(5):94-103.

Johnston, Norman (1994). *Eastern State Penitentiary: Crucible of Good Intentions.* Philadelphia: Philadelphia Museum of Art.

Jolowicz, H.F. (1957). *Roman Foundations of Modern Law.* London: Oxford University Press.

Kaestle, Carl F. (1976). "Between the Scylla of Brutal Ignorance and the Charybdis of a Literary Education: Elite Attitudes Toward Mass Schooling in Early Industrial England and America." In *Schooling and Society: Studies in the History of Education*, edited by Lawrence Stone, 177-191. Baltimore: Johns Hopkins University Press.

Kent, James (1827). *Commentaries on American Law.* 4 vols. Reprint. New York: Da Capo Press, 1971.

Langsam, Miriam Z. (1964). *Children West: A History of the Placing-Out System of the New York Children's Aid Society, 1853-1890.* Madison: State Historical Society of Wisconsin.

Lemert, Edwin M. (1970). *Social Action and Legal Change: Revolution Within the Juvenile Court.* Chicago: Aldine.

Lindenmeyer, Kriste (1997). *"A Right to Childhood: The U.S. Children's Bureau and Child Welfare, 1912-46."* Urbana: University of Illinois Press.

Lindsey, Ben B., and Harvey J. O'Higgins (1911). *The Beast.* Garden City, NY: Doubleday.

Mack, Julian W. (1925). "The Chancery Procedure in the Juvenile Court." In *The Child, the Clinic and the Court*, 310-319. Reprint. New York: Johnson Reprint, 1970.

Manfredi, Christopher P. (1998). *The Supreme Court and Juvenile Justice.* Lawrence: University Press of Kansas.

Mennel, Robert M. (1973). *Thorns and Thistles: Juvenile Delinquents in the United States, 1825-1940.* Hanover, NH: University Press of New England.

Paulsen, Monrad G. (1963). "The New York Family Court Act." *Buffalo Law Review* 12:420-441.

Paulsen, Monrad G. (1979). "Current Reforms and the Legal Status of Children." In *The Future of Childhood and Juvenile Justice*, edited by LaMar T. Empey, 211-233. Charlottesville: University Press of Virginia.

Pisciotta, Alexander W. (1994). *Benevolent Repression: Social Control and the American Reformatory-Prison Movement.* New York: New York University Press.

Platt, Anthony M. (1977). *The Child Savers: The Invention of Delinquency*, 2nd ed. Chicago: University of Chicago Press.

Prescott, Peter S. (1981). *The Child Savers: Juvenile Justice Observed.* New York: Knopf.

Radzinowicz, Leon (1948). *A History of English Criminal Law and Its Administration from 1750: The Movement for Reform, 1750-1833.* London: Stevens and Sons.

Report of the Governor's Special Study Commission on Juvenile Justice. (1960). Sacramento: California State Printing Office.

Ryerson, Ellen (1978). *The Best-Laid Plans: America's Juvenile Court Experiment*. New York: Hill and Wang.

Sanders, Wiley B., ed. (1970). *Juvenile Offenders for a Thousand Years: Selected Readings from Anglo-Saxon Times to 1900*. Chapel Hill: University of North Carolina Press.

Schlossman, Steven L. (1977). *Love and the American Delinquent: The Theory and Practice of "Progressive" Juvenile Justice, 1825-1920*. Chicago: University of Chicago Press.

Schneider, Eric C. (1992). *In the Web of Class: Delinquents and Reformers in Boston, 1810s-1930s*. New York: New York University Press.

Schneider, Eric C. (1999). *Vampires, Dragons, and Egyptian Kings: Youth Gangs in Postwar New York*. Princeton, NJ: Princeton University Press.

Schwartz, Ira M. (1989). *(In)Justice for Juveniles: Rethinking the Best Interests of the Child*. Lexington, MA: D.C. Heath.

Singer, Simon I. (1996). *Recriminalizing Delinquency: Violent Juvenile Crime and Juvenile Justice Reform*. Cambridge, England: Cambridge University Press.

Sutton, John R. (1985). "The Juvenile Court and Social Welfare: Dynamics of Progressive Reform." *Law and Society Review* 19:107-145.

Sutton, John R. (1988). *Stubborn Children: Controlling Delinquency in the United States, 1640-1981*. Berkeley: University of California Press.

NOTES

1 B.C.E. and C.E. replace B.C. and A.D., respectively. B.C.E. stands for "Before Common Era" and C.E. stands for "Common Era."

2 Radzinowicz (1948).

3 Abbott (1938), vol. II, 344.

4 Ibid., 348.

5 Schneider (1992).

6 Cogan (1970), 174

7 Brace (1880), 29.

8 Jackson (1986), 101.

9 Mack (1925), 14.

10 Lindsey & O'Higgins (1911), 82-83.

11 Ibid., 86-87.

12 15 Idaho at 127 (1908).

13 260 N.Y. 171 (1932), cert. den. 289 U.S. 709 (1933).

14 Ryerson (1978).

[15]   Report of the Governor's Special Study Commission (1960), 12.

[16]   387 U.S. 1.

[17]   Ibid., at 28.

[18]   Ibid., at 79-80.

[19]   397 U.S. 368.

[20]   Paulsen (1979), 219.

9

The Front Gate to the Juvenile Justice System

In the last chapter, we examined the background of the American juvenile justice system, including key events and issues in the development of its central institution, the juvenile court. We are now ready to consider it in operation, that is, to look at what happens to youths who are processed by it. The starting point for that discussion, because of its critical screening role, is the police as a social institution. While police encounters with juveniles are typically precipitated by the complaints of other people rather than by direct observation, the police are the central "gatekeepers" of the juvenile justice system in determining who does and who does not enter. If, after a given encounter, an officer decides to open the gate to the justice system, referral goes to a probation or court intake officer, who independently evaluates the case. Traditionally, the probation or court intake officer decides whether to petition the juvenile (or family) court for a hearing. In some states, however, that role has been given to the office of the prosecuting attorney, who "represents the people" at the hearing. The intrusion of the prosecuting attorney into the processing chain in recent years stems from public (and, therefore, political) distress about the extent and seriousness of juvenile crime (as mentioned in the preceding chapter). Along with many other measures, it represents one aspect of the attempt to "get tough" with young criminals, a tendency that has become quite strong in recent years.

The juvenile court may send a youngster to a custodial institution if the allegations in the petition are sustained. (We shall use the term "juvenile court" in a generic way to encompass all courts devoted to juvenile matters; in some states, juvenile offenses are handled in "family courts.") As another alternative, the court may place the youngster under formal supervision in the community by a probation officer. For a youngster sent to an institution, the final step in justice system processing may be interaction with a parole officer. The aim of parole is to facilitate transition between institutional life and full return to the community.

THE COMMUNITY

Factors Affecting the Decision to Call the Police

A man steps out of his front door one evening and observes neighborhood boys finishing the task of wrapping a substantial amount of toilet tissue around one of his trees. The boys run off, but he has recognized them. What does he do? Although he may call the parents of one or more of the boys, if he knows them, the chances are reasonably good that he will not notify the police.

On the other hand, if the man under similar circumstances had observed a group of boys assaulting an old lady and then running off with her purse, he would almost certainly notify the police. There are two principal reasons for the differing reactions in the two settings. First, the man would feel revulsion by the abuse of the lady and impelled to take some action, whereas the toilet tissue would produce no more than a "what a nuisance" reaction. Second, the man would realize that the police are too busy with more serious matters to respond to the relatively trivial prank of wrapping tissue around a tree.

A person could call the police upon being disturbed by a youth who is playing a radio too loudly while washing a car, or a call may result from concern about a youth who seems to be showing psychotic behavior. These reactions illustrate that the police are the 24-hour security blankets for much of the public. There is hardly a disturbing state of affairs in the community from which they are excluded from consideration as initial corrective agents. In order to examine various factors that enter into the decision to call or not call the police, we will assume that a citizen has observed a criminal act (or what seems to be the result of a criminal act) by a youth.

Certain factors affecting the decision whether to involve the police are functions of the criminal act, the context in which it occurs, and the characteristics of the offending youth or youths. Clearly, the degree of seriousness of the act or its outcome will influence the probability of its being reported. Assuming no risk to the informant (the presence of risk greatly complicates the issue), one is far more likely to report an offense like robbery than one like minor shoplifting. Further, the degree of repetitiveness of the behavior and the individual or institution against which it is directed also affect the likelihood of reporting. One may not notify the police (or some other individual who will in turn notify the police) on noticing that a youth has stolen a candy bar; however, the chances of such notification go up as the youth steals increasingly more over a period of time. The chances are greater, too, of reporting when the victim is an individual rather than an organization, particularly a large organization. What is more, the likelihood of calling the police when criminal behavior is observed may be different if the offender is the child of a neighbor rather than an unrecognized youngster, if the offender is black rather than white, if the offender is shabbily rather than tidily dressed, if the offender is a boy rather than girl, if the offender is a boy with long hair rather than a boy with neatly trimmed hair, and so on.

Other factors that enter into a decision regarding police notification are functions of the observer. The observer of a criminal act, for example, may be in a particularly bad mood as a result of a dispute with an employer and therefore more easily irritated by all external events. As a result, a youthful act that would have been shrugged off at another time may precipitate anger and police notification. It may seem strange that the question of whether a youngster is referred to the police and then enters the justice system is a function of something so irrelevant as the mood of the person who makes the original observation, but that can indeed be the case. Broader institutional and community factors have similar influences. For example, the array of outrageous shootings on school campuses in recent years has motivated educational officials to set policies that may lead to police involvement at any indication that a concealed object may be used as a weapon. The increased sensitivity of schools is reflected in the following news article dated September 7, 1999, the opening date for the area's 1999-2000 school year. About five months earlier, two teenage boys in Littleton, Colorado, shot and killed 12 of their classmates and a teacher before taking their own lives.

> As kids scramble back to classrooms across the nation, the jangle of school bells has some dissonant new accompaniments: the electronic beep of metal detectors, the robotic swivel of surveillance cameras, the crackle of walkie-talkies and the thwop-thwop-thwop of SWAT-team helicopters.

> After a sobering two years of school shootings, a growing number of school systems this fall has embraced measures designed to safeguard children against the armed rage of violent classmates or deranged adults.
>
> In communities large and small, urban and rural, violence-plagued and crime-free, police departments and special intervention teams have spent the summer mapping school grounds and plotting responses to violent incidents. Mock drills, complete with "victims" playing out their roles, have been conducted at schools from Berkeley to Pasadena, Md.; Pittsburgh even used helicopters to evacuate the "wounded."[1]

It is thus clear that features of people and society, perhaps far removed from the context in which a child misbehaves, can determine what is deviant and who is to be considered a deviate for exhibiting such behavior. A youth who has brought a pocket knife to school over many years without incident may, in the new context, be referred to the police for that possession and, perhaps, be taken into custody.

For a particular observer of a youthful criminal act or its outcome, the picture becomes even more complex when one considers that people differ markedly in personal characteristics and change markedly over short time periods (as in mood fluctuations). A given person may be particularly sensitive to all evidence of youthful misbehavior and eager to report it; another may show concern only when a youth commits a very serious assaultive crime.

Beyond such varying sensitivities, people differ in tolerance for different types of deviant behavior, in ethical and moral standards, in racial prejudice, in expectations based on the sex of a youngster, in attitudes toward the standards of the communities in which they live, and in attitudes toward law enforcement in general and the local police department in particular. Their reactions to crime will be influenced accordingly.

The Importance of Community Members in the Specification of Deviance

The importance of citizens in the specification of deviance was shown by Donald J. Black and Albert J. Reiss Jr., who systematically observed police encounters with juveniles in three cities. They noted that, excluding traffic violations, 78 percent were initiated by calls from citizens and only 22 percent by the police. Moreover, they found that the decision of an officer in regard to custody or release was strongly influenced by the preference of the complainant: "Hence, it would seem that the moral standards of the citizenry have more to do with the definition of juvenile deviance that do the standards of policemen on patrol."[2] The same conclusion was reached subsequently in a study of a very large metropolitan area. The following comment was based on the results of that study: "In addition to citizens' exercise of discretion in the context of calling the police about a delinquent act they have witnessed, in their roles as complainants, citizens influence arrest rates by their willingness to remain at the scene of an offense until the police arrive and by making their dispositional preferences manifest. . . . *Citizens, therefore, largely determine official delinquency rates* [italics in original]."[3]

The general reluctance of people to report a crime like shoplifting was demonstrated in a study by Steffensmeier and Terry in which incidents of shoplifting were staged in an obvious fashion so that the event would be observed by nearby shoppers. The person who observed the staged event was then given an opportunity to report the "offense" to a nearby "employer" (who was actually another accomplice in the study); only 29.2 percent of the observers did so. Even when another accomplice acting as a second store worker asked the nonreporters if they had seen an offense take place and pointed out that the "offender" was a suspicious person, a large number of people refused to report the occurrence.

Although the results are interesting, it is difficult to generalize conclusions to the diverse array of juvenile offenses and the different environmental conditions in which they occur. There is a bit more information when the observer is a victim of a crime. In the 1998 National Crime Victimization Survey (NCVS), we find that victims reported to the police 46 percent of violent crimes and 35 percent of property crimes. Among violent crimes, robberies were reported most often at 62 percent and rape or sexual assaults least often at 32 percent. The rate of reporting violent crimes was higher for women than for men (51 versus 42 percent), but there was no difference in reporting rates for men and women for crimes of theft. Further, blacks were more likely than whites to report violent crimes to the police (52 versus 44 percent).

There are many reasons given by victims as to why they do or do not report crimes to the police. Violent crimes are most frequently reported to prevent further crimes of a similar sort by the same offender. Household crimes and thefts are most frequently reported so that the victim could recover property. The two most common reasons given for not reporting violent victimizations to the police are that the crime was a private or personal matter, and that the offender failed in the attempt at violence. In the case of household crimes and thefts, the most common reasons for failure to report to the police were: (1) the stolen object had been recovered, (2) the crime had been reported to another official, and (3) there was insufficient proof relating to the crime.

Further evidence of the importance of the victim in the generation of official delinquency (or criminality, more generally) has come from several studies of police discretion in which it has repeatedly been found that offenders are more likely to be released by the police when victims make statements indicating that they are against prosecution.

The community, therefore, is the first step in the process whereby the behavior of a youth is escalated to the status of deviant, delinquent, or even criminal. Behavior that is ignored, no matter how repellent it may seem in the abstract, takes on no meaning beyond the interpretations of any immediate participants, observers, and victims. Realization of the importance of social response in the production of deviance led Frank Tannenbaum to lay the foundation for what later became labeling theory. He pointed out that boys in a slum area engage in a wide variety of mischievous, destructive, and possibly injurious behaviors. The behaviors are accepted as normal boys' activities by the boys themselves—it is only when the community takes responsive action (followed by the police, probation, the court, etc.) that the process of escalation and possibly labeling starts (see Chapter 6).

The Police

First Major Decision: To Release or Take Into Custody

It has been found over years of research that between 85 and 95 percent of the offenses of youths that have required police attention were relatively minor in nature. The offenses were, in other words, misdemeanors (or even less serious acts).

The Limits of Police Discretion

When a police officer confronts a youth who has been observed or is suspected of committing an offense, the officer must gather enough information at the scene to decide what to do with the youngster. If interrogation of the youth and other available people, together with observation of any possible evidence, serve to convince the officer that the youth committed no offense, the youth will generally be released with only the filing of a report that the incident occurred, usually called a field interrogation (FI) report. If that conclusion is not reached, the juvenile law of the state contains statements of the options available to the officer. In other words, the law specifies the amount of police discretion when there is good reason to believe that the youth committed an offense. In legal codes, good reason to believe that an offense was committed by a person or persons is referred to as probable cause or reasonable cause for so believing.

One option available to all officers is to deprive the youth of his or her liberty for a short period of time. The word "arrest" is generally used when an adult is deprived of liberty in that manner, but in formal and legal writing dealing with juvenile justice, the phrase "take into temporary custody" is used. (It should be pointed out again, however, that operating personnel use the term "arrest" in referring to the process for all ages, and the authors will do so frequently for ease of expression.) The different phrasing is part of an overall effort, starting with the first juvenile court in 1899, to differentiate the juvenile from the criminal process. There have been problems as well as gains from the phrasing. One advantage is that a person who was taken into temporary custody as a youth, no matter how many times, can accurately state that he or she had not been arrested. The problems stem from the applicability of the huge body of laws dealing with the arrest process. Davis has pointed out that "some courts have taken the position that the law of arrest does not apply to juveniles. That position finds potential support in legislative statements that taking a juvenile into custody does not amount to an arrest."[4]

The body of laws dealing with the arrest process (commonly called the law of arrest) contains important protections for citizens from abuse by the police. To make sure that these protections apply equally to the process of taking a youth into temporary custody, some states have wording in their codes such as the following recommendation of the Uniform Juvenile Court Act: "The taking of a child into custody is not an arrest, except for determining its validity under the constitution of this state or of the United States."[5]

A court in New Jersey stated that criteria for lawful arrest in the case of adults apply equally to the taking into custody of juveniles, although the New Jersey code states, "The taking of a juvenile into custody shall not be construed as an arrest. . . ."[6] Generally, courts have not specifically addressed the issue, leading to the assumption by some experts that the lack of judicial decisions on the question is due to general acknowledgment that the law of arrest is so clearly applicable to the juvenile process that the issue does not require special attention.

The following California code exemplifies a juvenile law that allows wide police discretion in deciding whether to take a youth into custody:

> A peace officer may, without a warrant, take into temporary custody a minor:
>
> 1. Who is under the age of 18 years when such officer has reasonable cause for believing that such minor is a person described in Section 601 [that is, has committed a status offense] or 602 [that is, has committed a criminal offense], or

2. Who is a ward of the juvenile court or concerning whom an order has been made [in regard to detention or disposition] when such officer has reasonable cause for believing that person has violated an order of the juvenile court or has escaped from any commitment ordered by the juvenile court, or

3. Who is under the age of 18 years and who is found in any street or public place suffering from any sickness or injury which requires care, medical treatment, hospitalization, or other remedial care.

In any case where a minor is taken into temporary custody on the ground that there is reasonable cause for believing that such minor is a person described in Section 601 or 602, or that he has violated an order of the juvenile court or escaped from any commitment ordered by the juvenile court, the officer shall advise such minor that anything he says can be used against him and shall advise him of his constitutional rights, including his right to remain silent, his right to have counsel present during any interrogation, and his right to have counsel appointed if he is unable to afford counsel.[7]

That statute clearly gives an officer a good deal of discretion in the decision regarding custody. The officer may take into custody any youth when it is reasonable to believe that the youth has committed an offense, either status or criminal. On the other hand, the comparable New York Family Court Act is more restrictive in specifying that "an officer may take a child under the age of sixteen into custody without a warrant in cases in which he may arrest a person for a crime."[8] In contrast to the California statute, by which a youth may be taken into custody when there is probable cause that he or she has committed a status offense, the New York statute limits the process to criminal offenses. That is, a police officer in New York is not authorized to take a youth into custody (without a warrant) when there is reasonable cause to believe the youth is in need of supervision (i.e., has committed a status offense). If the officer believes that custody is important for a youth who has not committed a crime, he or she must convince a magistrate that the youth needs supervision so that a warrant (summons) may be issued.

Davis illustrated the "potential abuse inherent in the broad jurisdictional power to take a child into custody, specifically in situations involving noncriminal conduct" by presenting a case from California in which an "appellate court expressed no concern over the fact that [a] juvenile has been taken into custody with neither warrant nor probable cause." Accordingly, he argues for the more restrictive New York approach, by which a magistrate's decision is necessary for noncriminal behavior, in the following way:

Most states grant very broad authority to police officers to take juveniles into custody in situations involving noncriminal conduct, under circumstances in which they are, in the broadest sense, endangered by their surroundings. These statutes indicate . . . that the decision to take a youth into custody is regarded primarily as a police decision. However, should it be solely a police decision when the broad jurisdictional power is invoked to take into custody a youth who is *not* charged with a criminal violation but rather, for example, is "in danger of leading a dissolute life"? Police officers generally are poorly equipped to make this sort of decision and the possibility of abuse is too hazardous to allow them to exercise it unchecked. To be sure, juveniles "in trouble" should receive help, but someone other than the officer in the street ought to assume the *primary* responsibility in the decision-making process.[9]

Finally, it is important to note that in state codes, no matter how broad the jurisdictional power granted to the police for taking a youth into custody, the phrasing is typically in the form of "may" rather than "must" take a child into custody under the stipulated conditions. That, of course, provides the basis for police discretion at the first major decision.

Does that imply that an officer is permitted to release a youngster (meaning no further action) suspected of committing a very serious offense, for instance, murder or assault with a deadly weapon? The answer is: legally, yes, but practically, no. The actions of an officer are influenced by a large array of forces in addition to the bare statements in legal codes. These include the written policies of the police department, the general ethos of the department as determined by the attitude of the chief, various peer pressures, specific and implied guides for actions by police supervisors, general working conditions, and the broad expectations of the community regarding appropriate police behavior. We will consider the operation of these forces later in this chapter.

A police officer stops a youth suspected of a criminal offense. Police have a good deal of discretion in the decision regarding custody of a youth. *(Photo by Mark C. Ide)*

Requirements During Interrogation

According to some states' codes and according to almost all recent court rulings, interrogation of a youth taken into custody must satisfy *Miranda* requirements. These requirements, which stem from the decision of the U.S. Supreme Court in *Miranda v. Arizona*, must be met before any statement made by a person in police custody may be used at a criminal trial. The Court stated:

> To summarize, we hold that when an individual is taken into custody or otherwise deprived of his freedom by the authorities in any significant way and is subjected to questioning, the privilege against self-incrimination is jeopardized. Procedural safeguards must be employed to protect the privilege, and unless other fully effective means are adopted to notify the person of his right of silence and to assure that the exercise of the right will be scrupulously honored, the following measures are required. He must be warned prior to any questioning that he has the right to remain silent, that anything he says can be used against him in a court of law, that he has the right to the presence of an attorney, and that if he cannot afford an attorney one will be appointed for him prior to any questioning if he so desires.[10]

In the California code presented above, the *Miranda* requirement is explicitly stated: "The officer shall advise such minor that anything he says can be used against him and shall advise him of his constitutional rights, including his right to remain silent, his right to have counsel present during any interrogation, and his right to have counsel appointed if he is unable to afford counsel."

It must be emphasized that a necessary condition for the requirements of *Miranda* (the right to remain silent, the right to an attorney, and the warning that any statement made by the suspect may be used against him or her) is that the person being interrogated be in custody. The *Miranda* requirements do not apply in situations in which a person is free to leave, as when a youth is interrogated by a school principal.

Some state codes have more restrictive requirements than those given in *Miranda* or in subsequent Supreme Court decisions that deal with the police interrogation of children. Oklahoma, for instance, requires the parent, guardian, attorney, adult relative or caretaker, or legal custodian of the child to be present during the interrogation and to be advised of the constitutional and legal rights of the child; otherwise, statements, admissions, or confessions of the child may not be used in court.[11] In other states, more restrictive conditions have been set by judicial decisions based on state law. For example, the Louisiana Supreme Court, following the lead of Pennsylvania, Indiana, and Georgia, required consultation with an attorney or other fully advised adult before *Miranda* rights could be waived by a youth.[12] Several writers have strongly argued in favor of a requirement for parental presence during the police interrogation of children. There will, of course, be problems when the parent and child are adversaries (that is, when parent and child have opposing interests). In such cases, appointment of a temporary legal counsel may be in order.

Second Major Decision: What to Do with a Youth Taken Into Custody

The Limits of Police Discretion

As in the case of the first major decision, a state code defines the limits of police discretion in deciding what to do with a youth who has been taken into custody. As Davis has emphasized, "In terms of protecting a juvenile's rights, the decision-making process that begins immediately after he is taken into custody is perhaps an area of even greater concern than the decision to take into custody."[13]

The alternatives commonly available to the police at this phase include outright release or release unconditionally to the custody of parents (alternatives usually called "counsel and release"), release to parents with a recommendation that help be sought from a community agency (an alternative that may fall under the rubric of "police diversion"—see Chapter 12), detention and referral to court intake (probation) in continued custody, or release to parents with the stipulation that future appearance at court intake is necessary. It is common in state statutes to require immediate notification to parents or guardian whenever a child is taken into custody, whether or not there is immediate release. For example, in North Carolina, "[a] person who takes a juvenile into custody, without a court order . . . . shall proceed as follows: (1) Notify the juvenile's parent, guardian, or custodian that the juvenile has been taken into temporary custody and advise the parent, guardian or custodian of the right to be present with the juvenile until a determination is made as to the need for secure or nonsecure custody."[14]

Despite expressed preference in state codes for minimum interference in the lives of youths, it has often been argued that the police overuse detention of youths and referral to the court. The President's Commission's Task Force on Juvenile Delinquency pointed out that the detention-referral process "has sometimes been employed not so much for protection of the juvenile or the community as for its shock effect on an alleged offender."[15]

Juvenile Officers

While it is typically an officer on patrol who takes a youth into custody, most medium and large police departments have specialized organizational units that are dedicated to juvenile matters. Such units are variously called juvenile divisions, juvenile bureaus, or youth services divisions, and the officers in the units are known as juvenile officers. In many departments, juvenile units are components of investigative (detective) services. Typically, the juvenile specialist takes over in the processing of young suspects, including interrogation and investigation, after a patrol officer has taken a youth into custody. In some departments, only juvenile officers may send youths to court intake, but more often, arresting officers may refer directly to the court if circumstances warrant.

A number of advisory committees have recommended the establishment of specialized juvenile units in all but the smallest departments. For example, one such committee for the state of Wisconsin recommended:

> In recognition of the frequency, complexity, and duration of juvenile problems coming to the attention of law enforcement, every such agency shall establish specialized support positions, in proportion to need, to enhance law enforcement services to juveniles . . . For every complement of 13 sworn officers there shall be the equivalent of one full-time officer whose work is primarily to:
>
> 1. Keep abreast of the needs of juveniles in the community;
>
> 2. Handle all juvenile dispositions more restrictive than release;
>
> 3. Advise supervisors of appropriate juvenile policies;
>
> 4. Provide advice to patrol officers to assist them in improving the quality of their juvenile contacts.[16]

Beyond that, the committee recommended a certification process for juvenile officers that included a mandatory curriculum containing courses ranging in content from the laws of arrest and the rights of juveniles to the psychology of adolescent behavior and theories of delinquency. Clearly, the committee believed strongly that the decisions of the second stage (that is, disposition after arrest) should be in knowledgeable hands.

To end this discussion of juvenile divisions on an incidental note, in years prior to the current era of general acceptance of all types of police work for women, almost all policewomen were given primary assignments as juvenile officers. Walker has pointed out that the first female police officer, Lola Baldwin, was hired by the Portland, Oregon, police department in 1905 for duties in "child protection." By 1925, 145 police departments had female officers, all assigned to work with juveniles. Walker expresses the spirit of the era as follows:

> The leaders of the policewomen's movement, moreover, stressed the idea that policewomen should project a helping image. They would not wear uniforms, would not patrol regular beats, and would not arrest adults. Spokeswomen emphasized the traditional childrearing role of the women. According to Mary Hamilton, the first policewoman in New York City, "the position of a woman in a police department is not unlike that of a mother in a home. Just as the mother smoothes out the rough spots, looks after the children and gives a timely word of warning, advice or encouragement, so the policewoman fulfills her duty."[17]

Actual Decisions

The Uniform Crime Reports for 1997 contain a table showing the rates of varying police dispositions of juvenile offenders taken into custody. They are: handled within the department and released, 24.6 percent; referred to juvenile court jurisdiction, 66.9 percent; referred to welfare agency, 1.1 percent; referred to other police agency, 0.8 percent; and referred to criminal or adult court, 6.6 percent.

Factors That Influence Police Discretion

As has been pointed out, several investigators found that the complainant or victim is very influential in the police decision regarding whether to take a youth into custody. A former police officer, Adrian Kinnane, has described other ways that the community influences the police as follows:

> In a middle-class neighborhood the officer is not expected to intervene as often as he does in a poorer neighborhood. People see him more as a public servant than as "the Man." He is expected to overlook minor parking violations and crowds in front of bars (unless the crowd is teenage). People do not drink in alleys because they have enough money to buy a drink at the bar, and they do not spill over into the streets as easily as poorer people, for whom the "public" street is often an extension of their own limited private property. There are fewer opportunities for police intervention in a middle-class neighborhood, and thus less of a history that the officer must live up to. The major cause of his interventions in these neigh-

borhoods is teenagers, both delinquent and nondelinquent. And the mobility of these adolescents means that the "car stop" is going to be one of an officer's major discretionary decisions. Any "souped-up" car is fair game here. A raised rear end, a loud muffler, a squealing acceleration, a large number of passengers, or any of the countless safety equipment violations (taillights, taglights, insufficient tread on tires, dashboard lights, etc., etc., etc.) justify a car stop that often leads to an alcohol or narcotics arrest, a stolen car, or a person wanted on a warrant.[18]

Clearly, then, the nature of the community plays a critical role in the determination of whether the police choose to pass a youngster through the front door into the juvenile justice system. We will now consider several other factors affecting police discretion at the second stage of disposition that also influence decisions at the first stage of release or custody.

Administrative and Organizational Factors

We turn again to Kinnane, a former police officer, for an interesting anecdotal summary of important administrative and organizational factors that influence police discretion, the first of which involves interaction between the community and the police hierarchy:

Another administrative factor is as follows: Would anyone around complain to my superiors if I were to handle it? The role of crime fighter can be held over an officer's head, and every time he makes a decision not to arrest where an arrest could, legalistically, be made, he takes a chance that someone will complain about his alleged inaction . . .

It was 11:40 at night—less than twenty minutes to go before shift change. The officer received a call for a group of teenagers drinking on a corner in a residential neighborhood. Seconds later he pulled up to the corner, got out of his car, and approached the boys. By this time, of course, all the beer was sitting in the gutter so that each boy could repeat the litany of innocence: "It's not mine, I don't know whose it is." The officer picked up the beer, poured it out, and ordered the boys off the corner. "But I live right here," protested one. "I don't care where you live," was the reply. "I got a complaint" worked wonders and the boys moved on, speculating on which old lady in the neighborhood turned them in. As the officer radioed in "Complaint abated" to the dispatcher and noted the complaint number of the call on his log sheet, he looked up at the windows around the corner, just a bit worried that someone would be disappointed that six specimens of degenerate youth had not been arrested.

If the officer had been receiving a lot of pressure from his sergeant to "get arrest stats up," he might have decided differently.

A final factor to be considered in the exercise of discretion is . . . the pressure of one's peers. In police work the regard and respect of one's colleagues is vitally important. In order to earn and maintain this respect, he must occasionally choose a course of action that, among other things, meets with the approval of his fellow officers. He must not be "too soft," and while it is difficult to be considered "too hard" without bordering on outright brutality, he must confine his hardness to "hardened criminals." An officer who is excessively physical in his handling of juveniles, for example, will be suspected of cowardice or "bullyism." If he is excessively tolerant, the word will spread that "they're carrying away his post," i.e., getting away with much more than "they" should. Not only is his own reputation at stake, but the work patterns of his colleagues are at stake too. If a too-lenient officer has a beat for a week, the officer who inherits that beat from him has to work extra hard to repair the damage done to the system of mutual expectations between citizens and police in that neighborhood.[19]

Some police departments maintain written guidelines for the handling of juvenile offenders, but many more do not. Several advisory commissions and committees have stressed the importance of such guidelines for placing desirable bounds on police discretion. For example, the committee in Wisconsin referred to earlier recommended, "The Chief or Sheriff of every law enforcement agency in Wisconsin shall immediately begin to develop written policies governing the agency's involvement in the apprehension, detection, and prevention of delinquent behavior and juvenile crime . . . [and] interaction with juveniles in custody." The need for these written policies is summarized as follows: "Presently, decisions are not restrained by mechanisms comparable to the principles of due process and the rules of procedure governing police decisions regarding adult offenders. Consequently, prejudicial practices by police officers can escape notice more easily in their dealing with juveniles than adults."[20]

Wilson, from a study of eight communities, conceived of three broad types of police departments on the basis of what he considered the "operating code of the department."[21] The operating code is reflected in a style of policing that shapes the way officers interact with the public. In departments with a "legalistic style," the emphasis is on high arrest rates, minimum discretion, and vigorous action against illicit enterprises. A single standard for community behavior is assumed so that juveniles are treated the same as adults; that leads to a large number of arrests and detentions for juveniles. In departments with a "watchman style," there is emphasis on maintaining order rather than on regulating individual behavior. The seriousness of infractions is judged more by immediate consequences than by strict law interpretation. In this type of department, "Juveniles are 'expected' to misbehave, and thus infractions among this group—unless they are serious or committed by a 'wise guy'—are best ignored or treated informally."[22] Finally, in departments with a "service style," which are often found in middle-class communities in which there is a consensus regarding the "need for and definition of public order," the emphasis is on courtesy and responsiveness to citizens with a minimum of heavy-handedness. In the words of Wilson, "with regard to minor infractions of the law, arrests are avoided when possible (the rates at which traffic tickets are issued and juveniles referred to Family Court will be much lower than in legalistic departments), but there will be frequent use of informal, nonarrest sanctions (warnings issued to motorists, juveniles taken to headquarters or visited in their homes for lectures)."[23] Although Wilson's typology is dated in several important ways and is much too general and descriptive for predictive purposes, it does convey an important relationship between the tone or ethos of a police department and the decision-making tendencies of its officers in police–citizen encounters.

In another publication, Wilson compared two police departments that differed markedly in the degree of "professionalism" in their handling of juvenile offenders. High professionalism implies recruiting officers on the basis of achievement and ability, low graft and corruption, equality in the enforcement of laws, and continuing formal training of officers. Contrary to expectations, he found, "In Western City [high in professionalism], the discretionary powers of the police are much more likely than in Eastern City [low in professionalism] to be used to restrict the freedom of the juvenile: Western City's officers process a larger proportion of the city's juvenile population as suspected offenders and, of those they process, arrest a large proportion."[24] He pointed out the price a community may pay in achieving a highly professional police department: "A principal effect of the inculcation of professional norms is to make the police less discriminatory but more severe."[25]

Finally, other writers have stressed the manner in which subtle forces emanating from advocacy groups, including police officer associations (unions), affect the decisions of police chiefs, which in turn affect departmental policy and regulations. As an example, vigorous complaints of a group of outraged citizenry may pressure the chief to change a tolerant departmental policy regarding youthful mischievousness in an area in which such youths congregate. The ultimate result may be the taking into custody of one or more youths who would never have made it through the front gate of the justice system without that community pressure.

Officer Characteristics and Perceptions

In addition to the statements of law and the array of external pressures on the officer, an important contribution toward discretionary decisionmaking comes from the set of personal characteristics of that officer. Police officers, like citizens in general, have different temperaments, moods, attitudes, biases, levels of tolerance for various types of behavior, and ethical and moral standards that influence their daily decisions—including those regarding what to do with a young offender. Indeed, certain results indicate that the personal beliefs of the officer may override all other factors in importance. It has been shown, for example, that officers tend to perceive lower-class boys as more delinquency-prone than boys from higher socioeconomic classes, employing implicit personal theories linking social class, parental neglect, and delinquent behavior.

One study of police dispositions in California concluded, "no matter what the offense, some officers are more likely to request petitions [that is, refer to the juvenile court] than others, and this trend is consistent for each offense category."[26] In that study, the proportion of referrals to the juvenile court (rather than informal adjustments) varied over investigators from a low of 0 percent to a high of 90 percent. Finally, a study comparing two departments that differed in professionalism on the handling of youths found that a police officer's socioeconomic background and personal difficulties with the law as a youth affect his or her referral rate (as well as degree of racial discrimination).

Beyond individual differences, officers change over time in characteristics like mood and level of tolerance, with concomitant effects on decisions. Thus, an officer may be in a pleasant, forgiving mood at one time and release a youngster to his or her parents without further action—and in an irritable, vengeful mood at another time and send on to probation or the juvenile court another youngster behaving much the same way.

Moreover, external forces and personal characteristics of officers interact in two primary ways. First, a given external pressure may very well produce different effects on different officers. For example, while most officers comply with a directive from superiors, a feeling of hostility toward those superiors (perhaps as a result of a salary or advancement issue) might lead a certain officer to a decision regarding a young offender that is precisely the opposite of what would be expected on the basis of the directive.

The second way external forces and personal characteristics interact is by the actual molding of the working personalities of the police by the forces. An illustration of that process is embedded in the issue of the "police personality," a set of characteristics frequently associated with police officers. According to the results of several studies, police officers show a tendency to be biased, cynical, suspicious, conservative, and authoritarian. It has been variously argued that one finds those features widely over police officers because: (1) people of that type are more likely to choose police work as an occupation, (2) police officers come from a class in society in which these features are widespread, (3) the screening process into police work tends to select people who are cynical and authoritarian, or (4) the police setting molds the personalities of its employees. Whatever the separate contributions of such determiners, it appears that the socialization process of the police is the most powerful influence in producing this constellation of personality characteristics.

Characteristics of Suspected Offenders and of the Offense

A study conducted more than 35 years ago reported the results of nine months of observation of the interactions between police officers and youths in a large industrialized city. It was found that police decisionmaking was affected by an array of the personal characteristics and self-presentation mannerisms of youths, but that one factor stood out in importance: the demeanor of the youth. In particular:

> both the decision in the field—whether or not to bring the boy in—and the decision made at the station—which disposition to invoke—were based largely on clues which emerged from the interaction between the officer and the youth . . . . These clues included the youth's group affiliations, age, race, grooming, dress, and demeanor. Older juveniles, members of known delinquent gangs, Negroes, youths with well-oiled hair, black jackets, and soiled denims or jeans (the presumed uniform of "tough" boys), and boys who in their interactions with officers did not manifest what were considered to be appropriate signs of respect tended to receive the more severe dispositions.
>
> Other than prior record, the most important of the above clues was a youth's demeanor . . . . The clues used by police to assess demeanor were fairly simple. Juveniles who were contrite about their infractions, respectful to officers and fearful of the sanctions that might be employed against them tended to be viewed by patrolmen as basically law abiding or at least "salvageable." For these youths it was usually assumed that informal or formal reprimand would suffice to guarantee

their future conformity. In contrast, youthful offenders who were fractious, obdurate, or who appeared nonchalant in their encounters with patrolmen were likely to be viewed as "would-be toughs" or "punks" who fully deserved the most severe sanction: arrest.[27]

That contribution led to a large amount of research relating arrest rates to characteristics of offender and offense. In summary, research results indicated: (1) arrest and subsequent referral rates to the juvenile court are higher for the more serious offenses (felonies) than for the less serious offenses (misdemeanors and status offenses), (2) a youngster is more likely to be arrested and referred by a police officer if he or she is known to have committed several prior offenses, (3) older youths are more likely to be arrested and referred than younger youths, particularly pre-teen youths, (4) the attitude of the young suspect (cooperative and respectful or the opposite) is frequently critical in determining police action, (5) while there does seem to be differential disposition of youths on the basis of race in some departments, there is no evidence that it is a common or widespread phenomenon, and (6) for the more serious offenses, boys have historically been more likely to be arrested than girls (but the reverse is true for status offenses).

SUMMARY

In the large majority of instances, police action in the case of a suspected young offender starts with a complaint by a citizen who may have observed or been a victim of an offense. The decision to initiate the complaint will be influenced by such factors as the seriousness of the offense, characteristics of the victim, general attitude of the community toward the particular type of offense, the number of times the offense was repeated by the youth, the mood of the observer or victim and his or her tolerance of deviance, and characteristics of the offender. The importance of the complainant in defining deviance and who is to be considered deviant is further highlighted by the substantial influence he or she has in the police officer's decision of whether to take a youth into custody.

State codes generally allow a good deal of discretion to police officers in the handling of juveniles, although there are differences in specific allowances. For example, New York permits an officer to take a juvenile into custody without a warrant only when the officer could have arrested an adult for the same crime. California, however, permits custody of a juvenile when there is probable cause that he or she committed an offense.

Before a youth may be interrogated after being taken into custody, the youth must be given the *Miranda* warnings—that is, informed that he or she has the right to remain silent and have an attorney present (to be appointed if the youth cannot afford one), and that statements made during the interrogation may be used against him or her. In some states and court jurisdictions, there are restrictions beyond those in *Miranda* on interrogating youths, such as the required presence of a parent or guardian during interrogation.

Whether the interrogation and related investigation is brief or extensive, a decision must be made in regard to the disposition of the offender in custody. State codes permit outright release, release to parents or guardian without further action, release to parents or guardian with a stipulated requirement for appearance at court intake, and referral to court intake in continued custody. Police discretion enters here at its second major stage. The processing of youths in police custody prior to the dispositional decision and the decision itself are often in the hands of specialists called juvenile officers.

The decision whether to take a juvenile into custody and the decision regarding disposition are both influenced by an array of factors beyond community standards, complainant preferences, and the wording in state codes. These include the administrative style of the department; the mutual pressures of police officers upon each other; the personal characteristics of police officers and how these are affected by administrative and organizational pressures; the characteristics of suspected offenders—demeanor, sex, race, prior offense history, and attitude; and the nature of the offense.

REFERENCES

Black, Donald J., and Albert J. Reiss, Jr. (1970). "Police Control of Juveniles." *American Sociological Review* 35:63-77.

Bouza, Anthony V. (1990). *The Police Mystique: An Insider's Look at Cops, Crime, and the Criminal Justice System*. New York: Plenum.

Cicourel, Aaron V. (1968). *The Social Organization of Juvenile Justice*. New York: Wiley.

Criminal Victimization in the United States, 1995 (1998). Washington, DC: U.S. Department of Justice, Bureau of Justice Statistics.

Davis, Samuel M. (1980). *Rights of Juveniles: The Juvenile Justice System*. New York: Clark Boardman.

Greene, Jack R., and Carl B. Klockars (1991). "What Police Do." In *Thinking About Police: Contemporary Readings*, 2nd ed., edited by Carl B. Klockars and Stephen D. Mastrofski. New York: McGraw-Hill.

Kinnane, Adrian (1979). *Policing*. Chicago: Nelson-Hall.

Lohman, Joseph D., and Gordon E. Misner (1996). *The Police and the Community: The Dynamics of Their Relationship in a Changing Society*. 2 vols. Washington, DC: U.S. Government Printing Office.

Lundman, Richard J., Richard E. Sykes, and John P. Clark (1980). "Police Control of Juveniles: A Replication." In *Police Behavior: A Sociological Perspective*, edited by Richard J. Lundman, 130-151. New York: Oxford University Press.

McEachern, A.W., and Riva Bauzer (1967). "Factors Related to Disposition in Juvenile Police Contacts." In *Juvenile Gangs in Context: Theory, Research and Action*, edited by Malcolm W. Klein and Barbara G. Myerhoff. Englewood Cliffs, NJ: Prentice Hall.

Morash, Merry (1984). "Establishment of a Juvenile Police Record: The Influence of Individual and Peer Group Characteristics." *Criminology* 22:97-111.

Niederhoffer, Arthur (1969). *Behind the Shield: The Police in Urban Society*. Garden City, NY: Anchor Books.

Piliavin, Irving, and Scott Briar (1964). "Police Encounters with Juveniles." *American Journal of Sociology* 70:206-214.

The President's Commission on Law Enforcement and Administration of Justice (1967). *Task Force Report: Juvenile Delinquency and Youth Crime*. Washington, DC: U.S. Government Printing Office.

Steffensmeier, Darrell J., and Robert M. Terry (1973). "Deviance and Respectability: An Observational Study of Reactions to Shoplifting." *Social Forces* 51:417-426.

Tannenbaum, Frank (1938). *Crime and Community*. Boston: Ginn.

Tonry, Michael, and Norval Morris, eds. (1992). *Modern Policing*. Chicago: University of Chicago Press.

Walker, Samuel (1980). *Popular Justice: A History of American Criminal Justice*. New York: Oxford University Press.

Wilson, James Q. (1968a). "The Police and the Delinquent in Two Cities." In *Controlling Delinquents*, edited by Stanton Wheeler, 9-30. New York: Wiley.

Wilson, James Q. (1968b). *Varieties of Police Behavior: The Management of Law and Order in Eight Communities*. Cambridge, MA: Harvard University Press.

Wisconsin Special Study Committee on Criminal Justice Standards and Goals (1977). *Final Report*. Madison, WI: The Council.

NOTES

[1]   *Los Angeles Times*, September 7, 1999, Part I, 1.

[2]   Black & Reiss (1970), 67.

[3]   Lundman, Sykes & Clark (1980), 139.

[4]   Davis (1980), 33.

5   Uniform Juvenile Court Act, Section 13b, (drafted by the National Conference of Commissioners on Uniform State Laws), 1968.

6   N.J. Stat. §2A:4A-31 (1999).

7   Cal. Wal. & Inst. Code §625 (1999).

8   §305.2[2] (1999).

9   Davis (1980), 3-9, 10.

10   384 U.S. 478, 479 (1966).

11   10 Okl. St. §7303-3.1 (1998).

12   *State in the interest of Dino*, 359 So. 2d 586 (La. 1978).

13   Davis (1980), 3-34.

14   N.C. Gen. Stat. §7A-572 (1999).

15   President's Commission on Law Enforcement and Administration of Justice (1967), 13.

16   Wisconsin Special Study Commission on Criminal Justice Standards and Goals (1977), 36.

17   Walker (1980), 139.

18   Kinnane (1979), 139.

19   Ibid., 38.

20   Wisconsin Special Study Commission on Criminal Justice Standards and Goals (1977), 31, 32.

21   Wilson (1968b), 140.

22   Ibid., 140.

23   Ibid., 201.

24   Wilson (1968a), 15.

25   Ibid., 28.

26   McEachern & Bauzer (1967), 152.

27   Piliavin & Briar (1964), 159, 160, 210.

10

The Juvenile Court

In Chapter 9, we examined the police process, starting with initial contact between officer and youth, which usually results from the complaint of a citizen. At this point, the youth may be released without being referred to the juvenile court. In this chapter, though, we will continue the examination of the juvenile justice process by assuming that a court referral is made. Referral may be by written document, in which case the youth is immediately released to the custody of his or her parents, or by bringing the youth to a court facility while keeping him or her in police custody. The process, whether the youth is referred in custody or not, brings into operation an evaluative process by court officers. This process encompasses interviews with the referred youth, his or her parents, such people as police officers and witnesses who can provide relevant information about the case, and an attorney (if one is handling the case at this point). The evaluation is often referred to as intake screening because it occurs at the entry point to the juvenile court and its primary function is to determine who is referred to the court for a hearing by the filing of a petition and who is screened out.

A petition for a hearing in juvenile court starts a procedure similar to a trial for an adult accused of a criminal offense. The petition requests the court to "inquire into conditions and enter such an order as may be necessary for the child's welfare" for a youth who is "in need of care and planning by the court" (or appropriate variants of the language in quotations). The petition identifies the youth by name, birth date, sex, and address; identifies parents or guardians by names, marital status, and address; provides a statement of the facts and allegations of the case; and summarizes previous court orders concerning the minor in question.

A time for the hearing—called the adjudicatory or jurisdictional hearing—is then set. The purpose of the adjudicatory hearing is to determine whether the youth committed the offense(s) as stated, or in more formal terms, to determine the truth of the allegations in the petition with regard to misbehaving. If the "allegations are sustained," the child is considered the equivalent of "guilty" in the adult court.

In addition to adjudicatory hearings, juvenile courts conduct each of the following types of hearing: detention hearings, waiver or fitness hearings, and dispositional hearings.

When a youth is arrested by a police officer, delivered in custody to an intake officer, and then kept in custody in a locked facility, there must be a judicial determination of the appropriateness of detention within a period of time specified in the relevant state code. The judicial determination is called a detention hearing.

A juvenile court may waive jurisdiction to the adult criminal court when the youth does not seem amenable to its methods of rehabilitation. The assumed lack of amenability may stem from the seriousness of the crime, the repetitiveness of the youth's criminal behavior, previous failures of the court in preventing recidivism, the age of the youth, the attitude of the youth, or some combination of these factors. A decision on this matter is made in a waiver or fitness hearing. Because the juvenile court decides whether to waive its jurisdiction, the term "waiver hearing" is clear enough. The term "fitness hearing" stems from the alleged goal of the hearing to determine whether the youth is "fit" for the treatment methods of the juvenile court.

The dispositional hearing follows the adjudicatory hearing (often immediately) and involves determination of a program for rehabilitation. That program could be probation, placement in a foster home, institutionalization, or some other alternative. Clearly, there is no need for a dispositional hearing if the allegations in the petition are not sustained.

In 1996, juvenile courts processed about 1,757,000 delinquency cases,[1] which represented a 49 percent increase over the years 1987-1996. The most common offenses leading to referral to the juvenile court in 1996 were: larceny-theft (24 percent of the cases), simple assault (12 percent), drug law violation (10 percent), burglary (8 percent), obstruction of justice (7 percent), vandalism (7 percent), disorderly conduct (5 percent), and aggravated assault (5 percent). Seventy-seven percent of the referrals to juvenile court were male, 59 percent were under the age of 16, and 30 percent were African-American (as compared with a juvenile population that was 15 percent African-American).

Detention was used in 18 percent of the cases. It was used frequently for drug law violations (23 percent of the cases) as for personal offenses including assault, forcible rape, and robbery. About 20 percent of the cases were dismissed at intake, frequently because the legal basis for further action was insufficient. Another 24 percent were handled informally where the youth agreed to the terms of the disposition—as in, for example, informal (that is, not court-ordered) probation. The final 56 percent of delinquency cases were petitioned for an adjudicatory or waiver hearing. About 58 percent of juveniles who were referred to adjudicatory hearings were judged to be delinquent (in juvenile terms, the allegations in the petition were sustained). The dispositional hearings for those so judged led to the following outcomes: Fifty four percent were given formal (court-ordered) probation, 28 percent were given institutional placement, and the remaining cases were referred to an outside agency or required to perform community service, including restitution to the victims of the offense in question.

DETENTION

The Role of the Court Intake Officer

As discussed in Chapter 9, referral of a youth to the juvenile court by the police may be accomplished as the youth is transferred to court intake in full custody. Observers of operations in the Denver juvenile court described the process of transfer and reception while in custody as follows:

> Almost hourly, a patrol car will turn into the alley behind juvenile hall with a child or two for the admissions office. The door is locked, and a buzzer must be pushed to notify the counselor that another child is awaiting admission. The child will pass through the door into a poorly lit office area. Behind a large counter, a juvenile hall employee waits to get basic information from the child and to relieve him or her of all valuables. If an intake screening counselor is not readily available, the child will be placed in a small locked room across from the admissions office until an interview can be arranged which will aid in determining whether or not the child will be detained pending a detention hearing before the court.[2]

It is clear from the quotation that when a youngster is brought in custody to the court facility, an intake officer has the decision-making responsibility of release or continued detention until a detention hearing is held. The task is generally performed by a probation officer, who, in larger probation departments, is commonly designated an intake probation officer. While recognizing that the decision regarding continued detention is the task of people who are not probation officers in some jurisdictions, we will use the terms "court intake officer," "intake officer," and "intake probation officer" interchangeably in referring to these evaluators.

Justifications for Detention

Typical state laws allow detention for one or more of the following reasons:[3]

1. Release of the youth endangers the person or property of others.

2. The youth himself or herself would be subject to harm if released.

3. There is substantial danger that the youth will flee and not be available for the adjudicatory and dispositional hearings. This may be a particular concern because there is no constitutional requirement for release on bail in juvenile justice, and such release is not allowed in most states.

4. There is not adequate supervision available for the youth in the community.

5. The youth has fled from another jurisdiction and is being processed for return to that jurisdiction. The youth might be a runaway parole violator, or a runaway from an institution to which he or she had been committed.

Usually, state statutes are expressed in rather general terms rather than in the restrictive manner recommended by agencies like the National Council on Crime and Delinquency (NCCD). For example, while the NCCD recommendations include forceful language stating that children may be detained only if they are "almost certain" to run away or to commit a dangerous offense, state laws are commonly worded to include detention for children who are "likely" to flee or endanger the community.

Whatever the legal justifications for the detention of youths, it became obvious through studies of the detention process that there are many extralegal factors that affect decisions to detain. The legal criteria determine who should be detained, but studies of the process in operation show who actually was detained and the special factors that apparently led to the detention decisions. Several of these extralegal factors are the following:

1. The feeling by some police and some (fewer) probation officers that a short period in jail or in a juvenile hall is the equivalent to a kick in the pants that might straighten out a young offender (see Chapter 9).

2. The concern of probation officers that release of a youngster who is brought in custody by police officers will result in severe police displeasure and endanger future rapport. That this reason may not be an overwhelming one, especially from the perspective of the police, is the frequent complaint a person in the field hears from police officers, "Why, that little bastard was back on the streets before I even got back from delivering him to juvenile hall."

3. Concern in the general community for the safety of citizens during a period of high crime, particularly violent crime by young offenders, may put pressure on justice personnel to lower considerably the release probabilities of youths taken into custody.

4. The availability of intake personnel for a thorough evaluation on a 24-hour basis seems to lower the probability of detention.

5. There are variations over intake officers in personal bias and variations over courts in philosophy, leading to emphasis on such factors as demeanor of the youth or the kind of home the youth comes from or number of prior offenses in certain contexts.

The Detention Hearing

The detention hearing is the court's review of an intake officer's decision to detain a youth. This is required by code in most states. The specific maximum time allowance for the detention hearing varies from state to state, as does the moment that the "clock" starts. For example, the California code states that a minor taken into custody must be released within 48 hours (excluding the nonjudicial days of Saturdays, Sundays, and holidays) from the moment of initial custody (arrest) if a petition has not yet been filed for an adjudicatory hearing. Further, if a petition has been filed, the minor must be brought to court to determine whether further detention is warranted by the end of the judicial day following the filing. Thus, in California, if a youngster is taken into custody by the police on Monday afternoon and kept in custody, he or she must have a detention hearing by the end of Thursday, assuming the petition is filed on Wednesday. The allowed delay would, of course, be longer if the arrest took place on a Thursday or a Friday, which would have the intervention of nonjudicial days before the required time limitation took effect—or if a holiday intervened.

The Role of Attorneys

Many states have declared the right to counsel (including court-appointed counsel when the alleged offender cannot afford retained counsel) at every stage of the juvenile proceedings. This represents an extension of both the *Kent* and *Gault* decisions, which required counsel only at the waiver and adjudicatory hearings, respectively. (See the relevant discussion in Chapter 8.) Some states simply declare the right to counsel without specifying that the right applies at all stages, other states require a court-appointed counsel where the juvenile requests one but cannot afford the expense, and still other states declare that a judge may appoint counsel at his or her discretion. The following verbiage from the code of California illustrates the most definitive type of grant of the right to counsel at a detention hearing:

> Upon his appearance before the court at the detention hearing, such minor and his parent or guardian, if present, shall first be informed of the reasons why the minor was taken into custody, the nature of the juvenile court proceedings, and the right of such minor and his parent or guardian to be represented at every stage of the proceedings by counsel.[4]

Several courts and standards-setting bodies have argued that the right to counsel at detention hearings is critical. One body even stated that the right is so critical that it should be nonwaivable.

Bail

The U.S. Supreme Court has not granted juveniles the constitutional right to bail, although one federal district court ruling has granted juveniles in its domain the same right to bail that adults have in criminal proceedings.[5] A handful of states have codes denying juveniles the right to bail, while several states have enacted laws expressly granting it to juveniles. In the other states, it is either not mentioned at all or left to the discretion of the court.

Most courts have taken the position that the emphasis on release to parents at the various decision points in juvenile processing provides an adequate alternative to the bail system, or that bail would be a cumbersome imposition on the juvenile court. As Davis has concluded, "The protective function of the juvenile court requires that it exercise a special responsibility toward children that is not necessary or appropriate in the case of adults. . . . It sometimes happens that those circumstances warrant [their] detention."[6]

Selection Criteria for Detention

Research has not shown a pattern of preference for detention on the basis of race. While a few studies have found that blacks were detained at a significantly higher rate than whites, many others have found no such difference. The lack of a clear relationship between race and detention may be the result of such complicating factors as differential arrest patterns.

On the other hand, several studies have shown that children of low socioeconomic status (SES) are more likely to be detained than children of middle and high SES, with no difference between the latter two. Using family income and educational levels reported in the census tracts for residences of youths who were candidates for detention, Cohen concluded, "It appears then that . . . the socioeconomic status of individuals referred to each of our courts is not substantially related to the criterion, but that in each court a greater proportion of youths from low status tracts was detained than middle and high status youths."[7] Despite that and other findings of a relationship between low SES and a greater likelihood of detention, the result has not been uniformly obtained.

Contrary to what one might expect from the data in Chapter 1 that indicated the far greater seriousness and frequency of crime by boys as compared with girls, the available evidence shows that girls have historically been more likely to be detained than boys and to be held for longer periods. Contributing to this is the high proportion of girls who have been referred to court intake for status offenses, together with the surprisingly high tendency to detain status offenders in past years.

Highlighting the extent of that anomaly in previous decades, a 1969 study found that in all but one of 11 jurisdictions, status offenders were detained at a higher rate (usually a much higher rate) than youths who committed crimes against persons. A similar but less pronounced pattern occurred in the comparison of status offenders with those who committed crimes against property. Averaging over jurisdictions produced percentages of juveniles detained as follows: crimes against persons (7.9 percent), crimes against property (27.8 percent), and status offenses (42.0 percent). Furthermore, research reported in 1975 and 1976 found, respectively, "that over 60 percent of all secure detentions were for 'status offense' reasons"[8] and that only 11.7 percent of children in adult jails "were charged with serious offenses against persons." The latter report added, "The rest—88.3 percent—were charged with property or minor offenses. What is most alarming is that 17.9 percent of jailed children . . . had committed 'status offenses' . . . such as running away or truancy."[9]

The array of results indicating higher proportions of youths in detention for lesser offenses than for serious offenses in the 1960s and

1970s was not purely a function of the frequencies of the various offenses. This is evident in findings by Cohen during the early 1970s of detention decisions in three juvenile courts serving large communities: Denver County, Colorado; Shelby County, Tennessee; and Montgomery County, Pennsylvania. In Denver County, 22.1 percent of CHINS and 29.3 percent of those with alcohol offenses were detained, as compared with 22.2 percent of those who committed property crimes and 27.4 percent who committed violent crimes. In Shelby County, the detention percentages were as follows: unruly behavior (42.7 percent), alcohol offense (34.0 percent), property crime (42.0 percent), and violent crime (55.2 percent). Finally, in Montgomery County, the percentages were: unruly behavior (51.5 percent), alcohol offense (5.0 percent), property crime (10.2 percent), and violent crime (21.6 percent). Emphasizing the fact that detention was not used predominantly for the serious offender was the finding that across the three jurisdictions, 40 percent of the status offenders were detained as opposed to 38 percent of those who committed violent crimes, and 31 percent of those who committed either alcohol or property offenses. Another study of that era involved a random sample of more than 600 files from the records of juvenile courts in three New Jersey counties. Those data were supplemented with interviews with court personnel, lawyers, and police officers.

Perhaps most interesting are the great differences over the three courts in detention decisionmaking (as well as court decisionmaking at other processing points), despite the fact that they operated under the same state laws. For example, in one county, detention rates were uniformly high (about 85 percent) for status offenders and for criminal-type offenders who committed serious, medium, or even minor offenses. In another county, with a low detention rate (about 25 percent), status offenders were detained at a higher rate (54 percent) than serious criminal-type offenders (25 percent), medium offenders (19 percent), and minor offenders (25 percent). The former was reported as the wealthiest county in New Jersey and was generally residential, while the latter was described as a densely populated county containing the city of Trenton. The third county (containing the city of Newark) was between the others in detention characteristics (with an overall rate of 53 percent and a rate for status offenders of 63 percent).

Results showing the tendency to detain status offenders, even in comparison with violent offenders, were influential in leading to significant changes in the law during the 1970s—changes that restricted the placement of status offenders in secure facilities. These changes are discussed in Chapter 11.

While the pattern of detention decisionmaking has necessarily changed because of these legal restrictions, more recent studies have shown that such factors as family circumstances and the available means for control of a child are often more critical than seriousness of crime (except for the most serious crimes) in determining a decision to detain or release a child.

INTAKE SCREENING

Court intake screening involves the same sort of discretionary decisionmaking that is involved in the case of the police.

Decisionmaking at Intake Screening

The functions of intake screening are as follows:

(1) to determine whether the circumstances of the case bring it within the jurisdiction of the juvenile court;

(2) to determine whether the evidence is sufficient to warrant a court hearing;

(3) to decide whether the case is serious enough to require a court hearing;

(4) and to arrange for a process of informal supervision if that alternative seems desirable. The process starts with an explanation of rights (to an attorney and to remain silent), the role of the intake officer, the decisions available, and what effect those decisions could have.

The officer is expected to dismiss a case if the circumstances make it inappropriate for the juvenile court or if the evidence is not sufficient for adjudication. However, as the Task Force on Juvenile Delinquency of the President's Commission reported:

The jurisdictional grounds, however, are broad, and at intake most cases are potential subjects of the juvenile justice process—if not for specific delinquent acts, then as incorrigibility or neglect. Most commonly, therefore, the major task at this point is to determine which cases to handle formally rather than whether a case for intervention exists. The choice is generally among dismissal (with or without referral to community service resources), unofficial handling by the court, and filing of petitions. Making that choice may call for exploration of the facts of the offense, the juvenile's background, and other facets of the case. . . .The basic choice is between adjudication and the various nonjudicial alternatives. The selection is signified by filing a petition or deciding not to do so.[10]

Creekmore summarized the factors that should be used in intake decisionmaking as follows:

Once the process has been explained, the interview should proceed through a two-step process. First, the complaint needs to be read and examined in factual detail and the youth questioned about the allegations. If the youth admits to the substance of the complaint, informal and formal handling or dismissal are possible. If the youth denies the complaint, only formal handling or dismissal are possible. The circumstances surrounding the offense in question need to be examined to determine if the complaint accurately represents what happened and if sufficient reason exists to file a petition based on information about this offense alone. The youth's involvement in the planning and execution of the offense, delinquent intent, and likelihood of repeating this or other offenses must also be gauged. If grounds for a petition are not found, the case should be dismissed or referred to another agency.[11]

Filing a petition in juvenile court is the rough equivalent to filing a complaint in the adult criminal system—it brings proceedings of the court into operation. The result is an adjudicatory hearing in the juvenile justice system.

Are Probation Workers "Tough Enough"?

It is important to reiterate that society's extreme displeasure with juvenile criminal behavior, particularly violent behavior, has led to statutory changes aimed at hardening the process of handling juvenile offenders (see Chapter 8). In addition to general effects on court philosophy, the hardening process has consisted of reducing the role of probation (which is often viewed as the "social worker" or compassionate side of justice), increasing the severity of punishment for juveniles (though a euphemism is often used for punishment), increasing the adversarial role of the prosecuting attorney in juvenile hearings, and decreasing the age at which minors may be tried in adult criminal courts. Our focus at the moment is on changes that affect court intake. To illustrate, the decision-making power of probation officers in California was eliminated for youths as young as 14 who have committed serious offenses. The law now requires immediate referral of such cases to the prosecuting attorney for possible petitioning with no option for such alternative dispositions as immediate release or informal probation:

> [In] the case of an affidavit [typically from the police] alleging that the minor committed an offense described in Section 602 [that is, a criminal offense], the probation officer shall cause the affidavit to be immediately taken to the prosecuting attorney if it appears to the probation officer that the minor has been referred to the probation officer for an offense [such as murder, robbery with a firearm, forcible rape, and kidnapping] and that offense was allegedly committed when the minor was 16 years of age or older or an offense [like the preceding except for some deletion of those considered a bit less serious] and that offense was allegedly committed when the minor was 14 years of age or older.[12]

Modification of the code to include youths as young as 14 occurred as recently as 1994, indicating the continuing doubts about the "toughness' of probation officers and the overall hardening of the juvenile justice system. Prior to that enactment, the responsibility remained with probation for children below the age of 16 for all offenses.

Other states that have responded particularly harshly (in legislative changes) to public demand for greater severity in dealing with criminal offenders of all ages include Washington, Arkansas, Hawaii, Florida, Minnesota, Indiana, Virginia, West Virginia, and Texas. The change in Washington has been described as abandonment of "the rehabilitation or 'best interests' model of juvenile justice . . . in favor of an offense-based, 'just deserts' model focusing on punishment and accountability."[13] The code requires referral to prosecution for all intake cases in the juvenile court that allege the commission of a criminal offense.[14] The responsibilities of the prosecutor may be performed by a probation counselor in cases of misdemeanors if sufficient notice has been given to the juvenile court.

There are some indications that the demand for more emphasis on public safety (and due process) have in recent years led probation departments to skepticism and despair. Perhaps in defense against being perceived as too soft, probation departments are substituting just-deserts (punitive) approaches, even without statutory support, in lieu of the former rehabilitative ideal.

Patricia M. Harris considered the intake role of probation officers in her attempt to answer the question, "Is the juvenile justice system lenient?"[15] She suggested that probation officers may be far less lenient than it seems on casual observation for several reasons. First, many cases are dismissed at intake for valid reasons, such as lack of evidence, the failure of victims or witnesses to cooperate, or the lack of credibility of a witness, while the public (including the police) may perceive only the release of "young thugs." Moreover, she and others have pointed out that informal probation may be just as restrictive and punitive as the formal probation that follows court processing.

The role and status of probation in juvenile justice has been strengthened somewhat recently by a federal effort (and funding) described as a "focus on accountability." The effort emphasizes the types of probation interventions shown to be most effective in well-designed research, an acceptance of victims and the community as clients of the system, the uses of mediation and restitution aimed at convincing young offenders of the consequences of their actions and their responsibility for those actions, and the stringent use of program evaluation. The results of the overall effort seem promising at both levels of probation: informal and court-ordered.

Informal Probation

Informal probation or informal supervision is based on an agreement among the probation officer, the minor, the minor's parents, and sometimes an attorney for a program of supervision whereby certain behavior is expected in order to avoid formal court proceedings. The maximum time allowed for the supervision is stated in law (usually three to six months). Within the allowed time, the probation officer may petition the court for a hearing (or refer the case to the prosecuting attorney for petitioning) if the conditions of informal probation are not satisfied.

A probation officer, thus, has the opportunity for control over a child's life during the period of time that informal probation is allowed under state law. The child could be required to be home by a certain time every evening, attend school regularly, call the probation department every day and visit it once each week, avoid various people who may have negative influences on the child's behavior, or attend counseling sessions at a local service agency. Because that sort of supervision could significantly interfere with a child's liberty, yet occurs by an administrative procedure without judicial review, there have been many criticisms of the process of informal probation over the years. One such criticism states:

> Informal handling, though having the advantage of minimizing the consequences of an encounter with the police and the courts and providing a way of settling matters by an agreement, has some serious drawbacks. A child, who has never been found within the jurisdiction of the juvenile court, may be subjected to a serious interference with his freedom. In short, public authority over the life of a child can be exercised without any judicial determination that a basis for it exists.[16]

The inherent dangers of informal probation led one important judicial committee to recommend the complete elimination of "nonjudicial probation" as an alternative disposition at probation intake, allowing referral to a community agency as the only permissible "nonjudicial disposition." In short, the committee felt that informal probation was too susceptible to possible abuse by intake officers. On the other hand, evidence indicates that courts, in contrast to opinions expressed in legal articles, are not sympathetic to making informal probation an impermissible option. The courts seem to insist on judicial determination with the usual due process rights only when there is the possibility of profound loss of liberty, as in detention. The restriction on freedom that may come with informal probation seems to be considered minor, closer to the restrictions that accompany arrest than the loss that accompanies incarceration.

The Choice Among Alternatives

Several studies have shown a close relationship between the seriousness of current offense and prior record of offenses, on the one hand, and intake decision (to petition or not to petition) on the other. However, marked differences have been found over jurisdictions. For example, a study by Rubin in 1972 found the percentages for filing petitions in cases of offenses against property to be 59 in one city and only seven in another; the respective percentages for filing in cases of offenses against persons were 55 and 31.

The age of the juvenile has also been shown to be a relevant factor in decisions at intake in various jurisdictions. Terry, in 1967, found that age ranked with seriousness of offense in determining the severity of disposition in a midwestern city; older juveniles are more likely to be referred to court than younger juveniles.

Differences found in the treatment of boys and girls at probation intake seem attributable to their immediate offenses and to their prior records. Terry did find, as expected, that boys were treated more severely at intake for criminal-type offenses, but full analysis of the data showed, "The seriousness of the offense and the number of previous offenses appear to account for most of the relationship between the 'maleness' of the offender and the severity of the probation department disposition."[17] Finally, some, but not all, investigators have reported racial factors as influential in the determination of decisions at intake. The issue is complicated by an observed interactive effect between race and such other determinative factors as seriousness of immediate crime, prior record, and social support system.

The following are some of the conclusions reached after a thorough review (by Smith, Black, and Weir) of the literature on decisionmaking at intake:

(1) the juvenile's prior record—the number of prior court referrals or number of previous offenses recorded—appears to be most consistently influential across all jurisdictions.

(2) The role of the alleged offense . . . is less clear. . . . There are definite variations between jurisdictions in which offenses are most likely to result in dismissal, informal adjustment, or referral for a court hearing.

(3) Age appears to be somewhat related to intake screening decisions in that younger juveniles appear not to be referred on for a formal court hearing as frequently as are older juveniles.

(4) Family status appears to be somewhat influential.

(5) Socioeconomic status and the juvenile's school attendance or employment do not appear to have an impact on the decisions made at the intake level.

(6) The studies do not indicate any consistent or predominant pattern of discrimination on the basis of race or ethnicity or of sex.[18]

THE WAIVER HEARING

The purpose of the waiver hearing is to determine whether the juvenile court should relinquish its jurisdiction over a minor and transfer the case to the jurisdiction of an adult criminal court. As discussed in Chapter 8, the U.S. Supreme Court decided in *Kent v. United States* that waiver of jurisdiction is a "critically important" decision in the sense that it is accompanied by potentially serious consequences for the youth in question. Accordingly, the Court ordered a certain degree of procedural formality accompanied by a minimum of due process rights in waiver hearings.

Another Supreme Court decision (also mentioned in Chapter 8) that bears on waiver hearings is *Breed v. Jones.*[19] In this case, the Court ruled that waiver to and prosecution in an adult criminal court after an adjudicatory hearing in juvenile court is constitutionally invalid because the procedure violates the double jeopardy clause of the Fifth Amendment. This establishes a functional equivalence between a juvenile hearing and a criminal trial.

Waivers to criminal court occurred in about 1 percent of the cases in which petitions were filed for hearings in juvenile courts in 1996, a figure that remained relatively constant over the decade preceding that year.[20] The characteristics of the approximately 10,000 cases so waived in 1996 were as follows:

Most Serious Offense	
Person	43%
Property	37%
Drugs	14%
Public order	6%
Gender	
Male	95%
Female	5%
Age at Time of Referral	
Under 16	15%
16 or older	85%
Race/Ethnicity	
White	51%
Black	46%
Other	3%
Predisposition detention	
Detained	51%
Not detained	49%

Criteria for Waiving Jurisdiction

In an appendix to the *Kent* decision, the Supreme Court listed the following as suggestive criteria in the determination of waiver of juvenile court jurisdiction to adult criminal court:

1. The seriousness of the alleged offense to the community and whether the protection of the community requires waiver.

2. Whether the alleged offense was committed in an aggressive, violent, premeditated or willful manner.

3. Whether the alleged offense was against persons or against property, greater weight being given to offenses against persons especially if personal injury resulted.

4. The prosecutive merit of the complaint . . .

5. The desirability of trial and disposition of the entire offense in one court when the juvenile's associates in the alleged offense are adults who will be charged with a crime . . .

6. The sophistication and maturity of the juvenile . . .

7. The record and previous history of the juvenile . . .

8. The prospects for adequate protection of the public and the likelihood of reasonable rehabilitation of the juvenile . . . by the use of procedures, services, and facilities currently available to the Juvenile Court.[21]

Almost all states have statutes providing for waiver of jurisdiction from juvenile court to criminal court (as of late 1996, such transfer could not occur in the states of Massachusetts, Nebraska, New Mexico, and New York). In most states, statutes authorizing waiver specify threshold criteria modeled on the eight points listed above in the *Kent* decision. Generally, those statutes specify a minimum age, a specified seriousness of offense, and a sufficiently repetitive pattern of offending. However, 17 states allow waiver for any offense, at least for older age groups. Here is an example of one of the tougher statutes (Vermont's) authorizing discretionary waiver:

Transfer from juvenile court

(a) After a petition has been filed alleging delinquency, upon motion of the state's attorney and after hearing, the juvenile court may transfer jurisdiction of the proceeding to a court of criminal jurisdiction, if the child had attained the age of 10 but not the age of 14 at the time the act was alleged to have occurred, and if the delinquent act set forth in the petition was any of the following:

(1) arson causing death. . . .

(2) assault and robbery with a dangerous weapon. . . .

(3) assault and robbery causing bodily injury. . . .

(4) aggravated assault as defined in [another Vermont statute]. . . .

(5) murder. . . .

[and seven additional serious offenses].[22]

The allowance of waiver for a child as young as 10 is the lowest of the minimum transfer ages specified over all states; in most other states, the specified minimum age is 13 or 14 (which indeed would seem young enough for a criminal trial). The upper age (of 13) specified in the Vermont code does not imply that older children may not be tried in a criminal court. There are other paths. For one, Vermont specifies that the adult criminal court has original jurisdiction when the youth is 14 or older and has committed one of the previously specified serious offenses. (The law does, however, allow reverse waiver, that is, from criminal court to juvenile court—a process that will be discussed shortly.) Finally, another section of the above code (b) allows the "state's attorney of the county" to move the juvenile court to waive its jurisdiction for any age and any offense, but there are more restrictions placed on the hearings for such actions.

The preceding discussion of the Vermont code uses two of three paths of youths to criminal court: discretionary waiver and statutory exclusion (the criminal court has original jurisdiction for those 14 and above who allegedly committed serious crimes). The third path is "direct file," by which the prosecutor may file either in the juvenile or the criminal court, as he or she chooses. That option is available in Vermont for those who are at least 16 and are not subject to statutory exclusion (that is, have not committed one of the specific serious offenses for which the prosecutor has no choice but to file in criminal court). Direct file will be discussed in more detail later in this chapter.

A case before Maryland's Court of Special Appeals illustrates the limits in discretionary decisionmaking when a statute specifies the criteria that must be used to justify waiver.[23] Diane was accused of killing a two-year-old boy in a grossly negligent manner when she drove a car onto a sidewalk and struck three children (the other two children survived). She was 16 years old at the time of the accident and did not hold a license to drive; her inexperience in driving was shown in the cause of the accident—she put her foot on the accelerator when she intended to apply the brakes.

The state's attorney for Baltimore requested a waiver hearing under the argument that the safety of the public required a criminal trial. As stated in the decision:

> The legislature has mandated that five factors are to be considered by the juvenile judge in any waiver proceeding. The factors are:
>
> (1) Age of child.
>
> (2) Mental and physical condition of child.
>
> (3) The child's amenability to treatment in any institution, facility, or programs available to delinquents.
>
> (4) The nature of the offense.
>
> (5) The safety of the public.
>
> Not all of the five factors need be resolved against the juvenile in order for the waiver to be justifiable.[24]

At the waiver hearing, it was established that Diane was an above-average student who seemed responsible and reliable in school with no evidence of any behavioral problems. Furthermore, she was active in civic affairs and regularly attended church, where she was a member of the choir. Her minister testified at the hearing that she was "very concerned about what has happened" and that occasionally "she has been crying because of the death of the two-year-old."

The judge granted the state's request and waived the case from juvenile to criminal court with the comment, "She has not been in any difficulty and she has done well in school and has been active in school activities, has been active in community activities, but I base my decision on her age, almost seventeen when this occurred, and essentially on the very grievous nature of the offense."[25] The judge admitted that the decision to grant waiver was a very difficult one for him.

The decision was appealed on the basis that "the judge abused his discretion by granting waiver."[26] The Maryland Court of Special Appeals agreed and remanded the case back to juvenile court for an adjudicatory hearing. Its decision stated, "We think it apparent that the hearing judge was unduly influenced by the 'nature of the offense' to the extent that the amenability of the appellant to rehabilitation was cast aside and not considered, or, if considered, was not afforded its proper weight." In addition, the appeals court stated that all five legislative factors must be considered actively by the hearing judge, with a proper balancing among them in the arrival at a final decision. The court felt that this was not done in this case.[27]

The ruling of the appeals court hinted at the punitive element in the waiver decision because of the death of a two-year-old boy. The case raises the issue of the social pressure on a judge—direct or implicit—to make a harsh decision when his or her community is deeply offended by an act or the result of an act; communities are very deeply affected by a tragedy involving a young child. Appeals courts are more immune to that type of pressure.

In a fashion similar to the Maryland appeals decision, the Montana Supreme Court required that all criteria specified in the waiver statute be carefully considered and weighed in each individual case before arriving at a waiver order.[28] It should be emphasized, though, that not all courts have taken similarly restrictive positions.

Feld objects to the process whereby judges make waiver decisions on the basis of their clinical evaluations of youths' "amenability to treatment" or "dangerousness." He argues: "In short, judicial waiver statutes that are couched in terms of amenability to treatment or dangerousness are simply broad, standardless grants of sentencing discretion." Juvenile court judges are thus allowed "virtually unreviewable discretion by allowing selective emphasis of one set of factors or another to justify any disposition."[29] Feld is in favor of the widespread use of statutory exclusion, whereby certain offense categories or age/ offense/prior record categories are excluded from the jurisdiction of the juvenile court. Youths in those categories are no longer defined as "children" for immediate legal purposes. As noted above, Vermont has such an exclusion for those 14 years of age and older who have allegedly committed such offenses as arson (causing death), assault, robbery with a weapon or with bodily injury, and murder.

The toughening of juvenile justice in recent years has had its greatest effect in raising the likelihood that the case of an alleged young offender will be tried in adult criminal court rather than be heard in juvenile court. This direction is endorsed by Feld, who is perhaps the United States' leading advocate for doing away with the juvenile court entirely. He argues, "States should uncouple social welfare from social control, try all offenders in one integrated criminal justice system, and make appropriate substantive and procedural modifications to accommodate the youthfulness of some defendants."[30]

It does not seem likely that society will do away with the juvenile court despite Feld's arguments. However, the "get tough" movement is approaching that result anyway by lowering the age at which waiver may occur, broadening age and offense categories for statutory exclusion, and turning more of the responsibility over to prosecutors for the decision regarding juvenile or criminal court (by direct file and by the fact that the prosecutor determines the nature of the alleged offense, i.e., the charge).

Another approach to toughening in this area is referred to as presumptive waiver. Presumptive waiver has been well illustrated in California over the past several decades. A code change that went into effect in 1977 specifies that if a youth (of 16 or 17 years of age) is alleged to be an offender who committed any of a long list of serious crimes, "the minor shall be presumed to be not a fit and proper subject to be dealt with under the juvenile court law."[31] Thus, if the minor is accused of one of the listed serious crimes (e.g., murder, arson, or forcible rape), a *prima facie* case of unfitness for the juvenile process is created, and the burden of proof to show fitness falls on the minor. In contrast, and as is generally the case in waiver hearings (or fitness hearings, as they are called in California), when one of the listed crimes is not alleged, the burden of proof falls on the prosecutor to show unfitness (i.e., the unsuitability of the youth for the methods of rehabilitation available to the juvenile court).

Similarly, in 1980, legislation in Minnesota provided that if a youth is 16 or 17 years of age and is accused of certain serious offenses or there is a certain combination of offense and intent or sophistication, a *prima facie* case for certification for criminal processing is established.[32] The goal of the legislation was to specify the serious offender, for purposes of the waiver decision, on the basis of age, offense, and prior record. There was, in short, a presumption that a serious offender of that type was not suited for treatment by the methods of the juvenile court. Interestingly, the effects of this legislation were evaluated using demographic data and case history information from the juvenile court files in Hennepin County (Minneapolis). The investigators compared the number of waiver motions filed by the county attorney for periods before and after enactment of the new legislation and found no significant change. Still, after the legislation became effective in 1981, county attorneys chose to file waiver motions in only slightly more than one-half of the cases in which the presumptive criteria were satisfied. To make the legislation even more questionable, the investigators found that the presumptive criteria "single out many juveniles whose records do not appear to be very serious and fail to identify many juveniles whose records are characterized by violent, frequent, and persistent delinquent activity."[33] Clearly, then, the legislation did not have the desired effect of singling out serious offenders for criminal trials.

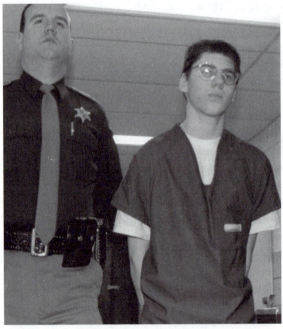

Fifteen-year-old Andrew Wurst is escorted by a sheriff's deputy to his waiver hearing in March 1999. The court heard testimony to decide whether Wurst, charged as an adult in the April 1998 killing of teacher John Gillette in Edinboro, Pennsylvania, should stand trial as an adult or juvenile. *(AP Photo/Gene J. Puskar)*

For that and other reasons, a 1992 law created a task force to study the operations of, and recommend changes to, Minnesota's juvenile justice system. The recommendations of the task force led (with minor changes introduced by the two branches of the legislature and by the governor) to a new juvenile code, effective January 1, 1995. The new law scrapped the previous criteria for certification, replacing it with one that, presumably, would make it more likely that the case of a serious offender (of 16 or 17) would be tried in criminal court. The new criteria placed greater emphasis on protection of the public. In addition (and incidental to the current topic), the new code created the new category of "extended juvenile jurisdiction" for serious young offenders whose cases remained in juvenile court. These juveniles have hearings in the juvenile court and potential dispositions with elements of adult trials, convictions, and dispositions. These elements include a jury, adult sentences, and hearings that are open to the public. The code includes an interesting diversion and threat combination as follows:

Subd.4. Disposition (a) If an extended jurisdiction juvenile prosecution results in a guilty plea or finding of guilt, the court shall:

(1) impose one or more juvenile dispositions . . .,

and

(2) impose an adult criminal sentence, the execution of which shall be stayed on the condition that the offender not violate the provisions of the disposition order and not commit a new offense.[34]

Actual Due Process Rights in Waiver Hearings

In arguing for the invalidity of the waiver order in the *Kent* case, due to the inadequacy of the procedure used by the juvenile court, the U.S. Supreme Court pointed out:

> We do not consider whether, on the merits, Kent should have been transferred; but there is no place in our system of law for reaching a result of such tremendous consequences without ceremony—without hearing, without effective assistance of counsel, without a statement of reasons. It is inconceivable that a court of justice dealing with adults, with respect to a similar issue, would proceed in this manner.[35]

That would seem to specify clearly the right to counsel in waiver hearings. However, because Kent had an attorney at his waiver hearing and because of references to that attorney in several parts of the written decision, there have been differences in interpretation of that elementary due process right. In one legal casebook, for example, we find, "Kent did not finally decide the issue of right to counsel at the waiver hearing, since the Court was not faced with that issue."[36] On the other hand, in another, equally sophisticated, legal casebook, we find, "Specifically, the Court [in *Kent*] set forth four basic safeguards required by due process during the waiver proceedings: . . . (2) The juvenile is entitled to representation by counsel at such hearings."[37]

There is another major difference in interpretation. Appellate courts have taken differing positions on whether the *Kent* rulings are derived from the U.S. Constitution or from the juvenile code of Washington, DC. Those differing positions determine the generalizability of the decision: if based on the Constitution, it governs waiver hearings in every court in the country, but if based on a local code, it has obviously more restricted generalizability. The tendency to use the constitutional interpretation has gained increasing weight in recent years, and that means minimum due process requirements for all waiver hearings.

OTHER PATHS TO THE CRIMINAL COURT

Given that this chapter deals with the juvenile court, the concentration has been on the hearings in that court (one being the waiver hearing). However, discussion of that type of hearing led to reference to two other types of law and process that produce the same end result of trial for a youth in an adult criminal trial: statutory exclusion and direct file. Even though they are tangential to juvenile court operations, they are important enough for elaboration in this chapter.

Statutory Exclusion

In response to serious juvenile delinquency, the state of New York passed harsh legislation in 1978 to deal with violent young offenders. Youths of ages 14 and 15 were made criminally responsible for such violent or potentially violent acts as murder, kidnapping, arson, rape, robbery, and burglary, giving original jurisdiction for trial to the criminal court. Thirteen-year-old youths were made criminally responsible for murder, again meaning original jurisdiction in the criminal court. (In this context, it is worth pointing out again that the age at which trial becomes the responsibility of the adult court in New York is 16.)

One motivation for that legislation in New York was the use of 13-, 14-, and 15-year-old youths by adults for crimes such as contract murders. Even if caught, the youths would be subject only to the (supposedly rehabilitative) methods available to the family court, whereas an adult would be subject to the more severe punishments available to the criminal court. As mentioned earlier in this chapter, there is no waiver in New York from family court to criminal court.

Under current law,[38] a youth of 13 or older charged for second-degree murder and one of 14 or older for first-degree manslaughter, first-degree rape, aggravated sexual abuse, or other serious crimes are assumed "criminally responsible" as "juvenile offenders" and tried in criminal court. (The juvenile offender designation does not affect the nature of the trial but does allow more lenient sentencing treatment.) However, reverse waiver is allowed in that the criminal court may waive jurisdiction to the family court if it finds, after considering various factors enumerated by statute but similar to the ones listed in the *Kent* decision as criteria for waiver in the other direction, that "to do so would be in the interests of justice." In the most serious cases, the district attorney must give consent to the waiver.

As noted and discussed above, Vermont has statutory exclusion, extending down to the age of 14. A total of 28 states now have statutes that remove certain age/offense categories from the jurisdiction of the juvenile court. The minimal age is usually 15 or 16, but Georgia, Oklahoma, and New York have a minimum of 13. Statutes vary from New Mexico's legislation, which specifies statutory exclusion only for murder and for those 15 or older, to that of Mississippi, which specifies statutory exclusion for any felony using a deadly weapon for those as young as 13. Twenty of the 28 states that have statutory exclusion also have provision for reverse waiver.

Direct File

As has been mentioned, Vermont does allow the prosecution to file in the criminal court rather than the juvenile court for a specified category of cases, if it so chooses. The distinguishing feature of direct file is that it depends on the concurrent jurisdiction of juvenile and criminal courts over specified kinds of cases. There are statutes in 15 states that present offense/age categories in which the prosecutor may decide in which court to file.

The following code from Arkansas illustrates this approach:

> A circuit [criminal] court and a juvenile court have concurrent jurisdiction and a prosecuting attorney may charge a juvenile in either court when a case involves a juvenile: (1) At least sixteen (16) years old when he engages in conduct that, if committed by an adult would be a felony; (2) Fourteen (14) or fifteen (15) years old when he engages in conduct that, if committed by an adult, would be: (A) Capital murder . . .; Murder in the first degree . . .; Murder in the second degree . . .; kidnapping . . .; Aggravated robbery . . .; Rape . . .; Battery in the first degree . . .; [and many other similarly serious offenses].[39]

Beyond authority of that sort, as stated above, prosecuting attorneys have the implicit power to choose the court in which a juvenile case will be heard in states where determination is based on the offense that is "charged." This may be illustrated most effectively by the District of Columbia code. A child is defined in it as "an individual who is under 18 years of age." Then, however, an exception is made whereby "The term 'child' does not include an individual who is sixteen years of age or older and—(A) charged by the United States Attorney with (i) murder, first-degree sexual abuse, burglary in the first degree, robbery while armed, or assault with intent to commit any such offense."[40] Thus, if the United States Attorney (the prosecutor) chooses to charge a 16- or 17-year-old with burglary in the second degree, the juvenile's case will be referred to juvenile court, but if the choice is burglary in the first degree, the case will go to criminal court because the juvenile is no longer defined as a "child."

Incidentally, another section of the D.C. code allows the "Corporation Counsel" to file a motion requesting transfer from juvenile court to criminal prosecution for a child of 15 who has committed any felony, and for various other conditions for which the prosecuting attorney has referred to the juvenile court.[41]

To determine the effectiveness of prosecutorial discretion, Gillespie and Norman examined the practice in Utah by which the prosecutor certifies juvenile offenders for waiver to a criminal court. They interviewed juvenile court personnel and analyzed official records over a four-year period. Certification was not widely used, and under 14 percent of all certifications were for the most serious offenses of murder and rape. Further indication that the citizens of Utah were not getting the results they may have expected from the process was in the finding that 53 percent of those certified were neither incarcerated in prison nor given lengthy periods of institutionalization.

Davis has vigorously objected to the determination of jurisdiction by prosecutors, original jurisdiction residing in the criminal court, and other deviations (such as concurrent jurisdiction) from the model of original jurisdiction in the juvenile court for the offenses of youths. After pointing out that the allowance of original jurisdiction in criminal court may represent social outrage at violent crime, he emphasized, "If the community's rage in response to the crime itself overcomes its sense of purpose in dealing with youthful offenders, this represents abandonment, or at least a suspension in certain cases, of the commitment to the rehabilitative ideal and a return to the purely retributive concepts prevalent in the nineteenth century."[42]

THE ADJUDICATORY HEARING

The adjudicatory hearing is functionally equivalent to the trial in criminal court in the sense that the goal is to determine the facts regarding the truth of allegations made about a person. In the criminal court, the allegations are contained in formal charges filed by a prosecutor or grand jury, while in the juvenile court, the allegations are contained in the petition for a hearing (as discussed earlier in this chapter). To help assure that decisions in adjudicatory hearings are based only on relevant facts regarding the allegations of offense, courts have prohibited the use of information in social reports until the fact finding is completed and an adjudicatory decision is reached. In particular, several state courts have ruled that a juvenile court's review of social and personal historical factors before the adjudicatory hearing is improper. The decision in an adjudicatory hearing, in short, is expected to be based on whether the youth did or did not do what is alleged, and such social characteristics as relationship to parents and academic performance are supposed to be irrelevant to that decision process.

Due Process Rights

In the *Gault* decision, the U.S. Supreme Court was unambiguous in its declaration that a juvenile who has violated a criminal statute and who may be committed to an institution (1) has a right to counsel, (2) must be given timely notice of factual allegations to be considered at the adjudicatory hearing, (3) has the right to confront and cross-examine witnesses, and (4) has the right to remain silent. There remains uncertainty about due process rights in the case of an adjudicatory hearing in which commitment to an institution is not a reasonable option for the court, as well as how widely and effectively the *Gault* rulings have been put into effect in juvenile courts throughout the country even when directly applicable.

An immediate question that might occur to the student of the *Gault* decision and its consequences might be: Do status offenders have the right to counsel in adjudicatory hearings? The *Gault* decision does not apply to them because they have not violated criminal statutes (so that their hearings are not normally considered "delinquency" hearings), and in most states (as we shall see in Chapter 11) they may not be committed to an institution.

The Assistance of an Attorney

As mentioned in the section devoted to detention hearings, some states have given the right to counsel "at every stage of the juvenile proceedings." That sort of wording has led some observers to argue that the right to counsel extends to cases of noncriminal offending, that is, status offenses. The codes of several jurisdictions specifically indicate that the right to counsel is applicable in the case of status offenses as well as in criminal offenses ("delinquency" cases). Finally, other states specify a general right to counsel or leave the decision of appointment of counsel to the discretion of the court.

In general, courts have not resolved the question of the right to counsel in nondelinquency cases. The few rulings so far indicate little willingness to grant a constitutional right to counsel in the hearings of status offenders who are not subject to institutionalization, regardless of the available alternative dispositions.

However, it is of interest to note, in a study of two juvenile courts in a southeastern area, that Marshall, Marshall, and Thomas found that there was little difference in the formality with which status and criminal-type offenders were processed. They stated that their analysis "indicates that statutory distinctions between legal categories (status versus criminal) have virtually no relevance for the degree of formality with which these cases are processed by the courts. Although the prosecutor appears to be somewhat more active when dealing with non-status offenders, there are hardly any differences with regard to the vigorousness of the defense activities."[43]

Other Due Process Rights

In addition to the right to counsel, the U.S. Supreme Court in *Gault* declared the rights to timely notice, to confront witnesses, and to remain silent in delinquency hearings that could lead to incarceration. Subsequent to *Gault*, the Court stated (in the case of *In re Winship*) that proof beyond a reasonable doubt was required during the adjudicatory phase of a delinquency proceeding.[44] In another important case (*McKeiver v. Pennsylvania*),[45] the Court drew a limit to constitutional rights, ruling that there was no right to a jury in adjudicatory hearings. It stated, "The imposition of the jury trial on the juvenile court system would not strengthen greatly, if at all, the fact-finding function, and would, contrarily, provide an attrition of the juvenile court's assumed ability to function in a unique manner."[46] Despite that strong statement, the decision did not prevent states from allowing jury trials. Indeed, we find the following position that seems to contradict its stated concern for maintenance of the court's uniqueness: "If in its wisdom, any State feels that the jury trial is desirable in all cases, or in certain kinds, there appears to be no impediment to its installing a system embracing that feature."[47]

A note in a law journal shortly after the *McKeiver* decision was released pointed out that 10 jurisdictions provided jury trial for juveniles in statutes and five others allowed jury trial by court mandate. An identical finding on the statutory right to jury trial was reported three years later, indicating no short-term retreat because of the Supreme Court's ruling. A similar picture was found more recently. The note questioned whether the right to a jury trial would continue in the state of Tennessee because the decision to grant the right was based on the federal Constitution (and the Supreme Court ruled that there was no such right in the U.S. Constitution). In 1978, however, the Tennessee Supreme Court ruled jury trial to be a matter of right under certain conditions.

Because the Supreme Court requires proof beyond a reasonable doubt in delinquency proceedings (that is, where there is criminal conduct with the possibility of confinement), what is the generally accepted standard of proof in the hearings of status offenders? In many states, the standard of proof is "preponderance of the evidence" or "clear and convincing evidence" for status offenders, as opposed to the stricter "beyond a reasonable doubt" for criminal-type offenders. A number of court rulings have upheld that difference but several states provide that proof beyond a reasonable doubt is the standard of proof in both delinquency and status offense cases.

Status offenders have not been alleged to have committed crimes. Therefore, by definition, they cannot be waived to adult criminal court. A double jeopardy issue did arise in one status offense case in which a petition was dismissed on the grounds of insufficient evidence. A petition was then filed for the same case and circumstances on the basis of allegations of violations of criminal law. An appeals court did not allow the hearing on the delinquency petition, arguing that it represented double jeopardy.

The issues of confrontation of witnesses, self-incrimination, and timely and effective notice of allegations have not generated much attention by courts beyond the requirements of *Gault*. Attention has been directed to more esoteric matters, such as the use of hearsay testimony, the need for corroborative evidence to support confessions, and whether the timely notice must satisfy the technical requirements of an indictment. The statutes of some states, however, confer on juveniles the rights to confrontation and cross-examination.

Due Process—Reality or Myth?

The title of this subsection is identical to the title of an article (published in 1976) that is part of a monograph devoted to research on the juvenile court. It reflects a debate among many commentators of the adjudicatory scene (and, secondarily, of preadjudicatory and postadjudicatory court processes). Several who take the position that due process in the juvenile court is myth rather than reality go on to argue for the court's dissolution and substitution of criminal trials in which due process is indeed reality.

In the article "Due Process—Reality or Myth?" Sosin and Sarri state, "If one looks only skin-deep, it appears that the Supreme Court mandates [for due process] have been almost universally adopted by juvenile courts. However, compliance becomes less complete the more deeply one looks at the operation of the court."[48]

Their look at the operation of the court consisted of a study based on two juvenile court samples. The first sample was obtained primarily by random selection from a listing of larger counties in the United States. Questionnaires were then sent to the selected courts for completion by key court personnel. The second sample, selected in a more directed manner, was targeted for more intensive study. That more intensive effort involved interviews, discussions, and observations in the seven selected courts to supplement the information obtained from the more broadly distributed questionnaires.

About 28 percent of the judges in the broad sample believed, "The Supreme Court has gone too far in protecting the rights of criminals."[49] About one-third of the judges did not believe that a petition should be dismissed even if there is not sufficient evidence to confirm the allegations. As the writers comment, "Perhaps even here it is indicative of the state of due process in many courts that roughly one-third of the judges do not agree with this very basic premise of the Supreme Court decisions."[50] Using a rough summary approach to measuring compliance with due process mandates of the Supreme Court, they found such compliance to be about 70 percent.

The survey results were generally confirmed in the intensive study in field sites. For example, they observed, "Seldom in the courts visited did it appear that lawyers were vigorously defending their clients"[51] and "lawyers seldom confront witnesses, and social reports are rarely used by lawyers to call witnesses." Thus, even when due process changes have been implemented, there was "only surface-level compliance from courts; there has been no due process revolution."[52]

Feld has argued that matters have not changed much up to 1999:

> Unfortunately, *In re Gault* constituted an incomplete procedural revolution, and a substantial gulf still remains between the law on the books and the law in action. States continue to manipulate the fluid concepts of children and adults, or treatment and punishment in order to maximize the social control of young people. For example, states use the adult standard of "knowing, intelligent, and voluntary under the totality of the circumstances" to gauge juveniles' waiver of rights . . . even though juveniles lack the legal competence of adults. Research on juveniles' waivers of *Miranda* rights . . . and waivers of their right to counsel provide compelling evidence of the procedural deficiencies of the juvenile court. On the other hand, even as juvenile courts have become more punitive, most states continue to deny juveniles access to jury trials or other rights guaranteed to adults. . . . Juvenile courts provide a procedural regime in which few adults charged with crimes and facing the prospect of confinement would consent to be tried.[53]

THE DISPOSITIONAL HEARING

The dispositional hearing in the juvenile court is comparable to the sentencing hearing in the adult criminal court. The goal is to decide what to do with a youth after it has been determined in a fact-finding hearing (the adjudicatory hearing) that he or she has offended in a manner that justifies court jurisdiction. That determination is equivalent to the determination of "guilt" in the adult criminal court.

In a substantial number of states, there is a bifurcated hearing process in which the adjudicatory and dispositional hearings are distinct and separate entities. The principal reason for the bifurcation lies in differing rules for the types and manner of presentation of evidence. Generally speaking, because the dispositional hearing is concerned with considerations of rehabilitation and correction rather than fact finding, virtually any information is admissible that bears on such matters as interpersonal relationships in general, family characteristics, health and medical history, academic achievement, types of friends, attitudes toward teachers and others in authority, and previous failures at adjustment. Thus, the social report, which (as mentioned earlier in this chapter) is not admissible in an adjudicatory hearing, is critical for the specification of individualized treatment aimed at meeting the youth's needs and protecting the public. The importance of the social report in dispositional decisions is illustrated by a court decision stating that disposition of a juvenile must be based on the characteristics of the offender rather than the gravity of the offense, as well as another decision ruling that a social history used in a dispositional hearing must be up to date. (One is not likely to encounter that first type of ruling in the current "get tough" atmosphere, in which there is frequently more emphasis on punishment and protecting the public than on rehabilitative disposition.) Some jurisdictions even have specific statements in their codes that require judges to use a social report in arriving at dispositional decisions.

The codes of some states specify that the dispositional hearing may begin immediately after the adjudicatory hearing, but delays of several weeks or longer are possible if there is a need for time to complete a social history or to receive evidence on a motion of the court or of a parent. In several states, there is a limit to the allowed delay between adjudicatory finding and the start of dispositional hearing, with special concern for youths who are being detained pending disposition. For example, in California, the delay may be up to 45 judicial days if the youth is not detained, but only 10 judicial days if he or she is detained.[54] (A judicial day is an ordinary working day for a court.)

A study of samples of cases from juvenile courts in Atlanta, Salt Lake City, and Seattle found that almost all dispositional hearings occurred on the same day as the corresponding adjudicatory hearing.

The median delay between time of filing the petition and final disposition was reported as follows: Atlanta, 41 days; Salt Lake City, 19 days; and Seattle, 70 days.

The Essence of the Hearing

In a manual prepared for training programs of the National Council of Juvenile Court Judges, it is stated, "The disposition hearing in the juvenile court may be the most complicated process of the entire Anglo-American judicial system."[55] That position is taken because it is an adversarial proceeding with a mixture of recommendations by probation and social workers; reports of social and academic histories; and interactions within the court among the legal participants, the offender and his or her family, probation staff, and, perhaps, psychologists and social workers. According to the manual, it is not simply a process of matching punishment to offense. "It is, rather, the matching of the needs of a complicated human being to every available facility and talent of the court and community which might best answer one particular individual child's needs, and the public's safety. It is a hearing, a judicial hearing, but with overtones of a discussion."[56]

That statement represents a surface view of operations. A more philosophically oriented (and franker) picture of the dispositional hearing is provided in the following quotation from a decision of the Supreme Court of Appeals of West Virginia:

> The dispositional stage of a juvenile proceeding is designed to do something which is almost impossible, namely, to reconcile: (1) society's interest in being protected from dangerous and disruptive children; (2) society's interest in nurturing its children in such a way that they will be productive and successful adults; (3) society's interest in providing a deterrent to other children who, but for the specter of the juvenile law, would themselves become disruptive and unamenable to adult control; (4) the citizens' demand that children be responsible for invasion of personal rights; and, (5) the setting of an example of care, love, and forgiveness by the engines of the state in the hope that such qualities will be emulated by the subject children. While retribution is considered an unhealthy instinct and, conceivably, an immoral instinct in an enlightened society, nonetheless, State imposed retribution has historically been the quid pro quo of the State's monopoly of force and its proscription of individual retribution. Retribution is merely another way of saying that children are to be treated as responsible moral agents.[57]

Due Process Rights

A dispositional hearing is obviously a critical stage in juvenile processing because it can lead to the most severe loss of liberty (institutionalization) and so it is widely accepted that it must be held in accordance with minimum due process standards. As juvenile codes are revised, they almost invariably require the provision of counsel at such hearings. Moreover, many legal experts have argued for (and several courts have affirmed) the right on constitutional grounds even where there was not a statutory requirement.

Prosecuting attorneys and counsels for the defense in dispositional hearings may be active advocates of the adversarial positions they represent or more passive in their approaches. In a more active role, a defense counsel, for example, may contest the harsher recommendations of the probation staff and argue for a more lenient disposition on the basis of mitigating circumstances stemming from interactions in the child's life. Similarly, the prosecutor may argue for the need to protect the public from a serious offender or one with a long history of offenses.

In accordance with the differences between adjudicatory and dispositional hearings in degree of formality and related uses of evidence, it is generally accepted that not all safeguards necessary in fact finding are required for dispositional decisionmaking. That includes the right to confront and cross-examine witnesses. Extrapolating from *McKeiver v. Pennsylvania*, there would seem to be no basis for a constitutionally based right to jury during a dispositional hearing. Even in the case of one state that has a codified right to jury during an adjudicatory hearing (Oklahoma), a court ruled that the right does not extend to disposition.[58]

Rubin lends a touch of reality to any discussion of due process rights in pointing out that it is common in many courts for a dispositional decision to be made before the dispositional hearing even starts. That may occur in an informal conference between judge and probation officer in the judge's chambers, in some other office, or even in a hallway. Understandably, he emphasizes, "This approach hardly comports with due process."[59]

Alternative Dispositions Available to the Court

In broadest terms, the available dispositional alternatives include treating a youth in his or her community or institutionalizing him or her. Return to the community is often accompanied by an order for supervision in formal probation (in contrast to the informal probation that may occur without a court order). However, it may involve only return to the parents or transferring custody to another person or agency under court supervision. The process of institutionalization may be a direct one by which the youth is sent by the court to a state training school or to a local facility that is subject to the court's direction (which may be operated by the probation department), or an indirect one by which the youth is sent to the appropriate state department, which in turn determines actual placement.

Type of Offender

In most jurisdictions, the specific alternatives available for disposition depend on whether the youngster was adjudicated as a criminal-type offender or as a status offender. Commonly, a status offender may not be sent to a secure institution—locally or state-run. (The development of that restriction since 1974 is discussed in the next chapter.) Some states, though, do not distinguish between youths who commit criminal offenses and those who commit status offenses (referring to both in some such form as "delinquent children") and specify equivalent dispositions for all as designated. Still other states allow institutionalization of children referred to in their codes as CHINS, PINS, or an equivalent designation for status offenders.

A West Virginia court objected to the practice of designating all offenders as delinquent children and allowing the same range of alternatives for a young serious offender as for a truant or a runaway. A West Virginia code stated that a child may be adjudicated a "delinquent child" if he or she commits an act that would be a crime if committed by an adult (short of the most serious crimes), is a habitual truant, is incorrigible or ungovernable, or is a runaway.[60] Another code permitted placing an adjudicated "delinquent child" in "an industrial home or correctional institution for minors."[61] As allowed by those statutes, a juvenile court in West Virginia sent a 16-year-old boy to a forestry camp because he had been absent from school for 50 days. The Supreme Court of West Virginia objected in resounding terms. The essence of the decision is shown in the following quotation:

> We find with regard to status offenders . . . [that] incarceration in secure, prison-like facilities, except in a limited number of cases, bears no reasonable relationship to legitimate state purposes, namely, rehabilitation, protection of the children, and protection of society. In view of the foregoing, and in view of the fact that there are numerous alternatives to incarceration for status offenders we hold that the State must exhaust every reasonable alternative to incarceration before committing a status offender to a secure, prison-like facility. Furthermore, for those extreme cases in which commitment of status offenders to a secure, prison-like facility cannot be avoided, the receiving facility must be devoted solely to the

custody and rehabilitation of status offenders. In this manner
status offenders can be spared contact under degrading and
harmful conditions with delinquents who are guilty of criminal conduct and experienced in the ways of crime.[62]

Concordant with that perspective, the court ordered the youngster
to be "discharged forthwith from custody and restored to his liberty."[63]
Further, it invited actions from other children held in state institutions
in violation of the guidelines enunciated in the decision, including
directing the superintendents of all juvenile institutions in the state to
post the opinion of the court in conspicuous places. The West Virginia
legislature reacted positively to the scolding on the part of its Supreme
Court by modifying the phrasing in its code by the amendment process.
The phrasing "juvenile is a status offender or a juvenile delinquent" was
substituted for "child is a delinquent child."

An earlier decision in New York anticipated later developments on
a national scale in its ruling that no person in need of supervision
(PINS) may be sent to a state training school for delinquent children.[64]
That ruling was based on interpretation of the New York Family Court
Act. (As an interesting aside, Ellery C., the youth in the preceding
PINS case, later stabbed and killed a 14-year-old boy. That led to a suit
against the state on the grounds that the public had not been adequately
protected and that the youth's problems had been exacerbated.)[65]

Harsher Penalties for Serious Offenders

Over the past decades, several states have legislated harsher alternatives for serious offenders as part of the general picture of "getting
tough on crime." To illustrate, the New York Juvenile Justice Reform
Acts of 1976 and 1978 called for the establishment of facilities that
were physically restrictive in construction, interior characteristics, and
procedures. Youths who committed certain designated felonies (such as
murder, assault, rape, manslaughter, kidnapping, and robbery in the
first degree) could be sent by the family court to restrictive placement
for up to 18 months, followed by mandatory placement in a secure residential facility. Restrictive placement was authorized for youths down
to 13 years of age on the basis of their criminal acts, and down to seven
years of age with two prior adjudications for felonious behavior. Further, once a restrictive order is placed by a court, it cannot be modified,
set aside, or vacated. There was, in short, no pretense that the acts were
not motivated by the desire for retribution and punishment for serious
young offenders within the juvenile system.

Similarly, in its Juvenile Justice Act of 1977, the state of Washington created the category of "serious offender" for youths 15 years of age and older who commit such crimes as murder, manslaughter, assault, and robbery. The act led to a set of sentencing standards that a court consults to determine commitment time. A disposition outside the allowed time range has to be justified by clear and convincing evidence.

In 1986, Pennsylvania added to its juvenile code the definition of a "dangerous juvenile offender."[66] A dangerous juvenile is a child of 15 years of age or older who has committed a serious violent crime (such as attempted murder, voluntary manslaughter, or rape) and who previously was adjudicated as delinquent, after turning 12, for a similarly serious violent act. The same law directed the Pennsylvania State Police to establish a repository containing the fingerprints and photographs of such dangerous juvenile offenders, together with the histories of their criminal activities.

The adoption of that type of categorization continued up to 1995, as discussed above, when Minnesota created its "extended jurisdiction juvenile." Prosecutors in that state may now designate certain 16- and 17-year-old serious offenders as extended jurisdiction juveniles. Their cases are heard in juvenile court, but they receive adult sentences (which are stayed pending good behavior) in adddition to juvenile dispositions. That process, it is worth pointing out, is a type of "blended sentencing." The expression refers, generally, to the imposition of juvenile and/or adult sanctions on serious young offenders who have been adjudicated in juvenile court or convicted in criminal court. By the end of 1995, 17 states had some form of blended sentencing. Other forms of blended sentencing are as follows: Oklahoma allows either a juvenile or an adult sanction in criminal court; Iowa allows both juvenile and adult sanctions in criminal court; Texas allows the juvenile court to impose a sentence that remains beyond its jurisdiction (first juvenile, then adult sanctions).

Two other ways in which disposition/sentencing practices have been made harsher over recent years are by mandatory minimum sentences and the extension of the jurisdiction of the juvenile court to older youths. To illustrate the former, in 1977, Arizona passed a law specifying that a juvenile of at least 14 adjudicated for a second felony must: serve mandated juvenile detention time, be incarcerated in a state correctional facility, or be placed under intensive supervision. Five states (Florida, Kansas, Kentucky, Montana, and Tennesse) set high ages for the jurisdiction of their juvenile courts, allowing the committing of juveniles to correctional facilities for longer periods of time.

The Death Penalty

The death penalty must be considered as a final dispositional alternative in the widespread national tendency to "get tough" in cases of serious juvenile crime. While there were relevant court decisions and discussions in scholarly journals in immediately preceding years, the issue reached prominence in 1985 when a 15-year-old Arkansas boy was sentenced to death by injection for the murder of two elderly women and their great-grandnephew. Although the sentence was eventually reversed, the case attracted nationwide attention. The interest and concern raised by the case were heightened because, less than a week earlier, the attorney general of the United States had declared that states are justified in executing young people who commit capital crimes when they are below the age of 18.

Writing two years before that decision, Streib argued that execution was in the process of emerging as a serious dispositional alternative for the capital offenses of children. In addition to the return to reliance in the United States on capital punishment for adults, Streib attributed the trend to more trials for juveniles in criminal courts. He emphasized that the phenomenon is not a new one, pointing out that of the 14,029 legal executions in American history up to 1983, 287 have been for crimes that were committed by youths below the age of 18. As surprising as it may seem, 192 of these uses of the death penalty took place after the inauguration of the juvenile justice system.

In the case of *Eddings v. Oklahoma*,[67] the U.S. Supreme Court vacated the death sentence of Monty Lee Eddings, who was 16 years old when he killed a highway patrol officer. The reversal was based on a technical error in the proceedings before the trial court. It is important to note that four members of the Court (including Chief Justice William H. Rehnquist) stated in their dissenting opinion that "the Court stops far short of suggesting that there is any constitutional proscription against imposition of the death penalty on a person under age 18 when the murder was committed."[68] Moreover, Justice O'Connor, even though voting with the majority to reverse the sentence, presented these views:

> The Chief Justice may be correct in concluding that the Court's opinion reflects a decision by some Justices that they would not have imposed the death penalty in this case had they sat as the trial judge . . . I, however, do not read the Court's opinion either as altering the constitutionality of the death penalty or as deciding the issue of whether the Constitution permits imposition of the death penalty on an individual who committed murder at age 16.[69]

While there remained doubt over subsequent years as to the constitutionality of the death penalty for children, the issue seemed to be reasonably well-settled in the final years of the 1980s. First, the U.S. Supreme Court, in *Thompson v. Oklahoma*, ruled, in effect, that execution of youths below the age of 16 at the time of their offenses was unconstitutional on the basis of the Eighth Amendment.[70] Second, in 1989, the Court decided in *Stanford v. Kentucky* that there was no Eighth Amendment prohibition of the death penalty for youths who committed their crimes at age 16 or 17.[71]

In 1994, there were 37 states (plus the federal system) with death penalty statutes. Over these jurisdictions, eight had no specified minimum age for a sentencing of death, 14 set the minimum age at 18, and 16 set the age of eligibility at between 14 and 17. In some cases, the minimum age was specified in the statutes authorizing waiver to criminal court down to a certain age.

Between 1973 and 1996, death sentences were given to 130 offenders who were below the age of 18 at the time of their crimes. More than one-third of those 130 offenders were sentenced to death in the states of Texas and Florida, although 24 states allow the death penalty for the crimes of minors. However, the reversal rate over all states is high; less than 10 percent of those so sentenced were actually executed. Moreover, all of those executed were 17 at the age of their crimes and in states in which the upper age for jurisdiction of the juvenile court was 16. On average, the executions took place 12 years after death sentences were initially imposed. The oldest at the time of execution was 33.

A columnist for the *Wall Street Journal* presented the following comment in mid-1999:

> In this decade, Amnesty International reports, only six countries are known to have executed people for crimes committed while under 18 years of age. They are Iran, Nigeria, Pakistan, Saudi Arabia, Yemen—and the U.S. In the last 21 months, the U.S. is the only country known to have executed any juvenile offenders.[72]

At the time the above column was written, there were 70 offenders (all men) on death rows in the United States for crimes that were committed when they were below the age of 18.

Factors Considered in Dispositional Decisionmaking

Because there have been significant effects on court decisionmaking as a result of changes over the past 20 years in juvenile law, public attitudes toward juvenile offenders, and modes of operation in the juvenile justice system, it seems reasonable to consider studies of dispositional decisions in segments. Accordingly, we will summarize the results of such studies in two categories: those completed before 1980 and those completed since 1980.

Summary of Pre-1980 Findings

The nature and seriousness of the offense were found to be factors in dispositional decisionmaking, but not as uniformly and strongly as one might expect. More important was prior record, which quite consistently affected outcomes, most especially when the record included court appearances. Judges tended to be more lenient in many jurisdictions when a juvenile had shown commitment to such conventional activities as attending school and working at a job. Status offenders were given surprisingly harsh dispositions but there is evidence that the result was a function of the impoverished family situations rather than the specific status offenses. Finally, there was thorough inconsistency in studies focusing on such factors as gender, race or ethnicity, age, and socioeconomic status. Those factors may be of significance in some jurisdictions (and perhaps in certain courts) but no general pattern was shown.

Summary of Post-1980 Findings

Several studies found no evidence that race, ethnicity, or social class affected dispositional decisions. On the other hand, a few studies did find such bias, indicating a pattern of differences over jurisdictions and courts such as that reported for pre-1980. Seriousness of offense and number of prior offenses were generally consistent determiners of dispositional outcome. Prior institutionalization was a particularly critical element in leading to a decision to incarcerate a given youth. Finally, it takes no formal study to conclude that youths in the twenty-first century who commit serious crimes—and particularly those who commit them repeatedly—will be treated more harshly than they would have been in the twentieth century. As pointed out in various parts of this chapter, all levels of the political and justice systems seem to be on a harshness crusade.

IMPORTANT ANCILLARY DEVELOPMENTS

Restorative Justice

The restorative response to juvenile crime is anchored by three critical elements: the victim, the offender, and the community. Its central theme is that young offenders must be held accountable for repairing the damage they have created. The issue is not one of deciding among the approaches to treatment and punishment, but to determine the extent of harm and who is responsible for that harm, and then to do what is necessary to make it as right as possible. Bazemore differentiates restorative justice from the usual approaches as follows:

> While current criminal and juvenile justice responses are driven by questions of guilt, lawbreaking, and the response to the needs and risks of offenders, restorative justice views crime through a lens that suggests that much more is at stake. . . . What is important about crime is that it causes harm to real people; crime injures individual victims, communities, offenders, and their families, and it damages relationships. If crime is more about peace breaking than lawbreaking, justice responses cannot focus simply on offender punishment or treatment. If crime can be viewed as a wound on the community, justice must focus on healing that wound.[73]

Transforming the juvenile justice system into a more restorative model entails providing services for crime victims, including victims and the community broadly in decisionmaking, actively involving the offender in repairing the harm created by the crime, and increasing the skills and abilities of the offender. At this time, many restorative programs operate more in the manner of juvenile diversion than as new approaches to juvenile justice, but several provide alternatives to the dispositions available to juvenile courts. For example, the Juvenile Reparation Program of Elkhart, Indiana, works with older juveniles who have shown repeated negative behavior that has not been corrected by the justice system. Staff members develop contracts with youths that include "accountability strategies such as restitution to the victim, volunteer service as symbolic restitution to the community, and specific self-improvement strategies. The contract may include face-to-face mediation with the victim."[74] Because these youths can be dangerous, they are restricted to their homes when not engaged in approved activities at school, at work, or in counseling. There is, finally, a crew of trained community volunteers who monitor the youths to provide encouragement and ensure that the rules are followed.

To show the impact of this conceptual structure, somewhat more than half of the states have incorporated restorative language in the clauses of their juvenile codes that specify purpose.

The Family Court Model

The first family court was established in Hamilton County (Cincinnati), Ohio, in 1914. The concept made little progress from there until 1959 when a model approach was published in the form of a "Standard Family Court Act." In that model, a state creates a family court, preferably through constitutional amendment or statute, which has jurisdiction over all legal matters that involve the family. That jurisdiction is indeed broad, including issues of divorce/dissolution, child custody, child abuse and neglect, juvenile delinquency, juvenile status offenses, guardianships and conservatorships, and domestic violence. The state of Rhode Island enacted the first statewide family court in 1961 based on that model. Hawaii followed in 1965 with a comprehensive version that was also based closely on the model.

The model presented in the Standard Act was subsequently adopted by other states such that by 1995, 13 states had family courts, 25 did not, and the remaining states were actively considering, experimenting with, or developing them.

Principal among the reasons for the continuation of adoptions of the family court model are the following: (1) there is substantial social interest in focusing on the family in the control of children, (2) the deprivations of children are most often associated with such family problems as divorce and spousal abuse, (3) there should be a "holistic" approach to family problems—indeed there is much recent stress on the concept of "one judge-one family," and (4) the needs for social support by courts dealing with such matters as divorce, delinquency, and domestic violence are vast, and consolidation fosters economy.

SUMMARY

A juvenile who is arrested by the police may be brought in custody to a court intake facility or released on condition that he or she appear at the facility at a future designated time or in accordance with later notification. The central goal of intake screening is to determine the most suitable action from among the following typical alternatives: release the youth to the custody of parents or guardian, perhaps with referral to a community agency for individual or family counseling; place the youth on informal probation; petition the court for an adjudicatory hearing; or refer the youth to prosecution for petitioning, as specified in the relevant state code. Several research studies indicate that the youth's prior record is most influential in determining severity of intake decision. The age of the youth, the nature of the immediate offense, and family status affect some decisions at certain times, but socioeconomic status (SES) and school attendance or employment seem to have little or no impact. Moreover, no consistent pattern of ethnic or racial discrimination has been found.

If the youth has been brought to court intake by the police while in custody, the intake officer must also decide whether he or she is to remain in custody. The legal justifications for continued detention encompass the goals of protecting the youth and the community and of keeping the youth from fleeing. However, there are several extralegal factors that affect the detention decision, including the personal biases of intake officers and pressures from the police or the community. Most states have a code that requires review of a decision to detain by a judicial officer at a detention hearing. While there is no constitutional right to an attorney at a detention hearing, the right exists by statute in many states. The right to release on bail has been codified in several states, but bail is not generally available in juvenile courts.

Several studies have shown that youths of low SES are more likely to be detained than youths of higher SES, but no clear pattern of a preference for detention on the basis of race has been found. Contrary to expectation, it has been shown repeatedly in studies through the 1970s that status offenders were detained at a higher rate than criminal-type offenders, even violent offenders. Because females were more likely than males to be brought into the system for status offenses, they have generally been detained at a higher rate.

Almost all states allow the transfer of a minor from juvenile court to adult criminal court by a process referred to as a waiver hearing. The formal grounds for waiver include the seriousness of the alleged offense, prior record, the degree of sophistication and maturity shown by the youth, and prospects for rehabilitation by methods available to the juvenile court. Although the U.S. Supreme Court, in its *Kent* decision, decided that waiver was an issue of critical importance that demanded minimum due process protection, various courts and legal scholars have, for technical reasons, interpreted the decision in different ways. The recent tendency is to regard the right to counsel (and similar rights) as constitutionally required in waiver hearings.

In addition to the method of waiver of jurisdiction from juvenile to criminal court, a juvenile's case may be tried in criminal court on the basis of statutory exclusion or by the direct filing of a prosecutor. In the former method, legislation makes youths above a certain age who commit serious offenses criminally responsible. Original jurisdiction, then, is assigned to the criminal court. In the latter method, state law allows prosecution the option to file in juvenile or criminal court for certain ages and offenses.

The adjudicatory hearing in the juvenile court determines whether the facts of the case support the allegations in the petition filed by probation or the prosecutor. The *Gault* decision firmly established the rights to counsel, to timely notice, cross-examination of witnesses, and to remain silent at adjudicatory hearings for criminal-type offenders when there is a possibility of incarceration. Such rights have not been extended to status offenders on constitutional grounds or to those not subject to institutionalization on other grounds. Moreover, the standard set by the Supreme Court for proof beyond a reasonable doubt in a delinquency hearing has not been extended to status offenders as a constitutionally based right. Beyond the absence of those required protections for status offenders, several observers have pointed out that the rights mandated in *Gault* and other Supreme Court decisions are not being implemented on a day-to-day basis in courts throughout the country.

A dispositional hearing for juveniles is equivalent to the sentencing hearing for adults. Unlike the adjudicatory hearing, which is aimed at fact finding, the dispositional hearing uses social reports directed at a youth's needs, relationships, coping skills, and deficiencies. The official goals in determining a disposition for a youth are rehabilitation and protection of the public, but punishment and retribution have been relevant concepts in the past and are coming more strongly into the picture. It is generally considered that there is a right to counsel during dispositional hearings, and that is being reflected in its inclusion in revised state codes. The principal alternative dispositions available to a juvenile court are return to the community with or without specific directives, return to the community under court-ordered probation, or placement in a local facility or a state institution (training school). In recent years, as punishment and retribution have become more prominent in response to violent juvenile crime, some states have added to their codes such harsher dispositions as placement in a facility more restrictive than a training school for minimum time periods. Another sign of increasing harshness has been an increasing emphasis on the death penalty for youths, in court sentencing if not in actual imposition of the sentences. The U.S. Supreme Court has effectively decided that execution of youths above the age of 15 is constitutional. Several studies have explored the array of factors that enter into dispositional decision-making, with the general conclusions that prior record is most consistently related to dispositional outcomes; that seriousness of immediate offense has some effect on decisions; that status offenders, perhaps because of social needs, were (prior to 1980) given relatively severe dispositions; and that the factors race, ethnicity, age, sex, SES, and present school or employment activity are important in some courts at some times, but not in others or at other times.

Two ancillary developments noted were an increasing emphasis on restorative justice and a model family court. The former emphasizes accountability and retraining of young offenders with involvement of victims and the community generally. The latter is based on the assumption that family matters should be dealt with holistically and that delinquency and status offending are primarily family matters.

REFERENCES

Arthur, Lindsay G., and William A. Gauger (1974). *Disposition Hearings: The Heartbeat of the Juvenile Court*. Reno, NV: National Council of Juvenile Court Judges.

Bazemore, Gordon (1999). "The Fork in the Road to Juvenile Court Reform." *Annals of the American Academy of Political and Social Science* 564(July):81-108.

Bazemore, Gordon (1998). "A Vision for Community Juvenile Justice." *Juvenile and Family Court Journal* 49 (4):55-88.

Binder, Arnold (1984). "The Juvenile Court, the U.S. Constitution and When the Twain Meet." *Journal of Criminal Justice* 1984:355-366.

Bortner, M.A., and Wornie L. Reed (1985). "The Preeminence of Process: An Example of Refocused Justice Research." *Social Science Quarterly* 66(June):413-425.

Braithwaite, John, and C. Parker (1999). "Restorative Justice is Republican Justice." In *Restorative Juvenile Justice: Repairing the Harm of Youth Crime*, edited by Gordon Bazemore and Lode Walgrave. Monsey, NY: Criminal Justice Press.

Chesney-Lind, Meda (1999). "Challenging Girls' Invisibility in Juvenile Court." *Annals of the American Academy of Political and Social Science* 564:185-202.

Chesney-Lind, Meda (1988). "Girls and Status Offenses: Is Juvenile Justice Still Sexist?" *Criminal Justice Abstracts* 20(March):144-165.

Children's Defense Fund (1976). *Children in Adult Jails*. Washington, DC: Washington Research Project, Inc., Children's Defense Fund.

Chused, Richard H. (1973). "The Juvenile Court Process: A Study of Three New Jersey Counties." *Rutgers Law Review* 26:488-589.

Cohen, Lawrence E. (1975a). *Delinquency Dispositions. An Empirical Analysis of Processing in Three Juvenile Courts*. Washington, DC: U.S. Government Printing Office.

Cohen, Lawrence E. (1975b). *Pre-adjudicatory Detention in Three Juvenile Courts: An Empirical Analysis of the Factors Related to Detention Decision Outcomes*. Washington, DC: U.S. Government Printing Office.

Creekmore, Mark (1976). "Case Processing: Intake, Adjudication and Disposition." In *Brought to Justice? Juveniles, the Courts, and the Law*, edited by Rosemary Sarri and Yeheskel Hasenfeld, 119-150. Ann Arbor: National Assessment of Juvenile Corrections, University of Michigan.

Dannefer, Dale, and Russell K. Schutt (1982). "Race and Juvenile Justice Processing in Court and Police Agencies." *American Journal of Sociology* 87:1113-1132.

Davis, Samuel M. (1980). *Rights of Juveniles: The Juvenile Justice System*, 2nd ed. New York: Clark Boardman.

Day, Jeffrey K. (1992). "Juvenile Justice in Washington: A Punitive System in Need of Rehabilitation." *University of Puget Sound Law Review* 16:399.

Feld, Barry C. (1999). "The Honest Politician's Guide to Juvenile Justice in the Twenty-First Century." *Annals of the American Academy of Political and Social Science* 5564:10-27.

Feld, Barry C. (1998). "Juvenile and Criminal Justice Systems' Responses to Youth Violence." *Crime and Justice: A Review of Research* 24:189-261.

Feld, Barry C. (1991). "The Transformation of the Juvenile Court." *Minnesota Law Review* 75:718.

Feld, Barry C. (1987). "The Juvenile Court Meets the Principle of Offense: Legislative Changes in Juvenile Waiver Statutes." *Journal of Criminal Law and Criminology* 78:471-531.

Feld, Barry C. (1984). "Criminalizing Juvenile Justice: Rules of Procedure for the Juvenile Court." *Minnesota Law Review* 69:141-276.

Feld, Barry C. (1981). "Juvenile Court Legislative Reform and the Serious Young Offender: Dismantling the 'Rehabilitative Ideal.'" *Minnesota Law Review* 65:167-242.

Ferster, Elyce Z., Edith N. Snethen, and Thomas C. Courtless (1969). "Juvenile Detention: Protection, Prevention or Punishment?" *Fordham Law Review* 38:161-197.

Flango, Carol R., Victor E. Flango, and H. Ted Rubin (1997). *How are Courts Coordinating Family Cases?* Alexandria, VA: State Justice Institute.

Gillespie, L. Kay, and Michael D. Norman (1984). "Does Certification Mean Prison? Some Preliminary Findings from Utah." *Juvenile and Family Court Journal* 35(3):23-34.

Griffin, Patrick, Patricia Torbet, and Linda Szymanski. (1998). *Trying Juveniles as Adults in Criminal Court: An Analysis of State Transfer Provisions.* Washington, DC: U.S. Department of Justice, Office of Juvenile Justice and Delinquency Prevention.

Harris, Patricia M. (1986). "Is the Juvenile Justice System Lenient?" *Criminal Justice Abstracts* 18:104-118.

Hufnagel, Lynne M., and John P. Davidson (1974). "Children in Need: Observations of Practices of the Denver Juvenile Court." *Denver Law Journal* 51:355-370.

Institute of Judicial Administration-American Bar Association Juvenile Justice Standards Project (1980). *Standards Relating to the Juvenile Probation Function.* Cambridge, MA: Ballinger.

Klein, Eric K. (1998). "Dennis the Menace or Billy the Kid: An Analysis of the Role of Transfer to Criminal Court in Juvenile Justice." *American Criminal Law Review* 35:371-410.

Kowalski, Gregory S., and John P. Rickicki (1982). "Determinants of Postadjudication Dispositions." *Journal of Research in Crime and Delinquency* 19:66-83.

Krisberg, Barry, Ira Schwartz, Gideon Fishman, Zvi Eiskovits, and Edna Guttman (1986). *The Incarceration of Minority Youth*. Minneapolis: University of Minnesota, Hubert H. Humphrey Institute of Public Affairs.

Kurlychek, Megan, Patricia Torbet, and Melanie Bozynski (1999). "Focus on Accountability: Best Practices for Juvenile Court and Probation." *OJJDP Bulletin*. Washington, DC: U.S. Department of Justice, Office of Juvenile Justice and Delinquency Prevention.

Levin, Mark M., and Rosemary C. Sarri (1974). *Juvenile Delinquency: A Study of Juvenile Codes in the U.S.* Ann Arbor: National Assessment of Juvenile Corrections, University of Michigan.

Marshall, Chris E., Ineke H. Marshall, and Charles W. Thomas (1983). "The Implementation of Formal Procedures in Juvenile Court Processing of Status Offenders." *Journal of Criminal Justice* 11:195-211.

Note (1971). "Juvenile Right to Jury Trial—Post McKeiver." *Washington University Law Quarterly* 605-614.

OJJDP Report (1998). *Guide for Implementing the Balanced and Restorative Justice Model*. Washington, DC: U.S. Department of Justice, Office of Juvenile Justice and Delinquency Prevention.

Osbun, Lee Ann, and Peter A. Rode (1984). "Prosecuting Juveniles as Adults: The Quest for Objective Decisions." *Criminology* 22:187-202.

Page, Robert W. (1993). "'Family Courts': An Effective Judicial Approach to the Resolution of Family Disputes." *Juvenile & Family Court Journal* 44(1):3-53.

Paulsen, Monrad G., and Charles H. Whitebread (1974). *Juvenile Law and Procedure*. Reno, NV: National Council of Juvenile Court Judges.

Phillips, Charles D., and Simon Dinitz (1982). "Labelling and Juvenile Court Dispositions: Official Responses to a Cohort of Violent Juveniles." *Sociological Quarterly* 23:267-279.

The President's Commission on Law Enforcement and Administration of Justice (1967). *Task Force Report: Juvenile Delinquency and Youth Crime*. Washington, DC: U.S. Government Printing Office.

Rubin, H. Ted (1985). *Juvenile Justice: Policy, Practice, and the Law*. New York: Random House.

Rubin, H. Ted (1972). *Three Juvenile Courts: A Comparative Study*. Denver: Institute for Court Management.

Schutt, Russell K., and Dale Dannefer (1988). "Detention Decisions in Juvenile Cases: JINS, JDs, and Gender." *Law and Society Review* 22:509-520.

Seib, Gerald F. (1999). "Capital Journal." *The Wall Street Journal* (June 16):A28.

Sickmund, Melissa, Howard N. Snyder, and Eileen Poe-Yamagata (1997). *Juvenile Offenders and Victims: 1997. Update on Violence*. Washington, DC: U.S. Department of Justice, Office of Juvenile Justice and Delinquency Prevention.

Smith, Charles P., T. Edwin Black, and Adrianne W. Weir (1980). *Reports of the National Juvenile Justice Assessment Centers. A National Assessment of Case Disposition and Classification in the Juvenile Justice System: Inconsistent Labeling. Volume II: Results of a Literature Search*. Washington, DC: U.S. Government Printing Office.

Sosin, Michael, and Rosemary Sarri (1976). "Due Process—Reality or Myth?" In *Brought to Justice? Juveniles, the Courts and the Law*, edited by Rosemary Sarri and Yeheskel Hasenfeld, 176-206. Ann Arbor: National Assessment of Juvenile Corrections, University of Michigan.

Special Study Committee on Criminal Justice Standards and Goals (1975). *Juvenile Justice Standards and Goals*. Madison: Wisconsin Council on Criminal Justice.

Stahl, Anne L. (1999a). "Offenders in Juvenile Court, 1996." *OJJDP Bulletin*. Washington, DC: U.S. Department of Justice, Office of Juvenile Justice and Delinquency Prevention.

Stahl, Anne L. (1999b) "Delinquency Cases Waived to Criminal Court, 1987-1996." *OJJDP Fact Sheet*. Washington, DC: U.S. Department of Justice, Office of Juvenile Justice and Delinquency Prevention.

Stephan, James J., and Tracy L. Snell (1996). *Capital Punishment 1994*. Washington, DC: Bureau of Justice Statistics, U.S. Department of Justice.

Streib, Victor L. (1995). "The Death Penalty Today: Present Death Row Inmates Under Juvenile Death Sentences and Executions for Juvenile Crimes, January 1, 1973 to June 30, 1995." Report from Cleveland State University, Cleveland-Marshall College of Law, Cleveland, OH.

Streib, Victor L. (1983). "Death Penalty for Children: The American Experience with Capital Punishment for Crimes Committed While Under Age Eighteen." *Oklahoma Law Review* 36:613-664.

Terry, Robert M. (1967a). "Discrimination in the Handling of Juvenile Offenders by Social Control Agencies." *Journal of Research in Crime and Delinquency* 4:218-230.

Terry, Robert M. (1967b). "The Screening of Juvenile Offenders." *Journal of Criminal Law, Criminology and Police Science* 58:173-181.

Thomas, Charles W., and Christopher M. Sieverdes (1975). "Juvenile Court Intake: An Analysis of Discretionary Decision-Making." *Criminology* 12:413-432.

Torbet, Patricia, and Linda Szymanski (1998). *State Legislative Responses to Violent Juvenile Crime: 1996-97 Update*. Washington, DC: U.S. Department of Justice, Office of Juvenile Justice and Delinquency Prevention.

Wadlington, Walter, Charles H. Whitebread, and Samuel M. Davis (1983). *Cases and Materials on Children in the Legal System*. Mineola, NY: Foundation Press.

Winner, Lawrence, Lonn Lanza-Kaduce, Donna M. Bishop, and Charles E. Frazier (1997). "The Transfer of Juveniles to Criminal Court: Reexamining Recidivism Over the Long Term." *Crime & Delinquency* 43:548-563.

Zehr, Howard (1990). *Changing Lenses: A New Focus for Crime and Justice*. Scottsdale, PA: Herald Press.

NOTES

1   Stahl (1999a).

2   Hufnagel and Davidson (1974), 355-356.

3   Cal. Wel. & Inst. Code §631, 632 (1999).

4   Ibid. §633 (1999).

5   *Trimble v. Stone*, 187 F. Supp 483 (D.D.C. 1960).

6   Davis (1980), 3-43.

7   Cohen (1975b), 25, 26.

8   Special Study Committee on Criminal Justice Standards and Goals (1975), 122.

9   Children's Defense Fund (1976), 3-4.

10   President's Commission on Law Enforcement and the Administration of Justice (1967), 15.

11   Creekmore (1976), 125.

12   Cal. Wel. & Inst. Code §653.1 (1999).

13   Day (1992), 399.

14   Rev. Code Wash. § 13.40.070(1) (1999).

15   Harris (1986).

16   Paulsen & Whitebread (1974), 127.

17   Terry (1967a), 225.

18   Smith, Black & Weir (1980), 243, 249.

19   421 U.S. 519, (1975).

20   Stahl (1999b).

21   *Kent v. United States*, 383 U.S. at 566, 567 (1966).

22   33 Vt. Stat. Ann. §5506 (1999).

23   *Matter of Johnson*, 304 A.2d. 859 (1973).

24   Ibid., 861.

25   Ibid., 863.

26   Ibid., 863.

27   Ibid., 863.

28   *In re Stevenson*, 538 P.2d. 5 (1975).

29   Feld (1987), 491.

30   Feld (1999), 19.

31   Ca. Wel. & Instit. Code §707 (1999).

32   Minn. Stat. §260, 135 (1980).

33   Osbun & Rode (1984), 199.

34   Minn. Stat. 260.126 (1999).

35   383 U.S. 554 (1966).

36   Wadlington, Whitebread & Davis (1983), 393.

37   Davis 1980, 393.

38   N.Y. Penal Law §30.00 (1999), 70.05; Crim. Proc. Law §1.20, 180.75, 210.43.

39   Ark. Stat. Ann. 9-27-318 (1997).

40   D.C. Code §16-2301 (1999).

41   Ibid., §16-2307.

42   Davis (1980), 2-17.

43   Marshall, Marshall & Thomas (1983), 208.

44   397 U.S. 358 (1970).

45   403 U.S. 528 (1971).

46   Ibid., 547.

47   Ibid., 547.

48   Sosin & Sarri (1976), 194.

49   Ibid., 193.

50   Ibid., 194.

51   Ibid., 196.

52   Ibid., 197.

53   Feld (1999), 14.

54   Ca. Wel. & Instit. Code §702 (1999).

55   Arthur & Gauger (1974), 54.

56   Ibid., 54.

57   *State ex rel. D.D.H. v. Dostert*, 269 S.E. 2d. 409 (1980).

58   *Alford v. Carter*, 504 P. 2d. 436 (1972).

59   Rubin (1985), 209.

60   W. Va. Code §49-1-4.

61   W. Va. Code §49-5-11.

62   *State ex rel. Harris v. Calendine*, 233 S.E. 2d. 329 (1977).

63   Ibid., at 331.

64   *Ellery C. v. Realich*, 347 N.Y.S. 2d. 51 (1973).

65   *Certo v. State*, 385 N.Y.S. 2d. 824 (1976).

66   42 Pa.C.S. §6302.

67   455 U.S. 104 (1982).

68   Ibid., 128.

69   Ibid., 128.

70   487 U.S. 815 (1988).

71   492 U.S. 361 (1989).

72   Seib (1999), A28.

73   Bazemore (1999), 86, 87.

74   *OJJDP Report* (1998), 12.

11

Detention, Institutionalization, and Parole

In preceding chapters, we have discussed various constitutional issues connected with the juvenile justice system's awesome power to deny a youth his or her liberty by confinement in a locked facility. In this chapter, we will look closely at the character and significance of that confinement process, which may be used as early as the very entry point to the system. As we discussed in Chapter 10, one option available to a police officer in dealing with a suspected young offender is to take the youth into custody (that is, arrest the youth) and then refer him or her to the juvenile court while the youth remains in custody. The youth may then, with concurrence of a judicial ruling coming in a short period of time (usually 24 or 48 hours), be held in continued custody up to and through adjudicatory and dispositional hearings. The process of keeping a youngster in a secure and restrictive facility up to adjudication and disposition is called detention. In contrast to that, institutionalization refers to the process of assignment of a youth to a facility for secure confinement by a court following a dispositional hearing; because of its presumed rehabilitative mission, a facility of this sort is often called a correctional institution.

DETENTION

Detention may be in a facility used exclusively for youths and associated with the juvenile court, or in a jail. The expression "juvenile hall" is often used to designate the former type of holding facility.

Numbers of Children in Detention

Available data from the Office of Juvenile Justice and Delinquency Prevention show that detention was used with youths referred to juvenile courts in 1995 as follows: about 324,000 youths who had committed criminal-type offenses and about 10,000 youths who had committed status offenses and were referred for adjudicatory hearings (petitioned). For delinquency cases, that represented an increase of 31 percent over the base year of 1986; for status offender cases, there was a decrease of 22 percent from the base year. Youths under the age of 16 accounted for 56 percent of the detained youths in 1995 (the same for delinquency and petitioned status offense cases). Males charged with delinquency offenses were more likely to be detained than females similarly charged by a ratio of 1.5 to 1; the detention rate was about the same for males and females in petitioned status offense cases. Blacks were more likely than whites to be detained in delinquency cases by a ratio of 1.8 to 1, while the ratio was only 1.3 to 1 in the case of status offenses.

In the mid-1990s, there were more than 500 juvenile detention facilities. The facilities have a capacity of about 22,000 youths, but actually have an average daily population of more than 23,000. The average length of stay was 15 days. However, it should be emphasized that there are substantial differences both over states and over counties within states in the use of detention. For example, a study found that 36 percent of the juveniles referred to 11 county probation departments in California were detained. The detention rate varied over counties from a low of 19 percent to a high of 66 percent. The highest likelihood of being detained was among those youths who offended while on probation; first offenders were detained only 25 percent of the time.

In 1996, the one-day count of youths under the age of 18 who were held in adult jails was 8,100—about 2 percent of the total jail population. Seven in 10 of these cases were heard in adult criminal courts. In this context, it would seem important to point out once again that in some states, 16- and 17-year-olds are considered adults from the perspective of the justice system (though not more generally). It has been estimated that 32 percent of juveniles (that is, those under 18) who are detained in jails are in states in which they are considered adults and fall under the jurisdiction of the criminal court.

An Era of Forceful Objections to the Detention of Children

Particularly vigorous opposition to the detention of young offenders, especially those in jails, began in the late 1960s and produced significant effects on operations of the juvenile justice system during the 1970s. One of the early expressions may be found in the report of the Task Force on Corrections of the President's Commission. The report states:

> Far too frequently detention, although justified on a variety of grounds, is utilized as a punishment device or to impose needless controls prior to adjudication. The National Survey of Corrections referred to a county in which about two-thirds of the youngsters detained prior to hearing were subsequently placed on probation in their own homes. Clearly, the great majority of these juveniles could have awaited a hearing without detention, with little risk of failure to appear in court.[1]

The opposition to detention stemmed from a general concern for human rights, particularly of the downtrodden; a specific concern for the fair treatment of youngsters in the system as reflected in *Kent*, *Gault*, and similar Supreme Court decisions; and specific research findings and descriptions of conditions in detention facilities (particularly jails) that reinforced those concerns. We will turn to the general and specific social concerns later in this chapter and consider at this point only the findings dealing with detention. One group of findings (see Chapter 10) contradicted the widely held belief that juvenile halls, jails, and other detention facilities have predominantly contained youths who committed serious crimes (a belief that is natural in view of the oft-stated position that a primary purpose of the system is to protect the public). Two other groups of findings deal, first, with the deplorable conditions in jails, and second, with the apparent misuse of detention generally.

Findings Indicating Deplorable Conditions in Jails

During the 1970s, reports of the surprisingly large number of children, even young children, in adult jails and the dangers to which they were exposed therein provided a source of particular concern about juvenile detention, as they had in earlier periods (see Chapter 8). For example, a survey undertaken by the National Council on Crime and Delinquency and reported by the Task Force on Corrections of the President's Commission found that there were 87,951 children detained in county jails during 1965 and at least another 1,300 in police jails (lockups). Furthermore, the report of the survey results notes:

Less than 20 percent of the jails in which children are held have been rated as suitable for adult Federal offenders. Nine states forbid placing children in jail, but this prohibition is not always enforced. In 19 states the law permits juveniles to be jailed if they are segregated from adults, but this provision is not always adhered to.[2]

During this same period, staff members of the Children's Defense Fund visited 449 jails in 126 counties and nine independent cities (most of which had populations of more than 50,000) in the states of Florida, Georgia, Indiana, Maryland, New Jersey, Ohio, South Carolina, and Virginia. They asked questions about the numbers of children jailed, the characteristics of jailed children, the services and conditions of the jails, and the legal process that preceded jailing. About one-half of the 449 jails held children regularly or occasionally. On the day of the visit, there were 257 children in jail who were under the jurisdiction of the juvenile court (that is, they had not been waived for criminal trial), and they were mostly white males. While minority children composed a smaller percentage (31.8 percent) of the jailed children, it was higher than their percentage in the general population of children. Finally, about one-third of the children were 14 or 15 years old, and more than 9 percent were 13 years old or younger.

Many of the articles and books that highlighted the deplorable conditions in jails presented vivid anecdotes of the effects of jailing on individual children. For example, the report of the survey of the National Council on Crime and Delinquency stated:

> In Arizona in January 1965, four teenage boys, jailed on suspicion of stealing beer, died of asphyxiation from a defective gas heater when they were left alone for 11 hours in a jail. In Indiana, a 13-year-old boy, who had been in five foster homes, drove the car belonging to the last of his foster fathers to a county jail, considered one of the finest in the State, and asked the sheriff to lock him up. The boy was well segregated from adults pending a hearing for auto theft. When he had been detained for about a week, his body was found hanging from one of the bars of his cell. Next to it was a penciled note: "I don't belong anywhere."[3]

The report of the Children's Defense Fund described jails visited by staff members as "very old, deteriorating, and unsafe" and failing to meet "minimal standards . . . for sewage disposal, plumbing and cleanliness." Moreover, the jails did "not provide inmates with such basic things as soap, toothpaste, toilet paper." Specific horror stories recounted include the following:

Jon was put in a cell alone. There was no sink and nothing to drink. No pillow. The sheets were sandy and dirty. There were two bunk beds with a toilet between them. "Rusty, grungy. I wouldn't use it. Anyway, everyone could see in. There were bars on two sides. I could see other cells. Could see a bunch of crazy-looking people. They looked mean. I just wasn't used to seeing people like that. One was beating on the bars to get attention. There was a lot of yelling. It took a long time to get to sleep."

Fred, not yet 13, was placed in a concrete cell with two small barred windows looking out on to the street. There was a mattress and one blanket, a sink, toilet, shower. There was one old dirty cup, too soiled to drink from. Fred slept badly. "The beds were mangy, with big stains on them. I felt kind of scared. I kept walking around the cell. There was just a big thick steel door and a little round window." The light was left on all night. When Fred asked to have it turned off "they said 'no.' They said they were afraid that I'd kill myself if it is dark. Once I threw a blanket over the light. It caught on fire."[4]

Other accounts of harshness, abuse, and dangerous conditions in jails describe unkempt, unsanitary cells in which youths were subjected to brutal beatings, homosexual rape, and even murder by other inmates and sometimes jail employees. To highlight the effects of jailing, Cottle interviewed children detained in jail and presented their profiles. There was, for example, the case of Bobbie (a fictitious name), a 15-year-old daughter of a prostitute, who was described as being among the group of youngsters "who have never experienced a tender friendship and therefore do not know the meaning of tenderness."[5] She was arrested along with another 15-year-old girl as an accomplice in the murder of a pimp; both were placed in jail. Bobbie spent 11 months awaiting trial in a jail where no one came to visit her.

The progression of life in jail for Bobbie was described as follows:

When she was first locked in her cell, she became violently ill. She felt her head getting warm as if the blood in her neck were being heated and rising hot into her brain. Then she felt as though her head was suddenly too heavy for her body to support. Her heart raced and perspiration appeared all over her body. She vomited violently, surprised that there had been no warning signs of nausea or abdominal pressure. Her fingers and toes tingled as though someone were sticking needles into them, and she was afraid that she was losing her sense of touch. Her eyesight too was affected; images became blurred and a strange scintillating arc appeared above everything she focused on, giving the impression of electrical interference. . . .

"I feel I'm getting sicker in here. Every day, just a little bit more. The place terrifies me. Sometimes I feel I'm screaming to get out, but it's all quiet. . . . I don't want to go mad. I fight against it, but it's like this large wall is moving in closer to me every day and I can't push it back anymore. There used to be a time when I thought I could, but not now. I don't know why it is either."

"I've been in this jail and another one for nine months! Nine months and one week. I went in on a Monday. Monday night. Like, the first couple of months I spent time getting used to the place—getting used to it, that's a laugh—and spending my time being angry 'cause they had no right keeping me in here. Then I started to change. Sometimes when you change you don't feel it happening. It just happens and one day you look back and say, I guess I've changed. But *this* time I really knew I was changing. Every day, twice a day, I would say, I'm not like me anymore. For a while I even stopped slouching over like I do. I wanted them to think they'd never break me. They got informers in here, you know. Ladies, maybe they're police, maybe they're real prisoners. They try to break you down, get you to confess things. One of them put a lighted cigarette on my ass one night. Honest to God, she held it closer and closer, they must have had six of them holding me down. She kept saying, 'I'll put a hole right in the middle of your goddam ass if you don't tell us what you did.' I always wondered how come the matrons let it go. . . ."

Three weeks before she was to be called to trial, Bobbie Dijon was found dead in her cell. She had swallowed more than a bottle of sleeping pills that she had asked a fellow prisoner to get for her. One rumor went that her brother Timmy knew about her plan to commit suicide but promised Bobbie he would never say anything. Timmy Dijon denied knowing anything of his sister's plan. Marianne Dijon did not cry upon hearing the news of her daughter's death. Her body grew stiff and she whispered, "I knew it would come." . . .

Six months after Bobbie Dijon's death, Patsy Monahan [Bobbie's social worker] received a letter from a man named Stuart Post who claimed to be Bobbie's father. The letter showed no return address. It contained a twenty-dollar bill and a note saying the money was to be given to Bobbie to use any way she wanted. She was to know it had come from her father. Marianne Dijon denied ever knowing anyone by the name of Stuart Post. "Besides," she added, "it's all too late for that."[6]

Important support for the condemnation of the use of jails for detaining children came from evidence indicating that the elimination of such jailing produced some positive effects but no negative ones.

Keve found that the prohibition of the jailing of children by Pennsylvania in 1979 had no perceptible effect on other aspects of the juvenile justice system in that state. Similarly, Allinson reported that, while the number of juveniles in Pennsylvania jails went from 3,196 in 1975 to zero in 1981, there was no corresponding increase in the number of youngsters detained in secure juvenile facilities. Both of these investigators noted an increase in the use of group home placement, foster care, and in-home detention as the use of jails decreased.

Findings Indicating the Unreasonableness of Detention

Another group of findings that reinforced negative attitudes about placing children in jails also raised questions about placing them in juvenile halls and similar secure detention facilities. One study found that up to 25 percent of juveniles who had been detained were released without a petition being filed for a court hearing. Another report noted that in one county only 5 percent of children who had been detained prior to a court hearing were eventually sent to an institution. While one can easily conceive of special cases in which conditions change so rapidly that a detained youngster does not need a court hearing or does not need institutionalization after adjudication, one must wonder about the need for secure custody when 25 percent of those so detained do not even have petitions filed and 95 percent of those detained are set free prior to or by the court hearings.

Several writers have pointed out that detention for the purpose of protecting the community is a slippery task at best because research indicates that future dangerousness is virtually unpredictable (especially from psychological states and personality features). It is worth noting that the U.S. Supreme Court was not sympathetic to expressions of opposition to juvenile detention on the basis of the high release rate following adjudication and the overwhelming difficulty of predicting future dangerousness. *Schall v. Martin* dealt with the constitutionality of a New York Family Court Act authorizing detention of a child if "there is a serious risk that he may before the return date commit an act which if committed by an adult would be a crime."[7] The law authorized "preventive detention" for juveniles.

A federal circuit court had earlier declared the act unconstitutional because the detention served as a punishment without a prior establishment of guilt in accord with due process standards. The circuit court relied heavily on statistical evidence that "the vast majority of juveniles detained under [the act] either have their petitions dismissed before an adjudication or are released after adjudication."[8] The Supreme Court was critical of that position in the following retort: "We are unpersuaded by the Court of Appeals' rather cavalier equation of detentions that do not lead to continued confinement after an adjudication of guilt and 'wrongful' or 'punitive' pretrial detentions. Pretrial detention need not be considered punitive merely because a juvenile is subsequently discharged."[9]

On the issue of predictability of future behavior, the Court commented:

> We have already seen that detention of juveniles . . . serves legitimate regulatory purposes. But appellees claim, and the district court agreed, that it is virtually impossible to predict future criminal conduct with any degree of accuracy. Moreover, they say, the statutory standard fails to channel the discretion of the Family Court [New York's juvenile court] judge by specifying the factors on which he should rely in making that prediction. . . .

> Our cases indicate, however, that from a legal point of view there is nothing inherently unattainable about a prediction of future criminal conduct. Such a judgment forms an important element in many decisions, and we have specifically rejected the contention based on the same sort of sociological data relied upon by appellees and the district court, "that it is impossible to predict future behavior and that the question is so vague as to be meaningless."[10]

Thus, the decision is clearly not responsive to arguments coming from the social sciences (indeed, the expression "the same sort of sociological data" clearly has a pejorative ring to it). The decision of the federal circuit court on the invalidity of preventive detention in New York was ultimately reversed with the accompanying statement, "We conclude that preventive detention under the Family Court Act serves a legitimate state objective, and that the procedural protections afforded pretrial detainees by the New York statute satisfy the requirements of the Due Process Clause of the Fourteenth Amendment to the United States Constitution."[11]

However, other people have been responsive to "sociological data" and to the arguments regarding the inequities in detaining youths, particularly in jails. One was Senator Birch Bayh of Indiana. His office instituted a four-year examination of the role of the federal government in the prevention and treatment of delinquency that culminated in the Juvenile Justice and Delinquency Prevention Act of 1974, an act aimed at reducing detention and other forms of juvenile incarceration. The Act discouraged putting juveniles in adult jails except when there were no alternatives available. When so necessary, the youths were to be confined entirely separately from adults. Six years later, the Act was amended to require that states could participate in the federal juvenile justice program (and thereby receive federal funds) only by prohibiting the confinement of youths with adults in jails by 1985, which was later extended to 1988. Regulations implementing the Act, however, exempted youths held in adult jails if their cases had been waived to criminal courts. Detention is permitted in local facilities if juvenile and adult inmates cannot see or converse with each other. Finally, there is a six-hour grace period (24 hours in rural communities) allowing alleged delinquents to be held in typical adult jails.

Despite those enactments in 1985 and 1988, many children remained confined in adult jails and lockups for considerably longer than six (or 24) hours. One case study found, for example, that during that era, Minnesota, despite being a state with enlightened human services and justice policies, remained one of the states in which substantial numbers of juveniles were incarcerated in adult jails. The major impediment to change was reported to be the lack of available alternatives. Another impediment was a widely held belief among professionals in juvenile justice that the matter was of trivial concern, especially considering the need for public safety and appropriate punishment.

On the other hand, in 1986, California, in conformity with the federal intent, adopted the strongest law over all states prohibiting placing children in adult jails. The law specified that by mid-1989 no minor under court jurisdiction could be confined in a county jail and that no minor could be held in a police jail (lockup) for more than six hours (and there were very strict conditions even for confinement for under six hours). The success of the effort to remove children from jails or restrict such confinement was attributed to the effectiveness of a lobbying effort and the respect among law enforcement agencies for the sponsoring state senator.

More Recent Developments

While the conditions of confinement for juveniles in detention centers have improved substantially over recent decades, a report published by the Office of Juvenile Justice and Delinquency Prevention in 1994 concerning a study of such centers found several conspicuous problems remaining. Using the minimum standards set by such organizations as the American Correctional Association, the study found substantial deficiencies in the areas of crowding, security, control of suicidal behavior, and the provision of health care. For example, only 33 percent of the surveyed juveniles were in detention centers that conformed to the four standards for suicide prevention.

Unfortunately, there is no similar information available on children in jails and police lockups, but there was a steady increase in numbers of youths in jails between 1983 and 1994.

The most recent report from the Office of Juvenile Justice and Delinquency Prevention provides an overall summary of detention caseloads up to 1996, but not many details. The principal features of that report are outlined as follows:

> The increase in the number of delinquency cases handled by the courts has driven the growth in the number of juveniles in the detention system. In 1987, 1.2 million delinquency cases were disposed in juvenile courts. By 1996, this number had risen 49%, to almost 1.8 million. This increase in the volume of juveniles in the justice system resulted in a 38% increase in the number of delinquency cases that involved the use of detention. The number of juvenile delinquency cases detained in 1996 was 89,000 more than in 1987. This has resulted in increased demand for juvenile detention bed space across the country. . . .

> In general, the courts' use of detention remained relatively steady between 1987 and 1996. Juveniles were detained in 20% of cases processed in 1987; in 1996, the proportion was 18%. However, there was a surge in the number of female cases entering detention (a 76% increase compared with 42% for males). The large increase was tied to the growth in the number of delinquency cases involving females charged with person offense crimes over this period (182%).

> Between 1987 and 1996, the increase in the number of cases involving detention was almost four times greater for black youth than for white youth. Contributing to this disproportionate increase was a 68% rise in juvenile court caseloads involving black juveniles, compared with a 39% rise for white juveniles. In 1996, 27% of cases involving black youth included detention between referral and disposition, compared with 14% for white youth.[12]

Finally, regulations effective in late 1996 modified the Juvenile Justice and Delinquency Prevention Act in the following ways (among others): "Expand the 6-hour hold exception to include 6 hours before and after court appearances" and "Allow adjudicated delinquents to be transferred to adult institutions once they have reached the State's age of full criminal responsibility where such transfer is expressly authorized or required by State law."[13]

INSTITUTIONALIZATION

The Development of Institutions

Predecessors

To provide an appropriate context for this section, it would be useful to review briefly previous material on the development in the United States of institutions for the custody of young offenders. As we saw in Chapter 8, the use of prisons to punish offenders (juvenile as well as adult) in England and America started toward the end of the eighteenth century. By 1825, concern about the imprisonment of children led to the first house of refuge in New York. The goal was to correct "vicious propensities" of the children in a broad effort at reformation.

Houses of refuge established shortly thereafter in Boston, Philadelphia, and elsewhere followed the New York model in being primarily dependent on private funding, in having private management, in accepting dependent and ungovernable children as well as young criminals, and in keeping their young charges for indeterminate periods of time. The houses of refuge provided operating examples when state-supported reform schools began to be established during the mid-nineteenth century. The earliest reform (or industrial or training) schools were established in Massachusetts, New York, and Maine. The first of these, the Lyman School for Boys, was opened in 1846 in Massachusetts. That was followed by the New York State Agricultural and Industrial School in 1859 and the Maine Boys Training Center in 1853. By 1900, virtually every state had a juvenile training facility. The early institutions used the congregate or dormitory system for housing delinquents in fortress-like buildings. Beginning in the mid-1850s, many facilities were built on the cottage model with its emphasis on family living style in agricultural settings (see Chapter 8).

Aims of Institutionalization

The working philosophies of juvenile institutions have been summarized as follows:

> The term "school of industry" or "reformatory" often designated the early juvenile training facilities, thus reflecting the relatively simple philosophies upon which their development was based. Their reform programs sought chiefly to teach the difference between right and wrong. Teaching methods were primarily on a precept level, tending to emphasize correct

behavior, formal education, and, where possible, the teaching
of a trade so that the trainee would have the skills to follow
the "right."[14]

Although, from the earliest period, the stated goal of these various
juvenile institutions was reformation, two developments in later years
produced particular reemphasis on reformation (or rehabilitation).
First, following a meeting in 1870, a group of influential reformers
denounced the predominant punishment philosophy in prison operations and advocated industrial training, education, rewards rather than
sanctions, and the cultivation of self-respect. In short, the reformers
argued that rehabilitation rather than punishment should be the primary goal in adult prisons; the day-to-day efforts should reflect that
goal. The second development that brought renewed emphasis on
reformation in juvenile institutions was the set of processes that surrounded the establishment of the juvenile court in 1899. As stated in
Chapter 8, the fundamental aim of all aspects of the new juvenile justice was to treat the young offender as a parent would.

Unfortunately, as Rothman has argued, the emphasis and reemphasis were often more at the verbal level than the operational level:

> The descent from the language of juvenile institutions to the
> reality of conditions is precipitous. No matter how frequent-
> ly judges insisted that confinement was for treatment, training
> schools did not fulfill this claim. "When is a school not a
> school?" asked one reformatory superintendent. "When it is
> a school for delinquents." Reformatories were not capable of
> administering a grade school or high school curriculum and
> they did no better at vocational training. As one observer
> reported: "Most of the large institutions have what they call
> trades departments, and use them mainly for repair and con-
> struction work about the plants. . . . This gives a small amount
> of instruction while utilizing the labor of the inmates in reduc-
> ing the expenses of the institution." Or, as the verdict of
> those who studied conditions at St. Charles, Illinois, put it:
> "Trade training of a quality which fits boys for self-mainte-
> nance is nonexistent."
>
> The cottages were almost invariably overcrowded with a staff
> that was at once undertrained and overworked. They bore no
> resemblance to a normal family life. And for child guidance,
> the most important service that institutional psychologists or
> psychiatrists performed was mental testing. IQ tests were
> prevalent. But there was really little that the training schools
> could do with the results. Classification was an absurdity
> when cottages were overcrowded and organized essentially by
> age and size. Thus, one answer to the question, "What good
> has psychiatry been in an institution for delinquents?" was

accurately enough: "To start surveys; to give us technical diagnoses and work out more and more elaborate records which no one uses."[15]

Numbers and Types of Institutions

According to various estimates, there were just under 170 public training schools for adjudicated young offenders in the United States at the start of the 1950s. That number includes institutions encompassed by such other names as "industrial school," "farm school," "agricultural school," and "reform school" as well as many schools that were simply given the names of benefactors or early superintendents. In addition, there were about 11 state reception and diagnostic centers, 42 forestry camps and ranches, and 135 private training schools, many run under the auspices of the Roman Catholic Church.

Formal surveys, called Children in Custody (CIC) surveys, were conducted over the time periods 1975-85 and 1985-95. Smith used the resulting data to provide a picture of juvenile correctional facilities and their inmates over a 20-year period.[16] The last CIC census was in 1995; a new method of approach, called Census of Juveniles in Residential Placement, was introduced in 1997 but has not provided data as of this date.

What Smith included under the rubric "juvenile correctional facilities" is quite broad, including training, industrial, farm, and reform schools; ranches and forestry camps; half-way houses; group homes; and all other institutions used to hold adjudicated youths (secure and nonsecure). The summary shows there were 874 public facilities and 1,277 private ones in 1975; these numbers increased to 1,059 and 1,989, respectively, in 1995. Over that 20-year period, there was a slight increase in the number of females in the correctional facilities on a given day (17,192 to 17,917) but a substantial increase in the number of males (57,078 to 89,720). The number of incarcerated youths per 100,000 youths in the population were 241 in 1975 and 381 in 1995. Finally, whereas 28 percent of the youths in custody were African-American in 1975, the rate climbed to 40 percent in 1995; an even greater climb was among Hispanic youths over those years: 9 percent to 17 percent.

Reception and diagnostic centers have been developed in several states to determine the likely causes of the personal difficulties of assigned wards, to determine reasonable approaches to treatment, to assess risks and security needs, and to select an appropriate facility for assignment. In California, for example, two reception centers were established for the evaluation of all new commitments to the state's Youth Authority. During a period of about six weeks, wards are given psychological tests, interviewed, and physically examined. This diagnostic process is intended to be directly responsive to the individualized, rehabilitative emphasis of the juvenile justice system.

As discussed in Chapter 8, the notion that the "country life" had curative properties for urban delinquents was advocated at least from the mid-nineteenth century. The Children's Aid Society of New York City put the notion into practice during a later era by placing big-city youths in rural homes, and several of the early schools had an agricultural emphasis. With that in perspective, it is easy to understand why there persistently has been the expectation of positive effects of sending youths to forestry camps or ranches.

In an early experimental camp opened in Los Angeles in 1931, boys were supervised by probation officers while working under the direction of employees of the Los Angeles County Forestry Department. That camp and others that followed were considered so successful in the treatment of young offenders that forestry camps became an established component of California's Youth Authority in 1943. In that year, "50 boys were transferred from county jails . . . to the Calaveras Big Trees Park where, under the supervision of skilled tradesmen, they built a camp of 100-boy capacity."[17] Portable buildings were used and the process of establishment was expedited because of severe overcrowding within urban institutions at the time.

However, the increasing interest in camps and ranches between the early 1950s and 1979 has not been sustained in subsequent years. There actually has been a decrease in numbers more recently.

Overview of Operations in Institutions

Institutional operations fall into one of three broad categories: treatment, management, and education/training.

Treatment

The treatment approaches used in juvenile correctional institutions have included each of the following: traditional insight psychotherapy by psychiatrists and clinical psychologists; evaluation and interpretation of interpersonal relationships in the manner of transactional analysis; emphasis on the achievement of basic needs by responsible actions in accord with the precepts of reality therapy; changing behavior according to the reinforcement procedures derived from operant learning theory; group psychotherapy oriented toward the achievement of insight and emotional control; psychodrama, in which participants are directed to act out their emotions; social therapy in cottage settings, in which the entire environment becomes a therapeutic community; and guided group interaction in nonauthoritarian cottage settings, in which group homogeneity is used in decisionmaking and the resolution of personal problems.

A review of studies that evaluated the successes and failures of various correctional treatments found that the majority of successful programs were derived from social learning models, while unsuccessful programs were generally based on "friendship" models that stressed open communication, or on medical models, according to which antisocial behavior could presumably be cured much like a disease. However, a survey of the evaluative literature on approaches to juvenile correctional treatment over the years 1975 to 1984 did not produce encouraging results on an overall basis. Only one of seven studies directed at institutional treatment showed that treatment was significantly better than control, and two others showed significance in the opposite direction. In contrast to previous studies, there were no indications of the greater effectiveness of behavioral interventions. The methods and results of that survey, however, were challenged in 1990. Reevaluation led to the conclusion that the effects of appropriate treatments (which were generally positive) were dampened in certain types of institutional settings.

More results will be presented later when attention is directed toward evaluation of institutionalization generally as well as the comparison of institutional and community treatment approaches.

Management

Management refers to the broad array of maintenance activities within an institution. While many of these activities may have rehabilitative potential, they are typically differentiated from treatment because the latter is most often derived from formal, usually theoretically based, modes of changing maladaptive behavior.

Education and Training

Formal education and training is an important class of activities within most institutions that falls neither under management nor under treatment in the above dichotomy. It is difficult to imagine a comprehensive rehabilitative program for young people without education in appropriate academic subjects and training in relevant vocational spheres.

Modes of Operation

The segmentation of institutional efforts into treatment, management, and education/training categories is in accord with general professional usage but carries no obvious implications for rehabilitative effectiveness. A warm relationship with a correctional officer or a shop teacher may very well lead to greater and longer-lasting change in attitudes and in behavior than the most dynamic of psychiatric therapies. On the other hand, it has become abundantly clear that the specific maintenance activities in many institutions are motivated more by convenience for the staff than for the rehabilitation of residents. Despite the ideal of a full effort made at rehabilitation, one often finds more destructive results than rehabilitative results in actual day-to-day operations.

Differences in management directions among correctional institutions led Cressey to place prisons on a continuum varying from authoritarian control to a rehabilitation orientation. On the side of authoritarian control, there is emphasis on custody and the prevention of escapes and on rigid relationships between staff members and inmates, but little interest in rehabilitation. At the other end of the continuum are institutions that follow the model for training schools given by the Children's Bureau, in which every staff member has a definite role in a broad therapeutic environment. Rather than coercion and control, there are collaborative efforts between staff members and inmates aimed at solving problems and bringing about long-term change.

As various observers have pointed out, most correctional institutions (prisons and training schools alike) fall between the ends of that continuum. There must almost always be control as a dominant consideration, but that may be more or less subject to amelioration by rehabilitative goals.

One study of staff decisionmaking in assigning youths to a cottage or treatment program at a state facility for male offenders found that decisions were based on the same array of variables as those used by the police and court intake officers rather than on more relevant personal characteristics. The results seemed contrary to treatment goals, but specific decisions were rationalized rather than modified when staff members became aware of information pointing to their apparent inappropriateness.

An investigation by Wooden of juvenile institutions in the late 1970s over a three-year period found two types of training schools in operation:

> The first is a miniature penitentiary with high walls surrounding the grounds. All the buildings and cell block wings therein are interlocked by long corridors. Not only are individual cell doors secured, but each wing is also locked at all

times. There is almost always a self-sufficient industrial complex on the grounds—laundry, hospital, maintenance shop and any other facility needed to keep strangers out and the children in. Dubious educational and religious services are available to the children, along with the standbys of solitary confinement and of bloodhounds to locate any who run away.

The second and more common type of training school is the cottage system. . . . Those in charge are "house parents" rather than "guards." The outside area is usually quiet and pleasant and bears little semblance to a penal facility. The cottages are usually small, aesthetically pleasing, dorm-like structures. . . . The windows are . . . secured with heavy wire and in the event of emergencies such as fire, escape would be impossible except through the front door.[18]

Miniature Penitentiaries

The miniature penitentiary has virtually the same array of management problems as an adult prison. The residents must be clothed, fed, guarded, protected, kept healthy, rewarded or punished when appropriate, provided leisure activities and recreation, and so on. The most critical players in the enterprise are the correctional or custodial officers, who are the line personnel in almost continual contact with inmates, and who are the central managers despite their relatively low status. While maintaining close daily contact with inmates, these officers must ordinarily keep substantial psychological distance from them because of various problems of control in penitentiary-like settings.

Cottages

The structure of the cottage makes it possible to be oriented less toward control and more toward rehabilitation. Residents are often made responsible for the care and maintenance of cottages in order to promote self-sufficiency. In addition, there is an atmosphere in which mutual problem solving and peer counseling is encouraged. Youths considered to be alike on important variables, as determined by the classification schemes of institutions, may be assigned to the same cottages in order to foster security or some other institutional goal.

Camps and Ranches

In forestry camps and ranches, youngsters spend the bulk of their time in such activities as fire control, road construction and maintenance, care of livestock, construction of buildings, reforestation, care of small trees in nurseries, and the processing of wood. There is little provision for formal education, although local schools do cooperate in offering special classes. Moreover, the entire working experience can be considered a form of vocational training. Supplementing the work activities are recreational and leisure programs ranging from individual and group sports to picnics and parties.

The living arrangement in one such facility has been described as follows:

> Emphasis is placed upon making community living a meaningful life experience. Each boy is expected to do his share of housekeeping and groundkeeping work. A boy's day begins when he arises at 6:30 A.M. After breakfast he cleans his room, and either attends school or goes to his work assignment. Upon completion of the school day there is a period of extracurricular activities, i.e., band, chorus, varsity sports, crafts, group counseling, and so forth.[19]

In addition, the facility offered both a formal educational program leading to a high school diploma (or, at least, to transferable high school credits) and a vocational program with training in such trades as printing, welding, automobile repair, drafting, and woodworking. Finally, although a social worker was assigned to form a "constructive relationship" with each boy, it was expected that the entire staff would interact with him in a therapeutic manner.

Boot Camps

Later in this chapter, we discuss the deinstitutionalization of young offenders in Massachusetts, where delinquents were moved from secure institutions to community-based facilities. Another alternative to traditional institutionalization in that state was founded there in 1973 by a former marine, George Cadwalader. This alternative, called the Penikese Island School, had disciplinary and responsibility features that resembled those of a "boot camp." Whereas the person behind deinstitutionalization in Massachusetts thought that all delinquent youths needed love and attention, the founder of the boot camp argued that young serious offenders had to learn, through a system of rewards and punishments (in a context of hard work), that their behaviors had consequences.

Although the model was launched in 1973, it was not until the 1980s that the concept of boot camps for both adult and juvenile offenders gained widely popular footing in the United States. The specific approaches of boot camp operations vary considerably over programs, but the essential element in all cases is military training and discipline. The key people are the drill instructors who rule firmly by dominance, harassment, and degradation. It has been argued, moreover, that "shock experience" is often a major component of life in boot camp. That experience may include shackling, herding, verbal abuse, and bullying.

It is important to add, though, that the programs in boot camps include educational and therapeutic components to supplement their harsh regimens. In addition, there must be provision for aftercare services, preferably coordinated with the program in the camp.

In 1997, Peters and his associates reported the results of evaluations of three experimental boot camp programs that were based on "public-private partnerships" in Cleveland, Denver, and Mobile. The evaluations were experiments in having random assignment of juveniles to experimental and control groups. Participation in the experiment was voluntary, with the understanding that the youth would either be sent to a boot camp or be treat-

Cadets maneuver an obstacle course at New Jersey's Wharton Tract Juvenile Boot Camp during a tour by Governor Christine Whitman. The camp for nonviolent juvenile offenders opened in February 1996. *(AP Photo/Charles Rex Arbogast)*

ed in accordance with the original disposition of the court. One important result was:

> [B]oot camp participants at all three sites were found to be no less likely to reoffend after release than their control group counterparts. These findings appear to be consistent with much of the research that has been conducted to date on adult boot camps . . .[20]

Based on that result in the context of the findings of other research, the concluding overview of Peters et al. is as follows:

> At this point in their development, boot camps do not appear to be the panacea that many hoped they would become. Nonetheless, boot camps do appear to offer certain practical advantages and future promise that warrant continued testing

and examination. . . . boot camps are a useful alternative for
offenders for whom probation would be insufficiently punitive,
yet for whom long-term incarceration would be excessive.[21]

That brings to mind the comment to one of us by the chief of
police of a medium-sized city adjacent to a Marine boot camp: "The
major contributors to property crime in the city are marines from the
base."

Benign Rhetoric Does Not Always Imply Benign Operations

As we saw in Chapter 8 and earlier in this chapter, juvenile institutions have been severely criticized from their earliest years. It would not
seem possible to select a decade, starting from those initial years, during which there was no substantial castigation of the institutions in articles and books. A summary of the criticisms by Teeters in 1950 stated,
"Many reports of reform schools present a bill of particulars regarding
the inadequate physical plant, the decrepit buildings, the untrained staff
or its frequent turnover, the poor food, poor sleeping arrangements,
overcrowding." Moreover, the institutions were reported to be "repressive and inhumane," with such "sadistic punishments" as flogging, ice-
cold baths, leg chains, bread-and-water diets, and shaving the hair off
the heads of girls as well as boys.[22]

The years between 1960 and 1977 saw major social stirring in the
United States, motivated to a large extent by concern for the rights and
needs of the poor, minority-group members, and women. That concern
was extended to other groups and individuals who were perceived as
similarly downtrodden by social processes, including juveniles incarcerated in institutions (particularly jails). Moreover, the concern in
the case of incarcerated juveniles was enhanced by several parallel
developments in sociology and in law. These included the rise of labeling theory and its emphasis on the social augmentation of deviant
behavior by the very processes used by society in attempts to eradicate
the behavior; the rulings by the U.S. Supreme Court in the *Kent* and
Gault decisions on the constitutional requirements of due process in the
juvenile justice system; and reports of the President's Commission on
Law Enforcement and Administration of Justice and its task forces that
were highly critical of institutional processes (which were strongly
influenced by the sociological thought of the day because of the predominance of sociologists on the staff of, and as consultants to, the
commission).

The era of 1960 to 1977 is marked by three important developments that resulted from the general concern about social underdogs
and specific concern about institutionalized youths: (1) the publication

of several semi-popular books that were lurid in their condemnation of juvenile institutionalization (as well as detention), (2) the federal Juvenile Justice and Delinquency Prevention Act of 1974, and (3) the deinstitutionalization of young offenders in Massachusetts.

Influential Books

Three books will be used to illustrate the powerful denunciation of institutionalization in the semipopular press: *The Concrete Cradle*, by Joseph Sorrentino (1975); *Weeping in the Playtime of Others: America's Incarcerated Children*, by Kenneth Wooden (1976); and *Children in Jail: Seven Lessons in American Justice*, by Thomas J. Cottle (1977). These were not initiators of concerns, but they reflected reactions to the concerns toward the end of the period. The titles themselves dramatically illustrate the negative attitudes of the authors toward institutionalization.

One may wonder why a book titled *Children in Jail* would occur in this context. Given the discussion in the first part of this chapter, the assumption might be that jails are used for the detention rather than the institutionalization of children. Jails are indeed so used in the vast majority of cases, but juvenile court judges have been known to use adult jails (or prisons) for the placement of children after dispositional hearings in juvenile courts (sometimes, according to authoritative sources, in violation of state law). In addition, a few states allow the transfer of a youth to a jail (or prison) if he or she is considered especially dangerous or inappropriate for the juvenile facility for other reasons, and in some cases it is possible for a youth to spend considerable time in jail awaiting transfer to a juvenile correctional institution. By far the largest proportion of juveniles in jails (or prisons) for long-range custody consists of youths committed there by criminal courts. The trial in criminal court could have come after a waiver hearing in the juvenile court that had original jurisdiction. Alternatively, the criminal court could have had original jurisdiction on the basis of seriousness of the crime or the age of criminal responsibility in a given state, or the waiver to criminal court could have been based on prosecutorial discretion.

1. *The Concrete Cradle*, by Joseph Sorrentino (1975).
Sorrentino, a juvenile court judge who had overcome the liabilities of a turbulent youth that included multiple institutionalizations for assault, dramatically contrasts the benign goal of rehabilitation with actual institutional operations.
On the one hand, he observed:

The Institute for Juvenile Court Judges states the credo that juvenile courts . . . are imbued with the goal of rehabilitation. . . . Special stress is given to providing the proper institutional environment to youthful offenders.

Customarily, institutions for juveniles publish statements setting forth their program objectives. They express elaborate psychological methods of reclaiming the wayward youth for constructive citizenship. At the O.H. Close School for Boys, transactional analysis, as developed by Dr. Eric Berne, has been adopted as the major treatment method. The Karl Hoeton School proudly boasts a "specific treatment approach for each ward using behavior modification principles." The Ventura School for Girls says it applies "reality therapy to change delinquent behavior." The Nelles School for Boys uses "principles of operant conditioning through contingency management." Whatever the method chosen, the uniformly stated aim of juvenile institutions is to reform, not punish, delinquents.[23]

In practice, however, during an inspection tour of institutional facilities, he found "deplorable conditions," the use of tranquilizing drugs to keep rebellious youths in a stuporous condition, overcrowded "cesspools," widespread violence and homosexual behavior, and little effort devoted to treatment or even to the most basic medical needs. Moreover, many youngsters were kept in locked facilities for minor offenses. Sorrentino encountered one girl who had been incarcerated for three months because she planned to marry her boyfriend against her mother's wishes and was defined as "incorrigible." The writer concluded, "It seems a bizarre legal system that permits a mother to jail a daughter to prevent her from getting married."[24]

2. *Weeping in the Playtime of Others: America's Incarcerated Children*, by Kenneth Wooden (1976).

Wooden found punitive isolation in nearly every facility he visited in 30 states. He described conditions as follows:

Solitary confinement is widely used in juvenile penal institutions throughout the United States. Just about every facility I have visited in thirty states has some form of punitive isolation for those children who break rules or are otherwise troublesome. In some tragic instances, isolation is even used for punishing the mentally retarded.

Solitary confinement consists in locking a child in a small, highly secure cell by himself for a period of time—it may be one day, it may be three months or longer. The rooms are dirty, damp, vermin-infested, vile-smelling, cold in the winter and hot in the summer. They usually have a bare mattress on the floor and a toilet or hole in the floor. Total silence is the rule. No talking, no reading, no visitations.[25]

Wooden found, on the one hand, that boys were frequently subjected to brutal physical punishment in institutions but that, on the
other hand, girls were more commonly subjected to extreme psychological indignities. The superintendent at the Indiana Boys School in
Plainfield told Wooden that in previous years when "any inmates ran,
they were beaten, then thrown into solitary." He showed Wooden the
leather straps used in the beatings. According to Wooden:

> They were 26 inches long, 3 inches wide and ½ inch thick. The
> handles were stained from sweat, the ends worn thin by those
> who administered the beatings. The youngsters who were to
> be disciplined were placed on wooden racks at an appointed
> time (4 P.M.) "with their ass up in the air." The big debate was
> "should they beat the boys with their trousers on or off."
> When the leather strap had no effect, the guards would "take
> them out in the cornfield and beat the piss out of them."[26]

As one illustration of the indignities to which girls were subjected,
he wrote:

> In matters of personal hygiene and cleanliness, once again,
> incarcerated girls suffer greater indignities than their male
> counterparts. Most female facilities have no individual toilets.
> An assortment of old pee pots, coffee cans, and other crude
> containers are issued for disposal of body wastes. At Artesia
> Hall, a private institution in Texas, the girls were forced to uri-
> nate in Coke bottles for punishment. The Texas Youth Coun-
> cil publicly hangs a "Monthly Menstruation Report" on the
> door of all female cottages which lists every inmate (regardless
> of whether she menstruates or not) and records the onset and
> finish of each menses. Physical examinations of girls being
> admitted to the Sheldon Farm for Girls in Pennsylvania deter-
> mine whether they are virgins or not. Virgins are assigned one
> color dress; all others wear a different color.

> Examinations for venereal disease are carried out with out-
> rageous frequency. Young ladies in custody have been known
> to undergo as many as three and four pelvic exams for the dis-
> ease. At some facilities, ten- and eleven-year-olds are forced to
> submit to "vaginals" each time they are transferred to a new
> facility, even though they have not been released between
> placements. In one town in Louisiana two detectives com-
> plained to me about the county coroner, who forcefully exam-
> ined all runaways: "You know when he is working because
> you can hear the young girls screaming at the other end of the
> hall."[27]

3. *Children in Jail: Seven Lessons in American Justice*, by Thomas J. Cottle (1977).

The final book in this trio of examples provides descriptions of children in jail based on several years of conversations with them. A case from the book, that of Bobbie Dijon who was being detained in jail, was presented earlier in this chapter. Another youth discussed, Fernall Hoover (again a fictitious name), was sentenced to three to five years in prison for breaking and entering and carrying a gun. He spent two and one-half years in prison and was placed in solitary confinement three times, the first time at the age of 16. The youth described the solitary experience to Cottle as follows:

> "First thing I realized, man, I didn't know the time. Room had no windows so I never could tell. Sometimes, you know, when you ain't sleeping you can sort of tell how many minutes passed you by. But when you're sleeping, you don't know. Ain't got no clock, ain't got no sounds to help you. You're in a cell. First I thought, I can dig it, they bring me my food, I'll make out, you know what I'm saying? But after a while they got you talking to yourself. I'd be standing in there yelling loud as I could, 'Tell me the time. Tell me the time.' Ain't no one going to answer you. You know this, but it don't stop you. You just keep yelling, 'Tell me the time. *Tell me the time.*' Ain't no one going to answer you. You know this, but it don't stop you. You just keep yelling, 'Tell me the time. Is it the day or the night?'
>
> Pretty soon, man, I figure I'm going crazy. I ain't even seen where I am. Suddenly the whole cell gets real light, you know, and I'm blinking my eyes so's I can get used to it. Then when I open 'em I can't see nothing. It's still black in there, 'cause I only *imagined* they turned the lights on. Then I start talking to myself, 'You ain't going crazy, man. You're doing all right. You're going to be all right. Believe me, you're going to be all right. Just hang in there.' So I tell myself, 'Think about the future, man, think about how it's going to be for you when you get out. Make it like a picture in your mind,' you know what I mean.[28]

Another youngster, Angela, age 15, was sentenced to a juvenile institution for a period of "no less than one year" for breaking into a food store and stealing money and food. She spent seven months in a county jail for women before being transferred to the correctional institution. Angela's experiences in the jail well illustrate the sexual dangers to which youngsters are exposed in adult facilities. She stated:

> "Another night this other woman comes up to me in the hall with a goddam tonic bottle. You believe this? I goes, 'What the hell you think you're going to do with *that*?' She goes, 'Come on baby lady, let's see what you got under there.' So she starts

to lift up my skirt and I push her away, only she laughs. Then she's coming at me again, only this time she's starting to take off her dress. No kidding. She ain't got anything underneath. So here I am, fifteen years old, standing in this goddam corridor of this goddam jail with a sex maniac coming at me with a root beer bottle in her hand. And she ain't kidding either. I ain't about to yell for no one 'cause when they caught you messing around like that they'd put you both in solitary for four, may five, days. And when you've been in there like I was—they put me in there the first time 'cause they heard I was going to try to escape after a show one night, which was a lie—you know you'll do anything, including getting raped, before you'll go back."[29]

After telling Cottle lurid details of various homosexual encounters, Angela asked, "So what else do you want to know about my days in the ladies' penitentiary?"[30] To show how resigned she eventually became to the whole state of affairs, there is the comment, "I figured, they're giving me clean clothes, they're giving me food, I'm only getting raped once every couple of weeks, what I got to complain about?"[31] Although matters improved greatly after Angela was transferred to the juvenile institution, there remained an "overriding feeling of hopelessness" with a fair degree of certainty that "she was destined to return to this or some other comparable institution."[32]

Your reaction after reading those descriptions of conditions in juvenile institutions might be something like, "But those books were written in the 1970s and probably have little current relevance." The following, from a newspaper article that appeared in late 1999, shows dramatically that harsh, even brutal, conditions still persist even in states that have benign reputations:

SACRAMENTO—The state's inspector general has uncovered a pattern of excessive force and abusive treatment of inmates at the California Youth Authority's flagship institution in Chino, where improper discipline regularly was meted out, according to a top state official.

A six-month investigation found that officers exercised their own brand of justice outside regular channels, allegedly slamming handcuffed inmates against walls; firing potentially lethal riot control guns at close range to remove inmates from cells; forcing unruly inmates into cells with urine and excrement on the floor; and ordering that disorderly inmates be injected with antipsychotic drugs.

One of the most disturbing disclosures, contained in what state officials describe as a status report to Gov. Gray Davis, is that guards would test the readiness of inmates to be sent to the facility's general population by forcing them to confront other inmates, often rival gang members, in what were referred to as "the Friday night fights". . . .

So far, investigators have found that one inmate was temporarily paralyzed and others experienced serious bruises and lacerations.[33]

The Juvenile Justice and Delinquency Prevention (JJDP) Act of 1974

The second major expression of concern about the institutionalization of juveniles was in the form of the Juvenile Justice and Delinquency Prevention (JJDP) Act of 1974. The chief sponsor of this act, as stated earlier, was Senator Birch Bayh, a strong proponent of human rights and welfare throughout his long political career. The act was far-reaching in its accomplishments; for example, it established the Office of Juvenile Justice and Delinquency Prevention in the Department of Justice; it authorized that office to make grants to state and local governments for the purpose of funding programs aimed at the reduction and control of delinquency; it created a center for evaluation and research by the name of the National Institute for Juvenile Justice and Delinquency Prevention; and it provided $350 million over a three-year period so that the preceding provisions could be carried out.

Most important for present purposes were the provisions in the act for preventing the placing of status offenders in locked facilities and requiring that delinquents be housed separately from incarcerated adults. Because Congress cannot dictate to the states in matters of criminal and juvenile justice under the federal system delineated in the U.S. Constitution, there was no way that compliance with those provisions could be mandated. Therefore, Congress used a carrot-and-stick approach made possible by its taxing and allocation powers—an approach used in such other areas as insistence on a maximum speed limit over all states (rescinded in 1995) and an attempt to set a minimum drinking age of 21 for alcoholic beverages. As mentioned earlier, Congress allocated a substantial amount of money for grants and other provisions of the JJDP Act. In order to receive funds, each state had to submit a plan to carry out the provisions of the act and related provisions in an earlier act. The state plan had to:

> (12) provide within two years after submission of the plan that juveniles who are charged with or who have committed offenses that would not be criminal if committed by an adult, shall not be placed in juvenile detention or correctional facilities, but must be placed in shelter facilities.[34]

The effort to keep youths out of locked facilities is commonly called deinstitutionalization, even though it may apply to detention facilities as well as correctional institutions. As important as the 1974 federal legislation was, it was not the initiator of the notion of deinstitutionalization of status offenders. For example, one year earlier, in 1973, the state of Maryland had forbidden the detention and institutionalization of status offenders. In that year, a national standards commission recommended prohibiting courts from sending status offenders to institutions for delinquents. (Several important organizations, it should be noted, have recommended going considerably beyond deinstitutionalizing status offenders by removing them entirely from the jurisdiction of the juvenile court.)

Clearly, there were many forces in society that created an appropriate zeitgeist for passage of legislation like the JJDP Act. However, because of various mediating factors, there was a softening of the provisions of the act over subsequent years, beginning in 1977.

We turn now to the results of the act and its amendments. A report in 1980 by Paul and Watt summarizing statutes relative to deinstitutionalization stated:

> Since the Act has been in effect, 47 states have agreed to the outlined requirements, including the deinstitutionalization of status offenders, and received funds appropriated under the Act. Nebraska, Oklahoma, and Wyoming have never participated, while South Dakota, North Dakota, and Nevada voluntarily withdrew from the Act after initial participation. The reasons for nonparticipation often involve fundamental disagreements with the federal deinstitutionalization and separation [of children from adults] requirements. Some states view the financial incentive as insufficient contrasted with the expenditure of state funds necessary to achieve compliance with the Act.[35]

A closer look at the various states indicates that the preceding summary may be somewhat misleading, because actual compliance with provisions of the act and its amendments cannot be assumed from agreement to abide by their provisions (and thereby receive federal funding). Thus, among the 44 states that agreed to participate and never withdrew, there was wide disparity in the actual degree of deinstitutionalization. For example, only 23 states enacted statutes prohibiting the committing of status offenders to secure institutions within the first six years following passage of the federal legislation. Moreover, in a 1992 assessment of compliance, it was found that only five states had achieved full compliance with the act and its amendments, while 29 others were in full compliance with the more critical requirements. (South Dakota did not begin participating in the 1974 act until 1991.) Some states have had disagreements with various aspects of the deinstitutionalization requirement and created statutes that generally prohibit placing status offenders in secure facilities but have language permitting secure detention or institutionalization under certain conditions. Disagreements of that sort led to a congressional change in 1980 that allowed, within the provisions of the act and its amendments, the institutionalization (that is, in locked facilities) of status offenders who have violated a court order—and a valid court order could be ordering a youngster to remain in an unlocked facility.

Thus, the JJDP Act of 1974 and its amendments did not seem to have a comprehensive, unambiguous effect on state legislation, even in the case of states that agreed to the requirements of the act and received funding. Nonetheless, several studies have made it clear that in general the placement of status offenders in secure facilities has decreased greatly since the first federal legislation in 1974, although the process of secure placement for them has not ended. Moreover, it is not clear, first, how many such youths are now sent to private facilities, including shelters and group homes, instead of the public institutions, and, second, whether appropriate services are being provided for misbehaving children when courts lose jurisdiction or lose interest because of the removal of their punitive tool of incarceration. Finally, it has been pointed out by several observers that status offenders are now being placed in locked psychiatric facilities for which their parents have insurance to cover the costs. No longer considered "bad," these offenders are considered "psychiatrically ill," but the locking up is the same.

Deinstitutionalization in Massachusetts

The third major expression of concern about the institutionalization of juveniles took the form of deinstitutionalization in Massachusetts. Deinstitutionalization refers to a process whereby all offenders, even serious delinquents, were released from state correctional institutions—and the institutions were subsequently closed permanently.

The process leading to such a radical deinstitutionalization started in the 1960s—as did many of the other processes that led to changes in juvenile justice. Several groups of citizens demanded reform of the state's juvenile correctional institutions. The groups charged that children were beaten and psychologically abused in the institutions, that solitary confinement was used extensively and brutally, and that unnecessary regimentation took such forms as shaving heads and marching in formation. Two of the institutions to which the reformers directed their attention, interestingly, were the Lyman School for Boys at Westboro, founded in 1846, and the Massachusetts Industrial School for Girls at Lancaster, founded in 1854. These were the first public correctional institutions in the United States for boys and girls, respectively.

Six major investigations of the institutions in the latter 1960s, including one by the U.S. Department of Health, Education, and Welfare, generally confirmed the criticisms of the advocates for reform. The Division of Youth Services (DYS), which administered the institutions, defended its methods, and the director of DYS was an articulate spokesperson for the general philosophy of the institutions.

The reform-minded governor of Massachusetts in 1969 displayed outspoken support for groups advocating change in juvenile institutions. He asked for the resignation of the director of DYS and set up a committee to find a qualified replacement. The committee selected Jerome Miller, a faculty member from the School of Social Work at Ohio State University. Before making the actual appointment, the governor strengthened Miller's position by making DYS an autonomous department and calling its head "commissioner" rather than "director." The governor indicated his strong desire for major change in these words: "I had been to some of the state and county [training schools] and God, I was repulsed—to think that we were paying something like $10,000 a year just to keep a kid in a cage without any type of rehabilitation. It was just really horrible. And I figured that if I didn't do any other damn thing while I was governor, I was going to [change] that system."[36]

Miller took on the job of commissioner with great gusto and issued a series of directives aimed at making the juvenile institutions more like therapeutic communities. One of his first directives was to allow the youths in institutions to wear their hair in any way they chose. Many other directives followed, including an order to permit youths to wear street clothes rather than institutional garb, one that forbade physical abuse and harsh sanctions even in the institution that housed the most disturbed and rebellious youngsters (corporal punishment was not against the law in Massachusetts at the time), one that removed control of cigarette allocation from staff members (who used that control for reward and punishment), and one that discontinued the policy of silent marching in formation between activities.

Those relatively minor changes were followed by such major ones as creating programs for boys and girls in the same institution, establishing coed cottages, reducing considerably the average length of stay for youths in the institutions (from eight months to three months), and recruiting and placing loyal adherents to Miller's philosophy of institutionalization. There was initial grumbling by a staff that had grown accustomed to the status quo. That mild resistance turned to open rebellion as it became clear that Miller intended to change the operations of the institutions radically. The rebellion took such forms as heckling Miller at public meetings and propagandizing people who had a stake in the system, such as judges, probation officers, police officials, and legislators.

In 1972, Miller decided that he would not be able to bring about the reform he intended because of staff opposition and because the controversy he created reduced considerably the time he could remain as commissioner. That led to the conclusion that the only way to change the system was to eliminate it:

> He [Miller] is quoted in a 1973 issue of the Boston Real Paper as saying: "my goal was to tear down the system to the point where Heinrich Himmler and the SS couldn't put it back together again." Unable to fire political appointees who had gained Civil Service status, he simply pulled the rug out from under them by abolishing their fiefdoms. In less than 2 years, Miller closed down all six training schools, whose population only a few years before had been 800.[37]

As reported earlier, the Lyman School for Boys in Westboro, Massachusetts, was the first public institution of its kind when it opened in 1846. According to one report, the closing of the Lyman School by Miller on January 17, 1972, "was a spectacular event, in which a caravan of cars and motorcycles descended on the institution, picked up thirty-nine remaining youngsters, and sped off to the University of Massachusetts at Amherst, where the youngsters stayed until homes were found for them."[38]

Closing institutions, of course, created the problem of finding other types of placement for the youths. A conference was organized at the University of Massachusetts to arrange for the transfer of a large number of youths to the community. In addition to formerly incarcerated youths and DYS staff members, college students from three colleges and universities in the area participated in the conference. The college students served as advocates for the youths while arrangements were being made for their placement. About two-thirds were placed in community settings as a result of deliberations at the conference; about equal numbers of the remaining youths were placed in a private facility, ran away, or were not placed. The youths sent to the private facility were considered too disturbed or too dangerous to be set free. Interestingly, it was reported that staff members at Lyman were so aghast at the whole undertaking that they circulated "rumors of mass escapes, chaos, and widespread sexual misconduct at the Conference."[39] The goal was to arouse the public so that there would be insistence that the youths be brought back to the institutions. That effort was at least partially deflated when one university official commented that the DYS youth had actually been "less trouble to the university than a convention of the American Legion."

The number of youngsters who remained in secure facilities after Miller's deinstitutionalization was about 50. Despite continuing opposition to the policy by judges, legislators, and police officers, the number of youths in secure facilities ranged between about 50 and 70 sub-sequently. The remaining youths committed to DYS were sent to a large array of nonresidential programs, to group homes, to foster homes, to a large boarding school, and to "concept houses" modeled on drug-free programs for adults. To avoid the difficulties of terminating incompe-tent people under civil service in future arrangements, private con-tractors were used in all components on a "payment-for-service" basis.

The model of mass deinstitutionalization introduced in Massachu-setts was not generally followed by other states. Utah, however, did dra-matically reduce the number of youths in secure facilities, and a few states did implement policies that were influenced by the Massachusetts effort. Massachusetts maintained a low custody rate up to the most recent report, dated 1997. According to that report, there were 21 adjudicated youths in public custody per 100,000 youths in the state between the ages of 10 and 16. Compare that with the figures from sev-eral other states: Louisiana, 218; South Carolina, 216; Illinois, 126; and Georgia, 141. The figure for the state of California was 385, but the basis for comparison was slightly different than for the preceding states.

The Right to Treatment

A development within the field of mental health that has had important implications for juvenile institutionalization is the right to treatment, a concept initially articulated in 1960 by Birnbaum, a physi-cian and attorney. Clearly, the juvenile justice system could easily have expected extrapolation of the concept, given the many criticisms of institutionalization. Several states have specifications in their codes giving mentally disturbed people the right to treatment if they are committed to public hospitals. As an example, the code of the District of Columbia stating that "a person hospitalized in a public hospital for a mental illness shall, during his hospitalization, be entitled to medical and psychiatric care and treatment"[40] led to an important court decision in 1966. A man by the name of Rouse was acquitted by reason of insan-ity on the criminal charge of carrying a deadly weapon, and was then committed to a mental institution. The misdemeanor offense implied a maximum sentence of one year, but Rouse remained hospitalized for three years. He filed a petition for release, contending that he did not receive the treatment that the D.C. law required during his three years at the mental hospital (which exceeded in length the maximum penal-ty for the misdemeanor offense). The ultimate decision by a federal appeals court (*Rouse v. Cameron*)[41] agreed with that contention but (perhaps more importantly) suggested that there may be a constitutional right to treatment based on due process requirements (Fourteenth Amendment) and the prohibition of cruel and unusual punishment (Eighth Amendment). (It should be pointed out that a constitutional right exists even though there is not a specification of that right in a code, as in the D.C. code above.)

In 1972, another court decision extended the thrust of *Rouse v. Cameron*. A complaint by residents in Alabama hospitals of the mentally ill led a federal district court to hold that there indeed was a constitutional right to treatment for patients involuntarily committed through civil proceedings (*Wyatt v. Stickney*).[42] The decision was affirmed by an appeals court ruling. It decreed that civil commitment occurs without the procedural safeguards (due process requirements) of a criminal trial and that treatment provides the justification, or quid pro quo, for involuntary commitment. The court went even further in specifying three fundamental conditions for effective treatment: (1) a humane physical and psychological environment, (2) a qualified staff that is large enough to administer adequate treatment, and (3) plans for treatment that are designed in accord with individual needs.

Historically, the philosophical basis for the juvenile court was *parens patriae* (as derived from equity or civil proceedings), as discussed in Chapter 8. The court was geared toward help and rehabilitation rather than toward punishment, and nonadversarial processes were presumably used without the usual due process standards. Accordingly, the juvenile proceeding was often conceptualized as civil rather than criminal. It is easy to see, therefore, how the arguments for the right to treatment in the case of mental health patients might be applied in the case of institutionalized juvenile offenders. In both cases, one sees involuntary commitment by a civil or civil-type proceeding, a goal of treatment rather than punishment, and the notion of a trade-off, or quid pro quo, between forfeiture of the due process requirements of a criminal trial and an informal proceeding aimed toward help and rehabilitation. The quid pro quo nature of the juvenile proceeding has, of course, been discussed throughout this century, but in 1961, Ketcham, a juvenile court judge, most directly anticipated the right-to-treatment arguments in his statement:

> [The mutual compact between delinquent and the state] can be regarded as an agreement whereby the state, through the juvenile court, is permitted to intervene, under broadly defined conditions of delinquency or violations of the law, in the lives of families who have given up certain of their constitutional safeguards. . . . Such an intrusion of governmental supervision is premised on the assumption that the state will act in the best interests of the child and that its intervention will affirmatively enhance the child's welfare. Applying the contractual analogy, it follows that unless the state satisfactorily performs its oblig-

ations under the compact, the juvenile and his parents should have the right to consider the agreement broken and to repossess their full constitutional rights.[43]

We now turn to the case that established the linkage directly between juvenile correctional institutionalization and the right to treatment. As discussed earlier in this chapter, Wooden reported on extremely cruel treatment at the Indiana Boys School in Plainfield. That cruelty led to a class action suit alleging violation of the Eighth Amendment (prohibition of cruel and unusual punishment) and the Fourteenth Amendment (requirement of due process to deprive a person of liberty) rights. The court agreed with the plaintiffs and ordered changes at the institution to eliminate the cruel practices. Of more relevance to current considerations, however, is that the court, in a separate judgment, declared that the boys had a right to adequate rehabilitative treatment. The decisions were appealed to a federal circuit court.

The appeals court agreed with the district court in *Nelson v. Heyne*:

> The district court decided that both Indiana law and the federal Constitution secure for juvenile offenders a "right to treatment," and that the School failed to provide minimal rehabilitative treatment. Defendants contend that there exists no right to treatment under the Constitution or Indiana law, and that if there is the right, the Quay Classification System used at the School did not violate the right. We hold, with the district court, that juveniles have a right to rehabilitative treatment.

> The right to rehabilitative treatment for juvenile offenders has roots in the general social reform of the late nineteenth century, was nurtured by court decisions throughout the first half of this century, and has been established in state and federal courts in recent years.[44]

The court went even further in stating that the right to treatment implied a minimum acceptable standard for individualized care and treatment.

Another case of significance in the right to treatment for incarcerated juveniles was originated by a class action suit on behalf of children committed to the custody of the Texas Youth Council (TYC). Wooden had such comments as the following to illustrate the brutality in TYC facilities:

> "Crumb" or "sitting on lost privileges" is usually reserved for weekends. The student is forced to sit facing a wall or fence all day, forbidden to speak or fall asleep. . . . at the Crockett School, female offenders are often placed in handcuffs and

beaten. . . For the boys the most fearsome threat is the constant reminder of Mountain View, the maximum security facility down the road from Gatesville. With its high double fence topped with massive rolls of barbed wire and patrolled by armed guards in jeeps, the facility is imposing and menacing. The reputation is deadly.

Here the guard administers blows to the child's bare back with the palm of his hand while the boy kneels with his head between the guard's legs. "Running in place" puts the youngster in the same position except the guard runs in place. The friction to the sides of the head causes burning and severe headaches.[45]

The plaintiffs in the class action suit complained not only of abuses such as those described above but of tear gas, mace, and similar chemicals used to control groupings of youths in many of the TYC facilities. The trial led to orders from a federal district court that proscribed the blatant abuses and set specific changes that were required for adequate care and treatment. In no uncertain terms, the court in *Morales v. Turman* (1974)[46] declared a constitutional right to treatment that included a set of minimum standards given in detail, as the following examples illustrate:

- A psychological staff, to consist of psychologists holding either Master's degrees or Doctorates in Psychology and experienced in work with adolescents, sufficient in number to meet the needs of the children.

- Provision of either individual or group psychotherapy for every child for whom it is indicated.[47]

A ruling by an appeals court in 1977[48] acknowledged the appropriate use of the Eighth Amendment's prohibition of cruel and unusual punishment to correct the abuses in TYC facilities, but it denied any constitutional right to treatment. In the words of the decision: "The case law has not universally accepted a right to treatment for the mentally ill . . . The argument for right to treatment is even less strong as related to juvenile offenders."[49] The appeals court was particularly disdainful of the specific treatment requirements given by the trial judge.

Although the issue of the right to treatment remains uncertain because of negative decisions at the appeals level and the Supreme Court's failure to decide, numerous recent federal trial court decisions[50] have affirmed that, in places where the policy behind juvenile corrections is rehabilitation, juveniles so institutionalized have a constitutional right to rehabilitative treatment. Those decisions, it should be pointed out, have relied on a U.S. Supreme Court decision requiring that conditions and programs in a juvenile correctional institution must be concordant with the purpose of the confinement. For technical reasons based on other arguments emanating from the Supreme Court, the quid pro quo component of the argument of the right to treatment has been rejected. Although the U.S. Supreme Court did establish a constitutional standard for adult prisons,[51] it is not clear at this time whether it is applicable to juvenile correctional institutions.

One obvious and persisting result of the right-to-treatment cases has been the imposition of court-ordered improvements in the care and handling of institutionalized juveniles (but the impact has been far from perfect, as was seen in the example from California noted above). As mentioned in the several cases reviewed above, arguments of cruelty and abusiveness on the part of staff have been components of all suits. The assertion of a constitutionally based right to rehabilitative treatment has been accompanied by demands for the cessation of cruel and unusual punishment (required by the Eighth Amendment). The validity of these demands has been acknowledged by appeals courts as well as trial courts; the result has been change, often court-supervised, in the day-to-day treatment of the youngsters. For example, there were extensive improvements in the training schools operated by TYC after the *Morales* decision, even given the serious reservations by the appeals court about the right-to-treatment arguments. Those improvements included significant personnel changes, the discontinuance of abusive practices, and the elimination of clearly inadequate facilities.

In addition, the initiative of the federal judiciary in the preceding actions, as well as in response to suits by institutionalized adults, led to the Civil Rights of Institutionalized Persons Act (CRIPA) in 1980. This act confers on the U.S. Attorney General the power to litigate on the basis of established constitutional and statutory rights. Important aspects of the Act were summarized in a report from the American Bar Association Juvenile Justice Center in 1998:

> A substantial body of law establishes the rights of detained and incarcerated youth and protects them from dangerous conditions and practices of confinement. CRIPA is . . . [a] method of ensuring that these laws are not violated in juvenile facilities. CRIPA's statutory language explicitly includes State or local facilities in which youth are detained or confined . . . and enables [the U.S. Department of Justice] to file a complaint against the State or local government when there are systematic violations of youth.[52]

It might be unreasonable to argue firmly for the right to treatment as an optimum resolution, given the dependence of right-to-treatment arguments on a medical model for delinquency. The issue has been summarized by Woody and Associates as follows:

While guaranteeing institutionalized juveniles a right to treatment is one step to ensure a rehabilitative milieu, there are
inherent problems in juvenile treatment that is based generally
on a medical model. The deviant juvenile is considered to be
someone who can be "cured" through proper treatment. In
point of fact, no one has developed a reliable treatment to cure
the "disease" of delinquency. Moreover, it is a dangerous
assumption that any type of treatment will benefit "sick"
delinquents more than allowing them to mature without institutional intervention.[53]

Is the System Effective?

During the 1970s, extensive reviews of institutional programs for
young (as well as for adult) offenders produced discouraging results.
"Nothing works" became the widely accepted expression of the era. Subsequent analyses, however, found so many methodological flaws in the
studies that formed the bases of those reviews that rethinking and
restudy replaced thorough disillusionment. Some newer, more sophisticated studies found that there are institutional programs that do reduce
recidivism significantly. Programs characterized as the very best use
behavioral and cognitive treatment approaches based on social learning
principles implemented with fidelity in youth-oriented settings.

Lipsey conducted an extensive review of the empirical research
dealing with the remedial effects of court-processisng and institutionalization of serious delinquents. He concluded:

> If one asks categorically, then, whether rehabilitative inter-
> vention works with juvenile offenders, the answer is essential-
> ly, yes. Not every intervention works in every application, but
> the research evidence, when carefully analyzed, unquestionably
> shows that, on average, those interventions subjected to study
> reduce recidivism . . . This evidence shows that optimal com-
> binations of program elements [noninstitutional as well as
> institutional] have the capability to reduce recidivism by 40-50
> percent, that is, to cut recidivism rates to very nearly half of
> what they would be without such programming.[54]

PAROLE

Regardless of the conditions that have led to the incarceration of a
youth, and whatever the conditions and interactions of the incarceration, the youth will eventually be released from the institution. In the

words of the Task Force on Corrections, President's Commission on Law Enforcement and Administration of Justice:

> Whatever rehabilitation they [offenders] have received, whatever deterrent effect their experience with incarceration has had, must upon release withstand the difficulties of readjustment to life in society and reintegration into employment, family, school, and the rest of community life. This is the time when most of the problems from which offenders were temporarily removed must be faced again and new problems arising from their status as ex-offenders must be confronted.[55]

Release from an institution may be unconditional (as when a state code specifies the discharge of a youngster when a certain age is reached) or conditional (as when the youngster leaves the institution with a set of behavioral requirements that will be supervised by an agent of the state). In most cases of unconditional release and in all cases of conditional release, various services will be made available to the youngster in the attempt to achieve a smooth reintegration into society. Historically, the expression "release on parole" had been used to specify conditional release under supervision because of the similarities with parole in the adult prison system. In the area of juvenile justice, however, the word "parole" eventually became the equivalent in usage to such others as "discharge," "aftercare," "release," "furlough," and "placement." Interestingly, beginning July 1, 1999, the state of North Carolina substituted the expression "post-release supervision" for "aftercare" in its statutes, as one of many changes in the state's juvenile code on that date.

Clearly emphasizing the service aspects rather than supervisory aspects following release from an institution, the federal Task Force on Corrections argued for the use of the term "aftercare" rather than "parole." The Task Force believed that the use of the term "aftercare" would separate juvenile matters from the language and concepts of adult parole. Regardless of the terminology, there are certain noteworthy elements in the process that lead from residence in a juvenile institution to life in the community: the release decision, parole supervision and services, and conditions of parole.

The Release Decision

A few states are determinate sentencing jurisdictions, while the great majority are indeterminate sentencing jurisdictions. Just under three-fourths of the jurisdictions with indeterminate sentencing have given the release decision to their juvenile correctional agencies. The others have assigned it to their parole boards or to juvenile court judges.

Assuming that the time of release is not fixed by law (as when a maximum sentence is completed or a certain age is reached), the release decision is based on estimates of the youth's progress toward rehabilitation and the likelihood of successful return to the community. In most cases, there is a minimum length of stay required for eligibility, which may be specified in a state code, but beyond that, some authorities use a formal credit system, some use a casework approach involving written evaluation, some base the decision primarily on completion of training or on completion of training in conjunction with other accomplishments, and some use an approach that considers the number and array of problems created by the youth in the institution. In addition, there is evaluation of such community factors as employment and educational possibilities, the home environment, and the attitudes of family members (or foster parents) and significant others. The use of community factors is illustrated in the following summary of the file of a youngster who was recommended for release from a juvenile institution:

> Although facing serious economic situations, the Browns are a relatively stable family . . . Jim is reported to be very sensitive to his problems—comes from a culturally deprived family who moved from a rural setting (to the city). The family was rejected by the community and Jim retaliated by drinking and becoming involved in delinquent associations. . . . a return home is not possible at this point, therefore, a foster home should be tried . . . Jim has expressed some interest in auto mechanics and this avenue should be pursued . . . he needs a strong expressive individual he can identify with—is presently too dependent on others. [The foster home] is well-furnished and well-kept . . . he will attend X school—has pre-registered and has been given a tour of the school.[56]

The body that determines when a youth is released from an institution may be referred to as the juvenile parole releasing authority. That authority has often consisted, fully or partly, of full-time staff members of juvenile correctional institutions. In other states, the decision regarding parole has been the responsibility of the youth commission to which youths are referred by the juvenile or family court, a board constituted for the sole purpose of parole decisions (this may be the same board responsible for the parole of adults), or the court that made the commitment leading to the incarceration.

In North Carolina, commitment is to the state's Office of Juvenile Justice for placement in a training school. The committing juvenile court, however, does maintain jurisdiction over delinquents in the custody of that office. Planning for release and for post-release supervision are to proceed as follows:

POST-RELEASE SUPERVISION PLANNING; RELEASE

(a) The Office [of Juvenile Justice] shall be responsible for evaluation of the progress of each juvenile at least once every six months as long as the juvenile remains in the care of the Office. Any determination that the juvenile should remain in the care of the Office for an additional period of time shall be based on the Office's determination that the juvenile requires additional treatment or rehabilitation. . . . If the Office determines that a juvenile is ready for release, the Office shall initiate a post-release supervision planning process. The post-release supervision planning process shall be defined by rules and regulations of the Office, but shall include the following:

   (1) Written notification shall be given to the court that ordered commitment.

   (2) A post-release supervision planning conference shall be held involving as many as possible of the following: the juvenile, the juvenile's parent, guardian, or custodian, court counselors who have supervised the juvenile on probation or will supervise the juvenile on post-release supervision, and staff of the facility that found the juvenile ready for release. The planning conference shall include personal contact and evaluation rather than telephonic notification.

   (3) The planning conference participants shall consider, based on the individual needs of the juvenile and pursuant to rules adopted by the Office, placement of the juvenile in any program under the auspices of the Office, including the juvenile court services programs that, in the judgment of the Office, would be appropriate transitional placement, pending release . . .

(b) The Office shall develop the plan in writing and base the terms on the needs of the juvenile and the protection of the public. Every plan shall require the juvenile to complete at least 90 days, but not more than one year, of post-release supervision.

(c) The Office shall release a juvenile under a plan of post-release supervision at least 90 days prior to:

   (1) Completion of the juvenile's definite term of commitment, or

   (2) The juvenile's twenty-first birthday if the juvenile has been committed to the Office for an offense that would be first-degree murder . . ., first-degree rape, ..., or first-degree sexual offense . . . if committed by an adult.

(3) The juvenile's nineteenth birthday if the juvenile has been committed to the Office for an offense that would be Class B1, B2, C, D, or E felony if committed by an adult. . . .

(4) The juvenile's eighteenth birthday if the juvenile has been committed to the Office for an offense other than an offense that would be a Class A, B1, B2, C, D, or E felony if committed by an adult.[57]

Actual supervision of a juvenile who is released from an institution is the responsibility of a court counselor, a person who has the combined responsibilities of probation and parole.

Returning to the general issue of parole, there was an interesting case on the right to parole decided by the Supreme Court of California in 1979 (*In re Owen E.*).[58] In 1974, Owen, who was 17 years old, shot and killed his father after a family argument. He admitted the killing in the adjudicatory hearing and was assigned in the dispositional hearing to the California Youth Authority (CYA) for custody. For 18 months, he participated fully in the institutional programs and was assumed to be making normal progress toward rehabilitation. He applied for parole, but it was denied by the CYA because "he had not yet accepted responsibility for his actions resulting in the commitment and did not fully appreciate his obligations to society."[59]

Shortly thereafter, an appeal to the juvenile court that committed Owen to the CYA resulted in an order that set aside the commitment and placed him on probation. The order of the juvenile court led to an appeal by the CYA and eventually to a decision by the state's highest court (which decided in favor of the CYA) stating that the law did "not authorize judicial intervention into the routine parole function of CYA."[60] Once a commitment is made, the CYA (as the state's youth commission) becomes the sole juvenile parole releasing authority, which may not be circumvented by the vacating of a commitment order by a juvenile court.

Parole Supervision and Services

Aftercare or post-release supervision and services are usually the responsibilities of an agent. This agent may be called a parole officer, though, as noted above, the person is designated a "court counselor" in North Carolina. Supervision requires monitoring school attendance or work habits, making sure that the parolee does not engage in criminal behavior, approving leisure-time activities and the people with whom the parolee associates while engaged in these activities, monitoring time away from home and broad movement patterns, and so on.

The variations in the approaches of aftercare or parole officers has been summarized as follows by Arnold:

> What parole officers actually do varies tremendously, just as different teachers, mechanics, and presidents vary in how well they do their jobs. One officer works sixteen hours per day in order to visit the homes and hangouts of all his parolees every month, whereas another confines his activities largely to his office, to which the parolees are expected to come (by mail if not in person) to report every month. Some officers are friendly; some are unfriendly. Some are very "concerned"; others seem a bit cynical. The most remarkable thing about these variations in work styles is that we do not really know which ones of them work "best."[61]

It has been estimated that the average time spent on each case by a parole officer is two hours per month, counting personal and telephone contact; contact with advisors, employers, and others; travel; and record keeping. That effort is supposed to encompass surveillance and treatment. Surveillance stems from the mission of parole officer as protector of society, and treatment or casework arises from the duty to continue the correctional efforts of the institution. Some have argued that it is impossible for a single person to act effectively both as police officer (in surveillance) and as a social caseworker. Matters are considerably complicated by a central function of the parole officer, which is to determine when to recommend the termination of parole, either by revocation of the parole or by discharge.

Given that state of affairs, it is perhaps not surprising that various evaluations have shown that parole is generally ineffective. In addition to the inherent complexities in the role of parole officer, there have been arguments that parole officers spend a disproportionate amount of time with parolees who cannot be helped at all, and that the typical social casework approach of parole officers is inappropriate and thus ineffective.

Conditions of Parole

When a youth is released from an institution under parole, certain conditions are imposed that could lead to revocation of parole if they are not followed to the satisfaction of the supervising officer. The conditions might include committing no illegal offenses; having no contact with certain individuals or certain groups; using no drugs or alcoholic beverages; maintaining a passing level of performance in school; keeping a job, or taking active steps toward making one likely in the future;

remaining in a specified geographical area; contacting the parole officer on a regular basis; and returning home each night no later than a certain hour.

Clearly there is some question as to how carefully these conditions can be monitored by a parole officer who spends so little time in relevant contacts per month (even though those contacts are usually supplemented by relationships with people like the police, school officials, and employers who will notify the officer or the parole agency if the parolee has conspicuous adjustment problems).

The discretionary power of the parole authority to revoke parole if the conditions are not fulfilled to its satisfaction have been limited by a decision of the U.S. Supreme Court and related decisions by lower courts. In *Morrissey v. Brewer* (1992),[62] the Court determined that a parolee's liberty was valuable and that its termination required an orderly process (at least a limited one).

In cases decided prior to that decision, several courts declared that youths were not entitled to special hearings when an authority revokes parole. For example, the Supreme Court of Minnesota[63] had concluded that procedural formalities would handicap the controlling authority and perhaps create obstacles to the operation of the entire parole process. Similarly, the Supreme Judicial Court of Maine[64] concluded that a hearing was not constitutionally required prior to revocation of a youth's parole and that a simple administrative ruling was all that is necessary.

In 1979 (after *Morrissey*), the Supreme Court of Appeals of West Virginia stated:

> The nature of the interest of the juvenile parolee is not less valuable than that of an adult parolee. The termination of liberty afforded by parole must be accomplished through some orderly process.[65]

In addition, the court ruled against a request for the full due process protections of a criminal prosecution. To strengthen the position of a need for procedural formalities prior to revocation of parole, many states now have a statement in their codes that specify that right. Here's the law in North Carolina by way of illustration:

REVOCATION OF POST-RELEASE SUPERVISION

(a) On motion of the court counselor providing post-release supervision or motion of the juvenile, or on the court's own motion, and after notice, the court may hold a hearing to review the progress of any juvenile on post-release supervision at any time during the period of post-release supervision. With respect to any hearing involving allegations that the juvenile has violated the terms of post-release supervision, the juvenile:

(1) Shall have reasonable notice in writing of the nature and content of the allegations in the motion, including notice that the purpose of the hearing is to determine whether the juvenile has violated the terms of post-release supervision to the extent that post-release supervision should be revoked;

(2) Shall be represented by an attorney at the hearing;

(3) Shall have the right to confront and cross-examine witnesses; and

(4) May admit, deny, or explain the violation alleged and may present proof, including affidavits or other evidence, in support of the juvenile's contentions. A record of the proceeding shall be made and preserved in the juvenile's record.

(b) If the court determines by the greater weight of the evidence that the juvenile has violated the terms of post-release suspervision, the court may revoke the post-release supervision or make any other disposition authorized by this Subchapter.

(c) If the court revokes post-release supervision, the juvenile shall be returned to the Office for placement in a training school for an indefinite term of at least 90 days.[66]

Success and Failure in Parole

On the basis of several studies, Arnold concluded that a youth is more likely to fail in parole if he or she is black rather than white, has been involved in crime for an extended period, has had substantial contact with the correctional system, and has committed predatory crimes (like burglary and forgery).

Chambers studied 239 youths released on parole in New York State. The youths had been convicted and sentenced by adult criminal courts as 13-, 14-, and 15-year-olds under that state's punitive legislation of 1978 (see Chapter 10). At the time of the investigation, the youths were between 17 and 19 years of age and 74 percent were black. In 12 percent of the cases, parole was revoked and the youth was returned to custody, but there was good adjustment to the community in 77 percent of the cases and marginal adjustment in the remaining 11 percent. The cases in which parole was revoked differed from those with good adjustments principally in the realm of productive activity—only 14 percent of the former were either employed or in an educational program, whereas fully 47 percent of the latter were so engaged. The investigator concluded that the probability of successful parole went up considerably when there was intensive prerelease preparation with active supervision during the first six months of parole that emphasized employment or an educational program.

Another study interviewed youths paroled from the California Youth Authority who had high rates of arrest and confinement. Almost one-fourth of them avoided arrest over a two-year follow-up period, and an additional 34 percent were arrested only for minor violations that did not lead to revocations of parole. While attitudes expressed during institutionalization were almost uniformly against the commission of more crimes, almost one-half admitted to criminal behavior during the early period of parole. A number of factors were useful in equations used to predict successful parole. These factors include having friends who are not delinquent, not belonging to a gang while institutionalized, having no problems with drugs or alcohol, living outside of the Los Angeles megalopolis, and spending a high proportion of time employed or in school while on parole.

Concern about the effectiveness of aftercare programs with serious offenders motivated the federal Office of Juvenile Justice and Delinquency Prevention, in 1987, to fund an "intensive aftercare project" aimed at assessing operating programs, developing model programs, and implementing and testing prototypes. Since then, several seemingly effective aftercare programs have been identified and studied; on that basis, a model intensive aftercare program has been proposed and is being tested in Colorado, Nevada, New Jersey, and Virginia. There are five basic principles on which the model is based: (1) preparing youths for increasing responsibilities in the community, (2) facilitating youth-community interaction, (3) enhancing community support systems, (4) developing additional resources as needed, and (5) monitoring the youths and their social interactions continuously.

Parole as conditional early release from a correctional institution has been attacked from both ends of the political spectrum. From the conservative direction, the process has been criticized as being too lenient and costly for offenders who deserve to be punished fully. From the liberal perspective, it has been pointed out that the evidence indicates that parole does not seem to lessen the amount of time served in an institution.

SUMMARY

Detention refers to the process whereby youths are kept in secure and restrictive facilities prior to the determination of disposition by a court. Youths are so detained for an array of legal reasons, which include protection of the youth and protection of the community, as well as an array of extralegal reasons, which include a desire to punish the youth and fear of antagonizing the police by releasing him or her. Institutionalization, on the other hand, refers to the process whereby youths are kept in secure and restrictive facilities as the result of dispositional decisions by juvenile courts. The historical purpose of institutionalization for youths has been rehabilitation, but punishment and protection of the community are increasingly becoming the predominant themes.

Youths may be detained in a locked facility designed for juveniles—often called a juvenile hall—or in an adult jail. Institutionalization may be in a cottage, a facility that is a miniature penitentiary (a state training school), a jail or prison, a camp or ranch, or a boot camp. The facility may be public or private. In some states, youths are sent to reception and diagnostic centers for evaluation prior to institutional placement.

Because the purpose of detention is secure holding prior to the court hearings, there is no emphasis on treatment. The rehabilitative goal of institutionalization, on the other hand, necessitates treatment and teaching programs of many types, including traditional group psychotherapy, social therapy, and both vocational training and academic education.

Although there have been questions about the practices of detention and institutionalization since the earliest days of juvenile justice, the questioning became more intense in recent decades because of a more compassionate social perspective regarding the downtrodden or underprivileged. Books, studies, and reports pointed out the deplorable conditions and abusive practices in many facilities, the personal degradations felt by many child inmates, and the widespread use of adult jails for detention. It was argued by many that detention was used far more frequently than needed and that institutionalization all too often did not include sincere efforts to rehabilitate. Arguments claiming that detention was overused included evidence that only a small proportion of detained youths were eventually institutionalized, that status offenders were locked up at least as frequently as serious offenders, and that the prediction of dangerous behavior (the threat to the community) was a very uncertain enterprise. It was noted that institutionalization frequently did not involve efforts to rehabilitate and that abusive, self-serving behavior was often evidenced by staff members.

Three important paths toward change occurred in the 1970S and 1980s. First, several class action court suits, some of which claimed a right to treatment for institutionalized children, led to court decisions that directed improvement in facilities, conditions, and day-to-day treatment of youths. Second, the federal government entered the picture in 1974 with its Juvenile Justice and Delinquency Prevention Act. The act had three principal components: (1) it created a federal agency devoted to juvenile justice and delinquency prevention, (2) it designated funds for programs aimed at reducing delinquency and rehabilitating offenders, and (3) it provided financial incentives to the states to stop putting status offenders in locked facilities (detained or institutionalized) or placing young offenders of any type in facilities that held adult offenders. (The process of keeping status offenders out of locked facilities is called deinstitutionalization.) Third, in the early 1970s, the state of Massachusetts deinstitutionalized all juvenile offenders; that is, all public institutions in the state were closed. Most of the former inmates were sent to their communities, but a small number (about 50) were sent to private locked facilities.

When a youth is released from an institution, he or she may be supervised for a period and provided various services in order to achieve smooth reintegration into society. The word "parole" emphasizes supervisory aspects, while the word "aftercare" focuses on the service aspects of the process. However, the two words are generally used interchangeably to refer to release from an institution and reentry into the community. A third expression becoming more widely used in recent years is "post-release supervision." This term seems to convey the same general meaning as parole without the latter's negative connotation. When the release is conditional, a parole officer evaluates the youth on a continuing basis and initiates a recommendation for discharge. A violation of the conditions of parole can lead to return to the institution for those on conditional release. Those on unconditional release, on the other hand, are not supervised and may not be returned to the institution for violation of parole, but are usually provided services to aid their readjustment.

REFERENCES

Allinson, Richard (1983). "There Are No Juveniles in Pennsylvania Jails." *Corrections Magazine* 9(3):13-20.

Altschuler, David M., and Troy L. Armstrong (1994). *Intensive Aftercare for High-Risk Juveniles: Policies and Procedures.* Washington, DC: U.S. Department of Justice, Office of Juvenile Justice and Delinquency Prevention.

Andrews, D.A., Ivan Zinger, Robert D. Hoge, James Bonta, Paul Gendreau, and Francis T. Cullen (1990). "Does Correctional Treatment Work? A Clinically Relevant and Psychologically Informed Meta-Analysis." *Criminology* 28:369-404.

Arnold, William R. (1970). *Juveniles on Parole: A Sociological Analysis.* New York: Random House.

Binder, Arnold, and Virginia L. Binder (1994). "The Incarceration of Juveniles from the Era of Crouse to that of Freud and Skinner." *Legal Studies Forum* XVIII:349-368.

Binder, Arnold, and Susan L. Polan (1991). "The Kennedy-Johnson Years, Social Theory and Federal Policy in the Control of Juvenile Delinquency." *Crime & Delinquency* 37:242-261.

Birnbaum, M. (1960). "The Right to Treatment." *American Bar Association Journal* 46:499-505.

Boyd, Neil (1983). "Juvenile Release Programs in British Columbia and Ontario: A Comparative Analysis." In *Current Issues in Juvenile Justice*, edited by Raymond R. Corrado, Marc LeBlanc, and Jean T. Trepanier, 603-614. Toronto: Butterworths.

Breed, Allen F. (1953). "California Youth Authority Forestry Camp Program." *Federal Probation* 17:37-43.

Cadwalader, George (1988). *Castaways: The Penikese Island Experiment.* Chelsea, VT: Chelsea Green.

Chambers, Ola R. (1983). *The Juvenile Offender: A Parole Profile.* Albany: Evaluation and Planning Unit, New York State Division of Parole.

Children in Custody, 1985-95 (1998). Washington, DC: U.S. Department of Justice, Bureau of Justice Statistics.

Children in Custody, 1975-85 (1989). Washington, DC: U.S. Department of Justice, Bureau of Justice Statistics.

Children's Defense Fund (1976). *Children in Adult Jails.* Washington, DC: Washington Research Project.

Cottle, Thomas J. (1977). *Children in Jail: Seven Lessons in American Justice.* Boston: Beacon Press.

Cressey, Donald R. (1965). "Prison Organizations." In *Handbook of Organizations*, edited by James G. March, 1023-1070. Chicago: Rand McNally.

Ferster, Elyce Z., and Thomas C. Courtless (1972). "Post-Disposition Treatment and Recidivism in the Juvenile Court: Towards Justice for All." *Journal of Family Law* 11:683-708.

Holden, Constance (1976). "Massachusetts Juvenile Justice: Deinstitutionalization on Trial." *Science* 192:447-451.

Ketcham, Orman W. (1961). "The Unfilled Promise of the Juvenile Court." *Crime & Delinquency* 7:97-110.

Keve, Paul W. (1984). *The Consequences of Prohibiting the Jailing of Juveniles.* Prepared for the Chicago Resource Center. Richmond: Virginia Commonwealth University.

Lab, Steven P., and John T. Whitehead (1988). "An Analysis of Juvenile Correctional Treatment." *Crime & Delinquency* 34:60-83.

Lipsey, Mark W. (1999). "Can Intervention; Rehabilitate Serious Delinquents?" *Annals of the American Academy of Political and Social Science* 564:142-166.

MacKenzie, Lynn Ryan (1999). *Detention in Delinquency Cases, 1987-1996.* Washington, DC: U.S. Department of Justice, Office of Juvenile Justice and Delinquency Prevention.

Martinson, Robert (1974). "What Works? Questions and Answers about Prison Reform." *Public Interest* 35:22-54.

Miller, Frank W., Robert O. Dawson, George E. Dix, and Raymond I. Parnas (1985). *The Juvenile Justice Process*, 3rd ed. Mineola, NY: Foundation Press.

1992 Compliance Monitoring Data (1992). *Summary of State Compliance with the Juvenile Justice and Delinquency Prevention Act of 1974*, as amended. (Preliminary Report, 1994). Washington, DC: U.S. Department of Justice, Office of Juvenile Justice and Delinqency Prevention.

Office of Juvenile Justice and Delinquency Prevention (1994). *Conditions of Confinement: Juvenile Detention and Corrections Facilities*. Washington, DC: Office of Justice Programs, U.S. Department of Justice.

Office of Juvenile Justice and Delinquency Prevention (1993). *Children in Custody: Census of Public Juvenile Detention, Correctional and Shelter Facilities 1990-1991* [machine-readable data file]. Washington, DC: Bureau of the Census [producer].

Ohlin, Lloyd E., Robert B. Coates, and Alden D. Miller (1974). "Radial Correctional Reform: A Case Study of the Massachusetts Youth Correctional System." *Harvard Educational Review* 44:74-111.

Paul, Warren N., and Helga S. Watt (1980). *Deinstitutionalization of Status Offenders: A Compilation and Analysis of State Statutes*. Denver: State Legislative Leaders Foundation.

Peters, Jean K. (1990). "*Schall v. Martin* and the Transformation of Judicial Precedent." *Boston College Law Review* 31:641-695.

Peters, Michael, David Thomas, Christopher Zamberlan, and Caliber Associates (1997). *Boot Camps for Juvenile Offenders*. Washington, DC: U.S. Department of Justice, Office of Juvenile Justice and Delinquency Prevention.

Pleune, F. Gordon (1959). "Effects of State Training School Programs on Juvenile Delinquents." In *The Problem of Delinquency*, edited by Sheldon Glueck, 711-721. Boston: Houghton Mifflin.

Poulin, John E., John L. Levitt, Thomas M. Young, and Donnell M. Pappenfort (1980). *Reports of the National Juvenile Justice Assessment Centers. Juveniles in Detention Centers and Jails: An Analysis of State Variations During the Mid 1970s*. Washington, DC: U.S. Government Printing Office.

President's Commission on Law Enforcement and Administration of Justice (1967). *Task Force Report: Corrections*. Washington, DC: U.S. Government Printing Office.

Puritz, Patricia, and Mary Ann Scali (1998). *Beyond the Walls: Improving Conditions of Confinement for Youth in Custody*. Washington, DC: U.S. Department of Justice, Office of Juvenile Justice and Delinquency Prevention.

Reichel, Philip L. (1985). "Getting to Know You: Decision-Making in an Institution for Juveniles." *Juvenile and Family Court Journal* 36:5-15.

Rothman, David J. (1979). *Incarceration and Its Alternatives in 20th Century America*. Washington, DC: U.S. Government Printing Office.

Schwartz, Ira M., Linda Harris, and Laurie Levi (1988). "The Jailing of Juveniles in Minnesota: A Case Study." *Crime & Delinquency* 34:133-149.

Serrill, Michael S. (1975). "Moving the Kids Out: A Unique Experiment." *Corrections Magazine* (2):29-40.

Sickmund, Melissa, Anne L. Stahl, Terrence A. Finnegan, Howard N. Snyder, Rowen S. Poole, and Jeffrey A. Butts (1998). *Juvenile Court Statistics 1995*. Washington, DC: U.S. Department of Justice, Office of Juvenile Justice and Delinquency Prevention.

Sickmund, Melissa, Howard N. Snyder, and Eileen Poe-Yamagata (1997). *Juvenile Offenders and Victims: 1997 Update on Violence*. Washington, DC: U.S. Department of Justice, Office of Juvenile Justice and Delinquency Prevention.

Smith, Bradford (1998). "Children in Custody: 20-Year Trends in Juvenile Detention Correctional, and Shelter Facilities." *Crime & Delinquency* 44:526-543.

Sorrentino, Joseph H. (1975). *The Concrete Cradle*. Los Angeles: Wollstonecraft.

Steinhart, David (1988). "California Legislature Ends the Jailing of Children: The Story of a Policy Reversal." *Crime & Delinquency* 34:169-189.

Sumner, Helen (1971). *Locking Them Up: The Study of Juvenile Detention Decisions in Selected California Counties*. New York: National Council on Crime and Delinquency.

Teeters, Negley K. (1950). "Institutional Treatment of Juvenile Delinquents." *Nebraska Law Review* 29:577-604.

Wiederanders, Mark R. (1983). *Success on Parole: The Influence of Self-Reported Attitudes, Experiences, and Background Characteristics on the Parole Behaviors of Youthful Offenders. Final Report*. Sacramento: Department of the Youth Authority.

Wooden, Kenneth (1976). *Weeping in the Playtime of Others: America's Incarcerated Children*. New York: McGraw-Hill.

Woody, Robert Henley, and Associates (1984). *The Law and the Practice of Human Services*. San Francisco: Jossey-Bass.

Wordes, Madeline, and Sharon M. Jones (1998). "Trends in Juvenile Detention and Steps Toward Reform." *Crime & Delinquency* 44:544-560.

Notes

[1] President's Commission on Law Enforcement and Administration of Justice (1967), 23.

[2] Ibid., 121.

[3] Ibid., 121.

[4] Children's Defense Fund (1976), 30-31.

[5] Cottle (1977), 2.

[6] Ibid., 16, 18, 20, 21

[7] 467 U.S. 255 (1984).

[8] Ibid., 262.

9   Ibid., 272.

10   Ibid., 278.

11   Ibid., 256. But see Peters (1990) for a stinging negative review of that decision.

12   MacKenzie (1999), 1.

13   Sickmund, Snyder & Poe-Yamagata (1997), 43.

14   President's Commission on Law Enforcement and Administration of Justice (1967), 141-142.

15   Rothman (1979), 58-59.

16   Smith (1998), 529-537.

17   Breed (1953), 705.

18   Wooden (1976), 28-29.

19   Miller et al. (1985), 896.

20   Peters et al. (1997), 31.

21   Ibid., 32-33.

22   Teeters (1950), 161.

23   Sorrentino (1975), 161.

24   Ibid., 166.

25   Wooden (1976), 129-130.

26   Ibid., 50.

27   Ibid., 121.

28   Cottle (1977), 35.

29   Ibid., 91.

30   Ibid., 93.

31   Ibid., 95.

32   Ibid., 93.

33   *Los Angeles Times*, September 26, 1999, Part I, 1.

34   Public Law 93-415, Title II, §223 [a].

35   Paul & Watt (1980), 1.

36   Serrill (1975), 30-31.

37   Holden (1976), 447.

38   Serrill (1975), 29.

39   Ohlin, Coates & Miller (1974), 96.

40   D.C. Code §21-562 (1981).

41   373 F.2d 4512 (1966).

42   344 F. Supp. 373 (1972).

[43]   Ketcham (1961), 100.

[44]   491 F.2d 358 (1974).

[45]   Wooden (1976), 8-9.

[46]   383 F. Supp. 53 (1974).

[47]   Ibid., 105.

[48]   *Morales v. Turman*, 562 F.2D 993 (1977).

[49]   Ibid., 998.

[50]   See particularly *Alexander S. v. Boyd*, 876 F.Supp. 773 (1995).

[51]   *Rhodes v. Chapman*, 452 U.S. 337 (1981).

[52]   Puritz & Scali (1998), 1.

[53]   Woody & Associates (1984), 95.

[54]   Lipsey (1999), 163.

[55]   President's Commission on Law Enforcement and Administration of Justice (1967), 60.

[56]   Boyd (1983), 309.

[57]   N.C. Gen. Stat. §7B-2514 (1999).

[58]   23 Cal. 3d 398.

[59]   Ibid., 400.

[60]   Ibid., 406.

[61]   Arnold (1970), 70.

[62]   408 U.S. 471 (1972).

[63]   *Loyd v. Youth Conservation Commisson*, 287 Minn. 12 (1970).

[64]   *Bernier v. State of Maine*, 265 A.2d 604 (1970).

[65]   *State v. MacQueen*, 163 W. Va. 623 (1979).

[66]   N.C. Gen. Stat. §7B-2516 (1999).

12

The Community as a Resource in the Treatment of Delinquency

At several points in the discussions of the preceding chapters we have seen examples in which community agencies and processes were important ancillaries to the juvenile justice system. For example, Chapter 9 pointed out that one alternative in police discretion is release of an arrested youth with referral to a community agency for appropriate treatment. As another example, Chapter 10 discussed the process of informal probation, in which a youngster is returned to his or her home rather than referred to court under various conditions that could include services from a community agency. As a final example, Chapter 11 discussed the closing of custodial institutions for young offenders in Massachusetts during the early 1970s and the transfer of the former inmates to community facilities.

The preference for informal, community-based treatment of young offenders has been a significant aspect of the juvenile justice system from the time it came into existence in 1899. The act establishing it specified that the newly created juvenile court should be biased toward probation and placement of a youth in his or her parental home or an equivalent family home (see Chapter 8). Such a preference was also part of the practice of Ben B. Lindsey in Denver during those early years, and it remained, at least in theory, a central characteristic of juvenile court law and juvenile justice operations over subsequent years.

Diversion

Historical Development

It became clear during the earliest years of the juvenile justice system that the system's operation included a bias (perhaps an absolute need) for informal handling before court appearance. There was discussion of prehearing settlement of cases by probation officers as early as 1904, well before informal probation was part of juvenile law. In 1926, the National Probation Association acknowledged the desirability of such incorporation when it proposed a Standard Juvenile Court Law. As discussed by Wallace and Brennan, justification of the act was presented by the recommending committee of the National Probation Association as follows:

> The act follows the procedure [of handling cases informally] in many of the best juvenile courts by providing for a preliminary inquiry and investigation before a petition is filed. It proceeds upon the theory that it is better for as many cases as possible to be adjusted without a formal court hearing. The system of handling cases informally, usually through the probation department, is well recognized and in many courts half or more of the cases are adjusted in this way. This can be done without explicit statutory authority, the court having an inherent right to exercise discretion as to taking official jurisdiction, but the system has grown so widespread and is so generally recognized as beneficial that the committee believes it should be recognized in the law.[1]

In the early 1930s, many police departments in larger cities developed programs for the informal handling of juvenile offenders in such forms as social investigations and casework-type treatment (where women police workers often played a role). The model for that type of program was the New York City Juvenile Aid Bureau, which was established in 1930, with a staff of police officers headed by an inspector. Closer to the approach of informal probation was a development (referred to as "police probation") during the same era in which the police entered into informal agreements with violators and their parents that specified required behavior. That behavior might include mandatory visits to the police station, restitution for victims, no truancy, and study at home for a certain number of hours each day.

When Passaic, New Jersey, established its Children's Bureau in 1937, there were four police officers assigned to the bureau who were expected to turn apprehended juvenile offenders over to bureau staff so that their problems could be analyzed and counselors assigned to guide readjustment.

The Recommendations of the President's Commission

The report of the President's Commission on Law Enforcement and Administration of Justice in 1967 led to profound changes in the pre-judicial handling of juveniles. Many prominent sociologists, in their capacities as commission staff members and consultants, were influential in the specifics of its recommendations. Moreover, during the era of the mid-1960s, when the commission did its work, labeling theory was at a high point of acceptance in sociology (see Chapter 6).

The report of the commission summarized the state of affairs in the juvenile justice system as follows:

> Informal and discretionary pre-judicial dispositions already are a formally recognized part of the process to a far greater extent in the juvenile than in the criminal justice system. The primacy of the rehabilitative goal in dealing with juveniles, the limited effectiveness of the formal processes of the juvenile justice system, the labeling inherent in adjudicating children delinquents, the inability of the formal system to reach the influences—family, school, labor market, recreational opportunities—that shape the life of a youngster, the limited disposition options available to the juvenile judge, the limitations of personnel and diagnostic and treatment facilities, the lack of community support—all of these factors give pre-judicial dispositions an especially important role with respect to juveniles.
>
> Consequently, the informal and pre-judicial processes of adjustment compete in importance with the formal ones and account for a majority of juvenile dispositions. They include discretionary judgments of the police officer to ignore conduct or warn the child or refer him to other agencies; "station adjustment" by the police, in which the child's release may be made conditional on his complying with designated limitations on his conduct; the planned diversion of alleged delinquents away from the court to resources within the school, clinic, or other community facilities, by such groups as mental health, social, and school guidance agencies; pre-judicial dispositions, at the intake stage of the court process, by probation officers or sometimes judges exercising a broad screening function and selecting among alternatives that include outright dismissal, referral to another community agency for service, informal supervision by the probation staff, detention, and filing a petition for further court action. In many courts the court intake process itself disposes of the majority of cases.[2]

The report went on to emphasize, "There are grave disadvantages and perils . . . in that vast continent of sublegal dispositions."[3] Among the disadvantages and perils it specified were the following: (1) the process existed outside the guidance, control, and scrutiny of the formal processes that protected constitutional rights; (2) the use of discretion was too often arbitrary, based more on bureaucratic convenience than on a thorough evaluation of the offender and careful consideration of available alternatives; and (3) it was too easy for illegal and discriminatory processes to intrude and for authority to be abused by the prejudiced and overzealous.

On balance, however, the commission argued that informal pre-judicial handling was widely preferable to formal treatment and should be continued in a modified form to control its various evils. The use of community approaches, according to the report, which shows the influence of labeling theory, "avoids the stigma of being processed by an official agency regarded by the public as an arm of crime control."[4] It recommended the following changes to achieve the acceptable modified form: complete elimination of police probation ("station adjustment"); the uniform use of written standards, at both police and probation levels, to guide decisionmaking among alternative dispositions for juvenile offenders; more in-service training for police and probation officers to further their understanding of the relationships among alternative dispositions, the needs of children, and the available community resources; and the elimination of the coercive features of informal probation.

Above all else, the commission recommended, "Communities should establish neighborhood youth-serving agencies—Youth Services Bureaus—located if possible in comprehensive neighborhood community centers and receiving juveniles (delinquent and nondelinquent) referred by the police, the juvenile court, parents, schools, and other sources." It made clear that the "bulk of the referrals could be expected to come from the police and the juvenile court intake staff" in a process of diversion of appropriate youths away from the formal path in the justice system.[5]

Reasons for the Rapid Expansion of Diversion

The commission's position laid the foundation for the transformation of a necessary and routine procedure in the pre-judicial handling of juveniles into a national passion for an enterprise that became uniformly known as diversion. Whereas, in the 1960s and earlier, the common practice was release and community referral, with more formal programs in some police and probation departments, by the mid-1970s there were hundreds of diversion programs, many of which called themselves Youth Services Bureaus or Youth Service Bureaus.

Many factors contributed to create that result. Of primary importance were federal acts that generated the appropriation of moneys aimed at putting the recommendations of the commission into effect. The first such legislation occurred in 1968. The federal funding generated by the legislation went to various components of the justice system and to community agencies through specially created federal bureaus.

Between 1968 and 1974, there was, as the process continued, a strengthening at the national level of the concept of community-based programs and services as a means of preventing delinquency and diverting youths from the juvenile justice system in general, and from detention and correctional facilities in particular. The process eventually led to the Juvenile Justice and Delinquency Prevention (JJDP) Act of 1974—the act that was described in Chapter 11 in terms of its attempt to prevent the placement of status offenders in locked facilities by threats of the loss of federal funds. Its statement of purpose was as follows: "It is therefore the further declared policy of Congress to provide the necessary resources, leadership, and coordination . . . to develop and conduct effective programs to prevent delinquency, to divert juveniles from the juvenile justice system and to provide critically needed alternatives to institutionalization."[6]

Accordingly, many millions of dollars were appropriated for the development of model diversion programs as a major priority of Congress. Guidance and additional incentives for the efforts were provided by two important monographs published early in the 1970s. The first, and clearly the more influential of the two, was titled *Instead of Court: Diversion in Juvenile Justice*. This work was written by Edwin Lemert, one of the consulting sociologists to the President's Commission, who differentiated between "primary" and "secondary" labeling processes. In it he discussed alternate models of diversion and provided the following perspective: "Ideally, the diversion of minors from juvenile court will become a state of mind, an unquestioned moral position held by all child and youth welfare organizations, considered as a good in itself rather than a means to an end."[7]

The second monograph, titled *The Youth Service Bureau: A Key to Delinquency Prevention*, was written by Sherwood Norman. It was published in 1972 by the National Council on Crime and Delinquency, of which Norman was a director. In the monograph, a Youth Service Bureau was defined as "a noncoercive, independent public agency established to divert children and youth from the justice system by (1) mobilizing community resources to solve youth problems; (2) strengthening existing youth resources and developing new ones; and (3) promoting positive programs to remedy delinquency-breeding conditions."[8] The recommended mode of operation of the Youth Service Bureau was service brokerage, whereby referrals to it by the police and probation officers were evaluated and then referred to other agencies for required services.

The National Effort

The Boom

A number of factors contributed to the rapid and great expansion of diversion during the 1970s: the excitement of a new effort that offered hope of helping troubled youths without the attendant faults of the juvenile justice system, the possibilities of mobilizing community resources to combat a social evil that had eluded all previous attempts at control, the supporting arguments by leading theorists of crime and delinquency, and (last but certainly not least) the lure of a substantial number of federal dollars. The extent of the boom is reflected in the opening sentence of a reader on diversion: "Seldom in the history of American criminal justice has a concept erupted on the scene and generated as much interest as that of diversion."[9]

To illustrate the typical operation of early diversion programs that received federal funds, we turn to the Sacramento 601 Diversion Project and its successor, the Sacramento 602 Diversion Project (as described by Baron and Feeney). The first of these was directed at status offenders (as described in Section 601 of the relevant California Code), who constituted more than one-third of all cases referred to the juvenile court of Sacramento County in the early 1970s. During the period of project operation, for four days each week diversion staff handled all status offenders referred to the Sacramento County Probation Department; regular probation intake officers handled comparable referrals on the other three days. This arrangement created a control group as a comparison yardstick for evaluating the degree of success of the experimental or diversion group.

The diversion staff members, consisting of a supervisor and six probation officers, used crisis intervention and family crisis counseling as their modes of approach. Prior to the start of service delivery, they received considerable training in those modes to achieve the goal of getting the family to approach the offense as a situation involving the whole family rather than as an issue of blame. There was a directed attempt to enhance family communication processes and to help the family face possible collective solutions.

Evaluation of the results, which involved comparison of experimental and control cases, indicated considerable success. Only 3.7 percent of the cases handled by project staff were referred to juvenile court, as compared with 19.8 percent of those handled in the usual way by the intake officers; the project cases spent fewer nights in detention than did control cases as a result of the initial referral, and fewer nights in detention during a year of follow-up; and the project reduced recidivism by 14 percent over all offenses and 40 percent for felonies.

Moreover, the success of the project was achieved at a considerably lower cost than that of usual probation operations.

Those results led to the second experimental program, the Sacramento 602 Diversion Project, in which youths referred for criminal-type behavior were accepted for diversion services (Section 602 of the relevant California Code deals with youths who violate criminal laws). The general procedure of the 601 Project was repeated for the new project, including special training of probation officers assigned to the program, the handling of a control group by regular intake staff, and an emphasis on family counseling. The evaluated accomplishments of the 602 Project were even more impressive than those of the 601 Project. There was a 99 percent reduction in court petitions, overall recidivism was reduced by 40 percent, and criminal recidivism was reduced by more than 50 percent.

Although the Sacramento projects were emulated widely, the proliferation of diversion programs involved a much broader diversity of approaches. Some programs were components of criminal and juvenile justice agencies, as was the case in Sacramento; others were components of social service agencies, public or private; and still others were independent, community-based operations. Some programs followed the brokerage format recommended by Norman and only made referrals to appropriate service-providing agencies, while others provided direct services to youths sent to them. Some programs accepted referrals only from the police, some only from probation, some from both police and probation, and some from a larger array of sources that included schools. Among the direct services provided by programs were family counseling, individual therapy, peer counseling, job development and counseling, drug counseling, advocacy, educational counseling and tutorial assistance, placement in recreational and craft activities, and short-term shelter.

Virtually all of the diversion programs were subjected to formal evaluations because such was required of social programs receiving federal funding. The results were generally significantly less positive than those found in Sacramento, although some successes that supported the optimism generated by the Sacramento findings did occur. In marked contrast to the report of Baron and Feeney, one of the most significant and comprehensive evaluations of the era found, "A diversion disposition was no more successful in avoiding stigma, improving social adjustment, or reducing delinquent behavior than normal justice processing or outright release."[10]

Contraction

In addition to challenging evaluative results of the sort just described, much criticism of diversion began appearing in the sociological literature almost as early as the enterprise was launched. The criticism was based on both theoretical and operational arguments, including some derived from a labeling perspective. Schur set the tone for the criticism in a book titled *Radical Nonintervention: Rethinking the Delinquency Problem*, in which he argued that society should be more tolerant of the diversity of youthful behaviors and attitudes and that children should be left alone by social agencies—including diversion programs—as much as possible. That position was expanded in subsequent arguments by many others to encompass several additional features that formed a theme for the negative comments. First, it was argued that diversion staff members spend most of their energies on youngsters who would have been counseled and released by the police or by probation officers if the programs were not available—which produces not genuine diversion but instead a "widening of the net" of social control. Second, it was argued that there was just as much labeling by a diversion program as there would have been if a youth had moved onward in the justice system, and considerably more labeling than if the youth had simply been counseled and released without referral. Third, it was argued that diversionary activities violate the due process requirements of the United States Constitution in subjecting a youth to social control without proper procedural protections. Finally, it was argued that there is discrimination in referrals to diversion programs—against lower-class youths, who were being denied these services although they could benefit from diversion's family services, and against females, who were disproportionately involved in diversion programs with the result that diversion could increase stigma and delinquency among the females in a process of "hidden sexism."

More Recent Developments

There was a marked decrease in the number of formal diversion programs over the 1980s. Although the negative evaluations and theoretical criticisms contributed to that decrease, more important was the entry into a politically conservative era and the concomitant decrease of federal funds for such purposes. The funding patterns during that era and their effects on diversion were discussed by Rubin as follows:

> A number of youth services bureaus failed to survive more than a few years; others have continued eight years or longer. In general, they have not been readily embraced by local funding bodies, since they lack the political clout of the court and other more primary social services. However, bureaus in some communities have built useful political relationships and appear to be on a stable funding course. Some state legislatures appropriate funds for the state to contract with a bureau for its services.[11]

Despite that contraction, early in the decade of the 1990s, David-son et al. published a monograph describing a mammoth research project (running almost 10 years) directed at evaluating diversionary approaches with delinquent youths. It was called the Adolescent Diversion Project. There were three intervention or treatment strategies having a primary goal of determining the effects of these strategies on recidivism, as predicted using such structures as labeling theory, social control theory, and social learning theory (discussed in Chapters 6 and 7). The results indicated that there was no "widening of the net." There was "true diversion" as a result of the interventions and all three approaches effectively reduced recidivism.

Another current approach to diversion is derived from the theory and practice of law-related education (LRE). The methods of LRE were initiated in the early 1960s, based on the concept that accurate knowledge of law, legal processes, and the legal system generally makes for better citizens. By the year 1978, there were almost 100 LRE programs, including statewide efforts in seven states. There was, then, a short leap from the notion of a method to create better citizenship among youths to the idea of using that method in a diversionary effort with offending youths.

An example of the use of LRE in diversion is provided by Williamson and Columbia. In a typical year of the mid-1990s, the state of Kentucky, processed about 46,000 cases in its court intake services; about one-half of that number were diverted. In each case of diversion, a contract was written that specified such required behavior as counseling, school attendance, community service, and restitution. The youth, though, had the right to request a formal court hearing instead of agreeing to the diversion contract. In addition, the victim of the offense, the arresting officer, and the prosecuting attorney were given an opportunity to object to the diversionary decision.

In the LRE part of the diversion program, "sessions [following a week of orientation] are devoted to rules, authority, responsibility, justice, juvenile justice, family law, environmental law, and community issues. Resource people (e.g. attorneys, social workers, and police officers) highlighting the Kentucky justice system participate in the sessions and engage youth in active learning strategies."[12] There are 11 weeks of these sessions, which are generally guided by Hirschi's control theory and its emphasis on social bonding. This includes continuing efforts to connect the learning in the sessions with field experiences.

There have been several formal evaluations of juvenile diversion programs in recent years, some using meta-analysis, with the general conclusion that diversionary approaches are less expensive than traditional ones but do not always produce comparative decreases in recidivism. The indications are that effective programs use a limited range of techniques, including behavioral approaches and the teaching of essential skills for living. What, then, is the status of diversion as we move along in the twenty-first century? In answering that question, one must distinguish between "traditional diversion" and "new diversion." Traditional diversion refers to the discretionary processes of the police and probation by which release of a youth from further processing is often accompanied by referral to a community agency. The American juvenile justice system could not operate effectively without that form of diversion. On the other hand, new diversion refers to the ideas that followed the President's Commission report in 1967, which stressed formalized programmatic approaches to diversion. The expectation was that the new programs would coordinate available services, create new services, and encourage police and probation to use those services instead of referral up the ladder of the justice system.

Traditional diversion, of course, will (and must) continue, but it should be modified by what has been learned over the years of the programmatic boom. There are many existing programs that offer new diversion, operating with renewed federal funding or with local funding, both public and private. Such programs must remain sensitive to the political realities of the twenty-first century and to reassessments dictated by research results. The major programmatic adjustments necessary are implied in Binder and Geis's summary of noted shortcomings:

> Many diversion programs, like many other human service programs, try to generate case loads. Sometimes, perhaps often, they involve themselves with youngsters who would likely be as well off if they were dispatched homeward after initial police contact. In addition, it seems unquestionable that diversion services are offered more in the affluent communities than in places where they might be more worthwhile by keeping minority youngsters from deeper involvement with the juvenile corrections system. Nor is there much doubt that the police are reluctant to refer "heavier" offenders to diversion agencies, though diversion might accomplish more positive results than eventuate from the traditional and more punitive dispositions.[13]

At this time, there are insufficient data to evaluate whether current diversion programs are abiding by those cautions, as well as the many others expressed in the conclusions of evaluative research over the years. The evidence, however, is not encouraging. It is clear that there are many active diversion programs in the programmatic sense, and that there is currently renewed federal funding that sustains them. Private communication from the Office of Juvenile Justice and Delinquency Prevention indicates that there were 315 allocations of federal funds (totaling just under $11 million) between 1993 and 1999 for police diversion programs. However, very few of these programs are subject to evaluation because the federal money is channeled through state agencies in a process called "sub-granting." There are also many local programs (an internet search found more than 600 of them with ties to the police, probation, or prosecution).

COMMUNITY-BASED PROGRAMS AND GROUP HOMES

Overview

Beyond the diversionary approaches just described, the most formal way in which community resources have been brought into play in the treatment of delinquency has been in the creation of programs, based within communities, that focus on using community ties and even community members as resources in the process of rehabilitation. Some of these programs might be called "group homes" in that they are based in residential facilities within the community in order to provide constant supervision and treatment to the young people referred to them. Others are nonresidential, representing efforts to divert troubled and delinquent young people from institutionalization. Some serve as settings not only for the treatment of delinquents but also for research on delinquency and rehabilitation.

Many such programs have been developed in the United States over the years. They exist in most states and in every major metropolitan area. Their work typically has been in close cooperation with the juvenile courts; many receive the bulk of their referrals from those courts. Although some were and are privately owned and operated, and some were and are profit-making ventures, many have been developed under the auspices of state and local government. As we shall see, the methods

Group homes for juvenile offenders exist in most states. These residential facilities provide supervision and treatment in a community setting. Treatment methods and success rates vary greatly. *(Photo by Ellen S. Boyne)*

these programs use to treat delinquents vary greatly, and the question of their efficacy is far from decided.

Although much of the most significant development of community-based programs occurred in the 1960s and 1970s, it is not difficult to see the roots of that development earlier in American history. Many of these programs stress the importance of creating a home-like setting for delinquents in a manner not unlike that found among the advocates of the "cottage system" in the middle of the nineteenth century. Others have developed techniques to encourage self-government among their charges, reminiscent of the "junior republics" of the early twentieth century (see Chapter 8). They may be thought of within the larger historical framework of efforts to find alternatives to institutionalization for young offenders.

It is also possible to identify more obvious precedents for modern programs from earlier in this century. One such predecessor was El Retiro, a school for girls in Los Angeles. In 1920, El Retiro came under the leadership of Miriam Van Waters, an important scholar in the early study of delinquency and a major leader in the effort to reform the treatment of delinquents. Van Waters focused her efforts on the reintegration of young women in her care back into their communities. At El Retiro, she established procedures for self-government among the young women, created a "halfway" club for those released from El Retiro, and even started an alumnae group.

One may also see a precedent for recent community-based programs in the Chicago Area Project (CAP) of the 1930s. Although this project was covered thoroughly in Chapter 6, it is worth stressing now the importance of its community basis. The key assumption of the project's leaders was that delinquency occurred within a community setting and therefore could best be brought under control by the people in that setting; the project, of course, drew much of its support because of that community orientation.

The CAP also directly inspired later community-based programs. One example is the Hard to Reach Youth Project of the 1950s. In this project, young indigenous leaders were employed on a part-time basis to work with gangs. These young men often took leadership roles within the gangs and served as liaisons between gang members and the community, as well as between gang members and the police.

These early precedents were fairly diverse in character, but all had in common the involvement of the community in the treatment of delinquents as well as the involvement of delinquents in the community as a basis for treatment. All sought to find viable alternatives to institutionalization as a response to delinquency.

Indeed, despite the diversity of those early programs, as well as that of more recent efforts, it is possible to see a common thread of assumptions and purposes that tend to tie community-based programs together. According to a perspective expressed in 1969 but still valid today in regard to community-based programs, delinquency is "a function not only of economically and socially depriving systems but of a community committed to the wrong values." These "wrong values" are part of "a series of extraordinarily intricate, dynamic, yet intractable patterns of community breakdown," including divisiveness, stigmatization and the failure of opportunities and services, among others.[14] Community-based programs seek to counteract these problems by building social networks, providing training, and (above all) inculcating new values in young offenders. Attachment to significant others, commitment to conventional lines of action, involvement in conventional activities, and belief in the moral validity of norms and the law involve social bonds, which can, accordingly, deter the juvenile from delinquent behavior.

Significant Programs and Homes

Many community-based programs and group homes that have existed in the United States have taken on special significance, either because of their impact on their communities or because of the wider influence they have had on the treatment of delinquency. We shall survey several of the more important ones.

Highfields

Among the first and most influential of the group homes with a strong community-based approach was that established at Highfields, New Jersey, in 1950. It grew out of the thinking of two men who had worked together during World War II on military-related rehabilitation programs and who sought to apply what they had learned to creating new treatment programs for young offenders. The overall purpose of Highfields was summarized as follows:

> (1) the informal and intimate living for a short period in a small group of about twenty boys in a noncustodial residential center, (2) the experience of a regular routine of work under supervision, (3) evening sessions of guided group interaction (GGI) designed to give the boys insight into the motivations for their conduct and incentive to change their attitudes, (4) continuing group discussion outside these sessions during their leisure time.[15]

The main assumption behind guided group interaction (GGI) was that "if the behavior of an individual delinquent is in fact maintained by a delinquent subculture, then effective rehabilitation should involve the peer group as an integral part of the treatment process."[16] Key interactions must, accordingly, be with other boys rather than with staff members. At Highfields, this meant the use of group discussions in order to help the boys understand their own behavior and to learn to value alternatives to the ideas and values that promote delinquency.

Boys of 16 and 17 years of age with no previous history of incarceration were referred to Highfields by juvenile courts. Most youths so referred were adjudicated for offenses against property; others were adjudicated for offenses ranging from incorrigibility to traffic violations to vandalism to statutory rape.

There were few formal rules at Highfields, but boys were not to leave the property unaccompanied by an adult. Days were full, beginning at 6:00 A.M. and not ending until after 10:00 P.M. Most of the boys worked at a nearby state hospital 40 hours a week, usually as farm laborers. This work itself was conceived to be part of the treatment program, teaching the boys responsibility. Evenings were taken up by GGI sessions.

Highfields inspired a number of similar efforts using GGI in the context of a community orientation.

The Provo Experiment

The Provo Experiment began in 1956 under the leadership of LaMar T. Empey, then of Brigham Young University in Utah. It was specifically designed to help habitual delinquent boys by giving them new values and a new approach to society. Empey and Rabow spelled out the basis for their approach in a 1961 account of the Provo Experiment:

1. Delinquent behavior is primarily a group product and demands an approach to treatment far different from that which sees it as characteristic of a "sick" or "well-meaning" but "misguided" person.

2. An effective program must recognize the intrinsic nature of a delinquent's membership in a delinquent system and, therefore, must direct treatment to him as a part of that system.

3. Most delinquents are affectively and ideologically dedicated to the delinquent system. Before they can be made amenable to change, they must be made anxious about the ultimate utility of that system for them.

4. Delinquents must be forced to deal with the conflicts which the demands of conventional and delinquent systems place upon them. The resolution of such conflicts, either for or against further law violations, must ulti-

mately involve a community decision. For that reason, a treatment program, in order to force realistic decision-making, can be most effective if it permits continued participation in the community as well as in the treatment process.[17]

As these four points indicate, the experiment was built on the theoretical basis that delinquency comprises a subculture. It used treatment methods intended to induce habitual offenders to reject that subculture in favor of a set of values, beliefs, and ideals inimical to delinquent activities.

The Provo Experiment was addressed to habitual offenders who were 15 to 17 years of age. Offenses included vandalism, trouble in school, shoplifting, car theft, burglary, and forgery. Highly disturbed and psychotic boys were not included in the experiment. No more than 20 boys at a time were assigned to the project—which depended on close contact with the juvenile court—and new boys could enter only when an older boy was released. The program was nonresidential, and the average length of attendance was somewhere between four and seven months.

Treatment took place in two phases. Phase I involved intensive treatment, focusing on the effort "to create a social system in which social structure, peer members, and authorities are oriented to the one task of instituting change."[18] There was little formal structure in the Provo Experiment, which was the result of a deliberate decision on the part of its creators. It was justified as follows:

> The absence of formal structure helps to do more than avoid artificial criteria for release. It has the positive effect of making boys more amenable to treatment. In the absence of formal structure they are uneasy and they are not quite sure of themselves. Thus, the lack of clear-cut definitions for behavior helps to accomplish three important things: (1) It produces anxiety and turns boys towards the group as a method of resolving their anxiety; (2) It leaves boys free to define situations for themselves: leaders begin to lead, followers begin to follow, and manipulators begin to manipulate. These are the types of behavior which must be seen and analyzed if change is to take place; (3) It binds neither authorities nor the peer group to prescribed courses of action. Each is free to do whatever is needed to suit the needs of particular boys, groups, or situations.[19]

As at Highfields, peer organization was central to the course of treatment at Provo.

Provo encouraged peer groups in several ways. One way was by deliberately omitting any staff-sponsored orientation for new boys.

Instead, newcomers were forced to learn the nature of the program from other boys. Another encouragement was through the use of guided group interaction, borrowed from the Highfields model. At Provo, as at Highfields, GGI was intended to get the youngster to question his own motivations in becoming delinquent, to suggest alternatives, and to get him personally involved in his own reformation and in the reformation of others. It was to make him part of a reformation group, working together to bring about change. Not incidentally, such an effort was also directed toward ridding the young offender of an "us versus them" mentality by placing sanctions for misbehavior in the hands of the boys themselves rather than in those of some "outside" authority figures.

A second major aspect of the Provo Experiment was its emphasis on work; boys were employed by the city to do public works. Those who refused to work could be sent back to the court and committed to the state reformatory. Others who refused to work on their city jobs (for which they were also paid) might be sent back to the experiment's center, Pinehills, and forced to work for nothing, usually scrubbing the floor, washing windows, mowing the lawn, or cutting weeds.

Phase II built on the experiences of Phase I and was designed to ease the transition of a Pinehills' alumnus back into the community. After release from Phase I, the youth continued to meet for discussions with his old group. The group was expected both to monitor his behavior and to provide a setting for the continuing discussion of problems. In addition, in an effort to reinforce good attitudes toward work and good work habits, every effort was made to find suitable employment for the boy and to make him a productive member of society.

The Provo Experiment was, in every sense, just that—an experiment. Though instituted with county support, it was chiefly the product of the efforts of concerned social scientists and laypersons who were interested in creating a setting in which to test innovative approaches to delinquency. The Provo Experiment was consciously intended to evaluate and originate techniques for changing the lives of its delinquent clients.

The Silverlake Experiment

The Silverlake Experiment, a California project that ran from 1964 to 1968, grew out of the Provo Experiment and was also under the leadership of Empey. There were many similarities between the Silverlake Experiment and the Provo Experiment, but Silverlake, run in cooperation with the California Boys' Republic, was a residential program using a former orphanage located in the Los Angeles area.

There were three main program components in the Silverlake Experiment. Like both Highfields and Provo, Silverlake made use of the techniques of guided group interaction in meetings held five evenings a week (boys were encouraged to go home on weekends). A second major program component was school attendance. Schooling was to serve as the primary institutional linkage for the program on the basis of the following arguments:

1.   the obvious and ever-increasing need for academic and vocational skills; . . .

2.   the fact that employment with any career potential is extremely difficult for a teenage adolescent without formal education to obtain; and . . .

3.   the importance of the school as the major societal institution for adolescents. [20]

This emphasis on education rather than work was one obvious difference between Silverlake and Provo. Indeed, the work experiences that comprised the third major component of the Silverlake Experiment chiefly involved the school.

Like the Provo Experiment, Silverlake took what was essentially a subcultural view of delinquency and sought to create a "program culture" to displace the old values and assumptions of delinquency. Silverlake also avoided formal structuring in order to place the key responsibility for order and behavior in the hands of the boys. Silverlake may best be thought of as an extension of the earlier Provo project, allowing Empey and his colleagues a new opportunity to test what had been learned from the earlier experiment in a new, somewhat different setting.

Achievement Place

Achievement Place began in Kansas in 1967. Designed both for the treatment of "predelinquent" youths referred by the court and for continuing research on rehabilitation, it was based not on subcultural theory but on approaches rooted in behavior modification (that is, using methods of positive and negative reinforcement directed toward changing the behavior patterns of its subjects). From three to eight boys were treated at any one time in the old home that served as the setting for Achievement Place. There they lived under the supervision of a pair of house parents—called "teaching parents"—whose function it was to supervise, treat, and manage them.

The key assumptions behind a behavior modification approach to delinquency have been concisely summarized by Whittaker as follows:

1. A child's psychological nature is his behavior; directly observable and measurable actions constitute the sum and substance of personality . . .

2. Behavior is largely controlled by the environment and, in the case of operant or active behavior, is either strengthened, maintained, or diminished by its immediate effects on the environment. Therefore, if the reinforcers for any given behavior can be identified and brought under control, the behavior itself can be similarly controlled.

3. The symptom of the troubled child is the entire problem; it is not simply an external manifestation of some underlying disease process, psychoneurosis, or character disorder. If the acting out of the delinquent, or the bizarre behavior of the psychotic child, is stopped, then the basic problem of delinquency or psychosis has been solved.[21]

Achievement Place embodied these assumptions in its approach to delinquent children. The principal distinguishing feature of Achievement Place was its use of what is called a "token economy." The tokens represented points that were earned for good behavior or lost for bad behavior. Points could be earned for such positively evaluated activities as keeping up with current events, cleaning one's room, a neat appearance, reading, doing housework, or keeping up with schoolwork. Points could be lost for such things as bad grades, aggressive or disobedient behavior, sloppiness, using poor grammar, stealing, lying, or cheating. Points were accumulated daily and could then be exchanged by the youngsters for various privileges, such as watching television, snacks, permission to leave Achievement Place, or even money. The goal was to use the incentives provided by the token economy to inculcate good behavior in program participants.

For most of its existence, Achievement Place contrasted sharply with other programs we have been discussing in the degree of responsibility placed upon the staff. In keeping with the emphasis on behavior modification rather than on the development of an alternative culture, there was little concern for peer organization and networks. In the early 1970s, however, some measures of self-government were introduced into Achievement Place, within the framework of the token economy. This involved, for one thing, the use of trials presided over by the boys themselves to deal with instances of misbehavior. It has also involved the institution of an elected "manager," whose job it was to assign tasks around the home, to supervise snacks and other activities, and to monitor social behavior. Initially, this was a position that could be purchased, at auction, using tokens. It was soon learned, however, that popular election was an arrangement much preferred by the boys themselves. Achievement Place, like Highfields, led to several other, similar projects.

House of Umoja

Unlike the projects we have been considering so far, the House of Umoja was not the product of any social scientific enterprise but was instead the outgrowth of concern on the part of a private citizen, Sister Falaka Fattah. It opened in 1968 in west Philadelphia after Sister Fattah, a journalist living in the area, learned that her 16-year-old son, Robin, had become involved in gang activity. Deciding that the only way to deal with the problem was to confront the entire gang, Sister Fattah invited the gang to live with her and her family in their home, which she named the House of Umoja ("umoja" means "unity" in Swahili). Her idea was to create an extended family of which every gang member could feel a member and thus to give each youth a place in a supportive network. The agreement she made with the youths was a simple one. The gang members were to avoid any illegal activity, and the Fattahs would help keep them out of jail (for past activities) and out of trouble.

The project grew significantly over subsequent years. It moved beyond the Fattah home to make use of other houses in the neighborhood acquired by the Fattahs. There were close connections with the juvenile courts in Philadelphia; the courts could refer young offenders to the House of Umoja for care and treatment.

The program to which young offenders had to submit at the House of Umoja sought to replicate a strong family life. Young men living in the house were required to rise at 6:00 A.M. and to participate in an early-morning conference on "goals for the day." They had to attend school and perform regular, assigned chores in the house. Their schoolwork was closely monitored. They were not to use rough language. They were also required to attend a weekly review session—called the Adella—at which they could be assessed fines for infractions of rules or for displaying a bad attitude. In return, they received not only Sister Fattah's efforts to create a family-like atmosphere but also a $10.00-per-week allowance—not to mention possible freedom from incarceration.

The House of Umoja sought to create a strong, prosocial peer group through the Adella meeting every Friday evening. This meeting was intended to resolve conflicts within the community as well as to deal with individual problems. Any member of the household was entitled to lead the discussion. An individual found guilty of misbehavior was given the responsibility of setting his own punishment, subject to the group's approval. Although fines were common, the most severe sanction was telling others on the street that the youth does not keep his word. Not unlike guided group interaction in terms of its use within the House of Umoja, the Adella was also used to settle hostilities between rival gangs.

The House of Umoja was not a venture of social scientists. Sister Fattah saw its basis primarily in black nationalism. In trying to create an extended family, Sister Fattah deliberately chose what she saw as an African model for extended kinship—for a feeling of kinship, as she saw it, that went beyond blood relationships. The very name Umoja refers to an ideal for unity among black people in order to inhibit the destructive and disruptive activities of gangs. The reported success of her program brought support and funding from a wide array of sources. It is interesting to note that Sister Fattah's son, who had been a gang member in the 1960s, wrote, as a social scientist, an article in 1987 describing the House of Umoja in a journal of distinction. Helping in the development of the House had an obvious effect on him.

VisionQuest

Founded in 1973 in Tucson, Arizona, VisionQuest was a private program enrolling young offenders from several states. Treatment at VisionQuest featured a 12- to 18-month program combining a range of experiences aimed at changing delinquent behavior. It included extensive wilderness training involving hiking, mountain climbing, and boating. It also featured a wagon train program, in which youths traveled for hundreds of miles in horse- and mule-drawn wagons under primitive, pioneer conditions. Vision-Quest used what is called "attack" therapy, in which experienced counselors shouted at and even physically restrained youngsters.

Buffalo Soldiers, part of the VisionQuest program for juvenile offenders, march at Arlington National Cemetery in Arlington, Virginia, during a ceremony to celebrate the African-American Civil War Memorial. *(AP Photo/Ruth Fremson)*

This program, like others we have discussed, was oriented toward habitual offenders. Although drug addicts and those found to have committed "premeditated" violence were not accepted into VisionQuest, most youngsters in the program had spent time in institutions or other programs prior to coming to VisionQuest. Some were referred by the courts, a few by their parents. The VisionQuest facility itself was open; there were no locked doors. As with other programs, the emphasis was on commitment, and young people placed in VisionQuest had to pledge not to run away.

The wilderness training that served as one component of the Vision-Quest treatment was difficult. Much of this training took place in two primitive camps operated by VisionQuest: one in New Mexico, the other in Pennsylvania. A stay at one of these camps included three weeks of training, during which campers lived in tepees, followed by a 19-day "quest" made of such trials as a "blind walk" (in which youngsters hiked blindfolded), rock climbing, and a six-mile run. Three days of the quest were devoted to a "solo," in which each young person had to seek a "vision," writing down his or her thoughts or reading a significant work.

The wagon train gave the program the most publicity. This component of wilderness training was introduced in 1976, when a Vision-Quest contingent joined the American Bicentennial Wagon Train. The apparent improvement in the behavior of participants was so noticeable that the wagon train was made a permanent part of the VisionQuest treatment. The covered wagons moved forward at a rate of 17 miles a day, and participants were responsible for making and breaking camp each day and for keeping the train in motion. They also had to handle the teams of horses and mules that pulled the wagons.

Certainly the most controversial feature of VisionQuest was its use of "attack" therapy (similar to a feature used in the boot camp approach described in Chapter 11). The confrontations this therapy involved occurred if a youngster failed to perform his or her commitments, became disruptive or angry, or tried to run away. They often appeared to be little more than shouting matches, as one staff member shouted at a youngster while both were surrounded by other staff members. Very often the confrontations involve what are called "physicals," in which senior staff physically restrained a youth. As described by one 16-year-old:

> When they go to restrain you, they act pissed off too . . . They surround you to make sure you don't hurt anyone. Then you're screaming and yelling and getting out frustrations and cussing them off the wall. Then they let you up off the ground, and you talk about things that are really bothering you. Usually things with your family.[22]

Physicals were not supposed to include slapping, punching, or similarly physically abusing a youth.

The St. Louis Experiment

This program was conducted in St. Louis between 1970 and 1974. In some ways, according to its creators, the St. Louis Experiment elaborated on such earlier programs as that at Provo. Experiment leaders Feldman, Caplinger, and Wodarski stated: "Like Empey and his colleagues, we believe that an adequate intervention program must make conventional and delinquent alternatives clear to youths, lead them to question the ultimate utility of delinquent alternatives, and help conventional alternatives assume more positive worth."[23] Unlike many other programs, however, the St. Louis Experiment stressed the importance of treating the young offender in the "open community." More than that, though, also in keeping with a subcultural model for delinquency, the experiment did not simply use peer pressure but deliberately sought to provide the specific peer orientation of "prosocial" young people. In St. Louis, young offenders were assigned to regular youth groups at a suburban community center. One or two such youngsters would be placed in a group that otherwise consisted of six to 12 "prosocial" peers. This meant that group interactions primarily involved young people who had no obvious behavioral problems rather than exclusively those who held to delinquent values and goals.

Youngsters were referred to the St. Louis Experiment from a variety of sources. The prosocial youths were those who normally participated in community center activities. Problem youths came from local mental health centers, juvenile courts, and residential treatment centers for children and youths, as well as from a special school district for learning disabled and physically handicapped children. The group activities also varied. Youths took part in arts-and-crafts activities, athletics, hikes and trips, and group discussions. Groups received the guidance of trained experimenters and students who served as group leaders. There was much to tie the St. Louis Experiment in with other programs we have been examining, particularly in its theoretical bases. Its use of "prosocial" peers in the treatment process, however, added a new element in community-based treatment strategies.

The Treatment Foster Care Program

The Treatment Foster Care (TFC) program was developed as an alternative to group residential programs for serious, chronic young offenders. Instead of placement in a group home, youths were placed in a foster-care family setting, on an individual basis or in pairs. The approach was motivated by two sets of research results: one indicating that group care treatment and the concomitant association with delinquent peers often leads to the learning of new modes of delinquent behavior, and another showing that properly selected and trained adults can be particularly effective in the socialization of chronic delinquents. The approach differs from the usual court-ordered foster placement in: (1) the great care taken in the selection of foster parents and the matching of parents and placed youths, and (2) the intensive preservice training given to parents. In addition, there is continuing case management involving meetings of parents with case manager, daily telephone contacts with parents, and crisis intervention as necessary.

The special, dedicated attention is not restricted to TFC parents:

> Because the youth[s] involved in the program have committed several delinquent acts prior to enrollment (an average of 13 arrests), a high level of supervision is required. Participating youth[s] are not permitted to have unsupervised free time in the community, and their peer relationships are closely monitored. Close monitoring at home and at school is a hallmark of the TFC model. Heavy emphasis is placed on teaching interpersonal skills and on encouraging positive social activities, including sports, hobbies, and other forms of recreation.[24]

Each youth, too, is assigned a therapist, but the individualized therapy focuses on the adjustments and skills required by the main thrust of treatment involving adults and peers.

Finally, the TFC program does not ignore the biological or adoptive parents of the youngsters in treatment. A family therapist is assigned to act as an educational and guidance source for teaching effective modes of interacting with and supervising the youths on their return to their homes.

The Effectiveness of Community-Based Programs and Group Homes

Up to this point, we have deliberately ignored specific questions of how effective these community-based programs and group homes were in treating delinquents. As noted in describing several of these programs, many were set up with strong research components, which have allowed investigators to evaluate continuously the effect they seemed to be having on the delinquent youths. Some have even been the setting for systematic experimentation, and, thus, provide the best possible insight into the effectiveness of community-based treatments. We will focus on the findings of investigators associated with such projects here. We shall also note that the question of effectiveness is of more than scientific interest, as in some places this question has taken on widespread social and political importance.

The Provo Experiment has provided the occasion for some of the most significant findings in regard to community-based treatment methods. In a book published in 1972, Empey and Erickson were able to report conclusions based on more than a decade's experience with the project. They acknowledged failures, but noted indications of success as follows:

> The evidence also indicated that significant reductions were made, not only in the number of postintervention arrests, but in the number of offenders who were arrested. In every program, those delinquents who committed fewer offenses after intervention far exceeded the number who committed more offenses. Even though delinquency was not totally cut off, like water through a spigot, the overall flow was diminished considerably.[25]

They go on to argue that, on balance, the Provo program was at least a modest success and a better method of handling delinquents than traditional methods of detention and incarceration.

This sort of cautious optimism is echoed in most other studies of community-based programs. Thus, a comparative evaluation of Highfields and conventional incarceration concluded:

> There is no reason to suppose that the primary goals or basic drives of either group were substantially changed. With the conventional reformatory group on the one hand, the goals remained distorted or unclear, the drives unrecognized or unaccepted. In contrast, among the Highfields group, there was movement toward a clearer view of primary goals and substantially increased acceptance of primary drives. The changes imputed to both the Highfields boys and the conventional reformatory group seemed clear in the sample studied. Moreover, they are congruent with what we know about reformatory life in general and with the letters written by the Highfields boys. Nevertheless, we cannot at this point wholly exclude the possibility that these changes in this particular group are the result of the happy coincidence of a new and surprising method of treatment, applied by an ingenious, sympathetic, industrious management, to a group of delinquents whose capacity for rehabilitation was inherently high.[26]

The evaluators did not think this "happy coincidence" to have been the case, but they were not prepared to dismiss it out of hand.

One may also see cautious optimism in the evaluational results involving such behavior modification programs as the one at Achievement Place. For example, studies comparing Achievement Place boys with those from the Kansas Boys' School and boys on probation (all of whom had been released for at least one year) show that more than one-half of those from the Boys' School and more than one-half of those who had been on probation had been readjudicated by the court and sent to a state institution. In contrast, less than 20 percent of the boys who had been through Achievement Place had gone back before the court, and those showed better school performances after release than boys treated traditionally. It is not entirely clear how much of the difference was due to the experience of the token economy and how much positive effect resulting from Achievement Place was due to other considerations, such as status within the Achievement Place community.

Those positive results have been repeated elsewhere, including a cross-cultural replication of Achievement Place in Holland. On the other hand, several other studies have shown markedly diminished effects as time on the streets following treatment increases.

Four studies, up to 1998, have evaluated the effectiveness of the TFC approach. The overall results were quite positive, indicating that in comparison with alternative community-based residential treatments, the TFC program was cost-effective and had more desirable outcomes in terms of such factors as program completion, subsequent arrests, and subsequent incarceration.

Overall, then, on the basis of direct evaluations, there would seem to be some basis for an optimistic view of the future of community-based programs and homes for juvenile offenders, even for serious and chronic offenders. Perhaps one indication of that optimism (as well as the potential profits) is the entry of several for-profit companies in the realm of residential treatment for juvenile offender. Some of these companies aggressively pursue possible sources of referral, such as juvenile and family court judges, at professional meetings and elsewhere.

There are skeptics, however. Murray and Cox, for example, while accepting the validity of the findings of such experiments as those at Provo and Silverlake, have argued that data taken in Chicago in the mid-1970s seriously question the hypothesis that community-based programs are superior. They urge that other factors may be at play in the kinds of differences other studies show. Further, Pabon, while favorable toward such programs, has nonetheless concluded: "Surveys of the results of large numbers of treatment projects have so far yielded little conclusive evidence that any of them work. The assumption that deinstitutionalization of juvenile offenders is more effective than incarceration is relatively untested." He describes arguments on behalf of most intervention strategies as "cherished assumptions."[27]

Doubt regarding the effectiveness of deinstitutionalization in favor of movement to community-based treatment comes also from a recent evaluation of a custodial institution in Maryland. While the cost was less in community treatment, the rate of subsequent criminal activity was higher than in a custodial institution.

Finally, an evaluation unit of a governor's commission in Minnesota reported that once differences in background variables were taken into account, there were no statistically significant differences between community-based residence clients and parolee or probationer control groups—that is, residential treatment, as such, seemed to be no more effective than traditional methods. Based on such findings, the unit recommended increased scrutiny on residential care programs and, more controversially, a halt to the funding of new residential community corrections facilities in that state.

The unit's report was opposed by community corrections groups and by the Minnesota Department of Corrections. For this reason, the governor's commission itself refused to accept the report and sent the questions back for further study and investigation. Some of the issues raised against the report were essentially methodological, focusing on questions of data collection and analysis. Others involved substantive issues of interpretation, as proponents of community programs argued that the evidence showed that community-based programs did, in fact, reduce recidivism. The key point here is that the results on both sides were far from conclusive, and this raised serious questions about the kind of support the state ought to give to community-based programs.

SUMMARY

This chapter discussed the major modes of treatment of juvenile delinquency in the community: diversion and such special programs as those offering residential care. Because diversion implies the redirection of youths from a path up the justice system ladder from the police through probation to the court, it has necessarily been a component of juvenile justice since the system started in 1899. Police and probation officers have been encouraged to use counsel and release, often with referral to a community resource, since the earliest days of the juvenile court.

That informal process was given a bit more structure during the 1930s, when police departments in the larger cities adopted specialized programs for treatment in the community in place of upward referral. One of these programs was police probation, which was similar to informal supervision by probation, but without the codified status in the law that informal probation had by that time.

It was not until the late 1960s that diversion moved from a routine component of justice system operations to a position that could evoke the following description by Carter and Klein: "Seldom in the history of American criminal justice has a concept erupted on the scene and generated as much interest as that of diversion."[28] The direct stimulus for that eruption was the report of the President's Commission on

Law Enforcement and Administration of Justice in 1967 and the considerable federal funding that the report generated. In its recommendation for the widespread adoption of Youth Services Bureaus to facilitate the diversionary process, the commission was influenced by labeling theory, which was then a theory of considerable importance in sociology. It was argued that handling youths informally in the community (in place of movement up the justice ladder) would avoid stigmatization. The Juvenile Justice and Delinquency Prevention Act of 1974 was important in furthering that aim of the commission and in the deinstitutionalization of status offenders. The sociological justifications for diversion were argued most eloquently by Lemert in 1971, who was also influential as a consultant to the President's commission.

The boom in diversion programs lasted until the late 1970s, when the process of severe contraction started. The prime reason for that contraction was the almost complete elimination of federal funding, which was motivated by many formal evaluations indicating that diversion was no more effective than the routine operations of the justice system, by legal and theoretical objections to diversion raised by lawyers and sociologists (including labeling theorists who now saw diversion as a labeling process in its own right), and by a general change in the climate of the federal government in regard to support for local social programs. Important evaluations of diversion were made for the Sacramento 601 and 602 projects and for other projects that received special federal funding. While the former found diversion to be a successful alternative, many others found diversion effective neither in avoiding stigma nor in reducing recidivism. However, diversion programs based on the models envisioned by the President's Commission continue to exist—apparently widely and with increasing support of federal funding.

Community-based treatment and rehabilitation programs and group homes also have something of an erratic history. There have been significant efforts over the last three decades to develop responses to juvenile delinquency that combine the same focus on community resources found in diversion programs with innovative, experimental techniques of treatment and, often, strong research components that are intended to evaluate the effectiveness of approaches. Sometimes privately funded, and occasionally created under state auspices, these programs and homes have been the subject of wide controversy and attention.

A substantial number of these homes relied for treatment on some form of guided group interaction (GGI). Pioneered at Highfields, in New Jersey, GGI combines peer pressure with counseling and mutual discussion of problems in an effort to make delinquents see for themselves the root causes of their behavior and to help them develop motivations for reformation and change. GGI, in one form or another, was not only used by Highfields but also served as the basis for treatment approaches in such varied programs as the Provo and Silverlake experiments and, with major variations, at the House of Umoja.

A second major approach, pioneered at Achievement Place in Kansas, is founded on the ideas of behavior modification. According to this approach, if one can develop rewards that lead to significant changes in behavior, then the delinquency will be overcome. At Achievement Place, this approach was maintained through what is called a "token economy," in which youths learned to act in ways that maximize rewards to them within a closed system.

A third significant basis for alternative residential care is social learning theory. In the Treatment Foster Care program, the learning involves foster parents, youths placed in foster homes, and the parents and guardians of the youths in their home settings.

While the results of evaluations have been mixed, there is some basis for optimism regarding community-based residential treatment. Clearly, there are differences in effectiveness across alternative approaches and even evidence that some community-based programs show no positive effect whatsoever in the reduction of subsequent delinquent behavior. Two factors that are important to keep in mind regarding the comparison of the future of community programs, on the one hand, and institutionalization, on the other, are: (1) the general social demands for punishment in the form of harsher treatment rather than a "soft" community approach, and (2) the consistent evidence that institutionalization is the most expensive alternative. It does seem that there will eventually be a decrease in the expectation of institutionalization among youths who are tried in juvenile rather than criminal courts.

REFERENCES

Alder, Christine, and Kenneth Polk (1982). "Diversion and Hidden Sexism." *Australian and New Zealand Journal of Criminology* 15:100-108.

Austin, James, and Barry Krisberg (1981). "Wider, Stronger, and Different Nets: The Dialectics of Criminal Justice Reform." *Journal of Research in Crime and Delinquency* 18:165-196.

Baron, Roger, and Floyd Feeney (1976). *Juvenile Diversion Through Family Counseling*. Washington, DC: U.S. Government Printing Office.

Binder, Arnold, and Virginia L. Binder (1982). "Juvenile Diversion and the Constitution." *Journal of Criminal Justice* 10:1-24.

Binder, Arnold, and Gilbert Geis (1984). "Ad Populum Argumentation in Criminology: Juvenile Diversion as Rhetoric." *Crime & Delinquency* 30:309-333.

Binder, Arnold, and Susan L. Polen (1991). "The Kennedy-Johnson Years, Social Theory, and Federal Policy in the Control of Juvenile Delinquency." *Crime & Delinquency* 37:242-261.

Blomberg, Thomas G. (1977). "Diversion and Accelerated Social Control." *Journal of Criminal Law and Criminology* 68:274-282.

Boone, George C. (1961). "The Passaic Children's Bureau." *Crime & Delinquency* 7:231-236.

Braukmann, Curtis J., and Montrose M. Wolf (1987). "Behaviorally Based Group Homes for Juvenile Offenders." In *Behavioral Approaches to Crime and Delinquency. A Handbook of Applications, Research, and Concepts*, edited by Edward K. Morris and Curtis J. Braukmann. New York: Plenum.

Carter, Robert M., and Malcolm W. Klein, eds. (1976). *Back on the Street: The Diversion of Juvenile Offenders*. Englewood Cliffs, NJ: Prentice Hall.

Chamberlain, Patricia, and John B. Reich (1987). "Comparison of Two Community Alternatives to Incarceration for Chronic Juvenile Offenders." *Journal of Consulting and Clinical Psychology* 66:624-633.

Chamberlain, Patricia (1994). *Family Connections: Treatment Foster Care for Adolescents with Delinquency*. Eugene, OR: Castalia.

Chamberlain, Patricia (1998). *Treatment Foster Care*. Washington, DC: U.S. Department of Justice, Office of Juvenile Justice and Delinquency Prevention.

Chinn, Jeffrey (1997). "The District of Columbia Street Law Diversion Program." In *Law-Related Education and Juvenile Justice; Promoting Citizenship Among Juvenile Offenders*, edited by Deborah Williamson, Kevin I. Minor, and James W. Fox. Springfield, IL: Charles C Thomas.

Coates, Robert B. (1981). "Deinstitutionalization and the Serious Juvenile Offender: Some Policy Considerations." *Crime & Delinquency* 27:477-486.

Davidson, William S. II, Robin Redner, Richard L. Amdur, and Christina M. Mitchell (1990). *Alternative Treatment for Troubled Youth*. New York: Plenum Press.

Dunford, Franklyn W., D. Wayne Osgood, and Hart F. Weichselbaum (1982). *National Evaluation of Diversion Projects: Executive Summary*. Washington, DC: U.S. Department of Justice, National Institute for Juvenile Justice and Delinquency Prevention.

Empey, LaMar T., and Maynard L. Erickson (1972). *The Provo Experiment: Evaluating Community Control of Delinquency*. Lexington, MA: D.C. Heath.

Empey, LaMar T., and Steven G. Lubeck (1971). *The Silverlake Experiment: Testing Delinquency Theory and Community Intervention*. Chicago: Aldine.

Empey, LaMar T., and Jerome Rabow (1961). "The Provo Experiment in Delinquency Rehabilitation." *American Sociological Review* 26:679-695.

Evaluation Unit of the Minnesota Governor's Commission on Crime Prevention and Control (1977). *Residential Community Corrections Programs in Minnesota: Summary and Recommendations*. St. Paul: author.

Fattah, David (1987). "House of Umoja as a Case Study." *The Annals of The American Academy of Political and Social Science* 494:37-41.

Feldman, Ronald A., Timothy E. Caplinger, and John S. Wodarski (1983). *The St. Louis Conundrum: The Effective Treatment of Antisocial Youths*. Englewood Cliffs, NJ: Prentice Hall.

Finestone, Harold (1976). *Victims of Change: Juvenile Delinquents in American Society*. Westport, CT: Greenwood Press.

Hoefler, Sharon A., and Philip H. Bornstein (1975). "Achievement Place: An Evaluative Review." *Criminal Justice and Behavior* 2:146-168.

Klein, Malcolm W. (1976). "Issues and Realities in Police Diversion Programs." *Crime & Delinquency* 22:421-427.

Lemert, Edwin M. (1971). *Instead of Court: Diversion in Juvenile Justice*. Washington, DC: U.S. Government Printing Office.

McCorkle, Lloyd W., Albert Elias, and F. Lovell Bixby (1958). *The Highfields Story: An Experimental Treatment Project for Youthful Offenders*. New York: Henry Holt.

Mennel, Robert M. (1973). *Thorns and Thistles: Juvenile Delinquents in the United States, 1825-1940*. Hanover, NH: University Press of New England.

Murray, Charles A., and Louis A. Cox, Jr. (1979). *Beyond Probation: Juvenile Corrections and the Chronic Delinquent*. Beverly Hills: Sage.

Norman, Sherwood (1972). *The Youth Service Bureau: A Key to Delinquency Prevention*. Paramus, NJ: National Council on Crime and Delinquency.

Pabon, Edward (1985). "A Neighborhood Correctional Program for Juvenile Offenders." *Juvenile and Family Court Journal* 36(2):43-47.

Palmer, Ted, and Roy V. Lewis (1980). *An Evaluation of Juvenile Diversion*. Cambridge, MA: Oelgeschlager, Gunn, and Hain.

Phillips, Elery L. (1968). "Achievement Place: Token Reinforcement Procedures in a Home-Style Rehabilitation Setting for 'Predelinquent' Boys." *Journal of Applied Behavior Analysis* 1:213-223.

President's Commission on Law Enforcement and Administration of Justice (1967). *The Challenge of Crime in a Free Society: A Report*. Washington, DC: U.S. Government Printing Office.

Rubin, H. Ted (1985). *Juvenile Justice: Policy, Practice, and Law*, 2nd ed. New York: Random House.

Schur, Edwin M. (1973). *Radical Nonintervention: Rethinking the Delinquency Problem*. Englewood Cliffs, NJ: Prentice Hall.

Sorrentino, Anthony (1977). *Organizing Against Crime: Redeveloping the Neighborhood*. New York: Human Sciences Press.

Spergel, Irving (1969). *Community Problem Solving: The Delinquency Example*. Chicago: University of Chicago Press.

Stanton, Cassandra A., and Aleta L. Meyer (1998). "A Comprehensive Review of Community-Based Approaches for the Treatment of Juvenile Offenders." In *Delinquent Violent Youth: Theory and Interventions*, edited by Thomas P. Gullata, Gerald R. Adams, and Raymond Montemayor. Thousand Oaks, CA: Sage.

Sweeney, Paul (1982). "VisionQuest's Rite of Passage." *Corrections Magazine* 8(1):22-32.

Wallace, J.A., and M.M. Brennan (1963). "Intake and the Family Court." *Buffalo Law Review* 12:442-451.

Weeks, H. Ashley (1958). *Youthful Offenders at Highfields: An Evaluation of the Effects of the Short-Term Treatment of Delinquent Boys*. Ann Arbor: University of Michigan Press.

Whittaker, James K. (1979). *Caring for Troubled Children: Residential Treatment in a Community Context*. San Francisco: Jossey-Bass.

Williamson, Deborah, and James R. Columbia (1977). "Law Related Education: A Diversion Option in the Kentucky Juvenile Justice System." In *Law-Related Education and Juvenile Justice: Promoting Citizenship Among Juvenile Offenders*, edited by Deborah Williamson, Kevin I. Minor, and James W. Fox. Springfield, IL: Charles C Thomas.

NOTES

[1]   Wallace & Brennan (1963), 444-445.

[2]   President's Commission on Law Enforcement and Administration of Justice (1967), 82.

[3]   Ibid., 82.

[4]   Ibid., 83.

[5]   Ibid., 83.

[6]   Sec. 102[b].

[7]   Lemert (1971), 92.

[8]   Norman (1972), 8.

[9]   Carter & Klein (1976), xi.

[10]   Dunford, Osgood & Weichselbaum (1982), 16.

[11]   Rubin (1985), 180.

[12]   Williamson & Columbia (1997), 121.

[13]   Binder & Geis (1984), 325.

[14]   Spergel (1969), 40.

[15]   Weeks (1958), viii.

[16]   Whittaker (1979), 67.

[17]   Empey & Rabow (1961), 683, 684.

[18]   Ibid., 685.

[19]   Ibid., 686.

[20]   Empey & Lubeck (1971), 88.

[21]   Whittaker (1979), 57,58.

[22]   Sweeney (1982), 30.

[23]   Feldman, Caplinger & Wodarski (1983), 37.

24   Chamberlain (1998), 4.

25   Empey & Ericson (1972), 222.

26   McCorkle, Elias & Bixby (1958), 126.

27   Pabon (1985), 43.

28   Carter & Klein (1976), xi.

13

Treatment of Young Offenders in Other Countries

We have examined how the juvenile justice system in the United States operates, but how does this system compare with those found in other countries? Juvenile delinquency occurs in every nation in the world. All nations have found ways to cope with young people who break the law, but methods differ greatly. Some societies treat delinquency as primarily a legal problem; others, as a problem of social welfare; still others, as a problem that must be handled with a combination of legal and welfare remedies.

JUVENILE DELINQUENCY IN COMPARATIVE PERSPECTIVE

Although crimes are committed by juveniles in every country, the degree to which juvenile delinquency is considered a problem varies greatly. Statistics can only suggest the extent and significance of delinquency in different countries, because the variance in ways that nations keep track of crime makes it difficult to compare levels of criminal activity.

Nevertheless, statistics do indicate that in some places juveniles comprise a major proportion of those who break the law; in others, only a small percent. In most Western industrial societies, about one-eighth to one-quarter of crimes are committed by juveniles, whereas in many nonwestern countries, juveniles account for as little as 4 percent of reported crimes. A few countries report notably high rates. In Japan, for example, nearly one-half of reported crimes are ascribed to juveniles.

Statistics also indicate some differences in patterns of juvenile crime itself. In most countries, thefts make up the bulk of juvenile offenses. However, violent crimes make up a larger proportion of offenses in Russia and in Argentina (which appear to have rates comparable to those of the United States) than they do in Sweden, Hungary, or Japan, where violent crime appears to be relatively rare. Although such figures are not fully comparable, the differing levels are suggestive (and perhaps not entirely artifacts of reporting).

Social and Cultural Forms: Trends in Delinquency

What are some of the factors that appear to account for varying levels of delinquency around the world? Unfortunately, comparative research is not extensive, and only a few suggestions may be readily offered.

In societies within the Western orbit (in Western Europe, for example, or Australia), levels of delinquency appear to be roughly comparable. They also tend to be understood in roughly similar ways, although, as we shall see, the juvenile justice systems sometimes have striking differences from those in the United States.

Students of many nonWestern nations, on the other hand, noting that such countries do experience lower rates of juvenile delinquency in relation to adult crime (and lower rates of crime generally), have argued that this has to do with the distinctive characteristics of those societies, particularly the degree to which many nonWestern countries are characterized by stronger forces directed toward integrating young people into the larger society.

There is much to support such an argument. In India, for example, both the overall crime rate and the proportion of juvenile crimes among all offenses tend to be quite low. The murder rate is about one-third that of the United States. Juveniles account for less than 1 percent of all arrests, compared with more than 30 percent in the United States. According to at least one study, the main reason for this is that a number of factors serve to reinforce a sense in Indian young people that they are part of a larger community. Traditions of social and kinship ties remain strong; economic necessity creates an important role for children and young people who must contribute to their families' survival. There is no counterpart to the "youth culture," which, some have argued, contributes to delinquency in Western industrial nations.[1]

Studies from other countries tend to support such a view. In fast-growing Lagos, Nigeria, for example, social and kinship networks also tend to inhibit delinquency, and to provide alternative mechanisms for controlling potential problems among young people. Delinquency tends to be most common in heterogeneous neighborhoods, those in which traditional kinship ties and patterns of deference have been most severely undermined, including those chiefly occupied by the middle-class families who have moved farthest from traditional forms. Moreover, when problems involving young people do develop in close-ly knit communities, they tend to be relatively minor, and informal net-works of relatives and local leaders are able to prevent them from growing serious enough to come to the attention of the authorities. In addition, victims of delinquency in neighborhoods with a high level of homogeneity tend to try to work things out with the offender's family rather than resorting to more formal legal mechanisms such as the police or the courts.

Finally, there has long been a tendency to explain the lower rate of crime (including delinquency) in Japan on the basis of that society's homogeneity and, especially, its emphasis on corporate values and ideals. Individuals in Japan, it is often argued, are encouraged to place identity with the group above personal ends and to place primary value on those activities that further rather than disrupt group harmo-ny and cooperation. Many scholars suggest that such values and ideals serve to inhibit the antisocial impulses and individual aggressiveness embodied in much delinquent behavior.

The argument is also supported, paradoxically, by what appear to be important increases in delinquency, particularly where Western, individualistic values are coming to displace older, traditional ties of community and kinship. Significant increases in juvenile crime have been noted in such diverse societies as Japan, China, and Nigeria—all of which have traditionally shown very low juvenile delinquency rates. In all these countries, juvenile crime has traditionally accounted for only a small proportion of the total crimes committed. For example, in China, juvenile delinquency comprised only about 7 percent of crimes in 1980; by 1989, it was nearer the typical Western level of 20 percent.

This change has been especially notable in Japan, where delin-quency (especially violent crime and drug abuse by juveniles) appears to have been growing at an alarming rate (though remaining well below Western levels). Many Japanese have attributed this increase to an American influence on the society; some have even referred to it as the "American disease." Particularly important have been tendencies toward American-style individualism that have served to weaken the community ties and corporate values that, in the past, may have helped to inhibit antisocial, delinquent behavior. Others have suggested that the enormous demands for individual achievement and success that arise in a society experiencing great economic and technological growth—especially school pressures in a society that places enormous emphasis on education—have produced severe emotional tensions that tend to be released through disruptive, even violent, behavior.

Similar processes have also been cited to explain an increase in delinquency in the nations of the former Soviet Union and Eastern Europe, following the introduction of Western-style political and economic institutions. Many scholars agree that the disruptions created by urbanization, industrialization, and the increasing role of Western forms of culture are helping to create an atmosphere encouraging what they see as Western styles of delinquency. Violent crime, in particular, has increased to a remarkable extent, especially among young people in Russia (as much as 500 percent, according to some sources).

Cultural factors alone cannot explain such apparent increases in juvenile crime. In many countries, for example, delinquency appears to be on the rise because of the increasing prevalence of drugs (especially hard drugs). As Russia and Eastern Europe have entered more fully into the world economy, one price of their economic integration appears to have been integration into the world drug trade, with an accompanying rise in delinquency. In China, economic integration has likewise meant a greater prevalence of drugs (especially heroin) reaching even children in their early teens. Japanese officials have reported what they see as an alarming increase in drug use in that country, citing it as a factor in growing problems of delinquency.

Still, despite the increase in delinquency in many parts of the world, variation remains an important fact. It should be stressed that, even in such nations as China, Nigeria, or Japan, where delinquency has shown significant increases, both the amount and the general seriousness of the crimes tends to remain well below American and many Western European levels.[2] Whether the social and cultural factors that may help account for variation will provide useful clues for addressing delinquency in the United States remains to be seen, but further research may help illuminate not only the character of delinquency around the world but in our own society as well.

MAJOR LEGAL APPROACHES TO DELINQUENCY

Legal approaches to juvenile delinquency also vary greatly from country to country. Even the ages at which young people can be considered delinquent and the reasons for their being so considered vary markedly. In general, most nations recognize a minimum age, below which a child is not considered to have sufficient capacity for distinguishing between right and wrong, for being held liable for what would be considered a delinquent act if committed by someone above that age. Although there may be welfare measures available when such children get into trouble, their behavior is not to be dealt with as delinquency. No nation has an age below seven as a minimum age, but many have set higher ages for adjudging a young offender as delinquent. In Japan and in Italy, for example, the age of legal responsibility is 14. In Sweden, the age is 15. Other nations are within this general range. Nigeria has set 10 as the age of legal responsibility; Poland and France, 13. In Israel, the minimum age is nine by law, but 12 by practice.

The age beyond which an offender is no longer eligible for treatment as a juvenile also varies. In many countries, the maximum age for treatment as a child is 18, but in Japan and Germany it is 21. In Cuba, by contrast, the maximum age for such treatment is 16, having been lowered from 18 two decades ago in response to a serious rise in the nation's delinquency rates. In many countries, as in the United States, there are also provisions for trying juveniles accused of serious crimes in adult criminal courts.

Nations also differ from each other in defining delinquency. In France, England, Sweden, and elsewhere, there is great concern for status offenses and for preventive work with those juveniles who are "at risk" as well as those who commit acts that would be considered criminal regardless of the offender's age. In a few nations, juveniles are governed by the same criminal code that governs adults. Although they may be treated differently from adults by the criminal justice system, there are no status offenses for which juveniles may be detained and treated or tried.

General Tendencies in International Juvenile Justice

There are also some general international trends that one may identify in looking at approaches to juvenile justice around the world. Although these trends are far from universal, they do characterize some fairly widespread tendencies in approaches to juvenile crime.

One trend is the continuing spread of institutions and procedures designed specifically for juvenile offenders. Although such institutions have existed in many parts of the world since the nineteenth century (as in the United States) they have only recently entered other areas. Nevertheless, there has been a steady interest in tailoring juvenile justice to the juvenile offender. As Third World nations have achieved independence since World War II, they have established distinctive facilities and procedures for juvenile delinquents, even as older nations have sought refinements to make their systems more responsive to what are believed to be the special characteristics of young offenders. In some cases, this has meant the creation of separate courts for juveniles, or even of alternative forms of adjudication, while in others it has meant the creation of special protections for juveniles within the larger criminal justice system. Since the mid-1980s, this trend has been strongly encouraged internationally by such documents as the United Nations (UN) Standard Minimum Rules for the Administration of Juvenile Justice (Beijing Rules, 1985) and the UN Convention on the Rights of the Child (1989), which urges separate systems of justice for children, and by other UN documents intended to provide a framework for juvenile justice cross-nationally.[3]

Also encouraged by the UN and other organizations has been an international tendency toward the widespread acceptance of treatment rather than punishment as the appropriate response to juvenile crime. Virtually all juvenile justice systems include important rehabilitative emphases based on an assumption that state intervention into the socialization of young people during adolescence can produce a reformation in character.

Related to this has been an effort in many places to create comprehensive approaches to juvenile justice, involving educational institutions, social workers, and even the police in the work of rehabilitation. In France, for example, a Juvenile Protection Unit organized within the Paris police force in 1976 is engaged not only in the normal work of criminal investigation but also in preventive work, including investigations of family life and attempts to counsel at-risk young people and their families.

At the same time, as in the United States, issues of due process have come to be part of the debate in other parts of the world. In England and other nations belonging to the Common Law tradition, the American *Gault* decision (discussed in Chapter 8) had impact in sensitizing people to the procedural shortcomings of existing juvenile justice systems. Outside the English-speaking world, due process concerns also have had some impact, again in part through the influence of the United Nations, which has sought to make its member states aware of the legal rights of children in any response to juvenile crime, whether the system is oriented toward a welfare or justice approach to responding to crime.

It is in part because of the concern for due process that one other general international tendency has been evident: widespread efforts (since about the mid-1980s) to rewrite juvenile codes so that they take due process more fully into account. In many countries, this has meant more clearly distinguishing between status offenders and delinquents, with the creation of separate institutions to deal with each. In others, this has meant that noncriminal offenders have been removed from the juvenile justice system altogether, as has happened in parts of the United States.

Countertendencies

While the general tendencies identified above have been strong, there have also been significant countertendencies visible in many parts of the world. Just as one can identify a "get tough" movement in the United States, for a variety of reasons, other nations have also sought to "harden the process" for juvenile offenders, particularly where juvenile crime has appeared to undergo a significant increase. In many places, despite the official emphasis on the diversion of juveniles from incarceration, rates of incarceration have gone up. This has been the case, for example, in Germany, despite a 1990 code, established after reunification, that set forth a wide range of alternative dispositions for juvenile cases. It has also become the case in Scotland, despite a long tradition there of welfare-oriented responses to juvenile problems.

Furthermore, it should be noted that, despite the emphasis on treatment that characterizes most of the world's juvenile justice systems, harsh forms of punishment for juvenile offenders are hardly unknown in other parts of the world. In South Africa, for example, where juvenile justice retains close ties to the adult criminal justice system, corporal punishment (i.e., whipping) remained the most common disposition for juvenile cases until 1995, when the practice was banned for youths under 18 by the nation's Constitutional Court. In 1994, many people in the United States were shocked when an 18-year-old American, convicted of vandalism in Singapore, was sentenced to a "caning" (strokes from a thick cane that are capable of breaking the skin and leaving scars) in keeping with Singapore law. Many Americans, it should be noted, not only approved of the case's disposition, but sought to introduce similar sentencing into American juvenile law. In England, the "get tough" movement has been extremely strong, particularly following the brutal murder of a two-year-old child by two 10-year-old boys in 1993, an act for which the two boys received life sentences.

As noted in Chapter 10, even the death penalty for juveniles is not unknown in other parts of the world. In China, during what was called a "severe blows" campaign against crime in 1983, authorities made widespread use of executions as a response to what many took to be an outbreak of juvenile delinquency, particularly in the form of gang-related crime. In Pakistan, early in 1995, a 14-year-old boy, convicted of blasphemy, was sentenced to death by hanging. (He was ultimately able to flee the country).

Such countertendencies are significant. They help to indicate the extent to which, at this point, juvenile justice systems internationally are in a state of flux, undergoing significant change in response to changing conditions and evolving legal and social concerns.

Still, despite the ongoing processes of change, it is possible to identify several distinctive approaches to juvenile justice that provide a useful comparison to what is found in the United States.

Focusing on Welfare

Although it is possible to identify few juvenile justice systems that
are oriented wholly toward legalism or toward welfare, in many cases
the emphasis on one or the other is so strong as to create clearly iden-
tifiable types. For example, in the systems of France and Scotland, the
orientation toward a welfare-based approach to addressing problems of
delinquency is so strong as to set them apart from many other systems
in the world.

The French system, in place since 1945, is remarkable for its tendency to avoid the use of punishment as a response to juvenile crime,
and for its significant avoidance of incarceration. Its rates are only 3 to
5 percent of those commonly found in North America, even though
under French law, incarceration is an option available to judges
responding to delinquency. Choice and cooperation are central features
of French juvenile justice.

In France, when a young person is arrested, the case is referred to
a *procureur*, a prosecutor, who can then decide to drop the case or to
send it to a juvenile court judge. Most cases are handled within the
judge's chambers, and because French law prohibits the incarceration
of young offenders whose cases are handled that way, the delinquent is
subject primarily to an array of welfare-oriented treatments. These
may include supervision by a social worker (an *educateur*) or, occasionally, placement in a group home. In either case, the juvenile must
agree to the disposition. Those failing to live up to it face little in the
way of sanctions. For cases that do proceed to a juvenile court (mainly those involving more serious offenders over the age of 16), a welfare
focus remains important. Dispositions tend to bear this out. Although
a young offender may be sentenced to a juvenile wing of a prison (and
usually for a very short period), incarceration is a last resort that
occurs in fewer than 5 percent of cases. Welfare provisions account for
the vast bulk of dispositions. Thus, for example, the French system
made news in Britain when, at about the same time the two English 10-
year-olds received life sentences for the murdering of an infant, three
French teenagers who were found guilty of killing a homeless man were
released to the custody of their parents.

The judge's obligations in a case maintain the system's welfare orientation. The offender, not the offense, is considered central, and a
judge is expected to be well-informed about a young person's background and situation. The *educateur* is expected to be similarly

informed and, while providing supervision, tends to focus more on help than control. Even the French police have developed programs focusing as much on intervention and prevention as on the apprehension of juveniles committing crime.

The French system preserves its welfare-focused approach largely through the informality with which it treats most juvenile crimes. A more formalized version of a welfare-oriented approach (though it is one currently in a state of flux) is found in Scotland. Scotland's system began to take shape in the mid-1960s, when, under the leadership of Lord Kilbrandon, Scotland passed the Social Work (Scotland) Act of 1968 (modified by Criminal Procedure Acts of 1975 and 1995), which removed juveniles under 16 from the criminal justice system and created an alternative system for them. The crucial component of that system is the "Children's Hearing," in which juvenile offenses are heard by a panel of concerned citizens, relying heavily on reports from social workers and other professionals. The panel has the power either to dismiss a case or to make a supervision order for the young person. Although the Act identified several categories of children who could come before the panels, by far the greatest number have faced the system as a result of having committed an offense.[4]

The crucial figure in the hearings system is an individual known as the "reporter." When a juvenile is charged with a crime, the police must take the case to the reporter. The reporter investigates the charges and may then decide either to take no further action, to refer the child to a voluntary supervision program, or, if the child appears "in need of compulsory measures of care," to refer the case to a hearing. Should the child plead innocent, there is also the option of referring the case to a "sheriff's court," in which the accused can still receive a regular trial. Some serious offenses (including murder, rape, and manslaughter) are usually not referred to hearings but are treated by the criminal courts. For these crimes, there is no welfare-oriented response available. For example, juveniles ages 16 to 18 who are found guilty of murder receive a mandatory life sentence, to be served initially in secure units for juveniles and, after age 21, in adult prisons.

Should the case be referred to a hearing, the reporter is responsible for organizing the hearing and providing necessary information for the panel, including reports from social workers, school workers, and other professionals. The hearings take place informally and last about 30 minutes. Panel members are expected to work with the child and his or her family in order to find the right treatment for the offender. The dominant style of the hearing is supposed to be encouraging and sympathetic. This ideal is not always met, however; panel members often confront young people angrily and questioning is sometimes sarcastic and abusive. There are often class tensions because panel members tend to be middle-class and young offenders more commonly have lower-class backgrounds. The social welfare focus remains crucial, though, as it does in dispositions, which can include supervision by a social worker or commitment to a "residential establishment" (including a number run by voluntary and religious organizations). For many years, detention was fairly rare in cases coming before the panels, but there is some evidence that it has become more common recently, particularly as the panels must deal with persistent offenders.

Law panels have been used in some Scandinavian countries, especially for very young offenders. They have also been used in Marxist states, notably Cuba, which tend to treat juvenile crime as a threat to the social fabric—one deserving a community response. Such panels are particularly relevant, however, to approaches to juvenile delinquency that stress welfare-based interventions as a basis for reformation.

The Legalistic Approach

At the exact opposite pole in procedure are those systems in which the juvenile justice system is more or less integrated into the criminal justice system as a whole (though often with special provisions for juveniles in court composition and sentencing). In the People's Republic of China, which lacked a code of substantive or procedural criminal law until 1979, juvenile courts date only to the mid-1980s and were not codified until the passage of the Juvenile Protection Act of 1991. Under Chinese law, offenders over age 18 are to be treated as adults, although for more serious crimes, young offenders between 14 and 17 are also criminally liable. In keeping with international conventions, the law does provide for private court proceedings and confidentiality in juvenile cases, and for separate pretrial detention. Unlike most Western systems, Chinese law also defines legal obligations for parents and other adults, and juvenile courts can hear cases against adults for corruption of minors and abuse or neglect. In all cases, though, including those involving juvenile offenders, China's juvenile courts follow procedures similar to those of adult courts. Each case is heard by a three-judge panel, and the law (more clearly for juveniles than adults) requires the presence of an attorney. Hearings are "inquisitorial" (rather than adversarial, as they are in American tradition) and are intended to establish factual guilt or innocence, as is also the case in adult courts. Moreover, the law provides that young offenders should receive mitigated sentences based on age. There are some facilities for young offenders and they often face fines and imprisonment. China prohibits the death penalty for offenders whose crimes were committed prior to age 18, but it does provide, in the case of serious crimes, for the possibility of death sentences for young people over 16, with a two-year suspension of execution (an option frequently exercised during the "severe blows" campaign of the mid-1980s).[5]

China's legalistic system provides some alternatives in responding to juvenile crime. Most important are local (even neighborhood) committees that are intended to respond to crime, including juvenile crime. These are mediating committees, which serve in place of the courts and seek to bring neighborhood and workplace pressure upon an offender to mend his or her ways and publicly to avow remorse and future conformity. China has more than 800,000 such committees, and they have played an important role in responding to juvenile crime as well as to offenses committed by adults. Nevertheless, the thrust of China's response to juvenile crime remains mainly within the larger criminal justice system, and increasing numbers of juvenile offenses are being referred to the courts rather than to less formal committees.

Legalistic systems are also found in other parts of the world. Argentina and Germany have both traditionally taken such an approach. In South Africa, children over the age of seven are initially taken before a magistrate's court. This court decides whether the case should be transferred to a children's court for welfare procedures or to a regular criminal court in which the child will be treated as an adult. However, only about 2 to 4 percent of cases go to a children's court, so that, even though they are tried in separate proceedings, most young South Africans accused of crimes receive a trial identical to that of an adult. Lengthy pretrial detention is common, usually in jails in which adult offenders are also housed. For those adjudged guilty, sentences may be mitigated, but fines, imprisonment, and (until recently) whippings are the usual dispositions. Since South Africa's first democratic elections in 1994, and the nation's ratification of the UN Convention on the Rights of the Child in 1995, there have been significant attempts to revise South Africa's approach to juvenile justice. However, these have not received implementation. Crime control remains a key concern in South Africa, and juvenile offenders continue to be treated mainly through the criminal justice system.

"Divided" Approaches to Juvenile Justice

In many countries, legalistic approaches and welfare approaches exist side-by-side. They are invoked separately to respond to specific juvenile problems, depending on their seriousness. Some essentially legalistic systems have moved in this direction. For example, Argentina, despite a generally legalistic approach, has excluded some offenses from the courts when they are committed by juveniles.

Some countries, such as Denmark, have maintained the classic separation, offering welfare-oriented approaches for some problems and treating others within the context of the criminal justice system. Danish law distinguishes between "juvenile delinquents," those age 15 to 18, and "delinquent children," those below the age of 15. It prescribes social welfare procedures for dealing with problems of the latter but subjects juvenile delinquents to the same criminal justice system as adults. There are no separate juvenile courts in Denmark, and since 1973, there have been no separate juvenile prisons (although delinquents do receive mitigated sentences).

In Sweden, juvenile offenders under the age of 15 are similarly referred to social welfare agencies and to lay panels for treatment, with young people between 15 and 17 being referred by the police to the prosecutor for further disposition. The prosecutor may choose to waive prosecution (as happens in about one-half of the cases), may issue a summary punishment (usually in the form of a fine), or may recommend disposition by a lay panel. The prosecutor may also refer the case (especially if it involves a serious or violent crime) to the criminal court for disposition, using the same procedures employed for adults.

Treatment and Punishment in Tension

England and Wales

No less common than either welfare-oriented or legalistic systems are those in which, as in the United States, treatment and punishment exist in a state of tension, and in which the orientation of the system itself is a matter of conflict and debate. This is true in England and Wales, where the juvenile justice system has developed in ways fairly closely connected to that of the United States.

Much of the background to the contemporary English system of juvenile justice is similar to that of the United States. Many of the developments in juvenile justice in the United States were paralleled, if not anticipated, in England; the Common Law tradition and the doctrine of *parens patriae* had their origins there. Finally, through the Children Act of 1908, England established a distinctive system of juvenile justice at about the same time that such systems were being established in many parts of the United States. This act established juvenile courts that were to be special sittings of magistrates' courts, focusing on neglected or abused children and on juvenile offenders between the ages of seven and 15. It also made provision for "juvenile-adults" from age 16 to 20, who could be committed to special institutions, which came to be known as "borstals."

Since 1908, the English system has undergone tremendous change. A 1933 Children and Young Persons Act raised the minimum age to eight and established a body of "approved schools" for young offenders from 10 to 17. The Criminal Justice Act of 1948 further refined the English system by seeking to ensure that no children should be sent to prison. It created a group of "Attendance Centres," whereby young offenders could receive "deprivation of leisure" without removal from home, school, or work. It also abolished corporal punishment.

Through the 1960s, under Labour Party government, English juvenile justice policy came increasingly under the influence of reformers who sought to establish a welfare orientation in the nation's response to juvenile crime. In 1963, a Children and Young Persons Act encouraged the diversion of young offenders from the juvenile courts, raising the age of criminal responsibility from eight to 10. Later in the decade, the Labour government issued two White Papers (i.e., reports), each stressing decriminalization and treatment as opposed to criminal justice approaches and incarceration in handing young offenders.

A 1969 Children and Young Persons Act sought to establish the welfare orientation more fully in law. The act required consultation between police and local social service agencies and major changes in possible dispositions. Although many older institutions (including borstals and Attendance Centres) remained intact, the 1969 Act encouraged an increasing use of probation (under the supervision of a social worker rather than a probation officer) and even the ultimate phasing out of older institutions or their transformation into community houses.

The results of the 1969 Act were not all that reformers had hoped. The Act allowed for the referral of cases to two kinds of proceedings: (1) a "care" proceeding, or (2) a criminal proceeding. The decision was based in large part on the discretion of the police, and English juvenile justice quickly began to take on the character of a divided system with two distinct orientations rather than one based primarily on ideas of social welfare.

Some would argue that the Act's welfare orientation never really caught on in English juvenile justice. In their operations, the courts tended to show something less than enthusiasm for welfare-oriented provisions, and some of the provisions were never implemented at all (including the one that raised the age of criminal responsibility). There was no massive intervention by social workers in the juvenile justice system. Furthermore, although the 1969 Act officially discouraged incarceration, evidence indicates that by the mid-1970s incarceration was being used more frequently for sentencing in criminal cases involving juveniles than had been the case before.[6]

Such tendencies were strengthened after the 1979 general election in Britain, when the Conservative Party took power on a "law-and-order" platform, inaugurating (as in the United States) a "get tough" approach to crime in general, including juvenile crime. In 1980, the Conservative government issued its own White Paper, which urged a more custodial approach for juvenile offenders.[7] The recommendation written into law by a 1982 Criminal Justice Act gave juvenile court judges increased discretion in sentencing young offenders to borstals and other institutions.

There were some counterbalances to the "get tough" approach of the 1982 Act. Most importantly, the 1980s did see some increasing diversion of juvenile offenders (especially below the age of 17) from the juvenile court system altogether. This was chiefly because of a more frequent use of police cautions in response to minor offenses. The 1980 White Paper on which the Act was based had recommended on expanded use of cautions. The use of cautions, further encouraged by Home Office Circulars of 1985 and 1990, appears to have become increasingly common through the 1980s and into the 1990s, especially for younger offenders and for girls. By the end of the 1980s, cautions were issued in almost 75 percent of the cases involving boys between the ages of 14 and 16 and in more than 80 percent of those cases involving girls the same age.[8]

The English system continues to evolve and to show a somewhat confusing mixture of welfare- and justice-oriented approaches. A 1989 Children Act, for instance, sought to decriminalized certain offenses that had previously been in the purview of the juvenile court system. On the other hand, though, the 1991 Criminal Justice Act set up a new "youth court" to focus entirely on criminal proceedings involving young offenders between the ages of 10 and 17. That Act included a series of provisions placing young offenders more within the confines of the criminal justice system.

More recently, government actions have continued to shape the system in complex directions. A 1994 Criminal Justice and Public Order Act tended to extend the justice-oriented approach. The act provided for a new custodial sentence for persistent offenders from age 12 to 14. It also extended the possibility of detention to 10- to 13-year-olds convicted of such "grave offenses" as murder, manslaughter, robbery, and rape, and lengthened maximum detention terms for 15- to 17-year-olds.

The courts also responded to the kinds of concerns these changes represent. In 1994, a Court of Appeals ruled that children ages 10 to 13 were capable of criminal intent and thus subject to criminal prosecution. Although the decision was overturned in 1995 by the House of Lords, the reversal was made on technical grounds, and with a proviso encouraging legislation to create such a policy.[9]

In 1998, such legislation was put into effect in the form of a new Crime and Disorder Act. The result of several studies and commissions created by the government in 1996 and 1997, the act provided (among other things) that children from age 10 to 13 were to be treated the same as 14- to 17-year-olds for purposes of prosecution. It also strengthened the use of detention as a response to juvenile offenses. At the same time, the act incorporated preventive measures aimed at reducing juvenile crime. These included the institution of "parenting orders" (including possible required counseling sessions) to aid parents in dealing with their children's behavior and the creation of neighborhood-based "Youth Offending Teams" to work with troubled young people. The latter provisions were scheduled to take effect during the years 2000 and 2001.[10]

Such developments raised a storm of controversy in England, focusing especially on the extension of criminal responsibility to children as young as 10 years of age. The conflict is longstanding; it is unlikely to be resolved in the near future.

Australia

Among the more complex and revealing developments in juvenile justice systems in recent years have been those taking place in Australia. Like the United States, Australia is composed of several different states, each with its own system of juvenile justice. However, the states of Australia exhibit certain trends and tendencies that show some of the dilemmas of juvenile justice in the modern world.

Certainly the most striking example of change in Australian juvenile justice comes from the state of South Australia, which has laid claim to establishing the world's first juvenile court, in 1890.[11] South Australia was also a pioneer in creating a welfare-oriented approach to juvenile justice. In 1971, the approach was enshrined in a Juvenile Courts Act establishing "Juvenile Aid Panels" to provide welfare-oriented alternatives to court proceedings, especially for first offenders between 10 and 16 years of age.

Nevertheless, beginning in 1979, with the passage of the Children's Protection and Young Offenders Act, South Australia began to move toward a two-tiered approach to juvenile justice. This act created a new procedure in which alleged offenders were brought to a "screening panel" first, which was expected to decide how a case should be disposed. Taking an array of factors into account, and not addressing issues of guilt or innocence, the screening panel could refer a case to a "children's aid panel," consisting of a police officer and a social worker, which (like panels in Scotland or the Scandinavian countries) sought a welfare-oriented response to delinquent behavior. Alternatively, the screening panel could refer the case to a children's court, especially if it involved a serious offense or the child entered a not-guilty plea. Influenced partly by the *Gault* decision in the United States, the 1979 Act explicitly incorporated due process guarantees into the Children's Court.

Dissatisfaction with the 1979 Act developed relatively quickly. For one thing, it had been hoped that the screening panels would themselves weed out less serious offenders, urging no further action. The effect, though, appeared to be the opposite, as both aid panels and children's courts saw increasing caseloads. In addition, in South Australia, as in other parts of the world, there was a widespread impression that juvenile crime was increasing and that welfare-oriented approaches were proving ineffective to stop it. From a somewhat different direction, there was also concern about bias on the part of the screening panels themselves, particularly in regard to a tendency to recommend harsher treatment for Aboriginal youth who ran afoul of the system than for whites accused of the same offenses.

Thus, in 1994, the South Australian system underwent a major revision through the implementation of a new Young Offenders Act. The children's court was replaced by a new youth court, intended to focus less on the offender than the offense, and which encouraged greater concern for victims and victims' rights. A "get tough" approach was incorporated in a provision to treat repeat offenders over 16 as adults, providing for the imprisonment of such offenders in adult facilities.

The 1994 Act also broke new ground through an effort to institutionalize provisions based on what is sometimes called "restorative justice" (see Chapter 10). Drawing on the shaming theory of John Braithwaite (Chapter 6), the Act seeks to divert at least some offenders from the youth court by providing for the possibility of family conferences in which principles of reintegrative shaming are put into practice. In these conferences, the offender meets with victims, parents, and a "justice coordinator" to find a mutually satisfactory solution to the offense (such as making reparations to the victim). Aimed particularly at Aboriginal youth, as noted in Chapter 6, the approach (which was pioneered in New Zealand, in an effort to apply traditional Maori forms to delinquency among Maori youth) has inspired a significant amount of controversy. Nevertheless, since 1994, similar processes have been instituted in other states, including Western Australia, New South Wales, and the Australian Capital Territory. In many parts of the world, efforts to balance welfare- and justice-oriented approaches to juvenile crime should become a matter of great interest for students of juvenile justice.

SUMMARY

The character and significance of juvenile delinquency varies greatly throughout the world. In the United States and in other industrial nations, delinquency is—and has long been—a serious social problem. In some other nations, delinquency seems to be less common. Although the methods by which statistics are kept makes comparisons risky, the rate of juvenile crime seems to be remarkably low in those nations.

There may be several reasons for such differences in the rates of juvenile crime, but the one most often cited has to do with the relative strength of traditional social and family institutions. Where these remain strong, they may serve to inhibit juvenile delinquency. Where they are weak or where (under the impact of urbanization and industrialization) they become weak, they can no longer serve to inhibit delinquent behavior. Such changes have already been noted in many parts of the world.

If one can find variations in the significance of delinquency, one can also find variations in approaches to juvenile justice internationally. There has been a general recognition of juvenile delinquency as a distinctive species of lawbreaking and of a need to respond to juvenile crime separately from the adult system of criminal justice. This recognition has been encouraged by such world-wide organizations as the United Nations. There has been a general introduction of social welfare concerns into juvenile justice, and an effort toward the use of probation, supervision, and other dispositions of juvenile cases that avoid incarceration. At the same time, there has also been something of an increase, in recent years, of two-tiered systems, particularly to deal with serious crimes committed by juveniles. In many parts of the world, there has been a rethinking of existing systems to incorporate both welfare- and justice-based approaches to juvenile crime.

For all the general tendencies, however, it is still possible to categorize juvenile justice systems in three broad groups. Some systems are clearly based primarily on a welfare-oriented approach. In such places as France or Scotland, most young offenders are kept out of any proceedings resembling those of the criminal justice system. They are dealt with by lay panels or by judges who are expected to put the welfare of the young person above the demands of criminal law and punishment. Although such systems are far from consistent in their adherence to the welfare approach, and provide for the institutionalization of some young offenders, they nevertheless seek to move as far as possible toward the decriminalization of delinquency.

In a few nations, the approach to juvenile crime is highly legalistic. While some provisions are made for age, these provisions are inconsistently applied and juveniles are treated within the general confines of the criminal justice system. In such nations as China or South Africa, which take the legalistic approach, it is often true that the disposition of a case will involve the same possibilities for punishment as those confronted by adult criminals.

Increasingly common, however, is a divided system, one that focuses on welfare-oriented approaches for status offenses and minor offenses but uses a criminal procedure for juveniles accused of more serious crimes. This has long been the case in Denmark and Sweden (in Denmark, more serious offenders are removed from the juvenile justice system altogether). More recently, other systems are similarly adopting a divided model. In England, where juvenile crime has been a major topic of debate and shifting policies since at least the 1960s, the establishment of youth courts and other recent proposals have served to move juvenile justice in the direction of a divided model. Similar developments have taken place in Australia in recent years.

The American model for responding to juvenile justice must not, therefore, be thought of as the only way in which a society may handle juvenile delinquency. Perhaps a consideration of alternatives—and of the range of problems other nations have faced—will help to give us a fuller understanding of American institutions as well.

REFERENCES

Bakken, Børge (1993). "Crime, Juvenile Delinquency and Deterrence Policy in China." *Australian Journal of Chinese Affairs* 30:29-58.

Blatier, Catherine (1999). "Juvenile Justice in France: The Evolution of Sentencing for Children and Minor Delinquents." *British Journal of Criminology* 39:240-52.

Booth, Tim, ed. (1991). *Juvenile Justice in the New Europe.* Sheffield, England: Social Service Monographs, Research in Practice.

Ebbe, Obi N.I. (1989). "Crime and Delinquency in Metropolitan Lagos: A Study of 'Crime and Delinquency Area' Theory." *Social Forces* 67:751-65.

Evans, Roger (1991). "Police Cautioning and the Young Adult Offender." *Criminal Law Review* (August):598-609.

Finckenauer, James D. (1995). *Russian Youth: Law, Deviance, and the Pursuit of Freedom.* New Brunswick, NJ: Transaction.

Fionda, Julia (1999). "New Labour, Old Hat: Youth Crime and the Crime and Disorder Act 1998." *Criminal Law Review* (January):36-47.

Hackler, James C. (1988). "Practicing in France What Americans Have Preached: The Response of French Judges to Juveniles." *Crime & Delinquency* 34:467-85.

Hartjen, Clayton A., and D. Priyadarsini (1984). *Delinquency in India: A Comparative Analysis.* New Brunswick, NJ: Rutgers University Press.

Hartjen, Clayton A., and Sesha Kethineni (1996). "India." In *International Handbook on Juvenile Justice,* edited by Donald J. Shoemaker, 175-190. Westport, CT: Greenwood Press.

Juvenile Justice in Australia. (1992). *Criminology Australia* 4:1.

Klein, Malcolm W., ed. (1984). *Western Systems of Juvenile Justice.* Beverly Hills: Sage.

Klein, Malcolm W., ed. (1989). *Cross-National Research in Self-Reported Crime and Delinquency.* Dordrecht, The Netherlands: Kluwer.

Lee, Carl (1994). "Preliminary Study of China's Juvenile Delinquency." *British Journal of Criminology* 34:502-505.

Lernout, Yves (1996). "The French Trial System." In *Children Who Kill: An Examination of the Treatment of Juveniles Who Kill in Different European Countries*, edited by Paul Cavadino, 162-173. Winchester, England: Waterside Press.

Littlewood, Paul (1996). "Secure Units." In *Children and Young People in Conflict with the Law*, edited by Stewart Asquith, 155-168. London: Jessica Kingsley, 1996.

Martin, F.M., Sanford J. Fox, and Kathleen Murray (1981). *Children Out of Court*. Edinburgh: Scottish Academic Press.

Morris, Allison M., and Henri Giller (1981). "Young Offenders: I. Law, Order and the Child-Care System." *Howard Journal of Penology and Crime Prevention* 20:81-89.

Muncie, John (1984). *The Trouble With Kids Today: Youth and Crime in Post-War Britain*. London: Hutchinson.

Nichols, Helen. (1981). "South Australia." In *Justice and Troubled Children Around the World*, edited by V. Lorne Stewart, 141-174. New York: New York University Press.

Parker, L. Craig (1986). *Parole and the Community-Based Treatment of Offenders in Japan and the United States*. New Haven, CT: University of New Haven Press.

Pitts, John (1988). *The Politics of Juvenile Crime*. London: Sage.

Ren, Xin (1996). "People's Republic of China." In *International Handbook on Juvenile Justice*, edited by Donald J. Shoemaker, 57-79. Westport, CT: Greenwood Press.

Sarneckie, Jerzy (1989). *Juvenile Delinquency in Sweden: An Overview*. Stockholm: National Council for Crime Prevention.

Sarre, Rick (1994). "Juvenile Justice in South Australia: An Update." *Criminology Australia* 5:13-16.

Schreiber, Mark (1997). "Juvenile Crime in the 1990s." *Japan Quarterly* 44(2):78-88.

Sereny, Gitta (1998). *Cries Unheard: Why Children Kill: The Story of Mary Bell*. New York: Henry Holt.

Seymour, John (1996). "Australia." In *International Handbook on Juvenile Justice*, edited by Donald J. Shoemaker, 1-19. Westport, CT: Greenwood Press.

Tubbs, Walter (1994). "The Roots of Stress-Death and Juvenile Delinquency in Japan: Disciplinary Ambivalence and Perceived Locus of Control." *Journal of Business Ethics* 13:507-522.

Wagatsuma, Hiroshi, and George A. De Vos (1984). *Heritage of Endurance: Family Patterns and Delinquency in Urban Japan*. Berkeley: University of California Press.

White, Rob, and Christine Alder, eds. (1994). *The Police and Young People in Australia*. Cambridge, England: Cambridge University Press.

Wilkinson, Christine, and Roger Evans (1990). "Police Cautioning of Juveniles: The Impact of Home Office Circular 14/1985." *Criminal Law Review* (March):165-176.

Wong, Dennis S.W. (1999). "Delinquency Control and Juvenile Justice in China." *Australian and New Zealand Journal of Criminology* 32:27-41.

NOTES

[1]   Hartjen & Priyadarsini (1984); Hartjen & Kethineni (1996).

[2]   Lee (1994).

[3]   Booth (1991).

[4]   Martin, Fox & Murray (1981).

[5]   Bakken (1993).

[6]   Pitts (1988).

[7]   Morris & Giller (1981).

[8]   Evans (1991).

[9]   Littlewood (1996).

[10]   Fionda (1999).

[11]   Nichols (1981).

14

Female Juvenile Delinquency

Advocates of women's rights have fought for equal privileges and responsibilities. They have pressed the doctrine that women should be treated in the same manner as men and that there are no differences between the genders that ought to translate into discriminatory actions. If premises such as these are being translated into public attitudes and public policy, why, then, should a separate chapter be devoted to female delinquency?

As we saw in Chapter 1, there are very significant differences in the rate and the kind of delinquent behavior committed by girls and young women in contrast to that of boys and young men. Such differences undoubtedly reflect to a great extent the manner in which females are trained and the values they come to adopt. However, the gender distinctions are so striking and so fundamental to an analysis of delinquency that they demand special treatment.

It is possible that as full equality of boys and girls and men and women is achieved, the pattern of female delinquency will come to look much more like that of males. Vedder and Somerville anticipate such a development: "Considering the direction our modern society is taking," they have written, "it will not be unreasonable to expect more serious female delinquency in the future."[1] Some scholars maintain that the liberation movement has caused some women to shed their traditional inhibitions about engaging in acts such as burglary and robbery. Others insist that there has been no significant increase in female participation in street crimes, in part because female criminal offenders are virtually the last group to be reached by the ideas of the women's movement, which at this time is primarily a middle-class campaign.

Statistics indicate that the only notable crime increases among women offenders are in larceny and in white-collar offenses. These upswings are largely insignificant in terms of any serious threat to society. The larceny is primarily shoplifting, which traditionally (though much less so nowadays) has been a female crime. The white-collar offenses, though tabulated officially as embezzlement, usually are nothing more sinister than checks written with insufficient funds behind them or on nonexistent accounts.

Some persons argue that males will be significantly changed by the women's rights movement and that they will in time show lower levels of aggression and other forms of predatory behavior. Others insist that women, after being released from the bonds that have historically governed their behavior, will come to act just as men do; they will kill and steal much more often. Finally, there are those who adhere to a third (and seemingly most unlikely) position: that the liberation of women from age-old restraints will give rise to a wave of much worse delinquent behavior than that of males, because females will go to extremes to try to prove their equality.

Adherents of this last position point to the common belief among workers in juvenile detention centers that facilities for girls pose more serious control problems than those housing boys. They insist that girls "don't play by the rules" (meaning the rules regarded by males as sensible and sporting). They claim that girls will throw tantrums when upset (while boys more often will withdraw and contain their emotions) and girls will fight "unfairly" when outraged (scratching, biting, pulling hair, and otherwise employing "outrageous" tactics).

Some verification of this viewpoint recently was supplied by two Australian researchers who interviewed male and female juvenile justice workers in Victoria, Australia. Their clients were between the ages of 12 and 15. They uniformly supported the notion that young women were the more difficult of the genders with whom to work. One worker explained why she found female delinquents particularly trying:

> One of the things is that often you get tired of a girl who's threatened to kill herself. That sounds terrible, but you just go, "For heaven's sake." We've had kids in the laundry sort of holding knives against their breasts, and you know that they're not going to do it, but they've been in there yelling and screaming and it's been very, I'll use the loaded term, hysterical.[2]

A prominent writer of detective fiction, Dorothy Sayers, has offered an additional expression of the view that women are at least as vicious as men but more skilled at camouflaging their meanness. Sayers has a police inspector say: "When a woman is wicked and unscrupulous, she is the most ruthless criminal in the world—fifty times worse than a man, because she is more single-minded about it." Sayers's hero answers: "They're not troubled with sentimentality, that's why. We poor mutts of men stuff ourselves up with the idea that they're romantic and emotional. All punk, my son." It is debatable whether Sayers, who was a distinguished theologian and modern language scholar besides being a mystery writer, accepted this viewpoint or was satirizing male ideas.

Those who believe that liberation will uncork terrible outbreaks of female delinquency cite several notorious cases in recent decades in which young women participated in gruesome crimes. Most memorable was the group associated with Charles Manson who were involved in the murder of a motion picture actress as well as a variety of other terrorist acts in southern California. Women were also prominent in the so-called Symbionese Liberation Army (SLA), which kidnapped Patricia Hearst and persuaded her to join in at least one bank robbery. Two women, Lynette "Squeaky" Fromme (who had been a member of the so-called Manson "family") and Sara Jane Moore, independently attempted to assassinate President Gerald Ford. It is arguable, however, whether the acts of the women associated with the SLA and Manson would have taken place without the leadership of charismatic males.

THE HISTORICAL RECORD

Otto Pollak: Hidden Female Crime

The first major book on female crime and delinquency, written in 1950 by Otto Pollak, offered a number of statements that today are regarded as patently incorrect. Pollak maintained that women commit as much crime as men but that their crime is more sneaky and therefore less readily detected. Pollack stated, for instance, that women tend to use poison for murder, taking advantage of their control over meal preparation. Poisoning could be difficult to detect, especially in earlier times, when the Roman Catholic church banned autopsies. Today, however, despite its regular appearance in mystery novels, poisoning is extremely uncommon. Pollak also speculated that female dominance of nursing the sick offers opportunities for doing away with weak and susceptible persons without being detected.

Pollak's views have been effectively challenged. One critic points out that Pollak offered no proof for many of his statements. "The likelihood that women are poisoning untold numbers of sick husbands is ridiculous," notes Eileen Leonard. "How could Pollak possibly know that such crimes are taking place?"[3] This position is supported by FBI statistics that show that of the more than 20,000 killings each year, only about 10 are by poison—and as many of these are committed by men as by women.

Emphasizing the point that social and psychological considerations are fundamental to an understanding of the striking variations in male and female delinquency is the fact that the ratio of male-female delinquency varies (1) from one nation to another, (2) with the social position of the sexes in different countries, (3) with the size of the community, (4) with age, (5) with areas of residence, (6) with time, and (7) with the degree of integration into the family. If Pollak was right about the biological determinism of delinquency, gender alone would dictate delinquency rate differences, and the variations in cultures would not be as distinctive as they are.

PHYSIOLOGY AND DELINQUENCY

A proponent of any of the numerous positions on the relationship among gender, feminism, and delinquency has to grant that there are physiological distinctions between males and females that influence certain behaviors. For instance, women cannot commit forcible rape (though approximately 200 women are arrested each year in the United States as accessories in such cases, usually having cooperated with a male companion in employing a ruse or using force to assault the victim). Women are less likely to undertake crimes of violence that involve physical confrontations with male victims, such as unarmed muggings, because they are not likely to fare as well as men in such physical confrontations. They can, in general, pick on other women, youngsters, or the aged, but this limits their range of targets.

Biological gender differences tend to be less pronounced in younger persons than in older persons, though girls weigh less than boys at birth, and this differential grows until about the age of 20, when there is a 20 percent difference between the sexes. Girls have less muscle than boys, and by age 20 they are 10 percent shorter than males. Girls also are not as well coordinated as boys, with the exception of fine muscle coordination. As infants, girls sleep more and are less vigorous than boys. These differences may play into the pattern of juvenile delinquency—some rather directly, others more subtly.

Hysteria and Premenstrual Syndrome

Two particular matters alleged to be related to female juvenile delinquency—hysteria and premenstrual syndrome (PMS)—merit attention. Hysteria is a condition, perhaps based in physiology but more likely in psychology, that often is related to tactics used by medical science to put a stigma on women. Premenstrual syndrome (PMS) tends to be based in hormonal action. The importance accorded to PMS varies considerably. It will be downplayed as having little, if any, significance by those countering the viewpoint that women require special treatment because of PMS (which could be a way of saying that they should be confined to lesser roles). Girls and women who are charged with serious offenses, however, sometimes rely upon a defense of premenstrual syndrome to obtain a verdict based on diminished responsibility. According to that defense, they were suffering so much stress and anxiety prior to their menstrual period that they were not in control of their emotions or behavior and could not appreciate the gravity of the criminal offense they had committed. Christine English, who killed her lover in Britain by driving her car over him, was acquitted after a medical expert witness maintained that she had been suffering from PMS for the past 13 years.

Hysteria

The belief in early medicine regarding the roots of hysteria are instructive. The word comes from a Greek stem meaning "womb," and it was believed at that time that hysteria was the result of the wandering of the womb from its proper place in the female body upward into the stomach and the throat. Hysterical women who could not speak properly were believed to be strangling from suffocation by the meandering womb. The condition was said to affect young girls and widows particularly. The explanation by physicians was that the patient's womb was discontent because of neglect. What was required was regular sexual intercourse; then the womb would return to its place, particularly if the woman became pregnant. Absent that resolution, doctors prescribed what, given the basis of their diagnosis, were obvious remedies. Noxious substances should be placed by the mouth and pleasant ones at the genitals. The abhorrent smells would drive the womb downward and the attractive ones would further impel it in the direction it ought to be moving. As one seventeenth-century physician indicated: "Apply evil smells to the nostrils, and sweet smells beneath. Let the bodies be kept upright, straight laced, and the belly and throat held down with one's hand."[4]

Hysteria continues in many medical circles to be regarded as a disorder apt to be located among girls. The standard definition is that it is characterized by the presence of "gross, often dramatic, bodily symptoms, unexplainable on an organic basis." Many persons believe that when males experience precisely the same difficulties, doctors are inclined to explain their problem with terms other than hysteria. Others argue that women are trained by their parents and by social rules to react to difficulties in ways that have come to be defined as hysterical, while men tend to respond to difficulties in other ways. Finally, there are those who believe that is no such medical entity as hysteria, that it is a grab-bag diagnostic category for moral assessments, usually by males, of manifestations of anxiety by females.

The phenomenal overrepresentation of young girls in two kinds of hysterical phenomena indicate that there is some basis for the early caricature of the sexual roots of the phenomenon. In virtually all recorded episodes of mass hysteria, it has been young girls who were most affected. In one study, researchers found that 89 percent of the 1,223 persons who suffered hysterical symptoms in 23 separate incidents were females. They note, however, that job boredom may have contributed significantly to the episodes; many occurred in factories and other places where mind-numbing work was routine for the young women afflicted. In a typical outbreak, 22 young women in a rural southwestern Louisiana school experienced hysterical symptoms or what they called "blackouts." Medical investigators thought that they had suffered an attack of anxiety after a rumor began to circulate that the students, most of whom were sexually active, were to undergo pregnancy tests.

Premenstrual Syndrome

About one in seven women are believed to suffer from difficulties prior to their menstrual period that are severe enough to interfere with their daily activities. It remains arguable whether such problems are biologically determined or whether they represent a condition associated with contemporary civilization or present-day social attitudes.

The term "premenstrual syndrome" was first coined more than 50 years ago by a medical doctor who described it as being marked by breast swelling and tenderness; headaches; edema (an accumulation of fluids) in the eyelids, cheeks, and extremities; abdominal discomfort; and "uncontrollable irritation and depression which manifests itself in manic or melancholic crises."[5] He maintained that the number of female suicides was highest during the time immediately prior to menstruation.

Many feminists and others challenge what they regard as simplistic notions of the doctor and his followers. They point out that the norm against which the behavior of women is measured is one of passivity, amiability, and good-naturedness. They resent the tendency to write off behavior with deep and complicated origins as related to menstruation. Suicide, they point out, is the consequence of a large number of circumstances that are more significant than any cyclical mood shift, presuming that such a shift exists at all. A girl may be oppressed, overwhelmed, physically ill, or otherwise in severe trouble when she kills herself, and it is insensitive and stupid, some writers say, to override such fundamental problems with a banal physiological "explanation." It is pointed out that after a search of anthropological records, one group of researchers found many cultural myths, taboos, and superstitions associated with menstruation, but located no report of premenstrual distress as such.

Many writers believe that PMS is at least as much a political issue as a medical one. According to some, doctors could just as readily suggest that there is a condition known as "pre-breakfast syndrome." This syndrome would be found among people who stagger out of bed, depressed at the dawn of a new day, feeling wobbly and uncertain, at least until they have some food, and perhaps coffee, to stimulate their circulation. Such a syndrome exists, but it is not notably important, just as the PMS syndrome may exist for some persons at some times but has been accorded too much significance and allows people to belittle female behavior. An example of such extreme thought is found in the opinion of Katharina Dalton, a British medical doctor, and the most prominent supporter of the importance of PMS as an influence on juvenile delinquency:

> Among PMS women, increased libido is occasionally noticed in the premenstruum. All too often it is this nymphomanian urge in adolescents which is responsible for young girls running away from home, or custody, only to be found wandering in the park or following the boys. These girls can be helped, and their criminal career abruptly ended with hormone therapy.[6]

Professional medicine remains uncertain about how to regard PMS. After reviewing 400 articles, the compilers of the fourth edition of the American Psychiatric Association's *Diagnostic and Statistical Manual of Mental Disorders* (1994) decided to keep its discussion of the subject in an appendix rather than in the main body of the manual. The condition is labeled "premenstrual dysphoric disorder (PMDD)" and is said to represent a disturbance in serotin metabolism similar to that found in mood disorders. Symptoms are reported to be fairly common in 20 to 30 percent of American women, while only 3 to 5 percent are believed to suffer from PMDD so severe that the symptoms are similar to a state of depression.

The APA Manual sells nearly one-half a million copies and is translated into about a dozen languages. Its listing of PMDD as a mental disorder has produced in many women, as one notes, "a huge loss in terms of their faith in 'science,' and a growing distrust of the APA as a neutral proponent of the scientific study of mental disorder."[7]

Summing Up

What can we conclude from our review of material on hysteria and PMS as these conditions (and other matters specifically tied to girls and women) relate to juvenile delinquency? The answer, at least for the moment, has to be, "Not much." Certainly, the absurd notion of Hippocrates and his followers—a notion that survived for centuries—that hysteria was caused by the womb wandering about the body can be taken as a view rooted in a dismissive if not hostile attitude toward women. The evidence is perhaps less certain with regard to PMS, but we are inclined, pending better data, to regard research such as that by Pauline Slade as pointing in a persuasive direction. Slade had 118 student nurses report their mood and their physiological condition on a regular basis, with the subjects not aware that this was a study of the relationship between their feelings and their menstrual cycle. She found that psychological changes occurred randomly throughout the cycle. Slade points out that women who experience negative moods during the premenstrual period tend to associate such moods with PMS. When they experience precisely the same moods at other times, they tend to attach them to personal or environmental factors.

In essence, then, it is clear that the subject of female delinquency affords an opportunity to examine issues of upbringing and biology and consequent illegal behavior. Evidence connecting delinquency to biological aspects of gender remains inconclusive, but the topic should benefit from further examination.

THE DOUBLE STANDARD

The investigation of relationships between gender and delinquency is deeply involved with what is called "the double standard," a definition for which is supplied by an eminent Oxford University social historian:

> Stated simply, it is the view that unchastity, in the sense of sexual relations before marriage or outside marriage, is for a man, if an offense, nonetheless a mild and pardonable one, but for a woman a matter of utmost gravity.[8]

Obviously, the double standard no longer prevails with the intensity and importance that once surrounded it, but its heritage is significant in current considerations of female juvenile delinquency. Basic to the double standard is the fact that sexual intercourse for females might result in pregnancy. In earlier times, whether a woman conceived after sexual intercourse often was something like a lottery. Moreover, conception outside of marriage in bygone days was often a fearsome social condition.

The biological snare for women, of course, was that maternity was readily established, while paternity was more doubtful and arguable. At least as important has been the millennium-old tradition that women are and should remain "purer" than men. Sex consistently was portrayed to women as "dirty" or, alternatively, as a treasure that a young woman can bestow upon the man of her choice. For men, on the contrary, sex has been regarded as a strong biological drive, demanding satisfaction, preferably through marriage or (failing that) through involvement with a déclassé group of "available" females who offer service for money or who are regarded as sexually wayward and therefore outside the mainstream of decent society.

Sociobiologists, who find functional attributes in social customs, insist that the double standard allows the fittest females—the healthiest, the prettiest, the smartest—to locate the most suitable fathers for their children, thereby constantly improving the gene pool of the group. If women were to be as sexually promiscuous as men, without abortion or birth control, they would be "trapped" into giving birth to children with less desirable fathers, genetically speaking. Therefore, according to these sociobiologists, women trade sexual access for the "best" male traits they can acquire for their offspring in the mating marketplace. The process presumably operates as it does in many animal groups, in which the strongest and most aggressive male collects a group of females and allows no other male to mate with them.

Contemporary Themes

Changes in the relationships between boys and girls and men and women hold an important key to our understanding of female delinquency. At the moment, as we enter the 2000s, women are moving into the work arena in increasing numbers, partly because they want to and partly because they feel that they must do so for financial reasons. Nor does there appear to be any doubt that women will succeed in gaining further opportunities to be treated equally with men in terms of hiring policies, compensation, and advancement.

How males and females ultimately will come to relate to each other in various spheres—work, sex, play, and family, among others—seems much less certain. Sexual relations, the issue at the core of the double standard and an item lying at the heart of female delinquency, are in a state of flux. More young and unmarried women are engaging in sexual intercourse more frequently and with more partners than was true a few decades ago, though the fear of AIDS has had a dampening effect on this trend. Some women now are as casual about sex as many men traditionally have been, though many others are more restrained.

The Good Girl/Bad Girl Dichotomy

The good girl/bad girl distinction has been noted by Meda Chesney-Lind and Randall Shelden as playing a prominent part in female juvenile delinquency. The concept was first identified in analyses of pre-World War II motion pictures. Strict censorship rules governed the making of such films. In almost all of them, the heroine was portrayed as an exciting, sexy, available creature. The male hero, though attracted to this apparently fast-living, beautiful person, also was put off by her seeming lack of decent morals. Only as the story developed did it turn out that the original conception was incorrect, the leading lady only appeared to be fast and loose: in truth, she was a decent, courageous, and thoroughly proper person, only pretending to be racy in order to achieve some desirable end. In *Notorious*, for instance, Ingrid Bergman seems to be wicked, and, because of this, Gary Cooper rejects her. It turns out, however, that she is a spy, working for the good guys. When Cooper comes to understand this, a romance between them blossoms.

According to Chesney-Lind and Shelden, the same phenomenon exists in the realm of female delinquency. "Good girls" do their work, go to school, are "feminine," virginal, pure, and polite. Good girls, however, often are not very popular. They are often defined as "weird," and some come to define their lives as "boring." A 17-year-old discussed her transformation from good to bad in the following terms:

> My parents got divorced about two years ago. That's when I started to get radical, but I did it on purpose. In a way I wanted to because it was too boring being a good little girl. I got all good grades. I would never think of smoking a cigarette. I used to go to church every Sunday. Oh, I used to be a real good little girl.[9]

Being "bad" carries for some a sense of recklessness and excitement. Bad girls boasted of their daring, toughness, and trickery. These girls tended not to be prom queens or cheerleaders, and could not afford the wardrobes that often accompany high school popularity. They could not compete in the middle-class arena. The authors note: "The one option that remains is to be the stoney, tough, 'bad' girl. The image may not fit with their career hopes, but it brings recognition and status today."

Is Unmarried Teenage Pregnancy Also Delinquency?

As a result of changing attitudes about sexual relations, more girls and young women are having children out of wedlock and raising the children by themselves. The most rational (and perhaps the only possible) defense of continuing to regard such sexual waywardness among girls as juvenile delinquency is that, unless it is curbed, the consequences for some of those who indulge in it can be detrimental.

Boys can walk away from a partner's pregnancy—perhaps nonchalantly, perhaps with some emotional damage—but it is rarely likely to interfere with their lives unless they elect to have it do so. Girls, on the other hand, even if they choose to have an abortion or give their child up for adoption, are likely to experience dramatic changes in their emotional lives when they undergo a pregnancy. Some contend that the strong reaction to female sexual waywardness represents an attempt to protect girls from an experience that they will wish they had not had, if not now, then when they look back on it later. An obvious counterargument is that how people choose to run (or ruin) their lives is their own business and that it is a girl's option whether to indulge in sex or to have children out of wedlock.

Two responses are common. One is that the girls are too young to know adequately what is in their own best interests. The second is that unmarried girls who bear children very often end up on welfare because they cannot earn enough to support themselves and the child. Therefore, they become a burden on the taxpayers, who are entitled to try to protect themselves by penalizing sexual activity in order to seek to control it.

The most comprehensive study of unwed teenaged mothers concluded (contrary to popular belief) that the "problem" has been created in recent years as part of a campaign to stigmatize those who do not abide by behavioral rules that govern middle-class lives. Kristin Luker determined that there has been no significant increase in teenage childbearing by unwed mothers and that, overwhelmingly, having a child represents a reasonably sensible decision by the teenagers who do so. These girls appreciate that they are going nowhere financially and socially and that, because of their lack of education and skills, they will at best be able to obtain dead-end jobs. They usually are well aware that they do not have the wherewithal to improve their lot, whether or not they become mothers. This cold-blooded appraisal of their situation is what irritates those above them on the social ladder, who insist—despite compelling evidence to the contrary—that anybody, anywhere, can with adequate motivation and dedication improve their lot. Luker notes that a particular impetus to having children early is that the girls realize that they can still rely on their relatively young parents for assistance in raising the infants. She provides strong evidence that welfare costs have not notably risen because of child-bearing by unwed teenagers. Luker's theme is summarized in the following quote:

> The idea that young people would be better off if they worked harder, were more patient, and postponed their childbearing is simply not true—and it is unlikely to become true in the foreseeable future—for a great many people at the bottom of the income scale. Even when poor people obtain more education, for example, they only displace other people at the end of the queue, and the problem of poverty and childbearing among young people continues.[10]

These cross-currents are intimately connected to the phenomenon of female delinquency. In the following pages, we will indicate some of the characteristics of that delinquency and will link these characteristics with the wider social changes discussed earlier.

THE EXTENT AND NATURE OF FEMALE DELINQUENCY

A brief review and extension of the discussion in Chapter 1 about differences in male and female delinquency will be useful at this point. Males under the age of 18 commit about three to seven times more offenses that come to the attention of the authorities than do females. Self-report studies, however, show a much lower ratio, generally between 1.2 to 1 and 2.5 to 1. Statistics indicate that boys are primarily involved in property offenses, while girls' misbehavior involves sex- and home-related acts.

A comprehensive analysis of information acquired by the National Youth Survey on self-reported delinquency offers an inventory of distinctions between males and females in delinquent behavior. Data came from interviews with 1,725 adolescents, ages 11 to 17. Statistically significant greater male participation was found for the following property offenses: damaging the property of others, stealing a motor vehicle, stealing more than $50, evading payment, breaking and entering, and joyriding. For stealing less than $50 and buying stolen property, the difference (though still showing higher male involvement) was less sharp.

As expected, boys also were more involved in the violent crimes of gang fighting, strong-arming others, and aggravated assaults. In addition, boys were 45 times more likely than girls to carry a hidden weapon.

The National Youth Survey found more alcohol and heroin use among males but equivalent recourse by boys and girls to marijuana and other illegal drugs. The study confirmed the general belief among research scholars that delinquency patterns have not altered much during the decades after the mid-1960s, the period during which the women's rights movement began to take hold.

Summarizing available evidence, Gary Jensen and Raymond Eve point out that "girls may be less willing to acknowledge delinquent acts than boys, and hence only 'appear' to be less delinquent." They find little reason to accept such a skeptical position, and instead point out that the evidence on high male delinquency rates is very persuasive:

> All we can say is that numerous investigations carried out at different points in time, in different regions of the nation, in a variety of different cities and sociodemographic groups, using a variety of alternative measures of delinquency (both official and unofficial) have discovered a sex differential in delinquency. It seems fairly safe to conclude that girls are "really" less involved in delinquency than are boys.[11]

Several forms of delinquency, most notably female prostitution and running away, will be discussed here as illustrative of how the double standard operates. The casting of specific law violations into the broader categories of incorrigibility, running away, and sexual delinquency has been labeled by Carol Smart as the "sexualization of offenses."[12] Smart notes that juvenile courts routinely impose pretrial physical examinations, often involving lengthy detention periods, upon girls and young women who are apprehended for delinquent behavior (see the related discussion in Chapter 11). These examinations seek to detect pregnancy and sexually transmitted diseases (neither of which is a law violation).

THEORY AND FEMALE DELINQUENCY

Especially telling was a sharp interchange at a recent meeting of the American Society of Criminology between a male, a former president of the Society, and a female, a well-known ardent feminist scholar. "In what ways has feminist theory and scholarship influenced your work and thinking?" she asked. "Not at all," he replied. "Girls and women commit such a small proportion of the total amount of crime that it diverts attention from the essence of the issue to deal with the offenses of girls and women." This viewpoint is rapidly disappearing, however, as those who seek to understand delinquency come to appreciate that the distinctive patterns and the varying degrees of male and female lawbreaking activities offer a valuable field for exploration.

Theories of delinquency traditionally have been concerned solely with the behavior of males. These earlier theories then have been used to explain females. The new feminist effort, as enunciated by Chesney-Lind and Shelden, is to "construct explanations of female behavior that are sensitive to its patriarchal context."[13] Today, there are hundreds of studies of female delinquency and crime, while 20 years ago the number could be counted on the fingers of two hands.

John Hagan: Power-Control Theory

Among the more persuasive theories of female crime is the power-control position propounded by John Hagan. Simply put, the theory suggests that, in a patriarchal society such as that in the United States, girls are protected by their family—that is, they are monitored and supervised—so that they typically do not become involved in activities that could lead them into delinquent associations and behavior. This is because of beliefs about the "proper" personal traits and behavior that will lead to female success in later life. Boys, on the other hand, are encouraged to engage in riskier, more daring endeavors and, for some, these lead to illegal acts. Independence tends to be encouraged for boys, and unsupervised time is more readily tolerated.

The theory focuses on how close or far apart the delinquency rates for males and females are in terms of three family forms. There are "unbalanced" families, in which the father's occupational and family authority exceeds that of the mother and child rearing is generally delegated to the mothers (who protect their daughters and train them to assume the roles that the mothers play). Males will show a much higher rate of delinquency in such families. In "balanced" families, where fathers and mothers have comparable authority, mothers still will play the leading role in socializing children, boys and girls will be handled in much the same ways, and their delinquency rates will be rather similar. The same is true, Hagan maintains, for single-parent families, because the lone parent holds all the reins.

The strongest criticism of power-control theory is by Meda Chesney-Lind, who argues that it focuses on the participation of mothers (particularly high-status women) in the labor force as a significant factor in the rise in female delinquency. Chesney-Lind maintains that there is no evidence to support this supposition. A feminist perspective, she says, should make an extensive and intensive examination of the actual lives of female delinquents and pay adequate attention to racism, poverty, and physical and sexual abuse as prominent contributing factors to delinquent behavior. Others point out that single-parent families differ greatly (in part depending on whether the child caretaker is a widow or widower, a divorcee, or an unmarried mother) and that these variations will play into the way male and female children are treated. A review of a variety of studies indicates that the Hagan postulation requires some refinement before it is likely to mesh with research results.

Charles Tittle: Control Balance Theory

Control balance theory is a recent entrant in the theoretical sweepstakes. The theory seeks to explain all crime, delinquency, and deviance. It is discussed in this chapter because it has a passing proximity to Hagan's ideas and because, unlike most theories of delinquency, which are totally male-based, control balance explicitly addresses female waywardness.

Control balance theory is unusually complex and some critics find its ingredients so numerous that they despair of being able to formulate research that might adequately determine whether the theory is on target. Stripped to its essentials, the theory focuses on whether a person's situation is marked by a lack of control (called a control deficit), a condition that is based on the person's ability to exercise power. Depending on a host of other circumstances, such as psychic and bodily needs and motivation and opportunity, an individual with a control deficit is said to be likely to engage in what are called "repressive" acts—acts of predation, defiance, and dependence. High levels of control (control surplus) are said to lead to "autonomous" acts, such as exploitation, plunder, and decadence. Conformity results when a person's control ratio is balanced; that is, the amount of control the person can exercise equals the amount of control to which the person is subject.

Tittle predicts that changes in control balance will be accompanied by changes in forms of behavior. Females almost always have more control exercised over them than they exercise, but they sometimes have resources that allow them to raise their control ratio. He identifies three such resources specifically: (1) their supervision of children, (2) their potential ability to control men in the sexual realm, and (3) the skills and abilities of some females that enable them, increasingly in these days, to escape male repression and exercise control.

The first published attempt to test control balance theory pared it down to a few elements and examined these ideas by distributing questionnaires to students in which they responded to several vignettes, a tactic that arguably addresses the ingredients of Tittle's theory. The results were reported to be "mixed," showing in particular, contrary to the theoretical claim, that both high and low levels of control deficit predicted predation and deviance.

RUNAWAYS

The rationale for the strong focus on female runaways in the enforcement of juvenile delinquency statutes is that such behavior is assumed to be a herald of more serious lawbreaking. The following three cases represent instances in which young girls were committed to correctional facilities after a finding that they were "wayward minors," either because they were "morally depraved" or "in danger of becoming morally depraved":

> Esther was living alone because her mother had been committed to a state mental hospital. Esther was expelled from school; the principal had charged her with "sexual promiscuity." She then was deemed a wayward minor and placed in a foster home. After her mother was released from the hospital, Esther wanted to return home, but her social worker refused to give her permission to do so. Esther ran away.
>
> Marion had lived in foster homes since she was five years old. When she was seventeen, she bore an illegitimate child. Marion's social worker wanted Marion to give her child up for adoption, but when she refused to do so, she too was adjudicated a wayward minor. Previously Marion had run away from her foster home when she was not permitted to see the father of her child.
>
> Dominica, the oldest of eight children, had a confused family life. Her mother, an alcoholic, had been married four times. Her mother was found to be unfit, and all the children were placed in foster homes. Then Dominica ran away, and her mother requested that a warrant be put out for her arrest. Dominica was then allowed to stay home, but she was placed under a curfew. She had no recollection of being placed on probation, but after she left home without permission (she was suspected of having attended a drug party), Dominica was charged with violating probation.[14]

There are two female runaways for each male runaway, a figure that may reflect the tighter restraints upon young girls by their parents. Runaway girls tend to come from families with an array of problems (with physical abuse being a leading determinant). Most of the runaways return or are returned to their homes within 48 hours after they depart, but about 10 percent remain absent either permanently or for long periods of time. Younger girls tend to be "running to" some thing or somebody; older girls or young women to be "running from" something with which they cannot cope (often physical or sexual abuse).

Running away is not an uncommon precursor of teenage prostitution. The girls (and, increasingly, boys as well) often believe that they have no other means by which to support themselves. If they look for legitimate work, their employer or fellow workers may detect that they are underage and report them to the authorities. Besides, they are not likely to have legitimate marketable skills.

For some juveniles, running away from home results in a continuing life on the streets, where there is a constant and sometimes desperate hunt for sustenance and shelter.

Prostitution is a common way for teenage runaways to make a living. Police have traditionally tended to arrest the prostitute but not the customer. *(Photo by Mark C. Ide)*

John Hagan and Bill McCarthy point out that these street youths are overlooked in what they call "school criminology." Self-report studies of crime and drug use, for instance, invariably are based on youngsters who are attending school and readily available to fill out questionnaires. Hagan and McCarthy believe that the neglect of "street criminology" is in part the result of the fact that the homeless are not as accessible to researchers. They point out that there are about 100 million homeless youths throughout the world, with about two-fifths of that total located in Latin American countries, particularly Brazil.

A study of homeless youths in Toronto and Vancouver by Hagan and McCarthy found that the youths constantly engage in a search for food, clothing, and a place to sleep. They sometimes receive help from their family or from work, social service agencies, hostels, and food banks, or engage in panhandling. Theft and prostitution are criminal options for survival. Homeless youths may "dine and dash" (eat at a restaurant and then bolt out of it without paying) or make a "bun run" (stealing food from trucks.) They note of their field study among homeless youth:

This book paints a mostly grim picture of the daily lives of urban street youth. While most people invest the largest part of their daily lives in the relatively benign worlds of school or work, homeless youth spend most of the time less profitably and more dangerously on the streets and in parks, social assistance offices, shelters, and abandoned buildings. . . . [Most spend] their time hanging out, panhandling, partying and foraging in the shadow economy of the street.[15]

Teenage Female Prostitution

In contrast to the dramatic coloration they often are given on stage, in films, and in novels, most prostitutes have rather drab lifestyles. In describing her work, a typical prostitute might say that it is "a little less boring" than her former job as a file clerk. One writer, noting an increase in juvenile prostitutes from "affluent and overindulged" backgrounds, explains what she believes is the relationship between the values the girls have learned at home and the attraction of prostitution:

Along with succumbing to intense pressure to be sexual and to measure self-worth in direct relationship to money-making ability, middle-class life yields other conditions that make prostitution alluring. It appears that for middle-class prostitutes it is basically entertaining to dress up with your friends and go down on the street and con, cajole, and be the aggressor. The extravagant sensation from the illegality, projected immorality, and danger of prostitution is a relief from the neutrality of suburbia. It is just something to do—another high.[16]

This theme is underscored by the observation of columnist Maureen Dowd, who notes that "prostitution is now an instrument of upward mobility."[17] Dowd points out this trend in motion pictures: Julia Roberts in *Pretty Woman* and Melanie Griffith in *Milk Money* were both rewarded for their sexual sins, and notes that Divine Brown, the real-life street prostitute arrested for engaging in paid sex with actor Hugh Grant in his car, became an instant celebrity.

Interviews with 200 current and former prostitutes in the San Francisco Bay Area, of whom 69 percent were 16 years of age and under (with many reported to be 10, 11, and 12) found that more than three out of five of the girls and women had been beaten (differentiated from being spanked) by at least one of their parents. The beatings took place once a month or more often for 45 percent of those who were hit. A similar percentage reported being victims of incest or sexual abuse when they were between the ages of three and 16, with 10 being the average age of first sexual victimization. Initial intercourse took place at an average age of 13.5 years; for most of the girls, it was not a good experience. As one noted: "I thought it would make someone like me, but it backfired." Before they began prostituting themselves for money, the girls on the average had sexual intercourse with 13 different men. The interviews are summarized in the following terms:

> The primary picture of entrance into prostitution is one of juveniles running away from impossible situations at home, who are solicited for prostitution, and start working for a pimp because they have no other means of support due to their age, their lack of education, and lack of necessary street sense to survive alone.[18]

Most major cities have pockets of illegal prostitution (in 14 of Nevada's 17 counties, the behavior is legal). Rather typical of prostitution in large cities is this depiction by a San Francisco investigating committee:

> The range of prostitution in San Francisco is fantastic. Practitioners may be male or female, black, white, or Oriental. They may be 14-year-olds hustling as part of a junior high school "syndicate" operation; they may be supporting the drug habits of their "old man" (or their own habits); they may be moonlighting secretaries who sell their favors on a selective basis through legitimate dating services. Places of assignation run from rundown hotels to luxurious hilltop apartments.[19]

Adolescent prostitutes in San Francisco tend to prefer older customers, largely because they pose less threat than younger ones and, for some, because they are easier to rob.[20]

Pimps and Prostitutes

Pimps (or "street sex trade managers," as James Hodgson calls them) typically approach young women who look a bit bewildered in places such as a bus arrival depot by inquiring if they require any assistance. It takes only a few questions to determine if a girl is a likely recruit. "They're just looking for a pimp like me," one man said. "They're practically carrying a help wanted sign." Flattery often is used. One 17-year-old was approached in a mall and asked if she were a model. The pimp acted surprised that she was not and suggested that with her body (and his supervision), she could make a lot of money, and after a year or so of work could buy a Mercedes.

Sometimes pimps will employ a more indirect approach, having their "wife-in-law" (usually the most senior and most trusted woman in the pimp's "family") seek out prospects for the pimp's stable. An 18-year-old wife-in-law tells how this is accomplished:

> I spent most of my time looking for new girls for Jason. Because he was older, he did not get along well with the young kids. He couldn't compete with all the young bucks showing their magic. I would usually introduce the girls to Jason after I talked with them for a few hours. I had to get their trust. I would tell them he will look after us. Jason was always so proud of me when I brought another one back to the motel.[21]

Pimps often initially show young recruits a good time and give them a great deal of attention and affection. Then the pimp may turn moody, saying that money is running low and he cannot afford to keep up their style of living unless the girl begins bringing in some money by prostitution. A 14-year-old remembered how this tactic played out for her:

> Billy said that we need money and that he had to go back to Philadelphia if he couldn't get more money. He more or less said he couldn't afford to keep looking after me. We suddenly didn't even have enough money for food or for cabs. Billy became miserable. He asked me to help out by turning a few tricks. I did feel somewhat obligated. I mean I needed to help out. I mean he helped me so much. I knew he would have to leave if I didn't help. It didn't seem so bad at the time.[22]

Training the girls for the sex trade involves the transmission of a set of rules. The most important is that they are not to tell the police that they have a pimp. The second is not to hold back "trap" (that is, money). The girls are also instructed not to talk with other pimps. They are trained in how to recognize plainclothes officers and "bad" (dangerous) customers, and how to perform various sex acts. They also are told that they must see that condoms are used and are informed about how to get paid and how much to charge. They generally are expected to make between $500-$700 a night.

The process by which pimps persuade young girls to enter prostitution has also been carefully described by Christina Milner and Richard Milner. Successful pimps isolate young girls from their previous associations and place them in an environment in which there are no contradictions of the lifestyle that the pimp is pushing. As a successful pimp put it:

> It's like going into the Army where they take you away from all your friends. You create a different environment. It's a brainwashing process. . . . When you turn a chick out, you take away every set of values and morality she had previously and you create a different environment. You give her different friends. You give her instead of squares or bookkeepers or secretaries, clerks, and so forth for friends, you give her professional hos [whores].[23]

Milner and Milner, trying to explain the willingness of young girls to remain in what objectively often appears to be a dismal and degrading existence, liken the situation of ghetto prostitution to that of lobsters in a basket. Fishers, they point out, never have to cover lobster baskets, because if one lobster tries to crawl out, the rest will pull it back in.

Pimps provide protection, a sense of worth and love, and an opportunity to make a considerable amount of money (though few teenage prostitutes retain much of their earnings). An interview with a runaway teenage prostitute in New York demonstrates the flavor of the relationship between a girl and her pimp, a relationship that most persons would find puzzling. The questions posed in the following paragraphs are those of a writer seeking to comprehend teenage prostitution:

> Did he ever beat her, as some of her later pimps had? "He never laid a hand on me, no. He looked after me—he was worried about me. He was concerned about me going on the streets." But it was he who put her there. "Yes," she said, matter-of-factly. "That's his job."

> And she never got any indication that he felt there might be something wrong in sending a twelve-year-old girl out on the street? "He was concerned for me," she repeated, steadfast in her loyalty to the thirty-two-year-old man who had started her in prostitution.

> Did she herself feel anything wrong with it? "At first, before I was doing it, of course I didn't know anything much about it; it was something I thought I wouldn't like to do. But then, after I got myself into it, it didn't seem so bad. It was kinda fun."[24]

Upbeat evaluations of hustling such as the foregoing typically turn sour after the youngsters have been working for a while. They usually learn that their pimp is feeding them a practiced line and exploiting them mercilessly. Most pimps work three or four different women—their "stable"—and are adroit at pretending that each is their favorite. While the charade lasts, it can keep the young prostitute at work. "I thought I was in love with him," says one teenager, who later returned to home and school. "I didn't look at it as prostitution, you know I looked at it as doing him a favor because he took care of me, and gave me so much attention and so much affection, you know. I'd do anything for him, you know."[25]

This particular girl was disillusioned when she learned that her pimp actually had sold her to a colleague and then skipped out on her. Sickness (particularly sexually transmitted diseases), beatings by customers, and numerous arrests can forcefully bring home the message that teenage prostitution is a dead-end enterprise. Some teenagers persist in "the life," as they call it, in part because they find discipline and routine intolerable.

GIRLS IN GANGS

Though their offenses were much more serious, the female law-breakers in the Manson "family" and Symbionese Liberation Army were repeating a common pattern found among young female gang members in inner-city areas. The interactions between girls and boys in gangs have been described in the following terms:

> The girls sometimes assist boys in gang fights by concealing weapons such as knives and fingernail files. Girls have been used by boy gangs to waylay leaders of rival gangs—the traditional "decoy" technique. These seem to be the principal activities of even those girls who organized their own female gangs such as the "Shangrila-Debs," "Robinettes" and others.[26]

That female gang members can be as hostile to authority as their male counterparts is illustrated by Kitty, a delinquent girl who expressed the common idea that adult disapproval drives them into deviancy:

> Wherever you look, wherever you turn, authority is there in the shape of parents, teachers, priests and policemen, social workers and truant officers—a great Greek chorus of do's and don'ts chanting about how you goofed and where you've failed. And man, you can't stand that for long. After a while you've got to cut or go nuts—or turn it all around and tell yourself that it's you who are right and the Greek chorus that is wrong. That's easy enough to do because half the time the chorus doesn't practice what it preaches anyway.[27]

Females are likely to join gangs at a younger age than males and to leave earlier. Irving Spergel and his colleagues report that "contrary to myth, female gang members are more likely to play a positive role, tempering the behavior of male gang members rather than inciting male gang members to violent or criminal activity."[28]

In a detailed investigation of girl gangs in the East Los Angeles area, Lee Bowker and Malcolm Klein reported that each gang averaged from 10 to 15 active members and an equal number of inactive members. The age range was more limited than in male groups (14 to 16 years). All female gangs were affiliated with male groups. The girl gangs tended to be organized by siblings and girlfriends of male gang members and then to expand membership by recruiting friends of the members.

The initiation of a girl into the Tiny Diablas, a Hispanic girls' gang in the South Central area of Los Angeles, has been described by a writer who was allowed to witness the rite. Shadow, the new inductee, was dressed in the current gang fashion: corduroy pants, a purple sweatshirt (purple is the gang's color), extravagantly teased hair, and exaggerated black-red makeup. Twenty gang members, ages 14 to 18, stood about counting off 13 seconds while three gang members ("Giggles," "Shygirl," and "Rascal") performed the initiation that they called a "court-in," a beating that ended with Shadow's hair being tangled and her nose bloody. At the court-in, each girl is christened with her gang nickname. If a member fails to live up to the group norms, she may have to undergo a "court-out," in which there is no time limit for the beating. The Tiny Diablas are affiliated with a local male gang, though they maintain that they plan to become less dependent.

New York Girl Gangs

Anne Campbell's research concentrated on the relationships among members in three New York gangs. First were the Sandman Ladies, who were predominantly Puerto Rican. They wore the trappings of an outlaw biker gang, including Nazi and Satanic symbols. Some had children and regarded themselves as good mothers, regardless of their gang activity. The Sex Girls were a former auxiliary of a male gang that was falling apart at the time of Campbell's field work. The gang was mixed, with Hispanic and African-American members, and members were involved in robbery, burglary, and drug dealing. The Five Percent Nation was comprised of African-Americans, organized around a neighborhood religion and frequently involved in crime.

Campbell believes that all of the girl gang members can best be viewed as "sisters" instead of "molls." She pinpoints the intense camaraderie and the strong dependency that exist among the gang girls. Nonetheless, she reports that girl gangs generally remain an adjunct to male gangs and that the range of possibilities open to their members are controlled by the boys. Girls are told how to dress and are encouraged to be good mothers and faithful wives. Their principal focus is on their men. In New York, the gang girls' uniform is denim sleeveless jackets with combat boots. However, if the boys object to these outfits as too "butch," the girls will reserve the full outfit only for encounters with rival gang members.

When both sexes are present, the girls tend to remain quiet, allowing the boys to do most of the talking. They may occasionally defy the males, often argue with them, and sometimes patronize them, but, according to Campbell's research, the men remain indisputably in control.

Campbell notes that the first edition of her study of girl gangs evoked criticism both from the right and left sides of the political spectrum. Those on the right maintained that she was too sympathetic to the gang members, and that she should have concentrated on their antisocial behavior rather than offering so much material about how they viewed their situation. Campbell argues that such a position is part of a conservative doctrine that seeks to isolate and control without understanding. "Never mind their poverty, their struggles to raise children, their victimization by fathers and lovers, their need to belong and be accepted," she writes. Those on the right don't want to hear their problems—they, the girls, are the problem for conservatives. What they blindly desire is to "count up their crimes and show us how to spot them early."[29]

A different kind of criticism arose from the other end of the political spectrum, one that accused Campbell of failing to provide a socialist analysis of the girl gang members. "In stressing their conservatism, their consumerism, their adherence to the romantic vision of finding the right man," Campbell writes, "I had not told many radical criminologists what they wanted to hear." What they wanted to hear, she says, is that the gang girls were naive revolutionaries, duped by ruling-class propaganda. Campbell says that to take such a position would misrepresent what the girls truly believed when they talked about their love affair with conventional society. To say they had been fooled would have been for the author to set herself up as having some direct line to truth that the gang girls themselves were unable to share.

Chicago Girl Gangs

The Black Sisters United (BSU) of Chicago, studied by Sudhir Alladi Vanketesh, was a leadership group that coordinated the activities of African-American girl gangs (or "sets," as Vanketesh prefers to call them, so as to avoid preconceptions associated with the term "gang"). The Black Sisters United provided social activities, such as large parties, barbecues, fashion shows, and beauty workshops for the sets, whose membership ran from about 20 to 100 young women. They turned the girl sets toward political activism as they sought to gain the support of churches, various office holders, and social service agencies. However, the BSU fell apart as the lure of money to be made from the drug trade was held out to members of the girl sets by the Saints, a powerful male gang in Chicago.

At first, the girl sets had largely avoided the kinds of behavior typically believed to be characteristic of gang alliances. They infrequently engaged in street fighting and petty theft, but instead sought to improve their financial condition, particularly that of those of them who were young, unmarried mothers. Conditions deteriorated, however, in the late 1960s, as America became segmented between persons enjoying high wages in the corporate sector and those whose only opportunities lay in the low-wage service jobs. Inner-city schools deteriorated and many opportunities for low income youth to enjoy a satisfying and legitimate way of life evaporated. The gang turned to the drug trade to make money.

The BSU leaders tried to negotiate with the Saints, the male gang that controlled drugs, so that the girl sets could keep their independence even though they might participate in the drug trade. They arranged contracts about splitting drug profits and allocating territories, but the males and many of the women ignored these agreements. The Saints extracted about 75 percent of the girls' earnings from them as "taxes." In time, the female sets that profited from the drug trade began to segregate themselves from those who had avoided it, and the Black Sisters United could no longer hold the coalition together.

Venkatesh substantiates the conclusion that girl gangs tend to find much of their meaning in their association with male gangs, but he emphasizes that his research points to the importance of economic concerns that might bind the gender groups to each other, though these too result in the subordination of the females to the males.

After reviewing field studies of girl gangs in different cities, Randall Shelden and his co-authors reached the following conclusion:

> The case studies of girl gang members in New York, Detroit, Hawaii, Fort Wayne, San Francisco, and East Los Angeles reveal the common circumstances in their lives. The crimes that they commit are for the most part attempts to survive in an environment that has never given them much of a chance in life. Most face the hardships that correspond to three major barriers—being a member of the underclass, being a woman, and being a minority. The gang, while not a total solution, seems to them a reasonable solution to their collective problems.[30]

SUMMARY

The most intriguing aspect of the phenomenon of female delinquency is that girls and young women commit so much less law-violative behavior than boys and young men. Of the major correlates of delinquency (such as age, gender, race, intelligence, ethnic background, and social class), it is gender that stands out most prominently as the best predictor of the likelihood of illegal acts. Either what they are or what they learn contributes profoundly to the way females behave in regard to the law. If men could be induced to act in the same manner—by whatever tactics work with women—we would have gone a very long way toward a solution to the problem of delinquency.

Female delinquency also offers interesting insights into the changing relationships between men and women in the United States. Eased sexual controls may ultimately lead to the reduction or the disappearance of female prostitution, as the demand for sex-for-pay lessens. However, this does not seem to be a likely short-term prospect because the ravaging effect of AIDS has had a strong impact on sexual permissiveness.

At present, it does not appear that the women's rights movement is having a considerable effect on either the extent or the form of juvenile delinquency. In part, this is because girls and young women committing delinquent acts are not part of the mainstream of the feminist movement, nor do they participate to a significant extent in the role changes that the movement advocates.

Biology exerts an influence on different patterns of male and female delinquency, particularly with regard to degree of strength. Girls and women traditionally have been penalized (or protected, depending on your viewpoint) by the sexual double standard, which abhorred sexual waywardness by women while overlooking the same behavior on the part of men. Delinquency statutes, backed by public opinion and concern with possible teenage pregnancy, reinforce the double standard by singling out girls for punishment when they violate sexual norms.

Prostitution by teenage girls is another area in which the different official response to delinquencies of young females compared to those of young males is illustrated. The police are much less interested in trying to arrest and hassle teenage male prostitutes than they are in dealing with females. For one thing, police officers tend to be squeamish about interacting with other men in ways that have homosexual overtones, and almost all male prostitutes traffic in homosexual services. For another, law enforcement personnel (reflecting social values) are less concerned with male sexual waywardness than they are with female sexual waywardness.

At the same time, law enforcement officers historically have not bothered to arrest the male customers of juvenile prostitutes, although some change in policy is becoming apparent. The reluctance stems in part from the perception that customers are engaging in an "understandable" transaction and in part because the customer is needed to testify against the prostitute (though there is no reason why the situation could not be reversed, with the prostitute implicating her patron). Police sometimes try to enforce the law against pimps, under statutes outlawing the living off the wages of a prostitute, but such efforts tend to be frustrated by the unwillingness of most prostitutes to testify against their pimps—either because of fear or because of affection.

Girl gangs invariably are closely tied to their male counterparts, though field studies show that their members may have close and supportive relationships among themselves. As women gain further independence, and as the ideas of the women's movement trickle down through the class structure, it will be interesting to determine what impact, if any, the doctrines of female independence will exert on the nature of gangs of delinquent girls.

REFERENCES

Alexander, Ruth M. (1995). *The "Girl Problem": Female Sexual Delinquency in New York, 1900-1930*. Ithaca, NY: Cornell University Press.

Baines, Margaret, and Christine Alder (1996). "Are Girls More Difficult to Work With? Youth Workers' Perspectives in Juvenile Justice and Related Areas." *Crime & Delinquency* 42:467-483.

Bart, Pauline B., and Diana Scully (1979). "The Politics of Hysteria: The Case of the Wandering Womb." In *Gender and Disordered Behavior: Sex Differences in Psychopathology*, edited by Edith Gumberg and Violet Ranks, 102-134. New York: Brunner/Mazel.

Bowker, Lee H., and Malcolm W. Klein (1983). "The Etiology of Female Juvenile Delinquency and Gang Membership: A Test of Psychological and Social Structural Explanations." *Adolescence* 18:739-751.

Campbell, Anne (1991). *The Girls in the Gang*, 2nd ed. Cambridge, MA: Blackwell.

Chesney-Lind, Meda (1997). *The Female Offender: Girls, Women, and Crime*. Thousand Oaks, CA: Sage.

Chesney-Lind, Meda (1973). "Judicial Enforcement of the Female Sex Role: The Family Court and the Female Delinquent." *Issues in Criminology* 8:51-69.

Chesney-Lind, Meda, and Randall G. Shelden (1992). *Girls, Delinquency, and Juvenile Justice*. Pacific Grove, CA: Brooks/Cole.

Colligan, Michael J., James W. Pennebaker, and Lawrence R. Murphy, eds. (1982). *Mass Psychogenic Illness: A Social Psychological Analysis*. Hillsdale, NJ: Lawrence Erlbaum Associates.

Dalton, Katharina (1982). "What is this Premenstrual Syndrome?" *Journal of the Royal College of Practitioners* 32:713-723.

Dowd, Maureen (1995). "The Rise of the Fallen." *New York Times* (September 21):A23.

Figert, Anne E. (1996). *Women and the Ownership of PMS: The Structuring of a Psychiatric Disorder*. New York: Aldine de Gruyter.

Frank, Robert T. (1931). "The Hormonal Causes of Premenstrual Tension." *Archives of Neurology and Psychiatry* 26:1053-1057.

Gold, Judith H. (1997). "Premenstrual Dysphoric Disorder. What's That?" *Journal of the American Medical Association* 278:1024-1025.

Hagan, John (1990). "The Structuration of Gender and Deviance: A Power-Control Theory of Vulnerability to Crime and the Search for Deviant Role Exits." *Canadian Review of Sociology and Anthropology* 27:137-156.

Hagan, John, and Bill McCarthy, in collaboration with Patricia Parker and Jo-Ann Climenhage (1997). *Mean Streets: Youth Crime and Homelessness*. New York: Cambridge University Press.

Hanson, Kitty (1964). *Rebels in the Streets: The Story of New York's Girl Gangs*. Englewood Cliffs, NJ: Prentice Hall.

Hodgson, James F. (2000). "Pimping: Sex-Trade Managers." In *Encyclopedia of Sexual Deviance*, edited by Nanette J. Davis and Gilbert Geis. Philadelphia: Taylor & Francis.

James, Jennifer (1978). *Entrance into Juvenile Prostitution*. Washington, DC: National Institute of Mental Health.

Jensen, Gary F., and Raymond Eve (1976). "Sex Differences in Delinquency: An Examination of Popular Sociological Explanations." *Criminology* 13:427-448.

Jorden, Edward (1603). *A Brief Discourse of a Disease Called the Suffocation of the Mother*. London: John Windet.

Laws, Sophie, Valerie Hey, and Andrea Eagan (1985). *Seeing Red: The Politics of Premenstrual Tension*. London: Hutchinson.

Leiber, Michael J., and Mary-Ellen Ellyson Wacker (1997). "A Theoretical and Empirical Assessment of Power-Control Theory and Single-Mother Families." *Youth and Society* 28:317-356.

Leonard, Eileen B. (1982). *Women, Crime, and Society: A Critique of Theoretical Criminology*. New York: Longman.

Luker, Kristin (1996). *Dubious Conceptions: The Politics of Teenage Pregnancy*. Cambridge, MA: Harvard University Press.

Maxson, Cheryl L., Margaret A. Little, and Malcolm W. Klein (1988). "Police Response to Runaway Children: A Conceptual Framework for Research and Policy." *Crime & Delinquency* 34:84-102.

Miller, Jody (1998). "Gender and Victimization Risk Among Young Women in Gangs." *Journal of Research in Crime and Delinquency* 35:429-453.

Milner, Christina, and Richard Milner (1972). *Black Players: The Secret World of Black Pimps*. Boston: Little, Brown.

Odem, Mary E. (1995). *Delinquent Daughters: Protecting and Policing Adolescent Female Sexuality in the United States, 1885-1920*. Chapel Hill: University of North Carolina Press.

Piquero, Alex R., and Matthew Hickman (1999). "An Empirical Test of Tittle's Control Balance Theory." *Criminology* 37:319-341.

Pollak, Otto (1950). *The Criminality of Women*. Philadelphia: University of Pennsylvania Press.

Riback, Linda (1971). "Juvenile Delinquency Law: Juvenile Women and the Double Standard." *UCLA Law Review* 19:313-342.

San Francisco Committee on Crime (1971). *A Report on Non-Victim Crime in San Francisco. Part II: Sexual Conduct, Gambling, Prostitution*. San Francisco: San Francisco Committee on Crime.

Sayers, Dorothy (1955). *Unnatural Death*. New York: Avon.

Sereny, Gitta (1985). *The Invisible Children: Prostitution in America, West Germany, and Great Britain*. New York: Knopf.

Shelden, Randall G., Sharon K. Tracy, and William B. Brown (1997). *Youth Gangs in American Society*. Belmont, CA: Wadsworth.

Silbert, Mimi, and Ayala M. Pines (1982). "Entrance into Prostitution." *Youth & Society* 13:471-500.

Slade, Pauline (1984). "Premenstrual Emotional Changes in Normal Women: Fact or Fiction?" *Journal of Psychosomatic Research* 28:1-7.

Smart, Carol (1976). *Women, Crime, and Criminology: A Feminist Critique*. London: Routledge and Kegan Paul.

Spergel, Irving A. (1995). *The Youth Gang Problem: A Community Approach*. New York: Oxford University Press.

Thomas, Keith (1959). "The Double Standard." *Journal of the History of Ideas* 20:195-206.

Tittle, Charles R. (1995). *Control Balance: Toward a General Theory of Deviance*. Boulder, CO: Westview.

Vedder, Clyde B., and Dora B. Somerville (1970). *The Delinquent Girls*. Springfield, IL: Charles C Thomas.

Venkatesh, Sudhir Aladi (1998). "Gender and Outlaw Capitalism: A Historical Account of the Black Sisters United 'Girl Gang.'" *Signs* 23:683-698.

NOTES

[1]   Vedder & Somerville (1970), 164.

[2]   Baines & Alder (1996), 476.

[3]   Leonard (1982), 51.

[4]   Jorden (1603), 7.

5   Frank (1931), 1054.

6   Dalton (1982), 219.

7   Figert (1996), 147.

8   Thomas (1959), 195.

9   Chesney-Lind & Shelden (1992), 172.

10   Luker (1996), 107.

11   Jensen & Eve (1976), 429.

12   Smart (1976), 22.

13   Chesney-Lind & Shelden (1992), 186.

14   Riback (1971), 313-314.

15   Hagan & McCarthy (1997), 200.

16   James (1978), 53.

17   Dowd (1995), A23.

18   Silbert & Pines (1982), 488-489.

19   San Francisco Committee on Crime (1971), 3.

20   Ibid., 73.

21   Hodgson (2000), 3.

22   Ibid., 7.

23   Milner & Milner (1972), 95.

24   Sereny (1985), 38.

25   Ibid., 46.

26   Vedder & Somerville (1970), 39.

27   Hanson (1964), 125.

28   Spergel (1995), 7.

29   Campbell (1991), xiii.

30   Shelden, Tracey & Brown (1997), 177.

15

Media Violence and Delinquency

As we have seen, most efforts to explain juvenile delinquency (including many theories) indicate that learning and the nature of the social environment play an important role in the development of delinquent behavior. As noted in Chapter 7, among the factors that some scholars have focused on—and one which has played a major role in popular thinking—is the ubiquity of violence in movies, television, popular music, and other forms of mass media, as well as the relationship between exposure to such violence and the problem of delinquency.

Representations of violence have long been a part of entertainment and popular culture in the United States, and many people have worried about the effects of those representations on society as a whole, and especially on young people. Is it possible to trace the cause of at least some delinquency—particularly that involving crimes of violence—to the influence of the violent stories and scenes to which children are exposed from a very early age? If so, how important a factor is it in producing juvenile crime?

HISTORICAL OVERVIEW

Concern about media violence goes back a long way in American history. In the urban setting within which concepts of delinquency arose, the availability of entertainment and its character (particularly of a theatrical world that, in the eyes of early reformers, was not entirely

439

respectable) developed early as a matter of concern, although less in regard to issues of violence than as a general source for the corruption of the morals of youths.

The issue of violence entered the discussion around the middle of the nineteenth century. This occurred as literacy grew, especially in the North, and as a market developed for a variety of forms of popular fiction that were inexpensively printed and priced, and designed for a youthful audience. Especially notable were the "dime novels," which were rapidly written, in almost assembly-line fashion, and published in the thousands. These short works told sensational stories of the Wild West, urban crime, daring outlaws, clever detectives, and the rise from rags-to-riches. Young people read them avidly, but not surprisingly, they were controversial. By the latter part of the nineteenth century, such reformers as Anthony Comstock were raising concerns about the effects of dime-novel reading on young minds, suggesting that many a youth had been turned to crime by their influence. In several states, efforts were made to regulate the sales of dime novels and similar materials to minors.

Concern about potentially problematic printed materials was to remain high on the agenda in the United States. Through the twentieth century, fears of the negative, potentially antisocial influence of even such major literary works as J.D. Salinger's *Catcher in the Rye* (1951) have continued to occupy parents, school officials, and political figures, resulting in efforts to regulate, if not ban, access to them by teenagers.

The Movies

Even before the end of the nineteenth century, however, the focus for those fearful of the impact of media violence began to be less on print than on the more graphic and direct portrayals of violence provided in the visual entertainment arts—initially by movies and later by television.

From the point of their introduction into American life (especially urban life) in the 1890s, movies provided a major form of entertainment for young people, who were attracted by their accessibility and cheap price of admission. With the development early in the twentieth century of theaters devoted exclusively to films, both viewing and uneasiness grew apace. Many turn-of-the-century reformers believed that movies attracted precisely the kind of urban, working-class boys and girls who were also prone to delinquency, and these reformers worried about the time young people were devoting to movie-going as well as the images they were seeing.

Even before the end of the first decade of the twentieth century, organized efforts against what was seen as the corrupting influence of movies (including movie violence) had begun to take shape in many parts of the United States. Several cities, including Chicago, passed ordinances providing for the censorship of movies that might appear to encourage crime and delinquency. By the end of the decade, a National Board of Review was formed in New York to censor those films its members found morally objectionable, particularly films portraying crime scenes so vividly as to possibly encourage the actual commission of criminal acts, especially by juveniles. That cinema violence could lead to actual violence was an article of faith for board members and others concerned about the directions in which movies appeared to be headed.

During the 1920s and 1930s, this concern became even greater, as film-making techniques became more sophisticated, especially with the rise of the gangster film as a major genre. After at least one case in which two boys, having seen a gangster film, played cops-and-robbers with a loaded gun, resulting in the shooting death of one of the boys, there was a national outcry against screen violence and its apparent role in increasing juvenile crime. In the early 1930s, some of the first serious research on the topic also began to appear. Prolonged efforts by such groups as the Catholic Legion of Decency and the motion picture industry's own Hays Office also focused on minimizing both the violence and its effects, even as they sought to control explicit sexuality in films.

MEDIA IN THE "GREAT DELINQUENCY SCARE"

The concern about movies and other media reached its height during the "delinquency scare" of the late 1940s and early 1950s (see Chapter 8). Increasingly, public clamor and Congressional interest focused on the role of the media in producing what many people saw as a post-World War II increase in juvenile crime, inaugurating debate, discussion, and a program of research that has continued to the present.

Although the discussion of media violence shaping up in the years following World War II was multifaceted, among the key figures by the early 1950s was the psychiatrist Frederic Wertham. Wertham's best-selling book, *The Seduction of the Innocent* (1954), did much to increase public awareness about media violence. Initially, he focused not so much on movies or other media as on comic books, which were successors to the dime novels that had developed a strong market among young readers. Later, however, he broadened his focus to film and television. Basing his conclusions on clinical analyses, Wertham not only decried the ubiquity of violence in entertainment directed toward children but argued that such entertainment was leading children to idealize violence—to glamorize it—in ways that contributed to later acts of aggression and even to violent crime.

Wertham's importance and his ideas about the media received their most significant encouragement in 1955, as Senator Estes Kefauver assumed the chair of the Senate Subcommittee to Investigate Juvenile Delinquency and launched a series of hearings on the mass media and delinquency (Chapter 8). Wertham appeared before the committee, where his views were taken seriously and the issue was broadened to address not only the role of comic books but of movies and television as well. Overall, expert opinion on the power of media to create delinquents was divided, but the committee nevertheless concluded that there was good reason to be concerned about the possibility.[1]

Some of this concern was enhanced by the directions movies were taking during this era, notably by the emergence of the "J.D. [juvenile delinquent] film." The three of the most important J.D. films were released in 1954 and 1955—*The Wild One*, *Blackboard Jungle*, and *Rebel Without a Cause*. Though not unprecedented, these films, featuring such charismatic stars as Marlon Brando, Sidney Poitier, and James Dean, appeared to romanticize teenage violence and delinquency in ways that excited significant public opposition, and significant public interest in relationships between the media and the problems of juvenile crime. The opposition was not enough to prevent a host of successors in the genre, over the next decade and a half, and those successors in themselves did much to keep the issue alive.

The rise of rock-and-roll at about this same time added to the controversy. Associated by many with unacceptable forms of dance, dress, and behavior, this music also came to be identified with that emerging "youth culture," which, in its independence from adult guidance, appeared to contribute to growing levels of delinquency (see Chapter 2).

Television Enters the Scene

Such concerns were also enhanced by the rapid growth of television during this same period. Commercial television had begun to gain ground in the United States immediately after World War II, spreading rapidly after about 1950. As early as 1951, critics began to worry about the frequently violent content of television programs and about the impact of such violence on young viewers. The Kefauver subcommittee considered the issue and issued a report concluding that television violence could have a negative influence.

Over the past three decades, interest in possible links between television violence and delinquency has remained high. Following the Kefauver hearings, subsequent congressional committees (in 1961 and 1964), spurred by an increase in television violence, investigated the issue and reached a similar conclusion regarding television's impact. Most significant, perhaps, were the findings of a National Commission on the

Causes and Prevention of Violence. This commission was appointed by President Lyndon Johnson in 1968 in the wake of the assassinations of Senator Robert Kennedy and Dr. Martin Luther King, Jr. (and the riots following the King assassination). The Commission's final report documented a significant level of media violence, especially on television, emphasizing the influence of television on young viewers. While recognizing that actual violence was the product of many factors, the report concluded that television has an "adverse effect" on such viewers.

The findings of the Commission were further supported by an extensive research report issued under the auspices of the United States Surgeon General in 1972. Compiling research efforts by some of the leading figures in the field, the report documented the persistence of violence in popular entertainment, especially on television, and reported on a number of studies investigating possible links between media violence and actual behavior. Although qualified in its conclusions, the weight of the research appeared to confirm that, at least for some people, and especially for children and young adolescents, media violence could be a contributing factor to actual violent behavior, including violent crime and delinquency.

A decade later, the National Institute of Mental Health (NIMH) assessed subsequent research and documented a continuing pattern of findings relating media violence to actual aggression, despite some contrary evidence adduced by a few careful studies. Subsequent reports by the Centers for Disease Control and Prevention in 1991 and the American Psychological Association and the National Academy of Science in 1992 reached similar conclusions. The link between media and actual violence—and, thus, between media and such problems as juvenile delinquency—was portrayed as fairly strong.

These conclusions have not gone unanswered. Throughout the 1970s, research sponsored by the three major television networks (some of which appeared to blunt the force of the research published in government reports) suggested that, while there were possible links between television violence and aggression, those links were by no means as strong or as clearly causal as the government reports suggested. Nevertheless, during this same period, a variety of organizations, ranging from the American Medical Association to the National PTA to Action for Children's Television (ACT), continued to attack the networks' continuing presentation of violent programming.

Recent Trends

In recent years, interest in the influence of media violence has, if anything, increased. Congress has maintained a focus on the issue, not just in regard to television violence but in regard to media violence generally, and has continued to do so to the present. Hearings through-out the 1980s and 1990s have addressed the issue as it arises in film, in television, and even in popular music. In the late 1980s, Congress passed legislation that exempted the networks from antitrust laws in order to allow them to collaborate in developing guidelines designed to lessen violent programming. Additional legislation, including measures banning violent programming during hours when children were most likely to be watching television, continued to be proposed through the 1990s.

Widespread public concern has continued to be significant as well. Several spectacular crimes committed by juveniles have been inspired by—or even copied from—violent episodes in films or television shows, as when, in 1995, a New York subway toll-taker was burned alive by a group of juveniles, apparently imitating a similar act in a just-released movie.[2] Such "copy-cat crimes" helped to increase public perceptions of the power of media violence to encourage juvenile crime and delinquency. In addition, in at least a few cases, young people accused of crimes have offered what is sometimes called the "television defense," claiming to have been inspired to violent action as a result of watching televised violence, and thus to have had diminished capacity to judge the significance of their crimes. Such defenses have had mixed results but have, again, tended to reconfirm public perceptions of the powerful influence media violence can have.

In addition, the level of violence in films and on television has been increasing both in its prevalence and its brutality, raising further fears about the impact of such violence on young audiences. Also drawing concern has been the popularity of programs portraying adolescent violence, such as the controversial "Beavis and Butthead." Major political figures, including President Bill Clinton, Attorney General Janet Reno, and former Surgeon-General Jocelyn Elders, have joined in expressing fears about the effects of media on American society.

Lawrence Lien, CEO of Parental Guide Inc., points out how the "V-chip" is used for blocking the television programs containing violence, sex, and/or inappropriate language in Omaha, Nebraska, in 1998. Omaha was the second city in the United States to utilize the "V-chip" codes. *(AP Photo/Cynthia J. Kohll)*

Such concern has been strong enough that, even as they cited the dangers of "censorship" in efforts to limit violence, the television networks did adopt a series of voluntary guidelines on television violence in 1992. Moreover, in 1993, they agreed to attach parental advisory labels to violent programs. Critics have argued that such measures have done little to change network programming and have not produced a serious reduction in either the amount or character of violence in the medium. As a result, at the beginning of 1997, major broadcasters considered the implementation of a ratings code, similar to that used by the motion picture industry. In addition, legislation was passed requiring the incorporation of a "V-chip" into newly manufactured television sets, a device that automatically blocks certain kinds of violent programming. Whatever their impact, these efforts have helped to maintain interest in the issue and to acknowledge at least the possibility that television violence is a major factor increasing the level of violent crime and delinquency in American society.

Some New Issues

Since the mid-1980s, especially, new forms of entertainment have raised additional issues. Trends in popular music (particularly the success of heavy metal and rap music, particularly "gangsta rap") in both recordings and videos have sparked widespread concern. The violent, sexist language and imagery found in heavy metal and gangsta rap has been well-documented, as has the apparent celebration (in at least some song lyrics) of criminal acts, including "cop-killing." The genre's reputation has not been improved by the fact that some of the best-known musicians have themselves been charged with violent crimes.

The popularity of such music forms has led a number of groups, including the Parent-Teacher Association (PTA), the Parents' Music Resource Center (PMRC) (led by Tipper Gore, wife of then-Senator Albert Gore), and the National Political Congress of Black Women—as well as recording company stockholders—to express strong fears over their impact on young people. As early as 1985, Gore's group and others helped to bring about a series of Senate committee hearings on "the contents of music and the lyrics of records," investigating links between rock music, in particular, and problems of juvenile crime and delinquency. These hearings focused mainly on gathering information, rather than on any possible legislation, but resulted in negotiations involving the PMRC, the national PTA, and the record industry providing for warning labels on recordings that the industry itself designated as having sexually explicit or violent lyrics.

More recent efforts to curtail media violence also occurred in the wake of the killings of 15 people in April of 1999, at Columbine High School in Littleton, Colorado. Accounts linking the two teenage killers to popular violent video games drew attention to the games themselves and their potential influence on young people. This led to a wave of criticism of the games' creators from an array of political and other figures, including President Clinton. Such criticism was supplemented by federal efforts to address issues of media violence, including a Federal Trade Commission inquiry into the entertainment industry's marketing of violent movies, video games, and music, along with calls for stricter enforcement of the motion picture industry's rating system for violent and sexually explicit films.

Such efforts have increased the popular impression of the potential danger of contemporary mass media. These more recent entertainment forms have done much to augment the popular belief that the United States has produced a violent media culture, one that contributes significantly to a violent tenor of life and that has significant implications for American social life generally and for the problem of juvenile delinquency in particular.

RESEARCH ON MEDIA VIOLENCE AND DELINQUENCY

The impression of a link between media violence and actual violence (and, hence, between media violence and delinquency) is, as we have seen, strong in American thinking. In Congressional hearings and government reports, scholarly conclusions that violence is a contributing factor in producing both violence and delinquency have been widely reported, with the weight of such major professional organizations as the American Psychological Association and the American Medical Association behind them.

What kinds of research have produced such conclusions? What does research tell us about the link between media violence and aggression? What role can we assign to media violence in creating, or at least helping to create delinquency itself?

Serious research on such questions goes back to the 1930s, to the work of W.W. Charters, who conducted massive initial research on movie violence, resulting in a nine-volume report. The report's conclusions were modest: Movie violence could have a negative influence on some children, especially those who were already at risk. On others, there was likely to be no harmful influence at all.

More concentrated efforts, however, are datable to the delinquency scare of the post-World War II period, and, especially, to the mid-1950s. The basic approaches that were developed then continue to guide researchers and have led to an enormous body of literature, including literally thousands of individual studies examining the potential effects of media violence on behavior. Within this substantial body of literature, however, several distinct theoretical perspectives have emerged, and scholars have drawn a series of conclusions that are widely held.

Laboratory Studies

Probably the greatest amount of research on media violence and aggressive behavior has focused on what might be termed the short-term effects of exposure to representations of violence—on whether such exposure produces more (or stronger) aggressive impulses in those who are exposed to it compared to those who are not. A number of such studies have suggested possible short-term or "priming" effects resulting from exposure to media representations of violence.

Most important are those that propose that violence in the media can produce an arousal in viewers that leads to aggressive impulses or to a decreasing inhibition to committing an aggressive act, or that even provides a model for aggressive action that viewers (children in particular) are inspired to follow. A number of laboratory experiments have been devised to test such short-term effects In some of these experiments, subjects are shown violent film clips and then tested for aggressiveness, based on a willingness to administer sharp electric shocks or on tendencies to mimic the observed behavior. Some are based on information gathered in questionnaires, through word association tests, or other means, in a controlled situation. Usually such experiments also involve the use of a control group, exposed either to nonviolent films or none at all, and tested according to the same measures.

One of the most influential of these experiments was conducted in the early 1960s by Albert Bandura and his associates. In this experiment, children were presented various kinds of models—live, on film, and even in cartoon form—behaving aggressively toward a plastic figure, with two control groups seeing either nonaggressive models or none at all. The children were then "mildly frustrated" and given a variety of play materials. Those exposed to aggressive models tended to act more aggressively toward the play materials than those in the control group, and were also more likely to engage in imitative aggressive responses to what they had seen the models do.[3]

Bandura and his associates concluded that exposure to media violence thus worked at two levels to encourage violence in its viewers: first, in weakening inhibitions to aggressive action as such, and, second, in teaching viewers new modes of aggression.

Other laboratory studies have similarly identified a relation between violence in media and actual aggressiveness. For example, Christine Hall Hansen and Ronald D. Hansen have created an experimental situation in which they showed that rock music videos containing antisocial content tended to make experimental subjects, in this case university students, more favorable toward an observed antisocial act (an obscene gesture) in an experimental situation, supporting the same conclusion that what people see in the media can desensitize them to violent, antisocial acts in the real world.[4]

Such a connection has not been universally found. A few studies have indicated that exposure to television or film portrayals of violence may actually reduce aggression. This has been labeled the "catharsis" effect, the argument being that the opportunity to view violence provides an opportunity to release tension on the part of the viewer—to dissipate hostility through a vicarious experience of aggressive action. A few researchers have also suggested that in cases in which the violence portrayed is especially disturbing, it may actually serve to inhibit any impulses toward actual aggression in the viewer.

Such negative associations are not, however, a common outcome to laboratory research on the effects of media violence. Some experiments have shown a fairly strong positive relationship between media violence and aggression. The preponderance have indicated at least a weak association between media violence and aggression, and have indicated a stronger effect on children than on adults—an effect that, some suggest, could have implications for later behavior.

Some reservations have been raised about how closely such experimental results can be linked to the "real world." In life, critics have pointed out, viewers rarely see violence in the kind of abbreviated form that tends to be used in experiments—in film clips, for example— nor is it clear that in routinely looking at movies and television, or listening to music, individuals (especially children) give it the kind of undivided attention an experimental situation tends to entail. More crucially, researchers have questioned whether the short-term, immediate responses produced in a laboratory setting have any significance for understanding non-immediate, long-term patters of behavior, despite the frequent suggestion that modes of behavior learned early in life are likely to influence later behavior.

Nevertheless, most of the evidence based on laboratory experiments tends to confirm that media violence probably has some influence on tendencies toward aggression, at least for some people.

Field Experiments

Field experiments have similarly sought to test the short-term effects of media violence, while addressing some of the shortcomings that may affect laboratory studies. These experiments have chiefly involved exposing subjects to violent media events in relatively natural settings, over a long period of time, and trying to observe the effects of media violence. Here, too, results have been mixed, most indicating increased interpersonal aggressiveness on the part of subjects but a few showing little or no positive relationship.

One of the most frequently cited field experiments, conducted in the late 1970s, was related directly to issues of juvenile delinquency. Using an institution for juvenile offenders as the research site, the experiment took place in several phases. Experimenters first sought to determine normal behavior. Then, after introducing such violent movies as *The Chase, Death Rides a Horse*, or others to one group of boys, and such nonaggressive films as *Ride the Wild Surf* or *Beach Blanket Bingo* to a control group, researchers measured both short-term and long-term differences. The evaluation was complex but it did show some increase in aggressive behavior on the part of those who saw aggressive movies as opposed to those in the control group. A series of follow-up studies, including both laboratory and field experiments, appeared to support the findings, indicating that exposure to movie violence increased aggressive behavior.[5]

Other field studies, conducted with a range of age groups, have similarly found an association between exposure to media violence and increased aggression. Others, building on the same idea but looking in a slightly different direction, have shown that giving subjects a diet of "prosocial" programming—showing young children *Mr. Roger's Neighborhood*, for example—may actually moderate aggressive behavior.

At least a few studies have also sought to examine the effects of media violence by making direct comparisons of the television or music preferences of delinquent and nondelinquent young people, as well as by measuring the impact of exposure to representations of violence on each group. Here, too, results have been mixed. Examinations of such musical forms as rap and heavy metal, in particular, have shown no clear-cut directions, although the tendency of the evidence indicates the encouragement at least of more favorable attitudes toward anti-social behavior.

At the same time, there have been some contrary findings, as in one study in which a group of institutionalized boys actually became more aggressive after a six-week diet of nonaggressive television, a result the researchers explained in terms of the catharsis hypothesis. However, critics pointed out that because the boys had already declared a preference for aggressive shows, their response may have been more an expression of anger and frustration than a matter of any direct influence from the shows they were allowed to see.

Thus, field experiments, like laboratory experiments, tend to confirm some association between media violence and aggression. As both approaches have been refined in response to specific criticisms, the understanding of that association has itself become increasingly sophisticated. For example, a few researchers have shown that the kind of violence portrayed is itself an important factor in the influence of media violence. Research has suggested that when the violence portrayed goes unpunished, or is rewarded, it tends to increase the likelihood of aggressiveness in experimental subjects, as does the portrayal of violence as justified. Violence in which the perpetrator is similar to the subjects tends to produce positive associations, as does violence that is presented as realistic rather than fictional. Science fiction violence and violent comedy, for instance, appear to have little effect.

"Naturalistic" Studies

For the study of juvenile delinquency, studies focusing on the immediate impact of media violence are inherently limited. While exposure to media violence may produce an aggressive response, does it lead to some longer-term disinhibitions to acting aggressively? Does this also mean it can produce the kinds of antisocial or violent acts that come under the purview of the law? That is, can it have effects that encourage crime and delinquency? Some research suggests that early-childhood aggressiveness may be a good predictor of later delinquency, but the link between media violence and later delinquency has been only occasionally tested.

Some scholars, recognizing the difficulties in relating controlled experiments to the ways in which people actually watch movies or television or listen to music, have seen a need to study the impact of media violence as it might be observed in day-to-day life, and as it might take place over time. Some of these "naturalistic" studies have related viewing or listening habits in a variety of ways to behavioral problems. Several such studies have compared children from homes with or without televisions in regard to aggressiveness and even delinquency. One of the most significant of these studies, conducted in England at the behest of CBS, related actual television viewing habits of individual boys to actual violent behavior by those boys in daily life. It found that heavy viewing (especially heavy viewing of realistic violence) did appear to encourage aggressiveness, including serious violence.

As Belson's study and others have shown, heavy viewing appears to comprise an important variable in trying to determine whether an individual may be moved to actual aggression—especially to criminal violence—as a result of exposure to some representations of violence through television, film, or music. This in itself may provide an important link between media violence and delinquency. There is at least some indication that juvenile delinquents tend to be heavier consumers of media culture than nondelinquents.

A few long-range studies of the impact of media have begun to explore this possibility in more detail, especially in regard to television. Historically, the varying dates at which television has been introduced into some communities has allowed for some testing of its impact, particularly in regard to levels of crime and delinquency. Observing levels of violent crime, especially on the part of young people, prior to and after the introduction of television in a community, has suggested that television can have a major impact. Significantly higher levels of aggressiveness have been found in young people since television's introduction.

Such studies have been enlarged to address, directly, questions of crime and delinquency. Brandon S. Centerwall has, for example, taken advantage of the fact that television was not introduced into South Africa until 1975 to do comparative research focusing on the United States, Canada, and South Africa in an effort to measure television's impact on violent crime. Noting substantial increases in homicide rates in the United States and Canada between 1945 and 1974, following the introduction, and spread, of television, he noted the absence of a similar increase in South Africa, where television was banned. He notes also that, within the United States, where television was introduced in different areas at different times, those regions that acquired television first also saw the earliest increases in homicide rates.[6]

More controlled longitudinal studies have also suggested that television can play a role in encouraging aggressive behavior. One of the most influential of these studies compared findings for the United States with those from such countries as Finland, Poland, and Australia, beginning in the late 1970s. Although the investigators found some variation from country to country, they also found a consistently positive association between television viewing and aggressiveness in children.[7]

Another widely cited study surveyed a five-year period, relying heavily on mothers' reports of their children's viewing habits, and sought to correlate an array of demographic variables with behavioral problems (including delinquency) and to analyze the role of television and television violence in contributing to such problems. While eschewing any clear causal relationship between watching television violence and delinquency, the authors similarly found a strong association between heavy viewing of violence and delinquency among the subjects they surveyed.[8]

Not all findings are so clear, however. For example, serious reservations about Brandon Centerwall's findings have been raised by Franklin E. Zimring and Gordon Hawkins, who argue from a much broader set of international comparisons that no clear association occurs between television ownership and levels of violence. Similar studies in the United States and Canada have similarly shown negative results. A long-term study based on interviews with prison inmates tried to sort out such variables as family violence, television, and other adolescent experiences in producing subsequent violent criminal behavior. The findings indicated some association between television violence and subsequent criminality, but the association was weak—far less significant, for example, than the character of family life and schooling.[9]

More pointed has been the work of J. Ronald Milavsky and his associates, one of whose projects was reported in the 1982 NIMH report. Undertaking a three-year study of children and adolescents in Minneapolis and Fort Worth, the project sought to measure the relationship between television exposure and aggressiveness, including delinquency. While they did find some short-term "arousal" effects that television violence appeared to have on aggressive behavior, they concluded that these did not necessarily translate into long-term influences and (in particular) that no clear, causal relationships appeared between television violence and delinquency.

The bulk of naturalistic studies has tended to find at least some association between television violence and aggressiveness, including the serious aggressiveness of violent crime. Nevertheless, the issue of causation remains much debated: Does media violence "cause" aggressiveness, or are aggressive children, influenced mainly by such other factors as class and family life, simply more likely to like violent entertainment? In 1961, in a classic overview of the effects of television on children, Wilbur Schramm, Jack Lyle, and Edwin B. Parker concluded that delinquent children who blame television for their crimes tend to have other serious problems apart from anything television might create—a conclusion supported by at least some continuing study in the field. The precise role of television thus remains an open question.

EXPLAINING MEDIA VIOLENCE AND ITS ROLE

Despite the uncertainties, most studies agree that the impact of media violence on human behavior cannot be ignored, particularly for young people. Whereas scholars have found an important role for media violence in encouraging actual violence, they have also suggested that the problem is not merely one of its immediate potential to encourage aggressive action but also of its long-term impact—its effect in producing violent dispositions, in fostering an approach to life in which violence itself may appear acceptable or even "normal" as a response to social situations. How could such an effect come about?

Desensitization

At the simplest level, and as we have seen in the laboratory experiments, many students of media violence have hypothesized that repeated exposure to violent films, television shows, video games, and other media desensitizes people to the brutality of violent acts and to the suffering violence creates. Under such circumstances, individuals become more willing to act in violent ways, and to accept violent behavior in other people. Although research in this area has produced mixed results, there is at least some evidence that repeated exposure to media violence can lead to a loss of sympathy for victims of real violence and to a callousness that makes people less sensitive to violence and its consequences.

Social Learning Theory

Another approach applies social learning theory (see Chapter 7) to suggest that media violence provides persuasive, powerful models (or "scripts") for young people as they seek to define, interpret, and develop strategies for handling the situations they confront. Because these models are so compelling (especially for young people) and because, for heavy viewers, they may appear to be the major alternatives available for understanding (or learning to understand) their world, the violence that such models seem to recommend comes to seem an acceptable part of life.

The theory is important for providing a link between laboratory or field experiments and possible long-term effects for media violence, especially in the work of such influential scholars as Albert Bandura. Some studies of the impact of television, rap music, and music videos have supported such an interpretation, not only in regard to violence but also in regard to gender and racial stereotypes—and even to personal identity.

The "Mean World"

No less influential than social learning theory has been one of the most compelling and discussed theories regarding media violence since the 1960s: the "mean world" hypothesis, which is often identified with the work of George Gerbner and his associates. Gerbner's work has focused mainly on television. One of his major contributions to the field was helping to define and document, through content analysis, the nature and the varying levels of television violence. Noting, several years ago, that by the time the average child graduates from high school, she or he will have seen at least 13,000 violent deaths on television, Gerbner suggested that the effects of such portrayals must be understood in terms of the deeper influences they can have on the child. While imitative aggression or short-term arousal may be important, more significant are the ways in which the symbolic world of television helps mold children's conceptions of what the real world is like.

Relying on survey research designed to test the attitudes of television watchers, Gerbner and his associates concluded that heavy viewing of television violence cultivates a strong, even exaggerated sense of vulnerability in viewers. Gerbner's approach is often identified as the "cultivation hypothesis." Those who view heavy doses of television violence view the world as more dangerous, with more distrust, and with a greater sense of personal risk than do those whose viewing is lighter. Children who are heavy viewers tend to believe that violence is easily justified and is an appropriate response to anger or fear.

Another aspect of the argument is that heavy viewers also tend to live in what Gerbner has called a "television world." Asked, for example, about the pervasiveness of crime, heavy viewers have tended to overestimate both the number and seriousness of crimes. They have also tended to overestimate the frequency with which police must themselves respond violently to crime (reflecting the television picture of law enforcement more than the reality). The heavy viewer's world is, thus, a scary place—one that helps to inculcate a strong sense that violence is an inescapable fact of life. Hence, there tends to be a greater acceptance of violence and a willingness to use violence on the part of young people heavily exposed to television representations.

The mean world hypothesis, like other approaches to television violence, has inspired a great deal of research. This research has attempted to address such questions as the extent to which the sorts of fears Gerbner and his associates documented may be understood as media-provoked and the extent to which they rest on a fairly realistic assessment of risk (especially in difficult environments). Many studies, especially those conducted in urban areas, have identified a range of factors that can contribute to the kinds of anxieties the "mean world" hypothesis addresses, making the exact role of media problematic.

Research on the cultivation hypothesis continues, including research addressing an array of demographic variables, issues of context, and forms of media violence. In addition, comparative research has sought to address the significance of the cultivation hypothesis by focusing on societies in which violence appears to be less a part of the national tradition than in the United States. The research has produced mixed results. Intervening variables appear to play a major role in how people perceive and respond to what they see. Clearly, such results complicate any assessment of the role of media violence in contributing to problems of crime and delinquency.

Research and Recommendations

Despite the problems evident in research on the subject of media violence, most researchers (with a few important exceptions) agree that some association between media violence and aggressiveness exists, however unclear its strength. Surveys have suggested that most studies show only a minority of those in any sample (as low as 2.25 percent and usually less than 10 percent) to be adversely affected by media violence. Hence, it is certainly reasonable to ask whether public policy regarding media violence needs be put on a crisis footing and how strong any measures limiting such portrayals need be.

Nevertheless, most of those who study media violence have argued for some kinds of constraints on its use, sometimes through voluntary guidelines to be followed by networks, filmmakers, and others in the entertainment industry. In movies, as in popular music, warning labels have been commonplace where violent content is strong, although, again, it is difficult to assess how effective such warnings have been (or even how strongly they have been observed).

Parental supervision has frequently been invoked as the best way to minimize children's exposure to violent media. Television control devices exist that block selected channels in order make parental policies more enforceable. Many studies indicate, though, that parents actually play only a minor role in their children's viewing habits—one that is likely to grow weaker rather than stronger as their children reach adolescence, and one that, in any case, is likely to be weakest in those families who engage in the sort of heavy viewing that appears to be associated with behavioral problems.

There have also been some attempts to involve the federal government in the control of media violence. This in itself has been a difficult area to address, because all major forms of entertainment—movies, television, popular music—can claim protection under the First Amendment to the Constitution, which guarantees freedom of press and freedom of speech. Any government interference with media content or efforts to censor that content can (and have) run afoul of constitutional guarantees. (However, in at least one case, a rap recording has been adjudged obscene in federal court, providing some grounds for restraint.)

Negotiations with networks and other entertainment organizations have led to some restraint on violent content, although recent years have seen still more difficulties arise, particularly as entertainment options have proliferated. In television alone, the network dominance that characterized the distribution of programming for several decades has been seriously diminished as a result of the technological changes affecting television itself. In recent years, cable services that provide 100 or more channels to home viewers, satellite dishes, and the large video-rental market have significantly expanded entertainment options within the home. Advances in computer technology and network services promise to expand such options even more. The possibility of even the weakest negotiated regulation becomes, in such a setting, even more problematic.

It is therefore likely that, whatever the effects of media violence, it will remain a significant part of American life and a major (albeit contested) issue in relation to problems of crime and delinquency.

SUMMARY

Since at least the nineteenth century, with the emergence of a clear-cut concept of juvenile delinquency, Americans have worried about the role of popular media in enhancing and reinforcing criminal tendencies in the young. Violence has long been a staple of American entertainment, and young consumers have not shied away from the entertainment industry's more violent offerings.

Several major forms of entertainment have historically attracted the interest of those concerned with counteracting the causes and effects of juvenile crime. From the dime novels of the nineteenth century to the early offerings of the movies, reformers have sought to find ways to constrain violent media offerings. This concern was increased by the great popularity of the "J.D." films of the 1950s, appearing at a time when public concern about delinquency was already at a high level. It was increased still further by the expansion of television virtually nationwide in the decade after World War II. Social scientists and government bodies alike sought to measure the effects of these new media forms in order to counteract what they saw as the dangers of those forms.

Such concern has never abated; if anything, it has been further encouraged by increasing violence in the media themselves, including movies and television, and by the emergence of such forms as heavy metal and rap music, both of which appear to celebrate violent acts in a violent world. All have drawn continuing attention from government and citizens alike.

Research has tended to reinforce such concern. Conclusions, though, have tended to be conservative, and acknowledgment has been made that associations among media violence, aggression, and delinquency are not as clear and strong as much popular thinking would assert. Laboratory and field studies have sought to document ways in which exposure to violent incidents in media have produced aggressive impulses or aggressive behavior in subjects, and have shown at least some associations between media violence and aggressiveness, although the strength of those associations remains unclear.

More naturalistic studies have similarly concluded that some association exists. Long-range studies assessing the impact of the introduction of television in specific communities have documented some increase in violence. Theoretical studies evaluating the cumulative impact of television viewing have indicated that, for at least some young people, media provide a means of learning that violence can (and even should be) an element in social situations. The effect of media on young people is likely to remain an object of extensive interest and investigation.

REFERENCES

Andison, F. Scott (1977). "TV Violence and Viewer Aggression: A Cumulation of Study Results, 1956-1976." *Public Opinion Quarterly* 41:314-331.

Bandura, Albert, D. Ross, and S. Ross (1963). "Imitation of Film-Mediated Aggressive Models." *Journal of Abnormal and Social Psychology* 66:3-11.

Belson, William A. (1978). *Television Violence and the Adolescent Boy*. Hampshire, England: Saxon House.

Binder, Amy (1993). "Constructing Racial Rhetoric: Media Depictions of Harm in Heavy Metal and Rap Music." *American Sociological Review* 58:753-767.

Black, Gregory D. (1994). *Hollywood Censored: Morality Codes, Catholics, and the Movies*. New York: Cambridge University Press.

Bok, Sissela (1998). *Mayhem: Violence as Public Entertainment*. Reading, MA: Addison-Wesley.

Bryant, Jennings, and Dolf Zillman, eds. (1986). *Perspectives on Media Effects*. Hillsdale, NJ: Lawrence Erlbaum.

Centerwall, Brandon S. (1993). "Television and Violent Crime." *The Public Interest* 111:56-71.

Chiland, Colette, and J. Gerald Young, eds. (1994). *Children and Violence*. Northvale, NJ: Jason Aronson.

Cohen, Ronald D. (1997). "*The Delinquents*: Censorship and Youth Culture in Recent U. S. History." *History of Education Quarterly* 37:251-270.

Comstock, George A., and Eli A. Rubinstein, eds. (1972). *Television and Social Behavior: A Technical Report to the Surgeon General's Scientific Advisory Committee on Television and Social Behavior.* 5 vols. Washington, DC: U.S. Government Printing Office.

Cook, Thomas D., Deborah Kendzierski, and Stephen V. Thomas (1983). "The Implicit Assumptions of Television Research: An Analysis of the 1982 NIMH Report on Television and Behavior." *Public Opinion Quarterly* 47:161-201.

Denning, Michael (1987). *Mechanic Accents: Dime Novels and Working-Class Culture America.* London: Verso.

Dubow, Eric F., and Laurie S. Miller. (1996). "Television Violence Viewing and Aggressive Behavior." In *Tuning In to Young Viewers: Social Science Perspectives on Television,* edited by Tannis M. Macbeth, 117-149. Thousand Oaks, CA: Sage.

Epstein, Jonathan S., David J. Pratto, and James K. Skipper Jr. (1990). "Teenage Behavioral Problems, and Preferences for Heavy Metal and Rap Music: A Case Study of a Southern Middle School." *Deviant Behavior* 11:381-394.

Felson, Richard B. (1996). "Mass Media Effects on Violent Behavior." *Annual Review of Sociology* 22:103-128.

Fowles, Jib (1999). *The Case for Televison Violence.* Thousand Oaks, CA: Sage.

Freedman, Jonathan L. (1984). "Effect of Television Violence on Aggressiveness." *Psychological Bulletin* 96:227-246.

Friedrich-Cofer, Lynette, and Aletha C. Huston (1986). "Television Violence and Aggression: The Debate Continues." *Psychological Bulletin* 100:364-371.

Gerbner, George (1996). "The Hidden Side of Television Violence." In *Invisible Crises: What Conglomerate Control of Media Means for America and the World,* edited by George Gerbner, Hamid Mowlana, and Herbert I. Schiller, 27-34. Boulder, CO: Westview Press.

Gerbner, George, Larry Gross, Michael Morgan, and Nancy Signorielli (1994). "Growing Up With Television: The Cultivation Perspective." In *Media Effects: Advances in Theory and Research,* edited by Jennings Bryant and Dolf Zillman, 17-41. Hillsdale, NJ: Lawrence Erlbaum.

Gilbert, James (1986). *A Cycle of Outrage: America's Reaction to the Juvenile Delinquent in the 1950s.* New York: Oxford University Press.

Gore, Tipper (1987). *Raising PG Kids in an X-Rated Society.* Nashville: Abingdon Press.

Hamilton, James T. (1998). *Channeling Violence: The Economic Market for Violent Television Programming.* Princeton, NJ: Princeton University Press.

Hansen, Christine Hall (1995). "Predicting Cognitive and Behavioral Effects of Gangsta Rap." *Basic and Applied Social Psychology* 16:43-52.

Hansen, Christine Hall, and Ranald D. Hansen (1990). "Rock Music Videos and Antisocial Behavior." *Basic and Applied Social Psychology* 11:357-369.

Hearold, Susan (1986). "A Synthesis of 1043 Effects of Television on Social Behavior." *Public Communications and Behavior* 1:65-133.

Heath, Linda, and Kevin Gilbert (1996). "Mass Media and Fear of Crime." *American Behavioral Scientist* 39:379-386.

Huesman, L. Rowell, and Leonard D. Eron, eds. (1986). *Television and the Aggressive Child: A Cross-National Comparison*. Hillsdale, NJ: Lawrence Erlbaum.

Kruttschnitt, Candace, Linda Heath, and David A. Ward (1986). "Family Violence, Television Viewing Habits, and Other Adolescent Experiences Related to Violent Criminal Behavior." *Criminology* 24:235-267.

McCarthy, Elizabeth D., Thomas S. Langner, Joanne C. Gersten, Jeanne G. Eisenberg, and Lida Orzeck (1975). "Violence and Behavior Disorders." *Journal of Communications* 25:71-85.

Medved, Michael (1996). "Hollywood's Four Big Lies." In *Screen Violence*, edited by Karl French, 20-34. London: Bloomsbury.

Milavsky, J. Ronald, Ronald Kessler, Horst Stipp, and William S. Rubin (1982). "Television and Aggression: Results of a Panel Study." In *Television and Behavior: Ten Years of Scientific Progress and Implications for the Eighties*, edited by David Pearle, Lorraine Bouthilet, and Joyce Lazar, vol. II, 138-157. Washington, DC: U.S. Government Printing Office.

Oskamp, Stuart, ed. (1966). "Television as a Social Issue." *Applied Social Psychology Annual* 8. Newbury Park, CA: Sage.

Palmer, Edward L., and Aimée Door, eds. (1980). *Children and the Faces of Television: Teaching, Violence, Selling*. New York: Academic Press.

Parke, Ross D., Leonard Berkowitz, Jacques P. Leyens, Stephen G. West, and Richard J. Sebastian (1977). "Some Effects of Violent and Nonviolent Movies on the Behavior of Juvenile Delinquents." *Advances in Experimental Social Psychology* 10:135-172.

Pearle, David, Lorraine Bouthilet, and Joyce Lazar (1982). *Television and Behavior: Ten Years of Scientific Progress and Implications for the Eighties*. 2 vols. Washington, DC: U.S. Government Printing Office.

Saunders, Kevin W. (1996). *Violence as Obscenity: Limiting the Media's First Amendment Protection*. Durham, NC: Duke University Press.

Schramm, Wilbur, Jack Lyle, and Edwin B. Parker (1961). *Television in the Lives of Our Children*. Stanford, CA: Stanford University Press.

Zillman, Dolf, and James B. Weaver, III (1999). "Effects of Prolonged Exposure to Gratuitous Media Violence on Provoked and Unprovoked Hostile Behavior." *Journal of Applied Social Psychology* 29:145-165.

Zimring, Franklin, and Gordon Hawkins. (1997). *Crime Is Not the Problem: Lethal Violence in America*. New York: Oxford University Press.

NOTES

[1]   Cohen (1997).

[2]   Medved (1996).

[3]   Bandura, Ross & Ross (1963).

[4]   Hansen & Hansen (1990).

5   Parke et al. (1977).

6   Centerwall (1993).

7   Huesman & Eron (1986).

8   McCarthy et al. (1975).

9   Kruttschnitt, Heath & Ward (1986).

16

Forms of Delinquency:
Gangs, Violence, and Drugs

In earlier chapters we have focused on a statistical portrait of the extent and nature of delinquency, looked at delinquency from a historical and cross-cultural perspective, discussed theoretical perspectives, and dealt with methods of control. In this chapter, we single out for closer scrutiny three particular aspects of juvenile lawbreaking: gangs, violent juvenile offenders, and juvenile drug offenders.

JUVENILE GANGS

What is a Gang?

There has been a great deal of debate about what constitutes a juvenile gang. The definition adopted will determine how many gangs you count and how serious a problem you believe gang behavior to be. Some researchers denote as gangs groups of youngsters who come together with some regularity, though almost exclusively for social events. Others apply the term to young people whose most serious misbehavior, at least as members of a group, involves spraying paint and posting graffiti throughout the neighborhood. Others reserve the term for collections of youths involved in more serious law infringements.

One of the most popular definitions, though it has many critics, is that offered by Walter Miller on the basis of a survey of youth service agency workers, judges, criminal justice planners, probation officers, educators, politicians, ex-convicts, and past and present gang members. These respondents named 1,400 different characteristics that they thought identified juvenile gangs. Eighty-five percent of them agreed on six items, which form the basis for Miller's definition:

> A youth gang is a self-formed association of peers, bound together by mutual interests, with identifiable leadership, well-developed lines of authority, and other organizational features, who act in concert to achieve a specific purpose which generally includes the conduct of illegal activity and control over a particular territory, facility, or type of enterprise.[1]

Some researchers maintain that one of the many problems with the Miller definition is that there are groups that meet all the foregoing criteria but in which there exists no clear leadership pattern. One person will take the lead in a particular activity, be it legal or illegal, while another will assume that role for a different activity, depending upon personal skills and group support. Critics also observe that a satisfactory definition of a phenomenon is not necessarily achieved by majority vote. One particularly astute social observer may do as well or much better than the consensus outcome of a large group.

Malcolm Klein's definition follows the same lines as Miller's, though the emphases are different:

> We shall use the term gang to refer to any denotable adolescent group of youngsters who (1) are generally perceived as a distinct aggregation by others in their neighborhood, (2) recognize themselves as a group (almost invariably with a group name) and (3) have been involved in a sufficient number of delinquent incidents to call forth a consistent negative response from neighborhood residents and/or enforcement agencies.[2]

The difficulty with this definition is that it confounds behavior with reaction to behavior. Can we reasonably say that a group is not a gang because its activities do not bestir a neighborhood, or because it commits its offenses in different places throughout a metropolitan area so that no one population becomes unnerved by its presence? At the same time, Klein's definition possesses important elements missing in Miller's, such as the group identification, which is usually accompanied by a gang name.

The following generalizations hold for most gangs: They are primarily male (though for a discussion of girl gangs, see Chapter 14), young, urban, lower class, and very often made up of members of minority groups. Carl Taylor attempted to differentiate gangs by concentrating on the motives that drive them. He distinguished three types:

1. Scavenger gangs, whose members often have no common bond beyond their impulsive behavior and their need to belong. Leadership changes occur often and members are "urban survivors who prey on the weak of the inner city." Acts of violence often are done just for fun;

2. Territorial gangs, which aim to defend their turf as in the classic movie *West Side Story*; and

3. Organized or corporate gangs, which have strong leaders and managers and ultimately blend into established organized crime groups such as Mafia organizations.[3]

In a comprehensive review of the books and articles on gangs, Herbert Covey, Scott Menard, and Robert Franzese add these as characteristics:

1. Gang members are primarily in their teens, with a smattering of young adults in their early twenties. Youths ages 12 to 14 generally are regarded as the best targets for recruitment.

2. Gangs are more likely to be found in areas in which the community is rapidly changing than in other areas of a city.

3. Traditional inner-city slum or barrio gang activity has begun to move out toward the suburbs; and inner-city gangs are beginning to engage in some of their delinquencies in suburban territory.

4. The mass media tend to print material that overestimates the prevalence and danger of gang activity. Press coverage can create an unreasonable "moral panic" over the alleged threat of gangs. William Chambliss noted that in the community he studied, the middle-class "Saints" were subject to less community censure than the lower-class "Roughnecks," although both groups were involved in similar kinds of activity. Malcolm Klein added that media exploitation of gang activity sometimes makes it difficult for members to back down from insults and attacks, because they feel compelled to uphold an image of toughness.

5. Gang violence tends to take four forms. The first involves fights between different gangs. The second type is victimization of nongang members from the same social

background as the gang members. The final two involve acts against the property of the general public, and violence against middle-class citizens.[4]

More recently, Richard Ball and David Curry have maintained that a gang is best viewed as a spontaneous, semi-secret, marginal system whose members share common interests. The gang functions with relatively little regard for legality, but regulates interactions among its members. It features a leadership structure and has processes for maintaining the organization and providing services for members. It also establishes tactics for dealing with other relevant social systems.

Chinese Youth Gangs in the United States

Many gangs, most notably the Chinese gangs in New York City, have strict rules that include physical punishment for members who use opiate drugs (e.g., heroin) because they believe that such usage is a threat to smooth gang operations and is more likely to bring the group to the attention of the police. Ko-Lin Chin's comprehensive study of Chinese gangs showed that more than one-third of their members had been born in America, but only one set of parents represented among the 62 males interviewed were born in the United States. Sixty-one percent of the gang members were either full- or part-time college or high-school students, a telling commentary on the emphasis among Asians on achieving educational credentials, even among those engaged in outlaw gang activities.

Initiation ceremonies among the Chinese gangs varied, with some rites (such as that for the Flying Dragons) duplicating those of the adult triad societies. New members of the Flying Dragons have to take oaths, drink wine mixed with the blood of other new recruits, and bow to the gods. The major New York City-based Chinese gangs are affiliated with adult tong members who are referred to as *ah kung* (grandfather) and *shuk foo* (uncle), who mentor the youngsters.

Extortion is the most prevalent form of Chinese gang activity. One type of extortion involves "protection." Gangs demand a fixed amount of money from businesses in their territory to ensure that the business will not be bothered by that gang or others. The amount is negotiated. The Chinese norm of ensuring harmony at all costs offers gang members culturally established opportunities for exploitation.

Finally, gang members sometimes refuse to pay for food and services or ask for heavy discounts. Although this type of behavior could be defined as theft, culturally it is regarded as "reciprocal face-giving" behavior between the offender and the victim. The material gain is secondary to the symbolic meaning.

South African Gangs

Patterns of American gang activity often are imitated in countries outside the United States. In South Africa, for instance, gangs typically adopt American names. They duplicate the dress and behavior they see in American movies and television programs and dub themselves with names such as Young Americans, Ugly Americans, L.A. Boys, Cool Boys, Dixie Boys, New Yorkers, and Laughing Boys. Most are well-armed and, as in the United States, they see one of their main jobs as protecting their turf. "There are thousands of gang members here in the Capetown area," a South African police officer says. "They are all about America." Some gang members cloak themselves in the American flag. Many gangs traffic in African-grown marijuana (known as dagga) and in buttons of mandrax, a synthetic sedative also known as methaqualone. The drug is crushed, mixed with tobacco and marijuana, and smoked in makeshift pipes.

GANG ORIGINS AND STRUCTURE

Malcolm Klein, one of the nation's authorities on juvenile gangs, suggests that gang activity is cyclical, that is, that there are periods of decline and periods of increase. He believes that the periodical decrease takes place primarily because gang members are scared off by the dangers posed by the ever-increasing levels of violence, which tend to be related to the growing availability of increasingly effective weapons. Klein estimates that today there are about 50,000 street gangs nationwide, with a total membership of about 400,000 youths.

Gangs usually are made up of members of similar ethnicity. Most use a variety of techniques to enhance and display their solidarity, including gang-specific insignias, colors, handshakes, and hand symbols. *(Photo by Mark C. Ide)*

Another gang researcher, Joan Moore, has traced the emergence of gangs in Milwaukee and in Los Angeles. The Milwaukee gangs were triggered in the 1980s by a youth fad for breakdancing and drill teams, which swept many black communities. In some instances, the transition from dance groups to gangs resulted from fights at dance competitions. In Los Angeles, gangs formed in the 1920s, faded out, and then were revived in the 1940s, precipitated by sweep arrests and the lodging of conspiracy charges by the police against minority youths (whose convictions later were overturned on appeal). This was followed by the notorious zoot suit riots in the early 1940s in which servicemen raged through East Los Angeles beating up gang members they identified by their zoot suits (distinctive draped garb that the gang members wore).

A similar pattern of gang development was found by Ronald Huff in two Ohio cities, Columbus and Cleveland. Gangs there traced their origin to three conditions:

1. Breakdancing or "rapping" groups evolved into gangs as a result of inter-group conflict involving competition. Dancing and skating contests often spilled over into adjacent parking lots and soon the groups coalesced into a more distinctive and lasting form;

2. Street corner groups which were almost exclusively social altered into a gang structure as a result of conflicts with other groups in the neighborhood; and

3. Persons who had moved to Columbus and Cleveland from Los Angeles became the core of gangs modeled on those in the site they had left. The newcomers, often charismatic because of the appeal of their experiences, readily recruited followers, but there was no direct affiliation between the midwest and west coast gangs.[5]

On the basis of his participant-observer work with the Diamonds, a drug-peddling gang of Puerto Rican youth in Chicago, Felix Padilla offers a typical tale of why youngsters find their way into the group. Note in his interview with one youth the stress on acceptance, comradeship, and a shared sense of what is proper behavior:

Padilla: You told me you knew things about the gang when you were in the eighth grade. What exactly were your thoughts of the gang at that time?

Elf: It was cool—a bunch of guys who cared for each other and who were having a good time.

Padilla: And that's what cool meant to you then?

Elf: Yeah, it said that you were part of a bunch of guys who trusted each other. There are some guys who don't know how to act cool. They are always showing off. They be lying and telling stories. In the gang you can't do that because the rest of the guys are going to think that you are a big jerk.

Padilla: Are you saying that other youngsters were not cool because they did not belong to a gang?

Elf: I guess they could be cool, but, you see, the gang forces you to always be cool, together. You know, this is your homey [fellow gang member], and brother, so take care of him, don't rat on him. That's what makes the whole thing cool, like a family. Everybody is a friend and brother.[6]

The members of the Diamonds found drug selling a lucrative source of income. They constantly expressed scorn for education and what they saw as the unappetizing legitimate work opportunities available to them. Said one: "We were supposed to go to school and receive an education? For what?" He answered his own questions. "To be employed in factory jobs. We were tired of that." Role models to be admired in the neighborhood were persons spending their profits from the drug trade. "We were watching those guys making a lot of money, so we said, 'Hey, let's follow those guys. Let's do what they are doing!'"[7]

Gang members sometimes form relationships with politicians in low-income communities. Their tasks can include obtaining signatures on petitions, putting up election posters and ripping down those of opponents, browbeating voters, and making certain that favorable voters get to the polling places. In return, the gangs are offered either money or protection if those they help are elected.

The ambivalence felt by family members about gang activity by their adolescent children was examined in a study of Latino gangs in Chicago. It was noted that the young people are not considered outsiders but are instead members of family networks in which they behave appropriately. At clan gatherings, for example, there is no fighting because the gang members appreciate that their parents and relatives and other established people in the community would be appalled by such behavior. When the family does learn of the street outrages committed by their children, they often find themselves uncertain about how to reconcile these reported actions with what they personally have experienced. The cultural concept of honor sometimes is invoked by parents to explain the street behavior; the assumption is that the young persons behaved as they did because there has been an insult to their ethnic pride.

Examining the reaction of community members to Latino youth violence and gang behavior, researchers have found that the greatest concern was with dropping out of high school, which was seen as a sign of or precursor to trouble. This concern was expressed by Hispanic respondents of both sexes and all ages, and in all counties of origin, educational level, and employment status. It was regarded as a more serious issue than either drug use or violence, which were ranked second and third. Blame for dropping out was placed on the failure of parents to become involved more effectively in the upbringing of their children.

Wilding

The pattern of "wilding" gang activity was studied by Scott Cummings in Rosedale Heights, a community in the greater Fort Worth (Texas) metropolitan area with a population of about 10,000 people. Cummings notes that wilding is a street term that refers to groups that seem to have no basic purpose, except to, in journalistic jargon, "run amok." Billy Hardin, an older member of such a gang in Rosedale Heights, was 20 years old when he turned himself in on a murder charge. He and three friends had jumped in front of a moving car and pulled the driver out. The four boys kicked the man, eventually beating him to death with his own cane, which had been lying beside him in the car. They then stole the dead man's wallet.

Billy's longest period of employment was only two months, though he was supposed to support his three-year-old child who lived in Kansas with her mother. Billy had prior arrests for burglary and a history of heavy drinking. He lost interest in school before he finished the elementary grades:

> The first time I missed school was about the fifth or sixth grade. Me and this girl just went off [to have sex] and I just got used to it. I just started doing it all the time. Then I started getting expelled. I used to get two whippings a day from my oldest brother for missing school. In the seventh grade, I ran away and left for about three years. I went to live with my sister.[8]

Billy Hardin was raised on the streets. He lived on the income from things he stole and pawned. He was unable to offer any explanation for the murder he committed. As Cummings notes of Billy: "Other than immediate gratification, he had no vocabulary to describe his actions."

Contrary to the view that gang members remain within the group for long periods of time, and that gang life substitutes for family living, Finn-Aage Esbensen and David Huizinga found that very few youths interviewed over many years during the Denver Youth Survey reported being in a gang for more than one year. Most members, it appears, are transitory, drifting in and out of the gang.

Curfew and RICO

For Americans, gang activity has come in many respects to symbolize an out-of-control condition that they find deeply threatening. Advocacy of tougher punitive measures is the most common reaction. Curfews are a popular response to gangs, though they have been attacked as discriminatory. In San Jose, California, a law forbidding persons under 17 to be on the street after dark saw the recent arrest of 2,011 Hispanics and only 788 Anglos. Ninety-six percent of the parents in the city supported the statute. Statutes also have been passed that outlaw the gathering together on specified inner-city streets of more than a minimum number of youths. Law enforcement has used the Racketeering Influenced and Corrupt Organization (RICO) statute to attempt to put gang members behind bars. RICO, which was enacted to control organized crime, outlaws "patterns of racketeering activity" engaged in by members of an "enterprise." It has been employed successfully against New York City's "Westies" gang, whose members engage in loansharking, narcotics traffic, and extortion.

Loitering Laws

Anti-loitering ordinances represent another approach that has been employed to attempt to harness gang activity. The laws seek to stop gang members from congregating on the streets and frightening and annoying people who live in the neighborhood. For the gangs, their street presence often is meant to convey their control over a particular stretch of urban territory.

Chicago led the way in 1992 by enacting an anti-loitering ordinance that banned gatherings on the street if someone in the group was a known or suspected gang member. Before law enforcement officers could take action, they would have to decide that the gathering had no apparent legal purpose. The police were authorized to tell such groups to disperse; if the groups failed to do so, the people there could be arrested. The offense was classified as a misdemeanor and carried a possible fine of $1,000 and six months in jail.

During the three years after the passage of the measure, 42,000 persons were arrested for its violation, almost all of them blacks and Latinos. In 1995, the Illinois supreme court ruled that the ordinance was unconstitutional. The city of Chicago, backed by the Department of Justice in Washington, appealed that ruling to the U.S. Supreme Court. In mid-June of 1999, in *Chicago v. Morales,* the Supreme Court ruled by a 6-3 vote that the ordinance was unconstitutional. The court's majority declared it was "impermissibly vague on its face" and that it was in contradiction to the right to freedom of assembly guaranteed to all citizens. Its reach also was said to be "inherently subjective," providing too much discretion to the police to hassle persons who were not in violation of any other law. Much quoted was the example offered by Justice Stevens, who noted that under the statute an arrest could ensue if a gang member and his father loitered near Wrigley Field, a Chicago baseball stadium, to rob an unsuspecting fan or if they were standing there to get a glimpse of superstar Sammy Sosa leaving the ballpark.

Attorneys for the city of Chicago told the Supreme Court that gang-related homicides had dropped 20 percent in 1995, the last year that the law had been in effect. The year following its invalidation, the homicide rate climbed 11 percent. Justice Stevens, however, unimpressed, pointed out that the year after that, without the law being in effect, the homicide rate dropped 19 percent. He sensibly concluded that available statistics did not allow the court to reach any firm conclusion about the impact of the ordinance.

Justice Scalia, in an angry dissent, argued that there was nothing in the constitution that specified that such a law did not meet its requirements. He insisted that the court majority had taken the side of gang members rather than serving law-abiding citizens who are preyed upon by outlaw brigands. "I would trade my right to loiter any day in exchange for the liberation of my neighborhood," Scalia declared.

Some people believe that juvenile gangs flourish in some measure because of the efforts of those who seek to tame them, such as those supporting anti-loitering laws. Malcolm Klein points out that gangs often are no more than a loose confederation of peers who rather aimlessly gather and disperse. Interveners establish programs through which they attempt to harness gang activity, but in doing so, Klein asserts, they provide a much more solid identification of gang membership, which is required to participate in the programs. Klein insists that outreach efforts, such as midnight basketball, scholastic tutoring, and similar programs, ought to be operated by parental or neighborhood associations rather than gang workers, and ought to be available to all youth, not only to those affiliated with a gang. Similarly, James Short notes that in Chicago having a "detached worker assigned to your gang gave the group status and could reinvigorate sagging morale. "Man, you ain't nothin' unless you got a worker," Short quotes one gang leader as saying.[9]

YOUTHFUL VIOLENCE

"We lost." When an attorney told his 10-year-old client the decision of the court in Fort Worth, Texas, the boy placed his head in his hands and wept. Seeing the little boy, an outsider would never have guessed that the court decision was based upon convincing evidence that he had severely beaten and stabbed a 101-year-old woman. The youngster, by his act, joined in the gory annals of crime by pre-teen perpetrators: a 10-year-old California babysitter who strangled the child in her care and a 12-year-old New York youth who had committed at least 27 felonies (including robbery, aggravated assault, and first-degree rape). Violence by youths takes a variety of forms, as evidenced by the examples that follow.

Drive-By Shootings

It is only recently that drive-by shootings became part of the repertoire of gang violence. Drive-by shootings, as William Sanders notes in a review of the activity in San Diego, California, is a hit-and-run tactic. Attackers usually remain inside the car. A "routine" drive-by shooting took this form:

> A member of the Neighborhood Crips was sitting on a wall when he heard a car drive up. He turned to look at the car and then turned back. At this point he was shot in the head. The victim ran into a friend's house, noting only that the shooter was wearing red [the color of the Crips' rivals, the Bloods/ Pirus].[10]

In gang warfare, the drive-by shooting is the military equivalent of getting hit by an unseen shell. In gang territory, it can happen anywhere, any time, though most shootings take place during the hours of darkness. Gang members involved in drive-by shootings talk about their feats in the same way that bomber pilots talk of hitting targets. Gang boys are proud that they had the heart to point the gun and pull the trigger to kill an enemy. Members of the rival gang persistently are depicted as cowardly, venal, and worthy of disdain. Sanders summarizes drive-by gang shootings in the following terms:

> As a strategy . . . the drive-by shooting is far superior to other forms of gang warfare. A gang can hit a target miles away from its home territory, and then speed away unscathed. In this situation, gang members can build an identity as having "heart" and live to tell about it. While risky in terms of counterstrikes by the rival gang and police apprehension, a drive-by shooting can be conducted by virtually anyone who can ride in a car and shoot a gun. As such, this type of violence is the most deadly and is likely to be a continuing source of gang power.[11]

Drive-by shootings, largely a California phenomenon that goes along with that state's car culture, have recently been joined in the array of gang violence by walk-by shootings. In Los Angeles, a member of the Temple Street Gang, a Hispanic group, told how he carries out such offenses: "I buy a box of mangoes and I just walk along the street looking like a border brother." By carrying the mangoes, he is seeking to be regarded as one of the Mexican immigrants who peddle fruit and ice cream on the streets. "Then I drop the box and shoot them—boom!— by surprise. Then I hop a fence and I'm gone."

Statistics show that killings among rival Hispanic gangs in Los Angeles, the city which reports the largest number of gang-related deaths in the country, outnumbered those of African-American gang members by a ratio of 2 to 1. Gangs are responsible for almost one-half of Los Angeles' violent deaths, up from about 20 percent two decades ago. Two-thirds of all child and teenage homicide victims in Los Angeles died at the hands of gangs. Yet, as in all types of warfare, there are some barriers that are not to be broken. Hispanic gang members will not attack a rival gang member if he is on the streets with his mother. Angel, a former gang leader in Los Angeles, notes: "I know I'm safe if I'm with my mom. You don't disrespect anybody if they are with their mom."

The Central Park Jogger Case

The "Central Park jogger case" in New York City stands, in the words of one report concerning the event, as "a shocking national symbol of personal fear and urban violence today." More than 30 teenagers swept into Central Park on a night of wilding, attacking anyone who looked vulnerable. Ultimately, six of the youths would be indicted for the savage assault on a 26-year-old female investment banker, who was beaten with a brick and lead pipe before being gang-raped and left for dead. She would in time emerge from her coma, though she suffered severe brain damage.

The predators, taken to a city precinct holding cell, whistled at policewomen and sang rap songs. The case led multimillionaire Donald Trump to take out full-page advertisements in city newspapers "decrying the breakdown of life as we know it" and calling for a return to the death penalty. "I want to hate these murderers," Trump wrote (though no murder had taken place in the Central Park case), "I want them to be afraid." Racial politics soon became entwined in the case, though a newspaper columnist saw it more in the nature of gender warfare: "The most critical element of this attack was they were male. She was female. They were predators. She was Bambi."

School Shootings

A number of episodes of shootings by students in public schools in recent years have been heralded in the mass media as a mournful sign of the deterioration of American culture—and particularly the failure of parents to train their children properly.

In 1998, there were five victims of a schoolyard shooting at Westside Middle School in Jonesboro, Arkansas. The murderers were 11 and 13 years old. Two years earlier, two students were killed in a Pearl, Mississippi, school. In another case, three students were shot to death and five wounded in a West Paducah, Kentucky, high school by a 14-year-old, the son of a respected lawyer. The boy fired as many as 12 shots from a .22 caliber automatic pistol into a student prayer group. The shooting stopped only when another student walked up to the killer and told him: "Put down that gun. Don't shoot anybody. What are you doing?"

What had made the 14-year-old slaughter his schoolmates? "It was kind of like I was in a dream," he said, "and then I woke up." He had brought several guns to school that day, wrapped in blankets, and told a teacher who asked about the package that it was his science project. Before he had begun shooting, the boy had stuffed plugs into his ears.

In one incident in 1999, 12 students and a teacher were killed and more than 20 wounded by two of their fellow students in Columbine High School in Littleton, Colorado. After the slaughter, the pair of perpetrators killed themselves. One of the Littleton killers had kept a hate-filled journal for more than a year in which he wrote about his intent to massacre classmates. He had previously been arrested for breaking into a van, and ran a website that bristled with profanity and wild threats against everyone and everything he did not like. Little of this was known to his parents or to neighbors, who saw the families of the two killers as essentially much like their own—having some problems, but generally under control. The parents of the two boys were described as "caring and conscientious" people who structured their lives around providing financial and emotional support to their children. One of the killers had seen a psychiatrist, who put him on an antidepressant drug regimen. After his parents found a homemade bomb in a closet, they took away the youth's computer and car privileges. In one case, the father was a retired Air Force Colonel and the mother took care of the home. The other father was a geophysicist; the mother, an artist. The parents' anguish is captured in the letter that the mother of one of the boys wrote to the families of the victims regarding her son's "moment of madness":

> We'll never understand why this tragedy happened or what we might have done to prevent it. We did not see anger or hatred in [our son] until the last moments of his life, when we watched [the television coverage] in helpless horror with the rest of the world.[12]

The Colorado high school slaughter also demonstrated vividly that such killings can have effects that extend beyond the immediate victims of the killings. Six months after the events in Littleton, the mother of a young girl seriously injured in the shootings walked into a pawnshop, asked to examine a .38 caliber revolver, and while the clerk was otherwise occupied put two bullets she had carried with her into the gun's chamber. She fired one bullet into a wall and the second into her head, killing herself. Her daughter, a senior in the high school, had been shot in the back and was paralyzed from the waist down. At about the same time, a 17-year-old Littleton student was arrested for proclaiming that he was going to "finish the job" started by the April massacre. In addition, many of the victims' families sued the school district and the parents of the killers for damages.

Each of the multiple killings garnered headlines and spurred media talk shows that sought to place blame and create remedies for the problem. A great deal of attention was focused on weapons. Some schools installed metal detectors and others began to demand that students carry their belongings in see-through bags, making it more difficult to conceal a weapon. The major conflict concerned the banning of gun sales and possession so that youngsters could not so readily obtain the types of weapons that had been used to kill their schoolmates. In addition, many commentaries blamed absent or indifferent parenting and poor teacher supervision: "It's this degree to which kids are being let on their own with very little involvement from teachers and other

adults," one commentator stated. Another thought that the common denominator in the shootings was that those who did the killing felt disrespected ("dissed") and that youth culture tells them to retaliate when they feel "dissed."

The argument has been made that rare episodes of school violence get enormous media attention. Such attention overshadows the fact that 52 million youths are in school each day and that a school setting may be the safest place they experience.

Tom Mauser holds up a pair of shoes belonging to his late son, Daniel, who was killed in the Columbine High School shooting, during an anti-handgun rally in Denver, on April 11, 2000. Mauser placed the shoes with over 4,000 other pairs, representing children killed by handguns in one year. *(AP Photo/Ed Andrieski)*

The Political Arena

Issues regarding youth violence overflowed onto the national political scene following the Littleton slaughter. During the summer of 1999, Congress authorized $1.5 billion for beefed-up school security programs, and proceeded to debate fiercely about what other measures might be taken to address youth violence. A proposal that would have made it a crime to expose children to movies, books, or video games containing explicit sex or violence was voted down, while permission was given to post the Bible's "Ten Commandments" in schools and other state and local facilities (a move that supporters declared would help promote morality).

Representative Tom DeLay of Texas, part of the Republican leadership team in the House, bitterly addressed the question of why the school killings had happened: "It couldn't have been that we place our children in day-care centers," he said sarcastically. "It couldn't have been that our children, once seen as blessings from God, are now considered mistakes when contraception fails."[13]

The possibility of tightened gun control laws was the subtext of the fiery House debate. The Senate had approved a measure that would further regulate sales at gun shows. In the House, a similar measure was backed by Representative Carolyn McCarthy of New York, whose husband had been killed (along with five other people) and her son critically wounded in a shooting on a commuter railroad six years earlier. In the end, those opposing the gun control provision prevailed on a vote of 218 to 211.

CORRELATES OF JUVENILE VIOLENCE

The rate of participation in violent acts by adolescent males is far higher than that for any other age group. Looking at victimization data and assuming that the assailants were about the same age as those they assaulted, Franklin Zimring found that the highest rates of violence were recorded by males in the 16- to 19-year-old group. "If a male ever will be involved in violence," Zimring observes, "adolescence is when it will happen."[14]

Despite the high levels of violent acts in adolescence, the death rate from adolescent violence is much lower than the death rates that result from similar behavior by adults. Zimring believes that part of the reason for this is that teenagers are less likely than adults to die from non-weapon assaults, and the use of guns and knives is less common in juvenile assaults than in those by adults. The third noteworthy factor associated with juvenile violence is group involvement. Whatever youths are doing in their teens, Zimring notes, they are likely to be doing it with others.

Studies conducted in particular geographic sites provide further details on juvenile violence. Columbus, Ohio, was the site of research on 1,138 people who had been arrested before the age of 18 for at least one violent crime. The offenders had committed 1,504 acts of violence over a 12-year period. The offenses varied from fist fights to murder. These were some of the characteristics of these young offenders:

1. Males outnumbered females by a ratio of six to one.

2. African-Americans were overrepresented by a ratio of four times their proportion in the relevant population.

3. Young violent offenders came to a great degree from specific areas in the city. Nearly a third of them lived in census tracts that contained only 7.8 percent of the area's population.

Nearly all of the 1,138 offenders had committed far more property offenses than crimes of violence. One-third of them had been arrested for five or more offenses, but they showed no progression from less serious to more serious offenses.

A New York City study looked at the characteristics of 500 youths brought before the juvenile court for "serious violent crimes" (that is, acts or attempts at homicide or rape, robbery in which a weapon was used or the victim was injured, and assaults in which there was an injury that had to be treated by a physician). As had the Ohio study, this inquiry found that only a small number of delinquents were chronically violent, though these relatively few were responsible for a large majority of the total number of violent crimes. The study found only a weak relationship between the socioeconomic status of the offender's family and juvenile violence. There were as many violent offenders from families on welfare as from those that were not receiving welfare funds. There was no evidence of severe psychological or emotional disturbance in the vast majority of offenders. Finally, the number of previous offenses that had been committed by a delinquent was of little use for predicting the occurrence of a later violent offense.

About 73 percent of students ages 12 to 17 report that violence and crime are major problems confronting teenagers. The percentage of students carrying a weapon to school is said to be higher in smaller cities than large cities (17 percent against 9 percent), an unexpected condition.

The importance of parental attitudes in the realm of violent crimes was captured by Peter G. Stringham, a medical doctor, who tells of the response of the mother of a 17-year-old who had been killed on the streets. "I don't believe he's dead," she kept repeating. "I mean he was really good with his hands—on the street. Everybody knew how he was. He got into a disagreement with this other kid, who knew how my son was, so he got a gun and shot him." Then the mother sadly repeats her lament: "I don't believe he's dead. He knew how to handle himself."[15] Reading her words, you get the sense that she comprehends but will not altogether face the fact that her son's ability to handle himself was the very thing that had led him to get caught up in violence and had prompted his opponent to use a weapon against him.

A 10-year follow-up study of 97 boys ages 12 to 17 who had been incarcerated for acts of violence examined the placements they were given after release. The only placement that appeared to have some beneficial effect was going home. This was true even though 78 percent of the homes to which they returned were deemed dysfunctional and violent. The research team suspected that even such a poor home setting was superior to an indifferent institution. In the home environment, they believed, at least one person usually cared something about the boy, be it an aunt, older sibling, or even the parent of a friend.

Research indicates that attitudes toward violence underlie a great deal of subsequent violence. Some kids learn tactics to avoid fights; they laugh things off, talk their way out of dangerous situations, and otherwise avoid trouble. Those who are violent tell interviewers that "violence is the best way to solve problems," that "if you are not violent, you are weak," and that the world is "essentially hostile and full of dangers."

Kids Who Kill

From 1985 to 1993, homicide by persons ages 14 to 17 rose dramatically compared to killings by adults. It also went up much more rapidly than other forms of juvenile lawbreaking. Homicide remains the second leading cause of death among young people 15 to 24 years of age, while accidents (particularly those involving motor vehicles) are the most common cause. Homicide is the third leading cause of death among children ages five to 15 (with accidents the first and cancer the second). Figure 16.1 illustrates a case of the bizarre character of some youth homicides. Chicago and Los Angeles now are the youth gang homicide capitals.

Since 1996, the youth homicide rate has dropped. This decrease has taken place in the face of estimates by leading criminologists that we were in for a tidal wave of juvenile killings. "So far it hasn't happened," noted James Q. Wilson, an eminent scholar who had predicted otherwise. "This is a good indication," Wilson observed, "of what little all of us know about criminology." Wilson thought that too much predictive reliance had been placed on demographics and too little on the perceptions of young people about the costs and benefits of crime.

In terms of victims, only 9 percent of juvenile offenders kill family members, compared to 22 percent of adult homicide offenders. The juvenile and adult groups are virtually similar in regard to victimizing acquaintances: 57 percent for juveniles, 58 percent for adults. Juveniles kill strangers (34 percent of their total homicides) much more often than adults do (21 percent of their total homicides). Criminal deaths inflicted by firearms on juveniles increased by 61 percent during the past decade. Homicides involving firearms have been the leading cause of death for black males ages 15 to 19 since 1969. In addition, the suicide rate for persons between 10 and 14 also doubled during the past decade.

Oddly, kids convicted of homicide generally show a lesser history of prior violence than those convicted of less serious assaults. The common interpretation is that the killers are marked by overcontrolled hostility; that is, they are angry people who bottle up their fury until it explodes in one murderous action.

The typical female juvenile homicide offender is nearly as likely to kill a family member (41 percent) as a friend or acquaintance (46 percent). Firearms are not used as often in female homicides as they are by males. About one-half of female juvenile offenders used a gun, while one-third killed with a knife.

James Sorrells studied 31 juveniles charged with homicide or attempted homicide. The following are sketches of two of the cases:

> Eddie, fifteen, had been in trouble quite a bit, mostly for a variety of thefts. He was attached to a particular girl, but they kept their relationship hidden. Learning that the girl was seeing another boy, Eddie took his rifle to her house, called her to the bedroom window and confronted her. When she confirmed his suspicions, he shot and killed her, saying: "If I can't have you, nobody else can."

> Manny, seventeen, had been arrested twice for auto theft and once for being drunk in public. One afternoon, when he and some friends were getting stoned on beer, marijuana, and PCP (crystal), someone said that one of the group had informed the police of drug sales and suggested that the informer be taught a lesson. Manny and two others forced the alleged informer into a car and drove to an irrigation canal, where one of the boys held the informer under water until he drowned.[16]

Sorrells concluded that the depiction of violence on television was the prime motivator of murder by the juveniles he studied. He pointed out: "One youngster who had stabbed a man to death commented that he didn't expect his victim to writhe and gasp while dying—people don't die like that on TV."[17] Sorrells believed that television not only promotes violence as the preferred method of resolving conflict but also distorts the viewer's appreciation of its true nature.

Cult-Related Killing

Cult-related killings, though only a very small number compared to the total number of murders involving youths, have been commanding considerable attention because of their often bizarre nature. One example is a torture and murder case in Nebraska committed by a 16-year-old boy whose father was the leader of a survivalist cult. The group, made up of 20 adults and children, had been stockpiling guns and ammunition. The leader claimed he spoke with God; he declared himself the "king" of the group and his son the "prince." The killing was of another cult member, who was to be demoted to the rank of "slave." The victim was chained to a post at night but allowed to work around the farm during the day. He died after five of the cult members took turns torturing him, inserting a greased shovel handle into his rectum and administering lashes with a bullwhip.

In New York, groups of reported devil worshippers brutally killed some of their peers during a so-called "satanic ritual." The cult called itself the "Knights of the Black Circle." In Missouri, saying that they were performing a human sacrifice to Satan, three 17-year-olds beat another boy to death with a baseball bat, tied a 200-pound boulder to his body, and dumped the body into a well. One of the murderers had been an honor student and altar boy until age 11. Thereafter, he entered into a period of drug abuse, temper outbursts, school problems, and extreme cruelty to animals. Friends reported watching him drive screws through a Barbie doll's head, then burn the plastic face and wish out loud that it were human.

Not all juvenile cults embrace violence. The Stoners, an East Los Angeles Satan-worshiping gang, are tied into the world of heavy metal music. They maintain that they know the true meaning of the lyrics, which they claim advocate sexual freedom, violence, occult practices, antiestablishment attitudes, and drug use. A study of the Stoners points out that some members join in order to establish an affiliation with a gang that avoids violence. Stoners will break into churches and destroy pews and vandalize whatever they can move. They also will enter mausoleums and steal coffins or urns containing human ashes. Satanists are frequently required to lie in the coffin with the skeletal remains while the lid is closed. A Stoner will write the lyrics of a favorite song backwards to give it an occult feeling. Figure 16.1, taken from a Stoner's journal, provides details of the "pact" between the gang member and Satan.

Figure 16.2
A Stoner's Pact with Satan

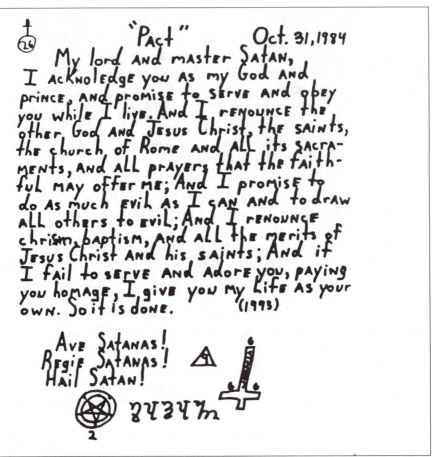

From a Stoner's journal. The inscription to the right of the inverted pentagram spells "Satan" in the witches' alphabet. The pact was written on Halloween.

The Case of Homicide and the Honor Student

A particularly notable instance of juvenile homicide and its controversial consequences arose in the mid-1990s when Harvard University withdrew its acceptance of Gina Grant after it learned that when she was 14 she had murdered her mother in Lexington, South Carolina. She used a kitchen knife that had been thrust so deep that the tip lodged an inch and a half into the victim's spinal column. The mother's hand had been wrapped around the knife to make the death appear to be suicide. The mother's skull also had been bashed at least 13 times with a lead candlestick. The murder had come after a quarrel between Gina and her mother. The mother had been drunk and abusive (as, apparently, she often was). The dispute was over the young girl's dating a football player who was a poor student and had a record of petty crime.

Gina Grant had been one of about 2,000 students admitted to Harvard out of 18,000 applicants. She had lied on her application, indicating that her mother had died in an accident. After killing her mother, Gina Grant had been incarcerated for six months in a juvenile detention center. She had pleaded no contest to a charge of manslaughter. After her release, she moved to Massachusetts to live with an aunt and uncle, and returned to school. She ranked near the top of her high school class, tutored underprivileged children, and was co-captain of the tennis team. Gina Grant's crime record came to the attention of the Harvard authorities after a batch of newspaper clippings arrived anonymously at the university admissions office in the wake of a story in the *Boston Globe* that portrayed her sympathetically as an orphan (her father had died of cancer when she was 11 years old) who had just been admitted to one of the nation's best schools.

Summarizing the case, a writer for *The New Yorker* noted how it bore intimately on the philosophical roots of the juvenile court movement:

> Gina Grant posed some uncomfortable questions: Should someone who took another person's life—whatever the circumstances were, and however reformed the taker of that life was said to be—be granted so spectacular a second chance? Should a young killer, even one of inarguable talent and accomplishment, be accorded the same opportunities as her peers to seek the rewards of society?
>
> In juvenile justice theory, the law says yes; rehabilitation is the primary goal of corrections. But theory and practice can be two different things.[17]

As for Gina Grant, she enrolled at Tufts University, a highly regarded school in the Boston area. Tufts had not known of her record of delinquency when it admitted her but decided to stick by its original decision.

DRUG USE BY JUVENILES

The money to be made by juveniles from drug connections can be substantial. A police officer in Los Angeles, for instance, said to a legislative committee: "How can you tell a kid who's making $500 a week guarding a rock house that he really ought to be in school or that he ought to be getting up at 4 A.M. every day to ride his bicycle around his neighborhood to deliver newspapers?"

It often is maintained, probably with a good deal of accuracy, that the widespread use of illegal drugs in the United States contributes significantly to juvenile delinquency. The dynamics are relatively simple. Drugs cost money; and to acquire that money, those who are habituated or addicted to the drugs very often need to break the law to be able to purchase them. Compounding this situation is the fact that the heavy use of some drugs incapacitates a person from gainful employment. In addition, the extraordinarily lucrative drug trade creates an underworld environment that generates crimes of its own (e.g., beatings and deaths of consumers who do not pay their debts and brutal fights over sales territories).

American adolescents overwhelmingly see drugs as the greatest problem they face, outranking by far issues such as crime, social pressure, grades, or sex. On the other hand, adults believe that drugs are more widely used by the young than the young people believe. Only 30 percent of the adolescents surveyed by the National Center on Addiction and Substance Abuse at Columbia University thought that it was easy to obtain heroin or cocaine, while 82 percent of the adults believed that these drugs were easily accessible to young people.

Drug Use Patterns

A survey conducted every year since 1975 by the Institute for Social Research at the University of Michigan on 45,000 eighth-, tenth-, and twelfth-grade students from what now is a total of 432 public and private high schools nationwide seeks to track changes in drug use within this age group in the United States. Readers of earlier chapters might recall the observation of Hagan and McCarthy that school surveys miss out on a significantly large group of youths who no longer attend school. The Michigan survey, nonetheless, has the advantage of looking at the same sample each year so that the findings reasonably can be said to represent trends in drug use among rather similar persons from year to year.

The survey determined that drug use among those it sampled had remained at fairly stable levels during the past year, despite the expenditure of more than $5 billion by the federal government for its "war on drugs."

Use within the past 30 days is the definition used in the survey for "current" use. Through 1999, current use of all drugs among twelfth graders was 25.9 percent, a very slight change from the previous year's 25.6 percent. Marijuana use had risen from 22.8 percent to 23.1 percent, while the use of other drugs declined from 10.7 to 10.4 percent. For tenth and eighth graders the patterns remained much the same as they had been the year before.

For some drugs, usage had dropped significantly by the end of 1999. Recourse to inhalants by high school seniors had decreased from a high of 3.2 percent in 1995 to 2.0 percent by the beginning of the year 2000. Likewise, the current use of LSD by twelfth graders has gone down during the past five years from 4.0 percent to 2.0 percent, though the figure remained slightly above the 1.9 percent reported in 1991. Black students reported the lowest rates of use for virtually all drugs. Overall, the level of illegal drug use today remains below that of the late 1970s and early 1980s.

Current marijuana use figures continued to show a quirky pattern. Since 1996, the use of marijuana has fallen from 11.3 percent to 9.7 percent among eighth graders, but it only declined from 20.4 percent to 19.4 percent among tenth graders during the same period. The trend flies in the face of many findings in the field of juvenile delinquency that young persons are becoming more precocious in regard to law-breaking behavior, that is, that they are doing more kinds of delinquent acts at younger ages.

Notable in this regard was the relationship among usage levels of different drugs. Those who reported using marijuana less than 10 times during the previous year, for instance, have virtually no likelihood of using cocaine. However, if a person reported using marijuana more than 100 times, or twice a week for a year, there was a 70 percent likelihood that the person also used cocaine.

In terms of usage during the past year in contrast to the past 30 days, for the high school seniors, 73.8 percent said that they had used alcohol and 43.8 percent had used an illicit drug other than alcohol during the previous year. Almost 31 percent had more than five drinks in a row, the survey's definition of "binge drinking," during the two weeks before the survey. Six percent reported using marijuana on a daily basis. For alcohol, that figure was 3.4 percent.

Methamphetamine use, though slight, had risen during the previous year in all the school grades surveyed. Also on the increase was recourse to MDMA ("Ecstasy"), known as a club drug because of its popularity at dance clubs and raves. Anabolic steroids also were used more often in 1999 than earlier. Heroin use remained fairly steady at all age levels, though the rate had approximately doubled between 1991 and 1995 (Institute for Social Research, 2000).

The survey of use patterns was accompanied by an inquiry concerning how serious the respondents believed the use of various drugs to be; that is, whether they saw them as involving "great harm." Between 1995 and the beginning of the new millennium, tenth graders became somewhat more convinced that marijuana use was not notably dangerous. However, the number of those concerned about the physical consequences of heroin increased somewhat in the same period (Institute of Social Research, 2000).

The political overtones of drug use are illustrated by the immediate reaction of General Barry McCaffrey, the federal government's "drug czar." McCaffrey interpreted the findings as demonstrating that all categories of drug use in the country remain "unacceptably high."

For his part, the director of the annual survey believed that the drug use statistics reflected a variety of factors, including peer pressure and a relaxation of efforts of major anti-drug organizations. Even more significant, he believed, was the constant theme in music and films that using drugs is acceptable, a trend that he labeled "the glamorization of drugs" by the entertainment industry (Institute for Social Research, 2000).

The solution to the drug-crime problem so far has been notably elusive. There are voices (an increasing number) who press for allowing drugs to be sold legally, though the precise nature of how this would be done remains unclear. Plans run from making drugs available in stores (as are cigarettes and alcoholic beverages) to blueprints that see the free distribution of drugs under the control of medical and public health authorities. The unknown item in all of these plans is their effect on the number of users. Will the number increase dramatically under such plans? Some say that we would become a country of zonked-out or hyped-up people who seriously imperil their health and other people's safety. Others insist that crime rates will decline dramatically and that in time people will be weaned from drug use by the same tactics that have dramatically reduced the smoking of cigarettes; that is, they will be convinced that it is in their own self-interest, in terms of their health and well-being, not to use drugs.

Puerto Rico: An Illustration

The island of Puerto Rico, with a population of 3.6 million people, offers a dramatic case study of the impact of drugs on juveniles. Since the 1980s, Puerto Rico has grown into a major gateway to the United States for drug smuggling from South America and the Caribbean. Puerto Rico is now regarded as second to Mexico in terms of being a corridor for drugs smuggled into America.

As drug traffic has expanded, youths from the elementary and junior high schools increasingly have been employed as lookouts and drug couriers. One 12-year-old said that he had asked a 19-year-old for drugs to sell at a neighborhood basketball court that functioned as a drug bazaar. The 19-year-old gave him 25 pieces of crack cocaine to sell for $1 each. Soon he was selling $500 worth of cocaine every week, splurging on clothes, sneakers, gold chains, and gifts for seven girl-friends. "I thought it would last forever," he said. Eventually, the young boy went from selling crack to using it. He said that many of his friends had been killed because of drug-associated violence: "Before, if you stole the drug, they would break your leg," he said. "Now they find you with 30 shots in your face."

In 1994, there were 980 homicides in Puerto Rico—the highest number ever, more than double the 1989 toll. At least 60 percent of them were said to be related to drugs. Among the uglier killings was the slaughter of a 12-year-old boy whose 88-pound body was found bound and gagged with duct tape. He had been shot at least eight times and dumped on the bank of a river.

Why Do Youths Become Drug Users?

After decades of sophisticated research, Denise Kandel concluded that the prediction of initiation into drug use can best be understood by looking at items in three categories: (1) parental and peer influence, (2) interpersonal attributes, and (3) sociodemographic factors.

Parental and Peer Influence

The most consistent finding in drug research is that there is a strong relationship between an individual's drug behavior and the concurrent drug use by that person's friends. Several studies also have shown the importance of the characteristics of parents in the initiation of drug use. This includes parental attitudes toward drugs as well as the nature and quality of parent-child interactions.

Intrapersonal Factors

There have been conflicting research results regarding the role of personality factors and other individual characteristics of the drug users. Some researchers have found that conditions such as psychological distress, depression, alienation, and low self-esteem precede the use of drugs, while others maintain that there are no such connections. Many studies have shown a pattern of falling school grades, increased absences, and declining academic motivation among high school students prior to their use of alcohol and marijuana.

Sociodemographic Factors

Variables such as gender, religion, family income, and father's education are not significantly related to the use of hard liquor or illicit drugs other than marijuana. While there may be a slight correlation between any of these items and drug use, their significance is far out-weighed by the preceding two—especially parental and peer influence—when sophisticated statistical analyses are carried out.

An accurate appraisal of one's position in the competitive life of American society undoubtedly also feeds into drug use. One study found that dispossessed black youngsters in the San Francisco Bay Area were painfully aware of the rejection and irrelevance of their labor. When efforts were being made to get them to stop smoking cigarettes, it was found that they resented attempts to discourage them from recourse to one of the few reasonably cheap pleasures easily available to them.

Detection and Treatment

There is intense debate regarding the most effective tactics for dealing with drug usage. On one side are those who believe that only tough retaliation against drug users will prove effective; on the other side, many persons advocate rehabilitative efforts, including counseling and an increase in job opportunities and other programs to enhance youths' self-esteem. As noted earlier, there also are people who insist that only legalization of drugs holds out much hope for any improvement. They argue that the "war on drugs," fought now for almost the entire twentieth century, has at best produced a stalemate, and that it has provided an opening for organized crime syndicates to engage in drug trafficking.

Efforts to introduce hair testing into the nation's schools to identify drug users typify the kinds of controversial issues that pervade the realm of drug use detection. In the United States, many employers now insist that the people who work for them must allow snippets of their hair to be taken and tested for telltale signs of illegal drug use. Drugs ingested into the body travel through the bloodstream and traces of them are deposited in hair follicles, where they can be detected for about 90 days after use.

In 1998, one New Orleans parochial school began testing its students at least once a year through the use of hair samples, adding $55 to their tuition to pay for the procedure; five other of the city's parochial schools soon followed its lead. Although private schools can legally mandate hair testing, the matter became more complicated when several New Orleans public schools sought to adopt the same testing procedure.

In the first parochial school to employ the hair testing, only 28 students out of a total of about 900 were found to be positive after having been given a three-month warning that hair samples would be tested. Most faculty estimated that a much higher percentage had been using drugs prior to the inauguration of the testing. Only the parents of those who failed the test were notified and each of the 28 students was referred for drug counseling. Several months later, only three of that group of 28 again was found to be using drugs.

Many students and parents in the New Orleans parochial schools approved of the new approach. One of their arguments was that the testing allowed youngsters to resist the overtures of peers who might try to introduce them to drug use or to persist in the habit. Students could now argue that they inevitably will be found out at school and that they do not want to embark on a no-win venture. Besides, concerned parents were pleased when their own children were found to drug-free. It was pointed out that the courts have approved drug tests for school athletes in Oregon and tests in Indiana and Arkansas for students desiring to engage in extracurricular activities.

As with many maneuvers to deal with drugs, mandatory hair sample testing has encountered strong opposition. For one thing, many researchers say that hair tests for drugs are far from accurate. They point out that drug traces bind more readily to black hair than to lighter hair and that this may lead to race and sex discrimination in the results. They also note that being near drug users can affect hair samples even if a person did not ingest any drugs. Others regard the testing procedure as an unacceptable invasion of a person's body and privacy.

SUMMARY

Crimes against the person—murder, manslaughter, forcible rape, robbery, and aggravated assault—are committed by youths between the ages of 10 and 17 at a rate considerably above their proportion in the population. Many homicides by youths are carried out as part of gang activity, but a considerable number of others are individual actions motivated by rage and jealousy. Gang homicide is preponderantly an activity of male minority-group members and generally involves youths younger than those involved in nongang homicides.

Research by Wolfgang, Figlio, and Sellin showed that serious crimes, particularly of the violent type, were mostly committed by a relatively small group of delinquents who they labeled "chronic offenders." Later research indicated, moreover, that such a pattern continued into adulthood. Because the menace persists, a critical question is: What, if anything, can and should society do about heading off these careers of violence? Answers vary greatly, and tend to depend upon the political position of the person addressing the question (whether to the right or to the left of the political spectrum). Those on the right tend to favor tougher responses; those on the left endorse measures that would improve the life conditions and chances of potential youthful offenders.

Research regarding the violent youngster has produced the following picture: first, a male minority-group member who lives in a depressed socioeconomic area of a large city; second, young violent offenders are not specialists (there are variations in the types of crimes they commit); third, there is no pattern of progression from nonviolent offenses to increasingly serious violent ones; fourth, contrary to many depictions on television and in movies, violent young offenders in general are not psychotic or otherwise psychologically disturbed (although they may come from homes in which there is a good deal of internal strife); and fifth, criminal tendencies of peers seem to encourage violent behavior even when there is no gang involvement.

It is widely believed that violence and other serious juvenile crime is highly related to the use of illicit drugs. However, several studies indicate that this belief is not factually accurate, at least in terms of drug use that does not reach the level of addiction. The research supports the opposite possibility, that drug use is a result of an earlier pattern of delinquency rather than a cause of such delinquency.

Interpersonal factors prove to be more important than either sociodemographic or personality factors in regard to drug use. The most consistent drug research finding is that there is a strong relationship between an individual's drug behavior and the use of drugs by that person's close friends. Parental characteristics, such as attitudes toward drugs, personal drug use, and degree of support for children, are also associated with a youngster's use of drugs.

REFERENCES

Ball, Richard A., and G. David Curry (1999). "The Logic of Definition in Criminology: Purposes and Methods for Defining Gangs." *Criminology* 33:235-245.

Bedard, Laura, Rudy Prine, and Marc Gertz (1994). "Crime and Delinquency Within the Hispanic Community: A Contemporary Description." *Latino Studies Journal* 5:22-39.

Belluck, Pam, and Jeffrey Wilgoren (1999). "Caring Parents, No Answer in Columbine Killers' Pasts." *New York Times* (June 29):A1, A16.

Chambliss, William (1975). "The Saints and the Roughnecks." *Society* 11:24-31.

Chin, Ko-Lin (1996). *Chinatown Gangs: Extortion, Enterprise, and Ethnicity*. New York: Oxford University Press.

Chin, Ko-Lin, Jeffrey Fagan, and Robert J. Kelly (1992). "Patterns of Chinese Gang Extortion." *Justice Quarterly* 9:625-646.

Clines, Francis X. (1999). "In a Bitter Cultural War, An Ardent Call to Arms." *New York Times* (June 17):1, 15.

Covey, Herbert, Scott Menard, and Robert J. Franzese (1992). *Juvenile Gangs*. Springfield, IL: Charles C Thomas.

Cummings, Scott (1993). "Anatomy of a Wilding Gang." In *Gangs: The Origins and Impact of Contemporary Youth Gangs in the United States*, edited by Scott Cummings and Daniel J. Monti. Albany: State University of New York Press.

Decker, Scott, and Barrik Van Winkle (1996). *Life in the Gang: Family, Friends, and Violence*. New York: Cambridge University Press.

Esbensen, Finn-Aage, and Delbert S. Elliott (1994). "Continuity and Discontinuity in Illicit Drug Use Patterns and Antecedents." *Journal of Drug Use* 24:75-97.

Esbensen, Finn-Aage, and David Huizinga (1993). "Gangs, Drugs and Delinquency in a Survey of Urban Youth." *Criminology* 31:565-589.

Hagan, John, and Bill McCarthy (1997). *Mean Streets: Youth Crime and Homelessness*. New York: Cambridge University Press.

Hagedorn, John M. (1994). "Neighborhood Markets and Gang Drug Organization." *Journal of Research in Crime and Delinquency* 31:265-294.

Hagedorn, John, and Perry Macon (1988). *People and Folks: Gangs, Crime, and the Underclass in a Rustbelt City*. Chicago: Lake View Press.

Hamparian, Donna, Richard Schuster, Simon Dinitz, and John P. Conrad (1978). *The Violent Few: A Study of Dangerous Offenders*. Lexington, MA: Lexington Books.

Hodgson, James F. (2000). *Pimping: Sex Trade Managers*. In *Encyclopedia of Sexual Deviance*, edited by Nanette J. Davis and Gilbert Geis. Philadelphia: Taylor & Francis.

Horowitz, Ruth (1983). *Honor and the American Dream: Culture and Identity in a Chicago Community*. New Brunswick, NJ: Rutgers University Press.

Howell, James C. (1999). "Youth Gang Homicides: A Literature Review." *Crime and Delinquency* 45:208-241.

Huff, C. Ronald, ed. (1990). *Gangs in America*. Newbury Park, CA: Sage.

Institute for Social Research (2000). *1999 National Teen Drug Statistics*. *www.monitoring thefuture.org*

Johnston, Lloyd D., Patrick M. O'Malley, and Jerald C. Bachman (1995). *Drug Use Among American High School Students, College Students, and Other Young Adults*. Washington, DC: U.S. Government Printing Office.

Kandel, Denise B., Ronald C. Kessler, and Rebecca Z. Margulies (1978). *Longitudinal Research in Drug Use: Empirical Findings and Methodological Issues*. Washington, DC: Hemisphere.

Klein, Malcolm W. (1995). *The American Street Gang: Its Nature, Prevalence and Control*. New York: Oxford University Press.

Klein, Malcolm W. (1971). *Street Gangs and Street Workers*. Englewood Cliffs, NJ: Prentice Hall.

Lewis, Dorothy O., Shelley S. Shanok, Jonathan H. Pincus, and Gilbert H. Glaser (1979). "Violent Juvenile Delinquents: Psychiatric, Neurological, Psychological, and Abuse Factors." *American Academy of Child Psychiatry Journal* 18:307-317.

Luker, Kristin (1996). *Dubious Conceptions: The Politics of Teenage Pregnancy*. Cambridge, MA: Harvard University Press.

Mayer, Jane (1995). "Rejecting Gina." *New Yorker* 71(June 5):43-51.

Miller, Walter B. (1975). *Violence by Youth Gangs and Youth Groups as a Crime Problem in Major American Cities*. Washington, DC: U.S. Government Printing Office.

Moore, Joan W. (1991). *Going Down to the Barrio: Homeboys and Home Girls in Change*. Philadelphia: Temple University Press.

Mydans, Seth (1995). "Hispanic Gang Members Keep Strong Family Ties." *New York Times* (September 11):A1, A8.

Mydans, Seth (1990). "Life in Girls' Gang: Colors and Bloody Noses." *New York Times* (January 29):A1, A12.

The National Drug Control Strategy, 1997 (1997). Washington, DC: The White House.

Navarro, Mireya (1995). "Puerto Rico Reeling Under Scourge of Drugs and Rising Gang Violence." *New York Times* (July 23):11.

Padilla, Felix (1992). *The Gang as an American Enterprise*. New Brunswick, NJ: Rutgers University Press.

Sanders, William B. (1994). *Gangbangs and Drive-Bys: Grounded Culture and Juvenile Gang Violence*. New York: Aldine de Gruyter.

Sheldon, Randall G., Sharon K. Tracy, and William B. Brown (1997). *Youth Gangs in American Society*. Belmont, CA: Wadsworth.

Short, James F., Jr. (1997). *Poverty, Ethnicity, and Violent Crime*. Boulder, CO: Westview.

Snyder, Howard N., and Melissa Sickmund (1995). *Juvenile Offenders: A Focus on Violence*. Washington, DC: National Center for Juvenile Justice.

Sorrells, James (1977). "Kids Who Kill." *Crime & Delinquency* 23:312-330.

Spergel, Irvine, et al., (1994). *Gang Suppression and Intervention: Problem and Response*. Washington, DC: Office of Juvenile Justice and Delinquency Prevention.

Stringham, Peter G. (1995). "What is Known About Changing Violence." *Smith College Studies in Social Work* 65:181-189.

Taylor, Carl (1993). *Girls, Gangs, Women and Drugs*. East Lansing: Michigan State University Press.

Trostle, Lawrence C. (1992). *The Stoners: Drugs, Demons, and Delinquency*. New York: Garland.

Venkatesh, Sudhir Alladi (1988) "Gender and Outlaw Capitalism: A Historical Account of the Black Sisters United 'Girl Gang.'" *Signs* 23:683-697.

Wolfgang, Marvin E., Robert M. Figlio, and Thorsten Sellin (1972). *Delinquency in a Birth Cohort*. Chicago: University of Chicago Press.

Zimring, Franklin E. (1998) *American Youth Violence*. New York: Oxford University Press.

NOTES

[1]   Miller (1975), 9.

[2]   Klein (1995), 13.

[3]   Taylor (1993), 46.

[4]   Covey, Menard & Franzese (1992), 112.

[5]   Huff (1990), 6.

[6]   Padilla (1992), 106.

[7]   Ibid., 114.

[8]   Cummings (1993), 56.

[9]   Short (1997), 86.

[10]   Sanders (1994), 66.

[11]   Ibid.

[12]   Belluck & Wilgoren (1999), A16.

[13]   Clines (1999), 15.

[14]   Zimring (1998), 27.

[15]   Stringham (1995), 187.

[16]   Sorrells (1977), 312-313, 319.

[17]   Ibid., 323.

Subject Index

Aboriginal juveniles, reintegrative shaming and, 162, 404
Abuse, in jails, 309-310
Achievement Place, 373-375, 380-381
Action for Children's Television (ACT), 443
Adjudicatory hearing, 258, 259, 280-284, 305
  due process rights and, 281-284
Adjustment problem, delinquency as solution to, 151
Administrative/organizational factors, police discretion in taking youths into custody and, 248-251
Adolescence, 41-46. *See also* Child; Childhood; Youth(s)
  age extension of, 48
  delinquency and, 44
  individuality and identity stressed in, 48
  as life stage, 42
  psychology of (Hall), 42-44
  weakening family role in, 48
Adolescence: . . . (Hall), 43
Adolescent Diversion Project, 365
Adoption studies, 104-105
Adult crime and criminals
  gangs and, 149
  young offenders and, 63
Adult focus, of childhood, 35
Advocacy groups, police discretion and, 250-251
African Americans. *See* Black nationalism; Black-to-white crime ratios; Minority groups; Race
Aftercare, 341. *See also* Parole
  programs, 348

Age
  adolescence extension and, 48
  delinquency and, 49, 63
  in international juvenile justice, 392-393
  juvenile delinquent categorization and, 3, 4, 5
  treatment at probation intake and, 269, 270
  in waiver of juvenile court jurisdiction, 272-273
Aggressive behavior. *See also* Media violence
  field experiments on media violence and, 449-450
  laboratory studies on media violence and, 447-448
  naturalistic studies on media violence and, 450-452
Agricultural school, 317
Akers' social learning theory, 181
Alcohol, usage by young people, 483
Alienation, 49
"American disease," 391
American juvenile system, 197. *See also* Juvenile justice system
American Medical Association, 443
American Psychological Association, 443
Ancient world, juvenile crime in, 198
Anomie theory (Cloward and Ohlin), 150-151
Anthropological theories, 62-63
Anti-loitering laws, gangs and, 469-470
Apes, Men and Morons (Hooton), 99
Apprenticeship, 199-200
Arapesh culture, 62-63

Name Index